S0-BZP-652

HAMPTON INSTITUTE HAMPTON VIRGINIA
23668

331
434 SHAW

Bizure April 13

LAW

OF

MASS COMMUNICATIONS

FREEDOM AND CONTROL OF PRINT AND BROADCAST MEDIA

by

HAROLD L. NELSON, Ph.D.
Professor of Journalism
University of Wisconsin

and

DWIGHT L. TEETER, JR., Ph.D.
Professor of Journalism
University of Kentucky

SECOND EDITION

Mineola, New York
The Foundation Press, Inc.
1973

COPYRIGHT © 1969 THE FOUNDATION PRESS, INC.

COPYRIGHT © 1973
By
THE FOUNDATION PRESS, INC.
All rights reserved.

Library of Congress Catalog Card Number: 73–89508

Nelson & Teeter Mass Com. 2d Ed. F.P.
3rd Reprint—1977

FOR ANN AND TISH

*

PREFACE

Rapid change has continued to characterize communications law during the five years since the first edition of *Law of Mass Communications*. The Supreme Court of the United States has expanded protection against libel judgments under the Times v. Sullivan doctrine. It has held that newsman's privilege is not to be found in the Constitution. It has issued, in the Pentagon Papers case, nine views on the old question of prior restraint. It has upheld the fairness doctrine in broadcasting with the flat statement that the First Amendment is meant first to protect the public's right to free expression. It has ruled that obscenity varies with the outlooks and mores of communities around the nation. Meanwhile, the Federal Communications Commission and the Federal Trade Commission have been highly active, producing new rules and interpretations. Those who know the first edition of this book will find many other changes.

Newsmen and civil libertarians widely view the past five years as a time of unusual threat to free expression. Many had presumed an almost unassailable First Amendment protection against being required to reveal sources of news, but the Supreme Court rejected the idea. Many had felt that the First Amendment made restraint in advance of publication unthinkable, but a deeply divided Supreme Court made it clear that such restraint could very well occur. The Florida Supreme Court ruled, to print media executives' dismay, that politicians criticized in news or editorial columns have a right of reply—a legal claim of access to the newspaper's columns. The worlds of magazines, motion pictures and books attacked the Supreme Court's 1973 decisions that obscenity is different from one community to another.

Apart from court decisions and administrative rules, many perceived an unparalleled assault on free expression, especially from the Executive Branch of government. The assault included heavy, prolonged attacks on the media by major figures in the Administration, plus recommendations that local broadcasters police the fairness of the network news they carry and correct imbalance, or face challenge to their licenses. Also, Congress considered adoption of a bill resembling Britain's "official secrets act" which would make it a crime to publish classified information. Important issues all, they stand largely outside the scope of this book, whose intent is to deal with existing law and regulations.

Determining that the present is more perilous to freedom than was some part of the past is hard to do. The authors would point out that striking retreats have occurred in legal restraint of the media in recent decades: civil and criminal libel, indirect contempt and sedition all are vastly weaker threats than they were, say, prior to 1940, and the past five years have seen some of the retreat.

This edition, like its predecessor, could not have been completed without the assistance of a large number of individuals, firms and institutions. Copyright holders who have generously allowed us to quote materials from their works include (in alphabetical order by author):

American Bar Association Project on Minimum Standards Relating to Fair Trial and Free Press (the Reardon Report), Text and Commentary Copyright © by the American Bar Association, 1966, 1967, 1968.

Carlson, John H., "Newspaper Preservation Act: A Critique," *Indiana Law Journal* Vol. 46:3 (Spring, 1971) pp. 392–412. Thanks are due to Fred B. Rothman & Co., publishers of law books.

Day, J. Edward, "Mailing Lists and Pornography," *American Bar Association Journal,* Vol. 52 (Dec., 1966) at p. 1103, Copyright © 1966 by J. Edward Day.

Friedman, Leon, "The Ginzburg Decision and the Law," *The American Scholar* Vol. 36:1 (Winter, 1966–67), Copyright © 1966 by the United Chapters of Phi Beta Kappa. Quoted by permission of the publishers.

Gerald, J. Edward, "Press-Bar Relationships: Progress Since *Sheppard* and Reardon," *Journalism Quarterly* Vol. 47:2 (Summer, 1970) p. 223.

Jinkinson, Earl A., "Negotiation of Consent Decrees," *Antitrust Bulletin* Vol. 9:Nos. 5–6 (Sept.-Dec. 1964) pp. 673–690, at pp. 676–677.

Johnson, Nicholas, "The Media Barons and the Public Interest," in *How to Talk Back to Your Television Set* (Boston: Little, Brown, 1970; New York: Bantam, 1970), pp. 52–55.

Earl W. Kintner, "Federal Trade Commission Regulation of Advertising," *Michigan Law Review* Vol. 64: No. 7 (May, 1966) pp. 1269–1284, at pp. 1280–1281.

Arthur R. Miller, *The Assault on Privacy: Computers, Data Banks, and Dossiers* (Ann Arbor: University of Michigan Press, Copyright © 1971.)

The Milwaukee Journal, "Guides for Advertising Acceptance." Special thanks are due to Mr. Jack Knake, Advertising Operations Manager of The Journal Company.

The New York Times, "Standards of Advertising Acceptability," and an editorial, "Freedom to Advertise," June 16, 1972, Copyright © 1972. Special thanks are due to Mr. John D. Pomfret, Assistant to the Publisher, *The New York Times*.

Pember, Don R., *Privacy and the Press* (Seattle: University of Washington Press, Copyright © 1972).

Pilpel, Harriet F. and Theodora S. Zavin, *Rights and Writers* (New York: E. P. Dutton & Co., 1960). Copyright © 1955 through 1959 by Harriet F. Pilpel and Theodora S. Zavin. All rights reserved. Printed in the U. S.

William L. Prosser, "Privacy," *California Law Review* Vol. 48:3 (August, 1960) pp. 383–423, at p. 389. Thanks are due to Fred B. Rothman & Co., publishers of law books.

Dwight L. Teeter, Jr. and Don R. Pember, "Obscenity, 1971: The Rejuvenation of State Power and the Return to Roth," *Villanova Law Review* Vol. 17 (Dec. 1971) pp. 211–245.

Robert S. Warren and Jeffrey M. Abell, "Free Press-Fair Trial: The 'Gag Order,' A California Aberration," *Southern California Law Review* Vol. 45:1 (Winter, 1972) pp. 51–99, at pp. 52–53.

The authors express special gratitude to Professor Richard A. Ek of the Mass Communications Department, California State University at Chico. His pathbreaking account of libel insurance is published as Appendix D of this volume. He offered to provide a brief summary of libel insurance, which ultimately expanded into his copyrighted study.

We are again in the debt of Representative Robert W. Kastenmeier of Wisconsin's Second Congressional District, for providing valuable information on the status of efforts to revise the now ancient copyright statute.

Other colleagues in the study of communications law who generously helped us include Professor and Dean Emeritus Fredrick S. Siebert of Michigan State University; Professors William B. Blankenburg, Charles Sherman and Mary Ann P. Yodelis of the University of Wisconsin; Professor William H. Fortune of the University of Kentucky College of Law; Prof. A. David Gordon of Northwestern University; Professor Paul Jess of the University of Michigan; Professor Don R. Pember of the University of Washington, and Professor Michael J. Petrick of the University of Maryland. Important also were Professors Maurice D. Leon and Paul A. Willis, Librarians respectively of the University of Wisconsin School of Law and the University of Kentucky College of Law. Our wives, Ann Nelson and Letitia Teeter, helped at every step.

Chapters 1, 3 through 5, 9, 10, 12 and 13 were written by Nelson; Chapters 6 through 8, 11, and 14 through 16 were written by Teeter. Both contributed to Chapter 2.

HAROLD L. NELSON, Madison, Wisconsin

DWIGHT L. TEETER, JR., Lexington, Kentucky

October, 1973

SUMMARY OF CONTENTS

Part I

PRINCIPLES AND DEVELOPMENT OF FREEDOM OF EXPRESSION

Part II

RIGHTS IN CONFLICT WITH FREE EXPRESSION

A. Free Expression and Citizens' Rights

B. Free Expression and the Rights of the State and Moral Order

Part III

FOR THE GREATEST GOOD: COMMUNICATIONS LAW AND THE PUBLIC INTEREST

APPENDICES

Appendix A

TABLE OF CONTENTS

Part I

PRINCIPLES AND DEVELOPMENT OF FREEDOM OF EXPRESSION

Part II

RIGHTS IN CONFLICT WITH FREE EXPRESSION

A. Free Expression and Citizens' Rights

TABLE OF CONTENTS

B. Free Expression and the Rights of the State and Moral Order

Part III

FOR THE GREATEST GOOD: COMMUNICATIONS LAW AND THE PUBLIC INTEREST

TABLE OF CONTENTS

APPENDICES

Appendix A

Appendix B

Appendix C

Appendix D

Appendix E

†

LAW OF
MASS COMMUNICATIONS

Part I

PRINCIPLES AND DEVELOPMENT OF FREEDOM OF EXPRESSION

Chapter 1

FREEDOM AND CONTROL

Sec.
1. The Worth of Freedom.
2. The Constitutional Guarantees.
3. Legal Boundaries for Speech and Press.
4. Control by Three Government Branches.

To self-governing societies, a major test of a nation's freedom is the degree of liberty its people have in speaking, writing, and publishing. Seventeenth and Eighteenth Century thought in much of Western Europe and America turned to faith in man's reason as the safest basis for government. And if man was rational, indeed, he needed access to a maximum flow of information and opinion as a basis for making decisions. Leaders of Enlightenment thought considered freedom of speech and press indispensable to the life of a public capable of self-government. In addition, it was widely considered that this freedom was essential to the individual's own development and realization, a "natural right" to which every man had claim in exploiting his faculties.

Even the age of faith in pure reason and natural rights, however, stopped short of granting men perfect freedom in all that they did or said. Men turned over to government the powers and rights which it needed in order to protect them in the enjoyment of their rights, in Lockean theory. Furthermore, though the outer boundaries of the freedoms enjoyed might be few and indistinct, some boundaries existed. To the mid-Twentieth Century, which grants at most that man possesses some elements of reason in his complex makeup, and which is skeptical indeed about the existence of "natural rights," boundaries continue to exist.

The hand of authority rests lightly on speech and press at some places and times, heavily at others. But its presence is felt everywhere, including the nations of the western world which generally consider themselves the most freedom-loving of all. Some degree of legal control over expression has been sought or permitted by the freest societies through history; for although the values of free speech and press may be considered paramount and be exalted, there are circumstances where other values may take priority and win in a conflict over rights. The individual's right to his good reputation limits verbal attacks through the penalties of the civil libel law; society's interest in morality denies legal protection to the obscene; a host of laws regulating business, industry, and trade applies fully to the commercial press and broadcasting.

SEC. 1.   THE WORTH OF FREEDOM

Major values underlying free speech and press are society's need for maximum flow of information and opinion, and the individual's right to fulfillment.

It is not always easy to separate society's need and the individual's right as the two grounds for freedom of expression. If the individual's right is thoroughly protected, the social good in confrontation of ideas presumably follows. John Locke, often called the philosophical father of the American Revolution, in the Seventeenth Century argued the individual's rights—the "natural right" of every person to life, liberty, and property. His ideological descendants included speech and press as one of these liberties, equally applicable to all men in all times and situations, they held.[1]

Almost half a century earlier, John Milton's seminal *Areopagitica* went straighter to the social good as the justification for expression. Arguing against pre-publication censorship in 1644, he cast his case in the religious context, and said that religious truth—so ubiquitously sought or asserted in that century when wars still were fought over whose god should prevail—was so essential to the fate of mankind that authority should open up

---

[1] Locke, John, Second Treatise of Government, ed. Thomas P. Peardon (N. Y., 1952); Strauss, Leo, Natural Right and History (Chicago, 1953).

the arena for debate.   Truth was the only safe basis for a society's life, he said: [2]

> And though all the winds of doctrine were let loose to play upon the earth, so Truth be in the field, we do injuriously, by licensing and prohibiting, to misdoubt her strength.   Let her and Falsehood grapple; who ever knew Truth put to the worse, in a free and open encounter?

There are men who would rather talk than live, no doubt, and without the protection of their individual right to do so, life would be empty to them.   Human beings are fulfilled in many ways, and for many none is more important than making their views known and felt.   To be allowed to express is central to the right to use one's faculties and to develop his personality—one way of defining liberty.   There are many who would deny that this freedom, or any other, constitutes a "natural right" as defined by the Enlightenment.[3]   But that it is real, important to human dignity, and worthy of far-reaching protection under law is widely agreed upon by societies of the West.

The social good has been more compelling to the Twentieth Century as a basis for freedom and control of expression than has natural right.   Society's stake in free speech and press is plain in the structure and functioning of a self-governing people: Only through a "clash of ideas in the open marketplace" can working truths be arrived at; the widest diversity of opinion and information must course through the channels of debate and discussion in arriving at solutions to problems and sound public policy.   If Milton found freer debate essential to religious "truth," modern man finds the confrontation of one idea with another, one set of facts with others, essential to all kinds of "truth," in social relations, politics, economics or art.

The individual and the society benefit alike, of course, in the rationale of the western world's practice of open debate.   Whether the goal is sound public policy, human beings' fulfillment of their potentialities, maintaining the kind of community where people do not need to live in suspicion and distrust of each other, or the fulfilling of the "duty of the thinker to his thought," free expression is held as crucial.

Jurists and lawyers alike have based their cases for freedom on both the social and the individual good.   Barrister Francis L. Holt, whose early Nineteenth-Century work on libel was one of the English texts heavily relied on by American law, put pri-

---

[2] Milton, John, Areopagitica (Chicago, 1953).

[3] Cohen, Morris R., Reason and Nature (Glencoe, Ill., 1953), 2d ed., Ch. 4.

mary emphasis on freedom of the press as one of the "rights of nature * * * that is to say, of the free exercise of our faculties"; but at the same time saw the common good in England's "system of liberty, equally remote from feudal anarchy, and monarchial despotism" as being "the fruit of a free press." [4]

Twentieth-Century jurists speak similarly. Justice Hugo Black of the United States Supreme Court pointed out in Braden v. U. S. that "There are grim reminders all around this world that the distance between individual liberty and firing squads is not always as far as it seems." [5] And in Bridges v. California, he wrote of society's stake: contempt of court citations for newspaper comment about a trial in progress, he warned, "produce their restrictive results at the precise time when public interest in the matters discussed would naturally be at its height." [6]

Yet to suggest that the worth of freedom to the individual and the society goes unchallenged, even in western democracies, is misleading. In any society, some hate and fear the expression of ideas contrary to their own. Is it permissible or proper to allow newspapers to attack my religion? To permit a socialist newspaper to publish in times of threat from "alien ideologies"? Even today, after almost two centuries in which the First Amendment to the Constitution has proclaimed free speech and press as a central American value, some Americans answer "no." [7]

One doubt expressed about free speech is that, for all its supposed power to bring about understanding and agreement, it really accomplishes little. Widespread discussion, freely engaged in, may in this view lead to no settlement of issues. Even scholars and social scientists, supposedly trained in coming to conclusions on the basis of evidence, find it hard to get agreement among themselves. And as for men in general, the argument continues, they are not really disposed to engage in the difficult process of hammering out serious issues, for they find mental effort the most onerous of work.[8]

[4] Holt, Francis L., The Law of Libel * * * in the Law of England, ed. Anthony Bleecker (New York, 1818), quoted in Nelson, H. L., Freedom of the Press from Hamilton to the Warren Court (New York, 1967), pp. 19–20.

[5] 365 U.S. 431, 445–446, 81 S.Ct. 584, 593 (1961).

[6] 314 U.S. 252, 268, 62 S.Ct. 190, 196 (1941).

[7] Swanson, Charles E., "Midcity Daily: What the People Think a Newspaper Should Be," 26 Journalism Quarterly 173 (June 1949); Cantril, Hadley, ed., Public Opinion 1935–1946 (Princeton, 1941), pp. 244–245.

[8] Knight, Frank, Ethics of Competition and Other Essays (New York: Harper & Brothers, 1935), pp. 302, 304, 353.

There is also the position that true "liberation" of societies cannot come about as long as toleration of aggression in national policies is practiced, or if racial, religious, or class hatred may be propounded. Some ideas and policies must be forbidden in this view, for to permit them free rein is to tolerate conditions that perpetuate servitude and unhappiness.[9]

The right to challenge or denounce the principle and worth of free expression is itself, of course, a rough measure of the extent of freedom in a society. " * * * [M]an can *seem* to be free in any society, no matter how authoritarian, as long as he accepts the postulates of the society, but he can only *be* free in a society that is willing to allow its basic postulates to be questioned." [10]

Protection, for the dissenters who challenge the worth of free expression as for those who cherish it, forms its front line in the organic law of the United States. The Federal and State constitutions unanimously give free expression a position of prime value.

SEC. 2.   THE CONSTITUTIONAL GUARANTEES

Federal and State Constitutions unanimously guarantee freedom of expression; most State Constitutions declare that citizens are responsible for the abuse of the right.

The Americans who wrote and in 1791 adopted the Bill of Rights of the United States Constitution served a theme in Anglo-American liberty that had surged to recurrent apogee. They wrought in the line of Englishmen who forced the Magna Charta from King John in 1215, dared to sign the Petition of Right in 1628, passed the Habeas Corpus Act in 1679 and the Bill of Rights in 1689, and in 1776 broke the bands connecting them with motherland by adopting the Declaration of Independence. The first provision in the 1791 Bill of Rights provided freedom of speech and press, and this First Amendment to the Constitution has since been the basic legal framework for protecting liberty of expression in the United States: [11]

> Congress shall make no law respecting an establishment of religion, or prohibiting the free exercise thereof; or abridging the freedom of speech, or of the press; or the

[9] Wolff, Robert P., Barrington Moore, Jr., Herbert Marcuse, A Critique of Pure Tolerance (Boston, 1965), pp. 87–ff.

[10] Wolfe, John B., in Schramm, Wilbur, Responsibility in Mass Communication (New York, 1957), 106.

[11] U.S. Constitution, Amendment 1.

right of the people peaceably to assemble, and to petition the government for a redress of grievances.

They did not say precisely what they meant by "freedom of
speech and press"—an ill-defined and much-debated concept in
England and America at the time. But while the best evidence
indicates that they were not thinking of a much broader freedom than that provided in their erstwhile motherland, they
stated a broad principle in firmly protective terms, and left it
to future generations to interpret.[12]

As the states adopted their own constitutions, each included
a provision for freedom of expression. A few made spare, un-
elaborated statements such as that of Massachusetts: "The liberty of the press is essential to the security of freedom in a
state: it ought not, therefore, to be restrained in this commonwealth. The right of free speech shall not be abridged." [13]

Many states, deeply aware of dangers in the old doctrine of
seditious libel which governments had used to silence their
critics, added further provisions. They denied to their governments the use of two legal instruments that they considered
especially hateful. One was based on the Eighteenth Century
reasoning that statements critical of government were only aggravated if they were true. On this basis, the English common
law had ruled that the accused was not to be permitted to try to
defend himself by pleading that his offensive words were true.

The second instrument barred to government was the practice
of giving judges, rather than juries, the power to decide whether
the particular criticism of government amounted to a crime—
was libelous. Juries in seditious libel cases had been restricted
to deciding whether the accused had, indeed, printed the illegal
statement—to deciding "the fact" of printing, but not "the law."
The overwhelming majority of state constitutions came to bar
these instruments to government's use. New York, an early
one, did so first with a law of 1805, and later placed the principles in its Constitution: [14]

> Every citizen may freely speak, write and publish his
> sentiments on all subjects, being responsible for the
> abuse of that right; and no law shall be passed to re-
> strain or abridge the liberty of speech or of the press.
>
> In all criminal prosecutions or indictments for libels,
> the truth may be given in evidence to the jury; and if

[12] Levy, Leonard, Legacy of Suppression (Cambridge, 1960) pp. 308–309.

[13] Constitution of Massachusetts, Part I, Art. XVI.

[14] Constitution of New York, Art. 1, § 8.

it shall appear to the jury that the matter charged as
libelous is true, and was published with good motives
and for justifiable ends, the party shall be acquitted;
and the jury shall have the right to determine the law
and the fact.

Denying governments the use of these instruments implied
that speech and press might be limited in some ways—although
not these. The freedoms were not "absolutes." This was recognized by most states' constitutions. Nearly all agreed that freedom of expression could be "abused," although they did not say
what "abuse" meant. Typically, the sentence in the state constitution that started with the guarantee of free expression,
ended with the qualification, as in Pennsylvania's: "The free
communication of thoughts and opinions is one of the invaluable
rights of man, and every citizen may freely speak, write and
print on any subject, being responsible for the abuse of that
liberty." [15]

As the Federal Constitution's First Amendment left the "freedom of speech and press" to future interpretation, the state
constitutions left "abuse" of free speech and press to future
interpretation. The principle resembled that expressed by Sir
William Blackstone, prestigious English legal authority whose
famous *Commentaries*, published in 1765–1769, influenced American law heavily. He had said: [16]

> The liberty of the press is indeed essential to the nature
> of a free state: but this consists in laying no *previous*
> restraints upon publications, and not in freedom from
> censure for criminal matter when published. Every
> freeman has an undoubted right to lay what sentiments
> he pleases before the public: to forbid this, is to destroy
> the freedom of the press: but if he publishes what is
> improper, mischievous, or illegal, he must take the con-
> sequences of his own temerity.

America was to part company with Blackstone not on the
principle that "abuse" was possible, but on what would be considered "improper, mischievous or illegal * * *." His ideas
of sedition and contempt of court, for example, although they at
times enjoyed strong and active lives in the United States, ultimately were widely rejected.

Each state's power to define what it considered abuse of free
expression long went unchallenged by the Federal courts. But
in 1925, the United States Supreme Court changed this situa-

[15] Constitution of Pennsylvania, Art. 1, § 7.

[16] 4 Blackstone Commentaries 151, 152.

tion.　It said that the Fourteenth Amendment to the U. S. Constitution protected freedom of speech and press from invasion by the states.　The amendment, which became effective in 1868, declares that no state shall "deprive any person of life, liberty or property, without due process of law　*　*　*." [17]　The "liberty" was not, until Gitlow v. New York, interpreted to include liberty of speech and press, and state courts' rulings on expression before that decision were allowed to stand without review by the U. S. Supreme Court.　In the Gitlow decision, however, the Court said: [18]

> *　*　* we may and do assume that freedom of speech and of the press—which are protected by the First Amendment from abridgment by Congress—are among the fundamental personal rights and "liberties" protected by the due process clause of the Fourteenth Amendment from impairment by the States.

Thereafter, states' punishment of expression that they considered abuse of freedom was subject to review by the U. S. Supreme Court.　The Fourteenth Amendment took its place with the First as a major protection for expression.

One other amendment to the Federal Constitution applies to expression.　This is the Fifth Amendment, which bars the Federal government from certain acts against expression in language similar to that of the Fourteenth: "No person　*　*　* shall be compelled in any criminal case to be a witness against himself, nor be deprived of life, liberty, or property, without due process of law." [19]

While the last part guarantees the liberty to speak or write, the first protects the right to silence, not only in criminal cases but also, by extension, in such encounters with government as appearances before committees of Congress.　It is protection for a witness against self-incrimination.　Its origins lie in the revulsion against the practice of forcing men to testify against themselves.　The practice was commonplace until the Seventeenth Century in England.　With it was associated torture to wring confessions from the accused.　"Freeborn John" Lilburne, one of the most contentious figures in the history of England's freedoms, won the day for the right "not to accuse oneself" in 1641.　Whipped and pilloried because he refused to take an oath before the Star Chamber to answer questions truly about his alleged importing of seditious and heretical books, he petitioned

[17] U.S. Constitution, Amendment 14.

[18] 268 U.S. 652, 666, 45 S.Ct. 625, 630 (1925).

[19] U.S. Constitution, Amendment 5.

Parliament for redress.   Parliament declared the sentence "illegal and against the liberty of the subject," and voted him indemnity of 3,000 pounds.[20]

The Fifth and Fourteenth Amendments and the state constitutions hold at bay government's acts against the freedoms of speech and press.   Yet the two amendments concede that persons may be deprived of liberty through due process of law.   The state constitutions widely agree that the right of free expression can be abused.   While the First Amendment contains no such specific limiting phrase, the courts have held consistently that even its sweeping command against suppression does not promise an "absolute" freedom of expression.   The Constitutional imperatives, libertarian in spirit and voice, yet provide certain boundaries to speech and press.

SEC. 3.   LEGAL BOUNDARIES FOR SPEECH AND PRESS

Although a few voices have urged an "absolute" freedom for speech and press, legislatures and courts have limited the freedom through various formulations.

Even in stating that "Congress shall make no law * * * abridging freedom of speech, or of the press * * *.", the First Amendment draws no exact, ruler-straight line between the permissible and the punishable.   American theorists, courts, legislators, and laymen have stated the boundaries of expression in various ways.   If a scale could be made with "freedom" at one end and "restraint" at the other, most American spokesmen would be found well toward the "liberty" pole.   Yet while clustering in that sector, they would insist on various ways of describing their positions.   Of all American spokesmen, Supreme Court Justice Hugo Black most flatly stated the position for the right of unlimited expression, for interpreting the First Amendment as an "absolute" command forbidding any restraint on speech and press: [21]

> It is my belief that there *are* "absolutes" in our Bill of Rights, and that they were put there on purpose by men who knew what words meant and meant their prohibitions to be "absolutes."

*   *   *   *   *   *   *   *   *

[20] Griswold, Erwin N., The Fifth Amendment Today (Cambridge, 1955), pp. 3, 4.

[21] Anon., Justice Black and First Amendment "Absolutes": a Public Interview, 37 N.Y.U.L.Rev. 548 (1962).

I believe when our Founding Fathers * * * wrote this [First] Amendment they * * * knew what history was behind them and they wanted to ordain in this country that Congress * * * should not tell the people what religion they should have or what they should believe or say or publish, and that is about it. It [the First Amendment] says "no law," and that is what I believe it means.

*   *   *   *   *   *   *   *   *

I have no doubt myself that the provision, as written and adopted, intended that there should be no libel or defamation law in the United States. * * *

*   *   *   *   *   *   *   *   *

I do not hesitate * * * as to what should be and what I hope will sometime be the constitutional doctrine that just as it was not intended to authorize damage suits for mere words * * * as far as the Federal Government is concerned, the same rule should apply to the states.

The late philosopher Alexander Meiklejohn, speaking of the realm of political affairs only, urged a similar absolute freedom of expression for all citizens of the United States. Speaking at a time when fear of domestic Communism was at its height in the nation and tendencies to curb Communists' freedom were strong, Meiklejohn declared: [22]

The first amendment seems to me a very uncompromising statement. It admits of no exceptions. It tells us that the Congress, and by implication, all other agencies of the Government are denied any authority whatever to limit the political freedom of the citizens of the United States. It declares that with respect to political discussion, political advocacy, political planning, our citizens are sovereign, and the Congress is their subordinate agent * * * men, as they endeavor to meet the public responsibilities of citizenship in a free society, are in a vital sense * * * beyond the reach of legislative control.

But the "absolute freedom" position, theoretically appealing to some, has not found official acceptance or widespread support. Three centuries ago, John Milton's extraordinary plea for expanded freedom yet drew the line when it came to those

---

[22] Meiklejohn, Alexander, Testimony of Nov. 14, 1955, U.S. Senate, Committee on Judiciary, Sub-Committee on Constitutional Rights, "Security and Constitutional Rights," pp. 14–15.

whose religion and morals he could not accept; and though religious toleration has long since dissolved the religious barriers
he supported, the case for freedom in England and America
ever since has been qualified in various ways as men have tried
to state principles, rules, and aphorisms that would confine or
enlarge the boundaries of legal control.

William Blackstone's Eighteenth-Century formula was adhered to for long periods of time in England and America:
government shall lay no restraint on writers *in advance* of publication, but may punish them *after* publication of anything that
violates the law. Sweeping in its restrictions as it was, his
rule has long since disappeared as a guide in American courts,
although in the early Twentieth Century, the United States Supreme Court quoted it with approval.[23]

An old dividing-line that rolls easily off the tongue but has
little operational content is stated as this: "Liberty is not the
same as licentiousness." It is impossible to say where one begins and the other leaves off.

In the law of criminal defamation of individuals, the rule was
laid down in state after state that the defendant could not have
protection from punishment unless he could prove that his
words were the truth, and spoken with "good motives and for
justifiable ends."

The intent of the writer—justifiable or malicious—was and is
used as a gauge for testing the degree of culpability of one accused of defamation. The "tendency" of words to cause a
breach of the peace, or to undermine government, or thwart
the process of justice in the courts, was for centuries a judgment to be made by the courts in deciding whether words were
criminal.

One formula which some have recommended is that freedom of
speech and press should be denied only to those who would deny
it to others. The principle was urged by some Americans in
the mid-Twentieth Century years when domestic Communists
were identified as those who demanded free speech but presumably would crush it if they came to power.[24]

Do the demands of freedom give First-Amendment protection
to advertising? Is the salesman's "pitch" to be given the same
protection afforded the aggrieved citizen who seeks political or

[23] Patterson v. State of Colo. ex rel. Attorney General, 205 U.S. 454, 462, 27
S.Ct. 556, 558 (1907).

[24] Eastman, Max, Freedom Must Defend Itself, in Bishop, H. M., and Samuel
Hendel, Basic Issues of American Democracy (New York, 1948), pp. 89–92.

social change, or the candidate for office who assails the incumbent? [25]

Is there a freedom not to speak when government demands testimony? [26]

Two famous formulations of Supreme Court justices attempt to state broad rules that may be applied to many situations. One is the test that was laid out by Justice Oliver Wendell Holmes, Jr.—the clear and present danger test. First articulated in Schenck v. U. S. in 1919,[27] the rule was an attempt, in part, to afford much greater freedom than the old "tendency" rule. Under it, before words can be punished it must be shown that they present a "clear and present danger," rather than merely a tendency, to bring about a serious evil.

The second, first propounded in the 1930's by various justices, speaks for a "preferred position" for First-Amendment freedoms of speech and press. The reasoning assumes that these are the paramount freedoms among all, the "indispensable condition of liberty." Therefore, where a law on its face restricts these freedoms, the Court should not grant it the normal presumption that laws reaching the Court for its scrutiny are valid. The government must prove that the law under question is constitutional, and that the speech or print under challenge by the prosecution endangers a major social interest.[28]

For radio and television broadcasting, legal formulas and principles are based considerably upon the limited capacity of the air waves—the nature of the physical universe—for establishing areas of freedom and control. The air waves belong to the public, not to broadcasters, and can carry only a restricted number of voices. Deciding who will be given access to frequencies, and under what conditions, was assigned to government by the Federal Radio Act of 1927 and the Communications Act of 1934. The Federal Communications Commission licenses broadcasters, choosing one rather than another, deciding whether a station will be re-licensed each three years, and occasionally rescinding a license. It is specifically denied powers of censorship by the Communications Act. Thus while First Amendment protection is provided for broadcast as well as for

[25] Anon., "Developments in the Law—Deceptive Advertising," 80 Harv.L.R. 1005, 1027–38 (1967).

[26] U. S. v. Rumley, 345 U.S. 1, 73 S.Ct. 543 (1953); West Virginia State Board of Education v. Barnette, 319 U.S. 624, 63 S.Ct. 1178 (1943).

[27] 249 U.S. 47, 39 S.Ct. 247 (1919).

[28] West Virginia State Board of Education v. Barnette, 319 U.S. 624, 63 S.Ct. 1178 (1943); Thomas v. Collins, 323 U.S. 516, 530, 65 S.Ct. 315 (1945).

printed communication, special conditions for broadcasting qualify the right in special ways.[29]

Encompassing principles like some of the foregoing have attempted to state broadly how much freedom an open society
wants its people to have. Less general statements have tried to
index or compile the limits which law has placed on expression.
A group of specific boundaries has been stated this way: [30]

> Freedom of the press * * * means prior to publi-
> cation the absence of censorship, but following publi-
> cation, no prosecution for free expression other than
> on widely accepted principles of the general law of the
> jurisdiction, and the guaranty of non-interference with
> lawful circulation; abuse of such freedom, by means
> of defamation, violation of privacy, in some jurisdic-
> tions, interference with the administration of justice,
> or the government in the prosecution of war, in any at-
> tempt to overthrow the government by violent and un-
> lawful means, or non-conformance with post office or
> other administrative regulations, subjects the offend-
> ing individual or organization to the potentiality of
> legal controls.

In the sequel, the reader will meet most of these legal and
philosophical boundaries as they have been applied in specific
cases.

SEC. 4.   CONTROL BY THREE GOVERNMENT BRANCHES

**Pre-publication censorship and licensing of printed media have
ceased, but continue in application to other media in special
circumstances; all branches of government have powers of
control after publication.**

For 200 years, English printers presented their copy to church
or state authorities before setting it in type. The censor approved, disapproved, or modified the manuscript according to
his notions of what was legal and moral. As a further safeguard to the protection of the state or religion against attack,
printers were licensed in order that government could more
easily check on their orthodoxy and obedience.[31] This was control of expression in its classic forms: licensing and censorship

---

[29] Emery, Walter B., Broadcasting and Government (East Lansing, Mich.,
1961), Ch. 3.

[30] Thayer, Frank, Legal Control of the Press, 4th ed. (Brooklyn, 1962), pp.
89–90.

[31] Siebert, Fredrick S., Freedom of the Press in England, 1476–1776 (Urbana:
Univ. of Ill. Press, 1952), Chaps. 2, 12.

in advance of publication. It persisted in oppressive and cumbersome form through the Sixteenth and Seventeenth Centuries in England, and until the 1720's in the American colonies.

Freedom from the censor and licensor—urged by John Milton in 1644 and made real by Parliament in 1695—was basic to the American statesmen who wrote the First Amendment, adopted in 1791. For the printed media today, censorship and licensing have all but vanished, existing more as a theoretical possibility under the law than as an actuality.[32] For movies, however, carefully drawn ordinances providing for previewing and cutting by the censor before public showing, have been held to be constitutional under the First Amendment.

And in a special application, licensing by government administrative agency applies to all broadcasters. Frequencies for access to the public ear, as we have seen, are limited in number. After years of intolerable overcrowding of desirable wave-bands, switching at will from one frequency to another by many stations, and conditions that could only be acknowledged as chaotic, the Federal Radio Act of 1927 provided that government would choose among applicants, licensing the chosen. Censorship, however, was specifically prohibited by the same Act.

While the censor and licenser were ejected from the realm of printing in the United States more than two centuries ago, the state retained the procedure of prosecution in the courts for criminal words. On the theory that the state had the right to preserve itself, the crime of seditious libel—illegal verbal attack on government—was recognized in the late Eighteenth Century and again in the Twentieth. The Christian religion was protected by blasphemy statutes. Breach of the peace is punishable under the criminal libel law, and so is defamation. The moral order is the "social good" presumably protected by the threat of punishment under the obscenity statutes. Where there is a clear and present danger that criticism of the courts or comment on a pending case will harm the process of justice, an action for criminal contempt of court may be brought.

It is the court action, of course, by which most control of speech and press ultimately takes place, and in addition to actions for criminal words, civil actions are many in which one citizen's use of words brings him into conflict with another citizen's rights. To preserve his reputation, the citizen may bring a suit for libel or slander against a newspaper or broadcasting station that has defamed him. Or he may sue for violation of copyright and seek an injunction against further violation, or for invasion of privacy.

[32] Near v. State of Minn. ex rel. Olson, 283 U.S. 697, 51 S.Ct. 625 (1931).

Major actions in the courts have confronted all mass media charged with attempts to monopolize or restrain trade, under the anti-trust laws. State laws provide for prosecution for fraudulent or unfair advertising practices. All commercial media of communication are subject to economic regulation, and general laws apply as much to the mass media, as to any business: labor laws, tax laws, health and safety ordinances, contracts, workmen's compensation—these and many others are in full effect for the newspaper as for the merchant.

Along with criminal and civil actions in the courts, legal restraint is applied by way of administrative agencies and the executive branch, most notably the Federal Communications Commission, the Federal Trade Commission, and the Post Office. We have already seen the FCC's power to license, to discontinue a license, or refuse renewal. The FTC monitors and investigates complaints about advertising, and when it finds evidence in advertising of unfair trade practices or fraudulence, may order a halt or bring an action in the courts. The Post Office Department regulates the format of printed communications that are to be mailed, rejects material that advertises lotteries, and on some occasions interrupts delivery of periodicals or other printed material.

Congress and the state legislatures, of course, are the main source of the laws which the courts, executive branch, and administrative agencies interpret or apply. The common law, established by judges in England through centuries of making and following precedent and adopted in many aspects by the American courts, also continues to furnish rules and principles in such fields as libel and slander, but more and more is replaced by legislative statutes. The legislative branch, it should be added, has a little-used direct control of the press at its disposal—the power to cite for contempt, for example when a newsman refuses to answer questions put to him by a congressional investigating committee.

Every branch of the government, at all levels, contributes thus to legal control of the mass media, but at the same time, each branch may contribute to freedom of expression. The courts and administrative agencies issue decisions that protect and uphold free speech and press, as well as decisions that limit it. Legislative acts may provide punishment for criminal words, but they also state protections which bar prosecutions. All branches of government deny public access to certain kinds of information, but federal and state laws, as well as court decisions, declare that public policy demands that secrecy be the exception, not the rule. Law facilitates expression as well as restraining it.

HISTORICAL BACKGROUND

The delicate balance between control and freedom of expression under the law has been most violently disrupted, over the centuries, when government has sought to arm or protect itself against attack by the press. Libertarians have viewed struggles for freedom of expression as crucial when government, acting in its own interest, has been the press' adversary. This is not to minimize struggles over control stemming from sources other than government's acting in its own behalf. Major battles have involved civil suits for damages brought by citizens against the media. Major contests have settled principles of freedom and control where government has taken the part of the public against the press, as in prosecutions of the media for monopolizing and restraint of trade. To view the clash between freedom and control in its most basic and often most dramatic form, however, is to examine the head-on confrontation when government believes itself threatened by the press and acts to bring it in check. Elemental aspects of the growth of political liberty are accentuated in this collision. The historical context develops the story best.

SEC. 5. SEVENTEENTH CENTURY ENGLAND

John Milton's thought and contentious martyrs' action helped unshackle printing; insistent printers' economic demands were the main factor in the death of licensing and censorship.

Stephen Daye, the first American colonial printer, pulled his first impressions from a hand press while the authoritarianism of divine right monarchy was still strong in the mother country. The year was 1638, the place was Harvard College, and the work was "The Freeman's Oath," approved for printing by the theocracy of Massachusetts Bay colony which had no more concept of freedom of the press than did Charles I who ruled in

London.　Yet by the time the first colonial newspaper appeared some 65 years later, major battles and major ideas had intruded upon the intricate network of press control in England, and the tiny group of American printers which began to grow in number after 1700 owed much to their brothers of the press and to contentious speakers across the Atlantic.　Advance toward freedom of the press, unthinkable in Seventeenth-Century America, had occurred in England and had saved the Eighteenth-Century colonial printers some of the hard work and pain of breaking free of authority.

The ingenious system of control established in the Sixteenth Century by the Tudor monarchs, Henry VIII and Elizabeth I, and perpetuated by the Stuart kings of the Seventeenth century, had largely disappeared by the close of England's Glorious Revolution of 1689.　Gone was the Stationers Company policing of the printers of England, first required by Elizabeth in return for economic protection, monopolies, and privileges for this printing guild's members.　The arbitrary Courts of the Star Chamber and the High Commission had died amid rejoicing.　Torture for criminal offenses, officially at least, was over.　Weakened and about to collapse was the system of licensing and censorship in advance of publication; the demands of business-oriented printers for release from its strictures, and the impossibility of managing the surveillance as the number of printers and the reading needs of the public grew, had more to do with the death of the system than did the high principle of Milton's *Areopagitica*.　Licensing and censorship in England died in 1695 when the House of Commons refused to renew the law for it.[1]

There was much left in the art and craft of government to overcome before a broad liberty would be accomplished.　Criminal prosecutions for sedition would thrive through the next century and beyond.　Control of newspapers and magazines through taxes would be tried repeatedly by Queen Anne and her successors.　Parliament would punish speakers and printers for contempt of its august stature, and would continue to refuse access to newsmen seeking to report it.　Yet this robust and oppressive body of restrictive instruments, available to the law for keeping printers in line, was hardly the equal of its predecessors.　American colonial printers and newsmen would face all these remaining controls, and also, for a time, the persistence in the colonial setting of some of those that England had shed.　They would

---

[1] Siebert, Fredrick S., Freedom of the Press in England 1476–1776 (Urbana: Univ. of Ill. Press, 1952).　This is the fullest and best-ordered treatment of the instruments of control.　See especially parts 2 and 4.

also be spared many of the grim restrictions of absolute monarchy.

A detailed account of the advance toward the relative freedom of the Eighteenth Century in England is beyond the scope of this work. But some Seventeenth Century English names, some ideas and drifts in government and society, must be accounted for. America took her law and her ideas of government largely from England.

The base of national authority was broadened somewhat when Parliament asserted its supremacy over the power residing in the individual monarch, with the Glorious Revolution and its Bill of Rights. William and Mary came to the throne of England in a position subordinate to Parliament; their predecessors for two centuries had acknowledged themselves subordinate only to God. Representing a few people who elected them, members of the Commons had some responsibility to a constituency, even though universal suffrage was centuries away. The Commons, thus, held new power and responsibility in relation to a segment of the public that chose it.[2] This may be seen as a step on the way to the ascendancy of the public in a self-governing society. A century or more later, the constituency—the public—would hold the position of ascendancy. The relationship may be seen in terms of a people's right of expression as well as in their power to elect and remove their officials:[3]

> Two different views may be taken of the relation between rulers and their subjects. If the ruler is regarded as the superior of the subject, as being by the nature of his position presumably wise and good, the rightful ruler and guide of the whole population, it must necessarily follow that it is wrong to censure him openly; that even if he is mistaken his mistakes should be pointed out with the utmost respect, and that whether mistaken or not no censure should be cast upon him likely or designed to diminish his authority.
>
> If on the other hand the ruler is regarded as the agent and servant, and the subject as the wise and good master who is obliged to delegate his power to the so-called ruler because being a multitude he cannot use it himself, it is obvious that this sentiment must be reversed. Every member of the public who censures the ruler

[2] Taswell-Langmead, T. P., English Constitutional History (London: Street & Maxwell, Limited, 1929), 9th ed. by A. L. Poole, pp. 594–599.

[3] Stephen, Sir James Fitzjames, History of the Criminal Law of England. (London: Macmillan, 1883), II, p. 299.

for the time being exercises in his own person the right which belongs to the whole of which he forms a part.

He is finding fault with his servant. If others think differently they can take the other side of the dispute, and the utmost that can happen is that the servant will be dismissed and another put in his place, or perhaps that the arrangements of the household will be modified.

The new structure of government, then, implied that behind the supremacy of Parliament lay at least a segment of the public, empowered to choose new governors in the Commons if it wished. And thorny, difficult men had been pressing throughout the Seventeenth Century—and indeed before—for recognition that members of the public ought to have this kind of power as well as its necessary concomitant, freedom of expression. It was part of the widespread re-casting of thought in the Western world that came to be known as the Enlightenment and the age of faith in man's reason.

John Milton's matchless prose is a starting point in the thinking of Seventeenth Century England about increased freedom of expression. Others of his time, less known today, sought a wider freedom that he; others never violated that which they advocated as he did in accepting a position as a censor of the printed word. Others' actions were more important than his arguments in bringing the death of censorship in 1695.[4] Yet Milton's *Areopagitica*, written in 1644, was to serve as a standard and banner for centuries to come in England's and America's annals of free expression.

Milton wrote just after Charles I had been driven from his throne in England's Civil War. He wanted a divorce, and had written a tract that he hoped would lead to authority's relaxing of the strict legal barriers forbidding it. Under deep official disapproval for publishing it without license, Milton addressed to Parliament a plea for unlicensed printing, the *Areopagitica*. Wide in its sweep, it argued that licensing was unworkable, was an indignity to those engaged in it, and was socially undesirable because of its strictures on the spread of truth. Let falsehood grapple with truth, he argued: "Who ever knew Truth put to the worse in a free and open encounter?"[5]

Milton's position on any scale measuring freedom today would be far from liberal. His argument was made within the frame-

---

[4] Siebert, pp. 195–197, 260–263; Levy, Leonard, Legacy of Suppression (Cambridge: Harvard Univ. Press, 1960), pp. 93–105.

[5] Milton, John, Areopagitica (Chicago: Henry Regnery Co., 1949), p. 58.

work of religious freedom; he was a Puritan, and religion was a central issue in the nation's Civil War. He would not tolerate Catholicism in his argument for freedom of expression. Nor would he permit atheism to have the freedom he sought. Yet viewed in the light of his time, his work was a clear advance over the prevailing authoritarianism of the Stuarts and over that of Parliament as well. Licensing, of course, was perpetuated through the life of the Long Parliament and Cromwell's reign, and lasted with short interruption from the Stuart Restoration of 1660 to 1695.

While Milton pleaded, others in England defied authority in their insistence on speaking. Most of them sectarians of Protestant stripe, their troubles stemmed from their intransigence in attacking the Romanism of which they suspected the Stuart kings and in propagating their own faiths. The law of seditious libel, the law of treason, and the procedures of the arbitrary Court of the Star Chamber were used against them, and some suffered maiming and torture.

William Prynn's book, *Histrio-Mastix*, propounded a strict Puritanism in behavior: he execrated such pastimes of people as dancing, play-going, hunting, Christmas-keeping and dressing up the house with green-ivy, and public festivals. He was brought before the Star Chamber on charges of seditious libel, his attack on government being inferred from Prynn's writing, shortly after the Queen had taken part in a pastoral play at Somerset House, that lewd women and whores were accustomed to act in plays. He was fined £10,000 and given life imprisonment, in addition to being pilloried, and having his ears cropped off.[6] During the year 1637, two other men, Dr. John Bastwick and Henry Burton, were handled similarly by the Star Chamber for their attacks on the Pope. Mob demonstrations against authority followed a public sentencing; Prynn was released by the Long Parliament on the ground that his trial had been illegal, after the abolition in 1641 of the Court of the Star Chamber.[7]

Treason in England had been defined by law since 1352, in Edward III's time. It included "compassing" or imagining the king's death, levying war against the king or giving aid and comfort to his enemies. Writing was included as part of compassing the king's death, and in 1663 at the session of Old Bailey, printer Twyn was indicted and tried for this crime by printing a book called *A Treatise on the Execution of Justice*. The book held

---

[6] 3 Howell's State Trials 561 (1632–3).

[7] Siebert, pp. 123–125.

to the view that the ruler is accountable to the people, and that the people may take up arms against a king and his family and put the king to death if he refuses accountability. John Twyn did not write the book, but he refused to say who did. The court's vengeance and the law's brutality were in the pronouncement of sentence: [8]

> [T]he country have found you guilty; therefore the judgment of the court is, and the court doth award, "that you be led back to the place from whence you came and from thence to be drawn upon an hurdle to the place of execution; and there you shall be hanged by the neck, and being alive, shall be cut down, and your privy-members shall be cut off, your entrails shall be taken out of your body, and you living, the same to be burnt before your eyes; your head to be cut off, your body to be divided into four quarters and your head and quarters to be disposed of at the pleasure of the king's majesty. And the Lord have mercy upon your soul."

Thirty years later, William Anderton printed books that were called treasonable in their intent to incite rebellion and the return to the throne of James II. Anderton refused to name the author, and was hanged in 1693. [9]

Martyrs to the principle of free expression had their impact and spokesmen for a new philosophy such as Milton and John Locke had theirs. Yet it was the independent printing and book-selling trade itself, according to the scholar Fredrick S. Siebert, that forced the end of licensing and censorship. Economic goals and profit were the central interest of the growing numbers of these tradesmen in the late Seventeenth Century; hedged and bound by the Regulation of Printing Act, cut out of the privileges still granted guild printers of the Stationers Company, they sought relief from Parliament. Unsuccessful in 1692, they continued pressing, and with help from people of power including philosopher John Locke, won their way in 1695. The House of Commons, offering a long list of reasons for its refusal to renew the Printing Act, focused on the restraint of the trades as the main factor, saying nothing about the principles of freedom of the press. [10] The classic instrument for press control was dead in England.

[8] 6 Howell's State Trials 513 (1663).

[9] 12 Howell's State Trials 1246 (1693).

[10] Siebert, pp. 260–263.

SEC. 6.   EIGHTEENTH CENTURY AMERICA

Colonial assemblies' control of the press persisted after governors' and courts' control was neutralized; in spite of the adoption of the First Amendment to the Constitution by the new nation, prosecutions for seditious libel rose again under the Alien and Sedition Acts.

American colonial printers never had to contend with the searches and seizures of a Stationers Company empowered with police functions. The courts they faced were scarcely the sinister and threatening bodies that the Courts of the Star Chamber and the High Commission were in the homeland. The punishments they received for illegal printing were far short of mutilation, life imprisonment, or hanging. Yet the first newspaper printers had to contend with licensing and censorship as a remnant of the English system, for some 30 years after the Commons rejected its renewal in 1695.

Newsman Benjamin Harris of Boston managed in 1690 to print his single, famous issue of *Publick Occurrences, Both Foreign and Domestick* without the authorities' stopping him. But the licensing power of the Massachusetts Bay authorities prevented another issue, and it was not until 1704 that there was a second attempt at a newspaper. This, by John Campbell also of Boston, was licensed, subsidized, sterilized, and blessed by the colonial government, and Campbell never offended. Governors licensed by order of their monarch in England, who was supreme in colonial affairs, and not until the 1720's did they yield the power in the face of reality: There had been no Regulation of Printing Act in England for about 30 years, and there was no power in the monarch to enforce the observance of licensing.[11] Barring Ben Harris, it was the first bold newspaperman in the colonies, James Franklin, who defied the demand that he submit to licensing. Though this printer of the *New England Courant* was made to suffer twice in jail for his belittling of authority, licensing had to be acknowledged dead after his release in 1723. The direct power over print held by the Governor and his Council was neutralized.[12]

Next in order to face the challenge of a contentious printer was the power of the courts to try for seditious libel, the crime

---

[11] Duniway, Clyde A., The Development of Freedom of the Press in Massachusetts (Cambridge: Harvard Univ.Press, 1906), pp. 104–105.

[12] Ibid.

of criticizing government. This instrument for control had advanced to major proportions in England in the late Seventeenth and early Eighteenth Centuries. At least four colonial Americans faced sedition actions for printed words before the most celebrated criminal trial in the colonial period occurred in 1735. This was the trial of John Peter Zenger, printer of the *New York Weekly Journal* whose work was given much to the cause of undermining Governor William Cosby. Courage was the ingredient that Zenger brought to the attack; he had neither the schooling nor the knowledge to launch and sustain the political assault planned and executed by James Alexander of the powerful Lewis Morris faction which opposed the grasping and autocratic Cosby.[13] What Zenger had to fear was going to jail for the attacks that labeled Cosby a tyrant and oppressor of the colony.

And to jail Zenger went in late 1734, under an information filed by the governor's attorney general after fruitless efforts to get a grand jury to indict the printer. For eight months he awaited trial for seditious libel, while Alexander managed to keep the Journal printing and the campaign against Cosby simmering. And Alexander, disbarred by Chief Justice De Lancey (a Cosby appointee), turned to lawyer Andrew Hamilton of Philadelphia as the best man to plead Zenger's case.

The original "Philadelphia lawyer," Hamilton had built a reputation as the ablest attorney in the colonies. The dignity of age, his utter confidence, and his bold advocacy that the court discard old patterns of thinking about sedition came to bear in an irresistible way with jurors already sympathetic to Zenger's cause. The law of sedition had long held that the defendant was not to be permitted to plead that his offending words against government were true; the truth, it was held, only aggravated the offense, for it was more likely than falsehood to cause the target to seek violent revenge and breach the community's peace. Furthermore, the law had given the jury only a minor role in a sedition trial: its job was to decide whether the accused had, indeed, printed the words; it was up to the court to decide whether they were illegal words.

Jockeying with De Lancey, Hamilton urged the jury to recognize truth as a defense for Zenger, and argued that the jury should decide "the law"—the libelousness of the words—as well as the fact of printing. Blocked by the judge from pursuing

---

[13] Katz, Stanley (ed.), A Brief Narrative of the Case and Trial of John Peter Zenger (Cambridge: Harvard Univ.Press, 1963), pp. 2–9.

these points far, he shifted his tactic and went to the importance of permitting men to criticize their governments: [14]

> Men who injure and oppress the people under their administration provoke them to cry out and complain, and then make that very complaint the foundation for new oppressions and prosecutions. I wish I could say there were no instances of this kind. But to conclude, the question before the Court and you, gentlemen of the jury, is not of small or private concern; it is not the cause of a poor printer, nor of New York alone, which you are trying. No! it may, in its consequences, affect every freeman that lives under a British government, on the main of America. It is the best cause; it is the cause of liberty; and I make no doubt but your upright conduct, this day, will not only entitle you to the love and esteem of your fellow citizens, but every man who prefers freedom to a life of slavery, will bless and honor you as men who have baffled the attempts of tyranny; and by an impartial and uncorrupt verdict, have laid a noble foundation for securing to ourselves, our posterity, and our neighbors, that to which nature and the laws of our country have given us a right—the liberty—both of exposing and opposing arbitrary power in those parts of the world at least, by speaking and writing truth.

Hamilton ended his plea in an emotion-charged courtroom; De Lancey delivered a confusing charge to the jury, which retired to deliberate; and in a short time the jury emerged with the "not guilty" verdict. There were celebrations in the streets that night; there were printings and re-printings of the Hamilton plea for years to come, more even in England than in the colonies; and the court trial for seditious libel was finished for the colonial period as an instrument for control of the press. Not for 40 years or more would it be used again in America.[15]

It was the elected Assembly, or lower house of the colonial legislature, that was the most successful and most active force in official control of Eighteenth Century colonial printers. Jealous of its powers under the view that it was Parliament in miniature, and unwilling to have its acts criticized, this agency of government disciplined printer after printer. Even as it emerged as the main check on the powers of the Crown's gov-

[14] Ibid., p. 99.

[15] Nelson, Harold L., Seditious Libel in Colonial America, 3 Am.Journ. of Legal History 160 (1959).

ernors, even as it showed itself as the seat of government support for the movement for independence, the Assembly demonstrated its aversion to popular criticism. Its instrument for control was the citation for contempt ("breach of privilege"), and it haled a long line of printers before it for their "seditious" attacks on its performance. The legislative contempt citation was a legislative sedition action.

Levy has demonstrated the relative power and activity of the Assemblies in respect to the press. Up and down the seaboard, printer after printer was brought to the legislative bar, there to be forced to kneel and beg the pardon of the stern law-makers, swear that he meant no harm by his writings, and accept rebuke or imprisonment. James Franklin's irony put him in jail; he had speculated that the Massachusetts government might get around to outfitting a ship to pursue a pirate "sometime this month, wind and weather permitting." New Yorkers James Parker and William Weyman were jailed for an article on the poverty of Orange and Ulster counties; the Assembly construed it as a reflection upon their stewardship. These were only a few actions among many, and they continued to the eve of the Revolutionary War in some colonies.[16]

The great article of faith that heads America's commitment to free expression was written in 1791 by men who had not yet thought through all that "free speech and press" implies. The founders stated in the First Amendment to the Constitution that "Congress shall make no law * * * abridging freedom of speech, or of the press * * *." while still arguing over precisely what they meant by the words. Behind them lay the great pamphleteering and newspapering that had done much to bring the colonists to revolt against the Mother country; the founders were convinced that the printed word had been indispensable in bringing down the most powerful nation on earth. Yet the axioms of centuries were with them; it still seemed to many that no government could stand if it could not at some point punish its critics, and their new government was meant to last. Some words surely were illegal. Not, perhaps, in the realm of religion, where James Madison, among others, argued an unlimited freedom to speak and write; but could sedition be given such scope? It was the party of Thomas Jefferson that gave an answer, in the debates and sequel of the Alien and Sedition Acts of 1798–1800.

The Acts were written at a time of high public and official alarm. With France and England in conflict through the 1790's,

16 Levy, pp. 20–63.

America had been pulled by both toward war. The Republicans —Jefferson's party—had favored France, while the Federalists sided with England. Angered at Jay's Treaty of 1794 with England, which she felt placed America on the side of her enemy, France had undertaken the raiding of American shipping. America's envoys, sent to France to negotiate a settlement, were faced with a demand for an American war loan to France, and a bribe of a quarter-million dollars. This unofficial demand as a price for negotiations was revealed to Americans as the famous "X, Y, Z Affair." Now most of America was incensed; President John Adams called for war preparation, which his Federalist Congress set about furnishing in 1797.[17]

The Republicans, though suffering heavy political losses in the nation's war fever, did not abandon their support of France. Stigmatized in the refusal to do so, associated by the Federalists with the recent French Revolution and its Terror, and beleaguered on all sides for their continued opposition to Britain, the Republicans were in deep trouble. And in this context, the Federalist Congress passed the Alien and Sedition Acts as measures to control opposition to America's war policy and to the Federalist majority party.

It was the Sedition Act that struck most lethally at opposition and at the Republicans. The Act made it a crime to publish or utter false, scandalous, and malicious criticism of the President, Congress, or the government with the intent to defame them or bring them into disrepute.[18]

Fourteen indictments were brought under the Act, all against Republican newspapermen and publicists, and all 14 resulted in convictions.[19] The first action put Rep. Matthew Lyon in jail for four months and cost him a fine of $1,000. He had implied that under President Adams, the Executive branch showed "an unbounded thirst for ridiculous pomp, foolish adulation, and selfish avarice," and that the public welfare was "swallowed up in a continual grasp for power." Anthony Haswell, Republican editor of the (Bennington) *Vermont Gazette*, came to Lyon's defense while the latter was in prison. He wrote that Lyon was held by "the oppressive hand of usurped power," and said that the federal marshal who held him had subjected him to indignities that might be expected of a "hard-hearted savage." Haswell's fine was $200 and his term in federal prison two months.[20]

---

[17] Smith, James M., Freedom's Fetters (Ithaca: Cornell Univ.Press, 1956), Chap. 2. This is the leading work on the Alien and Sedition Acts.

[18] Ibid., Chap. 6.

[19] Ibid., p. 185.

[20] Each trial is treated in Smith, Chaps. 11–17.

Its back to the wall under the attempt of the Federalists to proscribe it as a party of disloyalty and subversion, the Republican Party put forth spokesmen who declared that the idea of sedition was unacceptable to a self-governing society. The Acts, they said, were unconstitutional in making it a crime to criticize the President and government. No matter that the Acts permitted the defenses for which Andrew Hamilton had argued in defending Zenger: truth was of little use in defending opinions (how prove the truth of an opinion?); and jury power to find the law could be circumvented by judges in various ways. A people, they argued, cannot call itself free unless it is superior to its government, unless it can have unrestricted right of discussion. No natural right of the individual, they contended in the Lockean framework, can be more important than free expression. They rested their case on their belief in reason as the central characteristic of men, and on the people's position of ascendancy over government.[21] The radical Thomas Cooper, friend of Joseph Priestley, dissected one by one the arguments for permitting a sedition power in government.[22] Calmly and systematically, lawyer Tunis Wortman worked out the philosophical groundwork for unlimited freedom in the fullest statement of the group.[23] Madison, St. George Tucker, Albert Gallatin and others drove home the arguments.

The unpopularity of the Alien and Sedition Acts and outrage at the prosecutions of Republican printers helped defeat the Federalist Party and President John Adams in 1800. President Jefferson was committed to letting the Acts lapse, and they died in early 1801. The nation would see no federal peacetime sedition act again for 140 years. Furthermore, the alternative route of using the common law as a basis for federal sedition actions was closed to the government only a few years later. The Supreme Court ruled in cases of 1812 and 1816 that federal courts had been given no authority over common-law crimes by the Constitution, and that whatever question there had been about the matter had been settled by public opposition to such jurisdiction.[24]

[21] Levy, Chap. 6.

[22] Political Essays (Phila.: Printed for R. Campbell, 1800), pp. 71–88.

[23] Treatise Concerning Political Enquiry, and the Liberty of the Press (New York: Printed by George Forman, 1800).

[24] U. S. v. Hudson and Goodwin, 11 U.S. (7 Cranch.) 32 (1812); U. S. v. Coolidge, 14 U.S. (1 Wheaton) 415 (1816).

SEC. 7. WAR POWER, CONTEMPT OF COURT, AND CRIMINAL LIBEL

The federal government in the Nineteenth Century controlled its critics under martial law during the Civil War; states used criminal libel and contempt of court actions into the mid-Twentieth Century.

The fear and hatred of French revolutionary doctrine had been real factors in the passage of the Alien and Sedition Acts. Different fears, different hatreds led to suppressive laws in the South about a generation later, when states began passing laws to silence Abolitionists. The anti-slavery drive, coupled with incidents such as Nat Turner's slave rebellion, caused paroxysms of Southern fear that their "peculiar institution" and the shape of society and government would be subverted and destroyed. Laws were passed making it a crime to advocate the abolition of slavery or to argue that owners "have no property" in slaves, and denying abolitionist literature access to the mails.[25] The suppression of anti-slavery argument became almost total in most of the South by 1850.

When the Civil War came, the crisis in the North was accentuated by the anti-war, anti-Lincoln "Copperhead" press.[26] Savage attacks on government from major newspapers of general circulation became commonplace. Persistent demands to stop fighting, violent language denouncing the North's war aims, and hammering assaults on Lincoln went on month after month. Angry citizens mobbed Copperhead papers of the North time after time. Federal conspiracy laws were passed. Grand juries urged prosecution or suppression of newspapers. But the legal suppressions that took place were accomplished under martial law and under the President's extraordinary wartime powers.[27]

General Ambrose E. Burnside, Commanding General of the Department of the Ohio, issued General Order No. 38, warning Copperheads. Clement L. Vallandigham, a leading Copperhead newspaper owner, kept up his anti-war theme in the *Dayton* (O.) *Empire*. He was arrested, tried by the military, and sentenced

---

[25] Three Virginia laws passed between 1832 and 1848 are in Nelson, pp. 173–178.

[26] The best account of the Copperheads is Klement, Frank, The Copperheads in the Middle West (Chicago: Univ. of Chicago Press, 1960).

[27] American Annual Cyclopaedia and Register of Important Events (D. Appleton and Company, 1867), I, pp. 328–330; Chafee, Zechariah, Jr., Free Speech in the United States (Cambridge: Harvard University Press, 1954), pp. 36–37, 146.

to prison.　President Lincoln intervened and changed the sentence to banishment behind the Confederate lines.[28]　Later in 1863, Burnside issued General Order No. 84, directing the suppression of the *Chicago Times*.　Lincoln immediately stopped the Burnside action: [29]

War Department, Washington, June 1, 1863

Maj. Gen. A. E. Burnside,
Commanding Department of the Ohio.

General　*　*　*　the President has been informed that you have suppressed the publication or circulation of the Chicago Times in your department.　He directs me to say that in his judgment it would be better for you to take an early occasion to revoke that order.　The irritation produced by such acts is in his opinion likely to do more harm than the publication would do.　The Government approves of your motives and desires to give you cordial and efficient support.　But while military movements are left to your judgment, upon administrative questions such as the arrest of civilians and the suppression of newspapers not requiring immediate action the President desires to be previously consulted.

Edwin M. Stanton,
Secretary of War.

In 1864, the immense forbearance of Lincoln in regard to the Copperheads was finally stretched beyond limit.　The *New York World* and the *New York Journal of Commerce,* anti-administration newspapers both, published the text of a presumed presidential proclamation announcing a new draft of 400,000 men for the war.　It was a bogus document; the two newspapers were the victims of a hoax.　But the government had no knowledge that the newspapers had been victimized, and it knew that such news at this stage of the war would cause intense opposition, probably riots and violence.　Lincoln ordered the arrest of the editors and proprietors of the two newspapers, and the occupation by the military of their offices.　The manager and operators of the Independent Telegraph Co. in New York also were arrested and their office seized.　The arrests were made May 18; by May 20 reporter Joseph Howard of the *New York Times* was identified as the perpetrator of the hoax and the

---

[28] Emery, Edwin, The Press and America (New York: Prentice-Hall, Inc., 1962), pp. 292–293.

[29] War of the Rebellion, Official Records of the Union and Confederate Armies, Series 2, Vol. 5, pp. 723–724.

World and Journal of Commerce men were released. Howard confessed that he had "planted" the fake proclamation in the hope of profiting from the stock market reaction to the announcement.[30]

Besides the Sedition Act and extraordinary military powers in wartime, the federal government possessed in its early years another potential control over criticism of its officials. This was the power of judges to punish their critics for contempt of court. There was no question that judges were masters over all that occurred in their courtrooms, and might cite, try, and convict those who interfered with the administration of justice in the presence of the court. But it was less clear that a newspaper attack on a judge, especially one delivered while the case under attack was pending, might warrant a criminal contempt citation. Did such out-of-court attack actually interfere with justice? English precedent was weak for punishment of an out-of-court ("constructive") contempt.

Before 1800, a few state-court cases had brought home to newspapermen the danger of attacking judges. Soon after 1800, both Pennsylvania and New York passed laws curbing their judges' contempt power over printed criticism. In 1831, Congress followed suit. The impetus for its action came from a determined attorney, Luke Lawless, who sought for four years the impeachment of Federal Judge James H. Peck. With deep financial interests in questionable claims of speculators to lands once part of Spain's Upper Louisiana, Lawless had attacked Peck in newspaper articles for the judge's decision placing the claims in doubt. He delineated at length "some of the principal errors" of Peck's decision. The judge cited him for contempt, tried him, and punished him by suspending him from practice for eighteen months. Lawless asked Congress to impeach Peck, and though it took years to accomplish the impeachment, he succeeded. Almost endless debate in the Senate aired every phase of the subject of punishmnt for constructive contempt. Its resemblance to sedition actions, in the eyes of many of the senators, was striking. Finally the Senate voted, exonerating Peck by the narrowest of margins.[31]

But Congress wanted no more punishment of the press for criticism of federal judges. Only a month after the impeachment, it passed an act which said that federal judges might punish only for that misbehavior which took place "in the pres-

---

[30] Ibid., Series 3, Vol. 4, pp. 386–395.

[31] Stansbury, Arthur J., Report of the Trial of James H. Peck (Boston: Hilliard, Gray and Company, 1833).

ence of the * * * courts, or so near thereto as to obstruct
the administration of justice." [32]

Many states' judges were far less ready to permit criticism.
The main line of cases from the mid-Nineteenth Century until
1941 found judges asserting their "immemorial power" to cite
and try for newspaper criticism that took place far from their
courtrooms, as well as for misbehavior in the courtroom.[33]
They were upheld by the Supreme Court of the United States in
two early Twentieth-Century cases, Patterson v. State of Colorado ex rel. Attorney General, and Toledo Newspaper Co. v.
U. S. [34] But in 1941, the Supreme Court looked afresh at the
judicial contempt power. It ruled in Bridges v. State of California [35] that words must present more than a "tendency" to
obstruct justice before there may be a contempt citation; they
must present, rather, a clear and present danger to justice.
Since then, contempt convictions for news media's comment
have been rare.

If it was in the states, then, that the contempt power over the
press was developed and wielded, it was also in the states that
sedition actions persisted after the federal government vacated
the field in 1801. By and large, the Jeffersonians had somewhat warily accepted this power when held by the states.[36]
Supposedly, citizens could control their local, state affairs and
check tendencies toward oppression within that sphere much
more easily than they could check a remote, centralized national
government. Under the common law and under statutes, the
new states provided that libel could be a crime whether it was
aimed at plain citizens or government men. That the laws went
under the name "criminal libel" laws instead of under the rubric
of the hated "seditious libel" made them no less effective as
tools for prosecution of those who attacked officials.

The states drew up safeguards against some of the harshest
features of the old English law of libel. The principles that Andrew Hamilton pleaded for in defending Zenger, and that the
Alien and Sedition Acts had provided, emerged as important ones
early in the Nineteenth Century as states embarked upon prosecutions. Truth was established as a defense in criminal libel
actions, and juries were permitted to find the law under grow-

[32] 4 U.S. Statutes 487.

[33] Nelles, Walter, and Carol Weiss King, Contempt by Publication in the
United States, 28 Col.Law R. 401–431, 525–562 (1928).

[34] Respectively, 205 U.S. 454, 27 S.Ct. 556 (1907), and 247 U.S. 402, 38 S.Ct.
560 (1918).

[35] 314 U.S. 252, 62 S.Ct. 190 (1941).

[36] Levy, pp. 264–267.

ing numbers of state constitutions and statutes as the century progressed. A celebrated early case in New York encouraged the spread. It stemmed from a paragraph reprinted by Federalist editor Harry Croswell from the *New York Evening Post* attacking President Thomas Jefferson: [37]

> Jefferson paid Callender [a Republican editor] for calling Washington a traitor, a robber, and a perjurer; for calling Adams a hoary-headed old incendiary, and for most grossly slandering the private characters of men who he well knew to be virtuous.

The great Federalist leader, Alexander Hamilton, took up Croswell's case in 1804 after he had been convicted of criminal libel in a jury trial in which he had not been permitted to show the truth of his charge. Hamilton argued that "the liberty of the press consists of the right to publish with impunity truth with good motives for justifiable ends though reflecting on government, magistracy, or individuals." This, of course, made the intent of the publisher crucial. He also urged that the jury be allowed to find both the law and the facts of the case. He lost, the appeals court being evenly divided; but the result was so repugnant to people and lawmakers that the New York Legislature in 1805 passed a law embracing the principles that Hamilton urged.

In the states' adoption of Hamilton's formula (a few, indeed, made truth a defense no matter what the motives of the writer) there was an implied rejection of an ancient justification for punishing libel as a crime against the state. The old reasoning was that the truer the disparaging words, the more likely the insulted person to seek revenge and resort to violence, breaching the peace. If the words were false, the logic ran, they could be demonstrated as such, and the defamed would be more easily mollified. Thus the legal aphorism of the Eighteenth Century: "the greater the truth, the greater the libel."

But once admit truth to a protected position in the law, once make it public policy that the public needs to know the truth, and the aphorism crumbles. As states accepted truth as a defense in libel actions, they in effect undermined breach of the peace as an excuse for punishing libel. Few statutes or constitutions retained the possibility of breach of the peace as a basis for criminality in libel.[38]

Criminal libel actions were few through most of the Nineteenth Century. They surged in number in the 1880's and held

---

[37] People v. Croswell, 3 Johnson's Cases 337 (N.Y.1804).

[38] See below, Chap. 3.

at some 100 reported cases per decade for 30 years or more before going into a sharp decline after World War I. Not all, by any means, were brought for defamation of public officials in the pattern of seditious libel actions.[39] But criticism of police, governors, mayors, judges, prosecutors, sheriffs, and other government officials was the charge in scores of criminal libel cases.

Of all of them, the most famous by all odds was that stemming from the abortive attempt of President Theodore Roosevelt to punish the *New York World* and the *Indianapolis News* for charging deep corruption in the nation's purchase of the title to the Panama Canal from France. Enraged especially by the World and its publisher, Joseph Pulitzer, President Roosevelt delivered a special message to Congress. He charged that Pulitzer was responsible for libeling the United States Government, individuals in the government, and the "good name of the American people." He called it "criminal libel," but his angry words carried all the implications of sedition. He said of the articles and editorials: [40]

> In form, they are in part libels upon individuals
> * * *. But they are in fact wholly, and in form partly, a libel upon the United States Government. I do not believe we should concern ourselves with the particular individuals who wrote the lying and libelous editorials * * * or articles in the news columns. The real offender is Mr. Joseph Pulitzer, editor and proprietor of the World. While the criminal offense of which Mr. Pulitzer has been guilty is in form a libel upon individuals, the great injury done is in blackening the good name of the American people * * *. He should be prosecuted for libel by the governmental authorities * * *. The Attorney-General has under consideration the form in which the proceedings against Mr. Pulitzer shall be brought * * *.

For the charges brought against Pulitzer in federal court in New York, the indictment was quashed on grounds that the federal government did not have jurisdiction. The action was upheld by the United States Supreme Court. Charges against the *Indianapolis News,* also pushing the attack on the Panama Canal purchase, were brought before Judge A. B. Anderson who decided the case on its merits. The government sought to have News officials sent to Washington for trial. Judge Anderson

[39] Stevens, John D., et al., Criminal Libel as Seditious Libel, 43 Journalism Quar. 110 (1966); Leflar, Robert A., The Social Utility of the Criminal Law of Defamation, 34 Texas L.Rev. 984 (1956).

[40] House of Rep.Docs., 60 Cong., 2 Sess., § 1213 (Dec. 15, 1908), pp. 3–5.

Nelson & Teeter Mass Com.2d Ed. F.P.—3

said he had deep doubts that the newspaper articles were libelous, and thought they might be privileged as well as non-libelous. But it was on other grounds that he refused to send Newsmen to Washington for trial. He said that the Sixth Amendment governed, in guaranteeing trial in the state or district where the alleged crime was committed: [41]

> To my mind that man has read the history of our institutions to little purpose who does not look with grave apprehension upon the possibility of the success of a proceeding such as this. If the history of liberty means anything, if constitutional guaranties are worth anything, this proceeding must fail.
>
> If the prosecuting officers have the authority to select the tribunal, if there be more than one tribunal to select from, if the government has that power, and can drag citizens from distant states to the capital of the nation, there to be tried, then, as Judge Cooley says, this is a strange result of a revolution where one of the grievances complained of was the assertion of the right to send parties abroad for trial.
>
> The defendants will be discharged.

There is no indication that the failure of Roosevelt's action deterred lesser officials in state and municipal governments from bringing libel actions for words critical of them; the decline in number of criminal libel cases did not begin until a decade later.

What caused the rise and fall of prosecutions is not clear, but even the low incidence of cases that held after World War I was checked in 1964, when Garrison v. State of Louisiana [42] was decided by the United States Supreme Court.

Prosecuting attorney Jim Garrison of Orleans Parish, Louisiana, had attacked judges of the state for inattention to their judicial duties and laziness. He was charged and convicted of criminally libeling them. His case reached the Supreme Court, and there the prosecution for criminal libel was subjected to a new malice rule stated by the Court only a few months earlier in New York Times Co. v. Sullivan.[43] Criticism of public officials in their public acts, the Court said, is protected by the Constitution unless the prosecution can show that the criticism was made with malice. And it defined malice as knowledge by the pub-

---

[41] U. S. v. Smith, 173 F. 227 (D.C.Ind.1909).

[42] 379 U.S. 64, 85 S.Ct. 209 (1964).

[43] 376 U.S. 254, 84 S.Ct. 710 (1964).

lisher that the defamatory words were false, or reckless disregard of whether they were false or not.   Diverse and slippery definitions of malice of legal antiquity, and technical rules under which convictions had been gotten for generations, were reduced to harmlessness in criminal libel.   Garrison's conviction was reversed.

SEC. 8.   SEDITION IN THE TWENTIETH CENTURY

The urging of radical economic and political change, opposition to World War I, and the advocacy of violent overthrow of government were proscribed as criminal under sedition legislation of the Twentieth Century.

While seditious libel traveled under the disguise of criminal libel through the Nineteenth and into the mid-Twentieth Century, it also emerged uncloaked early in the 1900's.   Actions to punish verbal attacks on the form of government, on laws, and on government's conduct, found new life at the federal level some 100 years after they had been discredited by the Alien and Sedition Act prosecutions of 1798–1800.   The actions focused on a new radicalism, flourishing in the poverty and sweat-shop conditions of industrial cities and in the lumber and mining camps of the West.   Whether seeking an improved life for the deprived, driving for power, or fostering revolution, socialists, anarchists, and syndicalists advocated drastic change in the economic and political system.   Laws and criminal prosecutions rose to check their words.[44]

In the aftermath of the assassination of President William McKinley in 1901, the states of New York, New Jersey and Wisconsin passed laws against anarchists' advocating the destruction of existing government.   Congress passed the Immigration Act of 1903, barring from the country those who believed in or advocated the overthrow of the United States government by violence.   Industrial turbulence, the growth of the Industrial Workers of the World, the surge of right- and left-wing socialism, contributed to alarm in the nation.   And as the varied voices of drastic reform and radical change rose loud in the land, the coming of World War I increased their stridency: This, they insisted, was a "Capitalists' war," fostered and furthered for industrial profit.   By 1918, national alarm was increased by the victory of revolutionary communism in Russia.[45]

[44] Preston, William, Jr., Aliens and Dissenters, Federal Suppression of Radicals, 1903–1933 (Cambridge: Harvard Univ.Press, 1963).

[45] Ibid.;   Peterson, H. C., and Gilbert C. Fite, Opponents of War, 1917–1918 (Madison: Univ. of Wis.Press, 1957).

World War I brought a wave of legislation across the states to make criminal the advocacy of violent overthrow of government.   Yet it was the federal government's Espionage Act of 1917 and its amendment of 1918 to include sedition that put most muscle into prosecution for criminal words.   Foremost among proscribed and prosecuted statements were those that were construed to cause insubordination or disloyalty in the armed forces, or to obstruct enlistment or recruiting.[46]   Some 1,900 persons were prosecuted for speech, and possibly 100 newspapers and periodicals were barred from the mails.[47]   Polemics in pamphlet form, as well as books, also were the cause of prosecutions.

The best-known of the Socialist newspapers prosecuted under the Espionage Act were the *New York Call*, the *Masses*, also of New York, and the *Milwaukee Leader*.   In the last of these, editor Victor Berger had denounced the war, the United States government, and munitions makers.   Postmaster General Albert Burleson considered this the kind of opposition to the war forbidden by the Espionage Act, and excluded it from the mails as the Act provided.   Further, he said, the repeated attacks on the war effort in the Leader were evidence that it would continue doing the same in the future, and on these grounds, the Leader's second-class mail permit should be revoked.   He was upheld in his revocation of the permit by the United States Supreme Court, and the Leader was thus denied the low-rate mailing privilege from 1917 until after the war.[48]

Pamphleteers of the left were convicted under the Espionage Act and under state anarchy and sedition acts.   The famous case of Schenck v. U. S., in which Schenck was prosecuted for polemics that actually went to the matter of resisting the draft, brought Justice Oliver Wendell Holmes' articulation of the famous clear and present danger test: [49]

> We admit that in many places and in ordinary times the defendants in saying all that was said in the circular would have been within their constitutional rights.   But the character of every act depends upon the circumstances in which it was done * * *.   The question in every case is whether the words used are used in such circumstances and are of such a nature as to create a clear and present danger that they will bring

[46] 40 U.S. Statutes 217.   For state laws, see Chafee, pp. 575–597.

[47] Chafee, p. 52.

[48] U. S. ex rel. Milwaukee Social Democratic Pub. Co. v. Burleson, 255 U.S. 407, 41 S.Ct. 352 (1921).

[49] 249 U.S. 47, 39 S.Ct. 247 (1919).

about the substantive evils that Congress has a right
to prevent. It is a question of proximity and degree.
When a nation is at war many things that might be
said in time of peace are such a hindrance to its effort
that their utterance will not be endured * * *.

The new test did not free Schenck, nor was it to be used by
Supreme Court majorities in support of free expression for
two decades to come. Its plain implications, however, were that
old tests were too restrictive for the demands of freedom under
the First Amendment. As elaborated and developed in subsequent opinions by Holmes and Justice Brandeis against restrictive interpretations of free expression,[50] the test helped force
the Court to think through the meaning of the First and Fourteenth Amendments, and served as a rallying-point for libertarians for decades to come.

Another milestone in the Supreme Court's consideration of
sedition cases was reached in a post-war case, Gitlow v. People
of New York.[51] Here the 1902 New York statute on anarchy
was invoked against the publication of the "Left Wing Manifesto" in a radical paper called *Revolutionary Age*. It advocated
and forecast mass struggle, mass strikes, and the overthrow of
the bourgeoisie after a long revolutionary period. Convicted,
business manager Benjamin Gitlow appealed to the Supreme
Court. It upheld his conviction under an old test of criminality
in words—whether the words have a tendency to imperil or sub-
vert government.

But even as it upheld conviction, the Court wrote a single
short paragraph accepting a principle long sought by libertarians: It said that the Fourteenth Amendment's barrier to states'
depriving citizens of life, liberty, or property without due process of law protected liberty of speech and press against invasion
by the states. Heretofore, the Supreme Court had tightly restricted the scope of the "liberty" protected by the Fourteenth
Amendment; it had left it up to each state to say what liberty
of speech and press was. Henceforth, the Supreme Court would
review state laws and decisions on free expressions, under the
Gitlow case pronouncement that read: [52]

[W]e may and do assume that freedom of speech and
of the press—which are protected by the First Amend-

[50] Notably Abrams v. U. S., 250 U.S. 616, 40 S.Ct. 17 (1919); Gilbert v.
State of Minn., 254 U.S. 325, 41 S.Ct. 125 (1920); Gitlow v. People of State
of New York, 268 U.S. 652, 45 S.Ct. 625 (1925); Whitney v. People of State
of Cal., 274 U.S. 357, 47 S.Ct. 641 (1927).

[51] 268 U.S. 652, 45 S.Ct. 625 (1925).

[52] Ibid., 268 U.S. 652, 666, 45 S.Ct. 625, 630 (1925).

ment from abridgment by Congress—are among the fundamental personal rights and "liberties" protected by the due process clause of the Fourteenth Amendment from impairment by the States.

Although Gitlow went to jail, his case had brought acceptance of a principle of high importance. The confining interpretation of free expression fostered in many states over many decades now would be brought to the scrutiny of the United States Supreme Court.

Immediately after World War I, the thrust of revolutionary communism had spurred the Attorney General of the United States to urge the passage of a federal peacetime sedition act. His call for such a peacetime measure (the Espionage Act of 1917 had applied only to war) brought concerted opposition; the move was stopped although widespread deportation of Russians and other aliens for their ideas and words was accomplished. But 20 years later, similar fears engendered with the coming of World War II and the activity of domestic communists brought success for a similar bill. This was the Alien Registration Act of 1940, known as the Smith Act for Rep. Howard W. Smith of Virginia who introduced it.[53] For the first time since the Alien and Sedition Acts of 1798, America had a federal peacetime sedition law. The heart of its provisions, under Section 2, made it a crime to advocate forcible or violent overthrow of government, or to publish or distribute material advocating violence with the intent to overthrow government.

Upon the mass media of general circulation, the Act was to have little or no impact; they advocated the *status quo*, not radical change or revolution. But for speakers, teachers, and pamphleteers of the Communist Party, the Smith Act came to mean a great deal. Fewer than 20 persons had been punished under the Alien and Sedition Acts of 1798–1801; it is estimated that approximately 100 persons were fined or imprisoned under the Smith Act between 1940 and 1960.[54] In one sense, the Smith Act was less suppressive than its ancestor: the Alien and Sedition Acts had punished criticism of government officials, an everyday exercise of the press, but the Smith Act limited the ban to advocating violent overthrow.

The government made its first move in 1943. Leaders of a revolutionary splinter, the Socialist Workers Party which followed Russia's banished Trotsky, were the target. They were

---

[53] 54 U.S. Statutes 670.

[54] Chafee, Zechariah, Jr., The Blessings of Liberty (Phila., N.Y.: J. B. Lippincott Co., 1954), p. 22.

brought to trial in Minneapolis and convicted for the advocacy of violent overthrow in their printed polemics. The Court of Appeals sustained the conviction, and the United States Supreme Court refused to review the case.[55]

But the Communist Party was much more the target of government prosecution than the little group of Trotskyites. In the context of the cold war between the United States and the U.S.S.R. following World War II, almost 10 years of prosecution took place. The first case, Dennis v. United States, brought major figures in the Communist Party to trial and convicted 11 of them.[56] The charges were that they had reconstituted the American Communist Party in 1945, and conspired to advocate violent overthrow of the government.

For almost nine months the trial went on in federal district court under Judge Harold Medina. The nation was fascinated and bored in turn as the defense introduced complex legal challenges to the trial and the prosecution introduced exhibit after exhibit. Newspapers, pamphlets, and books were employed as evidence of the defendants' intent, from the *Daily Worker* to *The Communist Manifesto*. Scores of pages were read into the record, as the government sought to show conspiracy by publishing and circulating the literature of revolutionary force. Judge Medina followed the doctrine of the Gitlow case in instructing the jury that advocacy or teaching of violent overthrow of the government was not illegal if it were only "abstract doctrine." What the law forbade was teaching or advocating "action" to overthrow the government.[57] The jury found that the 11 did, indeed, conspire to advocate forcible overthrow. The Court of Appeals upheld the conviction and the case was accepted for review by the Supreme Court of the United States.

The justices wrote five opinions, three opinions concurring in conviction and two dissenting. Chief Justice Vinson wrote the opinion that carried the most names (three besides his). He said that free expression is not an unlimited or unqualified right, and that "the societal value of speech must, on occasion, be subordinated to other values and considerations." [58] But a conviction for violation of a statute limiting speech, he said, must rest on the showing that the words created a "clear and present danger" that a crime would be attempted or accomplished. Thus

[55] Dunne v. U. S., 138 F.2d 137 (8th Cir. 1943).

[56] 341 U.S. 494, 71 S.Ct. 857 (1951).

[57] U. S. v. Foster, 80 F.Supp. 479 (D.C.N.Y.1949). Upon appeal, this case became U. S. v. Dennis et al., 183 F.2d 201 (2d Cir. 1950).

[58] Dennis v. U. S., 341 U.S. 494, 71 S.Ct. 857 (1951).

he went to the famous Holmes rule first expressed in the Schenck case in 1919, and interpreted it as follows: [59]

> In this case we are squarely presented with the application of the "clear and present danger" test, and must decide what that phrase imports. We first note that many of the cases in which this Court has reversed convictions by use of this or similar tests have been based on the fact that the interest which the State was attempting to protect was too insubstantial to warrant restriction of speech * * *. Overthrow of the Government by force and violence is certainly a substantial enough interest for the Government to limit speech. Indeed, this is the ultimate value of any society, for if a society cannot protect its very structure from armed internal attack, it must follow that no subordinate value can be protected. If, then, this interest may be protected, the literal problem which is presented is what has been meant by the use of the phrase "clear and present danger" of the utterances bringing about the evil within the power of Congress to punish. Obviously, the words cannot mean that before the Government may act, it must wait until the *putsch* is about to be executed, the plans have been laid and the signal is awaited. If Government is aware that a group aiming at its overthrow is attempting to indoctrinate its members and to commit them to a course whereby they will strike when the leaders feel the circumstances permit, action by the Government is required * * *. Certainly an attempt to overthrow the Government by force, even though doomed from the outset because of inadequate numbers or power of the revolutionists, is a sufficient evil for Congress to prevent. The damage which such attempts create both physically and politically to a nation makes it impossible to measure the validity in terms of the probability of success, or the immediacy of a successful attempt.

Having thus rejected the position that likelihood of success in committing the criminal act is the criterion for restricting speech, Chief Justice Vinson adopted the statement of the Court of Appeals in interpreting the clear and present danger test. Chief Judge Hand had written: "In each case [courts] must ask whether the gravity of the 'evil,' discounted by its improbability, justifies such invasion of free speech as is necessary to

[59] Ibid., 508–509.

avoid the danger." [60]   Vinson was arguing that the danger need
not be immediate when the interest (here, self-preservation of
government) is important enough.

Deep disagreement in the Court over thus limiting the scope
of free expression appeared in the dissents of Justices Black
and Douglas. The latter could see no clear and present danger
to the government and state in the words and papers of the 11
Communists. Neither as a political force nor as a disciplined
corps of poised saboteurs did Justice Douglas see them as a
threat: [61]

> Communists in this country have never made a respect-
> able or serious showing in any election * * *. Com-
> munism has been so thoroughly exposed in this country
> that it has been crippled as a political force. Free
> speech has destroyed it as an effective political party.
> It is inconceivable that those who went up and down
> this country preaching the doctrine of revolution which
> petitioners espouse would have any success.
>
> *   *   *   *   *   *   *   *   *
>
> How it can be said that there is a clear and present dan-
> ger that this advocacy will succeed is, therefore, a mys-
> tery. Some nations less resilient than the United
> States, where illiteracy is high and where democratic
> traditions are only budding, might have to take drastic
> steps and jail these men for merely speaking their
> creed. But in America they are miserable merchants
> of unwanted ideas; their wares remain unsold. The
> fact that their ideas are abhorrent does not make them
> powerful.
>
> *   *   *   *   *   *   *   *   *
>
> * * * Free speech—the glory of our system of gov-
> ernment—should not be sacrificed on anything less than
> plain and objective proof of danger that the evil ad-
> vocated is imminent.

Through most of the 1950's, cases under the Smith Act continued to move through the courts. But with the decision in
Yates v. United States in 1957, prosecutions dwindled and died
out. In this case, the Supreme Court reversed the conviction of
14 Communist Party leaders under the Smith Act. Its decision
turned in large part on the difference between teaching the need

[60] Ibid., 510.

[61] Dennis v. U. S., 341 U.S. 494, 71 S.Ct. 857 (1951).

for violent overthrow as an abstract theory or doctrine, and teaching it as a spur to action. The Court said: [62]

> We are * * * faced with the question whether the Smith Act prohibits advocacy and teaching or forcible overthrow as an abstract principle, divorced from any effort to instigate action to that end, so long as such advocacy or teaching is engaged in with evil intent. We hold that it does not.

> The distinction between advocacy of abstract doctrine and advocacy directed at promoting unlawful action is one that has been consistently recognized in the opinions of this Court * * *.

> *   *   *   *   *   *   *   *   *

> * * * The legislative history of the Smith Act and related bills shows beyond all question that Congress was aware of the distinction between the advocacy or teaching of abstract doctrine and the advocacy or teaching of action, and that it did not intend to disregard it. The statute was aimed at the advocacy and teaching of concrete action for the forcible overthrow of the Government, and not of principles divorced from action.

Since the trial court had not required the jury which found the defendants guilty to make the distinction, the conviction was reversed. There was no reference to the famous clear and present danger doctrine, nor have court majorities used it in any sedition case since Dennis, where it was so variously interpreted by the five opinions that its usefulness was eroded.

The Warren Court—so called for Chief Justice Earl Warren who had been appointed in 1953—had grown less and less willing to uphold convictions under the Smith Act, and with the Yates decision, charges against many other defendants in pending cases were dismissed in lower courts. The Smith Act, nevertheless, remained in force, and none could say when some old or new political ideology might cast up advocates who would feel the Act's embrace under a less libertarian court in some future time of national alarm.

[62] Yates v. U. S., 354 U.S. 298, 77 S.Ct. 1064 (1957).

SEC. 9.   PRIOR RESTRAINT: FROM NEAR v. MINNE-
SOTA (1931) TO THE PENTAGON PAPERS (1971)

Pre-publication censorship is permissible only when the Government successfully "carries the heavy burden of showing justification for the imposition of such a restraint."

For journalists and for libertarians the term "prior restraint" is one of the most despised of phrases. Prior restraint—censorship at the source, before publication—had a long and ignoble history in England, where printers struggled during the Sixteenth and Seventeenth Centuries against a system which demanded official approval before publication was allowed.[63] Prior restraint is hated with good reason. If government gains the power to silence its critics before they can speak, it has power to hide its errors forever. Governments, as do all human institutions, make errors. The communications media, when free from prior restraints, are the prime exposers of such errors and are important initiators of corrective action.

NEAR v. MINNESOTA (1931)

For some 40 years after 1931, scholars termed Near v. Minnesota the Supreme Court's landmark decision forbidding prior restraint. That decision grew out of scruffy origins; Howard Guilford and J. M. Near were publishing partners in producing *The Saturday Press,* a Minneapolis "smear sheet" which vilified Jews and Catholics and exuded contempt for law enforcement authorities. *The Saturday Press* had published strong stuff, charging, among other things, that Jewish gangsters were in control of Minneapolis gambling, bootlegging and racketeering, and that the city law enforcement and government agencies and officers were derelict in their duties. Disgusting personalities, but important people nonetheless: Guilford and Near wrote and published the articles that eventually required the Supreme Court of the United States to make one of its most notable descriptions of the extent of freedom of the press in America.[64]

Publication of *The Saturday Press* was halted when a Minnesota statute authorizing prior restraint of "nuisance" or "undesirable" publications was invoked. That statute declared that any person publishing a "malicious, scandalous and defamatory newspaper, magazine or other periodical" could be found guilty

[63] See earlier sections of this Chapter; see also Fredrick Siebert, Freedom of the Press in England, 1476–1776, Urbana, Ill., 1952.

[64] Harold L. Nelson, "Prior Restraint Outlawed: Action Essential to Press," The Michigan Journalist, Oct. 21, 1968, p. 10.

of creating a nuisance and could enjoin the publishers from future wrongdoing.[65]   Near and Guilford were indeed brought into court after a temporary injunction ordered cessation of all activity by their paper.   After the hearing, the injunction was made permanent by a judge, but with the provision that the *Saturday Press* could resume publication if the publishers could persuade the court that they would run a newspaper without objectionable content described in the Minnesota "gag law" statute.[66]

Near and Guilford appealed to the Supreme Court, which found in their favor by the margin of five votes to four.   Speaking for the Court, Chief Justice Charles Evans Hughes noted the importance of this case: "This statute, for the suppression as a public nuisance of a newspaper or periodical, is unusual, if not unique, and raises questions of grave importance transcending the local interests involved in the particular action." [67] Hughes, relying on the *Gitlow* decision discussed in the preceding section of this chapter, declared: [68]

> It is no longer open to doubt that the liberty of the press and of speech is within the liberty safeguarded by the due process clause of the Fourteenth Amendment from invasion by state action.   It was found impossible to conclude that this essential personal liberty of the citizen was left unprotected by the general guaranty of fundamental rights of person and property.
>
> *   *   *   *   *   *   *   *   *
>
> If we cut through mere details of procedure, the operation and effect of the statute in substance is that public authorities may bring the owner or publisher of a newspaper or periodical before a judge upon a charge of conducting a business publishing scandalous and defamatory matter—in particular that the matter consists of charges against public officers of official dereliction—and, unless the owner or publisher is able and disposed to bring competent evidence to satisfy the judge that the charges are true and are published for good motives and for justifiable ends, his newspaper or periodical is suppressed and further publication is made

[65] Chapter 285, Minnesota Session Laws of 1925, in Mason's Minnesota Statutes, 1927, Sections 10123–1 to 10123–3.

[66] Near v. Minnesota ex rel. Olson, 283 U.S. 697, 702–707, 51 S.Ct. 625, 626–628 (1931).

[67] 283 U.S. 697, 707, 51 S.Ct. 625, 627–628 (1931).

[68] 283 U.S. 697, 707, 713, 51 S.Ct. 625, 628, 630 (1931).

punishable as a contempt. This is of the essence of censorship.

Chief Justice Hughes then turned to history-as-precedent to answer the question of whether a statute authorizing such proceedings in restraint of publication was consistent with the concept of liberty of the press. Hughes quoted Blackstone's declaration that the chief purpose of a constitutional guaranty of protection for the press is to prevent prior restraints upon publication.[69]

Hughes then embarked upon a two-fold modification of Blackstone. Blackstone would have had *no prior restraint*, period. The Chief Justice, however, conceded that such a prohibition against all prior restraint might be "stated too broadly," and said that " * * * the protection even as to previous restraint is not absolutely unlimited." In a few exceptional cases, limitation of the principle of "no prior restraint" could be recognized. Prior restraint, the Chief Justice asserted, could be allowed when publications involved a threat to the nation in time of war, or were obscene, or were incitements to violence or the overthrow of government by force.[70]

> No one would question but that a government might prevent actual obstruction to its recruiting service or the publication of sailing dates of transports or the number and location of troops. On similar grounds, the primary requirements of decency may be enforced against obscene publications. The security of the community life may be protected against incitements to acts of violence and the overthrow by force of orderly government. The constitutional guaranty of free speech does not "protect a man from an injunction against uttering words that may have all the effect of force."

Although Blackstone's "no prior restraint" was thus modified by the majority opinion in Near v. Minnesota, another aspect of Blackstone was liberalized. Blackstone had been a strict believer in the principle of seditious libel, and would have punished publication of criticisms of government or government officials. Chief Justice Hughes insisted that the press had a right—and perhaps even a duty—to discuss and debate the character and conduct of public officers.[71]

---

69 283 U.S. 697, 713–714, 51 S.Ct. 625, 630 (1931).

70 283 U.S. 697, 716, 51 S.Ct. 625, 631 (1931).

71 283 U.S. 697, 719–720, 51 S.Ct. 625, 632 (1931).

The general principle that the constitutional guaranty of the liberty of the press gives immunity from previous restraints has been approved in many decisions under the provisions of state constitutions.

The importance of this immunity has not lessened. While reckless assaults upon public men, and efforts to bring obloquy upon those who are endeavoring faithfully to discharge official duties, exert a baleful influence and deserve the severest condemnation in public opinion, it cannot be said that this abuse is greater, and it is believed to be less, than that which characterized the period in which our institutions took shape. Meanwhile, the administration of government has become more complex, the opportunities for malfeasance and corruption have multiplied, crime has grown to most serious proportions, and the danger of its protection by unfaithful officials and of the impairment of the fundamental security of life and property by criminal alliances and official neglect, emphasizes the primary need of a vigilant and courageous press, especially in great cities.

The fact that the liberty of the press may be abused by miscreant purveyors of scandal does not make any the less necessary the immunity of the press from previous restraint in dealing with official misconduct. Subsequent punishment for such abuses as may exist is the appropriate remedy, consistent with constitutional privilege.

As Professor J. Edward Gerald has noted, the dissent in the *Near* case by Justice Pierce Butler, in which Justices Willis Van Devanter, George Sutherland, and James C. McReynolds joined, "seemed oblivious of the unconstitutional nature of prior restraint and assumed that a state court operating by summary procedure was freed of the obligations of due process of law." [72] Despite the four dissenting votes, Near v. Minnesota has stood since 1931 as one of the most important decisions of the Supreme Court. Near was the first case involving newspapers in which the Court applied the provisions of the First Amendment against states through the language of the Fourteenth Amendment. [73]

During the 1950s and 1960s, the Supreme Court of the United States followed up suggestions made in the *Near* decision, ruling

[72] J. Edward Gerald, The Press and the Constitution, 1931–1947 (Minneapolis: University of Minnesota Press, 1947) p. 129.

[73] William A. Hachten, The Supreme Court on Freedom of the Press: Decisions and Dissents (Ames, Iowa: Iowa State University Press, 1968) p. 43.

in a number of obscenity cases that obscenity was not speech protected by the First Amendment, and that prior restraint constitutionally could be used to control obscenity.[74]   But in 1971, one key prior restraint case involved not obscenity but a neighborhood housing dispute.

ORGANIZATION FOR A BETTER AUSTIN
v. KEEFE (1971)

The Organization for a Better Austin (OBA), a racially integrated community group in the Austin neighborhood of Chicago, brought about another "prior restraint" case through its activities.   The OBA, which said that its purpose was to "stabilize" the racial ratio in the Austin area, opposed real estate tactics known as "blockbusting" or "panic peddling."   The OBA claimed that real estate dealer Jerome M. Keefe had been dealing in such tactics, arousing "the fears of the local white residents that Negroes were coming into the area, and then, exploiting the reactions and emotions so aroused, was able to secure listings and sell homes to Negroes." [75]

Several meetings were arranged between OBA and Keefe, with OBA trying to persuade the real estate dealer to change his business practices.   Keefe, however, consistently denied that he was engaged in "blockbusting" or "panic peddling" dealings, and refused to sign any sort of an agreement with OBA.   Thereafter, during the fall of 1967, members of OBA distributed leaflets in Keefe's home neighborhood of Westchester, a Chicago suburb seven miles from the Austin area.   The leaflets criticized Keefe's real estate practices in the Austin neighborhood, with one of the leaflets quoting Keefe as saying, "I only sell to Negroes" and also citing a Chicago Daily News article which called Keefe a "panic peddler."   Another OBA leaflet declared, "When he signs the agreement, we stop coming to Westchester."   Other leaflets urged recipients to call Keefe at his home phone number and urge him to sign an agreement with OBA not to do business in the Austin suburb.   The leaflets were distributed in a peaceful and orderly manner, being given out to persons in a Westchester shopping center on several days, and were also left at the doors of his neighbors and were handed out to some parishioners on their way to or from Keefe's church in Westchester.[76]

---

[74] See also Roth v. United States, 354 U.S. 476, 77 S.Ct. 1304 (1957); Times Film Corp. v. City of Chicago, 365 U.S. 43, 81 S.Ct. 391 (1961); Freedman v. Maryland, 380 U.S. 51, 85 S.Ct. 734 (1965); Interstate Circuit, Inc. v. Dallas, 390 U.S. 676, 88 S.Ct. 1298 (1968).

[75] Organization for a Better Austin v. Keefe, 402 U.S. 415, 416, 91 S.Ct. 1575, 1576 (1971).

[76] 402 U.S. 415, 416–417, 91 S.Ct. 1575, 1576–1577 (1971).

Keefe then sought and won a temporary injunction in the Circuit Court of Cook County, Illinois, enjoining the OBA "from passing out pamphlets, leaflets or literature of any kind, and from picketing, anywhere in the City of Westchester, Illinois." [77]

OBA appealed against the injunction, but an Illinois appellate court upheld the trial court's finding of fact that the OBA's leafleting activities in Westchester had violated Keefe's right of privacy.[78] The Appellate Court based its holding on the belief that public policy of Illinois favored protection of home and family from encroachment by activities of the sort engaged in by the Organization for a Better Austin. The Appellate Court appeared to view the leafleting activities as coercive and intimidating rather than informative; therefore, in the view of the Appellate Court, the activities of the OBA were not entitled to First Amendment protection.

The Supreme Court, by a vote of 8 to 1, disagreed with the appellate court's upholding of the injunction. Writing for the Court Chief Justice Burger said: [79]

> It is elementary, of course, that in a case of this kind the courts do not concern themselves with the truth or validity of the publication. Under Near v. Minnesota. * * * the injunction, so far as it imposes prior restraint on speech and publication, constitutes an impermissible restraint on First Amendment rights. Here, as in that case, the injunction operates, not to redress alleged private wrongs, but to suppress, on the basis of previous publications, distribution of literature "of any kind" in a city of 18,000.

Chief Justice Burger declared that the Supreme Court had often recognized that peaceful pamphleteering is a form of communications protected by the First Amendment.[80] He was not impressed by arguments that the leaflets distributed by the Organization for a Better Austin were not to inform the public but were meant to "force" Keefe to sign a no-solicitation agreement.[81]

---

[77] 402 U.S. 415, 417, 91 S.Ct. 1575, 1577 (1971).

[78] Keefe v. Organization for a Better Austin, see 115 Ill.App.2d 236, 253 N.E.2d 76 (1969).

[79] Organization for a Better Austin v. Keefe, 402 U.S. 415, 418, 91 S.Ct. 1575, 1577 (1971).

[80] 402 U.S. 415, 419, 91 S.Ct. 1575, 1577 (1971), citing Martin v. City of Struthers, 319 U.S. 141, 63 S.Ct. 862 (1943); Schneider v. State, 308 U.S. 147, 60 S.Ct. 146 (1939), and Lovell v. City of Griffin, 303 U.S. 444, 58 S.Ct. 666 (1938).

[81] 402 U.S. 415, 419, 91 S.Ct. 1575, 1578 (1971).

The claim that the expressions were intended to exercise a coercive impact on respondent [Keefe] does not remove them from the reach of the First Amendment. Petitioners [OBA] plainly intended to influence respondent's conduct by their activities; this is not fundamentally different from the function of a newspaper. * * * Petitioners were engaged openly and vigorously in making the public aware of respondent's real estate practices. Those practices were offensive to them, as the views and practices of petitioners are no doubt offensive to others. But so long as the means are peaceful, the communication need not meet standards of acceptability.

Chief Justice Burger ordered that the injunction issued by the Illinois court must be overturned. He noted that any situation smacking of prior restraint would receive the most careful and suspicious scrutiny from the Court: [82]

Any prior restraint on expression comes to this Court with a "heavy presumption" against its constitutional validity. * * * Respondent thus carries a heavy burden of showing justification for the imposition of such a restraint. He has not met that burden. No prior decisions support the claim that the interest of an individual in being free from public criticism of his business practices in pamphlets or leaflets warrants use of the injunctive power of a court. Designating the conduct as an invasion of privacy, the apparent basis for the injunction here, is not sufficient to support an injunction against peaceful distribution of informational literature of the nature revealed by this record. Rowan v. United States Post Office Dept., 397 U.S. 728, 90 S.Ct. 1484, 25 L.Ed.2d 736 (1970), relied on by respondent, is not in point; the right of privacy involved in that case is not shown here. Among other important distinctions, respondent is not attempting to stop the flow of information into his own household, but to the public. Accordingly, the injunction issued by the Illinois court must be vacated.

THE PENTAGON PAPERS DECISION (1971)

"VICTORY FOR THE PRESS" said the headline on *Newsweek's* cover. "The Press Wins and the Presses Roll" said a headline in *Time* in the wake of the Supreme Court's June 30,

---

[82] 402 U.S. 415, 419–420, 91 S.Ct. 1575, 1578 (1971).

1971, decision in New York Times Co. v. United States.[83] These triumphant headlines were tied to the "Pentagon Papers" case. Early in 1971, New York *Times* reporter Neil Sheehan was given photocopies of a 47-volume study of United States involvement in Vietnam titled *History of the United States Decision-Making Process on Vietnam Policy.* On Sunday, June 13, 1971, the New York *Times*—after a team of reporters had worked with the documents for three months—published a story headlined: "Vietnam Archive: Pentagon Study Traces 3 Decades of Growing U. S. Involvement." Within 48 hours after publication, Attorney General John Mitchell sent a telegram to the *Times*, urging that no more articles based on the documents be published, charging that the series would bring about "irreparable injury to the defense interests of the United States." [84] The *Times* chose to ignore Attorney General Mitchell's plea, and columnist James Reston angrily wrote: "For the first time in the history of the Republic, the Attorney General of the United States has tried to suppress documents he hasn't read about a war that hasn't been declared.[85]

After the *Times'* refusal to stop the series of articles, the Department of Justice asked U. S. District Court Judge Murray I. Gurfein to halt publication of the stories. Judge Gurfein, who was serving his first day as a federal judge, issued a temporary injunction on June 15, putting a stop to *Times'* publication of the articles. But silencing the *Times* did not halt all publication of the "Pentagon Papers." The Washington *Post*—and a number of other major journals—also weighed in with excerpts from the secret report. The Justice Department likewise applied for —and was granted—a temporary restraining order against The Washington *Post*.[86]

After two weeks of uncertainty, the decision by the Supreme Court of the United States cleared the papers for publication. New York *Times* Managing Editor A. M. Rosenthal was jubilant: "This is a joyous day for the press—and for American society." *Time* added, "Certainly the Justice Department was slapped down in its efforts to ask the courts to enjoin news-

[83] *Newsweek, Time,* July 12, 1971.

[84] Don R. Pember, "The Pentagon Papers Decision: More Questions Than Answers," Journalism Quarterly 48:3 (Autumn, 1971) p. 404; New York *Times,* June 15, 1971, p. 1.

[85] *New York Times,* June 16, 1971, p. 1.

[86] For a clear account of how the cases involving the New York *Times* and the Washington *Post* worked their way through the federal courts to the Supreme Court of the United States, see Don R. Pember, op. cit., p. 404–405.

papers, and will not likely take that route again.[87]　Despite such optimism, some observers within the press were disturbed by the outcome of the *"Pentagon Papers" case:*

1. For what may be the first time in American history, federal court injunctions imposed prior restraint upon American newspapers.　Tom Wicker of the *New York Times* argued that "it must never be forgotten that for two long weeks the presses were in fact stopped by court order, on government application."

2. The 6–3 decision was by no means a ringing affirmation of First Amendment rights or of "the public's right to know."　The Court was by no means as positive in denouncing prior restraint as it had been in Organization for a Better Austin v. Keefe, which the court had decided only six weeks before it ruled in the *Pentagon Papers* Case.[88]　The Court's *per curiam* statement, agreed to by six justices, said merely that the government has a heavy burden of proof in prior restraint cases, and that the government has not "met that burden."

3. In addition, three of the concurring opinions which agreed that the injunctions should be lifted from the *Times* and from the *Washington Post* nevertheless expressed severe doubts about supporting the press.

The Court's *per curiam* decision was short and to the point. It refused to leave in effect the injunctions which the Justice Department had secured against the *New York Times* and the *Washington Post,* and quoted Bantam Books v. Sullivan:[89]

"Any system of prior restraints of expression comes to this Court bearing a heavy presumption against its constitutional validity."　Bantam Books, Inc. v. Sullivan, 372 U.S. 58, 83 S.Ct. 631 * * * (1963); see also Near v. Minnesota ex rel. Olson, 283 U.S. 697, 51 S.Ct. 625 * * * (1931).　The Government "thus carries a heavy burden of showing justification for the imposition of such a restraint."　Organization for a Better Austin v. Keefe, 402 U.S. 415, 91 S.Ct. 1575, 1578 (1971).

With those words, a six-member majority of the Court ruled that the government had not shown sufficient reason to impose

---

[87] *Time,* July 12, 1971, p. 10.

[88] See 402 U.S. 415, 91 S.Ct. 1575 (1971).　Organization for a Better Austin v. Keefe is discussed at length earlier in this Section.

[89] New York Times Co. v. U. S., 403 U.S. 713, 714, 91 S.Ct. 2140, 2141 (1971).

prior restraint. However, only three members of the six-justice majority in the case—Justices Hugo L. Black, William O. Douglas, and William J. Brennan, Jr.—could be called willing supporters of the press. Black and Douglas were the only Justices who gave unequivocal support to the *Times* and to the *Post*. Both expressed abhorrence for prior restraint, with Douglas saying: [90]

> Secrecy in government is fundamentally anti-democratic, perpetuating bureaucratic errors. Open debate and discussion are vital to our national health. On public questions there should be "uninhibited, robust and wide-open debate." New York Times Co. v. Sullivan, 376 U.S. 254, 269–270, 84 S.Ct. 710 * * * (1964).
>
> *   *   *   *   *   *   *   *   *
>
> The stays in these cases that have been in effect for more than a week constitute a flouting of the principles of the First Amendment as interpreted in Near v. Minnesota ex rel. Olson.

Justice William J. Brennan, Jr., although not subscribing to the absolutist position on the First Amendment adhered to by Black and Douglas, nevertheless gave considerable latitude to the press. Brennan declared that prior restraint was permissible in only a "single, extremely narrow" class of cases, as when the nation was at war or when troop movements might be endangered. He added that even if it could be assumed that disclosure of massive movements of United States weapons might touch off a nuclear holocaust, the Government had not presented (or even alleged) that publication of the Pentagon Papers would cause such an event. Brennan concluded: [91]

> *   *   *   therefore, every restraint issued in this case, whatever its form, has violated the First Amendment —and none the less so because the restraint was justified as necessary to examine the claim more thoroughly. Unless and until the Government has clearly made out its case, the First Amendment commands that no injunction may issue.

Justices Byron White and Potter Stewart also joined in the judgment of the Court, but with reluctance. Justice Stewart (with whom White concurred) wrote that effective international diplomacy and national defense require both confidentiality

[90] 403 U.S. 713, 724, 91 S.Ct. 2140, 2146 (1971).

[91] 403 U.S. 713, 727, 91 S.Ct. 2140, 2147–3148 (1971).

and secrecy. Stewart said he was convinced that the Executive branch of government was correct in attempting to suppress publication of some of the documents. He added, however, that he joined with the Court's majority because he could not say "that disclosure of any of them [the "Pentagon Papers"] will surely result in direct, immediate, or irreparable damage to our Nation or its people." [92]

Justice White (with whom Stewart concurred) was Blackstonian in his discussion of the kinds of post-publication punishment which could be applied to the press.[93]

> If any of the material here at issue is of this nature [that is, falls within certain sections of the Espionage Act of 1917], the newspapers are presumably now on full notice of the position of the United States and must face the consequences if they publish. I would have no difficulty in sustaining convictions under these sections on facts that would not justify the intervention of equity and the imposition of a prior restraint.

Justice Marshall's concurring opinion concentrated upon separation of powers considerations. Marshall argued that Congress had twice (in 1971 and 1957) rejected proposed legislation that would have given the President, in time of war (or threat of war), the authority to "directly prohibit by proclamation the publication of information relating to national defense that might be useful to the enemy." [94] Marshall declared that it would be utterly inconsistent with the concept of separation of powers for the Court to use its contempt power to prevent behavior that Congress had specifically declined to prohibit.

In dissent, Justice Harlan bemoaned the lack of time available to give issues in the case proper consideration, and listed seven issues imbedded in the case which he considered to be of grave constitutional significance. "With all respect," Justice Harlan wrote, "I consider that the Court has been almost irresponsibly feverish in dealing with these cases." [95]

Beyond that, Harlan expressed concern that the Court was violating the principles of federalism when the judiciary overrode the executive department's determination that the secret papers should not be published. He said he could find no evidence that the executive department had been given "even the deference

[92] 403 U.S. 713, 730, 91 S.Ct. 2140, 2149 (1971).

[93] 403 U.S. 713, 735–738, 91 S.Ct. 2140, 2152–2153 (1971).

[94] 403 U.S. 713, 746, 91 S.Ct. 2140, 2157 (1971).

[95] 403 U.S. 713, 753, 91 S.Ct. 2140, 2161 (1971).

owing to an administrative agency, much less that owing a co-equal branch of the Government." [96] Justice Harlan added that he could not believe that the doctrine of prohibiting prior restraints "reaches to the point of preventing courts from maintaining the *status quo* long enough to act responsibly in matters of such national importance as those involved here." [97]

Mr. Justice Blackmun also complained about the haste involved in the case: Two federal district courts, two United States Courts of Appeal, and the Supreme Court of the United States were forced into "hurried decision of profound constitutional issues on inadequately developed and largely assumed facts * * *.[98] Expressing fear that the case might result in great harm to the nation, Justice Blackmun added this shrill indictment of the press: [1]

> If, however, damage has been done, and if, with the Court's action today, these newspapers proceed to publish the critical documents and there results therefrom "the death of soldiers, the destruction of alliances, the greatly increased difficulty of negotiation with our enemies, the inability of our diplomats to negotiate," to which list I might add the factors of prolongation of the war and of further delay in the freeing of United States prisoners, then the Nation's people will know where the responsibility for these sad consequences rests.

Journalist and scholar Herbert Brucker has said that a basic question raised by the *Pentagon Papers* case is this: "Who owns the news? Does news belong to the American people, or to Government?" He argued that Government attempts to keep hold of power by suppressing information. Brucker added that the unsuccessful prosecution during 1973 of Daniel Ellsberg and Anthony J. Russo, Jr. for their role in revealing the Pentagon Papers was a political case, not a legal case. Ellsberg and Russo were charged with theft, conspiracy, and espionage, with the Government claiming that publication of the papers had endangered national security. Not so, said Brucker: the Pentagon Papers were historical facts to which the public is entitled, and Government was simply trying to keep facts from the public;

---

[96] 403 U.S. 713, 758, 91 S.Ct. 2140, 2163 (1971).

[97] 403 U.S. 713, 759, 91 S.Ct. 2140, 2164 (1971).

[98] 403 U.S. 713, 760, 91 S.Ct. 2140, 2164 (1971).

[1] 403 U.S. 713, 763, 91 S.Ct. 2140, 2166 (1971). Justice Blackmun was quoting the dissent of Judge Wilkey in the Pentagon Papers involving the Washington *Post* in the Court of Appeals for the Second Circuit, 446 F.2d 1327 (1971).

hence the effort to punish Ellsberg and Russo for revealing embarrassing information.[2]

In addition to the Ellsberg-Russo trial, another event troubling to journalists and to other advocates of a free flow of information came in the submission to Congress of "Senate Bill 1400," a bill otherwise known as the Nixon Administration's proposed new criminal code. Embedded in this 366-page bill, which was drafted by the Department of Justice and approved by the White House, was a proposed new system to prosecute persons who leak classified information.[3]

It should be recognized that no new legal course was charted by the *Pentagon Papers* case. After a delay of two weeks—a prior restraint imposed by lower federal courts at the insistence of the Department of Justice—the Supreme Court allowed the press to resume publication of the documents. By a 6 to 3 margin, the Supreme Court precariously held on to Near v. Minnesota, that classic 1931 case which forbade prior restraint except in time of war, or when the materials involved were obscene, or when there was incitement to violence or to the overthrow of the Government.[4]

New York Times Co. v. United States was a hastily tried case, one in which the lawyers literally had to work through the night to prepare their briefs. As Don R. Pember has noted, the defense attorneys wished to win the case, not to make constitutional law. As a result, they "played safe," conceding that on occasion, in certain circumstances, prior restraint was constitutionally permissible. The case then became a squabble over whether or not the publication of the papers was a sufficient threat to national security to allow the imposition of prior restraint.[5]

<hr />

[2] Herbert Brucker, "Who Owns the News?", speech at Carnahan House Freedom of Information Seminar, University of Kentucky, April 13, 1973.

[3] Warren Weaver, Jr., "Justice Department Bill Asking New Code for Prosecuting Classified-Data Leaks Stirs Wide Attack," New York Times, April 22, 1973. The code proposes that in order to convict a person of leaking government information, all that would have to be proven was that the documents involved had received a security classification from an authorized official. The necessity or propriety of such a classification, according to the proposed code, could not be raised in court by persons accused of the leaks. Violators of the code, should it become law, would be subject to a $100,000 fine and 15 years in prison if the violation occurred during wartime or during a national emergency. The code is drawn so that reporters who gain possession of or who have a hand in publishing or broadcasting classified information could be punished, whether or not there was any real threat to national security.

[4] 283 U.S. 697, 51 S.Ct. 625 (1931).

[5] Pember, op. cit., p. 41.

No great declarations of legal principle were made in such a setting. The press won by the margin of 6 to 3, but this was by no means a resounding victory. As noted earlier, only three justices—Brennan, Douglas, and Black—stood firmly with the press. The other three members of the majority—White, Stewart, and Marshall—ruled in favor of the press on other grounds, with White and Stewart declaring that they could not rule in favor of the Government because it had not been proven that publication would cause "irreparable damage to our Nation."

Changes in the membership of the Supreme Court should be considered. Obviously, a change of only two votes would have meant a 5–4 defeat for the press instead of a 6–3 victory. Since the *Pentagon Papers* case was decided on June 30, 1971, two new justices have ascended to the Court. Hugo Black, the staunchest of fighters for freedom of expression during his 34 years on the Court, retired September 17, 1971; eight days later, he was dead of a stroke. John Marshall Harlan, who had voted against publication of the classified documents, retired from the Court on September 23, 1971, and died December 29 of that year. On January 7, 1972, two men appointed by President Richard M. Nixon were sworn in as associate justices of the Court: Lewis F. Powell, Jr., and William H. Rehnquist. Two other Nixon appointees were on the Court during the *Pentagon Papers* case, Chief Justice Warren Burger and Justice Harry Blackmun. They revealed in that case that they do not accord the First Amendment a preferred position when the press comes into conflict with bureaucratic classification of documents.

As this book goes to press late in 1973, Justice William O. Douglas is the only remaining member of the Court who believes that the First Amendment provides an absolute protection for the press in its adversary relationship with Government. Douglas, it should be added, is now the Court's elder statesman. New faces on the Court are always a possibility, and a change of two votes could bring a ruling in favor of prior restraint should a similar fact situation arise.

The *Pentagon Papers* case underlines an important truth, that no freedom is ever won, once and for all. Consider this statement:

> Some people may think that leaders of the free press
> would perhaps accomplish more if their claims of con-
> stitutional right were less expansive. I do not agree
> with this. I say it is their duty to fight like tigers right
> down the line and not give an inch. This is the way our

freedoms have been preserved in the past, and it is the way they will be preserved in the future.

No editor, publisher, or reporter said that. The quotation is from a statement by U. S. Senior Circuit Judge for the Second Circuit, Harold R. Medina. Judge Medina's words emphasize an obvious but necessary history lesson. Each freedom has to be rewon by each succeeding generation. And sometimes, as is apparently true during the latter third of the Twentieth Century, freedom has to be fought for again and again within one generation.

Part II

RIGHTS IN CONFLICT WITH FREE EXPRESSION

A. FREE EXPRESSION AND CITIZENS' RIGHTS

Chapter 3

DEFAMATION: LIBEL AND SLANDER

SEC. 10.   DEFAMATION DEFINED

Defamation is communication which exposes a person to hatred, ridicule, or contempt, lowers him in the esteem of his fellows, causes him to be shunned, or injures him in his business or calling.   Its categories are libel—broadly, printed or written material; and slander—broadly, spoken words.

The legal hazard that lurks most unfailingly in newsmen's employment of words and pictures lies in the damage that these basic "tools of the trade" may do to the reputations of individuals in the news.   The damage is defamation—libel or slander. The law classifies defamation as a tort, a civil wrong other than breach of contract for which the legal remedy is a court action for damages.[1]   Under various circumstances, one citizen may recover money from another who harms his reputation with the symbols of communication.

A great new avenue of protection against defamation judgments opened for the mass media in the decision in New York Times Co. v. Sullivan in 1964.   Here for the first time, the United States Supreme Court ruled that where public officials and public

---

[1] Prosser, William, Law of Torts (St. Paul: West Publishing Co., 1964), 3rd ed., p. 2.

issues are involved, the First Amendment clears a broad path for free expression through the thickets and jungles of centuries-old libel law. The court said that "a profound national commitment to the principle that debate on public issues should be uninhibited, robust, and wide-open. * * * " [2] prevents recovery for libel in words about the public acts of public officials unless actual malice is present. The offspring of this case broadened the protection further, until by 1970 courts held that the same protection applied to expression dealing with any subject of general public concern or interest. The next chapter details the progression.

Broad new shield for newsmen that these decisions are, it is not the case that the threat of defamation is dead except for the expense and trouble involved in hiring lawyers to defend against a defamation suit that is sure to be won by the news medium if taken to a high enough court. Libel judgments continued to be won in 1971 and 1972, with state and federal courts finding various circumstances where the Times v. Sullivan line of cases did not protect media.[3] While the newsman who does his work with a professional's standards has far less to fear than before 1964, he has no blanket protection against defamation judgments.

The *New York Times* decision cut through the confusion of centuries of development in the law of libel and slander. Defamation traced a tortuous course through the medieval and early modern courts of England. Feudal and then ecclesiastical courts had jurisdiction over the offense before it moved haltingly into the common law courts. The Court of the Star Chamber took part during the first half of the Seventeenth Century, until it was dissolved during the Civil War, by punishing libel of political figures as a crime in its arbitrary, sometimes secret, and generally hated procedures.[4] Difficulties arose when printing became common, for some distinction seemed important to separate damage done by the spoken word, which was fleeting, from damage by the printed word, which might be permanent and much

[2] 376 U.S. 254, 84 S.Ct. 710 (1964).

[3] For the view that "the libel laws have almost been repealed," see Gillmor, Donald M., "The Residual Rights of Reputation and Privacy," The Future of Press Freedom (Racine, Wis., Johnson Foundation, May 1972), p. 25; Coonradt, Frederick C., "The Courts Have All But Repealed the Libel Laws," Center Report, Dec. 1971, p. 26. For cases in which liability has been found since New York Times Co. v. Sullivan, see Chap. 4, infra.

[4] Kelly, John, Criminal Libel and Free Speech, 6 Kans.L.Rev. 295, 299, 1958; Anon., Developments in the Law, Defamation, 69 Harv.L.Rev. 875, 887, 1956.

more widely diffused than that which was spoken. Rules resulted which, if appropriate for their time, have long since become anachronisms that persist into the age of television and communication satellites.[5] The law of defamation carries much of its tangled past with it today.

The most-used definition of defamation is that it is a statement about an individual which exposes him to "hatred, ridicule, or contempt, or which causes him to be shunned, or avoided, or which has a tendency to injure him in his office, profession, or trade." [6] While that definition takes in a wide reach of words, it is nevertheless probably too narrow. Prosser points out that words which would cause most people to sympathize with the target have been held defamatory, such as an imputation of poverty, or the statement that a woman has been raped.[7] If a person is lowered in the estimation or respect with which he is held in the community, he is not necessarily hated, held in contempt, or shunned.

To have definitions such as the above is by no means always to be able to predict what will be held defamatory. The legal axiom which says that "every definition in the law is dangerous" most certainly applies to defamation. Customs and attitudes vary from one area of the nation to another; and while in the North it is not defamatory to call a white man a Negro, southern courts continue to recognize the social prejudices of centuries and consider it defamation.[8] Political attitudes of a nation may change over time: while it was probably not defamation to falsely call a man a Communist in the 1930's, a decade and more later, it was.[9] Under one set of circumstances, Wisconsin courts have ruled that it was libelous to call a man "a swine"; under others, the Washington Supreme Court has said it was not libelous to call a man a "hog." [10]

Anyone who is living may be defamed, and so may a corporation or partnership where its business standing or practices are impugned. A voluntary association organized for purposes not connected with profit or the self-interest of the organizers has

---

[5] Prosser, pp. 754, 769.

[6] Fraser, Sir Hugh, Libel and Slander (London: 1936), 7th ed., p. 3.

[7] Prosser, p. 756.

[8] Natchez Times Pub. Co. v. Dunigan, 221 Miss. 320, 72 So.2d 681 (1954); Strauder v. State of West Virginia, 100 U.S. 303 (1880).

[9] Spanel v. Pegler, 160 F.2d 619 (7th Cir. 1947); Levy v. Gelber, 175 Misc. 746, 25 N.Y.S.2d 148 (1941).

[10] Cf. Solverson v. Peterson, 64 Wis. 198, 25 N.W. 14 (1885); Urban v. Helmick, 15 Wash. 155, 45 P. 747 (1896).

been defamed.[11]   Ordinarily, however, it is not possible for one to be defamed through an insult or slur upon someone close to him, such as a member of his family.[12]   Nor can a group be defamed, except under the law of criminal libel which is outside the realm of torts.

A person does not need to be lowered in the esteem of an entire community, or even of a majority, to be defamed.   "It is enough that the communication tend to prejudice him in the eyes of a substantial and respectable minority of them   *   *   *." [13]

In the division of defamation into libel and slander, the mass media of communication are much more concerned with libel, which was originally printed defamation.   Slander, largely spoken defamation, arises as a problem in some cases involving broadcast media, and will be treated there.

SEC. 11.   LIBEL

Libel is defamation by written or printed words, by its embodiment in physical form, or by any other form of communication which has the potentially harmful qualities characteristic of written or printed words.

Libel took form in England as a crime, presided over by the Court of the Star Chamber which sought to curb the political attacks on authority that were increasing with the growth of printing.[14]   It soon was embraced in the civil law, however, and was distinguished from the older civil offense of spoken defamation—slander—on the grounds that the printed word was potentially more damaging than the spoken.   Print, of course, could be spread much further than speech, and in a shorter time;   furthermore, print was a permanent form of expression whereas speech was evanescent.   Print's greater capacity for harm brought courts to hold that that libel deserved

[11] Americans for Democratic Action v. Meade, 72 Pa.D. & C. 306 (1951); New York Society for Suppression of Vice v. MacFadden Publications, 129 Misc. 408, 221 N.Y.S. 563 (1927), affirmed 222 App.Div. 739, 226 N.Y.S. 870 (1928); Mullins v. Brando, 13 Cal.App.3d 409, 91 Cal.Rptr. 796 (1970).

[12] Wildstein v. New York Post Corp., 40 Misc.2d 586, 243 N.Y.S.2d 386 (1963); Ryan v. Hearst Publications, 3 Wash.2d 128, 100 P.2d 24 (1940); Security Sales Agency v. A. S. Abell Co., 205 F. 941 (D.C.Md.1913); But "daughter of a murderer" has been held libelous: Van Wiginton v. Pulitzer Pub. Co., 135 C.C.A. 483, 218 F. 795 (1914).

[13] American Law Institute, Restatement of the Law of Torts, III (St. Paul, 1938), p. 141; Herrmann v. Newark Morning Ledger Co., 48 N.J.Super. 420, 138 A.2d 61, 71 (1958).

[14] Kelly, op cit.

fuller redress than speech, and rules of law more favorable to the defamed person than did slander.

It has long been recognized, however, that writing and printing are not the only carriers of potential libel. In the celebrated case of People v. Croswell of 1804, pictures and signs were included in the definition of libel.[15] With new means of communication, it was held that motion pictures could be libelous.[16] As broadcasting brought radio, and later television, debate arose as to whether this should be treated as slander because it was speech rather than print, or as libel because its capacity for spreading defamation to huge audiences deserved the heavier penalties and stricter rules that libel provided.[17] State statutes and court decisions where there were no statutes brought differing conclusions as to whether broadcast was libel or slander.

One definition of civil libel attempts to take into account varying forms of communication that have specially great possibilities for harm to reputations. The American Law Institute defines libel as publication of defamatory matter "by written or printed words, by its embodiment in physical form, or by any other form of communication which has the potentially harmful qualities characteristic of written or printed words." [18] Imprecise though this remains, it does attempt to establish a logical basis on which to account for damage by Twentieth Century means of mass communication in determining what is libel. It also apparently embraces defamation outside the concern of the mass media, such as by effigies or statues, or by open and obvious "shadowing" of an individual.[19]

It should be remembered that civil libel is an offense against an individual or person or a specific entity such as a corporation, partnership, or certain voluntary organizations. There must be identification of the individual or entity. Large groups such as businessmen in general, or labor, or a political party, or the legal profession, or an ethnic group of a large city, cannot sue for libel, although under some circumstances the crime of "group libel" has been recognized (see below, Chap. 9).

When, however, a charge is levied against a small group, each member may be considered by the law to be libeled, and the

15 3 Johns. Cases 337 (N.Y.1804).

16 Youssoupoff v. Metro-Goldwyn-Mayer Pictures, 51 L.Q.Rev. 281, 99 A.L.R. 864 (1934); Kelly v. Loew's, 76 F.Supp. 473 (D.C.Mass.1948).

17 Haley, A. G., The Law on Radio Programs, 5 George Wash.L.Rev. 157, 183, 1937.

18 Restatement of Torts, p. 159.

19 Schultz v. Frankfort Marine, Accident & Plate Glass Ins. Co., 151 Wis. 537, 139 N.W. 386 (1913).

individuals may bring separate suits even though no one has been named or singled out. It is by no means clear what the upper limit of a "small group" that warrants such treatment is; twenty-five has been suggested.[20] Courts have held that each member of a jury can be defamed,[21] or all four officers of a labor union,[22] or all salesmen in a force of 25 employed by a department store.[23]

SEC. 12. LIBELOUS WORDS CLASSIFIED

Five categories or kinds of words may be identified in organizing the field of libel. Libel may also be classified according to libel *per se*, or words defamatory on their face; and libel *per quod*, or words defamatory when facts extrinsic to the story make them damaging.

Danger signals for the newsman who is trying to avoid libel can be raised by grouping the kinds of statements and the circumstances which have brought suits into classes. Five of these are identified here in helping clarify that which can bring hatred, ridicule, contempt, loss of esteem, or damage in one's trade or profession.

Damage to the Esteem or Social Standing in Which One is Held.

Of the various ways in which a person may be lowered in the estimation in which he is held, probably none has brought more libel suits than a false charge of crime. The "public principle" of New York Times Co. v. Sullivan, of course, is especially protective of the media where crime is reported, because crime is a matter of public or general concern if any subject is.[24] But, as the next chapter will show, there remain circumstances in which the protection is not given.

The news media cover the police and crime beat daily; the persistent possibility of a mistake in names and addresses is never absent. And the courts hold everywhere that it is libel to charge one erroneously with a crime. It is easy to get a libel case based on such a charge into court, even though it has become much harder to win it.

[20] Prosser, p. 768; Schutzman & Schutzman v. News Syndicate Co., 60 Misc.2d 827, 304 N.Y.S.2d 167 (1969).

[21] Byers v. Martin, 2 Colo. 605 (1875).

[22] DeWitte v. Kearney & Trecker Corp., 265 Wis. 132, 60 N.W.2d 748 (1953).

[23] Neiman-Marcus Co. v. Lait, 13 F.R.D. 311 (D.C.N.Y.1952).

[24] Cerrito v. Time, Inc., 302 F.Supp. 1071 (D.C.Cal.1969).

The print falsely that one has been arrested for larceny,[25] or that a person is held in jail on a forgery charge,[26] or to say incorrectly that one has illicitly sold or distributed narcotics,[27] is libelous on its face. To say without legal excuse that one has committed arson,[28] bigamy,[29] perjury,[30] or murder [31] is libelous.

There is no substitute as a protection against libel suits for the ancient admonition to the reporter: "Accuracy always." [32] Failure to check one more source of information before writing a story based upon a plausible source has brought many libel suits.

The *Saturday Evening Post* published a story titled "They Call Me Tiger Lil" in its Oct. 26, 1963 issue. The subject was Lillian Reis Corabi, a Philadelphia night club owner and entertainer. The article connected her in various ways with murder and theft, quoting a police captain as saying she and others were responsible for a death by dynamite, and in other ways connecting her with burglary and an apparent drowning. The *Post* argued that the words complained of were not defamatory, but the Pennsylvania Supreme Court upheld the trial judge in his finding some 18 paragraphs of the article "capable of defamatory meaning." It defined defamation as that which "tends so to harm the reputation of another as to lower him in the estimation of the community * * * ".[33] The court's decision thus found the elements of libel present in the story, although it agreed with the lower court that because of a grossly excessive award of damages by the jury—$250,000 in compensatory and $500,000 in punitive damages—[34] there should be a new trial.

---

[25] Thomas v. Bowen, 29 Or. 258, 45 P. 768 (1896); Porter v. News & Courier Co., 237 S.C. 102, 115 S.E.2d 656 (1960); Aku v. Lewis, 52 Hawaii 366, 477 P.2d 162 (1970).

[26] Oklahoma Pub. Co. v. Givens, 67 F.2d 62 (10th Cir. 1933); Barnett v. Schumacher, 453 S.W.2d 934 (Mo.1970).

[27] Snowden v. Pearl River Broadcasting Corp., 251 So.2d 405, (La.App. 1971).

[28] McAuliffe v. Local Union No. 3, International Brotherhood of Elec. Workers, 29 N.Y.S.2d 963 (Sup., 1941).

[29] Taylor v. Tribune Pub. Co., 67 Fla. 361, 65 So. 3 (1914); Pitts v. Spokane Chronicle Co., 63 Wash.2d 763, 388 P.2d 976 (1964).

[30] Milan v. Long, 78 W.Va. 102, 88 S.E. 618 (1916); Riss v. Anderson, 304 F.2d 188 (8th Cir. 1962).

[31] Shiell v. Metropolis Co., 102 Fla. 794, 136 So. 537 (1931); Frechette v. Special Magazines, 285 App.Div. 174, 136 N.Y.S.2d 448 (1954).

[32] For a classic mixup in names: Francis v. Lake Charles American Press, 262 La. 875, 265 So.2d 206 (1972).

[33] Corabi v. Curtis Pub. Co., 441 Pa. 432, 273 A.2d 899, 904 (1971).

[34] Corabi v. Curtis Pub. Co., 437 Pa. 143, 262 A.2d 665, 670 (1970).

Nor was the *Post* successful in arguing that libel was not present in a story on Mafia activities on Grand Bahama Island, in which it carried a photo of a group of people including Holmes, a tourist.   The photo caption referred to "High-Rollers at the Monte Carlo club," and said that the club's casino grossed $20 million a year with a third "skimmed off for American Mafia 'families'."   Holmes, the focal point of the picture and a man in no way connected with the Mafia, sued for libel.   The *Post*, saying the story was not defamatory, moved for a judgment on the pleadings; but the court held that a jury case was called for and that a jury might find libel.[35]

The Supreme Court of Hawaii found defamation in statements by a television sportscaster about Earle E. Aku, who launched a fund-raising television show to raise money for the Kaneohe Bantams Football Team of the Hawaii Pop Warner League. Tickets were sold by phone solicitation, the callers mentioning Earle Aku by name as he had organized the team and coached it for four years.   Soon after the solicitations began, the newsroom of station KGMB–TV received two phone calls from listeners who had long known radio personality Hal Lewis as "Aku," from his much-used pseudonym "J. Akuhead Pupule." They asked whether Aku were, indeed supporting the benefit program.   A sportscaster for the station went on the air later in the day, and according to Earle E. Aku, said that "There is a man of ill-repute who is posing as Aku, raising funds for a football team.   This is a fraud, and not true, so watch out."   Afterward, some would-be ticket purchasers returned their tickets and others failed to remit payments.

Earle E. Aku sued the station and Lewis for defamation.   The trial court gave a summary judgment to the defendants, but the Supreme Court of Hawaii reversed, saying that the case should have gone to a trial.   It said that the alleged statements were defamatory, and upon a trial they might be found unprotected.[36]

The news story which states incorrectly that a person has been *convicted* of a crime may be more dangerous than the one which wrongly suggests or states that he is *accused* of crime.   But whatever the difference, the latter can cause libel suits, as we have seen above in the *Corabi* and *Aku* cases, the one suggesting that Lillian Corabi was associated with major crimes and the other that Earle E. Aku had perpetrated fraud.

Not every suggestion of liability, however, has resulted in judgment against the defending news medium.   This story, for

[35] Holmes v. Curtis Pub. Co., 303 F.Supp. 522 (D.C.S.C.1969).

[36] Aku v. Lewis, 52 Hawaii 366, 477 P.2d 162 (1970).

example, was held by the court to contain nothing defamatory and capable of meaning that a fire was of incendiary origin and set by the owner of the burned building: [37]

THRICE BURNED

The Daniels & Cornell Block Again Visited by Fire— Damage Largely by Water, and Estimated at $70,000, Covered by Insurance

At 10:15 o'clock last night R. A. Reid, of the printer's firm of J. A. & R. A. Reid, while working at his desk on the top floor of the tall Daniels & Cornell Building on Customhouse street, discovered smoke and flame issuing from the composing room in the rear of the office * * *. He immediately descended to the street, and notified Patrolman Hartwell * * *. The fiery element completely invaded the entire fifth floor, which was all occupied by the Messrs. Reid, who claim complete loss from fire and water. They were insured for $55,000. The fire extended from this room to the roof, the northwest portion of which was destroyed. The fire is the third to have occurred in this building in the past thirteen years * * *. Every fire in this building has started on the upper floor, and twice in Reid's printing establishment.

Sometimes but not always involving crime are words imputing to women sexual acts outside prevailing moral codes, or that falsely state that a woman has been raped. Esteem and social standing, it is plain, are at stake where a woman is unjustifiably accused of adultery or unchastity, or is said to have been raped. Courts everywhere regard written or printed statements charging without foundation that a woman is immoral as actionable libel. The charge of indiscretion need not be pronounced; any statement fairly imputing immoral conduct is actionable.[38]

Esteem and social standing can be lowered in the eyes of others by statements concerning race and political belief, as well as by those grouped under crime and under sexual immorality in the preceding pages. To take political belief first, the salient cases since the late 1940's have largely involved false charges of "Communist" or "Red" or some variant of these words indicating

[37] Reid v. Providence Journal Co., 20 R.I. 120, 37 A. 637 (1897).

[38] Baird v. Dun & Bradstreet, 446 Pa. 266, 285 A.2d 166 (1971); Wildstein v. New York Post Corp., 40 Misc.2d 586, 243 N.Y.S.2d 386 (1963); Youssoupoff v. Metro-Goldwyn-Mayer, 50 Times L.R. 581, 99 A.L.R. 864 (1934).

that one subscribes to a generally hated political doctrine. But before these, a line of cases since the 1890's produced libel convictions against those who had anathematized others as anarchists, Socialists, or Fascists.

In the days of Emma Goldman and Big Bill Haywood, it was laid down by the courts that to call one "anarchist" falsely was libelous; [39] when socialism protested capitalism and America's involvement in World War I, "red-tinted agitator" and "Socialist" were words for which a wronged citizen could recover; [40] in the revulsion against Nazi Germany and Japan during World War II, false accusations of "Fascist" and "pro-Jap" brought libel judgments.[41]

Magazines, columnists, newspapers, and corporations have paid for carelessness indulged in by charging others as "Communist" or "representative for the Communist Party." The "basis for reproach is a belief that such political affiliations constitute a threat to our institutions * * *." [42]

The decisions holding false charges of communism as libelous largely began as America and the USSR entered the "cold war" period following World War II. One of the early cases stemmed from an article in the *Reader's Digest,* in which the author charged that the Political Action Committee of his union had hired Sidney S. Grant, "who but recently was a legislative representative for the Massachusetts Communist Party." Grant sued for libel, saying that the article was false. The magazine was unable to convince the court that "representative for the Communist Party" was not in the same category as a flat charge of "Communist," and Grant won the suit.[43]

Again, one organization charged in print that another was "communist dominated," and was taken to court on a libel charge by the second. The defendant gave evidence that the plaintiff organization's president had attacked the profit system and urged cooperative instead of corporate farming; that one of its pamphlets called the profit system vicious and unworkable;

[39] Cerveny v. Chicago Daily News Co., 139 Ill. 345, 28 N.E. 692 (1891); Wilkes v. Shields, 62 Minn. 426, 64 N.W. 921 (1895).

[40] Wells v. Times Printing Co., 77 Wash. 171, 137 P. 457 (1913); Ogren v. Rockford Star Printing Co., 288 Ill. 405, 123 N.E.2d 587 (1919).

[41] Hartley v. Newark Morning Ledger Co., 134 N.J.L. 217, 46 A.2d 777 (1946); Hryhorijiv v. Winchell, 180 Misc. 574, 45 N.Y.S.2d 31 (1943).

[42] Anon., "Supplement," 171 A.L.R. 709, 712 (1947).

[43] Grant v. Reader's Digest Ass'n, 151 F.2d 733 (2d Cir. 1945). And see Wright v. Farm Journal, 158 F.2d 976 (2d Cir. 1947); Spanel v. Pegler, 160 F.2d 619 (7th Cir. 1947); MacLeod v. Tribune Pub. Co., 52 Cal. 536, 343 P.2d 36 (1959).

and that several persons had been members of the accused organization and of the Communist Party at the same time. This was not convincing evidence to the court of communist domination, and the plaintiff was awarded $25,000, which was upheld upon appeal.[44]

Not every insinuation that a person is less than American, however, is libelous, as ruled in McAuliffe v. Local Union No. 3.[45] It is hard to draw a line, and the line has moved from decade to decade according to the currently feared political doctrine.

Where the courts hold an incorrect racial identification as libelous in America, the word at issue usually is "Negro" and the locale is below the Mason-Dixon line. The slur on Negroes inherent in a decision which says a white man can recover for being identified as a Negro has been no barrier to these decisions. At least as far back as 1791, cases in the South have asserted inferiority in the Negro race, and judgments have been upheld in which whites called Negro have been awarded damages.[46]

Under the heading "Negro News" and a picture of a Negro soldier, the *Anderson (S.C.) Daily Mail* printed an item saying that the son of a Mrs. Bowen had been transferred to a government hospital. Mrs. Bowen brought a libel suit, saying she had been named in the story as the mother, and that she was white. The newspaper asked the trial court for a directed verdict, arguing that it was not libel on its face to call a white person a Negro. The trial court gave the newspaper the verdict, Mrs. Bowen appealed, and the South Carolina Supreme Court reversed the verdict. It cited a line of South Carolina cases going back to 1791, and said: [47]

> The earlier cases were decided at a time when slavery existed, and since then great changes have taken place in the legal and political status of the colored race. However, there is still to be considered the social distinction existing between the races, since libel may be based upon social status.

*   *   *   *   *   *   *   *   *

[44] Utah State Farm Bureau Federation v. National Farmers Union Service Corp., 198 F.2d 20 (10th Cir. 1952).

[45] 29 N.Y.S.2d 963 (Sup.1941); McGaw v. Webster, 79 N.M. 104, 440 P.2d 296 (1968).

[46] Eden v. Legare, 1 Bay 171, (1791); Strauder v. W. Va., 100 U.S. 303 (1880); Jones v. R. L. Polk & Co., 190 Ala. 243, 67 So. 577 (1915).

[47] Bowen v. Independent Pub. Co., 230 S.C. 509, 512–513, 96 S.E.2d 564, 565–566 (1957); Natchez Times Pub. Co. v. Dunigan, 221 Miss. 320, 72 So.2d 681 (1954).

Although to publish in a newspaper of a white woman that she is a Negro imputes no mental, moral or physical fault for which she may justly be held accountable to public opinion, yet in view of the social habits and customs deep-rooted in this State, such publication is calculated to affect her standing in society and to injure her in the estimation of her friends and acquaintances.

Finally, there are many words among those lowering esteem or social standing that defy classifying. Appellations that may be common enough in the excited conversation of neighborhood gossips can turn to actionable libel when reduced to print or writing. It is actionable on its face to print and publish that one is "a liar," [48] "a skunk," [49] or "a scandalmonger"; [50] "a drunkard," [51] "a hypocrite," [52] or "a hog"; [53] or to call one heartless and neglectful of his family.[54] Name-calling where private citizens are concerned is occasionally the kind of news that makes a lively paragraph, but the alert as well as the responsible reporter recognizes it for what it is and takes it or leaves it on better grounds than its titillation value.

Damage Through Ridicule.

It is fruitless to try to draw too narrow a line between words that ridicule and those treated previously, that lower esteem and social standing. That which ridicules may at times have the effect of damaging social standing. Yet that which attempts to satirize, or which makes an individual appear uncommonly foolish, or makes fun of misfortune has a quality distinct enough to serve as its own warning signal.

Ridicule must be more than a simple joke at another's expense, for life cannot be so grim that the thin-skinned, the solemn, and the self-important may demand to go entirely unharried. But when the good-humored barb penetrates too deeply or carries too

[48] Paxton v. Woodward, 31 Mont. 195, 78 P. 215 (1904); Smith v. Lyons, 142 La. 975, 77 So. 896 (1918); contra, Bennett v. Transamerican Press, 298 F.Supp. 1013 (D.C.Iowa 1969); Calloway v. Central Charge Service, 142 U.S.App.D.C. 259, 440 F.2d 287 (1971).

[49] Massuere v. Dickens, 70 Wis. 83, 35 N.W. 349 (1887).

[50] Patton v. Cruce, 72 Ark. 421, 81 S.W. 380 (1904).

[51] Giles v. State, 6 Ga. 276 (1848); cf. Smith v. Fielden, 205 Tenn. 313, 326 S.W.2d 476 (1959).

[52] Overstreet v. New Nonpareil Co., 184 Iowa 485, 167 N.W. 669 (1918).

[53] Solverson v. Peterson, 64 Wis. 198, 25 N.W. 14 (1885).

[54] Brown v. Du Frey, 1 N.Y.2d 649, 151 N.Y.S.2d 649, 134 N.E.2d 469 (1956).

sharp a sting, or when a picture can be easily interpreted in a deeply derogatory manner, ridicule amounting to actionable libel may have occurred.

Mary and Letitia Megarry objected to the repeated parking of a car in violation of parking rules near their business. They wrote a note and placed it on the car, saying that they'd call the matter to the attention of the police unless the practice were stopped. James Norton, the owner of the car, hung a sign in public view saying "Nuts to You—You Old Witch." The Megarrys sued for $5,000, and on appeal their suit was upheld.[55] The court said that the sign "was intended to subject appellants to contempt and ridicule," and that the words could not fairly be read to have an innocent interpretation. This was libel.

To sensationalize the poverty of a former gentlewoman so as to bring her into ridicule and contempt,[56] or to make a joke out of the desertion of a bride on her wedding day[57] have been held libelous.

Yet there is room for satire, burlesque and exaggeration. The columnist Jimmy Breslin of the former *New York Herald Tribune* has a fine talent for satire, and a libel suit based on his account of barkeep Hyman Cohen's encounter with murder was not successful. Cohen was a witness to the murder of one Munos at the Vivere Lounge in New York City, and fearing for his life if he talked to authorities about the killers, he denied for a time that the murder had happened at the Lounge or that he had witnessed it. He also fled the city. Breslin's column about Cohen was written after he had interviewed police, the district attorney and Cohen's employer, and had read about and inspected the scene of the murder. The column began:

> Among New Yorkers out of town for the week end, and out of town for a lot of week ends to come if he has his way, is Mr. Hyman Cohen, of the Bronx. His friends say that he went to the Catskills for the rest of the summer, but there is a feeling that the Catskills are not quite far enough away for Hy at present.
>
> 'The last time I saw Hy he asked me about the Italian Alps,' a detective was saying the other night.
>
> Hy is a man who once liked this city very much. Particularly, he liked the part of the city they make television shows about. Gunmen, action guys; they were

[55] Megarry v. Norton, 137 Cal.App.2d 581, 290 P.2d 571 (1955).

[56] Moffatt v. Cauldwell, 3 Hun 26, 5 Thomp. & C. 256 (N.Y.1874).

[57] Kirman v. Sun Printing & Pub. Ass'n, 99 App.Div. 367, 91 N.Y.S. 193 (1904).

Hy's idea of people. Then a couple of weeks ago, this little corner of life in our town grew too big for Hy to handle. He had a change of heart. A heart 'attack' might be a better word for it. And he left town thoroughly disillusioned.

Hy is a bartender, and it all started a couple of summers ago when he worked at a hotel in the Catskills and found himself pouring drinks for some underworld notables. He never really got over this. When the summer ended, Hy came back to New York and he was no longer Hy Cohen of the Bronx. He was Hy Cohen of the Rackets. He wore a big, snap-brim extortionist's hat, white on white shirts and a white tie. And when he would talk, especially if there were only a few people at the bar and they all could listen, Hy would begin talking about all the tough guys he knew. This was Hy's field.

The court held that though the article was not literally true in every detail, "it presented a fair sketch of a confident talkative bartender who was reduced to speechlessness, self-effacement and flight by gangsters * * *." [58] It explained why it was not libelous: [59]

With sardonic humor Breslin described Cohen's frantic flight to avoid the murderous gangsters as well as to escape the police who were hot on the killer's trail. The humor was not funny, except on the surface. Murder and terror are * * * the subjects of satire which superficially conceals a tragic or a solemn happening. Our courts have held that mere exaggeration, irony or wit does not make a writing libelous unless the article would be libelous without the exaggeration, irony or wit.

While a living man whose obituary has mistakenly been printed may feel annoyed and injured, and may attract unusual attention and perhaps a rough joke or two as he walks into his office the next morning, he has not been libeled. As one court said, death "is looked for in the history of every man," and where there is notice of a death that has not occurred, "Prematurity is the sole peculiarity." [60]

[58] Cohen v. New York Herald Tribune, Inc., 63 Misc.2d 87, 310 N.Y.S.2d 709, 725 (1970).

[59] Ibid., 724. See also Sellers v. Time, Inc., 299 F.Supp. 582 (D.C.Pa. 1969).

[60] Cohen v. New York Times Co., 153 App.Div. 242, 138 N.Y.S. 206 (1912); Cardiff v. Brooklyn Eagle, Inc., 190 Misc. 730, 75 N.Y.S.2d 222 (1948).

Damage Through Words Imputing Disease or Mental Illness.

The law has long held that diseases which may be termed "loathsome, infectious, or contagious" may be libelous when falsely attributed to an individual. That which is "loathsome" may change with time and changing mores, of course, but venereal disease, the plague, leprosy, and small pox seem to fit this description. Anyone alleged to be presently suffering from any of these diseases is likely to be shunned by his fellows. And if the disease carries the stigma of immorality, such as venereal disease or alcoholism or addiction, it may be libelous to say of a person that he formerly had it, although he has since been cured.

To charge without legal excuse that one has leprosy was held libelous in Lewis v. Hayes; [61] the imputation of venereal disease was held libelous in King v. Pillsbury. As for an incorrect assignment of mental impairment or of mental illness to a person, it is libel on its face.[62] The magazine *Fact* published in its September-October issue of 1964, an article billed as "The Unconscious of a Conservative: A Special Issue on the Mind of Barry Goldwater." Goldwater was the Republican Party's candidate for president and a senator from Arizona at the time. He was portrayed in one of two articles as "paranoid," his attacks on other politicians stemming from a conviction that "everybody hates him, and it is better to attack them first." A *Fact* poll of psychiatrists, asked to judge whether Goldwater was psychologically fit to serve as president, also was reported on. A jury found libel and awarded Goldwater $1.00 in compensatory damages and $75,000 in punitive damages. Its finding was upheld by the U. S. Court of Appeals for the Second Circuit.[63]

Damaging One in His Trade, Occupation, or Profession.

So long as a man follows a legal calling, he has a claim not to be traduced unfairly in the performance of it. The possibilities are rich for damaging one through words that impugn his honesty, skill, fitness, ethical standards, or financial capacity in his chosen work, whether it be banking or basket-weaving. Observe some of the possibilities: that a University was a "degree mill"; [64] that a contractor engaged in unethical trade; [65] that a

[61] 165 Cal. 527, 132 P. 1022 (1913); Simpson v. Press Pub. Co., 33 Misc. 228, 67 N.Y.S. 401 (1900); King v. Pillsbury, 115 Me. 528, 99 A. 513 (1918); Sally v. Brown, 220 Ky. 576, 295 S.W. 890 (1927).

[62] Cowper v. Vannier, 20 Ill.App.2d 499, 156 N.E.2d 761 (1959); Kenny v. Hatfield, 351 Mich. 498, 88 N.W.2d 535 (1958).

[63] Goldwater v. Ginzburg, 414 F.2d 324 (2d Cir. 1969).

[64] Laurence University v. State, 68 Misc.2d 408, 326 N.Y.S.2d 617 (1971).

[65] Greenbelt Co-op Pub. Ass'n v. Bresler, 253 Md. 324, 252 A.2d 755 (1969), reversed on other grounds, 398 U.S. 6, 90 S.Ct. 1537 (1970).

clergyman was "an interloper, a meddler, a spreader of distrust"; [66] that a schoolmaster kept girls after school so that he could court them; [67] that a jockey rode horses unfairly and dishonestly.[68]

Likewise, it was libel for a newspaper to criticize a farmer and organizer so as to hold him up to public hatred and contempt, thus affecting his business; [69] for one to print an article which charged an attorney with betraying confidence and with extortion; [70] to publish charges that an attorney induced a girl to sign a false affidavit; [71] to state in print that a physician is a quack; [72] to charge a teacher with having an unsound mind.[73]

The slurring adjective or noun that libels a professional may, of course, cast no reproach upon a laborer, and *vice versa*. To say of a physician or attorney that he has not kept abreast of the literature of his field could be damaging to him, but is scarcely a charge that would do damage to a shovel man in a construction gang. To incorrectly accuse the shovel man of chronic bursitis in the shoulders, on the other hand, might limit his employment opportunities, while the same charge would be harmless to the professional.

By no means every statement to which a businessman, tradesman or professional takes exception, however, is libelous. Thus Frederick D. Washington, a church bishop, sued the *New York Daily News* and columnist Robert Sylvester for his printed statement that Washington had attended a nightclub performance at which a choir member of his church sang. The bishop argued that his church did not approve of its spiritual leaders' attending nightclubs, and that he had been damaged. The court said the account was not, on its face, an attack on the plaintiff's integrity, and called the item a "warm human interest story" in which there was general interest. This was not libel on its face, and the court upheld dismissal of Bishop Washington's complaint.[74]

Nor did David Brown convince the court that there was libel in a pamphlet that opposed his attempt to get a zoning change

[66] Van Lonkhuyzen v. Daily News Co., 195 Mich. 283, 161 N.W. 979 (1917).

[67] Spears v. McCoy, 155 Ky. 1, 159 S.W. 610 (1913).

[68] Wood v. Earl of Durham, 21 Q.B. 501 (1888).

[69] Stevens v. Morse, 185 Wis. 500, 201 N.W. 815 (1925).

[70] Mannix v. Portland Telegram, 136 Or. 474, 297 P. 350 (1931).

[71] Corsello v. Emerson Bros., 106 Conn. 127, 137 A. 390 (1927).

[72] Brinkley v. Fishbein, 134 Kan. 833, 8 P.2d 318 (1932).

[73] Totten v. Sun Printing & Publishing Ass'n, 109 F. 289 (2d Cir. 1901).

[74] Washington v. New York News, 37 A.D.2d 577, 322 N.Y.S.2d 896 (1971).

from the City Council of Knoxville, Tenn. The pamphlet attacked a change that would have permitted Brown to build apartments in a residential district, and asked the question: "Have the 'Skids Been Greased' at City Council?" Brown sued for libel, arguing that the question suggested he had bribed the City Council and that it had accepted the bribe. But the court held that the question was clearly unambiguous and did not suggest bribery in its reasonable and obvious meaning; but rather, that pressure in the form of political influence had been brought to bear on certain Council members to expedite matters. This was not libel. Had the pamphlet said that "palms are greased at the City Council," that would have been libel on its face and actionable.[75]

A margin of protection also exists in the occasional finding by a court that mistakenly attributing a single instance of clumsiness or error to a professional man is not enough to damage him. Rather, such cases have held, there must be a suggestion of more general incompetency or lack of quality before a libel charge will hold. One court said:[76]

> To charge a professional man with negligence or unskillfulness in the management or treatment of an individual case, is no more than to impute to him the mistakes and errors incident to fallible human nature. The most eminent and skillful physician or surgeon may mistake the symptoms of a particular case without detracting from his general professional skill or learning. To say of him, therefore, that he was mistaken in that case would not be calculated to impair the confidence of the community in his general professional competency.

The "single instance" rule, however, does nothing to protect printed material that assigns questionable ethics or business practices to a person. The *Bristow Record* carried a story saying that L. M. Nichols had sold a building. While he owned it, the Record said,

> Nichols used the building for the purpose of attempting to destroy the value of the Record-Citizen publishing plant after he had sold that plant and collected the money from the sale.
> However, he later discovered that * * * business firms in the city * * * did not enjoy doing busi-

75 Brown v. Newman, 224 Tenn. 297, 454 S.W.2d 120 (1970).

76 Blende v. Hearst Publications, 200 Wash. 426, 93 P.2d 733 (1939); November v. Time, Inc., 13 N.Y.2d 175, 244 N.Y.S.2d 309, 194 N.E.2d 126 (1963); Holder Const. Co. v. Ed Smith & Sons, 124 Ga.App. 89, 182 S.E.2d 919 (1971).

ness with organizations that openly operate with shady ethics. In recent years his publishing activities have been maintained on a sneak basis.

Nichols sued for libel, and though he lost his case at trial, he won it on appeal. The Supreme Court of Oklahoma said that an article accusing one of "shady ethics" and of operating on a "sneak basis" tends "to deprive that person of public confidence, and tends to injure him in his occupation." [77]

Damage to a Corporation's Integrity, Credit, or Ability to Carry on Business.

Finally, it is possible to damage the reputation of a corporation or partnership by defamation that reflects on the conduct, management, or financial condition of the corporation.[78] To say falsely that a company is in shaky financial condition, or that it cannot pay its debts, would be libelous, as would the imputation that it has engaged in dishonest practices. While a corporation is an entity quite different from the individuals that head it or staff it, there is no doubt that it has a reputation, an "image" to protect.

Cosgrove Studio and Camera Shop, Inc., advertised in two community newspapers that it would offer a free roll of film for every roll brought to it for developing and printing. The next day its business competitor, Cal R. Pane, advertised in one of the same newspapers, in part as follows:

USE COMMON SENSE * * *

You Get NOTHING for NOTHING!

WE WILL NOT!

1. Inflate the prices of your developing to give you a new roll free!

2. Print the blurred negatives to inflate the price of your snapshots!

Cosgrove brought a suit for libel, alleging that Pane's advertisement was by implication a response to its advertisements to give free film, and implied that Cosgrove was dishonest in business practices and inflated its prices. The trial court said that the words of Pane's advertisement were not libelous in themselves, and found for Pane. Cosgrove appealed and the appeals

---

[77] Nichols v. Bristow Pub. Co., 330 P.2d 1044 (Okl.1957).

[78] Dupont Engineering Co. v. Nashville Banner Pub. Co., 13 F.2d 186 (D.C. Tenn.1925); Electric Furnace Corp. v. Deering Milliken Research Corp., 325 F.2d 761 (6th Cir. 1963).

court reversed the judgment, saying that Cosgrove did indeed have a cause of action. The words, it said, were libelous on their face. Any language which "unequivocally, maliciously, and falsely imputes to an individual or corporation want of integrity in the conduct of his or its business is actionable," it held.

In arriving at this decision, the appeals court made a point important in many cases: that identification of the defamed need not be by name—as indeed it was not in this case. "The fact that the plaintiff is not specifically named in the advertisement is not controlling. A party need not be specifically named, if pointed to by description or circumstances tending to identify him," it ruled.[79]

SEC. 13.   THE FORM OF THE LIBEL

Damage may be caused by any part of the medium's content, including headlines, pictures, and advertisements.

Whatever is printed is printed at the peril of the publisher, who cannot, for example, escape liability for libel in an advertisement on grounds that a company or advertising agency furnished him with the copy. A headline which carries a libelous meaning may bring about a successful libel suit even though the story itself modifies or negates the meaning of the head. And a picture does not escape the definition of "libel" merely because it is a mode of communication different from words.

A 1956 decision explains how headlines and closing "tag-lines" of a news story can be libelous (even though in this case the newspaper defended itself successfully). One story in a series published by the *Las Vegas Sun* brought a libel suit because of its headline and closing tag-line advertising the next article in the series. The headline read "Babies for Sale. Franklin Black Market Trade of Child Told." The tag-line promoting the story to appear the next day read "Tomorrow—Blackmail by Franklin." The body of the story told factually the way in which attorney Franklin had obtained a mother's release of her child for adoption. Franklin sued for libel and won. But the *Sun* appealed, claiming among other things that the trial judge had erred in instructing the jury that the words were libelous. The *Sun* said that the language was ambiguous, and susceptible of more than one interpretation.

There were other questions involved, and the Nevada Supreme Court reversed the decision on different grounds.[80] But on the

---

[79] Cosgrove Studio and Camera Shop, Inc. v. Pane, 408 Pa. 314, 319, 182 A.2d 751, 753 (1962). Also, Grove v. Dun & Bradstreet, Inc., 438 F.2d 433 (3d Cir. 1971).

[80] Las Vegas Sun, Inc. v. Franklin, 74 Nev. 282, 329 P.2d 867 (1958).

matter of whether the headline and tag-line were libelous, it said
that they were indeed. Under any reasonable definition, it said,
"black-market sale" and "blackmail" "would tend to lower the
subject in the estimation of the community and to excite derogatory opinions against him and to hold him up to contempt."
Then it explained the part that a headline has in creating a
libel: [81]

> Appellants contend that the headline and tag-line can-
> not be considered apart from the context in which they
> were used. Thus, they contend, the headline must be
> qualified by and read in the light of the article to which
> it referred and the tag-line must be qualified by and
> read in the light of the subsequent article to which it re-
> ferred.

> This is not so. The text of a newspaper article is not
> ordinarily the context of its headline, since the public
> frequently reads only the headline * * *. The same
> is true of a tag-line or leader, since the public fre-
> quently reads only the leader without reading the sub-
> sequent article to which it refers. The defamation of
> Franklin contained in the headline was complete upon
> its face * * *. The same is true of the tag-line.

> We conclude that the trial judge properly instructed the
> jury that the article was libelous *per se*.

The dangers of libel in advertisements, of course, have already
been illustrated in the case of Cosgrove Studio and Camera
Shop, Inc. v. Pane.[82] As for pictures, pictures standing alone,
without caption or story with them, would pose little danger of
defamation, but almost invariably in the media of communication, illustration is accompanied by words, and it is almost always the combination that carries the damaging impact. In an
issue of *Tan*, a story titled "Man Hungry" was accompanied by a
picture taken several years earlier in connection with a woman's
work as a professional model for a dress designer. With it were
the words "She had a good man—but he wasn't enough. So she
picked a bad one!" On the cover of the magazine was the title,
"Shameless Love."

The woman sued for libel, and the court granted her claim for
$3,000. "There is no doubt in this court's mind that the publica-
tion libeled plaintiff," the judge wrote. "The inference to be
drawn by the ordinary reading public of the magazine in question must be the criterion of measurement * * *." It added

[81] Ibid. at 869.

[82] 408 Pa. 314, 182 A.2d 751 (1962).

that "A publication must be considered in its entirety, both the picture and the story which it illustrates." [83]

Where an advertisement carries libel, the advertiser, the advertising agency, and the publisher may be held liable. There is no room for laxity in a news medium's handling of the paid matter that comes to it from other hands. It is not always the case that the newspaper, magazine, or broadcaster is one of those sued, but the liability is there and so is the need for care.

During a program broadcast in Albuquerque, N. M., over station KGGM–TV, the secretary of a Better Business Bureau was speaking to the problem of dishonesty among television repairmen. He held up to the camera a newspaper advertisement of the Day and Night Television Service Company, which offered low-cost service through long hours of each day. In making his point, the speaker said that some television servicemen were cheating the public:

> This is what has been referred to in the trade as the ransom. Ransom, the ransom racket. The technique of taking up the stuff after first assuring the set owner that the charges would only be nominal, and then holding the set for ransom much as the way you would kidnap an individual and hold that individual for ransom.

The New Mexico Supreme Court pointed up the effect of combining the picture and the words: "Standing alone, neither the advertisement nor the words used by Luttbeg could be construed as libel. But the two combined impute fraud and dishonesty to the company and its operators." [84]

The use of the wrong picture in an advertisement gives the foundation for actionable libel, as decided in Peck v. Tribune Co.[85] The use of false or unauthorized testimonials in advertisements may constitute libel, according to decisions in Pavesich v. New England Life Ins. Co.,[86] Foster Milburn Co. v. Chinn,[87] and Hart v. John H. Woodbury Dermatological Institute.[88]

[83] Martin v. Johnson Pub. Co., 157 N.Y.S.2d 409, 411 (Sup., 1956). See also Farrington v. Star Co., 244 N.Y. 585, 155 N.E. 906 (1927) (wrong picture); Wasserman v. Time, Inc., 138 U.S.App.D.C. 7, 424 F.2d 920 (1970) certiorari denied 398 U.S. 940, 90 S.Ct. 1844 (1970).

[84] Young v. New Mexico Broadcasting Co., 60 N.M. 475, 292 P.2d 776 (1956); Central Arizona Light & Power Co. v. Akers, 45 Ariz. 526, 46 P.2d 126 (1935).

[85] 214 U.S. 185, 29 S.Ct. 554 (1909).

[86] 122 Ga. 190, 50 S.E. 68 (1905).

[87] 134 Ky 424, 120 S.W. 364 (1909).

[88] 113 App.Div. 281, 98 N.Y.S. 1000 (1906).

SEC. 14.   BROADCAST DEFAMATION: SLANDER AND LIBEL

The rules of slander apply to broadcast defamation in some states, of libel in others, with that which is read from a script more often held libel and that which is extemporaneous more often held slander.

When radio broadcasting joined the printed media as a means of mass communication, new problems in the law of defamation began to unfold.   One of the first concerned the old distinction between slander and libel: Was broadcast defamation to be classified as slander because it was speech, not writing?   Or might it be treated as libel because, in reaching huge audiences, its potential for harm to reputation warranted the use of the looser rules and heavier penalties of libel as compared to those of slander?   Or was it to be treated as something apart from either slander or libel?   As the rise of printing had forced the law to adjust rules of defamation, now the birth of voice broacasting confronted the law with new questions.

For the broadcast media, it was plain, the favorable settlement would be to treat their lapses as slander.   Historic development and accident, congealed during several centuries' adjudication, closed the field of slander to various legal actions and results that would be open to injured persons if radio defamation were to be defined as libel.   Some of the historical development is in order here.

As slander actions moved into the common law courts of England in the Sixteenth and Seventeenth Centuries, judges held that plaintiffs could recover only if they could prove actual damages.   Hard words about another were not to be considered damaging "on their face" and actionable without proof of damage.   Exceptions to this rule came soon to be recognized.   Over the centuries it was agreed by courts that the following words were so patently harmful that plaintiffs would not have to prove actual damage (also called "special damage") to recover:

1.   Words which impute the commission of a crime;
2.   Words which impute that one has or has had a loathsome or contagious disease;
3.   Words which damage a person in his business, trade, office, profession or calling;
4.   Words that impute unchastity or immorality to a woman or girl.

Thus if a man could not show that spoken disparaging words had caused him actual pecuniary damage, he sometimes had an alternative: he could still sue for slander if the words fell into one of the special categories.

With the coming of widely-used printed communications, damaging words in print—libel—seemed to the courts much more serious. The reasons seem to have been that print was permanent, that it could be spread more widely than even a speech to a large audience, that printed defamation seemed more likely to be premeditated than spoken, and that a certain reverence for the printed word existed.[89] With this view of printed or written defamation, the courts did not require in a libel action that a plaintiff prove actual damage or show that the damaging words fell into one of the special classes. An action could be brought for many printed words which, if spoken, would not permit recovery. It might be very hard for a physician, say, or an accountant or businessman to sue or recover for a spoken charge of "coward" because he would have to either:

(a) Prove that he suffered actual pecuniary loss as a result, or

(b) Claim and show that it affected him in the practice of his business or profession (category 3 above).

If, however, the charge were made in print, the courts would not require that he show either of these; they came to hold that damage would be assumed to result from printed defamation. And they awarded larger damages for the presumably more harmful printed defamation than for the spoken.

As the law worked out, gross contradictions came to be perceived in the supposition that slander was less harmful than libel. Little has been done about the problem to this day. A single person besides the defamed might see a libel, perhaps in the form of a letter. Yet it was easier to get such a case accepted by a court than it was to get acceptance in court for some slanders uttered to large groups or audiences: unless the orally defamed could show special damages or that the words fell into one of the four special categories, he had no suit. And it was very difficult, ordinarily, to show special damages. The realities of libel to one person or slander to a host, moreover, were not always reflected in the size of the damages awarded to the defamed: the presumption that slander was of small harm at times prevented a reasonable level of recovery for real wrongs.[90]

---

[89] Hinsdale v. Orange County Publications, Inc., 17 N.Y.2d 284, 270 N.Y.S. 2d 592, 217 N.E.2d 650 (1960); Munafo v. Helfand, 140 F.Supp. 234 (S.D. N.Y.1956).

[90] Prosser, op. cit., 754, 769–781; Spring, Samuel, Risks and Rights (New York: W. W. Norton, 1956), pp. 42, 44; Grein v. LaPoma, 54 Wash.2d 844, 340 P.2d 766 (1959).

If the printed or written work was libel and the spoken word was slander, other forms of communication existed that did not fit neatly into either category. Signs and gestures, pictures, statues, effigies, all could be defamatory; generally, they came to be categorized as libel rather than slander. Communications which reach the eye, it was sometimes said, are libel; those that reach the ear are slander. As movies entered the communication picture, they became identified with libel, the words accompanying the filmed pictures which were permanent in form. And when radio broadcasting began to reach mass audiences, the problem arose in a new way. Some state legislatures realized that the young medium would present problems in the courts. They passed laws classifying broadcast defamation, some declaring that it was libel, others that it was slander.[91] The disagreement and the difficulties were plain by 1930. One view was that since what was broadcast ordinarily was read from a page of typed or written manuscript, defamation that it carried must be libel. More persuasive, however, was the plain fact that millions of people might hear the defamation on radio, and it was preposterous to consider its potential for harm as less than that of defamation by newspapers.

An early case set one course of judicial decision-making that has classified radio and television defamation as libel. This was Sorensen v. Wood.[92] Sorensen was running for re-election as attorney general of Nebraska, when Wood took to the radio to read from an article he had written: Sorensen, he said, was "a nonbeliever, an irreligious libertine, a mad man and a fool." While the court did not deliberate the question whether the words were slander or libel, it noted that "The radio address was written and read by Wood." Then it ruled that "There can be little dispute that the written words charged and published constitute libel rather than slander." [93] Decisions that followed generally took up this reasoning.[94] But many broadcasts did not flow entirely or even partly from scripted words: the interview, the panel discussion, the free-wheeling entertainment program all were likely to field at some time an uninhibited speaker who had no inclination to be bound by words on paper.

---

91 Remmers, D. H., Recent Legislative Trends in Defamation by Radio, 64 Harv.L.Rev. 727, 1951; California, Illinois, and North Dakota passed laws calling it slander; Oregon and Washington, libel.

92 123 Neb. 348, 243 N.W. 82 (1932).

93 Ibid., 243 N.W. 85 (1932).

94 Hartmann v. Winchell, 296 N.Y. 296, 73 N.E.2d 30 (1947); Charles Parker Co. v. Silver City Crystal Co., 142 Conn. 605, 116 A.2d 440 (1955); Christy v. Stauffer Pubs., Inc., 437 S.W.2d 814, 815 (Tex.1969). Slander: Brown v. W.R.M.A. Broadcasting Co., 286 Ala. 186, 238 So.2d 540 (1970).

The ad lib and the Interview in Radio and Television.

Radio personnel who can screen and edit the manuscripts of entertainers, politicians, news analysts, advertisers, and others before their words go on the air have some chance of spotting grossly defamatory words in advance of the broadcast. Where this is the case, radio management can sometimes convince the author of the words that they should be changed before broadcast time to avoid legal problems. But how about the radio funny man or freely spouting politician who does not stick to his script? The spontaneous ad lib, certainly, has always been an ornament in the array of some comedians' talents. Is the station to be liable for a defamation suit rising out of the spontaneously articulated wit of a gifted man in the middle of a broadcast program? Is the careless slur of an insensitive entertainer or interviewee injected without warning into the flow of his talk to be the basis for libel action against the station that is powerless to prevent the misfortune?

Before the 1930's were out, one answer had been provided by the Pennsylvania court in the famous case of Summit Hotel Co. v. National Broadcasting Co.[95] Here the great entertainer, Al Jolson, appeared on an NBC Program under the sponsorship of Shell Eastern Petroleum Products, Inc. He was paid by the advertising agency which Shell had hired, J. Walter Thompson. A golf champion appearing on Jolson's show mentioned that his first professional golf job was with the Summit Hotel. Jolson blurted out an unscripted ad lib: "That's a rotten hotel." Summit sued NBC.

Was NBC to be held to strict accountability for the words, as a newspaper is held strictly accountable for anything it publishes? Or would the nature of the communication process by radio, incompatible with total advance control by the broadcast company, permit a different treatment? The court took into account the special character of broadcasting, and held that the rule of strict accountability did not apply:[96]

> Publication by radio has physical aspects entirely different from those attending the publication of a libel or a slander as the law understands them. The danger of attempting to apply the fixed principles of law governing either libel or slander to this new medium of communication is obvious * * *.

    *   *   *   *   *   *   *   *

---

[95] 336 Pa. 182, 8 A.2d 302 (1939).

[96] Ibid., 336 Pa. 182, 185–205, 8 A.2d 302, 310, 312 (1939). See also Snowden v. Pearl River Broadcasting Corp., 251 So.2d 405 (La.App.1971).

A rule unalterably imposing liability without fault on
the broadcasting company under any circumstances is
manifestly unjust, unfair and contrary to every principle of morals * * *.

*   *   *   *   *   *   *   *   *

We * * * conclude that a broadcasting company
that leases its time and facilities to another, whose
agents carry on the program, is not liable for an inter-
jected defamatory remark where it appears that it exercised due care in the selection of the lessee, and, having inspected and edited the script, had no reason to believe an extemporaneous defamatory remark would be
made.   Where the broadcasting station's employe or
agent makes the defamatory remark, it is liable, unless
the remarks are privileged and there is no malice.

This lenient rule was not to be applied everywhere, however.
When William Remington was called a member of the Communist
Party on a radio-television broadcast by Elizabeth T. Bentley, he
sued her and the National Broadcasting Company for defamation. Miss Bentley had not been reading from a script. In giving judgment for Remington, the court ruled that "extemporaneous oral expression" by broadcasting is slander.[97] Since Remington was a government employee, the words reflected upon him
in his office, the judge said, and Remington did not have to prove
actual damages in order to recover.

In trying to find ground that avoids such unsatisfactory distinctions as words read from the written page versus those ad
libbed, courts have arrived at various positions. In Grein v. La-
Poma [98] the Supreme Court of the State of Washington held that
there is no distinction between oral and written defamation.
Georgia's court, after struggling with solutions, decided that a
new tort was called for and affixed to it the unbelievable name
"defamacast." [1] The rather flat ruling that defamation by television constitutes libel was made in Shor v. Billingsley.[2]

It is far from clear whether, in the long run, broadcasters will
have to live with the hard rules of libel or will enjoy the barriers

---

[97] Remington v. Bentley, 88 F.Supp. 166 (S.D.N.Y.1949); Locke v. Gibbons,
164 Misc. 877, 299 N.Y.S. 188 (1937), affirmed 253 App.Div. 887, 2 N.Y.S.2d
1015 (1938).

[98] 54 Wash.2d 844, 340 P.2d 766 (1959).

[1] American Broadcasting-Paramount Theatres, Inc. v. Simpson, 106 Ga.
App. 230, 126 S.E.2d 873 (1962).

[2] 4 Misc.2d 857, 158 N.Y.S.2d 476 (1956), affirmed without opinion 4 A.D.
2d 1017, 169 N.Y.S.2d 416 (1957).

to recovery provided by the rules of slander.[3] Fairness would seem to require that the broadcaster deserves special protection from the consequences of the shocking burst of ad libbed defamation. Just as important, it seems, is the claim of the citizen defamed on television before millions to be allowed a legal action uncluttered by the ancient, restrictive rules of slander. But whether the broadcast newsman eventually is to be cheered by the universal arrival of the first, sobered by the adoption in all states of the second, or left to cope with things as they are or with things more confusing, his motto may remain the same: Accuracy always, and develop an instinct for detecting the ad lib a-borning.

The Candidate for Public Office.

A special problem in broadcast defamation grew out of government's special relationship to the broadcast media. When the United States Congress passed the Federal Communications Act and established the Federal Communications Commission to regulate traffic on the airways, it laid down certain rules about political broadcasting (see Chap. 13). One, under the famous Section 315 of the Act,[4] said that if a station decided to carry a political candidate's message on the air, it must of necessity carry those of any of his political opponents who might seek air time. The station was permitted to refuse all candidates, but if it took one it must take his opponents. Further, it was specifically barred from censoring the candidate's copy.

This put the station in a delicate and difficult position. If it refused air time to all candidates, it could be justly criticized for refusing to aid the democratic political process, even though it was within the law in so doing. But suppose that it accepted the responsibility of carrying campaign talks: Then, if it spotted possible defamation in the prepared script of the candidate about to go on the air, it had no way of denying him access to its microphone and no power to censor. The law required it to go ahead with the broadcast, even though the station was liable for defamation along with the candidate.

The station could do two things: try to persuade the candidate to change the apparently defamatory passages, or, if he refused, hold its breath through his broadcast and after, hoping that no

---

[3] Cf. Prosser, op. cit., p. 772, "The recent trend * * * has been strongly in the direction of holding such defamation slander * * *" and Phelps, R. H. and E. D. Hamilton, Libel, New York: Macmillan, 1966, p. 333, "But the tendency has been, more and more, to consider all defamatory broadcasts as libel."

[4] 48 Stat. 1088, as amended, 47 U.S.C.A. § 315(a).

one would sue. The law in effect forced the station to carry material that might very well damage it.

Several cases arose in which campaign talk produced defamation for which stations were held liable.[5] But in 1959, a case from North Dakota reached the Supreme Court of the United States and the problem was settled in favor of the beleaguered broadcasters.

A. C. Townley, some 30 years after he had been a major political figure in North Dakota and other upper midwest states, returned to the political arena in 1956. He ran for the U. S. Senate in North Dakota. Under the requirements of Sec. 315 of the Federal Communications Act, radio station WDAY of North Dakota permitted Townley to broadcast a speech in reply to two other candidates. In it, Townley accused the Farmers Educational and Cooperative Union of America of conspiring to "establish a Communist Farmers Union Soviet right here in North Dakota." The FECUA sued Townley and WDAY for libel. The North Dakota courts ruled that WDAY was not liable and FECUA appealed.[6]

The Supreme Court held that stations did not have power to censor the speeches of political candidates. For with that power, it said, "Quite possibly if a station were held responsible for the broadcast of libelous material, all remarks evenly [sic] faintly objectionable would be excluded out of an excess of caution." Moreover, if censorship were permissible, a station could intentionally edit a candidate's "legitimate presentation under the guise of lawful censorship of libelous matter." [7] The Court was confident that Congress had intended no such result when it wrote Sec. 315.

FECUA also argued that Sec. 315 gave no immunity to a station from liability for defamatory statements made during a political broadcast even though censorship of possibly libelous matter was not permitted. The court said: [8]

> Again, we cannot agree. For under this interpretation,
> unles a licensee refuses to permit any candidate to talk
> at all, the section would sanction the unconscionable re-
> sult of permitting civil and perhaps criminal liability

[5] Houston Post Co. v. U. S., 79 F.Supp. 199 (S.D.Tex.1948); Sorensen v. Wood, 123 Neb. 348, 243 N.W. 82 (1932); Daniell v. Voice of New Hampshire, Inc., 10 Pike & Fischer Radio Reg. 2045.

[6] Farmers Educational and Cooperative Union of America v. WDAY, Inc., 360 U.S. 525, 79 S.Ct. 1302 (1959).

[7] Ibid., 530.

[8] Ibid., 531.

to be imposed for the very conduct the statute demands of the licensee.

In ruling that WDAY was not liable for defamation in campaign broadcasts under Sec. 315, the Supreme Court gave great weight to the principle of maximum broadcast participation in the political process. And it relieved stations of an onerous and difficult burden that they had formerly carried in the furtherance of that participation.

SEC. 15.   EXTRINSIC CIRCUMSTANCES, LIBEL PER SE, AND LIBEL PER QUOD

Facts extrinsic to the story itself sometimes are necessary to make out a defamatory meaning; such "libel per quod" is distinguished from "libel per se" which ordinarily means that the words are defamatory on their face.

In most cases of libel, the hard words that cause a suit are plain to see or hear in the written word or broadcast. They carry the derogatory meaning in themselves: "thief" or "swindler" or "whore" or "communist" is defamatory on its face if falsely applied to a person. Words that are libelous on their face are called libel *per se.* (The term "actionable *per se*" is used to mean words that are actionable without proof of damage, with the court assuming that damage has been done by publication.)[9]

But on some occasions, words that have no apparent derogatory meaning turn out to be libelous because circumstances outside the words of the story itself become involved. In the classic case, there was no apparent derogatory meaning in a brief but erroneous story saying that a married woman had given birth to twins. But many people who read the story knew that the woman had been married only a month.[10] Facts extrinsic to the story itself gave the words of the story a libelous meaning. Where extrinsic facts turn an apparently harmless story into defamation, it is called by many American courts libel *per quod.*[11]

In a vital statistics column in the *Spokane Chronicle,* this entry appeared on April 21, 1961: "Divorce Granted Hazel M. Pitts from Philip Pitts." In these words alone there was no defamation. But the divorce had taken place on Feb. 2, 1960, 14 months

---

[9] 33 Am.Jur.Libel and Slander § 5; Martin v. Outboard Marine Corp., 15 Wis.2d 452, 113 N.W.2d 135, 138 (1962); Prosser, p. 782.

[10] Morrison v. Ritchie & Co., 39 Scot.L.R. 432 (1902).

[11] 53 C.J.S. Libel and Slander § 8a; Prosser, p. 781; Electric Furnace Corp. v. Deering Milliken Research Corp., 325 F.2d 761, 764–765 (6th Cir. 1963).

earlier, and now Pitts had been married to another woman for several months. Some of his acquaintances and neighbors concluded that Pitts had been married to two women at once and was a bigamist. Extrinsic facts made the story libelous, and the Pittses were awarded $2,000.[12]

In some jurisdictions it is held that where extrinsic facts are involved in making out a libel, the words are not "actionable *per se*," and the court will not assume, as ordinarily, that damage has been done. Here the plaintiff must plead and prove special damage. These damages are specific amounts of pecuniary loss that one suffers as a result of a libel, such as cancelled contracts or lost wages.

> Where the defamatory nature of the writing does not appear upon the face of the writing, but rather appears only when all of the circumstances are known, it is said to be libel per quod, as distinguished from libel per se, and in such cases damages are not presumed but must be proven before the plaintiff can recover.[13]

The late magazine *Life* published a story on May 20, 1966, dealing with electronic eavesdropping. With it was a picture of Mary Alice Firestone, her estranged husband, and Jack Harwood who had a business in electronic "snooping," especially in connection with divorce suits. The story read: [14]

> TWO-WAY SNOOP. In Florida, where electronic eavesdropping is frequently employed in divorce suits, private eyes like Jack Harwood of Palm Beach shown above with some of his gear, do a thriving business. Harwood, who boasts, "I'm a fastastic wire man," was hired by tire heir Russell Firestone to keep tabs on his estranged wife, Mary Alice. * * * She in turn got one of Harwood's assistants to sell out and work for her and, says Harwood, "He plays just as rough with the bugs as I do." * * * A court recently ordered Russell and Mary to stop spying on each other.

Mrs. Firestone brought suit for libel per quod, saying that the story injured her in her pending marital litigation. The

---

[12] Pitts v. Spokane Chronicle Co., 63 Wash.2d 763, 388 P.2d 976 (1964).

[13] Electric Furnace Corp. v. Deering Milliken Research Corp., 325 F.2d 761, 764–765 (6th Cir. 1963); see also Solotaire v. Cowles Magazines, Inc., 107 N.Y.S.2d 798 (Sup.1951); Moore v. P. W. Pub. Co., 3 Ohio St.2d 183, 209 N.E.2d 412 (1965); Campbell v. Post Pub. Co., 94 Mont. 12, 20 P.2d 1063 (1933). For other uses of *"per quod,"* see Developments in the Law of Defamation, 69 Harv.L.Rev. 375, 889, 1956.

[14] Firestone v. Time, Inc., 414 F.2d 790, 791 (5th Cir. 1969).

trial court dismissed her complaint, but the U. S. Circuit Court of Appeals ruled that she had a case, reversing the trial court. It said: [15]

> We are of the opinion that appellant's allegations of injury to her pending marital litigation constitute allegations of "special damages" for libel per quod which are sufficient to withstand a motion to dismiss. While it may be difficult indeed [for Mrs. Firestone] to prove these damages, we are not convinced that they are so speculative that she could not prove them under any circumstances.

For the mass media, the "special damage" requirement is the much more favorable rule; it is seldom easy for a plaintiff to demonstrate specific money loss as a result of derogatory words.[16] Some courts have in recent decades accepted the position that the plaintiff must show special damage if he is to recover for libel requiring extrinsic facts; others hold that "all libels are actionable without proof of special damages." [17]

SEC. 16. INNOCENT INTENT

Defamation arising from accident, error, or carelessness is sometimes actionable; if malice is present, punitive damages may be assessed.

Once, the libeler claimed in court that his intent was innocent because it might hold down the amount of damages. Today, "innocent intent" may shield him totally, because to prove it is often to negate the accusation of actual malice: [18] knowing falsehood or reckless disregard of falsity under the New York Times v. Sullivan rule.

---

[15] Ibid.

[16] Eldredge, Laurence H., The Spurious Rule of Libel Per Quod, 79 Harv. L.Rev. 733, 755, 1966.

[17] Martin v. Outboard Marine Corp., 15 Wis.2d 452, 113 N.W.2d 135, 139 (1962). For two interpretations of recent trends, see Eldredge, op. cit., and Prosser, William L., More Libel Per Quod, 79 Harv.L.Rev. 1629, 1966.

[18] The term "actual" malice (also called "express malice") is to be distinguished from "malice in law" (also called "legal malice"). The latter term is a formality or technicality that persists in pleadings in some states, as a confounding holdover from libel requirements prior to 1825 when it was held that one must plead and prove that the defamer was moved by malice in order to have a case. Though the requirement has long since disappeared, the form lingers on as a legal fiction. It is not always necessary to liability in libel that malice be present. See Prosser, pp. 790–791; Chesapeake Ferry Co. v. Hudgins, 155 Va. 874, 156 S.E. 429, 438 (1931).

Yet problems remain. Courts sometimes find ways to apply old definitions of malice that for centuries befouled the law of defamation. A New York case says that malice can be inferred from "extravagance" of communications, or from "vituperation" [19]—terms that are hard to define and that could be fastened onto a hard-hitting editorial in which the writer's intent might be unimpeachable. A Maine decision calls malice a design or purpose to do injury.[20]

Again, one court has found "reckless disregard" in a radio station's failure to use a "delay device" in broadcasting defamatory statements of a person who called in on a talk show.[21] It can scarcely be said that the radio host had an intent to help air words about whose truth he had "serious doubts"—one way of defining reckless disregard.

Furthermore, it may develop that "personals and socials" such as news of births, weddings, divorces, social events and the common currency of gossip columns will not be shielded by the public principle. Here, possibly, the libeler will get no more than mitigated damages out of his plea of innocent intent.

There are certain exceptions even to the old rule that "innocence is no excuse." The question often arises as to just what persons in the chain of news writing, editing, printing, and dissemination, may be liable for a libel. Decisions are not entirely consistent. In World Pub. Co. v. Minahan, the court held that the managing editor who was actively in control of the administration and policy of the publication was equally liable with the owner of the paper for a defamatory story.[22] This was the case even though the editor had no knowledge of the particular article. On the other hand, a federal court has taken the position that a corporation was liable, not the editor-in-chief who acted merely as an agent of the owner, who knew nothing about the libelous story in point, and who was not on duty at the time the defamation was published. The court said that the editor could not be held liable "without disregarding the settled rule of law by which no man is bound for the tortious act of another over whom he has not a master's power of control." [23]

Is the linotype operator who sets a story in print liable? Is the newsboy who sells the offending paper liable? In Street v.

[19] Green v. Kinsella, 36 A.D.2d 677, 319 N.Y.S.2d 780 (1971).

[20] Cohen v. Bowdoin, Me., 288 A.2d 106, 112 (1972).

[21] Snowden v. Pearl River Broadcasting Corp., 251 So.2d 405 (La.App.1971).

[22] 70 Okl. 107, 173 P. 815 (1918).

[23] Folwell v. Miller, 75 C.C.A. 489, 145 F. 495 (1906).

Johnson, which concerned the liability of vendors of newspapers for libelous statements, the court said: [24]

> The authorities are to the effect that the mere seller of newspapers is not liable for selling and delivering a newspaper containing a libel * * * if he can prove upon the trial to the satisfaction of the jury that he did not know that the paper contained the libel, that his ignorance was not due to any negligence on his part, and that he did not know, and had no ground for supposing that the paper was likely to contain libelous material.

There was long a rule in libel that said the newspaper which printed a libelous wire service story was as liable as the wire service, even though it could not possibly check the accuracy of the wire story.[25] This rule has been eroded in the thrust of New York Times Co. v. Sullivan, and today the newspaper has little to fear in this respect, protected because printing that which arrives from distant points by wire service or syndicate rarely would suggest reckless disregard.[26]

SEC. 17.   LIBEL TO PROPERTY

Disparagement of property, products, and goods may result in an action for trade libel or slander of title, in which malice and special damage must be shown.

Although the terms libel and slander are ordinarily applied to defamation of individuals or specific organizations such as business corporations, they are applied also in the special case of disparagement of products and property. Employed under the general term "trade libel" are two other terms, slander of title and slander of goods. Distinction between oral and written disparagement is of no consequence in the law of trade libel.

A news medium is responsible for whatever it carries,[27] of course, and trade libel can insinuate itself into advertisements or

---

[24] 80 Wis. 455, 50 N.W. 395 (1891).

[25] Wood v. Constitution Pub. Co., 57 Ga.App. 123, 194 S.E. 760 (1937); Carey v. Hearst Publications, 19 Wash.2d 655, 143 P.2d 857 (1943). For long, the only state with a contradictory position was Florida: Layne v. Tribune, 108 Fla. 177, 146 So. 234 (1933).

[26] Washington Post Co. v. Keogh, 125 U.S.App.D.C. 32, 365 F.2d 965, 972 (1966).

[27] An exception is defamation spoken by a political candidate in a broadcast: above, Sec. 13, Farmers Educational and Cooperative Union v. WDAY, Inc., 360 U.S. 525, 79 S.Ct. 1302 (1959).

into quotes carried as an interview in news columns. In addition, it need hardly be pointed out, the newspaper or television station could itself originate words in disparagement of goods, for example in an editorial.

Trade libel can easily be confused with libel or slander of a person in his business, calling or trade. There are real differences. Trade libel refers specifically to the products, goods, or title to property. Defamation of a person in his business or calling refers to questioning his honesty, integrity, or skill in work, or to the fitness of a firm to carry on business.[28] It's quite possible to libel a manufactured product without libeling the manufacturer at the same time, and vice versa.

The law raises difficult barriers to recovery for trade libel, however, and criticism of the quality of goods ordinarily enjoys a wide leeway. A plaintiff who believes his product has been libeled must prove that the statement was untrue, that there was actual malice in the statement, and that he suffered special damages. Both malice and special damages are hard to prove. The New York Court of Appeals stated the requirements in Drug Research Corp. v. Curtis Publishing Co.[29] In this case, the *Saturday Evening Post* was sued for an article that called into question the worth of weight-reducing pills. Part of its story said this:

> About a year ago, the Wonder Drug Corporation, in a flood of full-page newspaper advertisements, heralded an allegedly new reducing discovery called Regimen, which required "no giving up the kinds of food you like to eat." In the box of green, pink, and yellow pills you got for three dollars, however, were instructions, warning you to avoid heavy gravies, oils, thick soup, rice, spaghetti, jam, jelly, noodles, nuts, ice cream, potatoes, cake, candy, chocolate, cereal, crackers, cream, custard, bread, butter, pastry, pudding, sugar and salt.

> Last June, after an investigation by postal inspectors, officials of the Wonder Drug Corporation voluntarily signed an "affidavit of discontinuance," agreeing to stop soliciting orders through the mail—after taking in $200,000 in six months, according to inspectors' estimates. Nevertheless, Regimen is still obtainable over the counter in some retail stores, where postal authorities have no jurisdiction.

[28] Above, Sec. 12.

[29] 7 N.Y.2d 435, 199 N.Y.S.2d 33, 166 N.E.2d 319 (1960).

In holding for Curtis, the Court of Appeals stated the rule as to trade libel, and made the special point that the manufacturer had not been libeled: [30]

> The rule is that, if a product has been attacked, the manufacturer may recover in a cause of action for libel, provided he proves malice and special damages as well as the falsity of the criticism * * *.

> Giving the pleading its most favorable construction, namely, that it states a libel on the product, it nonetheless must be dismissed for failure to allege special damages. A libel of the plaintiff's product is not necessarily a libel of the plaintiff.

Hard to prove as special damages are, there must be actual material or pecuniary loss incurred, shown in such ways as measurable amounts of money or loss of specific customers. When the loss of a sale of property is claimed in a suit for disparagement, it is necessary that the loss of the sale to a particular party be proved. General claims such as serious loss of business or damaged credit are ordinarily not enough unless supported by specific instances. It is possible for the plaintiff to show the court his books for the period before and after the alleged injury to show relative volumes of business, or the number of customers before and after the injury. One decision has held that in exceptional cases, special damages may be obtained for the loss of general business, but there is little to support this.[31]

The second difficulty in establishing trade libel is the proving of actual malice ("malice in fact") in the disparaging words. The protean character of the word malice in its travels through the courts is demonstrated well in the many definitions it has had in trade libel cases. One writer has even said that "In an action for disparagement, when brought against a stranger, the existence of 'malice in fact' is never an essential requisite to making out of a *prima facie* case." [32] Rather, he suggests, some cases have required no more than that malice be used in the formalistic fashion of "malice in law."

---

[30] Ibid., and see Marlin Firearms Co. v. Shields, 171 N.Y. 384, 64 N.E. 163 (1902).

[31] Erick Bowman Remedy Co. v. Jensen Salsbery Laboratories, 17 F.2d 255 (8th Cir. 1926). See also Pendleton v. Time, Inc., 339 Ill.App. 188, 89 N.E. 2d 435 (1950), and dissent.

[32] Smith, Jeremiah, "Disparagement of Property, Slander of Property", 13 Col.Law.R. 13, 25, 1913. See also Shaw Cleaners & Dyers v. Des Moines Dress Club, 215 Iowa 1130, 245 N.W. 231 (1932).

However, in the courts' common practice of requiring actual malice, it has been called the intent to injure business; [33] the publication of a false statement "without any regard to [its truth] and without having made proper inquiry to ascertain [the truth]"; [34] the showing of active malevolence by using extreme language in a single publication or by repeating the statement unduly; [35] "words recklessly uttered in disregard of the rights of those who might be affected by them." [36] It may be expected that trade libel will have to meet the relatively careful definition given malice by the United States Supreme Court: knowledge that the statement is false, or reckless disregard for whether it is false or not.[36]

In Bourn v. Beck, the court in giving judgment for the plaintiff stated: [37]

> If the defendants knowingly made false statements with the purpose of preventing the sale of the property for the purpose of gaining some financial advantage to themselves at the expense of the plaintiffs, their conduct was malicious in the sense here important, although they may have had no personal ill will toward them.

Having seen the special requirements in trade libel of malice and special damages, then, it should be noted that in some cases both goods and a person's reputation may be libeled. And if a businessman's reputation in his calling is involved, he ordinarily does not need to plead and prove either malice or special damages. It has been held libelous *per se* to publish that a person sold impure ice cream which caused the death of a child; [38] the charge against the man took precedence over the charge against the product, and the special requirements of trade libel did not have to be met. Likewise, it was held libel *per se* to charge that the plaintiff sold adulterated butter, made up of 40 per cent butter and the balance grease, as creamery butter.[39]

---

[33] Mowry v. Raabe, 89 Cal. 606, 27 P. 157 (1891).

[34] Houston Chronicle Pub. Co. v. Martin, 5 S.W.2d 170 (Tex.Civ.App.1928).

[35] Saxon Motor Sales, Inc. v. Torino, 166 Misc. 863, 2 N.Y.S.2d 885 (1938).

[36] New York Times Co. v. Sullivan, 376 U.S. 254, 84 S.Ct. 710, 726 (1964).

[37] 116 Kan. 231, 226 P. 769, 770 (1924).

[38] Larsen v. Brooklyn Daily Eagle, 165 App.Div. 4, 150 N.Y.S. 464 (1914), affirmed 214 N.Y. 713, 108 N.E. 1098 (1915).

[39] Dabold v. Chronicle Pub. Co., 107 Wis. 357, 83 N.W. 639 (1900); Waechter v. Carnation Co., 5 Wash.App. 121, 485 P.2d 1000 (1971).

SEC. 18. BRINGING A LIBEL ACTION

The plaintiff in a libel suit must plead that there was publication, identification and defamation.

Having taken care to meet the deadline set by his state's statute of limitations—in most, one year after publication and in others two or three—the party [40] filing a libel suit must make three allegations. These are that the derogatory statement was published, that the statement identified the plaintiff, and that the statement was defamatory. [41]

To start with publication, the statement may of course be printed or written or, in the case of movies and broadcasting, oral. [42] It must be made not only to the defamed, for a communicator cannot blacken a reputation unless he spreads the charge to at least one person besides the target. Although those in the mass media ordinarily publish to huge audiences, it is worth remembering that no more than a "third person" need be involved for publication to take place. In Ostrowe v. Lee, [43] a man dictated a letter to his secretary accusing the addressee of grand larceny. The stenographer typed the letter and it was sent through the mail. The accused brought a libel suit and the court held that publication took place at the time the stenographic notes were read and transcribed.

The newspaper that "picks up" and prints a story from another newspaper or from any other news medium is itself making a publication and likely to be liable for libel that may be in the original. The rule is that "every republication of a libel is a fresh publication;" an often-quoted maxim is that to the law "tale bearers are as bad as tale makers." [44]

For the printed media, courts of most states call the entire edition carrying the alleged libel one publication; an over-the-counter sale of back copies of a newspaper weeks or months after they were printed does not constitute a further publication. The

---

[40] See Sec. 10 for who may bring a libel action.

[41] Necessary allegations in trade libel include also untruth, actual malice, and special damages: Supra, Sec. 17. For allegations in criminal libel, see Chap. 9, Sec. 59.

[42] Signs, statues, effigies, and other communications that may carry libel are in Sec. 11, supra.

[43] 256 N.Y. 36, 175 N.E. 505 (1931). See also Arvey Corp. v. Peterson, 178 F.Supp. 132 (E.D.Pa.1959); Gambrill v. Schooley, 93 Md. 48, 48 A. 730 (1901).

[44] Billet v. Times-Democrat Pub. Co., 107 La. 751, 32 So. 17, 20 (1902); Cavalier v. Original Club Forest, Inc., 59 So.2d 489 (La.App.1952).

rule is known as the "single publication rule." [45]   Where this is
not the rule, there is a chance that a plaintiff can stretch the
statute of limitations indefinitely, perhaps by claiming a separate publication in a newspaper's selling a February issue the
following December.   In Tocco v. Time, Inc., it was held that the
publication takes place at the time a magazine is mailed to subscribers, or put in the hands of those who will ship the edition to
wholesale distributors.[46]   This rule has not been universally accepted;   Osmers v. Parade Publications, Inc., rejected it and
stated this as its rule for publication date: [47]

> * * *   what is really determinative is the earliest
> date on which the libel was substantially and effectively
> communicated to a meaningful mass of readers—the
> public for which the publication was intended, not some
> small segment of it.

Publication established, the plaintiff must also demonstrate
that he was identified in the alleged libel—that the statement
he complains of referred to him.   In most cases, this presents
little problem to the plaintiff.   His name and the derogatory
words are there, and one or more readers or listeners attach the
name to the person.

But it is not uncommon for identification of a totally unintended kind to occur in the mass media.   A typographical error,
wrong initials, the incorrect address, the careless work of a reporter or editor—and an innocent person may have been linked
with a crime, immorality, unethical business conduct, or another
activity that is a basis for a libel suit.   The courts hold the publisher to "strict liability" for associating a person with a damaging statement.   The publisher is liable, no matter how innocent
or unintended the error.[48]

In a celebrated English case, E. Hulton & Co. v. Jones,[49] the
Sunday Chronicle had published a story from a correspondent in
France concerning a supposedly fictitious person named Artemus
Jones.   He had been seen, the story said, in the company of a
woman who was not his wife.   The Chronicle soon learned, with
the filing of a libel action, that a real Artemus Jones did, indeed,

---

[45] Leflar, Robert A., The Single Publication Rule, 25 Rocky Mt.Law R.
263, 1953; Wheeler v. Dell Pub. Co., 300 F.2d 372 (7th Cir. 1962).   Restatement of Torts, § 578, Comment (b) does not accept the single publication
rule.

[46] 195 F.Supp. 410 (E.D.Mich.1961).

[47] 234 F.Supp. 924, 927 (D.C.N.Y.1964).

[48] See Chap. 3, Sec. 15.

[49] (1910) A.C. 20, 1909, 2 K.B. 444.

exist, and that he said that some of his friends believed that the story referred to him. The courts held that the identification was sufficient and awarded Jones, a lawyer, £1750 in damages.

Plaintiffs may, of course, allege identification but fail to establish it at trial. Harry Landau operated a business known as Credit Consultants. He brought a libel suit based on a television show titled "The Easy Way." The plot involved a newspaper photographer's attempt to expose a book-making ring headed by a character named Sam Henderson, whose private office door carried the printed legend, "Credit Consultant, Inc." Landau contended that the use of that name identified him as Sam Henderson, the head of an unlawful gambling syndicate.

But the court held that there was no identification of Landau in the television drama. There was no resemblance between Landau and Henderson, or between the televised office and Landau's office. The fictional Henderson was killed at the end of the play, and Landau was alive and suing. The defendant Columbia Broadcasting System, Inc., was given the judgment.[50]

In Oma v. Hillman Periodicals, a professional boxer sued for libel on the basis of a magazine article that attacked various practices in boxing, especially those of managers and promoters. The article portrayed fighters as victims who fight because of economic necessity or ambition. The plaintiff's picture and name were used on the back cover of the magazine, but he was not identified with the article in any derogatory way, and he lost the suit.[51]

Identification cannot be established by a person who says that an attack upon a large heterogeneous group libels him because he happens to belong to it. Derogatory statements about a political party, an international labor union, the Presbyterian church, the American Legion, for example, do not identify individuals so as to permit them to bring a libel action.

However, if the attack is on a small group such as the officers of a local post of the American Legion, or the presiding elders of a local church, or the directors of the Smith County Democratic Party, each individual of the group may be able to establish identification and bring suit.[52]

The case of Neiman-Marcus Co. v. Lait [53] involved the portion of a book entitled *U.S.A. Confidential* about a well-known depart-

---

[50] Landau v. Columbia Broadcasting System, Inc., 205 Misc. 357, 128 N.Y.S. 2d 254 (1954).

[51] 281 App.Div. 240, 118 N.Y.S.2d 720 (1953).

[52] Above, Chap. 3, Sec. 10.

[53] 107 F.Supp. 96 (S.D.N.Y.1952); 13 F.R.D. 311 (1952).

ment store in Dallas and its employees. An action for libel was brought by the Neiman-Marcus Co., operator of the store, nine individual models who were the entire group of models employed by the store, 15 salesmen of a total of 25 salesmen employed, and 30 saleswomen of a total of 382. The defendants moved to dismiss the complaint on the grounds that the individual plaintiffs were not capable of identification from the alleged libelous words. The court stated that the following rules were applicable:

(1) Where the group or class libeled is large, none can sue even though the language used is inclusive.

(2) When the group or class libeled is small, and each and every member of the group or class is referred to, then any individual member can sue.

(3) That while there is a conflict in authorities where the publication complained of libeled some or less than all of a designated small group, it would permit such an action.

In applying these rules to the facts, the court dismissed the suits of the saleswomen, but allowed the suits of the models and salesmen.

Identity may be in reference to a member of a board although no specific member of the board or no director is actually named,[54] to a "city hall ring," [55] or to a radio editor when there are only a few to whom the libel could refer.[56]

The third necessary allegation, that the statement was defamatory, says in effect that the words injured reputation. The allegation of defamation must be made in bringing the suit, although it, like publication and identification, can fail of proof at trial. The court decides whether a publication is libelous *per se;* but when the words complained of are susceptible of two meanings, one innocent and the other damaging, it is for the jury to decide in what sense the words were understood by the audience. Both court and jury, in their interpretation of the alleged defamatory statement, should give the language its common and ordinary meaning:[57]

What sense will be given to them by a reader of ordinary intelligence? Will the natural and proximate con-

---

[54] Children v. Shinn, 168 Iowa 531, 150 N.W. 864 (1915).

[55] Petsch v. St. Paul Dispatch Printing Co., 40 Minn. 291, 41 N.W. 1034 (1889).

[56] Gross v. Cantor, 270 N.Y. 93, 200 N.E. 592 (1936).

[57] Peck v. Coos Bay Times Pub. Co., 122 Or. 408, 418, 259 P. 307, 311 (1927).

sequence be to injure the person about whom they have
been published? Will such words tend to bring a person
into public hatred, contempt or ridicule? If the words
are plain and unambiguous and susceptible of but one
meaning, it is the duty of the court to determine from
the face of the writing without reference to innuendo,
whether the same are actionable *per se*. If the article
is not of such nature and character that the court can
say as a matter of law that damages will be presumed
as a consequence of its publication, then it cannot be
made so by innuendo.

Chapter 4

THE CONSTITUTIONAL DEFENSE AGAINST LIBEL SUITS

SEC. 19. THE PUBLIC PRINCIPLE

When the news media go to court to defend against libel suits, they make their claim heavily on principles whose ground is the media's service to the public, not on claims of their own private interest however much that may be involved. This "public principle" extends far back in the law of defamation, strengthening in America in the nineteenth century as new defenses arose, and in the 1960s reaching far beyond nineteenth-century reasoning. The public principle briefly stated is that in an open society whose citizens are expected to participate in decisions that affect their lives and to have the opportunity to choose, information and discussion are essential ingredients for that participation and choice. Defenses against those who complained that their reputations had been harmed by publication grew in this context. Where the publications furthered certain public goods and values, the news media had protection from those who claimed harm.

The principle received its fullest extension in defense against libel after the United States Supreme Court ruled that only malice—defined with precision—could render a publication about the public acts of a public official susceptible to a successful suit for damages. The Court laid down this rule as a constitutional principle under the First Amendment in 1964, long after the early- and mid-nineteenth century protections under the public principle had been developed through state statutes and decisions. One of these earlier protections was the defense known as qualified privilege, which provided that fair and accurate reports of public official proceedings could not be the basis for a successful libel suit. Another was the rule of fair comment and criticism, which said that publications criticizing the public offerings of those who sought public approval in their work were protected against successful libel suit. A third major defense was proof of the truth of the words complained of; and while here the public principle was not always so thorough-going as in the other two, it also carried obvious components of the public good as its rationale, for often the publication of a painful truth is important to the public weal.

So sweeping is the constitutional protection that today, only a decade after its adoption, the earlier statutory defenses are relatively little used. Qualified privilege retains a diminished life of its own, indeed; but fair comment and truth as defenses are becoming rare so far as the mass media are concerned.

SEC. 20. THE CONSTITUTION AS A DEFENSE

Under the expanding doctrine of New York Times Co. v. Sullivan, the First Amendment broadly protects the news media from judgments for defamation of persons involved in matters of public interest or general concern.

The Supreme Court of the United States handed down a decision in 1964 that added a great new dimension of protection to news media in the field of libel. It said that news media are not liable for defamatory words about the public acts of public officials unless the words are published with malice. It defined the word "malice" with a rigor and preciseness that had been lacking for centuries and in a way that gave broad protection to publication. Public officials, it said, must live with the risks of a political system in which there is "a profound national commitment to the principle that debate on public issues should be uninhibited, robust, and wide-open * * *." Even the factual error, it said, will not make one liable for libel in words about the public acts of public officials unless malice is present.

The case was New York Times Co. v. Sullivan.[1] It stemmed from an "editorial advertisement" in the Times, written and paid for by a group intensely involved in the struggle for equality and civil liberties for the American Negro. Suit was brought by L. B. Sullivan, Commissioner of Public Affairs for the city of Montgomery, Alabama, against the Times and four Negro clergymen who were among the 64 persons whose names were attached to the advertisement.

The since-famous advertisement, titled "Heed Their Rising Voices," recounted the efforts of southern Negro students to affirm their rights at Alabama State College in Montgomery and told of a "wave of terror" that met them. It spoke of violence

1 376 U.S. 254, 84 S.Ct. 710 (1964).

against the Rev. Martin Luther King, Jr. in his leadership of the civil rights movement: [2]

Heed Their Rising Voices

As the whole world knows by now, thousands of Southern Negro students are engaged in wide-spread, non-violent demonstrations in positive affirmation of the right to live in human dignity as guaranteed by the U. S. Constitution and the Bill of Rights. In their effort to uphold these guarantees, they are being met by an unprecedented wave of terror by those who would deny and negate that document which the whole world looks upon as setting the pattern for modern freedom * * *.

*   *   *   *   *   *   *   *   *

In Montgomery, Alabama, after students sang "My Country 'Tis of Thee" on the State Capitol steps, their leaders were expelled from school, and truck-loads of police armed with shotguns and tear-gas ringed the Alabama State College Campus. When the entire student body protested to state authorities by refusing to re-register, their dining hall was padlocked in an attempt to starve them into submission.

*   *   *   *   *   *   *   *   *

Again and again the Southern violators have answered Dr. King's protests with intimidation and violence. They have bombed his home almost killing his wife and child. They have assaulted his person. They have arrested him seven times—for "speeding," "loitering" and similar "offenses." And now they have charged him with "perjury"—a *felony* under which they could imprison him for *ten years*. Obviously, their real purpose is to remove him physically as the leader to whom the students and millions of others—look for guidance and support, and thereby to intimidate *all* leaders who may rise in the South * * *. The defense of Martin Luther King, spiritual leader of the student sit-in movement, clearly, therefore, is an integral part of the total struggle for freedom in the South.

Sullivan was not named in the advertisement, but claimed that because he was Commissioner who had supervision of the Montgomery police department, people would identify him as

[2] Ibid., facing 292.

the person responsible for police action at the State College campus. He said also that actions against the Rev. King would be attributed to him by association. Libel law, of course, does not require that identification be by name.

It was asserted by Sullivan, and not disputed, that there were errors in the advertisement. Police had not "ringed" the campus although they had been there in large numbers. Students sang the National Anthem, not "My Country, 'Tis of Thee." The expulsion had not been protested by the entire student body, but by a large part of it. They had not refused to register, but had boycotted classes for a day. The campus dining hall was not padlocked. The manager of the Times Advertising Acceptability Department said that he had not checked the copy for accuracy because he had no cause to believe it false, and some of the signers were well-known persons whose reputation he had no reason to question.

The trial jury ruled that Sullivan had been libeled and awarded him $500,000, the full amount of his claim. The Supreme Court of Alabama upheld the finding and judgment. But the Supreme Court of the United States reversed the decision, holding that the Alabama rule of law was "constitutionally deficient for failure to provide the safeguards for freedom of speech and of the press that are required by the First and Fourteenth Amendments * * *."

The Court said there was no merit to the claim of Sullivan that a paid, commercial advertisement does not ever deserve constitutional protection. Of this advertisement it said:[3]

> It communicated information, expressed opinion, recited grievances, protested claimed abuses, and sought financial support on behalf of a movement whose existence and objectives are matters of the highest public concern * * *. That the Times was paid for publishing the advertisement is as immaterial in this connection as is the fact that newspapers and books are sold * * *. Any other conclusion would discourage newspapers from carrying "editorial advertisements" of this type, and so might shut off an important outlet for the promulgation of information and ideas by persons who do not themselves have access to publishing facilities—who wish to exercise their freedom of speech even though they are not members of the press. The effect would be to shackle the First Amendment * * *.

3 Ibid., 266.

The Court said that the question about the advertisement was whether it forfeited Constitutional protection "by the falsity of some of its factual statements and by its alleged defamation of respondent."

The Court rejected the position that the falsity of some of the factual statements in the advertisement destroyed Constitutional protection for the Times and the clergymen. "[E]rroneous statement is inevitable in free debate, and * * * it must be protected if the freedoms of expression are to have the 'breathing space' that they 'need to survive,' * * * " it ruled. Quoting the decision in Sweeney v. Patterson,[4] it added that " 'Cases which impose liability for erroneous reports of the political conduct of officials reflect the obsolete doctrine that the governed must not criticize their governors * * * . Whatever is added to the field of libel is taken from the field of free debate.' "

Elaborating the matter of truth and error, it said that it is not enough for a state to provide in its law that the defendant may plead the truth of his words, although that has long been considered a bulwark for protection of expression: [5]

> A rule compelling the critic of official conduct to guarantee the truth of all his factual assertions—and to do so on pain of libel judgments virtually unlimited in amount—leads to a * * * "self-censorship." Allowance of the defense of truth, with the burden of proving it on the defendant, does not mean that only false speech will be deterred. Even courts accepting this defense as an adequate safeguard have recognized the difficulties of adducing legal proofs that the alleged libel was true in all its factual particulars * * * . Under such a rule, would-be critics of official conduct may be deterred from voicing their criticism, even though it is believed to be true and even though it is in fact true, because of doubt whether it can be proved in court or fear of the expense of having to do so * * * . The rule thus dampens the vigor and limits the variety of public debate.

This was the end for Alabama's rule that "the defendant has no defense as to stated facts unless he can persuade the jury that they were true in all their particulars." But the decision reached much farther than to Alabama: most states had

---

4 76 U.S.App.D.C. 23, 128 F.2d 457, 458 (1952).

5 New York Times Co. v. Sullivan, 376 U.S. 254, 279, 84 S.Ct. 710, 725 (1964).

similar rules under which public officials had successfully brought libel suits for decades. In holding that the Constitution protects even erroneous statements about public officials in their public acts, the Court was providing protection that only a minority of states had previously accepted.

Having decided that the Constitutional protection was not destroyed by the falsity of factual statements in the advertisement, the Court added that the protection was not lost through defamation of an official. "Criticism of their official conduct," the Court held, "does not lose its constitutional protection merely because it is effective criticism and hence diminishes their official reputations." [6]

Then Mr. Justice Brennan, who wrote the majority decision, stated the circumstances under which a public official could recover damages for false defamation: Only if malice were present in the publication: [7]

> The constitutional guarantees require, we think, a federal rule that prohibits a public official from recovering damages for a defamatory falsehood relating to his official conduct unless he proves that the statement was made with "actual malice"—that is, with knowledge that it was false or with reckless disregard of whether it was false or not.

That statement of the court not only gave the broadest protection to publications critical of public officials that had been granted by the "minority rule" states which had held similarly for almost 50 years. It also defined "malice" with a rigor and preciseness that it had seldom been given. Malice was not the vague, shifting concept of ancient convenience for judges who had been shocked or angered by words harshly critical of public officials. It was not the oft-used "evidence of ill-will" on the part of the publisher; it was not "hatred" of the publisher for the defamed; it was not "intent to harm" the defamed; it was not to be found in "attributing bad motives" to the defamed. Rather, the malice which the plaintiff would have to plead and prove lay in the publisher's knowledge that what he printed was false, or else disregard on the part of the publisher as to whether it was false or not.

The state courts, it was soon plain, were required to recognize and use the new malice rule. This was noted in the decision in a case brought in the District of Columbia by Senator Thomas Dodd of Connecticut against columnists Drew Pearson

6 Ibid., 273.

7 Ibid., 279–280.

and Jack Anderson. The federal district court decision said of Senator Dodd, his case, and the new rule as to malice: [8]

> * * * his rights in an action for libel have been limited by the decision in the *Sullivan* case. In this respect the law of libel now completely departs from the common law of libel that prevails in England and that existed in this country prior to 1964. The rule of the *Sullivan* case is predicated not merely on the law of libel but on a constitutional principle, namely, freedom of speech guaranteed by the First Amendment.
>
> *   *   *   *   *   *   *   *   *
>
> The fact that the *Sullivan* case is predicated on a constitutional principle makes it applicable not only to the federal courts but also to the States.

The Constitution's guarantee of freedom of speech and press, then, protects all that is said about a public official in his public conduct except the malicious. But did "public official" mean every person who is employed by government at any level? Justice Brennan foresaw that this question would arise, and said in a footnote in the *New York Times* case: "We have no occasion here to determine how far down into the ranks of government employees the 'public official' designation would extend for purposes of this rule, or otherwise to specify categories of persons who would or would not be included * * *. It is enough for the present case that respondent's position as an elected city commissioner clearly made him a public official * * *." [9]

As subsequent cases under the *New York Times* doctrine arose, some definition of the public official who would have to prove malice in bringing libel suit occurred. In 1966, Rosenblatt v. Baer helped the definition. Newspaper columnist Alfred D. Rosenblatt wrote in the *Laconia Evening Citizen* that a public ski area which in previous years had been a financially shaky operation, now was doing "hundreds of percent" better. He asked, "What happened to all the money last year? And every other year?" Baer, who had been dismissed from his county post as ski area supervisor the year before, brought a suit charging that the column libeled him. The New Hampshire court upheld his complaint and awarded him $31,500. But when the case reached the United States Supreme Court, it reversed

---

[8] Dodd v. Pearson, 277 F.Supp. 469 (D.C.D.C.1967). See also Beckley Newspapers Corp. v. Hanks, 389 U.S. 81, 88 S.Ct. 197 (1967).

[9] New York Times Co. v. Sullivan, 376 U.S. 254, 84 S.Ct. 710, fn. 23 (1964).

and remanded the case. It said that Baer did indeed come within the "public official" category: [10]

> Criticism of government is at the very center of the constitutionally protected area of free discussion. Criticism of those responsible for government operations must be free, lest criticism of government be penalized. It is clear, therefore, that the "public official" designation applies at the very least to those among the hierarchy of government employees who have, or appear to the public to have, substantial responsibility for or control over the conduct of governmental affairs.

The Court also said that the *New York Times* rule may apply to a person who has left public office, as Baer had, where public interest in the matter at issue is still substantial.

Meanwhile, cases that did not reach the United States Supreme Court were working their way through state courts. During the year of the *New York Times* rule, 1964, the Pennsylvania court applied the rule to a senator who was candidate for re-election.[11] Shortly, state legislators were included,[12] a former mayor,[13] a deputy sheriff,[14] a school board member,[15] an appointed city tax assessor,[16] and a police sergeant.[17]

PUBLIC FIGURES AND PUBLIC ISSUES

In the *Rosenblatt* case treated above, Mr. Justice William O. Douglas of the Supreme Court wrote a separate concurring opinion. In it he raised the question of what persons and what issues might call for an extension of the *New York Times* doctrine beyond "public officials." He said: [18]

> * * * I see no way to draw lines that exclude the night watchman, the file clerk, the typist, or, for that

[10] Rosenblatt v. Baer, 383 U.S. 75, 86 S.Ct. 669 (1966).

[11] Clark v. Allen, 415 Pa. 484, 204 A.2d 42 (1964).

[12] Washington Post Co. v. Keogh, 125 U.S.App.D.C. 32, 365 F.2d 965 (1966); Rose v. Koch and Christian Research, Inc., 278 Minn. 235, 154 N.W. 2d 409 (1967).

[13] Lundstrom v. Winnebago Newspapers, Inc., 58 Ill.App.2d 33, 206 N.E.2d 525 (1965).

[14] St. Amant v. Thompson, 390 U.S. 727, 88 S.Ct. 1323 (1968).

[15] Cabin v. Community Newspapers, Inc., 50 Misc.2d 574, 270 N.Y.S.2d 913 (1966).

[16] Eadie v. Pole, 91 N.J.Super. 504, 221 A.2d 547 (1966).

[17] Suchomel v. Suburban Life Newspapers, Inc., 84 Ill.App.2d 239, 228 N.E.2d 172 (1967).

[18] Rosenblatt v. Baer, 383 U.S. 75, 89, 86 S.Ct. 669, 678 (1966).

matter, anyone on the public payroll. And how about those who contract to carry out governmental missions? Some of them are as much in the public domain as any so-called officeholder. And how about the dollar-a-year man * * *? And the industrialists who raise the price of a basic commodity? Are not steel and aluminum in the public domain? And the labor leader who combines trade unionism with bribery and racketeering? Surely the public importance of collective bargaining puts labor as well as management into the public arena so far as the present constitutional issue is concerned * * *. [T]he question is whether a public *issue* not a public official, is involved.

In other words, wherever the public had a stake in the discussion and outcome of an issue, it seemed possible that a citizen involved in it would have to accept the *New York Times* rule. If libeled, he would then have to plead and prove actual malice on the part of the publisher. And in 1966, the decision in a suit brought by the noted scientist and Nobel Prize winner, Dr. Linus Pauling, indeed said that not only "public officials" would have to prove malice if they were to succeed with libel suits.

Pauling sued the *St. Louis Globe-Democrat* for alleged libel in an editorial entitled "Glorification of Deceit." It referred to an appearance by Pauling before a subcommittee of the United States Senate, in connection with Pauling's attempts to promote a nuclear test ban treaty. It read in part: "Pauling contemptuously refused to testify and was cited for contempt of Congress. He appealed to the United States District Court to rid him of the contempt citation, which that Court refused to do. The appeal from the lower court's affirmation of contempt is expected to be handed down by the Supreme Court today."

Pauling said that he had not been cited for contempt, that he had not appealed to any court to rid himself of any contempt citation, and that no appeal was expected because there had been no affirmation.

The federal court conceded that Pauling was not a "public official" such as the plaintiff in New York Times Co. v. Sullivan. But it added: [19]

We feel, however, that the implications of the Supreme Court's majority opinions are clear. Professor Pauling, by his public statements and actions, was projecting himself into the arena of public controversy and into

[19] Pauling v. Globe-Democrat Pub. Co., 362 F.2d 188, 195–196 (8th Cir. 1966).

the very "vortex of the discussion of a question of pressing public concern". He was attempting to influence the resolution of an issue which was important, which was of profound effect, which was public and which was internationally controversial * * *.

*   *   *   *   *   *   *   *   *

We * * * feel that a rational distinction cannot be founded on the assumption that criticism of private citizens who seek to lead in the determination of national policy will be less important to the public interest than will criticism of government officials. A lobbyist, a person dominant in a political party, the head of any pressure group, or any significant leader may possess a capacity for influencing public policy as great or greater than that of a comparatively minor public official who is clearly subject to *New York Times*. It would seem, therefore, that if such a person seeks to realize upon his capacity to guide public policy and in the process is criticized, he should have no greater remedy than does his counterpart in public office.

Pauling took his case to the United States Supreme Court, but that court denied certiorari, and the lower court's decision stood. Nor was Pauling successful in bringing suit against the *National Review* and its editor, William F. Buckley, Jr., who had called Pauling a "leading fellow traveler," partly in connection with the latter's public criticism of the United States' intervention in Vietnam. "It is clear," said the judge in applying the *New York Times* rule, "that if any private citizen has, by his conduct, made himself a public figure engaged voluntarily in public discussion of matters of grave concern and controversy, Dr. Pauling has done so." [20]

While public figure Linus Pauling was thus being embraced within the *New York Times* rules, another man who had formerly been a general in the United States Army was undertaking a set of "chain" libel suits. This was retired Maj. Gen. Edwin A. Walker, who after a storm of controversy over his troop-indoctrination program had resigned from the Army in 1961. Opposed to the integration of the University of Mississippi, he had in 1962 appeared on the scene there when rioting took place over the enrollment of Negro James H. Meredith. An Associated Press dispatch, circulated to member newspapers around the nation, said that Walker had taken command of a violent crowd and had per-

---

[20] Pauling v. National Review, Inc., 49 Misc.2d 90, 269 N.Y.S.2d 11 (1966).

sonally led a charge against federal marshals. Further, it described Walker as encouraging rioters to use violence.

Walker's chain libel suits totalled $23,000,000 against the *Louisville Courier-Journal* and *Louisville Times* and their radio station; against *Atlanta Newspapers Inc.* and publisher Ralph McGill; against the Associated Press, the *Denver Post*, the *Fort Worth Star-Telegram* and its publisher, Amon G. Carter, Jr.; against *Newsweek*, the Pulitzer Publishing Co. (*St. Louis Post-Dispatch*), and against the *Delta* (Miss.) *Democrat-Times* and its editor, Hodding Carter.[21]

Walker's case for recovery reached the Supreme Court of the United States through a suit against the Associated Press which he filed in Texas. He was awarded $500,000 by the trial court. The Texas Court of Civil Appeals upheld the judgment, and stated without elaboration that the *New York Times* rule was not applicable. The Supreme Court of Texas denied a writ of error, and the United States Supreme Court granted certiorari.[22]

The U. S. Supreme Court decided *Associated Press v. Walker* and *Curtis Publishing Co. v. Butts* in the same opinion.[23] Wallace Butts was former athletic director of the University of Georgia, and had brought suit against Curtis for a story in the *Saturday Evening Post* that had accused him of conspiring to "fix" a football game between Georgia and the University of Alabama. Neither Walker nor Butts was a "public official" and the late Justice John M. Harlan's opinion said explicitly that the Court took up the two cases to consider the impact of the *New York Times* rule "on libel actions instituted by persons who are not public officials, but who are 'public figures' and involved in issues in which the public has a justified and important interest." [24]

Four opinions were delivered by the Court. All agreed that Walker, a "public figure," did not have grounds for recovery. Justice Harlan wrote the opinion endorsed by the largest number of justices: Justices Clark, Stewart, and Fortas joined him, making a total of four. They agreed that a publication deserves constitutional protection under the First Amendment. But while Walker was a man of "some political prominence" and a public figure "by his purposeful activity amounting to a thrusting of his personality into the 'vortex' of an important public controversy," he was not to be treated in libel exactly the same as a "public

21 96 Editor & Publisher 10, Oct. 5, 1963.

22 Associated Press v. Walker, 393 S.W.2d 671 (1965).

23 Curtis Pub. Co. v. Butts, 388 U.S. 130, 87 S.Ct. 1975 (1967).

24 Ibid., 134.

official" would be. Justice Harlan rejected the *New York Times* malice rule as inapplicable to public figure Walker. Instead of using that rule requiring a plaintiff to show reckless disregard of falsity on the part of the publisher in order to recover, he expressed a new standard for a public figure: [25]

> We consider and would hold that a "public figure" who is not a public official may * * * recover damages for a defamatory falsehood whose substance makes substantial danger to reputation apparent, on a showing of highly unreasonable conduct constituting an extreme departure from the standards of investigation and reporting ordinarily adhered to by responsible publishers.

While this opinion did not define "highly unreasonable conduct constituting an extreme departure" from responsible reporting standards, it examined AP's work in this case and found no such departure: [26]

> [T]he dispatch [of the AP reporter] which concerns us in *Walker* was news which required immediate dissemination. The Associated Press received the information from a correspondent who was present at the scene of the events and gave every indication of being trustworthy and competent. His dispatches in this instance, with one minor exception, were internally consistent and would not have seemed unreasonable to one familiar with General Walker's prior publicized statements on the underlying controversy. Considering the necessity for rapid dissemination, nothing in this series of events gives the slightest hint of a severe departure from accepted publishing standards.

The Supreme Court reversed the judgment against the Associated Press, the group with Justice Harlan finding no "severe departure from accepted publishing standards" in the AP reporter's work, and Chief Justice Warren, with Justices Brennan and White, finding no "reckless disregard" of truth or falsity in his work, and hence no malice.

But both groups of justices found that the libel judgment against the *Saturday Evening Post* should stand. Athletic director Wallace Butts of the University of Georgia had won $460,000 in his suit against the Post. The magazine stated that Butts had revealed his school's football secrets to Alabama coach Paul Bryant just before a game between the schools. The article said that

[25] Ibid., 155.

[26] Ibid., 158–159.

one George Burnett had accidentally been connected, in using the telephone, to the conversation between the two in which Butts told Bryant the secrets. According to the article, Burnett made notes of the conversation as he listened, and the Post obtained his story.

Justice Harlan's analysis of the Post's methods of investigation —analysis that was noted with approval in the separate opinion of Chief Justice Warren—found the Post wanting. He said, in part: [27]

> The evidence showed that the Butts story was in no sense "hot news" and the editors of the magazine recognized the need for a thorough investigation of the serious charges. Elementary precautions were, nevertheless, ignored. The Saturday Evening Post knew that Burnett had been placed on probation in connection with bad check charges, but proceeded to publish the story on the basis of his affidavit without substantial independent support. Burnett's notes were not even viewed by any of the magazine personnel prior to publication. John Carmichael who was supposed to have been with Burnett when the phone call was overheard was not interviewed. No attempt was made to screen the films of the game to see if Burnett's information was accurate, and no attempt was made to find out whether Alabama had adjusted its plans after the alleged divulgence of information.

Justice Harlan found this kind of reporting to be "highly unreasonable conduct constituting an extreme departure from the standards of investigation and reporting ordinarily adhered to by responsible publishers." And in Chief Justice Warren's opinion, it was evidence of "reckless disregard" of whether the statements were false or not.

While a majority of the Court thus agreed that Butts should recover damages and Walker should not, they were of two opinions as to whether the *New York Times* malice rule applying to public officials should also apply to these "public figures." Justice Harlan, as described above, expressed and applied a different standard—"extreme departure" from responsible reporting standards by a news medium was enough to warrant recovery by the defamed, he wrote. But Chief Justice Warren felt that the *New York Times* malice rule should be applied to public figures as much as to public officials. This, of course, was what several

[27] Ibid., 157.

lower courts had said in other cases since New York Times Co. v. Sullivan. Chief Justice Warren wrote: [28]

> To me, differentiation between "public figures" and "public officials" and adoption of separate standards of proof for each has no basis in law, logic, or First Amendment policy. Increasingly in this country, the distinctions between governmental and private sectors are blurred * * *. This blending of positions and power has * * * occurred in the case of individuals so that many who do not hold public office at the moment are nevertheless intimately involved in the resolution of important public questions, or by reason of their fame, shape events in areas of concern to society at large.

> Viewed in this context then, it is plain that although they are not subject to the restraints of the political process, "public figures" like "public officials," often play an influential role in ordering society * * *. Our citizenry has a legitimate and substantial interest in the conduct of such persons, and freedom of the press to engage in uninhibited debate about their involvement in public issues and events is as crucial as it is in the case of "public officials."

> *   *   *   *   *   *   *   *   *

> [T]he *New York Times* standard is an important safeguard for the rights of the press and public to inform and be informed on matters of legitimate interest. Evenly applied to cases involving "public men"—whether they be "public officials" or "public figures"—it will afford the necessary insulation for the fundamental interests which the First Amendment was designed to protect.

> *   *   *   *   *   *   *   *   *

> Under any reasoning, General Walker was a public man in whose public conduct society and the press had a legitimate and substantial interest.

Chief Justice Warren also criticized the "extreme departure" formula which Justice Harlan substituted for the *New York Times* rule. He said he could not believe that "a standard which is based on such an unusual and uncertain formulation" could either guide a jury or afford "the protection for speech and de-

28 Ibid., 163–165.

bate that is fundamental to our society and guaranteed by the First Amendment." [29]

Since Justice Harlan's opinion lacked majority support in the Court of nine persons, it cannot be said to have the force of a Court-adopted rule. Yet his standard of "extreme departure" from responsible reporting has been picked up and used in several decisions since.[30]

It was the malice of the *New York Times* rule, however, that came to dominate rulings in libel suits and that quickly extended the reach of the public principle beyond public officials and public figures to anyone involved in matters of public interest or general concern. It was in a privacy case—not libel—that the Supreme Court first ruled that a private person thrust unwillingly into an event of public interest would have to prove the malice of the *New York Times* rule if he was to recover damages.

Time, Inc. v. Hill [31] stemmed from an article in *Life* magazine concerning a new play based on a book about a family held hostage in its home by escaped convicts. The article said that the novel was "inspired" by the true-life ordeal of the James Hill family which three years earlier had, indeed, been held hostage by convicts. Hill brought suit under the New York privacy statute. He said that the article was intended to give, and did give, the impression that the play "mirrored the Hill family's experience." *Life* knew that this was false, Hill said, yet referred to the play as a re-enactment of the Hills' ordeal.

Hill won the suit, but *Life*'s appeal to the Supreme Court was successful. The Court said first that the rule as to malicious publishing from New York Times Co. v. Sullivan was applicable to the privacy suit. The U. S. Constitution prevented applying the New York privacy statute in matters of public interest "in the absence of proof that the defendant published the report with knowledge of its falsity or in reckless disregard of the truth." [32]

Having brought the *New York Times* rule to bear in the field of privacy, the Supreme Court then made it plain that the rule

---

[29] Ibid., 163.

[30] Cerrito v. Time, Inc., 302 F.Supp. 1071 (D.C.Cal.1969); Fotochrome Inc. v. New York Herald Tribune Inc., 61 Misc.2d 226, 305 N.Y.S.2d 168 (1969); Holmes v. Curtis Pub. Co., 303 F.Supp. 522, 525 (D.C.S.C.1969); Buckley v. Vidal, 50 F.R.D. 271 (D.C.N.Y.1970); Cervantes v. Time Inc., 330 F.Supp. 936 (D.C.Mo.1971).

[31] 385 U.S. 374, 87 S.Ct. 534 (1967).

[32] Ibid., 388.

protects expression beyond the realm of politics and government: [33]

> The guarantees for speech and press are not the preserve of political expression or comment upon public affairs, essential as these are to healthy government. One need only pick up any newspaper or magazine to comprehend the vast range of published matter which exposes persons to public view, both private citizens and public officials. Exposure of the self to others in varying degrees is a concomitant of life in a civilized community. The risk of this exposure is an essential incident of life in a society which places a primary value on freedom of speech and of press. "Freedom of discussion, if it would fulfill its historic function in this nation, must embrace all issues about which information is needed or appropriate to enable the members of society to cope with the exigencies of their period." Thornhill v. State of Alabama, 310 U.S. 88, 102, 60 S.Ct. 736. We have no doubt that the subject of the Life article, the opening of a new play linked to an actual incident, is a matter of public interest. "The line between the informing and the entertaining is too elusive for the protection of * * * [freedom of the press]." Winters v. People of State of New York, 333 U.S. 507, 510, 68 S.Ct. 665.

Hill, the Court ruled, would have to prove that *Life* knew its story was false or showed reckless disregard for the truth of the article. He was not a public official, or a public figure except possibly as he was linked, by his unwilling experience as a hostage, to a new play that was a matter of public interest.

By 1968, the logic of Justice Douglas's 1966 opinion in the *Rosenblatt* case—that the question was whether a public *issue*, not a public official, was involved—and the thrust of the high court's *Hill* decision, were reaching to lower courts. CBS had investigated the findings of mail-order medical testing laboratories, and newsman Walter Cronkite said in one of a series of radio and television reports: [34]

> How typical are these [mail-order testing laboratory] results? We don't know, but a sick patient may get only

---

[33] Ibid.

[34] United Medical Laboratories, Inc. v. Columbia Broadcasting System, Inc., 404 F.2d 706, 713 (9th Cir. 1968), certiorari denied 394 U.S. 921, 89 S.Ct. 1197 (1969). For other very early cases resting on "public interest" see

one chance to find out. And * * * we'd like to underscore that the labs in question are all mail-order laboratories, not the community laboratories that do the bulk of the nation's medical testing.

United Medical Laboratories, a mail-order firm doing business in Portland, Ore., sued CBS, Cronkite and the series producer for libel damages totaling $11,000,000. The broadcasters argued that United Labs should meet the malice test of *New York Times*. The U. S. Circuit Court of Appeals agreed. Recognizing that neither "public official" nor "public figure" was bringing the suit against the broadcasters, the Court said that the area of public interest involved in the broadcast—namely, conditions affecting public health—"would seem to us to be one of such inherent public concern and state that there could be no possible question as to the applicability of the *New York Times* standard * * *." [35] It concluded with "no difficulty" that the First Amendment immunity properly extended to disclosure and discussion of professional practices and conditions in this health area. United Labs would have to meet the standard, proving with "convincing clarity" that CBS's statements were made with knowing or reckless falsity.

The rule that persons and firms involved in matters of general concern or public interest would have to prove the *New York Times* decision's malice in their libel suits spread quickly through the lower courts.[36]

Time, Inc., successful in the Hill privacy case, was establishing a remarkable record in the late 1960s in defending libel suits, many under the new scope of the public principle extended to matters of public interest. It was challenging suits brought against its magazines *Time, Life* and *Sports Illustrated* through motions for summary judgment—judicial rulings before suits reached the actual trial stage. By August 1969, it had been successful in at least five cases within less than two years in motions for summary judgment, on the argument that the plaintiff's pleadings and papers did not show the actual malice of the *New*

All Diet Foods Distributors, Inc. v. Time, Inc., 56 Misc.2d 821, 290 N.Y.S.2d 445 (1968); Bon Air Hotel, Inc. v. Time, Inc., 295 F.Supp. 704 (S.D.Ga. 1969).

[35] United Medical Laboratories, Inc. v. Columbia Broadcasting System, Inc. 404 F.2d 706, 711 (9th Cir. 1968).

[36] DeSalvo v. Twentieth-Century-Fox Film Corp., 300 F.Supp. 742 (D.C.Mass. 1969); Ragano v. Time, Inc., 302 F.Supp. 1005 (D.C.Fla.1969); Holmes v. Curtis Pub. Co., 303 F.Supp. 522 (D.C.S.C.1969); Lloyds v. United Press International, Inc., 63 Misc.2d 421, 311 N.Y.S.2d 373 (1970); Gertz v. Robert Welch, Inc., 322 F.Supp. 997 (D.C.Ill.1970).

York Times rule.[37]   The court in Ragano v. Time, Inc. called attention to the heavy burden on the plaintiff in defeating the motion for summary judgment: [38]

> Perhaps in no other area of civil litigation is the burden so ominous as in the law of defamation.   To survive summary judgment proceedings it is necessary that [plaintiff] offer some evidence upon which a jury could find convincing clarity * * * of actual malice or reckless disregard.   The decisions require that he come forward with evidence of the defendant's state of mind; in effect, he must prove a negative.

It was seven years after the New York Times Co. v. Sullivan standard of malice was enunciated that the Supreme Court of the United States gave its practical blessing to requiring private persons involved in matters of public interest to meet the standard in a libel case.   In 1971, the Court denied recovery in a libel suit of Philadelphia magazine distributor George A. Rosenbloom. While only three justices (writing the plurality opinion) did so on the ground that private citizen Rosenbloom, the subject of a police action, was involved in a matter of public interest and so would have to prove *New York Times* malice, lower courts effectively accepted their opinion as the Court's.[39]

The case arose after police arrested Rosenbloom, Philadelphia distributor of nudist magazines, searched his home and warehouse, and seized magazines and books.   Metromedia's radio station, WIP, was given a phone report by the police and broadcast twice a story referring to Rosenbloom's arrest on charges of possessing obscene literature and "obscene books" that had been seized.   Subsequent broadcasts referred to the "smut literature rackets."   Later, Rosenbloom was acquitted of obscenity charges. He brought action against Metromedia under the Pennsylvania libel statute.   The statute said that the media's privilege to report official proceedings may be defeated by "want of reasonable care and diligence to ascertain the truth, before giving currency to an untrue communication." [40]

---

[37] Bon Air Hotel, Inc. v. Time, Inc., 295 F.Supp. 704 (S.D.Ga.1969); Time, Inc. v. McLaney, 406 F.2d 565 (5th Cir. 1969); Sellers v. Time, Inc., 299 F.Supp. 582 (E.D.Pa.1969); Wasserman v. Time, Inc., No. 2925–66, unreported (D.C.1969); Firestone v. Time, No. 68–C–977, unreported (15 Jud.Cir. Fla.1968).

[38] Ragano v. Time, Inc., 302 F.Supp. 1005, 1010 (D.C.Fla.1969).   In this case, Time's motion for summary judgment was not successful.

[39] Matus v. Triangle Pubs., Inc., 445 Pa. 384, 286 A.2d 357 (1971); West v. Northern Pub. Co., 487 P.2d 1304 (Alaska 1971); Frances v. Lake Charles American Press, 262 La. 875, 265 So.2d 206 (1972).

[40] Rosenbloom v. Metromedia, Inc., 403 U.S. 29, 91 S.Ct. 1811, 1816 (1971).

Rosenbloom won at trial but lost on appeal. At the trial, the judge instructed the jury that to give Rosenbloom the judgment, it would have to find either that WIP intended to injure him personally or exercised its privilege to report official proceedings unreasonably and without reasonable care (as per the statute). The jury found for Rosenbloom, awarding him $25,000 in general damages and $725,000 in punitive damages (the latter reduced by the court to $250,000).[41]

The United States Circuit Court of Appeals reversed the finding, resting its decision on the reasoning that although Rosenbloom was a private individual, the broadcasts involved subject matter of public interest. It quoted Time, Inc. v. Hill:[42] "The guarantees for speech and press are not the preserve of political expression or comment upon public affairs, essential as these are to healthy government."

It did not matter to the Circuit Court that Rosenbloom was neither a "public official" nor a "public figure." It declared:[43]

> * * * we do not consider the absence of a public figure of controlling importance here. Considering the type of news broadcasts involved as well as the established public interest in the subject matter, we conclude that the fact that plaintiff was not a public figure cannot be accorded decisive importance if the recognized important guarantees of the First Amendment are to be adequately implemented.

Rosenbloom's status as a private individual thus did not free him from establishing that Metromedia published with the "knowing or reckless falsehood" of the *New York Times* rule, according to the Circuit Court.

The United States Supreme Court upheld the Circuit Court's reversal, three justices rejecting Rosenbloom's appeal on the "public interest" rationale used by the Circuit Court. Two others found other reasons for rejecting the appeal; three dissented from the finding; and one (Douglas) did not take part, making the decision 5 to 3.

Writing for the plurality of three, Justice William J. Brennan (Chief Justice Warren E. Burger and Justice Harry A. Blackmun concurring) said:[44]

> If a matter is a subject of public or general interest, it cannot suddenly become less so merely because a private

---

[41] Ibid., 1817–1818.

[42] Supra; at text footnoted 33.

[43] Ibid., 896.

[44] Rosenbloom v. Metromedia, Inc., 403 U.S. 29, 91 S.Ct. 1811, 1819, 1824 (1971).

individual is involved, or because in some sense the individual did not "voluntarily" choose to become involved. The public's primary interest is in the event; the public focus is on the conduct of the participant and the content, effect, and significance of the conduct, not the participant's prior anonymity or notoriety.

* * * * * * * * *

We thus hold that a libel action, as here, by a private individual against a licensed radio station for a defamatory newscast relating to his involvement in an event of public or general concern may be sustained only upon clear and convincing proof that the defamatory falsehood was published with knowledge that it was false or with reckless disregard of whether it was false or not.

Concurring in the result, Justice Hugo L. Black said, as in earlier cases, that the First Amendment does not permit recovery of libel judgments against news media even when statements are made with knowledge they are false.[45] Justice Byron R. White concurred in the result also, but said that it could be reached much more narrowly than through the plurality opinion: The media are privileged, without the actual malice of the *New York Times* rule, to report and comment on official actions of public servants (such as the police in the instant case) in full detail. He said that trying to protect everyone involved in an episode that centrally concerns the actions of public officials is constructing "artificial limitations" on discussion. When such actions are concerned, he said, there should be no requirement that the reputation of an individual involved in or affected by the official action be spared from public view.[46]

Justice Harlan dissented, saying that the "reasonable care" standard of the Pennsylvania statute adequately serves "those First Amendment values that must inform the definition of actionable libel * * *." While special circumstances made that standard insufficiently precise when applied to public officials and public figures, those circumstances do not obtain where the litigant is a private individual.[47]

Justice Thurgood Marshall (Justice Potter Stewart concurring) also dissented. He said that the threat to free expression in defamation law is that self-censorship will occur under it, and the size of the potential judgment that may be rendered

45 Ibid., 1826.

46 Ibid., 1827.

47 Ibid., 1829, 1833.

against the media is the most significant factor in producing self-censorship. (The jury in the *Rosenbloom* case had awarded $725,000 in punitive damages, and even when reduced by the judge, the sum was $250,000.) Further, general damages are awarded on the legal presumption that injuries "normally flow" from defamation without showing actual loss, suffering, or standing. He said that the threats to society's interest in freedom of the press can largely be eliminated by restricting damages to proven, actual injuries.[48]

Lower courts have taken the plurality opinion as ruling. The questions that rise for the newsman in this context are centrally: What is a "matter of public interest or general concern"? And what is "reckless disregard of truth"?

SEC. 21. MATTERS OF PUBLIC INTEREST OR GENERAL CONCERN

While many private citizens become newsworthy and associated with matters of public or general interest, not all must meet the requirement of proving malice in libel suits.

We have seen three sub-concepts within the public principle in defamation: public officials, public figures, and matters of public interest. The last is the broadest, embracing most media messages about public officials and public figures, as well as countless reported events concerning "private" persons like the Hill family and Rosenbloom.

Since the lower courts in 1968 began recognizing "matter of public interest" as the touchstone for specifying those who would have to prove actual malice in their libel suits, their decisions have illuminated what these matters are and are not. The newsman who grasps the sweep of the protection offered him may be at once reassured by this shield and sobered by the duty placed on him to use it responsibly.

We have seen above several kinds of news events that the courts have held to be "matters of public interest" that require the plaintiff to prove actual malice. Among stories about crime and police action, Lillian Corabi, a night-club entertainer and owner, was linked by police to various crimes; George Rosenbloom, a magazine distributor, was arrested on charges of possessing obscene books, though later exonerated. Many other cases involving police and crime could be cited, some of which are these:

Davis sued NBC for libel, saying a broadcast had identified him as one Clay Bertrand, a pseudonym for a homosexual of New

48 Ibid., 1836–1838.

Orleans who allegedly had involved himself in the defense of Lee Harvey Oswald, the accused assassain of President John F. Kennedy. The court granted NBC's request for summary judgment, saying that this was information of public interest, and Davis was under the rule that "A person may become a matter of public interest within the meaning of [the *New York Times* malice rule] although he does not seek to be one, and indeed avoids it." [49]

The Arizona Biomedical Co. sued the Hearst Corp. for libel, saying the *Albany Times Union* published articles associating the company with the Mafia, with paying "kickbacks" and with threats of violence against its competitors. The court granted Hearst its motion for summary judgment. It explained that the biomedical company by its own statement performed essential services for several communities, being for all practical purposes the sanitation department of several towns. "The operation of plaintiff's business is infected with the public interest," the court said. "It is * * * a matter of substantial public concern." [50]

West and Tate were owners of taxi cab companies in Nome, Alaska. Robert Zelnick, reporter for the *Anchorage Daily News*, wrote a series on "Justice in the Bush." He said in part: [51]

> The city of Nome is dominated economically, politically, and socially by the liquor merchants. It is the distribution center for legal and illegal liquor traffic throughout the northwest. Liquor interests control the city council. Some booze is furnished minors by cab companies, which in turn are owned by the liquor interests. Individual proprietors furnish liquor illegally on credit. They sell booze for money, ivory, and even federal food stamps.

West and Tate sued for libel, and the Northern Publishing Co. which owned the *Daily News* moved for summary judgment, which was granted at trial and upheld by the Alaska Supreme Court. The Court held that the *Rosenbloom* decision was controlling, quoting U. S. Supreme Court Justice Brennan's wording that " * * * a libel action * * * by a private individual * * * for a defamatory falsehood * * * relating to his involvement in an event of public or general concern * * * " requires proof of actual malice to succeed. There was no such proof here.

"There can be no doubt," as one court has put it, "that organized crime is a subject about which the public has an interest and a right to be informed." [52]

---

[49] Davis v. National Broadcasting Co., 320 F.Supp. 1070 (D.C.La.1970).

[50] Arizona Biomedical Co. v. Hearst Corp., 302 F.Supp. 412 (S.D.N.Y.1969).

[51] West v. Northern Pub. Co., 487 P.2d 1304 (Alaska 1971).

[52] Cerrito v. Time, Inc., 302 F.Supp. 1071, 1073 (N.D.Cal.1969).

What, apart from crime and police action, are matters of public interest that require a showing of actual malice? Is anything that the news media find "newsworthy" a matter of public interest? Probably not, but some courts have found a high degree of identity between the two. The late *Life* magazine published pictures of Goldman and Heckler, and captions reading "Young American Nomads Abroad," and "Two Californians at home in a cave in Crete." The article treated the nature and attitudes of various people in and about the caves of Matala, Crete. Heckler, who had left America with his girl after his budding business was closed, was quoted as saying "Maybe" he might some day return to America. The two did return, and sued for libel and privacy invasion, saying the article subjected them to ridicule, shame and disgust by their community, for it associated them with drug-users, draft-dodgers and others of social opprobrium.

The court said that one issue was "whether the subject matter of the article in question qualifies as being within the broad ambit of newsworthiness or public interest * * *." It found the article within that ambit: [53]

> The public interest is at once an expansive yet exclusive concept. Plaintiffs take the position that only concrete, specific events can constitute the basis of a story entitled to the protection of newsworthiness. Here, they continue, *Life* Magazine merely "manufactured" a story where none existed before in order to bolster a pre-conceived idea about youth abroad. Youth, claim the plaintiffs, is simply too broad an issue to qualify as being newsworthy without more being thrown into the pot.
>
> We disagree. Certainly discrete events of current interest are entitled to the protection of newsworthiness, but so are matters of more general scope, such as unemployment, the problems of the aged, hospital care, and * * * organized crime. The topic of youth traveling abroad is equally general, but equally deserving of being called newsworthy.
>
> The California courts have looked to several factors in determining whether a particular incident is newsworthy. Such factors include: (1) the social value of the facts published; (2) the depth of the article's intrusion into ostensibly private affairs; and (3) the extent to which the party voluntarily acceded to a position of public notoriety. Briscoe v. Reader's Digest Association, Inc., supra, 4 Cal.3d at 541, 93 Cal.Rptr. 866, 483

[53] Goldman v. Time, Inc., 336 F.Supp. 133, 138 (N.D.Cal.1971).

P.2d 34; Kapellas v. Kofman, supra, 1 Cal.3d at 36, 81 Cal.Rptr. 360, 459 P.2d 912.

Applying these three factors, we conclude that the subject matter of the *Life* Magazine article in question is entitled to the protection of newsworthiness. First, the article does present facts about a significant segment of the American population engaging in activities that would be interesting to many. Second, it cannot be said that the article delved deeply into seemingly private affairs. Relatively little mention was made of plaintiffs and the references to them were not in depth. Speaking physically, plaintiffs have not—and indeed could not —contend that they had a great expectation of privacy on Crete in view of the tourist nature of the activities there and the very openness or public nature of the caves. Third, and finally, it is obvious that plaintiffs did not resist and in fact made themselves readily available for both the text and photographs which eventually appeared in the *Life* Magazine article.

This court is well aware of the power of the public media to bring virtually any person, even the most insignificant event, into its ambit as "news." In one sense, of course, all news is manufactured, for the public would generally not know of or be interested in matters not brought to its attention by the media. Nonetheless, the right of the public to know, and of the media to tell, is so deeply entrenched in the American conscience that a great deal of latitude must necessarily be afforded the media in its selection and presentation of news.

The scope of "matters of public interest" has further definition. We have seen that a magazine's review of a play based in part on the Hill family's experience in being held prisoners by escaped convicts was a matter of public interest.[54] Thus news and criticism of the arts is clearly within the protection. So, as we have seen, is implied criticism of the standards of a firm involved in medical testing.[55] The public interest in sports was the basis for providing protection for a magazine article criticizing a hotel's accommodations for people at a golf tournament.[56] The career of a basketball player—"destroyed," ac-

[54] Time, Inc. v. Hill, 385 U.S. 374, 87 S.Ct. 534 (1967).

[55] United Medical Laboratories, Inc v. CBS, Inc., 404 F.2d 706 (9th Cir. 1968).

[56] Bon Air Hotel, Inc., v. Time, Inc., 426 F.2d 858 (5th Cir. 1970).

cording to a magazine article, by the skill of another—was a matter of public interest.[57]

What, then, has been found to be outside the great sweep of "matters of public interest" in libel cases since the Supreme Court's practical endorsement of its appropriateness in Rosenbloom v. Metromedia on June 7, 1971?

The Pennsylvania Supreme Court has held that a "patently anonymous plaintiff engaged in a one-man snow-plowing business" in a suburb did not come within the scope of "matter of public interest" for libel. Gerhart, a radio host on a talk show, said on the air that a company called "Matus or something like that" had charged his wife $35.00 to plow their driveway, and that "people like that shouldn't be in business." Matus denied that he had plowed the driveway or authorized anyone to do it, and sued for libel, winning on trial. The radio firm appealed, and the Pennsylvania Supreme Court upheld the verdict against it. Matus, the Court said, was a [58]

> patently anonymous plaintiff engaged in a one-man snow-plowing business as to whom a defamatory statement, established by the jury's verdict to be false, is uttered in a radio "talk show" * * *. The "announcer" states that his wife has been overcharged by plaintiff, calling him by name * * * and that "people like that shouldn't be in business." We have no doubt that Gerhart could with impunity * * * discuss the problem of snow removal. We see no justification, however, for the interjection of Matus' name into the discussion or for the expression of opinion as to his business ethics or fitness to be in business. This was no contribution to "robust debate on public issues"; it was by no stretch of the imagination a matter of public concern that Gerhart thought he or his wife had been bilked by Matus the evening before; it was but a matter of private pique. The great values of the First Amendment are not served by making it a haven for unprovoked and defamatory gossip-mongering of interest only to the speaker merely because he happens to be on the radio at the time of speaking. * * * We hold that the decision of the United States Supreme Court in Rosenbloom v. Metromedia, Inc. * * * does not require the application of the rule that the appellants'

[57] Time, Inc. v. Johnston, 448 F.2d 378 (4th Cir. 1971).

[58] Matus v. Triangle Publications, Inc., 445 Pa. 384, 286 A.2d 357, 364–365 (1971).

conditional privilege could be defeated "only upon clear and convincing proof that the defamatory false-hood was published with knowledge that it was false or with reckless disregard of whether it was false or not."

The U. S. Court of Appeals, Third Circuit, which had found that the "matters of public interest" standard applied to Rosenbloom as his case proceeded to the Supreme Court of the United States, shortly afterward denied that the same standard applied to a small business engaged in brick and tile brokerage. Dun & Bradstreet, Inc., a mercantile agency which supplies credit reports to its subscribers, had said in a report that Altoona Clay Products, Inc., had had a "confession of judgment in the penal sum of $60,000" entered against it. This was in error; a predecessor-firm of a similar name was the real subject of the judgment. Grove, owner of the firm, brought a libel suit and was awarded $110,000 by a jury. Dun & Bradstreet argued that the Altoona firm's credit was a matter of public interest, and that it should be required to prove actual malice in order to recover: Altoona sometimes involved itself in public projects such as sewerage plants, public school buildings, and post offices. But the Court of Appeals did not agree and upheld the jury verdict. It said: [59]

> We cannot accept the theory that plaintiff's business or credit standing is a matter of "real public interest." It may generally be true that "the modern business corporation by virtue of its pervasive influence on the political, economic, and social aspects of American life, has necessarily become a subject of public concern to the extent that the critics of its operations and behavior must enjoy constitutional protection for errone-ous statements made without actual malice." But those cases which have required that corporate plaintiffs meet the more difficult constitutional quantum of proof have all involved corporations engaged in activities of real public interest, and are grounded in that dis-tinction. We are not here dealing with a publication or broadcast alleging, for example, that plaintiff caused sub-standard building material to be used in these proj-ects. Such operative facts might constitute a matter of grave public interest. Our research discloses no case, however, which would support the application of the more rigorous standard to the covert reportage of the

[59] Grove v. Dun & Bradstreet, Inc., 438 F.2d 433, 436–437 (3d Cir. 1971).

credit standing of a small brick and tile brokerage firm, and we decline to do so now.

While the credit standing of the small brick and tile brokerage firm thus was not a "matter of real public interest," Dun & Bradstreet's case failed even more fundamentally on another consideration: The credit reporting publication itself did not constitute a "public" instrument, for it provided specialized information to a selective, finite audience, unlike a general-circulation newspaper or a broadcasting station.[60] The "private" character of its publication was made plain in the contract that subscribers agreed to in subscribing. The contract said that information in the publication "shall be held in strict confidence and shall never be revealed or made accessible in any manner. * * * " The New York Times malice doctrine was inapplicable to this confidential reporting service of Dun & Bradstreet.

The Louisiana Supreme Court revealed its concern about the sweep of Rosenbloom in a case of 1972, saying there were serious questions about the impact of that decision on the right of a private citizen to protect his reputation. In the case before the Court, Francis had signed an appearance bond of $100 for LaRue who was accused of being a "peeping Tom." LaRue (later exonerated) failed to appear for arraignment, and the trial court rendered judgment forfeiting the bond. Two days later the *Lake Charles American Press* carried the ancient error to which all reporters are heir: It got the names wrong, and published a story saying that Francis had failed to appear on a peeping Tom charge. It printed a retraction, but Francis, who had suffered injury with his employer and with acquaintances, sued and was awarded $15,000 by a jury. Though it reduced the award to $8,000, the Louisiana Supreme Court upheld the verdict, saying that Francis did not have to prove knowing falsehood or reckless disregard, for he was not involved in matter of public interest.

The Court rested this part of its decision on just what it means to be "involved" in a matter of public interest. It said that Francis was not involved: [61]

> The critical question here is whether plaintiff was involved in an event of public or general interest within the meaning of the constitutional pronouncement. We think not.

[60] Ibid., 437. See also Packaging Industries, Inc. v. Dun & Bradstreet, Inc., 67 Civil 4638 (S.D.N.Y.1969) ; cited at Ibid.

[61] Francis v. Lake Charles American Press, 262 La. 875, 265 So.2d 206, 218 (1972).

Plaintiff signed a small appearance bond in a misdemeanor case. Standing as a surety in such a case is citizen-action that the law views with favor. It is not, however, in defamation law, an event of general or public concern.

The only event of general concern here was the failure of the charged defendant to appear in court for his arraignment. The plaintiff was in no way involved in this dereliction. It is true that the news release identified him as the person who failed to appear to answer for his crime. The publisher, however, cannot build a privilege by joining a private individual with an event of public interest when there is no factual connection between the two. For this Court to validate a purely artificial connection would allow an offender to freely pierce the legal shield against defamation.

In Rosenbloom v. Metromedia, supra, the police arrested the plaintiff for distributing obscene magazines. The defendant's newscast related to this event.

*   *   *   *   *   *   *   *   *

The keystone of the privilege is actual involvement, not the unsupported association of a name and an event. We hold that the constitutional privilege is unavailable in the present case.

Is a divorce or separation suit a "matter of public or general interest," even considering the fact that it takes place in the official setting of a court? The New York Court of Appeals in 1970 delivered a 4–3 judgment which strongly suggests it is not under New York statutes. The *New York Daily News* and *Sunday News* carried a series of articles about Shiles, an airline executive, purporting to report a separation suit brought against him by his wife (headlines: "Wife Says Air Exec Had Harems," and "Wife Says Exec Built a Harem in the Sky"). Shiles sued for libel, and the News defended by saying that the stories were "privileged" (see Chap. 5) as a "fair and true report of a judicial proceeding" as provided by New York statute. The *News* won at trial, but New York's highest court reversed. It said that in most judicial proceedings "the public interest in having proceedings of courts of justice public, not secret [lies in] the greater security thus given for the proper administration of justice." But in matrimonial cases, it said, the state Legislature had made it plain that [62]

---

[62] Shiles v. News Syndicate Co., 27 N.Y.2d 9, 313 N.Y.S.2d 104, 107, 110, 261 N.E.2d 251 (1970).

in the case of papers filed in such actions the public
interest is served not by publicizing [the proceedings]
but by sealing them and prohibiting their examination
by the public.

*   *   *   *   *   *   *   *   *

[Former court decisions denying protection to reports
of matrimonial actions] were founded upon a recognition of the inherently personal nature of matrimonial
proceedings and the obvious desirability that records
of such proceedings not be "used to gratify private
spite or promote public scandal" * * *.

*   *   *   *   *   *   *   *   *

The records of proceedings in an action for divorce or
separation are kept sealed precisely because disclosure of their contents could cause great harm to the
persons involved without producing any countervailing public benefit.

Another question that has not yet, apparently, been considered in the light of Rosenbloom concerns the personal activities of those who often are involved in matters of public interest.   In Aku v. Lewis (1969), Policeman Aku was in no way
involved in his official duties but rather was serving as coach
of a youth football team when broadcasters allegedly defamed
him in the coaching capacity.   Was he so involved in a "matter
of public interest" that he would have to prove malice against
the radio station in order to recover damages?   The Supreme
Court of Hawaii, ruling before Rosenbloom became a guide,
said that he was acting as a private citizen when coaching, and
his activities were not within the purview of the New York
Times doctrine.[63]

And in Stearn v. MacLean-Hunter, Ltd., the federal court
held that criticism of author Stearn, in a *Macleans* article, in
part went to his personal conduct and motives.   It said that to
the extent that the criticism did not go to his public function
as a writer, "there is no reason to extend First Amendment
protection to non-malicious but defamatory statements." [64]

[63] Aku v. Lewis, 52 Haw. 366, 477 P.2d 162 (1970).

[64] Stearn v. MacLean-Hunter, Ltd., 46 F.R.D. 76, 78 (D.C.N.Y.1969).

SEC. 22.   ACTUAL MALICE

The United States Supreme Court has defined reckless disregard of truth as "high degree of awareness of probable falsity" and as "entertaining serious doubts as to the truth of publication"; knowing falsehood has required less definition and has seldom been found.

If a news medium can successfully demonstrate that its allegedly defamatory words were published of a person involved in a matter of public interest or general concern, its next move under the Constitutional protection is to defend against the charge of actual malice.   This term, as we have seen, is defined by the Supreme Court as reckless disregard for the truth or falsity of the publication, or knowledge that the publication was false.

Reckless Disregard of Truth.

Very soon after Times v. Sullivan had established the new definition of actual malice, the Supreme Court began the process of defining "reckless disregard."   In Garrison v. Louisiana,[65] a criminal libel action, it said that reckless disregard means a "high degree of awareness of probable falsity" of the publication and in 1968 in St. Amant v. Thompson, it said that for reckless disregard to be found, "There must be sufficient evidence to permit the conclusion that the defendant in fact entertained serious doubts as to the truth of his publication." [66]

The St. Amant wording is used more by lower courts in following the Supreme Court's rules.   In this case, St. Amant read, in a televised political campaign speech, the accusation by one Albin that Herman Thompson had had money dealings with another man accused of nefarious activities in labor union affairs.   Thompson sued for defamation, and the Supreme Court of Louisiana upheld a judgment in his favor.   It said there was sufficient evidence that St. Amant recklessly disregarded whether the statements about Thompson were true or false.   The United States Supreme Court reversed the decision.

Reviewing decisions since New York Times Co. v. Sullivan, it said that the outer limits of reckless disregard were not yet known, but: [67]

> These cases are clear that reckless conduct is not measured by whether a reasonably prudent man would have

65 379 U.S. 64, 74, 85 S.Ct. 209, 216 (1964).

66 St. Amant v. Thompson, 390 U.S. 727, 731, 88 S.Ct. 1323, 1325 (1968).

67 Ibid., 1325.

published, or would have investigated before publishing. There must be sufficient evidence to permit the conclusion that the defendant in fact entertained serious doubts as to the truth of his publication. Publishing with such doubts shows reckless disregard for truth or falsity and demonstrates actual malice.

But the decision added that a defendant may not count on a favorable verdict merely by *testifying* that he published with a belief that the statements were true: [68]

The finder of fact must determine whether the publication was indeed made in good faith. Professions of good faith will be unlikely to prove persuasive, for example, where a story is fabricated by the defendant, is the product of his imagination, or is based wholly on an unverified anonymous telephone call. Nor will they be likely to prevail when the publisher's allegations are so inherently improbable that only a reckless man would have put them in circulation. Likewise, recklessness may be found where there are obvious reasons to doubt the veracity of the informant or the accuracy of his reports.

In this case, the Supreme Court found, there was no evidence that St. Amant was aware of the probable falsity of Albin's statement about Thompson. Albin had sworn to his statements and St. Amant had verified some of them, and Thompson's evidence had failed to demonstrate "a low community assessment of Albin's trustworthiness."

As for the specifying of reckless disregard in Garrison v. Louisiana: Garrison, a Louisiana prosecuting attorney, had attacked several judges during a press conference, for laziness and inattention to duty. He was convicted of criminal libel, and the Supreme Court of the United States reversed the conviction. It said that the fact that the case was a criminal case made no difference to the principles of the *New York Times* rule, and that its malice would have to be shown. And the "reckless disregard" of truth or falsity of malice, it said, lies in a "high degree of awareness of falsity" on the part of the publisher. Nothing indicated that Garrison had this awareness of falsity when he castigated the Louisiana judges.[69]

Since the first case providing the Constitutional protection in libel, the courts have been at pains to distinguish between

---

[68] Ibid., 1326.

[69] 379 U.S. 64, 85 S.Ct. 209 (1964).

"reckless disregard of truth" and "negligence." [70]   The latter is not enough to sustain a finding of liability for libel.   In the leading case, the Court went to this point.   Errors in the famous advertisement, "Heed Their Rising Voices," could have been discovered by the *New York Times* advertising staff had it taken an elevator up a floor to the morgue and checked earlier stories on file.   Failure to make this check, the Supreme Court said, did not constitute "reckless disregard"; at the worst it was negligence, and negligence is not enough to indicate malice.[71]

In another case, a New York congressman sued the *Washington Post* for a story by columnist Drew Pearson which the Post carried.   The story accused the congressman of bribe-splitting.   The Post did not check the accuracy of the columnist's charges.   The Federal Court of Appeals held that the Post showed no reckless disregard in not verifying Pearson's charge, regardless of Pearson's reputation for accuracy.   The court held that to require such checking by the Post would be to burden it with greater responsibilities of verification than the Supreme Court required of the *New York Times* in the landmark case.   It discussed at length whether the newspaper could be held to the malice rule for not verifying syndicated news reports such as Pearson's: [72]

> Verification of syndicated news reports and columns is a time-consuming process, a factor especially significant in the newspaper business where news quickly goes stale, commentary rapidly becomes irrelevant and commercial opportunity in the form of advertisements can easily be lost.   In many instances considerations of time and distance make verification impossible.   Thus the newspaper is confronted with the choice of publication without verification or suppression.   Verification is also a costly process, and the newspaper business is one in which economic survival has become a major problem.   *   *   *   We should be hesitant to impose responsibilities upon newspapers which can be met only through costly procedures or through self-censorship designed to avoid risks of publishing controversial material.   The costliness of this process would especially deter less established publishers from

---

[70] Priestley v. Hastings & Sons Pub. Co. of Lynn, —— Mass. ——, 271 N.E. 2d 628 (1971); A. S. Abell Co. v. Barnes, 258 Md. 56, 265 A.2d 207 (1970).

[71] New York Times Co. v. Sullivan, 376 U.S. 254, 288, 84 S.Ct. 710, 730 (1964).

[72] Washington Post Co. v. Keogh, 125 U.S.App.D.C. 32, 365 F.2d 965, 972–973 (1966).

taking chances and, since columns such as Pearson's are highly popular attractions, competition with publishers who can afford to verify or to litigate, would become even more difficult. It is highly unlikely, moreover, that the form of journalism engaged in by Pearson and other columnists could survive in the face of a rule requiring verification to negate recklessness. Pearson and his fellow columnists seek and often uncover the sensational, relying upon educated instinct, wide knowledge and confidential tips. Verification would be certain to dry up much of the stream of information that finds its way into their hands. Whether or not this would please a number of us is irrelevant. What matters is that a rule requiring certification in the absence of evidence that the publisher had good reason to suspect falsity would curtail substantially a protected form of speech.

In Time, Inc. v. Hill, it was shown that a story said that a play "re-enacted" the ordeal of the Hill family, held as hostages in their home by convicts. Testimony in the trial showed that the *Life* editor possessed in his "story file" several news clippings that portrayed the real-life ordeal as non-violent and thus different from the play. The clippings also said that the author of the play had stated that it "was based on various news stories" of incidents in at least four states. Was it reckless disregard for *Life* to say incorrectly that the play "re-enacted" the Hill family experience, when a correct version of the experience was on hand for checking in the editor's story file? The Supreme Court did not say, but ruled that the question was a real one and should be decided by a jury in any retrial of the case.[73]

Turning now to cases in which libel suits have been won on grounds that the publisher showed reckless disregard for truth: The earliest was the 1967 case, Curtis Publishing Co. v. Butts, treated above, in which the former athletic director of the University of Georgia sued for a *Saturday Evening Post* story accusing him of conspiring to "fix" a football game between Georgia and Alabama. The *Post* had relied on the story of Burnett, a man serving on probation in connection with bad check charges, had not seen Burnett's notes about the alleged telephone conversation he said he had overheard, had not interviewed a man supposedly in the company of Burnett at the time of the phone conversation. Furthermore, the story was not

[73] Time, Inc. v. Hill, 385 U.S. 374, 393–394, 87 S.Ct. 534, 544–545 (1967).

"hot news" that demanded immediate publication. In the words of part of the Supreme Court, this was reckless disregard of whether the statements were true or false; to other members it was "highly unreasonable conduct constituting an extreme departure" from responsible reporting standards.[74]

Goldwater v. Ginzburg [75] was decided in 1969. Here Sen. Barry Goldwater, running as the Republican candidate for President of the United States, sued the publisher of *Fact* for libel. At issue was an article advertised as "The Unconscious of a Conservative: A Special Issue on the Mind of Barry Goldwater." One article portrayed him as "paranoid," and under "an inner conviction that everybody hates him and it is better to attack them first"; these statements were based on editor Ginzburg's own conclusion without benefit of expert psychiatric advice. Another reported the results of a "poll" of psychiatrists, using methods termed invalid by an expert witness at the trial and by many respondents in the survey. A jury found for Goldwater, $1.00 in compensatory damages and $75,000 in punitive damages. The Court of Appeals upheld the verdict, saying that a false charge of mental illness is libel per se in New York, place of publication, and that reckless disregard or knowing falsehood was proved.

In 1970, a divided court let stand a libel judgment in which a jury found reckless disregard. An inmate died in jail, and another inmate was convicted of beating him shortly before his death. The *Indianapolis Star* carried many stories on the matter. One said that a third inmate, McAdams, claimed that deputy sheriff King had actually administered the beating. Later, McAdams repudiated this story. The newspaper said that the sheriff, Fields, in trying to protect the deputy from facing or answering the charges, intimidated McAdams into repudiating his story of the deputy's involvement. The sheriff sued for libel, and the jury returned a $60,000 verdict.

In reviewing facts of the trial and the newspaper stories, two of the Indiana Supreme Court (made up of five members, one of whom disqualified himself in this case) said that the Star's reporter knew of evidence that contradicted McAdams' original story, but barely mentioned it only once. Further, some statements reported in the news stories indicated that other deputies were witnesses to the alleged beating by King, but the

---

[74] Curtis Pub. Co. v. Butts, 388 U.S. 130, 155, 87 S.Ct. 1975 (1967). Supra., fn. 30 for subsequent cases employing "extreme departure" standard.

[75] 414 F.2d 324, 331 (2d Cir. 1969).

deputies denied at the libel trial that they had told that to the reporter, or that King had performed the beating. All this, said the two justices, was sufficient evidence to sustain a jury finding that the Star published with reckless disregard of truth, or with knowledge of falsity.[76]

Actor Marlon Brando was sued for slander by three Oakland, Calif. police officers who had fired shots at Black Panther Bobby Hutton, killed during a police action. Brando, a guest on the Joey Bishop television program heard by millions, said he had set out to investigate "what it is to be black in this country," and "what this rage is all about." He went to the San Francisco-Oakland area, "a place which could be considered the center of rage." There he visited with some Black Panthers and listened to their thoughts and views. Two days later, Brando said, Hutton "was in a shoot-out with the police. He came out of the house with his hands up and he was told to run for the car and he was shot dead and killed." Brando added that he was told that "the police department was out to get the Panthers." The trial court found for Brando; but the Court of Appeal said that the "reckless disregard" of the Times malice definition was "the precise state of mind that the plaintiffs have pleaded," and reversed the lower court's grant of a demurrer.[77]

A Louisiana case decided in 1971 demonstrates the danger in a radio station's broadcasting a "call-in" show live, without a delay device. WBOX of Bogalusa had such a show. The announcer asked call-ins not to use specific names and places unless they were willing to identify themselves, in fairness to all people. On April 2, 1968, a call-in by an unidentified person associated the Pizza Shanty with narcotics, and said that Dr. Newman "is writing those prescriptions," and "Guerry Snowden [manager of a drug store] is filling them and they are selling them down there." The announcer broke in repeatedly, trying to get the name of the caller, but did not succeed. After the program, the Bogalusa police department was besieged with calls, so vehement that the police chief on April 4 issued a statement saying that characters of innocent persons were being slandered by rumors of trafficking. Snowden, Newman and Blackwell of the Pizza Shanty sued, and a jury awarded them $4,000, $5,000, and $2,500 respectively. The station appealed, and in upholding the judgments, the Louisiana Appeals Court

[76] Indianapolis Newspapers, Inc. v. Fields, 254 Ind. 219, 259 N.E.2d 651 (1970).

[77] Mullins et al v. Brando, 13 Cal.App.3d 409, 91 Cal.Rptr. 796 (1970).

explained in detail why the station's behavior was reckless disregard of truth or falsity: [78]

> The question here presented is whether a radio station, having invited the public to speak freely through its facilities on a matter of public interest, is impressed with the duty of preventing such persons from making defamatory statements over the air. We would have no difficulty in finding a station liable, if it received defamatory material from an anonymous source, and broadcast the report without attempting verification. The direct broadcast of such anonymous defamatory material, without the use of any monitoring or delay device, is no less reprehensible in our judgment. The publication, in either event, is done by the station, and we find that there is the same reckless disregard for the truth in each instance.

> The procedure employed amounted to an open invitation to make any statement a listener desired, regardless of how untrue or defamatory it might be, about any person or establishment, provided only that the declarer identify himself. The announcer's qualifying remarks did not even remotely indicate that unfounded remarks were out of order, or that statements and accusations should be based on personal knowledge, or that mere rumor, speculation, suspicion and hearsay would not be permitted. The clear import of the announcer's remarks was that an identified caller was free to make such accusations as he chose. To the uninitiated, at least, it extended both the privilege and opportunity to make any statement whatsoever, provided only that the declarer shed the cloak of anonymity. It also inferred that disclosure of identity would render a certain degree of respectability and propriety to such charges and accusations as might be made against named individuals. Appellant could have effectively monitored the program by the use of tape recorders or delayed broadcast equipment. For the reasons above noted, it did not choose to do so. It is contended the announcer terminated the anonymous call as soon as possible under the circumstances. The quoted excerpt from the broadcast does not support this argument. At no time was the caller informed that his interview would be terminated if he

[78] Snowden v. Pearl River Broadcasting Corp., 251 So.2d 405 (La.App.1971).

did not identify himself.   The announcer merely requested that the caller disclose his identity, and concluded by thanking the caller when the caller finished
his statement.   We find that the style utilized encouraged the utterance of defamatory statements with utter
disregard of their truth or falsity.   Appellant placed
itself in a position fraught with the imminent danger of
broadcasting anonymous unverified, slanderous remarks based on sheer rumor, speculation and hearsay,
and just such a result actually occurred.   Such an
eventuality was easily foreseeable and likely to occur,
as it in fact did.   In our judgment, the First Amendment does not protect a publisher against such utter
recklessness.

A decision of 1971, in Kent v. City of Buffalo and WBEN,
upheld a jury verdict for $5,000 in finding that station WBEN–
TV showed "reckless disregard of the rights of another," a
rubric used by some courts as an evidence of malice long before New York Times Co. v. Sullivan defined malice as "reckless
disregard of whether [a statement] was false or not."   Four
men had committed armed robbery at about 7 p. m. on July 1,
1961, and three were quickly arrested and handcuffed.   Kent,
a passerby not involved in the robbery, was arrested and handcuffed with the three as a suspect, and a WBEN–TV photographer photographed the four together.   Later, the fourth
man actually involved was found and by 8:30 p. m., Kent was
released.   At 11 p. m., the station broadcast film of four men
including Kent, and again the next noon, with a script saying
that "Buffalo police have captured four men with sawed-off
shotguns who held up the Hall Bakery * * *."   The script
gave the names, addresses and ages of the four actually involved, but not of Kent.   Kent sued for libel, and the jury found
for him and awarded $5,000.   The station appealed.

The appeals court held that the film portrayed the four as
the robbers, and this was false both times it was published because one shown was the innocent plaintiff.   The station should
have known this, the court said, and "Its failure to be aware
thereof could well have been found to be due to its reckless or
careless publication." [79]   Kent had been released at 8:30 p. m.,
"and defendant's failure to learn of his release in time to correct its 11 p. m. telecast and the noon telecast on the following
day could also have been found to have been due to its reckless-

---

[79] Kent v. City of Buffalo and WBEN, 36 A.D.2d 85, 319 N.Y.S.2d 305, 308
(1971).

ness or carelessness. The news editor testified that defendant's normal and established procedure was to verify the identity of the people in the file. This it failed to do, even after it had the names and addresses of the true culprits * * *." [80]

A dissenting judge argued that the station had not shown the reckless disregard defined by St. Amant ("high degree of awareness of probable falsity") or by Garrison ("entertained serious doubts as to the truth of publication"). But the majority—writing shortly before the United States Supreme Court's decision in Rosenbloom had reached out to "matters of public or general interest"—merely noted that since Kent was neither public figure nor public official, the Constitutional definitions did not apply. [81]

In 1972, a federal court found reckless disregard in the *Washington Star's* articles about the financing of the Airlie Foundation which operates a conference center in Virginia. *Star* reporter Robert Walters had gone to a press conference of one Higgs, who gave each reporter a 16-page handout. Higgs said that the foundation was secretly financed by government agencies, including the Pentagon, the Central Intelligence Agency (CIA) and the State Department. *Star* stories on two successive days carried these statements, and some that did not come from Higgs. Airlie brought suit, and the jury returned verdicts of $419,800 to the corporation and $100,000 to Head, founder of the foundation. The *Star* moved for a judgment notwithstanding the verdict.

The federal court found reckless disregard in the *Star's* stories and upheld the verdict, reducing the awards to $50,000 and $10,000. One point of evidence for reckless disregard was that the *Star's* editor-in-chief, Newbold Noyes, called a personal friend at the CIA the evening that the first story ran—the friend being Richard Helms, the director of the CIA. Helms told Noyes the story was false, and Noyes testified that this conversation left him "considerably shaken as to my original impression as to the validity of Mr. Higgs' charges." The second-day story repeated the charges, though emphasizing Head's denial, and added other details: that a "government source" denied the financing, but that "the CIA declined to comment on the charges * * *." Fresh details also said that there was a large discrepancy between Airlie's 1965 expenses ($49,-684) and its income ($561,205), when actually the expenses were $500,000 more than the story stated; and in this discrepancy,

[80] Ibid., 309.

[81] Ibid.

the reporter's testimony showed conflicts as to why he had included the figures.   In finding reckless disregard, the court said: [82]

> Faced with this testimony and evidence there was a basis established with convincing clarity upon which the jury might well have concluded these details were known by the *Star* to be false and were added by it to lend credence to the Higgs charges at a time when it entertained serious doubts as to the validity of those charges.   Accordingly, the Court concludes that the evidence was sufficient to go to the jury on the question of whether the *Star* published "with knowledge that it was false or with reckless disregard of whether it was false or not" as required by the *New York Times* case.

Knowledge of Falsity.

Rarely has it been shown that a news medium published defamation in the knowledge that it was false, the second aspect of actual malice.

In a Wisconsin case, banker Howard Meister was sued for libel by former Assistant Attorney General LeRoy Dalton.   Meister had been exonerated of charges of bribery and unlawful lobbying brought by Dalton, and at a press conference afterward released a statement calling Dalton a "gestapo leader" and charging that Dalton had campaigned to "smear" him.   Evidence in the case showed that Meister had tried through influence, political pressure and spending large sums of money to have Dalton removed from his job.   Ultimately, Dalton was removed from office by his supervisor, who said the removal was not the result of Meister's political influence—"a statement the jury apparently did not believe," the Wisconsin Supreme Court said.   The Court said that the evidence plainly showed a "persistent course of conduct on the part of Meister to 'get Dalton'."   The jury had found that Meister's statements had been made with malice and knowedge of their falsity, and the Court observed that "even a casual reading of this record would lead one to believe as a matter of law that the proof of malice and knowledge of falsity or reckless disregard of the truth was by clear and convincing evidence." [83]   Dalton was awarded $150,000, half in compensatory and half in punitive damages.

---

[82] Airlie Foundation, Inc. v. Evening Star Newspaper Co., 337 F.Supp. 421, 428 (D.C.D.C.1972).   See also Mahnke v. Northwest Publications, Inc., 280 Minn. 328, 160 N.W.2d 1 (1968).

[83] Dalton v. Meister, 52 Wis.2d 173, 188 N.W.2d 494, 500 (1971).

Dun & Bradstreet, in a credit report to subscribers, linked Joseph F. Morgan to his brother, Claude B., in a scheme of incorporating retail stores and defaulting on obligations due suppliers. The publication implied that Joseph F. was a deadbeat and fraud, and as a result his credit was terminated and finally his drug business was destroyed. Despite notices from Joseph to Dun & Bradstreet that he had not since 1959 associated with his brother in business, and responsible third parties' similar notices, the company republished the report in November 1965 and March 1966, "in the teeth of findings by [its own] agent Olney that there was no business connection between the Morgan brothers in 1965." The Court of Appeals held that "The subsequent publication of a libel with knowledge of its falsity is proof of malice." [84] Morgan's recovery included $25,000 punitive damages.

[84] Morgan v. Dun & Bradstreet, Inc., 421 F.2d 1241, 1242 (5th Cir. 1970).

Chapter 5

TRADITIONAL DEFENSES IN LIBEL

SEC. 23.   QUALIFIED PRIVILEGE AS A DEFENSE

News media may publish defamation from legislative, judicial or other public and official proceedings without fear of successful libel or slander action; fair and accurate reports of these statements are privileged.

Before the landmark year 1964 and New York Times Co. v. Sullivan, libel suits were usually defended under statutory and common law provisions termed *qualified privilege, fair comment and criticism*, and *truth*. While today most libel suits are met by the new constitutional defense, a news medium still may raise the traditional defenses; if a court rejects one defense it may accept another. Furthermore, an occasional news item may be shaky as "matter of public or general interest," as we have seen in the last chapter; and if it fails on that score, it cannot qualify for the constitutional protection. Also, if a court can decide a case under statutes or the common law—which embrace the old defenses—it will not ordinarily take up the higher Constitutional issues.[1]

As noted above, the theory that free expression contributes to the public good in a self-governing society underlies the older defenses as well as the constitutional defense. The older ones say there are certain kinds of events and ideas about which a democratic public has a need to know that overrides an individual's right to reputation; the newer expands the range of events and ideas, still in the name of the public. The older defenses ordinarily were defeated by a finding of malice; the newer by the same finding, but under a more rigorous definition of malice than courts previously used. Many terms of the older defenses run through decisions dealing with the new.

[1] Trim-A-Way Figure Contouring v. National Better Business Bureau, 37 A.D.2d 43, 322 N.Y.S.2d 154, 156 (1971).

In some circumstances it is so important to society that men be allowed to speak without fear of a suit for defamation as a result, that their words are given immunity from a finding of libel or slander. The immunity is called privilege. For purposes of the mass media, it is applicable especially in connection with government activity.[2] The paramount importance of full freedom for participants in court, legislative or executive proceedings to say whatever bears on the matter, gives all the participants a full immunity from successful libel action. If a person is defamed in these proceedings, he cannot recover damages. The public interest in unhampered conduct of public business outweighs the individual's right to reputation, even though he may suffer real harm.

The immunity for the participant in official proceedings is called "absolute" privilege. No words relevant to the business of the proceeding will support a suit for defamation. The only qualification is in the word "relevant": A witness in a trial is usually not immune, for example, if out of the blue he volunteers the accusation that Jones is a heroin-pusher when Jones has nothing to do with the trial.

Public policy also demands, in an open society, that people know to the fullest what goes on in the proceedings. For this reason, the reporting of what occurs in proceedings is also protected. Anyone who reports proceedings is given an immunity from successful suit for defamation; and for the public at large, "anyone" ordinarily means the mass media. The protection is ordinarily more limited for the reporter of a proceeding than for the participant in the proceeding. It is thus called "qualified" (or "conditional") privilege, and it is qualified in that it does not protect malice in reports.[3]

It has been held that any citizen has *absolute* immunity in any criticism he makes of government. The City of Chicago brought a libel suit against the *Chicago Tribune*, claiming damages of $10,000,000 through the *Tribune's* campaign coverage in 1920. The stories had said that the city was broke, that its credit "is shot to pieces," that it "is hurrying on to bankruptcy and is threatened with a receivership for its revenue." As a result, the city said, competitive bidding on materials used by the city was

---

[2] For other circumstances where it applies, see Prosser, pp. 804–805.

[3] A few states give absolute privilege to press reports of official proceedings, e. g. Thompson's Laws of New York, 1939, Civ.P. § 337, Wis.Stats.1931, § 331.05(1). And as we have seen in Ch. 3, Sec. 14, broadcasters are immune from defamation suits brought for the words of politicians in campaign broadcasts: FECUA v. WDAY, Inc., 360 U.S. 525, 79 S.Ct. 1302 (1959).

stifled, and it was unable to conduct business on an economical basis because of injury to its credit.

The court denied the city's claim. It said that in any libelous publication concerning a municipal corporation, the citizen and the newspaper possess absolute privilege: [4]

> Every citizen has a right to criticize an inefficient government without fear of civil as well as criminal prosecution. This absolute privilege is founded on the principle that it is advantageous for the public interest that the citizen should not be in any way fettered in his statements, and where the public service or due administration of justice is involved he shall have the right to speak his mind freely.

Qualified privilege in reporting official proceedings is the heart of the concern here. The privilege arose in the law of England, the basic rationale having been developed before the start of the nineteenth century in connection with newspaper reports of court proceedings.[5] While American courts relied on English decisions, America was ahead of England in expanding the protection for press reports. The immunity was broadened to cover the reporting of legislative and other public official proceedings by the New York legislature in 1854, 14 years before privilege for reporting legislative bodies was recognized in England.[6] Other states readily adopted the New York rule.

For America a famous figure in jurisprudence stated the heart of the rationale for qualified privilege in an early case that has been relied upon by American courts countless times since. Judge Oliver Wendell Holmes, Jr., then of the Massachusetts bench and later a justice of the United States Supreme Court, wrote the words in Cowley v. Pulsifer, 1884.[7] Publisher Royal Pulsifer's *Boston Herald* had printed the content of a petition seeking Charles Cowley's removal from the bar, and Cowley sued. Judge Holmes wrote that the public must have knowledge of judicial proceedings, not because one citizen's quarrels with another are important to public concern,[8]

> * * * but because it is of the highest moment that those who administer justice should always act under

[4] City of Chicago v. Tribune Co., 307 Ill. 595, 139 N.E. 86, 90, 91 (1923).

[5] Curry v. Walter, 170 Eng.Rep. 419 (1796); King v. Wright, 101 Eng.Rep. 1396 (1799).

[6] New York Laws, 1854, Chap. 130; Wason v. Walter, L.R. 4 Q.B. 73 (1868).

[7] 137 Mass. 392 (1884).

[8] Ibid., 394.

the sense of public responsibility, and that every citizen should be able to satisfy himself with his own eyes as to the mode in which a public duty is performed.

The advantage to the nation in granting the privilege of press report, he stressed, is "the security which publicity gives for the proper administration of justice."

The defense of qualified privilege still appeared rather frequently in cases published at the time of this writing (mid-1973). It may be that states' recognition of the plurality opinion in Rosenbloom v. Metromedia [9] (1971) will result in less use of qualified privilege and more of the constitutional defense.   Rosenbloom, of course, said that a story about persons involved in a matter of public interest would be protected by the requirement of proof of the actual malice of Times v. Sullivan; and official government proceedings are "matters of public interest" if anything is.   As of this writing, relatively few cases begun since the *Rosenbloom* decision had been published in court reports.

While the privilege is "qualified" in the sense that it will not hold if the report of the proceeding is made with malice, there are certain other conditions that must be met by the reporting news medium.   The story must be a fair and accurate account of the proceeding, and must not engage in comment.   And, most states hold, the story must be one of a "public and official proceeding," not a report of related material that emerges before, after, or in some way outside the proceeding.

Fair and Accurate Reports.

Errors can destroy qualified privilege: careless note-taking by a reporter at a court trial, the constant danger of a misspelled name, and all the slip-ups of life with tight deadlines.   Further, if the report of an official proceeding is not fair to people involved in it, the newsman can be in trouble.   The public interest in having a flow of official news stops short of protecting the news story that is not a "fair and true report."

Jones v. Commercial Printing Co.[10] is a recent case that illustrates one court's reasoning in retaining long-standing qualified privilege rules.   The *Pine Bluff Commercial* attempted to use the Constitutional defense in a libel suit on grounds that its news stories reported on a man "involved in a matter of public interest."   While Rosenbloom had not yet been decided, precedent from lower federal courts which had preceded the United States Su-

[9] 403 U.S. 29, 91 S.Ct. 1811 (1971).

[10] 249 Ark. 952, 463 S.W.2d 92 (1971).

preme Court in employing the "matter of public interest" doctrine in libel cases was available to the *Commercial*.

The *Commercial* had covered court proceedings at which attorney Jones petitioned with others for an order to allow them to inspect financial records in a bank in which they held stock. Jones interpreted the *Commercial's* three stories on the proceedings as an attack on his integrity. He sued for libel saying the stories were not true and fair reports of the proceedings, and thus not privileged. He lost and appealed.

The *Commercial* argued that Jones was "involved in matters of * * * public concern" in the court proceedings, and would therefore have to prove actual malice in the stories if he were to recover. It cited an early libel decision that had expanded the Times v. Sullivan doctrine to "matters of public interest" before the U. S. Supreme Court had ruled in *Rosenbloom*: Time, Inc. v. McLaney. But the Arkansas Supreme Court said no, the standing rules of the state on qualified privilege would apply, and if the stories were not fair and accurate, that was enough to defeat the Commercial's defense. Agreeing that trials are often of great public interest, the Court said "we do not think that this is sufficient reason to engraft an 'actual malice' requirement onto the rule presently applicable to reports of judicial proceedings * * *." It said that the reasons for protecting speech and press under the *New York Times* decision have [11]

> little significance relative to publications which purport to be reports of judicial proceedings. The major distinction in this regard between judicial proceedings and public figures (and perhaps other subjects of great public interest) is the former's peculiar susceptibility to exact reporting in every instance. An account of what transpired at trial is not contingent upon fallible or futile modes of investigation. Court records are available; and, insofar as reports of in-progress proceedings are concerned, the threat of a libel prosecution emanates only from incompetent reporting * * *. Since it is always possible for a report of a judicial proceedings to be complete, impartial and accurate, we decline to engraft the actual malice requirement onto our present rule, regardless of the notoriety of the subject matter or participants involved in the judicial proceedings.

The Arkansas Supreme Court said that the trial judge's instructions to the jury requiring proof of actual malice as the basis of recovery constituted prejudicial error.

[11] Ibid., 95.

A newsman who relied on second-hand information from persons in a court-room following a judge's charge to a grand jury wrote this story:

(Special Dispatch to the News)

ANNAPOLIS, Oct. 20.—Corruption in official circles of Annapolis and Anne Arundel County was strongly hinted at by Judge Robert Moss of the Circuit Court in his charge to the grand jury this morning. The judge's charge also included a stinging rebuke to Sheriff Bowie of the county. After declaring the increase of bootlegging was a disgrace to the county, Judge Moss said a clean up of conditions was in order. He referred to Garfield Chase * * * who was employed as a stool pigeon by the sheriff's office in running down bootlegs and said repeated attempts to tamper with Chase and make him useless as a state's witness had been made. He blamed Sheriff Bowie for permitting these attempts and intimated that a member of the city police force was responsible for them. The court insisted that Chase be indicted either for bootlegging or for perjury and urged the jury to go to the bottom of the plot to save those against whom Chase was to testify.

Taking a chance on the hearsay picked up from persons to whom he talked, and not checking with Judge Moss, the newsman had made major blunders. Sheriff Bowie sued for libel, and as the suit unfolded, it turned out that there was no evidence that Judge Moss had blamed the sheriff for increasing illegal liquor sales, for lax conditions in the county jail, nor for permitting inmates at the jail to be influenced or tampered with. It was by no means a fair and accurate report of a proceeding, and qualified privilege as a defense failed.[12]

Not every inaccuracy in reporting proceedings is fatal, however. Privilege did not fail in Mitchell v. Peoria Journal-Star,[13] merely because the news story of a court action for liquor ordinance violation got the violators' place of arrest wrong. In Josephs v. News Syndicate Co., Inc.,[14] the newspaper did not lose privilege because somehow the reporter incorrectly slipped into his story of a burglary arrest the statement that the accused had been found under a bed at the scene of the burglary.

[12] Evening News v. Bowie, 154 Md. 604, 141 A. 416 (1928).

[13] 76 Ill.App.2d 154, 221 N.E.2d 516 (1966).

[14] 5 Misc.2d 184, 159 N.Y.S.2d 537 (1957).

The story that is not "fair" often comes from an error of omission rather than one of commission. Given the complexity of some court proceedings, avoiding this is far from easy in many situations. An omission from the following story, rich in human interest and the kind that delights city editors, turned out later to be fatal to a newspaper's plea of privilege.

> Ninety-nine-year-old twin sisters, perhaps the oldest twins in the United States, Saturday had won their suit for 13 acres of oil-rich land in Starr County.
>
> The sisters, Inez Garcia Ruiz, and Aniceta Garcia Barrera, had alleged that the land was fraudulently taken from them by a nephew, Benigno Barrera, and Enrique G. Gonzalez, both of Starr County.
>
> The women said they signed a deed to the land when Barrera represented it as a document permitting him to erect a corral fence there. The sisters cannot read or write Spanish or English.
>
> Judge C. K. Quinn in 45th District Court last year returned the sisters the land, which had been in their family since a Spanish grant.
>
> Saturday it was announced the appeals court had ruled against Barrera and Gonzalez.

Unfortunately for the newspaper, the story did not carry the fact that the sisters' original charge against both men had been amended to leave Gonzalez out of it. Gonzalez brought suit for libel against the newspaper and won. The appeals court said that the story implied that Gonzalez had been found guilty of fraud, and that the newspaper could not successfully plead privilege.[15] It upheld an award of $12,500 to Gonzalez.

The reporter who has absorbed the lessons of accuracy and responsibility—important parts of a professional attitude—is unlikely to risk damaging reputations in a complex court trial by going into print without checking with specialists in the court for accuracy and fairness. Equally, he is unlikely to risk damaging his boss's bankroll.

Opinion and Extraneous Material.

One way to destroy immunity for a news story is to add opinion or material extraneous to the proceeding. It is necessary for reporters to stick to the facts of what comes to light under officials' surveillance. Radio station KYW in Philadelphia broadcast a "documentary" on car-towing rackets, and Austin

---

[15] Express Pub. Co. v. Gonzalez, 326 S.W.2d 544 (Tex.Civ.App.1959); 350 S.W.2d 589 (Tex.Civ.App.1961).

Purcell sued for defamation. The broadcast had used a judicial proceeding as a basis—a magistrate's hearing at which Purcell was convicted of violating the car-tow ordinance. (Purcell later was exonerated, on appeal.) But the producer of the documentary wove into his script all sorts of material that he had gathered from other sources—the voices of a man and a woman telling how they had been cheated, a conversation with detectives, and something from the district attorney. He added comment of his own to the effect that "the sentencing of a few racketeers is not enough." Said the court: [16]

> Thus through this manipulation of the audio tape and the employment of anonymous voices, the public was made to believe that Purcell was a "mug," a "thug," a "racketeer," one who "gypped" others, and one who "terrified" his victims who were afraid of "reprisals."
>
> * * * All the derogatory phrases and attacks on character employed in the broadcast were funneled by Taylor into a blunderbus which was fired point-blank at Purcell * * *.

That was defamation, the court said, and it was not protected by qualified privilege. The documentary lost the protection because it contained "exaggerated additions": [17]

> The fault lay in breaking the egg of the extra-judicial "investigation" and the egg of judicial hearing into one omelet and seasoning it with comment and observations which made the parentage of either egg impossible of ascertainment * * *.

Malice

New York Times Co. v. Sullivan gave the term "malice" a restricted—and for the newsman, a newly plain—meaning. The "malice" that the person involved in matters of public interest must plead and prove in a libel action is that the publisher knew his words were false, or had reckless disregard for whether they were false or not. Malice before the *New York Times* decision, at least, was defined in many ways—as ill will toward another, hatred, intent to harm, bad motive, lack of good faith, reckless disregard for the rights of others, for example. People who claimed that news stories of government proceedings libeled them, often charged "malice" in the stories, in terms such as

[16] Purcell v. Westinghouse Broadcasting Co., 411 Pa. 167, 191 A.2d 662, 666 (1963).

[17] Ibid., 668. See also Jones v. Pulitzer Pub. Co., 240 Mo. 200, 144 S.W. 441 (1912); Robinson v. Johnson, 152 C.C.A. 505, 239 F. 671 (1917).

these. Are such definitions still alive for libel that does not proceed under the Constitutional protection? Will such manifestations of malice destroy the defense of qualified privilege? One case since New York Times Co. v. Sullivan shows a court feeling its way in dealing with the question.

A news story in the *St. Paul Dispatch* told of a complaint filed in district court, which accused William and Frank Hurley of depleting almost the entire fortune of an aged woman during her last years of life when she was in an impaired state of mind. Some $200,000 was involved. The complaint had been filed at the order of the Probate Court, where the dead woman's estate was in process. The Hurleys sued for libel, saying among other things that the news report was malicious and thus not privileged.

But the court did not agree. It spoke of two malice rules: *New York Times* and *Restatement of Torts*. The court felt that the Restatement standard, which while it does not use the word malice, "states in effect * * * that actual malice will be present only if a publication was either an inaccurate report of the proceedings or 'made solely for the purpose of causing harm to the person defamed' ".[18] This, it said, seemed more difficult to prove than the *Times* rule, but "whichever standard is adopted, plaintiffs in this case must prove actual malice or its equivalent in order to remove the cloak of privilege." And under either standard, the court said, it could find no malice: the news story reporter did not know the Hurleys; the Hurleys could produce no evidence of malice at the trial; and the reporter was no more than slightly negligent in not seeking out the plaintiffs before writing his story, to get their version. And such negligence does not constitute malice, the court said, quoting New York Times Co. v. Sullivan.

Other courts are using old definitions of malice, where qualified privilege is pleaded, alongside knowing or reckless falsehood. Thus one says there is no malice in that which "the publisher reasonably believed to be true" and another speaks of malice as "intent to injure." [19]

Official Proceedings.

Especially before the Constitutional defense was expanded in *Rosenbloom* to embrace media accounts of people involved in a

---

[18] Hurley v. Northwest Publications, Inc., 273 F.Supp. 967, 972, 974 (D.C. Minn.1967).

[19] Bannach v. Field Enterprises, Inc., 5 Ill.App.3d 692, 284 N.E.2d 31, 32 (1972); and Brunn v. Weiss, 32 Mich.App. 428, 188 N.W.2d 904, 905 (1971). See also Orrison v. Vance, 262 Md. 285, 277 A.2d 573, 578 (1971).

"matter of public or general concern," newsmen needed to keep alert to another requirement of qualified privilege. This was the rule saying they were protected only in reporting that which happened in the official proceeding itself. Reports of official activity outside the proceeding—the trial, the hearing, the legislative debate or committee—were not protected. Some official activity had the color of official proceeding but not the reality. Today, protection for coverage of public officials' activity needs to meet only the far looser criterion of "matter of public or general concern," not the tighter one of "official proceeding."

It is true that at this writing cases have not been reported that require courts to deal with this distinction. That is, plaintiffs who might argue that libelous stories were unprotected because they were based on something less than a proceeding have not yet, in the reported decisions, had to face the new standard of *Rosenbloom*. However, the assumption in limiting the problem of "official proceeding" to rather brief treatment here, is that *Rosenbloom* apparently reduces it to a small problem.

To start with the courts: Any trial including that of a lesser court "not of record" such as a police magistrate's furnishes the basis for privilege.[20] The ex parte proceeding in which only one party to a legal controversy is represented affords privilege to reporting.[21] So does the grand jury report published in open court.[22]

In most states, the attorneys' pleadings filed with the clerk of court as the basic documents for joining issue are not proceedings that furnish protection. The judge must be involved; an early decision stated the rule that for the immunity to attach, the pleadings must have been submitted "to the judicial mind with a view to judicial action," [23] even if only in pretrial hearings on motions.

A New York decision, as so often in defamation, led the way for several states' rejecting this position and granting protection to reports of pleadings. Newspapers had carried a story based on a complaint filed by Mrs. Elizabeth Nichols against Mrs. Anne Campbell, claiming the latter had defrauded her of $16,000. After the news stories had appeared, Mrs. Nichols withdrew her suit. Mrs. Campbell filed libel suits. Acknowledging that near-

[20] McBee v. Fulton, 47 Md. 403 (1878); Flues v. New Nonpareil Co., 155 Iowa 290, 135 N.W. 1083 (1912).

[21] Metcalf v. Times Pub. Co., 20 R.I. 674, 40 A. 864 (1898).

[22] Sweet v. Post Pub. Co., 215 Mass. 450, 102 N.E. 660 (1913).

[23] Barber v. St. Louis Post-Dispatch Co., 3 Mo.App. 377 (1877); Finnegan v. Eagle Printing Co., 173 Wis. 5, 179 N.W. 788 (1920).

ly all courts had refused qualified privilege to stories based on pleadings not seen by a judge, the New York Court of Appeals said it would no longer follow this rule. It acknowledged that it is easy for a malicious person to file pleadings in order to air his spleen against another in news stories, and then withdraw the suit. But it said that this can happen also after judges are in the proceeding; suits have been dropped before verdicts. It added that newspapers had so long and often printed stories about actions brought before they reached a judge, that "the public has learned that accusation is not proof and that such actions are at times brought in malice to result in failure." [24] The newspapers won.

At least eleven jurisdictions follow this rule today; the filing of a pleading is a public and official act in the course of judicial proceedings in California, District of Columbia, Georgia, Kentucky, Nevada, New York, Ohio, Pennsylvania, South Carolina, Washington and Wyoming.

But most states have not chosen to follow this rule. Massachusetts specifically rejected it in 1945. The *Boston Herald-Traveler* had published a story based on pleadings filed in an alienation of affections case, had been sued for libel, and had lost. The state Supreme Court said: [25]

> * * * the publication of accusations made by one party against another is neither a legal nor a moral duty of newspapers. Enterprise in that matter ought to be at the risk of paying damages if the accusations prove false. To be safe, a newspaper has only to send its reporters to listen to hearings rather than to search the files of cases not yet brought before the court. The older doctrine * * * still seems to us well founded in principle and without injustice in its practical application. It is supported by the great weight of authority in other jurisdictions * * *. We adhere to it.

Stories based on the following situations were outside "official proceedings" of courts and did not furnish news media the protection of qualified privilege: A newsman's interview of ("conversation with") a United States commissioner, concerning an earlier arraignment before the commissioner; [26] a grand jury's statement put out in advance of its formal report

[24] Campbell v. New York Evening Post, 245 N.Y. 320, 327, 157 N.E. 153, 155 (1927).

[25] Sanford v. Boston Herald-Traveler Corp., 318 Mass. 156, 61 N.E.2d 5 (1945).

[26] Wood v. Constitution Pub. Co., 57 Ga.App. 123, 194 S.E. 760 (1937).

of findings in open court; [27] the words of a judge [28] and of an attorney [29] in courtrooms, just before trials were convened formally; the taking by a judge of a deposition in his courtroom, where he was acting in a "ministerial capacity" only, not as a judge.[30]

To shift now to news stories about the executive and administrative sphere of government, the dangers are similar and the decisions from state to state no less varying. Where the executive officer in government holds a hearing or issues a report, or even a press release, absolute privilege often protects him. And where absolute privilege leads, qualified privilege for press reports ordinarily follows. Yet there is not perfect consistency from one jurisdiction to another in granting the absolute privilege to the officer himself. While major and minor federal officials enjoy the privilege under federal decisions, state courts have not been unanimous in granting it.[31]

The formalized hearings of many administrative bodies have a quasi-judicial character, in which testimony is taken, interrogation is performed, deliberation is engaged in, and findings are reported in writing. The newsman can have confidence in such proceedings as "safe" to report. The minutes of a meeting and audits of a city water commission were the basis for a successful plea of privilege by a newspaper whose story reflected on an engineer.[32] The Federal Trade Commission investigated a firm and an account based on the investigation told that the firm had engaged in false branding and labeling; the account was privileged.[33] A news story reporting that an attorney had charged another with perjury was taken from a governor's extradition hearing, a quasi-judicial proceeding, and was privileged.[34]

Also, investigations carried out by executive-administrative officers or bodies without the dignity of hearing-chambers and the gavel that calls a hearing to order ordinarily furnish privilege. For example, a state tax commissioner audited a city's books and reported on his findings, which included the fact that there were irregularities in the city council's handling of

[27] Parsons v. Age-Herald Pub. Co., 181 Ala. 439, 61 So. 345 (1913).

[28] Douglas v. Collins, 243 App.Div. 546, 276 N.Y.S. 87 (1935).

[29] Rogers v. Courier Post Co., 2 N.J. 393, 66 A.2d 869 (1949).

[30] Mannix v. Portland Telegram, 144 Or. 172, 23 P.2d 138 (1933).

[31] Barr v. Matteo, 360 U.S. 564, 79 S.Ct. 1335 (1959); Prosser, pp. 802–803.

[32] Holway v. World Pub. Co., 171 Okl. 306, 44 P.2d 881 (1935).

[33] Mack, Miller Candle Co. v. Macmillan Co., 239 App.Div. 738, 269 N.Y.S. 33 (1934).

[34] Brown v. Globe Printing Co., 213 Mo. 611, 112 S.W. 462 (1908).

funds. A story based on the report caused a suit for libel, and the court held that the story was protected by privilege.[35]

Yet not every investigation provides a basis for the defense of qualified privilege; reporters and city editors especially need to know what the judicial precedent of their state is. In a Texas case, a district attorney investigated a plot to rob a bank, and obtained confessions. He made them available to the press. A libel suit brought on the basis of a news story that resulted from the district attorney's documents could not be successfully defended with a plea of privilege. The confessions were held insufficient executive proceedings to provide the protection.[36]

"Proceedings" that need especially careful attention by the reporter alert to libel possibilities are the activities of police. When arrests are made and charges are reported by the police to newsmen, privilege may well attach, but there is enough variation from state to state to call for constant caution. Police blotters, the record of arrests and charges made, are the source for many news stories. Their status as a basis for a plea of privilege varies from state to state.[37] Oral reports of preliminary investigations by policemen do not support a plea of privilege in some states. The *Rutland Herald* published a story about two brothers arrested on charges of robbery, and included this paragraph:

> Arthur was arrested on information given to police by the younger brother, it is said. According to authorities, Floyd in his alleged confession, stated that Arthur waited outside the window in the rear of the clothing store while Floyd climbed through a broken window the second time to destroy possible clues left behind.

A suit for libel was brought, and the court denied qualified privilege to the story. It reviewed other states' decisions on whether statements attributed to police were a basis for privilege in news, and held that "a preliminary police investigation" is not a proper basis.[38]

---

[35] Swearingen v. Parkersburg Sentinel Co., 125 W.Va. 731, 26 S.E.2d 209 (1943).

[36] Caller-Times Pub. Co. v. Chandler, 134 Tex. 1, 130 S.W.2d 853 (1939). But see Woolbright v. Sun Communications, Inc., 480 S.W.2d 864 (Mo.1972).

[37] Steigleman, Walter, The Legal Problems of the Police Blotter, 20 Journalism Quarterly 30, 1943; Sherwood v. Evening News Ass'n, 256 Mich. 318, 239 N.W. 305 (1931); Petrick, M. J., The Press, the Police Blotter and Public Policy, 46 Journal Quarterly 475, 1969.

[38] Lancour v. Herald & Globe Ass'n, 111 Vt. 371, 17 A.2d 253 (1941); Burrows v. Pulitzer Pub. Co., 255 S.W. 925 (1923); Pittsburgh Courier Pub. Co. v. Lubore, 91 U.S.App.D.C. 311, 200 F.2d 355 (1952).

The State of New Jersey has provided by statute that "official statements issued by police department heads" protect news stories, and Georgia has a similar law.[39]   In other states, courts have provided the protection through decisions in libel suits. In Kilgore v. Koen,[40] privilege was granted to a story in which deputy sheriffs' statements about the evidence and arrest in a case involving a school principal were the newspaper's source.

The legislative branch, the third general sphere of government, remains now to be examined in its proceedings that provide privilege in news.   State statutes have long declared that the immunity holds in stories of the legislative setting; a New York law led the way in this declaration even before the privilege was recognized in England.[41]   For debates on the floor of Congress or of a state legislature, there has been no question that protection would apply to news stories.   A few early cases indicated that stories of petty legislative bodies such as a town council [42] would not be privileged; but today's reporter need have little fear on this count as long as his reports stick to the proceeding itself and are fair and accurate.

In news stories about a New Jersey municipal council meeting, the city manager was quoted as saying that he was planning to bypass two policemen from promotion because they were insubordinate and "I should have fired them."   There was some question as to whether the meeting was the regular one, or a session held in a conference room later.   The New Jersey Supreme Court said that that didn't matter.   It was not only an official but also a public meeting, at which motions were made by councilmen, sharp discussion was held, and the city manager was queried by councilmen.   Privilege held for the newspaper.[43]

A series of "chain" libel suits in the 1920's by Charles C. Cresson against several major newspapers settled any question about immunity in news reporting of committees of legislative bodies: immunity holds for press reports of committees.   The suits were based on news stories of a report by a House of Representatives committee that investigated the escape of a World War I draft dodger, millionaire Grover Cleveland Bergdoll.   Bergdoll fled to Germany, and the news stories said that

[39] Angoff, p. 134;   Rogers v. Courier Post, 2 N.J. 393, 66 A.2d 869 (1949); Code of Ga.1933, § 105–704.

[40] 133 Or. 1, 288 P. 192 (1930).

[41] New York Laws, 1854, Chap. 130;   Wason v. Walter, L.R. 4 Q.B. 73 (1868).

[42] Buckstaff v. Hicks, 94 Wis. 34, 68 N.W. 403 (1896).

[43] Swede v. Passaic Daily News, 30 N.J. 320, 153 A.2d 36 (1959).

Cresson played a leading part in the conspiracy that led to his escape. In Cresson v. Louisville Courier-Journal,[44] the court held the story an accurate summary of the committee's report, and privileged as the account of the activity of a committee of the House of Representatives.

Legislative committees have a long history of operating under loose procedural rules.[45] Irregular procedures raise the question whether committee activity always meets the requirements of a "legislative proceeding" that gives the basis for immunity in news reports.[46] In reporting committee activity, the alert newsman will sense danger signals if the committee:

Holds hearings without a quorum;

Publishes material that its clerks have collected, without itself first investigating charges in the material;

Has not authorized the work of its subcommittees;

Has a chairman given to issuing "reports" or holding press conferences on matters that the committee itself has not investigated.

Where he is uncertain about regularity in a committee's procedure, the newsman can help protect his report. He can ask the committee chairman for the authority by which the committee activity takes place.

When state and congressional investigating committees relentlessly hunted "subversion" in the 1940's and 1950's, thousands of persons were tainted with the charge of "communist" during the committee proceedings. High procedural irregularity was common. Yet only one libel case growing out of these irregular proceedings has reached the highest court of a state, and the newspaper successfully defended with a plea of privilege. The case, Coleman v. Newark Morning Ledger Co.,[47] is treated in the next section.

A single case from the early 1900's gives support for qualified privilege in reports of committees with doubtful authority. Almost 800 citizens had petitioned a Michigan county board for an investigation of a public officer, and the board ordered a committee to investigate. The committee did so but it refused to re-

[44] Cresson v. Louisville Courier-Journal, 299 F. 487, 491 (6th Cir. 1924).

[45] Gellhorn, Walter (ed.), The States and Subversion (Ithaca: Cornell Univ. Press, 1952); Eberling, Ernst, J., Congressional Investigations (New York: Columbia Univ.Press, 1928).

[46] Nelson, H. L., Libel in News of Congressional Investigating Committees, 1961, Ch. 1, 2.

[47] 29 N.J. 357, 149 A.2d 193 (1959).

port the findings of its investigator as ordered by the board. Currie, the committee chairman, finally took matters into his own hands and reported to the public by way of a story released to a newspaper. He was sued for libel alleged to be in the report, but the court held that he was protected by qualified privilege. Currie and the public, it said, had a common interest and duty in this situation.[48]

Public Proceedings.

The laws of at least ten states provide that qualified privilege applies to news reports of "public" proceedings.[49] In some other states, the same rule has been applied under common law principles.[50] The word "public" has in almost all cases meant "not secret" rather than proceedings which have a strong element of "public interest" or "public concern."[51] In several cases, immunity has been lost where a newspaper obtained access to secret proceedings of government bodies and reported libelous stories based on these proceedings.

In an Alabama case, a newspaper story of grand jury proceedings was made before the grand jury formally reported its findings to the court. The newspaper was sued for libel that it took from the report, and was unsuccessful in pleading privilege. The court said that the immunity "does not attach at all until the report has been duly published by the grand jury itself in open court."[52] In another case, a news story was based on a complaint to a deputy district attorney, and was held not to deserve the privilege. In McCurdy v. Hughes,[53] a newspaper reported on the secret meeting of a state bar board in which a complaint against an attorney was considered. The attorney brought a libel suit for derogatory statements in the story and won.

The state of New York denied privilege to news reports of secret proceedings repeatedly, under its ground-breaking statute of 1854. The statute provided privilege to a "fair and true re-

---

[48] Madill v. Currie, 168 Mich. 546, 134 N.W. 1004 (1912).

[49] Angoff, passim, shows Arizona, California, Idaho, Louisiana, Minnesota, North Dakota, Oklahoma, South Dakota, Utah and Wisconsin besides New York which in 1956 deleted the word "public" from its statute.

[50] Parsons v. Age-Herald Pub. Co., 181 Ala. 439, 61 So. 345 (1913); Switzer v. Anthony, 71 Colo. 291, 206 P. 391 (1922).

[51] A rare exception is Farrell v. New York Evening Post, 167 Misc. 412, 3 N.Y.S.2d 1018, 1022 (1938) where the word "public" was held to mean "of general interest or concern," and a story based on the report by an executive officer of his secret proceeding was held privileged.

[52] Parsons v. Age-Herald Pub. Co., 181 Ala. 439, 61 So. 345, 349 (1913).

[53] McCurdy v. Hughes, 63 N.D. 435, 248 N.W. 512 (1933).

port * * * of any judicial, legislative, or other public official proceeding." [54]   But in 1956, after 102 years under the "public" provision of the statute, New York changed its law and eliminated the word "public."   *Editor & Publisher,* trade publication of the American daily newspaper world, reported that the legislature made this change "at the behest of newspaper interests." [55]   The change was "drafted as the aftermath to two successful libel suits against New York City newspapers," the magazine said, and added that with the change, it had become possible for a newspaper to publish with immunity news of an official proceeding even though the proceeding was not public.

But as we have seen above (Sec. 21), the New York Court of Appeals ruled in a 4–3 decision in 1970 that elimination of the word "public" from that statute does not mean that news stories of matrimonial proceedings—secret under New York law—are protected by qualified privilege.   Matrimonial proceedings are "inherently personal," the Court held, and "the public interest is served not by publicizing but by sealing them and prohibiting their examination by the public." [56]

With the New York law, there is the New Jersey decision mentioned above, Coleman v. Newark Morning Ledger Co. [57]   In 1953, the late Senator Joseph McCarthy of Wisconsin was investigating the Army Signal Corps laboratory at Fort Monmouth, N. J.   Sitting as a one-man subcommittee of the Senate Permanent Subcommittee on Investigations, McCarthy repeatedly held secret executive-session hearings.   Occasionally he emerged from them to give oral "reports" to waiting newsmen, portraying a sensational "spy ring" in operation at Fort Monmouth, associated with Julius Rosenberg who had been executed for espionage.

On October 23, 1953, the *Newark Star-Ledger* ran a story from the previous day's oral report by McCarthy.   McCarthy, the story said, reported that his secret investigation had learned that an ex-Marine officer, suspended from his Fort Monmouth job in 1949 after military intelligence found classified documents in his apartment, had once roomed with Rosenberg.   Keys to the apartment were in the possession of known Communists, Mc-

---

54 New York Laws, 1854, Chap. 130; McCabe v. Cauldwell, 18 Abb.Pr. 377 (N.Y.1865); Danziger v. Hearst Corp., 304 N.Y. 244, 107 N.E.2d 62 (1952); Stevenson v. News Syndicate Co., 276 App.Div. 614, 96 N.Y.S.2d 751 (1950).

55 May 5, 1956, p. 52.   See New York State Legislative Annual, 1956, pp. 494–495.

56 Shiles v. News Syndicate Co., 261 N.E.2d 251, 27 N.Y.2d 9, 313 N.Y.S.2d 104, 107 (1970).

57 29 N.J. 357, 149 A.2d 193 (1959).

Carthy said. Then on December 9, 1953, the *Star-Ledger* identified the ex-Marine as Coleman, in reporting a public hearing held by McCarthy.

Coleman sued the *Star-Ledger* for libel. He said that the statements were false and were unprotected because they were spoken outside the proceeding. McCarthy was among the witnesses at the libel trial. He said that the newspaper story was an accurate report of his report of the secret proceeding. He also said that he had been authorized by the subcommittee, in executive session, to make reports to the press as to what transpired during executive sessions.

The court accepted McCarthy's testimony, and held that the newspaper's plea of qualified privilege was good. It denied that the secret nature of McCarthy's subcommittee session destroyed qualified privilege for McCarthy as a reporter or for the newspaper as a reporter. Secret sessions often are indispensable, it said, and "this does not preclude the publication of such information as the committee may in its discretion deem fit and proper for the general good." [58]

Chief Justice Joseph Weintraub of the New Jersey Supreme Court was the only dissenter in the 5-to-1 decision for the newspaper. He said that qualified privilege depends everywhere on a "fair and accurate report" of the proceedings; but who could say whether McCarthy gave the fair and accurate report required? In his words, "There is no way to measure a report against this standard when the proceedings are secret," and "The secret nature of the hearing negates the reason for the privilege." [59]

A final note about the word "public" in connection with qualified privilege: The immunity has been held to apply for news reports of the "public meeting" or "public gathering" where people are free to attend for discussion of matters of public concern. This is the general rule in England. The reasons for it are similar to those protecting reports of official proceedings: It is important for the community to know what is happening in matters where the public welfare and concern are involved. The protection in this situation has been granted by a few courts in America.[60] And as for private gatherings of stockholders, directors, or members of an association or organization, they are no basis for privilege in news reports.

[58] Ibid., 205–206.

[59] Ibid., 209.

[60] Phoenix Newspapers, Inc. v. Choisser, 82 Ariz. 271, 312 P.2d 150 (1957); Pulverman v. A. S. Abell Co., 228 F.2d 797 (4th Cir. 1956).

SEC. 24.   FAIR COMMENT AS A DEFENSE

Fair comment on matters of public concern, a complete defense in libel, protects criticism of the work of persons and institutions who offer their work for public approval or whose work affects the public interest. Its use in law is giving way to the Constitutional defense.

The term "fair comment on matters of public concern" refers to a set of rules—varying somewhat from state to state—that formerly made up a fairly distinct defense to libel. Today, while the term "fair comment" continues to run through libel decisions, its content is largely absorbed by the Constitutional defense.

Alongside facts, comment permeates news and editorial pages and broadcasts, explaining, drawing inferences, reacting, evaluating. "Fair comment" arose to protect the public stake in the evaluation of public matters—whether the works of authors and musicians, the work of the hospital or public utility, or the work of a public official—through comment and opinion. Anyone was protected in commenting fairly on the public acts of public persons and institutions; all such entities involve the public interest whether in matters of taste and culture, health and daily living, or government. He who offered himself for public approval would also have to offer himself for public disapproval.

Such comment and criticism, of course, was very much part of the communication protected by the New York Times decision, which quoted with approval an earlier opinion: [61]

> "In the realm of religious faith, and in that of political belief, sharp differences arise. In both fields the tenets of one man may seem the rankest error to his neighbor. To persuade others to his own point of view, the pleader, as we know, at times resorts to exaggeration, to vilification of men who have been, or are, prominent in church or state, and even to false statement. But the people of this nation have ordained in the light of history, that, in spite of the probability of excesses and abuses, these liberties are, in the long view, essential to enlightened opinion and right conduct on the part of the citizens of a democracy."

The identity between the principles of the two protections became apparent as lower courts began applying the new doctrine in cases where the old previously applied; the terminologies of

[61] New York Times Co. v. Sullivan, 376 U.S. 254, 271, 84 S.Ct. 710, 721 (1964), quoting Cantwell v. Conn., 310 U.S. 296, 310, 60 S.Ct. 900, 906 (1940).

the two became interwoven in decisions. For example, a case of 1967 spoke of fair comment in applying the *New York Times* rule to a libel case brought by the principal of a Negro school in Mississippi.[62] An issue of a publication called *The Freedom Train* had called the principal an "Uncle Tom," the equivalent of traitor to his race. He won a $60,000 judgment in trial court, but the case was appealed and there he lost. The state Supreme Court ruled that the attacks on the principal were fair comment under the *New York Times* rule, and that only knowing false-hood or reckless disregard for falsity could meet the definition of malice that would destroy the publication's defense. It said that hatred for the principal, ill will toward him, intent to harm him, or negligence in publishing, would not meet the definition of malice.

The doctrine of fair comment was less protection than the Constitutional protection, to begin with precisely because a Constitutional shield has more strength than a statutory or common law shield. But furthermore, certain provisions in the former varied from state to state, and the protection was applied unevenly.

1. Most states said that the protection for comment did not extend to that which was falsely given out as "fact." This presented at the outset the often difficult problem of distinguishing fact from comment; where one left off and the other started was sometimes an arbitrary finding, better suited to philosophers than jurists. But beyond that problem of making an often cloudy distinction was the diversity from state to state. Most insisted on the rule of "no protection for misstatement of fact," Oregon's Supreme Court, for example, saying "it is one thing to comment upon or criticize * * * the acknowledged or proved act of a public man, and quite another to assert that he has been guilty of particular acts of misconduct." [63]

California had long held to this view when in 1921 its Supreme Court reversed its position in deciding a libel suit brought by the Los Angeles police chief against the *Los Angeles Record* for a cartoon of him. He said it suggested he was receiving money secretly for illegal purposes. The court held that even if false, the cartoon was protected as fair comment: [64]

> [T]he right of the publisher to speak or write is complete and unqualified, under the Code, except that he must speak or write "without malice." When under

[62] Reaves v. Foster, 200 So.2d 453, 458 (Miss.1967).

[63] Marr v. Putnam, 196 Or. 1, 246 P.2d 509, 524 (1952).

[64] Snively v. Record Pub. Co., 185 Cal. 565, 571, 198 Pac. 1, 5 (1921).

these conditions he honestly believes that the person of whom he speaks or writes is guilty of a crime of a nature that makes the fact material to the interests of those whom he addresses, it is as much his right and duty to declare to them that fact as it would be to tell them any other fact pertinent to the occasion and material to their interests. If the publisher of a newspaper honestly believes that a public officer has committed a crime of a nature which would indicate that he is unfit for the office he holds, we think he is not liable for damages * * *.

A second problem involving "fact" faced the writer: the comment must be based on facts—facts stated with the comment, or facts that are known or readily available to the reader. The Fisher Galleries asked art critic Leslie Ahlander of the *Washington Post* to review an exhibition of paintings by artist Irving Amen. Later, Mrs. Ahlander's column carried this comment:

The Fisher Galleries are showing about 20 oils by the noted printmaker, Irving Amen. The paintings are warm in color and expressionist in tendency, but lack the distinction of the prints. They are so badly hung among many commercial paintings that what quality they might have is completely destroyed. The Fisher Galleries should decide whether they are a fine arts gallery or a commercial outlet for genuine "hand-painted" pictures. The two do not mix.

Fisher sued for libel, and the *Post* defended on the grounds of fair comment and criticism. Fisher argued that in order for opinion to be protected by the fair comment doctrine, the facts upon which it is based must be stated or referred to so that the reader may draw his own conclusions. The court acknowledged that that is the rule in some jurisdictions.[65] But it followed instead the view adopted by the *Restatement of Torts*,[66] that the facts do not necessarily have to be stated in the article, but may be facts "known or readily available to the persons to whom the comment or criticism is addressed * * *." The court said: [67]

We believe that this is the better view, for criticism in the art world may be based on such intangibles as experience, taste, and feeling. It is often impossible for

[65] A. S. Abell Co. v. Kirby, 227 Md. 267, 176 A.2d 340 (1962); Cohalan v. New York Tribune, 172 Misc. 20, 15 N.Y.S.2d 58 (1939).

[66] # 606.

[67] Fisher v. Washington Post Co., 212 A.2d 335, 338 (D.C.App.1965).

the critic to explain the basis for his opinion; to require him to do so would tend to discourage public discussion of artistic matters. So long as the facts are available to the public, the criticism is within the doctrine of fair comment. The Amen show was open to the public both before and after publication, and the facts upon which Mrs. Ahlander based her conclusions were readily accessible to any who wanted to test them.

A final warning to critics and commentators that fell in the realm of "fact" was this: There is danger in assigning corrupt and dishonorable motives to a person; many courts have held this is to be treated as fact, not as comment, and will not be protected by the defense of fair comment but must be defended by a plea of truth. This principle goes far back in the libel law, as expressed in a famous nineteenth-century case, Campbell v. Spottiswoode, where the court held: [68]

> A line must be drawn between criticism upon public conduct and the imputation of motives by which that conduct may be supposed to be actuated; one man has no right to impute to another, whose conduct may be open to ridicule or disapprobation, base, sordid and wicked motives, unless there is so much ground for the imputation that a jury shall find, not only that he had an honest belief in the truth of his statements but that his belief was not without foundation.

2. Besides the problem of "fact," the ancient question of what constituted "malice" entered the picture and had much to do with what was "fair." Malice would destroy the protection of fair comment; and malice for centuries before New York Times Co. v. Sullivan had been defined in various ways. Furthermore, various characteristics of "unfair" expression were sometimes treated as suggesting malice. Thus from state to state and jurisdiction to jurisdiction, malice could be pretty much what the court felt it ought to be: ill-will, enmity, spite, hatred, intent to harm; "excessive publication," [69] vehemence, [70] words that were not the honest opinion of the writer, [71] words which there was no "probable cause to believe true," [72] words showing reck-

---

[68] 32 L.J.Q.B. 185, 3 B. & S. 769, 776 (1863). See also Cross v. Guy Gannett Pub. Co., 151 Me. 491, 121 A.2d 355 (1956).

[69] Pulliam v. Bond, 406 S.W.2d 635, 643 (Mo.1966).

[70] England v. Daily Gazette Co., 143 W.Va. 700, 104 S.E.2d 306 (1958).

[71] Russell v. Geis, 251 Cal.App.2d 560, 59 Cal.Rptr. 569 (1967).

[72] Taylor v. Lewis, 132 Cal.App. 381, 22 P.2d 569 (1933).

less disregard for the rights of others,[73] words which a reasonable man would not consider fair.[74]   Malice still can be "adduced" [75] from such qualities of expression in some jurisdictions where qualified privilege or fair comment is at issue.

Thus the West Virginia Supreme Court held in denying fair comment's protection to the *Charleston Gazette* which had tongue-lashed several legislators who sued it for saying, among other things, that they had sold their votes: [76]

> While it is very generally held that fair comment as to matter of public affairs is not actionable, where sufficient facts exist on which to ground such comment, it appears to be definitely settled that if such comment is unfair or unreasonably violent or vehement, immunity from liability is denied. "Matters of public interest must be discussed temperately. Wicked and corrupt motive should never be wantonly assigned. And it will be no defense that the writer, at the time he wrote, honestly believed in the truth of the charges he was making, if such charges be made recklessly, unreasonably, and without any foundation in fact * * *. [T]he writer must bring to his task some degree of moderation and judgment."   Newell, Slander and Libel * * *.
>
> * * *   [T]he charges and imputations contained in the editorial complained of are very different from mere comment.

But in another state—Iowa—there was no suggestion in a Supreme Court decision that "Matters of public interest must be discussed temperately."   Journalists everywhere know the case of the Cherry sisters, one of the most famous in the annals of libel in America. The *Des Moines Leader* successfully defended itself in their libel suit, using the defense of fair comment. It started when the Leader printed this:

> Billy Hamilton, of the *Odebolt Chronicle,* gives the Cherry Sisters the following graphic write-up on their late appearance in his town: "Effie is an old jade of 50 summers, Jessie a frisky-filly of 40, and Addie, the flower of the family, a capering monstrosity of 35. Their long skinny arms, equipped with talons at the

---

[73] Campbell v. Spottiswoode, 32 L.J.Q.B. 185 (1863).

[74] James v. Haymes, 160 Va. 253, 168 S.E. 333 (1933).

[75] Goldwater v. Ginzburg, 414 F.2d 324, 342 (2d Cir. 1969).

[76] England v. Daily Gazette Co., 143 W.Va. 700, 104 S.E.2d 306, 316 (1958).

extremities, swung mechanically, and anon waved fran-
tically at the suffering audience. The mouths of their
rancid features opened like caverns, and sounds like the
wailing of damned souls issued therefrom. They
pranced around the stage with a motion that suggested
a cross between the *danse du ventre* and fox trot,—
strange creatures with painted faces and hideous mien.
Effie is spavined, Addie is stringhalt, and Jessie, the
only one who showed her stockings, has legs with calves
as classic in their outlines as the curves of a broom
handle."

There was nothing moderate about Billy Hamilton's criticism of
these three graces, but the Iowa Supreme Court said that that
did not matter. What Hamilton wrote about the three sisters,
and the Leader reprinted, was fair comment and criticism: [77]

One who goes upon the stage to exhibit himself to the
public, or who gives any kind of a performance to which
the public is invited, may be freely criticized. He may
be held up to ridicule, and entire freedom of expression
is guaranteed to dramatic critics, provided they are not
actuated by malice or evil purpose in what they write.
Fitting strictures, sarcasm, or ridicule, even, may be
used, if based on facts, without liability, in the absence
of malice or wicked purpose. * * * Ridicule is often
the strongest weapon in the hands of a public writer;
and, if fairly used, the presumption of malice which
would otherwise arise is rebutted, and it becomes necessary to introduce evidence of actual malice, or of some
indirect motive or wish to gratify private spite.

The actual malice that will destroy a newsman's privilege of
fair comment is narrowing in the light of the United States
Supreme Court's restrictive definition of the term in 1964 in
New York Times Co. v. Sullivan. One court has said that the
defense of fair comment and criticism raised against a newspaper columnist's libel suit will prevail unless the new definition
of malice can be proved. This case rose from editorials appearing in the *Fairbanks* (Alaska) *Daily News-Miner*, attacking
columnist Drew Pearson for his belittling of Alaska Governor
Mike Stepovich in the drive for Alaska statehood. One editorial
was titled "The Garbage Man of the Fourth Estate." A few
weeks later, the *News-Miner* said it was dropping Pearson's
column because it did not wish to distribute garbage with its
newspaper. Pearson sued for libel, lost, and appealed to the

[77] Cherry v. Des Moines Leader, 114 Iowa 298, 86 N.W. 323 (1901).

Alaska Supreme Court. The court said that the privilege of fair comment and criticism existed in this case, because the subject of Alaska statehood was a matter of public interest and concern. The privilege extended to the newspaper, it said, unless the statements about Pearson were made with actual malice. It discarded its own earlier acceptance of malice as being ill-will, enmity, hatred, spite, or desire to injure, and said: [78]

> We adopt for this jurisdiction the meaning of "actual malice" as given by the United States Supreme Court in the case of New York Times Co. v. Sullivan. Actual malice exists when it is proved that the defamatory statement was made with knowledge that it was false or with a reckless disregard of whether it was false or not. * * *

> The trial court found that there was no actual malice. We are obliged to sustain such finding unless it is shown to be clearly erroneous. We perceive no clear error. In referring to appellant as a "garbage man" and to his writings as "garbage", the imputation was that appellant was inaccurate and that his writings were worthless, that they were literary trash.

Cases continue to be adjudicated today under the rules of fair comment.[79] Occasionally, a decision will be written that separately takes account of the fair comment rules and the Constitutional defense.[80] The two have much in common although the latter's protection is much firmer, in cutting through the old confusions over the "facts" problem and the "malice" definition. Under either, the touchstone is the public's right to know about the public acts of public persons and agencies. Always, the newsman needs to remember that the private characters and acts of public persons retain protection, for although one's private character can deeply affect his public acts, there remains a sphere of life that is recognized as private. Going far back in the law of libel, it was long ago articulated thus: [81]

> In our opinion, a person who enters upon a public office, or becomes a candidate for one, no more surrenders to the public his private character than he does his private property. Remedy by due course of law, for injury to

[78] Pearson v. Fairbanks Pub. Co., Inc., 413 P.2d 711, 715 (Alaska 1966).

[79] Steak Bit of Westbury, Inc. v. Newsday, Inc., 70 Misc.2d 437, 334 N.Y.S. 2d 325 (1972); Miller v. News Syndicate Co., 445 F.2d 356 (2d Cir. 1971); Buckley v. Vidal, 327 F.Supp. 1051 (D.C.N.Y.1971); Christy v. Stauffer Publications, Inc., 437 S.W.2d 814 (Tex.1969).

[80] Griffin v. Clemow, 28 Conn.Sup. 109, 251 A.2d 415 (1968).

[81] Post Pub. Co. v. Moloney, 50 Ohio St. 71, 89, 33 N.E. 921, 926 (1893).

each, is secured by the same constitutional guaranty, and the one is no less inviolate than the other. To hold otherwise, would, in our judgment drive reputable men from public positions, and fill their places with others having no regard for their reputation; and thus defeat the object of the rule contended for, and overturn the reason upon which it is sought to sustain it.

Cases since New York Times Co. v. Sullivan have continued to point this out.[82]

SEC. 25.   TRUTH AS A DEFENSE

Showing the truth of the defamation, or truth with good motives and for justifiable ends, is a complete defense.

The defense of truth (often called "justification") in civil libel has ancient roots developed in the common law of England. It was taken up by American courts as they employed the common law in the colonial and early national periods, and was transferred from the common law to many state statutes. Its basis appeals to common sense and ordinary ideas of justice: Why, indeed, should an individual be awarded damages for harm to his reputation when the truth of the matter is that his record does not merit a good reputation? To print or broadcast the truth about a person is no more than he should expect; and in addition the social good may be served by bringing to light the truth about people whose work involves them in the public interest.

Perhaps the Constitutional defense vitiates this oldest of the traditional defenses even more than it does the other two. Falsehood will destroy the Constitutional protection of defamation only if it is made with actual malice. To the extent that truth continues to be used, most states provide that it is a complete defense. Others hedge, however, and provide that truth is a defense if it is published "with good motives and for justifiable ends." [83] The qualifying term was perhaps originated by Alexander Hamilton in his defense of newspaper editor Harry Croswell in a celebrated New York criminal libel case of 1804.[84]

---

[82] Zeck v. Spiro, 52 Misc.2d 629, 276 N.Y.S.2d 395 (1966); Stearn v. MacLean-Hunter, Ltd., 46 F.R.D. 76 (D.C.N.Y.1969); Standke v. B. E. Darby & Sons, Inc., 291 Minn. 468, 193 N.W.2d 139, 144 (1971).

[83] State statutes and constitutional provisions are collected in Angoff, Charles, Handbook of Libel, New York, 1946. See also Note, 56 N.W.Univ. L.Rev. 547, 1961; Ray, Roy R., Truth: A Defense to Libel, 16 Minn.L.Rev. 43, 1931.

[84] 3 Johns.Cas. 337 (N.Y.1818).

It moved from there into civil libel, persuasive in its implication that the printing of malicious words could be minimized by reminding the publisher to consider his motives before going into print.

The burden of proving truth is on the defendant, and it is also up to him to prove that his motives were good and his ends justifiable if his state requires the qualification. It is often a heavy burden. Although not so strictly required as formerly, the rule is sometimes phrased to say that the exact truth of the alleged libel must be proved if the plea of justification is to succeed.[85] A more common phrasing is that the truth must be as broad and as narrow as the defamatory accusation if it is to be a complete defense.[86] Neither of these rules, however, means that every detail of an allegedly libelous story must be proved accurate in order to have a good defense. No formula can measure just what inaccuracy will be tolerated by a particular court, but cases throw light on the problem.

The *New York World-Telegram and Sun* tried to establish truth of the following statement from its pages, but failed:

> John Crane, former president of the UFA now under indictment, isn't waiting for his own legal developments. Meanwhile, his lawyers are launching a $$$$$$ defamation suit.

Focusing on the word "indictment," Crane brought a libel suit against the newspaper and the columnist who wrote the item. He said that the defendant knew or could have learned the falsity of the charge by using reasonable care.

The defendants chose to try to establish the truth of the charge. They did not try to show that there had been a legal indictment by a grand jury. Instead, they said that the facts were widely published and commented upon by the press of the city. They claimed that Crane was "under indictment" in a nonlegal sense, that he had been accused of various crimes by others and was guilty of those crimes. They detailed findings from scandals and investigations involving the New York City Fire Department several years earlier; Crane had been president of an association of firemen at that occasion and was depicted as having been a prominent figure in the investigation.

[85] Pallet v. Sargent, 36 N.H. 496 (1858); Neigel v. Seaboard Finance Co., 68 N.J.Super. 542, 173 A.2d 300 (1961).

[86] Empire Printing Co. v. Roden, 17 Alaska 209, 247 P.2d 8 (1957); Stephens v. Columbia Pictures Corp., 240 F.2d 764 (9th Cir. 1957); Benn v. Lucks, 201 N.Y.S.2d 18 (Sup.1960).

But you cannot prove the truth of one charge against a man by showing that he was suspected or guilty in connection with another.[87]   The court held that "indictment" means the legal action, ordinarily carried out by a grand jury, and that use of the term to mean accusation by private persons is rare.   No reader, it said, would accept the looser usage as the intended one.[88]

Yet while the word "indictment" unquestionably has a clear meaning, a newspaper's loose usage of certain other technical terms does not always destroy a plea of truth.   This is what a court ruled when a Massachusetts newspaper said that a man named Joyce had been "committed" to a mental hospital when actually he had been "admitted" to the hospital at the request of a physician as the state law provided.   The newspaper's words that caused the man to bring a libel suit were that the man "charges * * * that his constitutional rights were violated when he was committed to the hospital last November."   In ruling for the newspaper which pleaded truth, the court said: [89]

> Strictly * * * "commitment" means a placing in
> the hospital by judicial order * * *.   But the words
> [of the news story] are to be used in their "natural
> sense with the meaning which they could convey to man-
> kind in general."   This meaning of the word "commit-
> ment" was placing in the hospital pursuant to proceed-
> ings provided by law.   In so stating as to the plaintiff
> * * * the defendant reported correctly.

Of course, the newsman who is highly attuned to nuances in word meanings may save his newspaper the expense and trouble of even a successful libel defense by avoiding gaffes such as confusing "commit" with "admit."   While news media continue to be staffed in part by writers insensitive to shades of meaning, however, they may take some comfort in the law's willingness to bend as in the Joyce case.

Courts frequently hold that a plea of truth will not be destroyed by a story's minor inaccuracies.   "Rather, it is sufficient to show that the gist or the sting of the defamatory imputation is true." [90]   Thus a plea of truth succeeded although a newspaper

87 Sun Printing and Pub. Ass'n v. Schenck, 40 C.C.A. 163, 98 F. 925 (1900); Kilian v. Doubleday & Co., 367 Pa. 117, 79 A.2d 657 (1951); Yarmove v. Retail Credit Co., 18 A.D.2d 790, 236 N.Y.S.2d 836 (1963).

88 Crane v. New York World Telegram Corp., 308 N.Y. 470, 126 N.E.2d 753 (1955).

89 Joyce v. George W. Prescott Pub. Co., 348 Mass. 790, 205 N.E.2d 207 (1965).

90 Mitchell v. Peoria Journal-Star, 76 Ill.App.2d 154, 221 N.E.2d 516 (1966).

had printed that the plaintiff was in police custody on August 16, whereas he had been released on August 15; [91] and it was not fatal to a plea of truth to report in a news story that an arrest, which in fact took place at the Shelly Tap tavern, occurred at the Men's Social Club.[92]

Sometimes a statement that may be taken in one sense as true, in another sense carries an implication that is much harder to prove as truthful. *Official Detective Stories* published a story dealing with the exploits of Jack Friday and his arrest. The story carried this statement:

> A search of police records yielded the names of several associates, as well as all Friday's relatives who live in West Texas. These persons were warned to notify police if they received any communication from Friday and their homes were placed under surveillance.

Twelve indignant West Texans, all relatives by blood or marriage of Jack Friday, brought libel suit. They complained that the term "police records" as understood by the ordinary reader means the records of arrests, convictions and sentences for offenses against the law. The statement thus accused the entire West Texas Friday connection of being criminals, they said.

Official Detective Stories argued that, on the contrary, "police records" referred to materials relating to Jack Friday in the hands of various law enforcement agencies. While the complaining relatives' names appeared in these materials, they were not thereby accused of crime, in the magazine's view. The magazine asked the judge to give a summary judgment in its favor. But the judge denied the motion, saying: [93]

> Truth, to be a solid defense, must extend to the innuendo, the libelous implications and insinuations, as well as the direct accusation in the statement. And the innuendo [in this story] admittedly is not true, for it is conceded by defendants that not all the plaintiffs had criminal records.

In accord with the maxim that "tale bearers are as bad as tale tellers," it is no defense for a news medium to argue that it reported accurately and truthfully someone else's false and defamatory statements. The broadcaster or newspaperman writes at his employer's peril; the words "it is reported by police" or "ac-

[91] Piracci v. Hearst Corp., 263 F.Supp. 511, affirmed 371 F.2d 1016 (4th Cir. 1966).

[92] Mitchell v. Peoria Journal-Star, 76 Ill.App.2d 154, 221 N.E.2d 516 (1966).

[93] Friday v. Official Detective Stories, 233 F.Supp. 1021 (D.C.Pa.1964).

cording to an absolutely reliable source" do not remove from the news medium faced with a libel suit the job of proving that the allegation or rumor itself is true.[94]

Nor does the fact that the publisher believed the damaging statement to be true protect him. The crusading newspaper that works hard at a prolonged exposé may well decide to go into print in its campaign with a charge that it fully believes true, but that it knows will be hard to prove. Risk-taking such as this sometimes is made over the impassioned objection of the newspaper's legal counsel, whose fears may be proved out with the filing of a libel suit against the crusaders. An authoritative decision stated the principle long ago: [95]

> In order to justify a publication, purporting to be made on the belief of the author that the fact was true, the defendant must prove the truth of the fact, and not merely that he believed it to be true. If one publish of another that he believes he was guilty of murder or arson, it is no justification to prove that he did in good faith believe it, but to make good the justification he must prove that the plaintiff was, in fact, guilty of murder or arson.

Belief in the truth of the charge may, however, be useful in holding down damages, if it can be established to the satisfaction of the court. Showing honest belief indicates good faith and absence of malice, important to the mitigation of general damages and the denial or lessening of punitive damages to the successful suit-bringer in a libel case.

The plea of truth always presents an uncomfortable possibility to the defendant in a libel case: If the proof fails, the attempt to prove it may be considered a republication of the libel and become evidence of malice.[96] And malice, as indicated earlier, may be reason for assessing punitive damages. There seems to be a tendency in recent decades, however, to examine the manner and spirit with which the defense of truth is made. If the plea of truth appears to have as its real object the defense of the case, rather than to repeat the defamation, evidence of malice is not necessarily concluded.

---

[94] Miller, Smith & Champagne v. Capital City Press, 142 So.2d 462 (La.App. 1962); Dun & Bradstreet, Inc. v. Robinson, 233 Ark. 168, 345 S.W.2d 34 (1961).

[95] Wilson v. Fitch, 41 Cal. 363 (1871). See John v. Tribune Co., 28 Ill. App.2d 300, 171 N.E.2d 432 (1960); Lindsey v. Evening Journal Ass'n 10 N.J. Misc. 1275, 163 A. 245 (1932).

[96] Hall v. Edwards, 138 Me. 231, 23 A.2d 889 (1942); Coffin v. Brown, 94 Md. 190, 50 A. 567 (1901).

The *Las Vegas* (Nev.) *Sun* pleaded the truth of this charge which it made in a headline concerning one Franklin: "Babies for Sale. Franklin Black Market Trade of Child Told." The judge instructed the jury that "Failure to prove a plea of truth may be considered as evidence of express and continued malice." The jury decided that the Sun had not proved truth, and awarded Franklin damages. The Sun appealed, and the Nevada Supreme Court ruled that the judge's instruction to the jury was in error. It said that although there is authority to support the judge's instruction,[97]

> * * * the better rule is that failure of proof of truth is not itself evidence of malice. Where malice appears a plea of truth may be considered in aggravation of damages as an unprivileged republication of the original libel. However, to constitute such aggravation it should appear that the defense of truth was not pleaded in good faith. When the defendant actually believes his plea to be true and offers evidence in support of it in good faith, the rule should not apply to penalize him simply because the evidence fails to convince the jury. Rather, in such a case, the evidence offered should operate in mitigation of damages.

In another case involving a newspaper's minor error in reporting a court proceeding in which three persons were fined $50 each for liquor law violation, the newspaper included the plea of truth in its defense. The trial court instructed the jury to consider whether this plea was made "with malicious intent." The jury found that it was so made, and awarded $12,500 in punitive damages to each of the three plaintiffs. But the appeals court reversed the finding, saying merely that "the record does not sustain the conclusion that this news report of the activity of a governmental agency was motivated solely by malice." [98]

SEC. 26. DAMAGES

Compensatory damages are granted for injury to reputation, special damages for specific pecuniary loss, and punitive damages as punishment for malicious or extremely careless libel.

Courts and statutes are not entirely consistent in their labeling of the kinds of damages that may be awarded to a person

[97] Las Vegas Sun, Inc. v. Franklin, 74 Nev. 282, 329 P.2d 867 (1958).

[98] Mitchell v. Peoria Journal-Star, Inc., 76 Ill.App.2d 154, 221 N.E.2d 516 (1966).

who is libeled. Generally, however, three bases exist for compensating the injured person.

The first is that injury to reputation ought to be recognized as real injury, even though it is impossible to make a scale of values and fix exact amounts due the injured for various kinds of slurs. Injury is presumed, and for this, damages are labeled "general" damages, or sometimes "compensatory" damages. Substantial amounts of money may be awarded for the presumed fact of injury, without the plaintiff's showing specific loss.

Besides the harm that is presumed and may be compensated for, there is harm of a more definable kind—actual pecuniary loss that a person may suffer as a result of a libel. It may be the loss of a contract or of a job, and if it can be shown that the loss is associated with the libel, the defamed may recover "actual" or "special" damages—the actual cost to him. It is plain, however, that some states use the term "actual damages" to cover both pecuniary loss and presumed loss that goes with injured reputations. Thus it was held in Miami Herald Pub. Co. v. Brown: [99]

> Actual damages are compensatory damages and include (1) pecuniary loss, direct or indirect, or special damages; (2) damages for physical pain and inconvenience; (3) damages for mental suffering; and (4) damages for injury to reputation.

The third basis for awarding damages is public policy—that persons who maliciously or carelessly libel others ought to be punished for the harm they cause. Damages above and beyond general and actual damages may be awarded in this case, and are called punitive or exemplary damages.

SEC. 27. RETRACTION

A full and prompt apology following the publication of a libel will serve to mitigate damages awarded to the injured.

The news medium that has libeled a person may retract its statement, and in doing so, hope to lessen the chances that large damages will be awarded to the injured. The retraction must be full and without reservation, and there should be no attempt to justify the libel. But while a full and timely apology will go to mitigate damages, it is in no sense a complete defense. The law reasons that many persons who saw the original story may not

---

99 66 So.2d 679, 680 (Fla.1953). See also Ellis v. Brockton Pub. Co., 198 Mass. 538, 84 N.E. 1018 (1908); Osborn v. Leach, 135 N.C. 628, 47 S.E. 811 (1904).

see the retraction.   The retraction must be given the prominence in space or time that the original charge received.

Generally, a full and prompt retraction will serve to negate punitive damages, for it is considered an indication that the libel was not published with malice.   Further, it may help reduce the award of compensatory damages.

Many states have had retraction statutes, some providing that punitive damages may not be awarded if retraction is made properly and the publisher shows that he did not publish with malice.   Others have gone further, providing that only special damages may be awarded following a retraction and demonstration of good faith on the part of the publisher.   California has the statute most favorable to publishers.   It provides that a proper retraction limits recovery to special damages, no matter what the motives of the publisher.[1]

Some retraction statutes have been attacked as unconstitutional, one reason being that they sometimes are applicable only to newspapers and as such are discriminatory.   Many persons may publish libel in non-newspaper form, but not have the advantage of retraction statutes in these states.   In Park v. Detroit Free Press, a Michigan retraction statute was held unconstitutional, the Court holding that "It is not competent for the legislature to give one class of citizens legal exemptions from liability for wrongs not granted to others." [2]   The Supreme Court of Kansas held that state's retraction provision unconstitutional. The decision went to the law's preventing recovery of general damages, and said: [3]

> The injuries for which this class of damages is allowed
> are something more than merely speculative * * *.
> In short, they are such injuries to the reputation as
> were contemplated in the bill of rights * * *.

Where punitive damages only are barred to the defamed, however, the constitutionality of the statute ordinarily has been upheld.[4]

---

[1] Newell, T. M., and Albert Pickerell, California's Retraction Statute: License to Libel?, 28 Journ.Quar. 474, 1951.   See also Wis.Stats. 895.05, 1967.

[2] 72 Mich. 560, 40 N.W. 731 (1888).

[3] Hanson v. Krehbiel, 68 Kan. 670, 75 P. 1041 (1904).

[4] Comer v. Age Herald Pub. Co., 151 Ala. 613, 44 So. 673 (1907); Meyerle v. Pioneer Pub. Co., 45 N.D. 568, 178 N.W. 792 (1920).

Chapter 6

THE LAW OF PRIVACY AND THE MEDIA

SEC. 28. DEVELOPMENT OF PRIVACY

Privacy—"the right to be let alone"—is protected by an evolving area of tort law and has been recognized as a constitutional right by the Supreme Court of the United States.

Privacy—roughly but usefully defined as "the right to be let alone"[1]—is in great peril during the 1970's. The peril exists, despite a great outpouring of apprehension by politicians, legal scholars, anthropologists, and just plain concerned citizens.[2] Infra-red telephoto lenses which "see in the dark;" super-sensitive directional microphones; dossier compilation by credit bureaus and by myriad government agencies—all are continuing phenomena in the further development of what Vance Packard termed "The Naked Society."[3] The great interest in privacy, and fear for its loss, is reflected by hundreds of popular and

[1] Thomas M. Cooley, A Treatise on the Law of Torts, 2d ed. (Chicago: Callaghan and Co., 1888) p. 29.

[2] See, e. g., Arthur R. Miller, The Assault on Privacy (Ann Arbor: University of Michigan Press, 1971); Don R. Pember, Privacy and the Press (Seattle: University of Washington Press, 1972); Alan Westin, Privacy and Freedom (New York: Atheneum, 1967); Subcommittee on Constitutional Rights of the Committee on the Judiciary, United States Senate, Ninety Second Congress, First Session ("The Ervin Subcommittee"), February 23–25, March 2–4, 9–11, 15 and 17, 1971, Parts I and II, pp. 1–2164, *passim*.

[3] Vance Packard, The Naked Society (New York: David McKay and Co., 1964.)

scholarly articles and books which complain, with considerable justification, about Americans' vanishing right to privacy.

"The right to be let alone," as Judge Thomas Cooley called privacy in 1888, now rides precariously at the confluence of many powerful currents in American society. Population increase is part of the problem; whether or not they like enforced nearness to their neighbors, people are simply being shoved closer and closer together. More worrisome than population increase, however, is the accelerating sophistication in electronic devices for listening or spying or storing or retrieving dossier information. It is becoming more and more difficult for anyone to make sure that he is not heard—or seen—or "on file"— when he wishes to be "let alone."

Americans' realization that they are being snooped at by credit bureaus as well as by police agencies and other arms of government has occasioned grim little jokes. "Smile," said one bit of graffiti in a men's room. "You're on 'Candid Camera.' And a few years ago, it was revealed that a person might not even be safe from eavesdroppers while enjoying a cocktail in an intimate little bar. Is the olive in that Martini glass nearby really an olive? Or is it a transistorized listening device? *Time* magazine straight-facedly recounted the doubtless apocryphal yarn about a shapely female investigator for the Internal Revenue Service whose brassiere contained a radio set for picking up conversations with men suspected of creative income tax return preparation.[4]

If a privacy-minded citizen cannot trust a Martini or a buxom young woman, recent studies by Professor Arthur R. Miller of Harvard University School of Law will make him feel even less secure. Professor Miller, who has emerged as a leading spokesman for protecting the privacy of American citizens, did not paint an encouraging picture in his best-selling study, *The Assault on Privacy*. Miller investigated the impact of the technological explosion upon the citizen's privacy, looking at topics ranging from the abuses of credit bureaus to the increasingly more sophisticated systems and devices for data collection and information storage and retrieval. Acknowledging that the new information-handling technology has "enormous long-range beneficial consequences for society," Miller then cautioned: "we must be concerned about the axiom—so frequently verified since

---

[4] Time, July 15, 1966, pp. 38–39. See also "Engineers Told of Bugging Boom," *New York Times*, March 21, 1968, p. 47M, quoting Mr. Ben Jamil, president of Continental Supply Co. of New York, as saying that there was a sevenfold increase in the purchase of bugging devices from 1966 to 1968.

the industrial revolution—that man must shape his tools lest they shape him." [5]   Consider some of Professor Miller's concerns:

> —"Today's laser technology already makes it feasible to store a twenty-page dossier on every American on a piece of tape that is less than 5000 feet long." [6]

*   *   *

> —"The seductive character of computerized information probably means that for some, success or failure in life may turn on what other people decide to put into their file and a programmer's ability—or inability—to evaluate, process, and interrelate that information." [7]

Computers *uber alles*?   Even successes in fighting against threats to privacy may turn out to be, as Professor Miller has said, "Pyrrhic victories."   Miller and other attorneys—plus a number of influential legislators—led the charge against the Federal National Data Center which was first recommended by the Bureau of the Budget in 1967.   The Bureau seemingly had no intent of enslaving America via such a proposal; "efficiency" was all that was sought.   For persons valuing their privacy, such a scheme seemed to come straight out of a George Orwellian nightmare, circa 1984. [8]   The National Data Center's computers were to simplify record-keeping by assigning each person a "birth number" which would serve as his social security, medical, draft, police record, and tax return identification, and which might even be the number for his telephone and credit cards.

Grave threats to freedom and privacy were seen;   such a central computer system might become the hub of a government surveillance operation which could reveal "our finances, our associations, our mental and physical health to government inquisitors or even to casual observers." [9]   In the end, the clamor was so loud that the National Data Center proposal was dropped. Miller, however, regards this as only an "apparent victory;" he expressed this fear: [10]

> The real tragedy that may emerge when the dust settles is that the failure to establish a data center under a

[5] Miller, The Assault on Privacy, pp. 7–8. © University of Michigan Press, Ann Arbor, 1971. Quotes from Professor Miller's book are used by permission.

[6] Ibid., p. 12. See also Alan F. Westin and Michael Baker, Databanks in a Free Society (New York: Quadrangle Books, 1972).

[7] Ibid., p. 38.

[8] George Orwell, 1984.

[9] Miller, "The National Data Center and Personal Privacy," The Atlantic, Nov. 1967, p. 53.

[10] Miller, The Assault on Privacy, p. 59.

legislative mandate directing the managers to take the
steps necessary to protect individual privacy actually
may serve to undermine individual privacy. This certainly will be the case if nothing is done to curb the
present tendency of each federal agency to "constitute
itself a data center."

Computers or data bank proposals are only part of the story
of the threat to privacy. During the 1972 Presidential election
campaign, the Democrats' Watergate Hotel campaign headquarters was discovered to be "bugged," and the men accused of
this political espionage had connections traced to the White
House. Democratic Campaign Manager Lawrence O'Brien—in
whose office hidden microphones were discovered—expressed
surprise that the discovery of the political espionage had not
outraged the mass of voters. Presidential Candidate George
McGovern's attempts to make a campaign issue of the bugging
of Democratic headquarters fell flat in the face of the public's
ho-hum, "all's fair in politics" attitude. "The people treat it
like a gang war, as if it was the Mafia settling things in its own
way," one McGovern aide said. "They shrug it off with, 'That's
got nothing to do with me,' when it has everything to do with all
of us. How would you like your bedroom bugged?" [11]

Although the political espionage story never really penetrated
public consciousness in time to aid McGovern's campaign, the
term "Watergate" has since become a shorthand term for political chicanery and invasion of privacy by wiretapping and bugging. Persons highly placed in President Nixon's "law and
order" Administration were shown to be involved in lawless
behavior: wiretapping, bugging, and even a break-in into the
office of the psychiatrist of Pentagon Papers case defendant
Daniel Ellsberg. The privacy issue had President Nixon in deep
trouble indeed: while certain Congressmen muttered about possible impeachment proceedings, one cartoonist suggested a new
version of the Presidential Seal: an eagle clutching a camera and
a (presumably tapped) telephone in its talons. [12]

A man far less famous than Daniel Ellsberg or President
Nixon found himself ensnarled by what he argued was an erroneous dossier in California's Bureau of Criminal Identification and Investigation. Gene Arthur White declared that he had

---

[11] Warren Rogers, "Democrats Amazed That Voters Not Outraged by
Bugging Case," (Chicago Tribune Service), Lexington (Ky.) Herald, Oct. 2,
1972, p. 1.

[12] *Newsweek*, April 30, 1973; *Time*, April 16, May 14, 1973.

repeatedly sought to have an incorrect reference to a "fictitious checks" incident pulled from his file, but to no avail. Failing to clear his name, he was denied jobs—ironically, as a policeman— because of the material in the file at the Bureau of Criminal Investigation. He sued the State of California for damages. A majority of the California Court of Appeals, Third District, did not believe White's story. The Court tossed aside White's libel suit against the State of California, saying: [13]

> There is no showing of malice on the part of the Bureau or its employees. It is true that the Bureau was advised by unsubstantiated statements that the information in plaintiff's [Gene Arthur White's] record was false. However, the Bureau was under no duty to change or alter its records on the basis of the unsubstantiated word of the concerned individual.

The Court's majority added that the Bureau had reasonable grounds for believing its statements to be true: the information had come from a law enforcement agency.[14]

Whether or not he believed White, Acting Presiding Judge Leonard M. Friedman dissented strongly from the decision of the court. In words which are also a dissent against America's diminishing "right to be let alone," Friedman declared: [15]

> Our nation's current social developments harbor insidious evolutionary forces which propel us toward a collective, Orwellian society. One of the features of that society is the utter destruction of all privacy, the individual's complete exposure to the all-seeing, all-powerful state. Government agencies, civilian and military, federal, state, and local, have acquired miles and acres of files, enclosing revelations of the personal affairs and conditions of millions of private individuals. Credit agencies and other business enterprises assemble similar collections. Information peddlers burrow into the crannies of these collections. Microfilm and electronic tape facilitate the storage of private facts on an enormous scale. Computers permit automated retrieval, assemblage, and dissemination. These vast repositories of personal information may easily be assembled into millions of dossiers characteristic of a police state. Our age is one of shriveled privacy. Leaky statutes im-

---

[13] White v. California, 17 Cal.App. 621, 630, 95 Cal.Rptr. 175, 181 (1971).

[14] Ibid.

[15] 17 Cal.App. 621, 631, 95 Cal.Rptr. 175, 181–182 (1971).

perfectly guard a small portion of these monumental revelations. Appellate courts should think twice, should locate a balance between public need and private rights, before deciding that custodians of sensitive personal files may with impunity refuse to investigate claims of mistaken identity or other error which threaten the subject with undeserved loss. The office of judges is to strike that balance rather than pursue sentiments of sympathy. It is obvious, nevertheless, that an unwarranted record of conviction, even of arrest, may ruin an individual's reputation, his livelihood, even his life.

While such a record explosion is cause for the gravest concern, the sense of privacy is being nibbled away, almost subliminally, even during a trip to the drug store. For example, parabolic mirrors—designed to detect shoplifters—make sure that merchants' eyes can follow shoppers around every aisle and counter in a store. Speaking of such devices—and closed circuit television cameras which have been installed in restrooms by some companies—American Civil Liberties Union Attorney Lawrence Speiser has asked: "Where do you go to scratch that irresistible itch?" [16] Business was not merely spying on its customers or employees: big firms were snooping for each other's trade secrets.[17]

But privacy is worth fighting for, against governmental stupidity or arrogance, or against the prying of businesses or private individuals. Louis D. Brandeis, one of the Supreme Court's greatest justices, once wrote that the makers of the American Constitution "sought to protect Americans in their beliefs, their thoughts, their emotions and their sensations. They [the Constitution's framers] conferred, as against the Government, the right to be let alone—the most comprehensive of rights and the right most valued by civilized man." [18]

Privacy is a problem for each citizen, a desired right to be fought for and zealously guarded. Privacy is also a communications media problem, one to be reported upon. And finally, privacy is a media problem in another sense because missteps by newspapers, magazines and radio and television stations have resulted in all too many of those privacy cases.

---

[16] Speiser Speech, Conference on the Right of Privacy, University of Wisconsin-Milwaukee, April 15, 1967.

[17] See footnote 4, *supra.*

[18] Olmstead v. United States, 277 U.S. 438, 48 S.Ct. 564 (1928).

What, then, is privacy? *Black's Law Dictionary* says, in pertinent part: [19]

> PRIVACY, RIGHT OF. The right to be let alone, the right of a person to be free from unwarranted publicity * * *. The right of an individual (or corporation) to withhold himself and his property from public scrutiny, if he so chooses.

Many of the more humorous—or tragicomic—American court decisions have come from contests involving privacy. When a landlord plants a microphone in the bedroom of a newly married couple, is that an invasion of privacy? [20] When a tavern owner takes a picture of a woman customer against her will—and in the women's restroom, later displaying the photograph to patrons at the bar—is that an invasion of privacy? [21]

Such cases, in their rather comical aspects, indicate growing pains in an area of law which is—in terms of legal gestation time—remarkably new. Privacy is nowhere mentioned in the Constitution, and its absence is understandable. In America during the Revolutionary generation, most people lived on farms. Urban residents made up not much more than 10 per cent of the new nation's population. When the Constitution was ratified, Philadelphia, then the nation's largest city, had little more than 40,000 residents. When people were out-of-doors, there was little felt need for any specific Constitutional statement of a right to privacy. Indoors, privacy was another matter. As Don R. Pember has written, [22]

> Paradoxically, while considerable physical distance existed between villages and residences, little privacy was possible within most homes and in most places of public accommodation and work. While man had progressed a long way from caves and tentlike dwellings, homes with living, eating and sleeping facilities in the same room where often the rule. In public inns, travelers shared many of the same facilities. If man could exalt his solitude, his isolation, his own little world in spacious colonial [or revolutionary] America, he might also regret on occasion his inability to find a place where he could withdraw within his own home.

[19] Henry Campbell Black, Black's Law Dictionary, Rev. 4th ed. (St. Paul, Minn., West Publishing Co., 1968) p. 1358.

[20] Such "bugging" was held to be an invasion of privacy. See Hamberger v. Eastman, 106 N.H. 107, 206 A.2d 239, 11 A.L.R.3d 1288 (1964).

[21] Yoeckel v. Samonig, 272 Wis. 430, 75 N.W.2d 925 (1956).

[22] Pember, Privacy and the Press, p. 5.

Although privacy was not mentioned by the Constitution by name, its first eight amendments, plus the Fourteenth Amendment, include the right to be secure against unreasonable search and seizure and the principle of due process of law. Taken together with the Declaration of Independence's demands for the right to "life, liberty and the pursuit of happiness," it can be seen that the men who founded the nation had a lively concern for something like the "right to be let alone."

Here, a useful distinction may be made between the *right* of privacy and the *law* of privacy. As Professor James Willard Hurst of the University of Wisconsin Law School has shown, American legal history is replete with evidence of concern for a broad *right* to privacy, represented by interests protected in the Constitution's Bill of Rights. Of this broad *right* to privacy, only small slivers have been hammered into the narrower *law* of privacy as enunciated by judges and legislatures.[23]

The narrower *law* of privacy is, as law goes, very new indeed. It has been traced to an 1890 *Harvard Law Review* article written by two young Boston law partners, Samuel D. Warren and future Supreme Court Justice Louis D. Brandeis. The article, often named as the best example of the influence of law journals on the development of the law, was titled "The Right to Privacy."

If this law journal article was the start of the formalization of a law of privacy in America, it should also be noted that the newspaper press was involved too. Standard accounts of the origins of the Warren-Brandeis article have it that Warren and his wife had been greatly annoyed by newspaper stories about parties which they gave. This irritation, so the story goes, led to the drafting of the article, which is now thought to have been written primarily by Brandeis. The co-authors asserted that an independent action for privacy could be found lurking within then-established areas of the law such as defamation and trespass to property. Warren and Brandeis wrote: [24]

> The press is overstepping in every direction the obvious bounds of propriety and of decency. Gossip is no longer the resource of the idle and of the vicious, but has become a trade which is pursued with industry as well as effrontery. To satisfy a prurient taste the details of sexual relations are spread broadcast in the columns of the daily papers. To occupy the indolent, column upon

[23] James Willard Hurst, Law and Conditions of Freedom (Madison, Wis.: University of Wisconsin Press, 1956) p. 8.

[24] Samuel Warren and Louis D. Brandeis, "The Right to Privacy," 4 Harvard Law Review (1890) p. 196.

column is filled with idle gossip, which can only be procured by intrusion upon the domestic circle.   The intensity and complexity of life, attendant upon advanc-
ing civilization, have rendered necessary some retreat
from the world, and man, under the refining influence
of culture, has become more sensitive to publicity, so
that solitude and privacy have become more essential
to the individual; but modern enterprise and invention
have, through invasions upon his privacy, subjected him
to mental pain and distress, far greater than could be
inflicted by mere bodily injury.

While this law journal article was indeed a catalyst toward
the development of a law of privacy, the article's evidence, at
some points, left something to be desired.   As Justice Peters of
the California Supreme Court noted in 1971,[25]

[t]ry as they might, Warren and Brandeis had a difficult time tracing a right of privacy to the common
law.   In many respects a person had less privacy in
the small community of the 18th century than he did in
the urbanizing late 19th century or he does today in the
modern   metropolis.   Extended   family   networks,
primary group relationships, and rigid communal mores
served to expose an individual's every deviation from
the norm and to straitjacket him in a vise of backyard
gossip, which threatened to deprive men of the right of
"scratching where it itches."

But as a judge in a Missouri appeals court noted in 1911, the
concept of a right of privacy was not new at all.   Privacy the
judge wrote, "is spoken of as a new right, when in fact it is
an old right with a new name.   Life, liberty, and the pursuit of
happiness are rights of all men." [26]

Long before 1890, when Warren and Brandeis added the word
"privacy" to the vocabulary of the law, England's William Pitt
gave ringing affirmation to the idea that "a man's home is his
castle."   Pitt said: "The poorest man may in his cottage bid de-
fiance to all the forces of the Crown.   It may be frail; its roof
may shake; the winds may blow through it; the storms may
enter,—but the King of England cannot enter; all his forces dare
not cross the threshold of the ruined tenement!"

[25] Briscoe v. Reader's Digest Ass'n, 4 Cal.3d 529, 93 Cal.Rptr. 866, 483 P.2d
34, 36–37 (1971).   Justice Peters cited Alan Westin, "Science, Privacy and
Freedom: Issues and Proposals for the 1970's," 66 Columbia Law Review
1003, at 1025.   See also John P. Roche's essay, "American Liberty: An
Examination of the Tradition of Freedom," in Shadow and Substance (New
York: Macmillan, 1964) pp. 3–38.

[26] Munden v. Harris, 153 Mo.App. 652, 659–660, 134 S.W. 1076, 1078 (1911).

From such beginnings has emerged an expanding law of privacy. Although Warren and Brandeis complained about the excesses of the news media, the first privacy cases involved other settings. In his pathbreaking study, *Privacy and the Press,* Professor Don R. Pember argued that the first privacy case appeared in 1881—nine years before the Warren and Brandeis article was published. In that case, *Demay v. Roberts,* a woman sued a doctor when she discovered that the doctor's "assistant," who had been present when the woman gave birth to a baby, had no medical training. The Supreme Court of Michigan held that the woman could collect damages from the doctor. The court declared that the moment of a child's birth was sacred and that the mother's privacy had been invaded.[27] And in an 1890 case, opera star Marion Manola got an injunction—based on her "right of privacy"—to prevent the use of her picture (when she was clad only in tights) in a poster advertising a production of "Castles in the Air." [28]

Twelve years later, misdeeds by advertisers led to an early—and famous—privacy case in New York. The judges of two New York courts were evidently readers of the Harvard Law Review, because they would have allowed recovery in a privacy lawsuit brought by Miss Abigail M. Roberson. She had sued for $15,-000 because—without her consent—her pretty likeness was used to decorate posters advertising Franklin Mills flour. But in 1902, New York's highest court—the Court of Appeals—ruled that she could not collect because there was no precedent which established a "right of privacy." Despite Miss Roberson's unwilling inclusion in an advertising campaign featuring the slogan of "The Flour of the Family," the Court of Appeals held that her injury was "merely" a mental one. The court added that if her claim were allowed, a flood of litigation would result, and that it was too difficult to distinguish between public and private persons.[29]

The *Roberson* decision, however, hinted broadly that if the New York legislature wished to enact a law of privacy, it could do so. Considerable public outcry and a number of outraged newspaper editorials greeted the outcome of the *Roberson* case. The next year, in 1903, the New York legislature passed a statute which made it both a misdemeanor and a tort to use the name, portrait, or picture of any person for advertising or "trade purposes" without that person's consent. Note that this was nar-

---

27 Pember, op. cit., pp. 50–51; 46 Mich. 160 (1881).

28 Ibid., p. 51, citing *New York Times,* June 15, 1890, p. 2, June 18, 1890, p. 3, and June 21, 1890, p. 2.

29 171 N.Y. 538, 64 N.E. 442, 447 (1902).

rowly drawn legislation, limited to the kind of fact situation which had arisen in *Roberson*.[30]

The New York statute, an amendment to the Civil Rights Law of the State of New York, has turned out to be a great generator of privacy law, and is responsible for about one-half of all the reported privacy decisions in the United States since 1903.[31] New York is a natural birthplace for such lawsuits: it is highly populous, and it is also the center of America's publishing and broadcasting industries.

In 1905, two years after the New York privacy statute was passed, the Georgia Supreme Court provided the first major judicial recognition of a law of privacy. An unauthorized photograph of Paolo Pavesich and a testimonial attributed to him appeared in a newspaper advertisement for a life insurance company. The Georgia court ruled that there is a law of privacy which prevents unauthorized use of pictures for advertising purposes.[32]

Since the 1905 *Pavesich* decision, the law of privacy has grown mightily. It has been recognized in at least 35 states: by statute in five states, and by common law by courts of 31 states.[33] Courts in Rhode Island, Texas, Nebraska, and Wisconsin have denied that there is a law of privacy. In Wisconsin, despite a woman's plea that her privacy had been disturbed in a tavern restroom by a flash camera, no right of privacy was found. The affronted woman, Mrs. Norma Yoeckel, declared that when she emerged from the restroom, men standing at the bar in Sad Sam's Tavern were passing pictures back and forth. No matter.

[30] New York Session Laws 1903, Ch. 132, Sections 1–2, now known as Sections 50–51, New York Civil Rights Law.

[31] Pember, op. cit., p. 67.

[32] Pavesich v. New England Life Ins. Co., 122 Ga. 190, 50 S.E. 68, 79 (1905).

[33] Privacy statutes have been passed in New York, Oklahoma, Utah, Virginia, and California. In 1971, the California Legislature added Section 3344 to the state's Civil Code. Section 3344 is similar to the New York privacy statute, New York Civil Rights Law §§ 50–51. The California Legislature specified $300 as the minimum amount recoverable. Courts in Wisconsin, Rhode Island, Nebraska and Texas have held that there is no right of privacy. Colorado, Minnesota, Massachusetts and Washington courts have had the opportunity to try cases under the law of privacy, but have decided those cases on other grounds. Many other states have recognized a common law of privacy by court decisions. The law of privacy has long been recognized as an action by the federal courts.

Cases in which state courts have rejected the law of privacy include: Wisconsin, Yoeckel v. Samonig, 272 Wis. 430, 75 N.W.2d 925 (1956); Rhode Island, Henry v. Cherry & Webb, 30 R.I. 13, 73 A. 97 (1909); Nebraska, Brunson v. Ranks Army Store, 161 Neb. 519, 73 N.W.2d 803 (1955); Texas, Milner v. Red River Valley Publishing Co., 249 S.W.2d 227 (Tex.1952). Privacy is recognized in the District of Columbia.

Wisconsin's Supreme Court declared that there was no right of privacy. The court said—in a decision which the late Dean William L. Prosser once termed an atrocity—that if there was to be such a law, the state legislature must enact it.[34] At this writing—nearly 20 years after Yoeckel v. Samonig—the state of Wisconsin has yet to enact a privacy statute.

When considering privacy law, two things should be kept in mind:

First, the law of privacy is not uniform. In fact, one judge once compared the state of the law to a haystack in a hurricane. There is great conflict of laws from state to state and from jurisdiction to jurisdiction.

Second, when courts or legislatures become involved with the law of privacy, they are attempting to balance interests. On one side of the scale, you have the public interest in freedom of the press and the right to publish. On the other side, you have the individual's right to privacy.

The late William L. Prosser, for many years America's foremost torts scholar, suggested that there are four kinds of torts included under the broad label of "invasion of privacy." [35]

1. Intrusion on the plaintiff's physical solitude.

2. Publication of private matters violating the ordinary decencies.

3. Putting plaintiff in a false position in the public eye, as by signing his name to a letter attributing to him views he does not hold.

4. Appropriation of some element of plaintiff's personality—his name or likeness—for commercial use.

It should be noted that these are not mutually exclusive categories: more than one of these four kinds of privacy actions may be present in the same case.

Professor Prosser noted that an action for invasion of privacy is much like *"libel per se:"* a plaintiff does not have to plead or prove actual monetary loss ("special damages") in order to have a cause of action. In addition, a court may award punitive

---

[34] Yoeckel v. Samonig, 272 Wis. 430, 75 N.W.2d 925 (1956).

[35] Barbieri v. News-Journal Co., 189 A.2d 773, 774 (Del.1963). The Delaware Supreme Court summarized Dean Prosser's analysis of the kinds of actions to be included by the law of privacy. For fuller treatment, see Prosser's much-quoted "Privacy," 48 California Law Review (1960), pp. 383–423, and his Handbook of the Law of Torts, 4th ed. (St. Paul, Minn., West Publishing Co., 1971) pp. 802–818.

damages. But while actions for defamation and for invasion have points of similarity, there are also major differences. As a Massachusetts court said, "The fundamental difference between a right to privacy and a right to freedom from defamation is that the former directly concerns one's own peace of mind, while the latter concerns primarily one's reputation." [36]

While such a distinction may exist in theory, in practice the distinction between defamation and invasion of privacy is blurred. As noted previously, Warren and Brandeis in 1890 drew upon a number of old defamation cases on the way to extracting what they called a right to privacy. Privacy, it would seem, may often be regarded as a close, if young, cousin of defamation. Some publications, indeed, may be both defamatory and an invasion of privacy, and shrewd attorneys have often sued for both libel and invasion of privacy on the basis of a single publication.[37]

Privacy actions also resemble defamation lawsuits in that the right to sue belongs only to the affronted individual. Relatives or friends cannot sue because the privacy of someone close to them was invaded, unless their own privacy was also invaded. In general, the right to sue for invasion of privacy dies with the individual.[38]

SEC. 29. "INTRUSION" AS INVASION OF PRIVACY

Invading a person's solitude, including the use of microphones or cameras, has been held to be actionable.

In the area which has been called "intrusion on the plaintiff's physical solitude," the media must beware of the modern technology which they increasingly call upon to gather and to broadcast news. Telephoto lenses on cameras—including television cameras—and microphones which can pick up quiet conversations hundreds of feet away—should be used with care by the media.

[36] Themo v. New England Newspaper Publishing Co., 306 Mass. 54, 27 N.E. 2d 753, 755 (1940).

[37] In general, although invasion of privacy and defamation are often included as elements of the same lawsuit, usually courts have not allowed a plaintiff to collect for both actions in one suit. "Duplication of Damages: Invasion of Privacy and Defamation," 41 Washington Law Review (1966), pp. 370–377; see also Brink v. Griffith, 65 Wash.2d 253, 396 P.2d 793 (1964), and Donald Elliott Brown, "The Invasion of Defamation by Privacy," Stanford Law Review 23 (Feb., 1971), pp. 547–568.

[38] Bremmer v. Journal-Tribune Pub. Co., 247 Iowa 817, 76 N.W.2d 762 (1956); Wyatt v. Hall's Portrait Studios, 71 Misc. 199, 128 N.Y.S. 247 (1911).

Back in 1765, Sir William Blackstone's *Commentaries* dealt with part of the problem of intrusion, naming eavesdropping as part of a list of nuisances which the law should control and punish. Eavesdroppers were defined as "people who listen under windows, or the eaves of a house, to conversation, from which they frame slanderous and mischievous tales." [39] Today, the tort subdivision of intrusion includes affront ranging from illegal entry into a person's dwelling to peeping into windows. Where intrusion cases are concerned, occasionally the camera has been a big troublemaker. Courts have held that it is not an invasion of privacy to take someone's photograph in a public place. Here, the media's cameramen are protected on grounds that they "stand in" for the public, taking pictures of what any persons could see if they were there.

It follows, of course, that photographers should beware of taking photos in private places. When a journalist or photographer invades private territory, he and his employer could be in trouble. A classic case of this sort is that of Barber v. Time. In 1939, Dorothy Barber was a patient in a Kansas City hospital, undergoing treatment for a disease which caused her to eat constantly but still lose weight. An International News Service (INS) photographer invaded her hospital room and took a picture of Mrs. Barber despite her protests. Such activities resulted in stories about Mrs. Barber's ailment appearing in Kansas City area newspapers for several days. *Time* purchased the picture from INS, and published it under the caption "Starving Glutton" along with a 150-word story drawn from the original INS account. The cutline under the picture said "Insatiable-Eater Barber; She Eats for Ten." Mrs. Barber won $3,000 in damages from Time, Inc. [40]

Although Barber v. Time is a famous case, it is—as privacy scholar Don R. Pember has argued—in some respects a bad decision, one which is out of step with the subsequent development of the law of privacy. [41] If the Missouri Supreme Court had limited tort liability to the International News Service— and to the photographer who took the picture over Mrs. Barber's protests—that would have squared with the law as it has evolved since the *Barber* decision in 1939.

[39] Sir William Blackstone, Blackstone's Commentaries on the Law, ed. by Bernard C. Gavit (Washington, D. C., Washington Book Co., 1892) p. 823.

[40] Barber v. Time, Inc., 348 Mo. 1199, 159 S.W.2d 291, 295 (1948). Time purchased the picture from "International," a syndicate dealing in news pictures, and mainly followed the wording of an account furnished by United Press.

[41] Pember, op. cit., p. 133.

Instead, the court ruled that Mrs. Barber's identity should not have been given by news accounts: "It was not necessary to state plaintiff's name in order to give medical information to the public as to the symptoms, nature, causes or results of her ailment." [42]

As Pember wrote, "the facts in the case seem to have overtaken the law."[43] The circumstances of the case were so extreme that the court ignored the fact that Mrs. Barber's identity was part of a public record, the admissions records of a public institution named Kansas City General Hospital.

Much more recently, in 1971, Time, Inc. lost a privacy lawsuit which again was one that may be labeled under the subdivision of intrusion.

Over the years, there have been few cases of the "intrusion" privacy lawsuits against the news media. Reporters for *Life* magazine, however, were guilty of intrusive behavior, and that cost the now defunct *Life's* parent corporation $1,000 in damages for invasion of privacy. Despite the small size of the judgment, the case of A. A. Dietemann v. Time, Inc. has sizable significance.

In its November 1, 1963, edition, *Life* published an article entitled "Crackdown on Quackery," depicting A. A. Dietemann as a quack and including two pictures of him. *Life* had done a reporting job with a difference—it had entered an agreement with the office of the Los Angeles District Attorney. "It had been agreed that Life would obtain pictures and information for use as evidence, and later could be used by Life for publication." [44] After this agreement, two *Life* reporters—William Ray and Mrs. Jackie Metcalf—went to Dietemann's home. They rang a bell at a locked gate at the front of Dietemann's yard, and Dietemann invited them in after the reporters said—as a ruse to gain admittance—that one of Dietemann's friends had sent them. Once inside Dietemann's house, the reporters were ushered into his den, where a number of other persons were sitting.

Mrs. Metcalf then told Dietemann that she had a lump in her breast. Dietemann, a journeyman plumber, then proceeded to examine her. Surreptitiously, without Dietemann's knowledge or consent, *Life* employee Ray photographed the "examination."

---

[42] 348 Mo. 1199, 159 S.W.2d 291, 295 (1948).

[43] Pember, op. cit., 134.

[44] Dietemann v. Time, Inc., 449 F.2d 245, 246 (9th Cir. 1971).

Life subsequently published one of these photos, showing Dietemann with his left hand on the upper part of Mrs. Metcalf's breast.   Meanwhile, Dietemann seemed to be looking at some gadgets and holding what appeared to be a wand (mercifully, not a plumber's friend) in his right hand.   After this diagnosis, Dietemann concluded that Mrs. Metcalf's complaint was caused by her having eaten some rancid butter 11 years, 9 months, and 7 days prior to that time.

There was more to Mrs. Metcalf's presence in Dietemann's den than met the eye or the touch.   Her purse contained a radio transmitter which relayed her conversation with the friendly plumber to a tape recorder in an automobile parked near Dietemann's house.   Keeping the tape recorder company in the car were *Life* reporter Joseph Bride, John Miner of the District Attorney's office, and Grant Leake, an investigator from the California State Department of Public Health.   Bride took notes on the radio transmissions reecived from Dietemann's house, although the recorded conversation was not used in *Life's* article.[45]

As the result of such sleuthing, Dietemann was arrested at his home on a charge of practicing medicine without a license. Dietemann, it may be noted, did not advertise, nor did he make charges when he attempted to diagnose illnesses or when he prescribed herbs and minerals.   He *did* accept contributions.[46]

As might be imagined, Dietemann was not overjoyed. He sued *Life* magazine for invasion of privacy, asking $100,000 general damages and $200,000 exemplary damages.   Employees of the magazine had gained admission to his home through subterfuge. They photographed him and electronically transmitted and recorded conversations in his home, without his knowledge or consent, resulting in emotional distress.   The trial court held that these circumstances amounted to a cause of action against the magazine for invading Dietemann's privacy.[47] A jury awarded Dietemann only $1,000 in general damages, and made no exemplary damage award. Writing for the trial court, District Judge Charles H. Carr said that although Dietemann was entitled to damages for injury to his feelings and peace of mind, "the injury is mental and difficult of ascertainment. * * * "[48] Judge

45 Ibid.

46 Ibid.

47 Ibid., p. 247; and at the trial level, 284 F.Supp. 925, 926 (D.C.Cal.1968).

48 284 F.Supp. 925, 932 (D.C.Cal.1968).

Carr, nevertheless, indicated that he was putting the magazine's conduct in the light most favorable to the press: [49]

> In view of the unusual facts of this case, it is concluded that the award of punitive damages is not warranted. It cannot be overlooked that defendant's efforts were directed toward the elimination of quackery, an evil which has visited great harm upon a great number of gullible people. Furthermore, if this decision correctly states the law, publisher will undoubtedly be guided accordingly in the future.

Attempting to defend the magazine's conduct, attorneys tried to find refuge in their version of the First Amendment. In upholding the judgment against *Life* magazine, Circuit Judge Shirley Hufstedler disagreed with those attorneys. She wrote: [50]

> The defendant claims that the First Amendment immunizes it from liability for invading plaintiff's den with a hidden camera and its concealed electronic instruments because its employees were gathering news and its instrumentalities "are indispensable tools of investigative reporting."

That was apparently to much for Judge Hufstedler to ignore. She proceeded to deliver a lesson in journalistic ethics—and privacy law—which *Life* should not have had to learn at the late date of 1971: [51]

> We agree that newsgathering is an integral part of news dissemination. We strongly disagree, however, that the hidden mechanical contrivances are "indispensable tools" of newsgathering. Investigative reporting is an ancient art; its successful practice long antecedes the invention of miniature cameras and electronic devices. The First Amendment has never been construed to accord newsmen immunity from torts or crimes committed during the course of newsgathering. The First Amendment is not a license to trespass, to steal, or to intrude by electronic means into the precincts of another's home or office. It does not become such a license simply because the person subjected to the intrusion is reasonably suspected of committing a crime.

[49] Ibid., pp. 932–933.

[50] 449 F.2d 245, 249 (9th Cir. 1971).

[51] Ibid.

Judge Hufstedler said that an actionable invasion of privacy had occurred during the reporting process as carried out by *Life's* employees; publication was not an essential part of plaintiff Dietemann's cause of action. Moreover, the judge added that the magazine could not shield itself from an invasion-of-privacy lawsuit by publishing a story and then saying that the intrusion was necessary to get that story. She declared:[52]

> No interest protected by the First Amendment is adversely affected by permitting damages for intrusion to be enhanced by the fact of later publication of the information that the publisher improperly acquired. Assessing damages for the additional emotional distress suffered by a plaintiff when the wrongfully acquired data are purveyed to the multitude chills intrusive acts. It does not chill freedom of expression guaranteed by the First Amendment.

Although Dietemann won his "intrusion" privacy lawsuit against Time, Inc., and *Life* magazine, Senator Thomas Dodd of Connecticut was not so fortunate in his suit against muckraking columnists Drew Pearson and Jack Anderson. Pearson and Anderson did great harm to the reputation and political career of Senator Dodd by publishing papers from Dodd's office files which showed an appropriation of campaign funds for personal purposes. The exposé of Dodd began during the summer of 1965 when two employees and two former employees of Senator Dodd removed documents from his files, photocopied them, and then replaced the originals in their filing cabinets. The copies were turned over to Anderson, who knew how they had been obtained. The Pearson-Anderson "Washington Merry-Go-Round" column proceeded to run six stories about the Senator, dealing—among other matters—with his relationships with lobbyists for foreign interests.

Dodd argued that the manner in which the information for the columns was obtained was an invasion of his privacy. After hearing Pearson and Anderson's appeal from a lower court judgment,[53] Circuit Court Judge J. Skelly Wright said:[54]

> The question then becomes whether appellants Pearson and Anderson improperly intruded into the protected sphere of privacy of appellee Dodd in obtaining the information on which their columns were based. In de-

[52] Ibid., p. 250.

[53] 279 F.Supp. 101 (D.C.D.C.1968).

[54] 133 U.S.App.D.C. 279, 410 F.2d 701, 704–705 (1969).

termining this question, we may assume, without deciding, that appellee's [Dodd's] employees and former employees did commit such an improper intrusion when they removed confidential files with the intent to show them to unauthorized outsiders.

* * *

If we were to hold appellants [Pearson and Anderson] liable for invasion of privacy on these facts, we would establish the proposition that one who receives information from an intruder, knowing it has been obtained by improper intrusion, is guilty of a tort. In an untried and developing area of tort law, we are not prepared to go so far.

Judge Wright commented that a person approached by an eavesdropper bearing information should perhaps "play the nobler part" and shut his ears. But this, the judge suggested, might place too great a strain on human weakness, holding a person liable for damages who merely gives in to temptation and listens.

Of course, Judge Wright noted, columnists Pearson and Anderson did much more than take and read copies of documents from Senator Dodd's files: they published excerpts from them in the national press. Judge Wright added:[55]

But in analyzing the claimed breach of privacy, injuries from intrusion and injuries from publication should be kept clearly separate. Where there is intrusion, the intruder should generally be liable whatever the content of what he learns. An eavesdropper to the marital bedroom may hear marital intimacies, or he may hear statements of fact or opinion of legitimate interest to the public; for purposes of liability, that should make no difference. On the other hand, where the claim is that private information concerning the plaintiff has been published, the question of whether that information is genuinely private or is of public interest should not turn on the manner in which it has been obtained.

A number of scholars have expressed consternation over this decision. Professor William H. Fortune of the University of Kentucky College of Law declared that the effect of the Dodd case is that journalists—as long as they do not actively participate in intruding in a search for damaging private documents—

---

55 133 U.S.App.D.C. 279, 410 F.2d 701, 705 (1969).

can receive the fruits of other person's illegal activity.[56]   Jack Anderson had met one of the documents' takers, sometime before the documents were copied, and that person described his knowledge of evidence of Dodd's misconduct.   According to that person, Anderson said, "If we can substantiate half of this it will be the most significant disclosure of misconduct in Washington for forty years, certainly in all my time as a reporter." [57]

In the excitement of "getting the goods" on Dodd, Anderson exaggerated the importance of the exposé.   As Professor Fortune suggested, the decision brings up some enormously perplexing problems of journalism law—and of journalism ethics. "What if the media know of information of public interest which cannot be obtained without committing a crime?   Is there a First Amendment defense under those circumstances to a private damage suit or to a criminal prosecution?" [58]   Although the late Drew Pearson and Jack Anderson successfully defended the invasion of privacy suit brought against them by Senator Dodd, the "Pentagon Papers Case"—United States v. New York Times, discussed in Section 9 of Chapter 2, suggests that no such First Amendment right exists.[59]

SEC. 30.   PUBLICATION OF PRIVATE MATTERS

With the law of privacy, "truth can hurt."   Unlike the law of defamation, truth is not necessarily a defense to a lawsuit for invasion of privacy.

The case of Dorothy Barber discussed in the last section was not only an incident of "Intrusion," but also involved a second sub-area of privacy law: "publication of private matters violating the ordinary decencies."   In this area of law, far more than in the category of "intrusion," missteps by the mass media have led to lawsuits.   In publishing details of private matters, the media may make scrupulously accurate reports and yet be found liable for damages.   A suit for defamation would not stand where the press has accurately reported the truth, but the press could nevertheless lose an action for invasion of privacy based on the same fact situation.   Here, the truth often hurts.

---

[56] Interview with Professor Fortune, Lexington, Ky., October 16, 1972.

[57] Note, "The Emerging Tort of Intrusion," 55 Iowa Law Review (1970) pp. 718–728, at p. 723n.   That case comment argued that the court was unimaginative; that Pearson and Anderson should have been held liable for the intrusion because it was a wrongful act done for their benefit.

[58] Fortune interview, Oct. 16, 1972.

[59] 403 U.S. 713, 91 S.Ct. 2140 (1971).

One of the most famous—and wrong-headed—cases involving the disclosure of embarrassing private facts came in the 1931 case of Melvin v. Reid, which for many years was regarded as a leading decision in the law of privacy. Gabrielle Darley Melvin sued when a 1924 motion picture—"The Red Kimono"—was made about her life as a prostitute and her trial for murder in 1918. But Gabrielle Darley had been acquitted of the murder charge, and thereafter led a changed life: she got married, found many friends who were not aware of her tawdry past, and became an accepted member of society.[60]

Although the court found that a movie could be made about Mrs. Melvin's life without penalty—because the facts were part of a public record—it was found that damages could be recovered for the use of her name, both in the motion picture and in advertisements for it. Strangely, the California Supreme Court— via a decision written by Justice Emerson J. Marks—said that privacy as a tort action did not then (in 1931) exist in California. However, Justice Marks found provisions in the California state constitution, such as Section 1, Article I: "men are by nature free * * * and have certain inalienable rights, among which are pursuing and obtaining safety and happiness." [61]

So it was that Mrs. Melvin won her lawsuit, even though Justice Marks denied the existence of the tort of invasion of privacy in California. From this unusual setting, Justice Marks wrote an oft-quoted list spelling out the following eight principles which that court found running through the law of privacy.[62]

1. The right of privacy was unknown to the ancient common law.

2. It is an incident of the person and not of property —a tort for which a right of recovery is given in some jurisdictions.

3. It is a purely personal action and does not survive, but dies with the person.

4. It does not exist where the person has published the matter complained of, or consented thereto.

---

[60] Melvin v. Reid, 112 Cal.App. 285, 297 P. 91 (1931).

[61] This was indeed a curious reading of the state's constitution. Usually, constitutions or bills of rights are seen as protecting individuals from the actions and powers of governments, rather than establishing protection against the actions of other individuals. See Pember, Privacy and the Press, p. 98.

[62] Melvin v. Reid, 112 Cal.App. 285, 297 P. 91 (1931).

5. It does not exist where a person has become so prominent that by his very prominence he has dedicated his life to the public and thereby waived his right to privacy. There can be no privacy in that which is already public.

6. It does not exist in the dissemination of news and news events, nor in the discussion of events of the life of a person in whom the public has a rightful interest, nor where the information would be of public benefit as in the case of a candidate for public office.

7. The right of privacy can only be violated by printings, writings, pictures, or other permanent publications or reproductions, and not by word of mouth.

8. The right of action accrues when the publication is made for gain or profit. (This however is questioned in some cases).

With the exception of the eighth point, the above list from Melvin v. Reid is quite an accurate summary of the "publication of embarrassing private facts" sub-area of the tort of invasion of privacy. Point 8 needs some explanation. If a publication is an advertisement, that is a publication for gain or profit. (See Sec. 33: Appropriation of a Person's Name or Likeness for in Advertising or for Commercial Use) Newspapers and magazines, of course, are generally published in the hope of making a profit. The fact that a newspaper makes a profit does *not* help to label its contents an invasion of privacy. In fact, as will be seen in Section 36, "newsworthiness" is the prime defense against a lawsuit for invasion of privacy.

One especially curious thing about Melvin v. Reid is that the California Supreme Court gave little heed to the qualified privilege attached to reports made from public records. But perhaps, in 1931, a movie such as "The Red Kimono" was not believed to be a defensible part of "the press" which is protected by the First Amendment.[63] The court suggested strongly that if the motion picture company had used only those aspects of Gabrielle Darley's life which were in the trial record or public record of her case, then the film would have been privileged. Even so, Gabrielle Darley's name surely was part of the public

---

[63] For years, courts were reluctant to accord First Amendment protection to motion pictures. See, e. g., Mutual Film Corp. v. Industrial Commission of Ohio, 236 U.S. 230, 35 S.Ct. 387 (1915); Burstyn, Inc. v. Wilson, 343 U.S. 495, 72 S.Ct. 777 (1952) was the case which first termed movies a significant medium for the expression of ideas.

record and it would seem that using it should have been "privileged."

In other cases, the existence of a public record has usually prevented recovery for invasion of privacy. Even if persons are embarrassed by publication of dates of a marriage or birth,[64] or information which is a matter of public record,[65] publications accurately based on such records have escaped successful lawsuits. The catch here seems to be that the basis of the report must be a record kept by a government agency and which is a record open to the public. Since some kinds of documents are public records in some states and not in others, knowledge of the statutes of various records in your state is imperative.

Where there is a legitimate public record—and the media's use of that record is not forbidden by law—the material may be used for publication without fear of suit. In 1960, the Albuquerque (N.M.) *Journal* published a story which said: [66]

> Richard Hubbard, 16, son of Mrs. Ann Hubbard, 532 Ponderosa, NW, was charged with running away from home, also prior to date, several times endangered the physical and moral health of himself and others by sexually assaulting his younger sister. Court ordered a suspended sentence to the New Mexico Boys' Home on the condition that he serve 60 days in the Juvenile Detention Home.

The younger sister, Delores Hubbard, sued for invasion of privacy, asserting that she had suffered extreme humiliation and distress and that the story "caused her to be regarded as unchaste, and that her prospects of marriage have been adversely affected thereby." Attorneys for the newspaper, however, brought proof that the *Albuquerque Journal's* story was an exact copy of an official court record. In upholding a lower court's judgment for the newspaper, the New Mexico Supreme Court ruled that because this was a public record, the newspaper enjoyed privilege. Although the plaintiff complained that the article was not newsworthy, the court held that the story was "accurate, newsworthy and exercised in a reasonable manner and for a proper purpose." The court added that the

---

[64] Meetze v. Associated Press, 230 S.C. 330, 95 S.E.2d 606 (1956).

[65] Stryker v. Republic Pictures Corp., 108 Cal.App.2d 191, 238 P.2d 670 (1951).

[66] Hubbard v. Journal Pub. Co., 69 N.M. 473, 474, 368 P.2d 147 (1962). New Mexico has no law forbidding publication of identities of rape victims. At least four states have statutes prohibiting such publications: W.S.A. (Wis.) 348.412; Ga.Ann.Code § 26–2105; S.C.Ann.Code § 16–81, and F.S.A. (Fla.) § 794.03.

girl, although an unwilling participant who did not seek publicity was in the unfortunate situation of being a person who might come to the notice of the public and have her misfortunes told to the world.[67]

In at least four states—regardless of whether Delores Hubbard was of an age where state law no longer regarded her as a juvenile—the kind of story run by the *Albuquerque Journal* could not have been used. In those states—Wisconsin, Florida, Georgia and South Carolina—the *identity* of a rape victim may not be published.[68]

In the law of privacy, as in the law of libel, the problem of *identification*—whether plaintiff was sufficiently identified by a publication to have a cause of action—can sometimes arise. In November, 1961, newsmen for a Florence, S. C., television station took pictures of a station wagon which had been abandoned in that city, and the pictures were used in TV newscasts. The station wagon was in the news because its former occupants, Patricia Nappier and Maxine Gunter, had been raped, and the rapist had fled in the station wagon the women had driven.

The televised news shows never used the women's names, but on the side of the auto was a sign closely associated with those women. They were puppeteers employed by the South Carolina State Department of Health; they traveled from school to school presenting shows about health and hygiene. Signs on the state-owned station wagon said "Little Jack, Dental Division, South Carolina State Department of Health." Because of this, the women had come to be known around the state as the "Little Jack Girls."

At the trial court level, it was held that a South Carolina statute specified that it was a misdemeanor and an invasion of privacy if a rape victim were to be *named.* Since the victims' names were not used, the court held that the women could not succeed in a lawsuit for invasion of privacy.[69]

Patricia Nappier and Maxine Gunter appealed this decision, arguing that the pictures of the label on the car in effect named them, and a United States Court of Appeals agreed with their contention. Circuit Judge Albert V. Bryan said that the statute's use of the word "name" was to be read as being synony-

[67] 69 N.M. 473, 474–475, 368 P.2d 147, 148–149 (1962).

[68] Wis.Code Annotated, § 348.412; Florida Statutes, § 794.03; Georgia Statutes, § 26–2105, and South Carolina Annotated Code § 16–81.

[69] Nappier v. Jefferson Standard Life Ins. Co., 213 F.Supp. 174 (D.C.S.C. 1963).

mous with "identity," and that the televised pictures "transgressed the statute and trespassed on the plaintiffs' privacy." [70]

The television station contended that the crime was newsworthy, and that the defense of newsworthiness should therefore overcome the lawsuit for invasion of privacy. Judge Bryan ruled, however, that South Carolina law specifically declared that identities of rape victims should not be published or broadcast, and that a statutory exemption to the defense of newsworthiness had thereby been created.[71]

Another person who did not seek publicity but who was found by it was William James Sidis. In 1910, Sidis was an 11-year-old mathematical prodigy who lectured to famed mathematicians. He was graduated from Harvard at the age of 16, and received a great deal of publicity. More than 20 years after his graduation, the *New Yorker* magazine—in its August 14, 1937—issue— ran a feature story about Sidis plus a cartoon, with the captions "Where Are They Now?" and "April Fool." The article told how Sidis lived in a "hall bedroom of Boston's shabby south end," working at a routine clerical job, collecting streetcar transfers and studying the history of American Indians. Sidis sued for invasion of privacy, but a United States Court of Appeals ultimately held that Sidis could not collect damages.

The court admitted that the *New Yorker* had perpetrated "a ruthless exposure of a once public character, who has since sought and has now been deprived of the seclusion of private life." Even so, the lawsuit did not succeed.[72]

> * * * [W]e are not yet disposed to afford to all of the intimate details of private life an absolute immunity from the prying of the press. Everyone will agree that at some point the individual interest in obtaining information becomes dominant over the individual's desire for privacy. * * * At least we would permit limited scrutiny of the "private" life of any person who has achieved, or has had thrust upon him, the questionable and indefinable status of a "public figure." * * *
>
> *   *   *   *   *   *   *   *   *
>
> The article in the *New Yorker* sketched the life of an unusual personality, and it possessed considerable popular news interest.

[70] Nappier v. Jefferson Standard Life Ins. Co., 322 F.2d 502, 503 (4th Cir. 1963).

[71] Ibid.

[72] Sidis v. F–R Pub. Corp., 113 F.2d 806 (2d Cir. 1940).

We express no comment on whether or not the news-worthiness of the matter printed will always constitute a complete defense. Revelations may be so intimate and so unwarranted in view of the victim's position as to outrage the community's notions of decency. But when focused upon public characters, truthful comments upon duress, speech, habits, and the ordinary aspects of personality will usually not transgress this line. Regrettably or not, the misfortunes and frailties of neighbors and "public figures" are subjects of considerable interest and discussion to the rest of the population. And when such are the mores of the community, it would be unwise for a court to bar their expression in the newspapers, books, and magazines of the day.

The court implied that the invasion of privacy must be so severe that it would cause more than minor annoyance to an hypothetical "average" or "reasonable" man of "ordinary sensibilities." William James Sidis was an unusually sensitive man, and it has been speculated that the *New Yorker* article was in large measure responsible for his early death.[73]

Despite circumstances such as those surrounding the *Sidis* case, American courts have generally given the media the benefit of the doubt. However, when the "embarrassing private fact" brought to light by publication was more painful to ordinary persons than Mr. Sidis's eccentricities, the media may be held liable.

In 1968, for example, *Readers Digest* magazine published an article titled "The Big Business of Hijacking," describing various truck thefts and the efforts being made to stop such thefts. Dates ranging from 1965 to the time of publication were mentioned throughout the article, but none of the hijackings mentioned had a date attached to it in the text.[74]

One sentence in the article said: "Typical of many beginners, Marvin Briscoe and [another man] stole a 'valuable-looking' truck in Danville, Ky. and then fought a gun battle with the local police, only to learn that they had hijacked four bowling-pin spotters."

There was nothing in the article to indicate that the hijacking had occurred in 1956, some 11 years before the publication of the *Reader's Digest* article. In the words of the California Supreme Court, "As a result of defendant's [*Reader's Digest's*] publication, plaintiff's 11-year-old daughter, as well as his friends, for

---

[73] Prosser, "Privacy," California Law Review, Vol. 48 (1960), at p. 397.

[74] Briscoe v. Readers Digest Ass'n, 4 Cal.3d 529, 93 Cal.Rptr. 866, 483 P.2d 34, 36 (1971).

the first time learned of the incident. They thereafter scorned and abandoned him." [75] Briscoe argued that he had since "gone straight" and that he had become entirely rehabilitated, and led an exemplary and honorable life, making many friends in respectable society who were not aware of the hijacking incident in his earlier life.

Briscoe conceded the truth of the facts published in the *Reader's Digest* article, but claimed that the public disclosure of such private facts humiliated him and exposed him to contempt and ridicule. He conceded that the *subject* of the article might have been "newsworthy," but contended that the use of his *name* was not, and that Reader's Digest had therefore invaded his privacy.

Writing for a unanimous California Supreme Court, Justice Raymond E. Peters agreed with Briscoe's arguments, saying: [76]

> Plaintiff is a man whose last offense took place 11 years before, who has paid his debt to society, who has friends and an 11-year-old daughter who were unaware of his early life—a man who has assumed a position in "respectable society." Ideally, his neighbors should recognize his present worth and forget his past life of shame. But men are not so divine as to forgive the past trespasses of others, and plaintiff therefore endeavored to reveal as little as possible of his past life. Yet, as if in some bizarre canyon of echoes, petitioner's past life pursues him through the pages of Reader's Digest, now published in 13 languages and distributed in 100 nations, with a circulation in California alone of almost 2,000,000 copies.
>
> In a nation built upon the free dissemination of ideas, it is always difficult to declare that something may not be published. But the great general interest in an unfettered press may at times be outweighed by other societal interests. As a people we have come to recognize that one of these societal interests is that of protecting an individual's right to privacy. The right to know and the right to have others *not* know are simplistically considered, irreconcilable. But the rights guaranteed by the First Amendment do not require total abrogation of the right to privacy. The goals sought by each may be achieved with a minimum of intrusion on the other.

Although the California Supreme Court was not in a position to actually award damages to Mr. Briscoe, it did send his case

---

[75] Ibid.

[76] 4 Cal.3d 529, 93 Cal.Rptr. 866, 483 P.2d 34, 41–42 (1971).

back to a lower court for trial. Justice Peters declared that although there was good reason to discuss the crime of truck hijacking in the media, there was no reason to use Briscoe's name. A jury, in the view of the California Supreme Court, could certainly find that Mr. Briscoe had once again become an anonymous member of the community.[77]

> Once legal proceedings have concluded, and particularly once the individual has reverted to the lawful and unexciting life led by the rest of the community, the public's interest in knowing is less compelling.

> Second, a jury might find that revealing one's criminal past for all to see is grossly offensive to most people in America. Certainly a criminal background is kept even more hidden from others than is a humiliating disease (Barber v. Time, Inc., *supra*, 348 Mo. 1199, 159 S.W.2d 291) or the existence of business debts (Trammell v. Citizens News Co., Inc., *supra*, 285 Ky. 529, 148 S.W.2d 708; Tollefson v. Price, *supra*, 247 Or. 398, 430 P.2d 990). The consequences of revelation in this case—ostracism, isolation, and the alienation of one's family—make all too clear just how deeply offensive to most persons a prior crime is and thus how hidden the former offender must keep the knowledge of his prior indiscretion.

> Third, in no way can plaintiff be said to have voluntarily consented to the publicity accorded him here. He committed a crime. He was punished. He was rehabilitated. And he became, for 11 years, an obscure and law-abiding citizen. His every effort was to forget and to have others forget that he had once hijacked a truck.

Despite such sweeping language, Mr. Briscoe did not win his lawsuit. The action was removed to a United States District Court for the Central District of California, where the judge granted a motion for summary judgment on behalf of the magazine. No published opinion was provided. The California Supreme Court's judgment was on a demurrer by *Reader's Digest*, with the magazine pleading that even if the facts were as alleged, they did not constitute a viable lawsuit. In such a situation, a court will give a highly favorable reading to plaintiff's statement of the facts. In the U. S. District Court trial, Briscoe evidently was unable to show "actual malice" required to sustain his suit. See the discussion of "actual malice" in Section 35, at pages 215–216.

---

[77] 4 Cal.3d 529, 93 Cal.Rptr. 866, 483 P.2d 34, 43 (1971).

SEC. 31. FALSE PUBLICATIONS WHICH INVADE PRIVACY

Putting a person in a false position before the public has proven costly for many publications.

A third sub-area of privacy law, "putting plaintiff in a false position in the public eye," is one which holds great dangers of lawsuits for the mass media.[78] The first invasion of privacy case dealing with the mass media to be decided by the Supreme Court of the United States involved the "false position in the public eye" area.[79]

This branch of privacy law has roots which go back to an outraged English poet, Lord Byron, who successfully sued to prevent the publication of inferior poems under Lord Byron's name.[80] In more recent years, the press—or people who use the press—have misrepresented the views of other people at their peril. For example, the New York *Herald* published a fake story on "stopping a Congo cannibal feast"—ostensibly written in a self-praising autobiographical style—which made fun of Antonio B. D'Altomonte, a well-known explorer. D'Altomonte collected damages as a result of this playfulness by the newspaper.[81] And in 1960, Rabbi Julius Goldberg received a judgment against a "romance" magazine. This publication had attributed to Rabbi Goldberg views on sex which he did not hold.[82]

The old saw that "photographs don't lie" is perhaps true most of the time, but photos—and especially their captions—must be carefully watched by editors. Pictures which would give, or are used in such a way that they give, a misleading impression of a person's character are especially dangerous. The *Saturday Evening Post* was stung by a privacy lawsuit in Peay v. Curtis Publishing Co. The magazine published an article about Washington,

---

[78] It should be noted that this third area of privacy overlaps a fourth area discussed later in this chapter, "appropriation of some element of plaintiff's personality for commercial use." This overlapping is especially apparent in cases involving spurious testimonials in advertisements. See, e. g., Flake v. Greensboro News Co., 212 N.C. 780, 195 S.E. 55 (1938) where a woman's picture was placed, by mistake, in an advertisement; Fairfield v. American Photocopy Equipment Co., 138 Cal.App.2d 82, 291 P.2d 194 (1955), where a plaintiff was labeled one of a number of law firms which used a certain brand of photocopying machine.

[79] Time, Inc. v. Hill, 385 U.S. 374, 87 S.Ct. 534 (1967).

[80] Lord Byron v. Johnston, 2 Mer. 29, 35 Eng.Rep. 851 (Chancery 1816).

[81] D'Altomonte v. New York Herald, 154 App.Div. 453, 139 N.Y.S. 200 (1913).

[82] Goldberg v. Ideal Pub. Corp., 210 N.Y.S.2d 928 (Sup.1960).

D. C., taxicab drivers titled "Never Give a Passenger an Even Break." The court noted that this article painted the city's drivers as "ill mannered, brazen, and contemptuous of their patrons * * * dishonest and cheating when opportunity arises." [83] The *Saturday Evening Post's* article was worth money to cab-driver Muriel Peay, whose picture had been used, without her permission, to illustrate the article.

The Curtis Publishing Company lost another invasion of privacy lawsuit only three years later, and the cause was again careless use of a picture. Back in 1947, ten-year-old Eleanor Sue Leverton was knocked down by a careless motorist. A news photographer snapped a picture of a woman helping the little girl to her feet. This photo was published in a Birmingham, Ala., newspaper. To this point, there was no action for invasion of privacy possible for young Miss Leverton.

But 20 months after the little girl was hit by the car, the *Saturday Evening Post* used her picture to illustrate an article headlined "They Ask to Be Killed." The little girl's picture was captioned, "Safety education in schools has reduced child accidents measurably, but unpredictable darting through traffic still takes its sobering toll." In a box next to the headline, these words appeared: "Do you invite massacre by your own carelessness? Here's how to keep them alive." A Federal Court of Appeals said: [84]

> The sum total of all this is that this particular plaintiff, the legitimate subject for publicity for one particular accident, now becomes a pictorial, frightful example of pedestrian carelessness. This, we think, exceeds the bounds of privilege.

The lesson, for photo-editors, should be plain: if a picture is not taken in a public place or if that picture—or its caption—places someone in a false light, don't use it. The exception, of course, would be when you have received permission, in the form of a signed release, from the persons pictured. Two invasion of privacy lawsuits of Mr. and Mrs. John W. Gill, one successful and one not, illustrate the point rather neatly.

Mr. and Mrs. Gill were seated on stools at a confectionery stand which they operated at the Farmer's Market in Los Angeles. Famed photographer Henri Cartier-Bresson took a picture of the Gills, as Mr. Gill sat with his arm around his wife. The photograph was used in *Harper's Bazaar* to illustrate an article titled

---

[83] Peay v. Curtis Pub. Co., 78 F.Supp. 305 (D.C.D.C.1948); Fowler v. Curtis Pub. Co., 78 F.Supp. 303, 304 (D.C.D.C.1948).

[84] Leverton v. Curtis Publishing Co., 192 F.2d 974 (3d Cir. 1951).

"And So the World Goes Around," a brief commentary having to do with the poetic notion that love makes the world go 'round. Although the Gills sued, they failed to collect from the Hearst Corporation, publisher of the magazine. The court held that the Gills had no right to collect since they took that voluntary pose in public and because there was nothing uncomplimentary about the photograph itself.[85]

Although they couldn't collect from the Hearst Corporation for invasion of privacy, Mr. and Mrs. Gill had already won damages from the Curtis Publishing Company. The *Ladies Home Journal*, a Curtis publication, had printed the very same photograph taken at the Farmer's Market but had made that photo an invasion of privacy by using faulty captions. The *Journal* used the Gills' picture to illustrate an article titled "Love." Underneath the picture was this caption, "Publicized as glamorous, desirable, 'love at first sight' is a bad risk." The story termed such love "100% sex attraction" and the "wrong" kind. The court held that the article implied that this husband and wife were "persons whose only interest in each other is sex, a characterization that may be said to impinge seriously upon their sensibilities." [86]

SEC. 32. FICTIONALIZATION

Addition of untrue materials to publications may prove actionable.

The misuse of pictures or photographs is one way to lose a privacy lawsuit. So is *fictionalization*. Fictionalization, as used by the courts, involves more than mere incidental falsity. Fictionalization appears to mean the deliberate or reckless addition of untrue material, perhaps for entertainment purposes or to make a good story better. Although the courts' rules for determining fictionalization are by no means clear, journalists should be warned to look to their ethics and accuracy. Jazzing up or "sensationalizing" a story by adding untrue materials so that a false impression is created concerning the subject of the story may be actionable.

Triangle Publications, which produced magazines such as *Timely Detective Cases* and *Uncensored Detective*, lost a privacy suit because of fictionalization. Robert H. Garner and Grace M. Smith had become legitimate objects of news interest because they were on trial for the murder of her husband. Mr. Garner and Mrs. Smith were convicted of the murder. Meanwhile, magazines pub-

---

[85] Gill v. Hearst Pub. Co., 40 Cal.2d 224, 253 P.2d 441 (1952).

[86] Gill v. Curtis Publishing Co., 38 Cal.2d 273, 239 P.2d 636 (1952).

lished by Triangle carried numerous articles about the crime, adding some untrue elements to their stories. The magazines claimed that Mr. Garner and Mrs. Smith had had "improper relations with each other." However, after the detective magazines had published their stories, the convictions of Mr. Garner and Mrs. Smith were reversed.

A Federal District Court held that there could be no liability for presenting news about a matter of public interest such as a murder trial. However, Triangle Publications could be liable for a privacy lawsuit because when the magazines

> enlarged upon the facts so as to go beyond the bounds of propriety and decency, they should not be cloaked with and shielded by the public interest in dissemination of "information." * * * It is no answer to say, as defendants do, that such interests, if they exist, can be adequately compensated for under the libel laws. If the articles violate rights of privacy, plaintiffs may bring their action under the privacy laws also.[87]

It appears, however, that minor errors in fact will not be sufficient to defeat the defense of newsworthiness, which will be discussed below. In the first media-related privacy case to reach the Supreme Court of the United States, it was held that Constitutional protections for speech and press forbid recovery for false reports "in the absence of proof that the defendant published the report with knowledge of its falsity or in reckless disregard of the truth." [88]

A more recent lawsuit for fictionalization involved the famed Warren Spahn, the left-handed pitcher who won more than 300 games during a long career with the Boston—and later the Milwaukee—Braves. Spahn was a hero to many baseball card collectors in the 1950s and early 1960s, and some people wanted to cash in on "Spahnie's" success. Writer Milton J. Shapiro and publisher Julian Messner, Inc., brought out a book titled *The Warren Spahn Story*. This book was aimed at a juvenile audience, and was assembled from the author's vivid imagination and a pastiche of secondary sources—newspaper and magazine articles, for example—about Spahn. Throughout this book, Spahn's feats were exaggerated. For one thing, Spahn was portrayed as

---

[87] Garner v. Triangle Publications, Inc., 97 F.Supp. 546, 550 (D.C.N.Y.1951). For similar holdings, see Hazlitt v. Fawcett Publications, Inc., 116 F.Supp. 538 (D.C.Conn.1953); Reed v. Real Detective Pub. Co., 63 Ariz. 294, 162 P.2d 133 (1945).

[88] Time, Inc. v. Hill, 385 U.S. 374, 388, 87 S.Ct. 534, 542 (1967). See also Binns v. Vitagraph Corp. of America, 210 N.Y. 51, 103 N.E. 1108 (1913); Stryker v. Republic Pictures Corp., 108 Cal.App.2d 191, 238 P.2d 670 (1951).

a war hero, which he was not.   An elbow injury finally brought an end to Spahn's career; author Shapiro consistently wrote about Spahn's "shoulder injury."   Such inaccuracies were topped off by page after page of fictional dialogue—words attributed to Spahn and his associates but which had been invented by author Shapiro.[89]

Shapiro and Julian Messner, Inc., argued strenuously that Spahn was a public figure who enjoyed no right of privacy.[90] Spahn v. Julian Messner worked its way through the courts of New York from 1964 to 1967.   Justice Charles Breitel of the Appellate Division, New York Supreme Court disagreed with contentions that Spahn no longer possessed a right of privacy. Justice Breitel said: [91]

> It is true * * * that a public figure is subject to being exposed in a factual biography, even one which contains inadvertent or superficial inaccuracies. But surely, he should not be exposed, without his control, to biographies not limited substantially to the truth. The fact that the fictionalization is laudatory is immaterial.

This was by no means the end of the *Spahn* case, which went up and down through the New York State and federal court systems, yo-yo fashion, from 1964 until it was finally settled out of court in the late 1960s.[92]

If, indeed, a writer cannot down the impulse to fictionalize, he would be more likely to avoid a lawsuit if he does not use the names of actual people involved in an event upon which he bases his fictionalization.   Where there is no identification, courts will not be able to find for the plaintiffs.[93]   But where there is both identification and fictionalization, the publisher is in some danger of losing a suit.[94]

---

[89] Spahn v. Julian Messner, Inc., 43 Misc.2d 219, 230–232, 250 N.Y.S.2d 529, 540–542 (1964).

[90] See Time, Inc. v. Hill, 385 U.S. 374, 87 S.Ct. 534 (1967).

[91] 23 A.D.2d 216, 221, 260 N.Y.S.2d 451, 456 (1965).

[92] Michael F. Mayer, Rights of Privacy (New York: Law-Arts Publishers, 1972), pp. 145–151 ; Pember, op. cit., 218–222.

[93] Bernstein v. NBC, 129 F.Supp. 817 (D.C.D.C.) affirmed 98 U.S.App.D.C. 112, 232 F.2d 369 (1955); Smith v. NBC, 138 Cal.App.2d 807, 292 P.2d 600 (1956).

[94] Mau v. Rio Grande Oil Co., 28 F.Supp. 845 (D.C.Cal.1939); Garner v. Triangle Publications, Inc., 97 F.Supp. 546 (D.C.N.Y.1951). But see Leopold v. Levin, 45 Ill.2d 434, 259 N.E.2d 250 (1970), where a fictional treatment of Nathan Leopold's participation in the famed 1924 murder of Bobby Franks was declared to be protected by the First Amendment despite the addition of fictional embellishments. See Mayer, op. cit., p. 151.

SEC. 33.   APPROPRIATION OF PLAINTIFF'S NAME OR PICTURE IN ADVERTISING OR FOR COMMERCIAL USE

The appropriation or "taking" of some element of a person's personality for commercial or other advantage has been a source of many privacy lawsuits.

Often, careless use of a person's name or likeness will be the misstep which results in a privacy action. The first widely known privacy cases, Roberson v. Rochester Folding Box Co.[95] and Pavesich v. New England Life Ins. Co.,[96] both discussed earlier in this chapter, turned on taking a person's name or picture for advertising purposes.

The use of a name, by itself, is not enough to bring about a successful lawsuit. For example, a company could publish an advertisement for its breakfast cereal and say that the cereal "gave Fred Brown his tennis-playing energy." There are, of course, many Fred Browns in the nation. However, should the cereal company, without explicit permission, identify a *particular* individual—such as "Olympic High Hurdle Champion Fred Brown"—then Mr. Brown, the hurdler, would have an action for invasion of privacy. Thus a *name* can be used, as long as a person's *identity* is not somehow appropriated.

A good example of this point is a suit which was brought by a Joseph Angelo Maggio, who claimed that the use of a name— "Angelo Maggio"—in James Jones' best-selling novel, *From Here to Eternity*, invaded his privacy. The court ruled, however, that although the name was the same as that of the plaintiff, the plaintiff's *identity* had not been taken. The fictional "Angelo Maggio" was held not to be the same individual as Joseph Angelo Maggio.[97]

Where the media are concerned, however, the great bulk of the trouble has come in cases involving advertising. There have been successful lawsuits, time and time again, when a person's identity or picture is used in an ad.[98] Even the fact that a per-

---

[95] 171 N.Y. 538, 64 N.E. 442 (1902).

[96] 122 Ga. 190, 50 S.E. 68 (1905).

[97] People on Complaint of Maggio v. Charles Scribner's Sons, 205 Misc. 818, 130 N.Y.S.2d 514 (1954). See also Uproar Co. v. National Broadcasting Company, 8 F.Supp. 358 (D.C.Mass.1934), affirmed 81 F.2d 373 (1st Cir. 1936); Nebb v. Bell Syndicate, 41 F.Supp. 929 (D.C.N.Y.1941).

[98] See, e. g., Flores v. Mosler Safe Co., 7 N.Y.2d 276, 196 N.Y.S. 975, 164 N.E.2d 853 (1959); Colgate Palmolive Co. v. Tullos, 219 F.2d 617 (5th Cir. 1955).

son's name or likeness appears in an advertisement through an innocent mistake will not provide a defense.   For example, the Greensboro, N. C., *News* advertised the appearance of Mademoiselle Sally Payne at the Folies de Paree Theatre through a joint advertising agreement with a bakery.   The published advertisement was intended to show a picture of Miss Payne in a bathing suit, but instead was printed with a picture of Miss Nancy Flake in a bathing suit.   The court held that Miss Flake had a property right in her name and likeness.   However, punitive damages were not allowed because the advertisement was a mistake made without malice and because the newspaper printed an apology.[99]

Persons who use the media should develop a kind of self-protective pessimism: it should always be assumed that if something could go wrong and result in a lawsuit, it might indeed go wrong. This is, of course, an overly pessimistic approach, but it can help to avoid much grief.   Take, for example, the case of Kerby v. Hal Roach Studios, Inc., where a simple failure to check as obvious a reference as a telephone directory led to a lost lawsuit.   A publicity gimmick boosting one of the *Topper* movies involved the studio's sending out 100 perfumed letters to men in the Los Angeles area.   These letters gushed:[1]

> Dearest:
>
> Don't breathe it to a soul, but I'm back in Los Angeles and more curious than ever to see you.   Remember how I cut up about a year ago?   Well, I'm raring to go again, and believe me I'm in the mood for fun.
>
> Let's renew our acquaintanceship and I promise you an evening you won't forget.   Meet me in front of Warner's Downtown Theatre at 7th and Hill on Thursday.   Just look for a girl with a gleam in her eye, a smile on her lips, and mischief on her mind!
>
> Fondly,
>
> Your ectoplasmic playmate,
> Marion Kerby.

Marion Kerby was the name of one of the characters—a lady ghost—portrayed in the movie.   Unfortunately for the Hal Roach Studios, there was a real-life Marion Kerby in Los Angeles, an actress and public speaker.   She was the only one listed in the Los Angeles telephone directory.   Miss Kerby, after being an-

[99] Flake v. Greensboro News Co., 212 N.C. 780, 195 S.E. 55 (1938).

[1] Kerby v. Hal Roach Studios, Inc., 53 Cal.App.2d 207, 127 P.2d 577, 578 (1942).

noyed by numerous phone calls and a personal visit, sued for invasion of privacy, and ultimately collected.[2]

Sometimes the out-and-out use of a person's name or likeness *is* permissible in an advertisement—*if* a court decides that the use of the name or likeness is "incidental."   Take Academy Award and Emmy Award winning actress Shirley Booth, who was vacationing in Jamaica some years ago.   A *Holiday* magazine photographer asked, and received, permission to take her picture, and that picture was later used in a *Holiday* feature story about Jamaica's Round Hill resort.   Several months later, however, the same picture appeared in full-page promotional advertisements for *Holiday* in *Advertising Age* and *New Yorker* magazines.   Beneath the picture of the actress were the words "Shirley Booth and Chapeau, from a recent issue of *Holiday*." [3]

Miss Booth sued *Holiday's* publisher, the Curtis Publishing Co., in New York, claiming invasion of privacy on the ground that *Holiday's* advertising use of that picture was impermissible.   New York's privacy statute, after all, prohibits use of a person's name or likeness "for purposes of trade" unless the person involved has given consent.[4]   Curtis Publishing responded that this sort of promotional advertising was needed to help magazine sales, thus supporting the public's interest in news.[5]

Miss Booth won $17,500 at the trial level, but that finding was reversed on appeal.   Finding for the Curtis Publishing Co., Justice Charles D. Breitel termed *Holiday's* advertising use of the picture "incidental," and therefor not prohibited by New York's privacy statute.[6]

Author-playwright A. E. Hotchner's attempt to write an intimate biography of the American literary giant Ernest Hemingway led to another privacy suit under the New York statute. Hemingway had died in 1961, and his widow, Mary Hemingway, sued to enjoin Random House from publishing Hotchner's manuscript.   Hotchner's biography covered the Nobel laureate's life from 1948, when Hemingway and Hotchner first met in a bar in

---

[2] Ibid., at 578.   It should be noted that this case is also a good example of the privacy tort category called "false position in the public eye."

[3] Booth v. Curtis Pub. Co., 15 A.D.2d 343, 223 N.Y.S.2d 737 (1962).

[4] Sections 50–51, New York Civil Rights Law, McKinney's Consolidated Laws, Ch. 6.   See 15 A.D.2d 343, 223 N.Y.S.2d 737, at 739 (1962).

[5] Booth v. Curtis Pub. Co., 15 App.Div.2d 343, 349, 223 N.Y.S.2d 737, 743–744 (1962).

[6] 11 N.Y.S.2d 907 (1962).   See also University of Notre Dame Du Lac v. Twentieth Century Fox, 22 A.D.2d 452, 256 N.Y.S.2d 301 (1965).

Havana, Cuba, up to the time of Hemingway's death. New York Supreme Court Judge Harry B. Frank wrote of Hotchner's book: [7]

> The format and narrative style of the work make immediately apparent that it is intended as a subjective presentation from the vantage of the friendship, camaraderie, and personal experiences that the younger author shared with the literary giant. Their adventures, their travels, their meetings are all set forth in detail and the portrait of Hemingway that emerges is shaded in terms of the unique self that he manifested and revealed in the course of his particular relationship with Hotchner.

Mary Hemingway's suit for an injunction complained, among other things, that the Hotchner manuscript violated her statutory right of privacy under Section 51 of the New York Civil Rights Law. Mrs. Hemingway was mentioned in various places throughout the book, and she charged that those references to her amounted to an invasion of her privacy.[8] Judge Frank rejected Mrs. Hemingway's privacy contentions and allowed Random House to publish the book: [9]

> The individual's security has fared best when pitted against naked commercial assault, and protection is afforded under the statute where the invasion has been solely for "advertising purposes, or for the purposes of trade." A book of biographical import such as is here involved, however, has been held not to fall within such category. Compelling public interest in the free flow of ideas and dissemination of factual information has outweighed considerations of individual privacy in conjunction with factual publications of such type, whether authorized or not, and as to such book the statutory proscription is ordinarily without relevance. * * * Moreover, plaintiff's status as the wife and widow of a man of celebrated prominence who was the recipient of both the Nobel and Pulitzer Prizes during his lifetime and her own activities incidental to such position have thrust her into the category of a newsworthy personality * * *.

In other lawsuits dealing with "appropriation," it has been held that the taking or appropriation need not be for a dollars-and-cents gain in most jurisdictions where the common-law right of privacy is recognized. Just as long as someone's identity or

---

[7] Estate of Hemingway v. Random House, Inc., 49 Misc.2d 726, 268 N.Y.S. 2d 531, 534 (1966).

[8] 49 Misc.2d 726, 268 N.Y.S.2d 531, 534 (1966).

[9] 49 Misc.2d 726, 268 N.Y.S.2d 531, 534 (1966).

likeness is used for some advantage, an action for invasion of privacy may succeed.   An example of this occurred when a political party used a man's name as a candidate when he had not given his consent.[10]   However, the five states which have privacy statutes—New York, Oklahoma, Virginia, Utah, and California—require proof of monetary advantage gained by the publication.[11]   It has often been urged that everything published by the mass media is done "for purposes of trade." [12]   If such a construction were allowed, the press might be greatly threatened by privacy suits brought by persons who objected to the use of their names, even in news stories.   In defense of press freedom, however, courts have repeatedly held that just because a newspaper, magazine, or broadcasting station makes a profit does not mean that everything published is "for purposes of trade." [13]

SEC. 34.   THE RIGHT OF PUBLICITY

Although the right to sue for invasion of privacy typically dies with the individual, one court has declared that a "right of publicity" is not so limited.

As a general rule, the right of privacy dies with the individual.[14]   As tort scholar William L. Prosser noted, "there is no common law right of action for a publication concerning one who is already dead."   However, as with most general rules, there are exceptions.   A viable lawsuit for invasion of privacy may exist after a person's death, "according to the survival rules of the particular state." [15]

Similarly, there is a general rule that relatives have no right of action for an invasion of the privacy of a deceased person. A satirical national television show, "That Was the Week that Was," included this statement in a broadcast over the National Broadcasting Company network: "Mrs. Katherine Young of

[10] State ex rel. LaFollette v. Hinkle, 131 Wash. 86, 229 P. 317 (1924).

[11] McKinney's N.Y. Civil Rights Law §§ 50–51; Virginia Code 1950, § 8–650; 15 Oklahoma Statutes Anno. § 839.1; Utah Code Ann. 1953, 76–4–8, and § 3344, California Civil Code.

[12] See Joseph Burstyn, Inc. v. Wilson, 343 U.S. 495, 501, 72 S.Ct. 777, 780 (1952); New York Times Co. v. Sullivan, 376 U.S. 254 at 266, 84 S.Ct. 710 at 718 (1964).

[13] See, e. g., Time, Inc. v. Hill, 385 U.S. 374, 87 S.Ct. 534, 546 (1967).

[14] Schuyler v. Curtis, 147 N.Y. 434, 42 N.E.2d 22 (1897); Lunceford v. Wilcox, 88 N.Y.S.2d 225 (City Ct.1949).

[15] William L. Prosser, Handbook of the Law of Torts, 4th ed., St. Paul, Minn.: West Publishing Co., 1971, at p. 815, citing the highly confusing decision in Reed v. Real Detective Pub. Co., 63 Ariz. 294, 162 P.2d 133 (1945).

Syracuse, New York, who died at 99 leaving five sons, five daughters, 67 grandchildren, 72 great grandchildren, and 73 great-great grandchildren—gets our First Annual Booby Prize in the Birth Control Sweepstakes." Two of Mrs. Young's sons sued for invasion of privacy, but failed because there is no right in relatives for invasion of privacy of a deceased person.[16]

In a 1972 decision by a Superior Court of the State of California, however, relatives were able to collect successfully in a privacy-related action. It might be said that the legal ghost of the late horror-film star, Bela Lugosi came back to haunt Universal Pictures Company. Lugosi, famed for his portrayal of Count Dracula, was one of a number of actors to take the role of that worthy vampire. Because of the popularity of various monster or horror motion pictures, Universal Pictures—beginning in 1960—entered into lucrative licensing agreements with a number of manufacturing firms. These agreements allowed production and sale of a number of items, including shirts, cards, games, kites, bar accessories and masks—all featuring the likeness of the character of Count Dracula as portrayed by Bela Lugosi.[17]

Lugosi's son, Bela George Lugosi, and his widow, Hope Linninger Lugosi, sued to recover the profits made by Universal Pictures in its licensing of the Count Dracula character to various manufacturers. In addition, Lugosi's son and widow sought to enjoin Universal Pictures from making any additional licensing arrangements without their consent. This lawsuit raised questions of whether Bela Lugosi's contracts with the film company granted the company merchandising rights in his portrayal of Count Dracula, and whether such rights, after Lugosi's death, descended to his widow and son.[18]

In part, the *Lugosi* case turned upon the peculiarities of a contract that the actor had signed in 1930 with Universal Pictures. The court held that Lugosi's contract allowed Universal Pictures Company to " 'use and exploit in connection with the said photoplay ["Dracula"] any and all of the artist's acts, poses, plays and appearances * * * in connection with the

---

[16] Young v. That Was the Week that Was, 423 F.2d 265 (6th Cir. 1970); accord: see Maritote v. Desilu Productions, Inc., 345 F.2d 418 (7th Cir. 1965); Ravellette v. Smith, 300 F.2d 854 (7th Cir. 1962).

[17] Bela George Lugosi v. Universal Pictures Co., No. 877875, Memorandum Opinion, Superior Court of the State of California for the County of Los Angeles, case published in full in Performing Arts Review, Vol. 3, No. 1 (1972), pp. 19–62.

[18] Ibid., p. 21.

advertising and exploitation of said photoplay.' " [19]   Judge Bernard S. Jefferson added: [20]

> The products such as kites and shirts which were licensed to carry the appearance of the Count Dracula character were not sold at all in connection with any advertising of the Dracula photoplay to appear on television or any theatre screen. Such use of the Count Dracula character was completely separate and apart from any *advertising* or *exploitation* of the photoplay "Dracula."

Once past such contractual language, the judge declared that Universal Pictures' merchandising of Bela Lugosi's likeness and appearance as Count Dracula constituted an invasion of the actor's rights, even though the actor had died in 1956, four years before Universal Pictures signed licensing agreements to allow production and sale of "Bela Lugosi" novelty items.[21]

"Right of Publicity"

But what rights were violated? Judge Jefferson decided that there was no violation of Lugosi's privacy, because such a right had ended with his death in 1956. Instead, the judge accepted the assertion of Lugosi's widow and son that there had been violation of a "right of property or a right of contract which, upon Bela Lugosi's death, descended to his heirs." [22]

For precedents, Judge Jefferson turned from the world of motion pictures to that of baseball players. Beginning with Judge Jerome D. Frank's 1953 decision in Haelan Laboratories, Inc. v. Topps Chewing Gum, several cases involving baseball players' photographs. He wrote of a "right of publicity" apart from a right of privacy which compensates a person for mental suffering because he has received unwanted publicity. Judge Frank said: "We think that in addition to an independent right of privacy * * * a man has a right in the publicity value of his photograph, i. e., the right to grant the exclusive privilege of publishing his picture * * *. This right might be called a 'right of publicity.' " [23]

Other "right of publicity" cases involved outfielder Ted Uhlaender and slugging first baseman Orlando Cepeda. Both

[19] Ibid., pp. 21–22, quoting Lugosi contract with Universal Pictures Co.

[20] Ibid., p. 26, emphasis the court's.

[21] Ibid., p. 27.

[22] Ibid., pp. 27–28.

[23] Haelan Laboratories v. Topps Chewing Gum, 202 F.2d 866 (2d Cir. 1953).

sued for compensation for the unauthorized use of their names for advertising or promotional purposes. In the *Uhlaender* case, a court decided that a public figure such as a baseball player has a property or proprietary interest in his public personality. This included his identity, as embodied in his name, likeness, or other personal characteristics. This property interest—in effect the "right of publicity" of which Judge Frank wrote in 1953 in the *Haelan Laboratories* case—was held in *Uhlaender* to be sufficient to support an injunction against unauthorized appropriation.[24]

After considering such cases, Judge Jefferson concluded that Bela Lugosi's "rights to his likeness and appearance as Count Dracula is a descendible property right and that the cause of action in favor of the plaintiffs rests upon the tort theory of an appropriation of such property right by defendant. Lugosi's heirs were entitled to collect from Universal Pictures.[25]

SEC. 35.   TIME, INC. v. HILL

The "malice rule" from the libel landmark case, New York Times v. Sullivan, was stirred into privacy law in Time, Inc. v. Hill.

When the Supreme Court weighed the right to privacy against the First Amendment freedom to publish, the freedom to publish was given preference. The 1967 case of Time, Inc. v. Hill was noteworthy in one respect because the losing attorney was Richard Milhous Nixon, more recently known as President of the United States.[26] Beyond that, Time v. Hill is a difficult case to understand and interpret because it melds together the concepts of privacy-as-tort and privacy-as-constitutional right. However confusing, this decision is important because it represents the first time that the Supreme Court decided a privacy case dealing with the mass media. Furthermore, Time v. Hill has become a key precedent in strengthening the media's defenses against lawsuits for invasion of privacy. Such defenses are discussed in Sections 36 to 38 of this chapter.

---

24 Uhlaender v. Henricksen, 316 F.Supp. 1277 (D.C.Minn.1970); Cepeda v. Swift & Co., 415 F.2d 1205 (8th Cir. 1969).

25 Lugosi v. Universal Pictures, published in Performing Arts Review, Vol. 3:1 (1972) pp. 59–61. The court ruled that considerations involving a two-year statute of limitations meant that Lugosi's heirs could recover those damages arising out of licensing agreements entered into by Universal Pictures for the two years before February 3, 1966, the date the lawsuit was filed against Universal Pictures.

26 385 U.S. 374, 87 S.Ct. 534 (1967).

In 1952, the James J. Hill family was minding its own business, living in the suburban Philadelphia town of Whitemarsh. Like most families, the Hills wanted to be left alone. On September 11, 1952, however, the Hills' anonymity was taken away from them by three escaped prisoners. The convicts held Mr. and Mrs. Hill and their five children hostage in their own home for 19 hours. The family was not harmed, but the Hills—much against their wishes—were in the news.[27] The Hills stayed in the news for some time; their story became even more sensational when two of the three convicts who had held them hostage were killed in a shoot-out with police.[28]

In 1953, Random House published Joseph Hayes' novel, The Desperate Hours, a story about a family which was taken hostage by escaped convicts. The novel was later made into a successful play and, subsequently, a motion picture.

The publicity which léd the Hills to sue for invasion of their privacy was an article published in 1955 by *Life* magazine. The article, titled "True Crime Inspires Tense Play," described the "true crime" suffered by the James Hill family of Whitemarsh, Pennsylvania.[29] The article said:[30]

> "Three years ago Americans all over the country read about the desperate ordeal of the James Hill family, who were held prisoners in their home outside Philadelphia by three escaped convicts. Later they read about it in Joseph Hayes's novel, *The Desperate Hours*, inspired by the family's experience. Now they can see the story re-enacted in Hayes's Broadway play based on the book, and next year will see it in his movie, which has been filmed but is being held up until the play has a chance to pay off.
>
> "The play, directed by Robert Montgomery and expertly acted, is a heart-stopping account of how a family rose to heroism in a crisis. LIFE photographed the play during its Philadelphia tryout, transported some of the actors to the actual house where the Hills were besieged. On the next page scenes from the play are re-enacted on the site of the crime."

Life's pages of photographs included actors' depiction of the son being "roughed up" by one of the escaped convicts. This

[27] 385 U.S. 374, 377, 87 S.Ct. 534, 536 (1967).

[28] Pember, Privacy and the Press, p. 210.

[29] Life, Feb. 28, 1955.

[30] 385 U.S. 374, 377, 87 S.Ct. 534, 536–537 (1967).

picture was captioned "brutish convict." Also, a picture titled "daring daughter" showed the daughter biting the hand of a convict, trying to make him drop the gun.[31]

The Joseph Hayes novel and play, however, did not altogether match up with *Life's* assertion that Hayes' writings were based on the ordeal of the Hill family. For one thing, Hayes' family was named "Hilliard," not Hill. Also, the Hills had not been harmed by the convicts in any way, while in the Hayes novel and play the father and son were beaten and the daughter was "subjected to a verbal sexual insult."

Hill sued for invasion of privacy under the privacy sections of New York's Civil Rights Law, which provides: [32]

"§ 50. Right of Privacy

"A person, firm or corporation that uses for advertising purposes, or for the purposes of trade, the name, portrait or picture of any living person without having first obtained the written consent of such person, or if a minor of his or her parent or guardian, is guilty of a misdemeanor."

In addition, the New York law provides that a person whose name or picture was so used "for purposes of trade" without his consent could "sue and recover damages for any injuries sustained by reason of such use.[33]

The Hills sought damages on grounds that the *Life* article "was intended to, and did, give the impression that the play mirrored the Hill family's experience, which, to the knowledge of defendant * * * was false and untrue." In its defense, Time, Inc., argued that "the subject of the article was 'a subject of legitimate news interest,' 'a subject of general interest and of value and concern to the public' at the time of publication, and that it was 'published in good faith without any malice whatsoever * * *.' " [34]

The trial court jury awarded the Hills $50,000 compensatory and $25,000 punitive damages. On appeal, the Appellate Division of the Supreme Court of New York ordered a new trial on the question of damages, but upheld the jury's finding that *Life*

31 Ibid.

32 Sections 50–51, New York Civil Rights Law, McKinney's Consolidated Laws, Ch. 6.

33 Ibid.

34 385 U.S. 374, 378, 87 S.Ct. 534, 537 (1967).

magazine had invaded the Hills' privacy. The Appellate Division bore down hard on the issue of fictionalization:[35]

> "Although the play was fictionalized, *Life's* article portrayed it as a reenactment of the Hills' experience. It is an inescapable conclusion that this was done to advertise and attract further attention to the play, and to increase present and future magazine circulations as well. It is evident that the article cannot be characterized as a mere dissemination of news, nor even an effort to supply legitimate newsworthy information in which the public had, or ought have a proper interest."

At the new trial on the issue of damages, a jury was waived and the court awarded $30,000 compensatory damages with no punitive damages.

When the *Hill* case reached the Supreme Court, it took up Constitutional issues of freedom of speech and press raised in the appeal by Time, Inc. Justice Brennan's majority opinion first dealt with the issue of whether truth could be a defense to a charge of invasion of privacy. Quoting a recent New York Court of Appeals decision, Brennan noted that it had been made "crystal clear" in construing the New York Civil Rights Statute, "that truth is a complete defense in actions under the statute based upon reports of newsworthy people or event."[36] Brennan added, "Constitutional questions which might arise if truth were not a defense are therefore no concern."[37]

Justice Brennan then wrestled with the issue of fictionalization. He noted that James Hill was a newsworthy person " 'substantially without a right to privacy' insofar as his hostage experience was involved." Hill, however, was entitled to sue to the extent that *Life* magazine "fictionalized" and "exploited for the defendant's commercial benefit." Brennan then turned to a libel case, New York Times v. Sullivan, for guidance.[38]

> Material and substantial falsification is the test. However, it is not clear whether proof of knowledge of the falsity or that the article was prepared with reckless disregard for the truth is also required. In New York Times Co. v. Sullivan * * * we held that the Con-

[35] 385 U.S. 374, 379, 87 S.Ct. 534, 537 (1967), quoting Hill v. Hayes, 18 A.D. 2d 485, 489, 240 N.Y.S.2d 286, 290 (1963).

[36] At the outset of his opinion, Justice Brennan relied heavily upon Spahn v. Julian Messner, Inc., 18 N.Y.2d 324, 274 N.Y.S. 877, 221 N.E.2d 543 (1966).

[37] 385 U.S. 374, 383–384, 87 S.Ct. 534, 539–540 (1967).

[38] New York Times v. Sullivan, 376 U.S. 254, 84 S.Ct. 710 (1964), used in Time, Inc. v. Hill, 385 U.S. 374, 386–388, 87 S.Ct. 534, 541–542 (1967).

stitution delimits a State's power to award damages for libel in actions brought by public officials against critics of their official conduct. Factual error, content defamatory of official reputation, or both, are insufficient to an award of damages for false statements unless actual malice—knowledge that the statements are false or in reckless disregard of the truth—is alleged and proved. * * *

* * * * * * * * *

We hold that the Constitutional protections for speech and press preclude the application of the New York statute to redress false reports of matters of public interest in the absence of proof that the defendant published the report with knowledge of its falsity or in reckless disregard of the truth.

The Supreme Court, however, did not appear to wish to tie all future privacy holdings to the "Times Rule" cited above. Justice Brennan carefully emphasized that the malice rule from New York Times v. Sullivan—"knowledge that it was false, or reckless disregard of whether it was false or not"—was here being applied only in the "discrete context" of the facts of the *Hill* case.[39] It was, however, important to Brennan's opinion that the trial judge, in Brennan's view, had failed to instruct the jury correctly. The instructions to the jury, Justice Brennan maintained, would have included a call for a verdict finding "knowing or reckless falsehood" to be able to assess damages against *Life* magazine.

It should be emphasized that Justice Brennan's opinion in Time v. Hill has not made truth an entirely dependable defense against a lawsuit for invasion of privacy. For one thing, the Supreme Court's adoption of the malice rule from New York Times v. Sullivan applies only to those privacy cases involving falsity. Furthermore, the Supreme Court was badly split in Time v. Hill; a five-Justice majority did vote in favor of *Life* magazine, but only two justices—Potter Stewart and Byron White—agreed with Brennan's use of the "Sullivan rule." Justices Hugo L. Black and William O. Douglas concurred in the decision, but on other grounds.

Brennan appeared to prize press freedom's benefits to society more than the individual's right to privacy.[40] And if incidental,

---

[39] 385 U.S. 374, 390–391, 87 S.Ct. 534, 543 (1967).

[40] See the dissent by Mr. Justice Abe Fortas, which was joined by Chief Justice Earl Warren and by Justice Tom C. Clark, 385 U.S. 374, 411, 416, 87 S.Ct. 534, 554, 556 (1967).

nonmalicious error crept into a story, that was part of the risk of freedom, for which a publication should not be held responsible. Justice Brennan wrote: [41]

> Exposure of the self to others in varying degrees is a concomitant of life in a civilized community. The risk of exposure is an essential incident of life in a society which places a primary value on freedom of speech and press.
>
> *   *   *   *   *   *   *   *   *
>
> Erroneous statement is no less inevitable in * * * [a case such as discussion of a new play] than in the case of comment upon public affairs, and in both, if innocent or merely negligent, * * * it must be protected if the freedoms of expression are to have the "breathing space" that they "need * * * to survive."
>
> *   *   *   *   *   *   *   *   *
>
> We create grave risk of serious impairment of the indispensable services of a free press in a free society if we saddle the press with the impossible burden of verifying to a certainty the acts associated in news articles with a person's name, picture or portrait, particularly as related to nondefamatory matter. Even negligence would be a most elusive standard * * *. A negligence test would place on the press the intolerable burden of guessing how a jury might assess the reasonableness of steps taken by it to verify the accuracy of every reference to a name, portrait or picture.

The "breathing space" mentioned by Justice Brennan—a phrase borrowed from New York Times v. Sullivan—indicated that the Court was giving the press a healthy "benefit of the doubt." Press freedom, Brennan declared, is essential to "the maintenance of our political system and an open society." Yet this freedom, he argued, could be dangerously invaded by lawsuits for libel or invasion of privacy.[42]

> Fear of large verdicts in damage suits for innocent or mere negligent misstatement, even fear of the expense involved in the defense, must inevitably cause publishers to "steer far wider of the unlawful zone."

Was the *Life* article done "for purposes of trade" under the terms of the New York statute? Or was it a legitimate, newsworthy job? Perhaps the best answer to these questions was giv-

[41] 385 U.S. 374, 388–389, 87 S.Ct. 534, 542–543 (1967).

[42] 385 U.S. 374, 389, 87 S.Ct. 534, 543 (1967).

en in a dissent at an earlier stage in the *Hill* case in New York's Supreme Court (an intermediate appellate court) by Presiding Judge Bernard Botein: [43]

> To hold * * * that a violation of Section 51 [of New York's Civil Rights Law] may be established by showing that a newsworthy item has been published solely to increase circulation injects an unrealistic ingredient into the complex of the right to privacy and would abridge dangerously the people's right to know. In the final analysis, the reading public, not the publisher, determines what is newsworthy, and what is newsworthy will perforce tend to increase circulation.

Despite the lower courts' contentions that the *Life* article was not legitimate news, but was fictionalized entertainment for purposes of trade, Justice Brennan quickly disposed of such arguments. "We have no doubt," Brennan wrote, "that the subject of the *Life* article, the opening of a new play linked to an actual incident, is a matter of public interest. 'The line between the informing and the entertaining is too elusive for the protection of * * * [freedom of the press]'." [44] Author Joseph Hayes had said that he did not consciously portray the Hill family's experience, but did admit that the Hills' ordeal "triggered" the writing of the book and the play. [45] Moreover, " 'That books, newspapers, and magazines are published and sold for profit does not prevent them from being a form of expression whose liberty is safeguarded by the First Amendment.' " [46]

Justice Brennan's language gave the longer-recognized right of freedom of the press precedence over the right of privacy. Even so, the concurring opinions of Justices Black and Douglas contained stinging assertions that Brennan had undervalued the liberty of the press. Black repeated his bitter disagreement with the "Sullivan rule:" "The words 'malicious' and particularly 'reckless disregard' can never serve as effective substitutes for the First Amendment words: ' * * * make no law * * * abridging the freedom of speech, or of the press * * *.' " [47] And Justice Douglas dismissed discussions of privacy as "ir-

43 Hill v. Hayes, 18 A.D.2d 485, 240 N.Y.S.2d 286, at 293 (1963).

44 385 U.S. 374, 388, 87 S.Ct. 534, 542 (1967), quoting Winters v. New York, 333 U.S. 507, 510, 68 S.Ct. 665, 667 (1948).

45 385 U.S. 374, 392–393, 87 S.Ct. 534, 544 (1967).

46 Quoting Joseph Burstyn, Inc. v. Wilson. 343 U.S. 495, 72 S.Ct. 777, 780 (1952).

47 385 U.S. 374, 398, 87 S.Ct. 534, 547 (1967). See also Justice Black's concurring opinion in New York Times v. Sullivan, 376 U.S. 254 at 293m, 84 S.Ct. 710 at 773 (1964).

relevant" in the context of Time v. Hill; the Hills' activities, he maintained, were fully in the public domain. "Once we narrow the ambit of the First Amendment, creative writing is imperiled and the 'chilling effect' on free expression * * * is almost sure to take place. That is, I fear, the result once we allow an exception for 'knowing or reckless falsity.' " [48]

Justice Abe Fortas, however, answered with a polished dissent complaining that the Court's majority "does not repeat the ringing words of so many of its members on so many occasions in exaltation of the right to privacy.[49]   Fortas added,[50]

> * * * First Amendment values are supreme and are entitled to at least the types of protection that this Court extended in New York Times v. Sullivan * * *.
>
> * * * * * * * * *
>
> For this Court totally to immunize the press—whether forthrightly or by subtle indirection—in areas far beyond the need of news, comment on public persons and events, discussion of public issues and the like would be no service to freedom of the press but an invitation to public hostility to that freedom. This Court cannot and should not refuse to permit under state law the citizen who is aggrieved by the type of assault which we have here and which is not within the specially protected core of the First Amendment to recover compensatory damages for recklessly inflicted invasion of his rights.

Fortas, in sum, did not believe that "the First Amendment precludes effective protection of the right of privacy—or, for that matter, an effective law of libel." [51]

Despite such recriminations, Justice Brennan's opinion carried the day. His opinion in Time v. Hill is rambling and hard to follow. Nevertheless, it is an important decision on several counts. First, this was the first case on the law of privacy involving the communications media which was decided by the Supreme Court. Second, the use of the malice rule from New York Times v. Sullivan—requiring proof that the defendant published material "with knowledge of its falsity or in reck-

---

[48] 385 U.S. 374, 401–402, 87 S.Ct. 534, 549 (1967).

[49] Fortas's dissent was joined by Chief Justice Warren and Justice Clark. 385 U.S. 374, 416, 87 S.Ct. 534, 556 (1967), citing Boyd v. United States, 116 U.S. 616, 630, 6 S.Ct. 524, 532 (1886); Mapp v. Ohio, 367 U.S. 643, 81 S.Ct. 1684 (1961); Griswold v. Connecticut, 381 U.S. 479, 85 S.Ct. 1678 (1965).

[50] 385 U.S. 374, 420, 87 S.Ct. 534, 559 (1967).

[51] 385 U.S. 374, 412, 87 S.Ct. 534, 554 (1967).

less disregard of the truth" [52] is highly significant. True, the Times v. Sullivan malice formula was to be applied "only in this discrete context." [53] But the context involved here appears to be in publications "of public interest," and not just political comment: [54]

> The guarantees for speech and press are not the preserve of political expression or comment upon public affairs, essential as those are to healthy government. One need only to pick up any newspaper or magazine to comprehend the vast range of published matter which exposes persons to public view, both private citizens and public officials.

A key question, of course, was how broadly the courts would construe the notion of "public interest." The central meaning of Time v. Hill is still emerging, and will become clearer only as the courts consider more privacy cases touching the mass media. Justice Brennan's majority opinion, for a severely divided court, must be considered only a beginning. But in this beginning, the Supreme Court cautiously extended constitutional guarantees of freedom of the press to law of privacy cases.

SEC. 36.   DEFENSES: NEWSWORTHINESS

The media's most useful defense against an invasion-of-privacy lawsuit is the concept of "newsworthiness."

The best defense in privacy cases is the concept of newsworthiness. What is news? While no two editors are apt to be able to agree on a definition of the term, courts, in numerous privacy cases, have attempted to present definitions of news and newsworthiness. But news has proved to be hard for courts to define too. One court has even called news "that indefinable quality of information which arouses public attention." Newsmen will often assert that "news is what we say it is" or that news is "whatever interests people." Fortunately for the media, where the defense of newsworthiness is concerned, the courts have tended to accept newsmen's definitions. [55]

---

[52] 385 U.S. 374, 393, 87 S.Ct. 534, 545 (1967). In a footnote, Justice Brennan added that it was for a jury, not for the Supreme Court, to determine whether there had been "knowing or reckless falsehood." Cf. New York Times Co. v. Sullivan, 376 U.S. 254, 284–285, 84 S.Ct. 710, 728–729 (1964).

[53] 385 U.S. 374, 391, 87 S.Ct. 534, 543 (1967).

[54] 385 U.S. 374, 388, 87 S.Ct. 534, 542 (1967).

[55] Sweenek v. Pathe News Co., 16 F.Supp. 746, 747 (D.C.N.Y.1936); Sidis v. F–R Pub. Co., 113 F.2d 806, 809 (2d Cir. 1940); Associated Press v. International News Service, 245 F. 244, 248 (2d Cir. 1917), affirmed 248 U.S. 215,

If an event falls within this loosely drawn concept of "newsworthiness"—in general, whatever interests the public—the media may be protected from successful privacy suits by the privilege to report the news. Here, the courts have reached a public policy which gives the media a kind of judicial benefit of the doubt. It has generally been held that news is what people *are* interested in, not what they *ought* to be interested in.[56]

Often, of course, people are caught up in the news when they would much rather retain the anonymity of private persons. But when an event is news, the courts have uniformly forbidden recovery for substantially accurate accounts of an event which is of public interest. A rather extreme case in point here involved the unfortunate John Jacova, who had bought a newspaper at a Miami Beach hotel's cigar counter. As Jacova innocently stood at the counter, police rushed into the hotel in a raid and mistook Jacova for a gambler. Jacova was taken into custody, but was released after he showed identification. Mr. Jacova was understandably annoyed, later in the day, to see himself on television being questioned by policemen. He sued the television station for invasion of privacy. He was not allowed to collect, however, because the court ruled that Jacova had become an "unwilling actor" in a news event.[57]

Mrs. Lillian Jones also—and much against her will—originated the "unwilling public figure" rule in a famous privacy case decided in 1929. Her husband was stabbed to death on a Louisville street in her presence. The Louisville *Herald-Post* published a picture of Mrs. Jones, and quoted her as saying of her husband's attackers: "I would have killed them." The court expressed sympathy and acknowledged the existence of a right to privacy, but added: [58]

> There are times, however, when one, whether willing or not, becomes an actor in an occurrence of public or general interest. When this takes place, he emerges from his seclusion and it is not an invasion of his right of privacy to publish his photograph with an account of such occurrence.

39 S.Ct. 68 (1918); Jenkins v. Dell Publishing Co., 251 F.2d 447, 451 (3d Cir. 1958).

56 Sidis v. F–R Publishing Co., 113 F.2d 806, 809 (2d Cir. 1940); Goelet v. Confidential, Inc., 5 A.D.2d 226, 230, 171 N.Y.S.2d 223, 227 (1958).

57 Jacova v. Southern Radio Television Co., 83 So.2d 34 (Fla.1955); see also Hubbard v. Journal Pub. Co., 69 N.M. 473, 368 P.2d 147 (1962); Elmhurst v. Pearson, 80 U.S.App.D.C. 372, 153 F.2d 467 (1946).

58 Jones v. Herald-Post Co., 230 Ky. 227, 18 S.W.2d 972 (1929).

As indicated earlier in this chapter in the discussion of Hubbard v. Journal Publishing Co.—the case in which a newspaper printed a court record saying that a girl had been sexually attacked by her brother—proof that the media have published a substantially accurate account of a public record will defeat a privacy lawsuit. In cases such as *Hubbard*, the courts have had to distinguish between legitimate news accounts which are in the public interest and the individual's right to privacy.

Such a case arose in Minneapolis in the late 1940s when the Minneapolis *Times* covered a sensational divorce trial and the related child custody hearings. Photographers took pictures of the husband, the wife, and the children during a break in the hearings, and the newspaper also published a story on the trial and the custody hearings. Carl A. Berg brought suit for invasion of privacy, although he admitted that the newspaper had been accurate in what it published. In finding for the newspaper, the judge ruled: [59]

> Undoubtedly * * * the courts should recognize the rights of privacy of the individual on one hand, and the rights of the press to disseminate news and the rights of the public to obtain legitimate news from the newspapers in their community on the other. When one assumes to determine what constitutes legitimate news, it is undoubtedly true that there may be a wide and marked diversity of opinion as to what should be so designated. Some people would like to see newspapers refrain from publishing any items of news regarding the intimacies disclosed in divorce cases or any salacious testimony divulged in matters before the courts, contending that, as stated by Warren and Brandeis, they only seem to satisfy a "prurient taste." Others feel that the public interest is such that citizens have a right to be informed as to that which takes place in the community, especially at a public trial, and if the news is true and not libelous, fit to print and newsworthy, it should be published.
>
> *   *   *   *   *   *   *   *   *
>
> Plaintiff probably does not fully appreciate that, through the force of circumstances, he was required to throw aside the mantle of privacy * * * in his divorce proceedings and his attempt to retain the custody of his children * * *. But the undeniable fact is

[59] Berg v. Minneapolis Star & Tribune Co., 79 F.Supp. 957, 960–962 (D.C. Minn.1949).

that he had made public the most intimate and indeed scandalous occurrences of his domestic life and had spread them on the public records of a court of his choosing, and, in so doing, he departed from his "quiet peaceable life free from the prying curiosity and unmitigated gossip which accompanies fame, notoriety and scandal" and in a sense became a quasi-public figure in the community * * *.

Certainly, this court should proceed with caution before it attempts to sit as a censor and to interfere with the traditional right of the press to print all printable news which appears in the public records of our courts * * *. [T]here are many people in the immediate community where the action is pending who look to the press for all such details, and it does not seem to avail that the more intelligent public deprecates that such details "usurp the place of interest in brains capable of other things." P. 196, 4 *Harvard Law Review.*

Moreover, it cannot be controverted that there is a widespread interest in this very kind of news and perhaps it is not strange that it should be so. Most people are interested in the weather because it generally concerns all classes of people. Domestic disputes, controversies between parents and others as to the custody of minor children, allowances of alimony, and the various acts and conduct recognized by the courts as grounds for divorce, are probably of interest to a large number of people because in their own immediate lives, to a greater or less degree, such problems have concerned their friends and acquaintances and sometimes their own immediate families.

*   *   *   *   *   *   *   *   *

[T]he publication of Berg's picture in connection with the legitimate news was within the scope of the accepted prerogatives assumed by the press, which is charged with the responsibility of furnishing news to the public.

If unwilling public figures have been so treated by the courts in privacy lawsuits, what of people who seek fame, public office, or otherwise *willingly* bring themselves to public notice? Public figures have been held to have given up, to some extent, their right to be "let alone." Persons who have sought publicity—actors, explorers, or politicians to give a few examples—have made themselves "news" and have parted with some of their privacy. In one case, a suit by a former husband of movie star Janet Leigh was unsuccessful despite his protestations that he had done everything he could to avoid publicity. Her fame rubbed off on him.[60]

Even so, when the media go "too far," celebrities can bring successful privacy lawsuits. The taking of a name of a public figure, for example, to advertise a commercial product without his consent would be actionable. Also, even newsworthy public figures can collect damages when fictionalized statements are published about them. Some areas of life are sufficiently personal and private that the media may intrude only at their peril. Private sexual relationships, homes, bank accounts, and private letters of an individual would all seem to be in a danger zone for the press.[61]

One way in which the privilege of newsworthiness is sometimes attacked in court involves the passage of time since an event was first reported. This argument runs that although an event may have been legitimate news when it occurred, say five years ago, the story is now out of the public eye and cannot be legitimately revived. A case in which a time lapse of seven years was crucial was the famed "Red Kimono" case discussed earlier in this chapter, Melvin v. Reid. Gabrielle Darley Melvin, the reformed prostitute, had been acquitted of a murder charge in 1918, and the movie, based upon her involvement in the "Red Kimono" murder trial, was brought out in 1925.[62] The time lapse argument, however, used by itself, almost uniformly has failed to rebut a defense of newsworthiness. But when a time lapse argument is coupled with a publication's dredging up a reformed ex-convict's 11-year-old misadventure as a truck hijacker, as in Briscoe v. Reader's Digest discussed earlier in this chapter, time lapse may be part of a privacy suit.[63]

[60] Carlisle v. Fawcett Publications, 201 Cal.App.2d 733, 20 Cal.Rptr. 405 (1962).

[61] See Garner v. Triangle Publications, 97 F.Supp. 546 (D.C.N.Y.1951); Bazemore v. Savannah Hospital, 171 Ga. 257, 155 S.E. 194 (1930); Baker v. Libbie, 210 Mass. 599, 97 N.E. 109 (1912); Pope v. Curll, 2 Atk., 341, 26 Eng. Rep. 608 (1741).

[62] 112 Cal. 285, 297 P. 91 (1931). However, more than mere time-lapse was involved in this decision. This case suggested that re-creating events might have been permissible, but that the unnecessary use of the name "Gabrielle Darley" in advertising and in the movie itself was not to be tolerated. More innocuous subject matter, however, has since been dealt with more leniently by the courts. See, e. g., Sidis v. F–R Pub. Corp., 113 F.2d 806 (2d Cir. 1940); Smith v. Doss, 251 Ala. 250, 37 So.2d 118 (1948); Smith v. NBC, 138 Cal.App. 2d 807, 292 P.2d 600 (1956).

[63] Briscoe v. Reader's Digest Ass'n, 4 Cal.3d 529, 93 Cal.Rptr. 866, 483 P.2d 34 (1971).

Even after Time, Inc. v. Hill, the newsworthiness of a publication will not always protect the publisher. The protection of newsworthiness may vanish suddenly if a careless or misleading caption is placed on a picture. Consider the case of Holmes v. Curtis Publishing Company.

"MAFIA: SHADOW OF EVIL ON AN ISLAND IN THE SUN" screamed the headline on a feature story in the February 25, 1967 issue of the *Saturday Evening Post*. Published along with the article was a picture of James Holmes and four other persons at a gambling table, evidently playing blackjack. This picture was captioned, "High-Rollers at Monte Carlo have dropped as much as $20,000 in a single night. The U. S. Department of Justice estimates that the Casino grosses $20 million a year, and that one-third is skimmed off for American Mafia 'families.' "

Holmes objected to publication of this article, and sued for libel and invasion of privacy, arguing that the picture and caption had placed him in a false light. Holmes was not mentioned by name in the article, but he was, however, the focal point of the photograph. A United States district court in South Carolina noted that the article dealt with subjects of great public interest—organized crime, the growth of tourism in the Bahama Islands, and legalized gambling.

The court refused to grant the Curtis Publishing Company's motions that the libel and privacy lawsuits by Holmes could not stand because of precedents such as New York Times Co. v. Sullivan [64] and Time, Inc. v. Hill.[65] Instead, the court declared that the libel and privacy issues would have to go to trial: [66]

> Certainly defendant's caption is reasonably capable of amounting to a defamation, for one identified as a high-stakes gambler or having a connection with the Mafia would certainly be injured in his business, occupation, and/or reputation.

> As to plaintiff's action for privacy, there appears no question that if it were not for defendant's caption beneath plaintiff's photograph, this court would be justified in dismissing plaintiff's invasion of privacy cause of action. But such is not the case. Conflicting inferences also arise from the record as it stands today which preclude disposition of this cause of action summarily.

[64] 376 U.S. 254, 84 S.Ct. 710 (1964).

[65] 385 U.S. 374, 87 S.Ct. 534 (1967).

[66] Holmes v. Curtis Pub. Co., 303 F.Supp. 522, 527 (D.C.S.C.1969).

Unwilling subjects of photographs or motion pictures caused considerable activity in the law of privacy in the wake of Time, Inc. v. Hill. Consider the case of Frank Man, a professional musician who made the scene at the Woodstock Festival in Bethel, N. Y. in August of 1969. At someone's request, Man clambered onto the stage and played "Mess Call" on his Flugelhorn to an audience of movie cameras and 400,000 people. Subsequently, Warner Bros., Inc. produced and exhibited a movie under the title of "Woodstock." Man claimed that the producers and distributors of the film included his performance without his consent, and brought suit in New York against Warner Bros.

A United States District Court said: [67]

> The film depicts, without the addition of any fictional material, actual events which happened at the festival. Nothing is staged and nothing is false. * * *
>
> There can be no question that the Woodstock festival was and is a matter of valid public interest.

Man argued that a movie depicting Woodstock could no longer be treated as news because of the lapse of time. The court replied that "the bizarre happenings of the festival were not mere fleeting news but sensational events of deep and lasting public interest." The court concluded that Frank Man, by his own volition had placed himself in the spotlight at a sensational event. He had made himself newsworthy, and thus deprived himself of any right to collect for invasion of privacy.[68]

It should not, however, be inferred that all factual reports of current events have been—or will be—held absolutely privileged. Film Producer Wiseman produced a film—"The Titicut Follies" —which showed conditions in a mental hospital, with individuals identifiable. The film showed naked inmates, forced feeding, masturbation and sadism, and the court concluded that Wiseman's film had—by identifying individuals—gone beyond the consent which mental hospital authorities had given him to make the film. The film was taken out of commercial distribution, but was not destroyed. The court ruled that the film was of educational value, and that it could be shown to special audiences such as groups of social workers, or others who might be moved to work toward improving conditions in mental hospitals.[69]

---

[67] 317 F.Supp. 51, 53 (D.C.N.Y.1970).

[68] Ibid.

[69] Commonwealth v. Wiseman, 356 Mass. 251, 249 N.E.2d 610 (1969). See also Daily Times Democrat v. Graham, 276 Ala. 380, 162 So.2d 474 (1964), where a woman collected for invasion of privacy after a newspaper used her identifiable picture as she emerged from a "fun house" where a jet of air blew her dress above her waist.

The defense of newsworthiness seems to have been greatly strengthened by courts' reliance on Time, Inc. v. Hill. The potency of the concept of newsworthiness may be seen in the outcome of a privacy lawsuit against Life magazine by two young travelers to Europe. During the summer of 1968, Life magazine ran a cover story picturing Rick Heckler and Cathy Goldman, with the captions "Young American Nomads Abroad" and "Two Californians at home in a cave in Crete." [70] Inside the magazine appeared an article entitled "CRETE: A STOP IN THE NEW ODYSSEY," subtitled, "A restless generation of U. S. youth roams abroad." The article's pictures showed people in and around the caves of Matola, Crete, making their homes in the caves. One picture showed Rick Heckler and Cathy Goldman, dressed in bathing suits, sitting in front of their cave. Life reporter Thomas Thompson's 5,000 word story included these paragraphs referring to Mr. Heckler and Ms. Goldman: [71]

> Rick Heckler, who was a champion sprinter at San Diego State, took a degree in English and then wondered what on earth it was good for, told me [Reporter Thompson] how it happened with him: "Four of us decided to open a restaurant in California at Big Bear Lake. We found an old place and cleaned it up, fixed it up—I mean from top to bottom—and we got our liquor license and we were going great. Then one of our partners—a Rhodes Scholar candidate by the way—got busted for smoking grass. They took away our liquor license and the restaurant folded.

> Rick's dream folded, too. So rather than try a new one, he and his girl, Cathy Goldman, 20, left America to wander.

> "Are you going back?"

> Shrugs. "Maybe," Rick said.

Plaintiffs Heckler and Goldman contended that they had been given the impression that Thompson was doing a travelog rather than an article on disenchanted American youth, and that they never expected to be front-page attractions. Further, and perhaps more important, they objected to the light in which the article placed them. They argued that the implied association with drug-users, draft-dodgers and "others of social opprobrium" subjected them to ridicule, shame and disgust by their community. They added that they had been on the island of Crete only two

[70] Life, July 19, 1968.

[71] Goldman v. Time, Inc., 336 F.Supp. 133, 135 (D.C.Cal.1971).

days when they first talked with reporter Thompson, and that they always intended to return to America after their travels overseas.

Rick Heckler and Cathy Goldman sued Life magazine under the "false light category" of privacy, but to no avail. Awarding the defendant magazine a summary judgment, Judge Knox wrote: [72]

It is now unquestioned that the *New York Times* rule, requiring plaintiff in a libel-type action to show actual malice, includes matters of newsworthiness or public interest, even where the plaintiff is not a public official or public figure. As the Court held recently in Rosenbloom v. Metromedia, 403 U.S. 29, 43–44, 91 S.Ct. 1811, 1819–1820, 29 L.Ed.2d 296 (1971):

"If a matter is a subject of public or general interest, it cannot suddenly become less so merely because a private individual is involved, or because in some sense the individual did not 'voluntarily' choose to become involved. The public's primary interest is in the event; the public focus is on the conduct of the participant and the content, effect, and significance of the conduct, not the participant's prior anonymity or notoriety. * * * We honor the commitment to robust debate on public issues, which is embodied in the First Amendment, by extending constitutional protection to all discussion and communication involving matters of public or general concern, without regard to whether the persons involved are famous or anonymous. [Footnotes omitted.]"

*   *   *   *   *   *   *   *   *

* * * "false light" claims are to be treated by the same standard; a plaintiff cannot avoid the impact of the *New York Times* rule merely by labelling his action as one for invasion of privacy rather than libel. See Time, Inc. v. Hill * * *

Youth's disenchantment—and travels and living abroad—was held to be of current interest and newsworthy, and the Life article in question presented facts about a significant segment of the American population. Plaintiffs Goldman and Heckler, the court added, could not have expected much privacy, in view of the tourism on Crete and the public nature of the caves in which they had taken up residence. Finally, they did not resist, "and in fact made themselves readily available for both the text and

[72] Ibid., pp. 137–138.

photographs which eventually appeared in the Life magazine article.[73]

Judge Knox said that in a "false light" privacy action, as in a libel case, there is [74]

> * * * a constitutionally required showing of clearly convincing actual malice on the part of the person or persons responsible for publishing the allegedly defamatory [or privacy invading] article. Such actual malice cannot be found simply from the language of the article alone * * * but must amount to the printing of a knowing falsehood or the printing of such matter with a reckless disregard for whether it is false or not. Reckless disregard is not measured by what a reasonably prudent person would have published or would have investigated before publishing. Rather, there must be sufficient evidence for the conclusion that the party responsible for publication in fact entertained serious doubts as to the truth of the published matter.

Because plaintiffs Goldman and Heckler were unable to show such "actual malice," their lawsuit failed.

SEC. 37.   DEFENSES: CONSENT

If a person has consented to have his privacy invaded, he cannot later sue to collect damages for that invasion.

In addition to *newsworthiness*, another important defense to a lawsuit for invasion of privacy is *consent*. Logically enough, if a person has consented to have his privacy invaded, he should not be allowed to sue for the invasion. As Warren and Brandeis wrote in their 1890 *Harvard Law Review* article, "The right to privacy ceases upon the publication of the facts by the individual or with his consent." [75]

The defense of consent, however, poses some difficulties. To make this defense stand up, it must be *pleaded* and *proved* by the defendant. An important rule here is that the *consent* must be as broad as the invasion.

A young man had consented to have his picture taken in the doorway of a shop, supposedly discussing the World Series. But the youth was understandably chagrined when *Front Page Detective* used this photograph to illustrate a story titled "Gang Boy."

[73] Ibid., p. 139.

[74] Ibid., p. 139.

[75] Warren and Brandeis, op. cit., p. 218.

The Supreme Court of New York allowed the young man to recover damages, holding that consent to one thing is not consent to another. In other words, when a photograph is used for a purpose not intended by the person who consented, that person may be able to collect damages for invasion of privacy.[76]

In the case of Russell v. Marboro Books, a professional model was held to have a suit for invasion of privacy despite the fact that she had signed a release. (In the states which have privacy statutes—New York, Oklahoma, Utah and Virginia—prior consent in writing is required before a person's name or picture can be used in advertising or "for purposes of trade.") Miss Russell, at a picture-taking session, had signed a printed release form:

MODEL RELEASE

The undersigned hereby irrevocably consents to the unrestricted use by * * * [photographer's name], advertisers, customers, successors and assigns of my name, portrait, or picture, for advertising purposes or purposes of trade, and I waive the right to inspect or approve such completed portraits, pictures or advertising matter used in connection therewith * * *.

Miss Russell maintained that her job as a model involved portraying an "intelligent, refined, well-bred, pulchritudinous, ideal young wife and mother in artistic settings and socially approved situations." Her understanding was that the picture was to depict a wife in bed with her "husband"—also a model—in bed beside her, reading. Marboro books did use the pictures in an advertisement, with the caption "For People Who Take Their Reading Seriously." Thus far, there was no invasion of privacy to which Miss Russell had not consented.

Marboro Books, however, sold the photograph to Springs Mills, Inc., a manufacturer of bed sheets which enjoyed a reputation for publishing spicy ads. The photo was retouched so that the title of the book Miss Russell was reading appeared to be *Clothes Make the Man*, a book which had been banned as pornographic. The advertisement suggested that the book should be consulted for suitable captions, and also suggested captions such as "Lost Weekend" and "Lost Between the Covers." The court held that Miss Russell had an action for invasion of privacy despite the unlimited release that she had signed. Such a release, the court reasoned, would not stand up "if the picture were altered sufficiently in situation, emphasis, background, or context * * *

---

[76] Metzger v. Dell Publishing Co., 207 Misc.2d 182, 136 N.Y.S.2d 888 (1955).

liability would accrue where the content of the picture had been so changed that it is substantially unlike the original." [77]

Even if a signed release is in one's possession, it would be well to make sure that the release is still valid. In a Louisiana case, a man had taken a body-building course in a health studio. This man had agreed to have "before" and "after" photos taken of his physique, showing the plaintiff's body in trunks. But 10 years later, the health studio used the pictures in an ad. The court held that privacy had been invaded. [78]

Also, it would be well to make sure that you have explicit consent. On occasion, courts have found that the circumstances of a publication were such that there was *implied consent*. One such instance was when a person published a personal letter himself, and then sued to prevent further publication of the letter. The court held that the man had forfeited his right to prevent the letter's appearing in another publication. [79]

The best rule is this: make sure that the consent or release is broad and explicit enough to cover any invasion of privacy which might be claimed. A casual, offhand consent may be taken back at any time before publication actually takes place. Even celebrities such as movie stars have brought suit when they felt that their performances had been put to uses which they did not intend. Comedienne Beatrice Lillie, for example, sued Warner Bros. Pictures, contending that her contract with the company did not include the use of her performances in "short subjects." However, the court held that Miss Lillie's consent to such use of the film was included in her contract. [80] Similarly, actor Douglas Fairbanks Sr. was defeated in an attempt to control the use of one of his films. The court decided that Fairbanks had given up control of the film. However, he could have had an action for damages if the film had been so garbled that Fairbanks' reputation was impaired. [81]

When a defendant does not have consent and does invade someone's privacy, good intentions are not a defense. It may be pleaded that the defendant honestly believed that he had consent, but this can do no more than to mitigate punitive damages. [82] Some of the consequences of a publication's not getting a clear and spe-

---

[77] Russell v. Marboro Books, Inc., 18 Misc.2d 166, 183 N.Y.S.2d 8 (1955).

[78] McAndrews v. Roy, 131 So.2d 256 (La.App.1961).

[79] Widdemer v. Hubbard, 19 Phil. 263 (Pa.1887), cited in Hofstadter and Horowitz, op. cit., p. 75.

[80] Lillie v. Warner Bros. Pictures, 139 Cal.App. 724, 728, 34 P.2d 835 (1934).

[81] Fairbanks v. Winik, 119 Misc. 809, 198 N.Y.S. 299, 301 (1922).

[82] Barber v. Time, Inc., 348 Mo. 119, 159 S.W.2d 291, 293 (1942).

cific consent from persons whose pictures were used in a magazine article may be seen in the case of Raible v. Newsweek. According to Eugene L. Raible, a Newsweek photographer visited his home in 1969, and asked to take a picture of Mr. Raible and his children in their yard for use in "a patriotic article." Then, the October 6, 1969, issue of that magazine featured an article—which was headlined on the cover, "The Troubled American—A Special Report on the White Majority." [83] Newsweek did use Mr. Raible's picture (with his children cropped out of it); he was wearing an open sport shirt and standing next to a large American flag mounted on a pole on his lawn. The article ran for many pages thereafter, with such marginal headlines as "You'd better watch out, the common man is standing up," and "Many think the blacks live by their own set of rules." [84] Mr. Raible sued for libel and for invasion of privacy.

Although Raible's name was not used in the story, the court said it was readily understandable that his friends and neighbors in Wilkinsburg, Pa., might consider him to be typical of the "square Americans" discussed in the article. Raible argued that his association with the article meant that he was being portrayed as a " * * * typical 'Troubled American,' a person considered 'angry, uncultured, crude, violence prone, hostile to both rich and poor, and racially prejudiced.' " [85]

District Judge William W. Knox granted *Newsweek* a summary judgment, thus dismissing Mr. Raible's libel claims. Judge Knox declared that since the article indicated that the views expressed are those of the white majority of the United States—of whom Mr. Raible was one—"then we would have to conclude that the article, if libelous, libels more than half of the people in the United States and not plaintiff in particular." [86]

Judge Knox declared, however, that Mr. Raible's invasion of privacy lawsuit appeared to stand on firmer ground. Directing that Raible's privacy lawsuit go to trial, Judge Knox wrote: [87]

> It is true that if plaintiff [Raible] consented to the use
> of his photograph in connection with *this article,* he
> would have waived his right of action for invasion of
> privacy. However, it would appear to the court that

[83] Raible v. Newsweek, Inc., 341 F.Supp. 804, 806, 809 (1972).

[84] Ibid., p. 805.

[85] Ibid., p. 806. See also De Salvo v. Twentieth Century Fox Film Corp., 300 F.Supp. 742 (D.C.Mass.1969).

[86] Ibid., p. 807.

[87] Ibid., p. 809.

the burden of proof is upon the defendant to show just what plaintiff consented to and the varying inferences from this testimony will have to be resolved by the trier of facts.

SEC. 38.   DEFENSES: LIMITATIONS AND PROBLEMS

Privacy is a new region of law which has seen much unplanned, chaotic growth in recent years in the areas of tort and constitutional law.   Complexities and confusions in the law affect defenses to privacy lawsuits.

Journalists should not take too much comfort in the defenses of newsworthiness and consent.   Although the courts have generally been most lenient in their interpretation of what constitutes a "newsworthy" story, the press has reason to be concerned. The concept of "newsworthiness" could prove to be so elastic that it might be dangerously subject to the whims of a judge or jury.   Although it must be emphasized that the courts have been careful lest their definitions of "news" and "public interest" become too restrictive, the fact remains that courts have what amounts to a power of censorship in deciding privacy cases.

Privacy is a new area of law, and has not had the centuries of trial-and-error development that attended the law of defamation. This relative newness is a great source of privacy law's danger for the media.   Over time, defenses to defamation were built up: for one thing, truth was made a defense.   And where slander is concerned, "special damages"—actual monetary loss—must generally be proved before a plaintiff can collect.   Where retraction statutes are in force, a plaintiff must prove special damages once a fair and full apology for the defamation has been published.[88]   But with the law of privacy, the media do not have such shields.   In only one of the privacy tort sub-groups discussed above—"putting plaintiff in a false position in the public eye"—would truth be a defense to a privacy action.   Also, a publication need not be defamatory to invade someone's privacy.

Small wonder, then, that some eminent scholars have viewed the law of privacy as a threat to freedom of the press.   Professor William L. Prosser has suggested that the law of privacy, in many respects, comes "into head-on collision with the constitutional guaranty of freedom of the press," and that privacy law

---

[88] When the fact situation giving rise to a privacy action also involves defamation, retraction statutes have been held to apply.   Werner v. Times-Mirror Co., 193 Cal.App.2d 111, 14 Cal.Rptr. 208 (1961).

may be "capable of swallowing up and engulfing the whole law of public defamation." [89]

If, for example, a newspaper were to be sued for *both* libel and invasion of privacy for the same article, difficulties in making a defense hold up might well arise. If the publication were defamatory, the newspaper might be able to plead and prove truth as a defense. But proving truth would not halt the privacy suit unless the article had to do with "putting plaintiff in a false position in the public eye." It would be possible, if a plaintiff alleged that a newspaper printed "embarrassing private facts," that proving the truth of an article might encourage a sympathetic jury to find against the newspaper for invasion of privacy.

This means that an article containing no defamation, based on true facts, and published with the best of intentions or through an innocent mistake could be the basis for a successful invasion of privacy lawsuit. If, indeed, it becomes easier to collect for an invasion of privacy suit than for a defamation action, it has been suggested that privacy suits may supplant libel actions.[90]

The foregoing discussion has concentrated on invasion of privacy as a tort. Privacy, however, is protected not only by tort law—where individuals may sue if their privacy is invaded. Since 1960, privacy has become a constitutional right, a right which to some extent protects citizens from intrusions by government or police agencies.[91]

[89] Prosser, Handbook of the Law of Torts, 3d. ed., p. 844; 4th ed. (1971), pp. 815–816; "Privacy," 48 California Law Review 383, 401 (1960).

[90] John W. Wade, "Defamation and the Right of Privacy," 15 Vanderbilt Law Review 1093, 1121 (1962); Prosser, "Privacy," *loc. cit.*

[91] See, e. g., Mapp v. Ohio, 367 U.S. 643, 81 S.Ct. 1684 (1961); Griswold v. Connecticut, 381 U.S. 479, 85 S.Ct. 1678 (1965).

Chapter 7

COPYRIGHT

SEC. 39. DEVELOPMENT OF COPYRIGHT LAW

Copyright is the right to control or profit from a literary, artistic, or intellectual production.

Mark Twain once declared that whenever copyright law was to be made or altered, then all the idiots assembled. Twain's harsh judgment was obviously formed by the fact that he was badly burned in several copyright disputes. Many years later, it may be ruefully admitted that as much as any body of law dealing with communications, the part of the law of literary property known as copyright needs to be modernized and clarified.

The basic federal copyright statute became law in 1909. It is sadly and perhaps hopelessly out-of-date, and amendments since 1909 have given little recognition to the enormous changes in technology since 1909.[1] Radio and motion pictures were then little more than novelty items or scientific curiosities. The gigantic scope of developments in the film industry, in telecommunications, and in computers was, of course, unforeseen by men in Congress who drafted the Copyright Act of 1909.

Repeated attempts have been made in Congress to revise the copyright law, including massive efforts by Congressional committees during the 1960s. These endeavors have been to little avail at this writing, but at least groundwork has been laid for needed revisions. One of the leaders in Congress working for copyright law revision, Representative Robert Kastenmeier of

---

[1] 17 U.S.C.A. §§ 1–216 (1964).

235

Wisconsin, has indicated some of the labyrinthine problems of this field of law.

Congress, as Kastenmeier has pointed out, is faced with an information and communication explosion of unimaginable proportions. Discussing a pending copyright revision bill, Kastenmeier said:[2]

> To relate the term information explosion to the great wealth of ideas and material embraced by the Copyright Revision bill, I think it must be understood to refer primarily to a communication explosion rather than solely an information explosion as currently identified with the developing computerized information disseminating technology. That surely is part of it, but it is only the latest manifestation of the broader communication explosion we have been experiencing since entering the 20th Century—* * *

> Today the patent and copyright systems face a critical dilemma. The great and growing proliferation of information—and of techniques for its dissemination—taxes our capacity to manage the systems. Meanwhile, the Federal Government's increasing involvement in research and development and in publishing further complicates the picture. We are warned, and it seems evident, that a collective national appraisal of our situation is imperative if we are to avoid structural and relational changes in our economy that are neither planned nor wanted, but that may be on their way.

> *   *   *   *   *   *   *   *   *

> The history of the pending copyright revision dramatically reflects our failure to keep the law abreast of economic and technological developments. The first copyright law, like the first patent law, was enacted in 1790. The third and most recent occurred in 1909. In that year, motion pictures and sound recordings had just made their appearance and radio was still in the early stages of development. Since that time significant changes in technology have affected the operation of the copyright law. A wide range of new techniques for communication information in the form of print, pictures, and sound have come into use. Television,

---

[2] Congressman Robert W. Kastenmeier, "The Information Explosion and Copyright Law Revision," Remarks before the American Patent Law Association, Sheraton Park Hotel, Washington, D. C., Jan. 24, 1967. Reprinted by permission.

computers and communications satellites have entered
the field. Entire new industries have appeared, using
new methods of reproduction, communication and distribution.

Despite concern about what copyright law might become,
the emphasis here must be with copyright law as it exists at
this writing.

Copyright Defined

Black's Law Dictionary defines copyright as: [3]

> The right of literary property as recognized and sanc-
> tioned by positive law. An intangible, incorporeal right
> granted by statute to the author or originator of certain
> literary or artistic productions, whereby he is invested,
> for a limited period, with the sole and exclusive priv-
> ilege of multiplying copies of the same and publishing
> and selling them.
>
> *   *   *   *   *   *   *   *   *
>
> International copyright is the right of a subject of one
> country to protection against the republication in an-
> other country of a work which he originally published
> in his own country.

Such definitions aside, journalists must have a basic understanding of this complicated, frustrating area of the law. Perhaps this area of law is so complex because it draws authority
from a number of bases: Anglo-American literary history and
common law, state and federal laws, court decisions, plus Article
I, Section 8 of the Constitution of the United States :[4]

> The Congress shall have power   *   *   *   to promote
> the Progress of Science and useful Arts by securing for
> limited Times to Authors and Inventors the exclusive
> Right to their respective Writings and Discoveries.

Passage of the first federal copyright statute as early as 1790
indicates that America's Revolutionary generation had a lively
concern about the need for copyright protection. Additional
copyright statutes were enacted during the 19th century.[5]

Underlying the words of the Fourth Amendment was the
principle of copyright, which had been known since ancient

[3] Black's Law Dictionary, Revised 4th ed. (St. Paul, Minn., West Publishing
Co., 1968) p. 406.

[4] Benjamin Kaplan and Ralph S. Brown, Jr., Cases on Copyright (Brooklyn,
Foundation Press, 1960) pp. 22–52.

[5] Thorvald Solberg, Copyright Enactments of the United States, 1783–1906.
Washington, 1906.

times. It is known that the Republic of Venice in 1469 granted John of Speyer the exclusive right to print the letters of Pliny and Cicero for a period of five years.[6]

The development of printing increased the need for some form of copyright. Although printing from movable types began in 1451 and although Caxton introduced printing into England in about 1476, the first copyright law was not passed in England until 1709 in the "Statute of 8 Anne." Before this time, the printing business was influenced in two distinct ways. First, printing gave royalty and government in England the opportunity to reward favored individuals with exclusive printing monopolies. Second, those in power recognized that printing, unless strictly controlled, tended to endanger their rule.

Hoping to control the output of the printing presses, Queen Mary I granted a charter to the Stationers Company in 1556. The Stationers Company, a guild of printers, was thus given a monopoly on book printing. Simultaneously these printers were given the authority to burn prohibited books and to jail the persons who published them.[7] The Stationers Company acted zealously against printers of unauthorized works, making use of terrifying powers of search and seizure. Tactics paralleling those of the Inquisition were used defending the doctrines of the Catholic Church against the burgeoning Reformation movement.[8]

The Stationers Company remained powerful into the seventeenth century, with its authority augmented by licensing statutes. The Act of 1662, for example, confined printing to 59 master printer members of the Stationers Company then practicing in London, and to the printers at Oxford and Cambridge Universities. The privileged position of the Stationers' Company in England during the sixteenth and seventeenth centuries underlies the development of the law of copyright of more recent times. Printers who were officially sanctioned to print by virtue of membership in the Stationers Company complained when their works were issued in pirated editions by unauthorized printers.[9]

6 R. C. DeWolf, Outline of Copyright Law (Boston: John W. Luce, 1925) p. 2.

7 Philip Wittenberg, The Law of Literary Property (New York: World Publishing Co., 1957), pp. 25–26; Fredrick S. Siebert, Freedom of the Press in England, 1476–1776 (Urbana: University of Illinois Press, 1952) pp. 22, 65, 249.

8 Siebert, op. cit., pp. 82–86; Mrs. Edward S. Lazowska, "Photocopying, Copyright, and the Librarian," American Documentation (April, 1968) pp. 123–130.

9 Siebert, pp. 74–77, 239.

In time the guild printers who belonged to the Stationers Company began to recognize a principle now known as "common law copyright." They began to assume that there was a common law right, *in perpetuity*, to literary property. That is, if a man printed a book, duly approved by government authority, the right to profit from its distribution remained with that man, or his heirs, forever.[10]

Authors, like England's printers, came to believe that they also had some rights to profit from their works. Authors joined printers in the latter half of the seventeenth century in seeking Parliamentary legislation to establish the existence of copyright. In 1709, Parliament passed the Statute of 8 Anne, believed to have been drafted, in part, by two famed authors, Joseph Addison and Jonathan Swift. This statute recognized the author's rights, giving him—or his heirs or persons to whom he might sell his rights—exclusive powers to publish the book for 14 years after its first printing. If the author were still alive after those 14 years, he could renew his copyright for an additional 14 years.[11]

This limitation of copyright to a total of 28 years displeased both authors and printers. They complained for many years that they should have copyright in perpetuity, forever, under the common law. In 1774, the House of Lords, acting in its capacity of a court of highest appeal, decided the case of Donaldson v. Beckett.

This 1774 decision is of enormous importance to American law, because it outlined the two categories of copyrights, *statutory copyright* and *common law copyright*. The House of Lords ruled that the Statute of 8 Anne, providing a limited 28 year term of copyright protection, had superseded the common law protection for *published* works. Only *unpublished* works, therefore, could receive common law copyright protection in perpetuity. An author was to have automatic, limitless common law copyright protection for his creations only as long as they remained unpublished. But once publication occurred, the author or publisher could have exclusive right to publish and profit from his works for only a limited period of time as decreed by legislative authority. The Statute of 8 Anne, as upheld by the House of Lords in Donaldson v. Beckett, is the progenitor of modern copyright legislation in the United States.[12]

---

10 Wittenberg, op. cit., pp. 45–46.

11 Siebert, op. cit., p. 249; Wittenberg, Ibid., pp. 47–48.

12 4 Burr. 2408 (1774); Lazowska, op. cit., p. 124.

When the first federal copyright statute was adopted in the United States in 1790, implementing Article I, Section 8 of the Constitution, it gave the federal government *statutory* authority to administer copyrights. Since there is no common law authority for federal courts, questions involving *common law* copyright have remained to be adjudicated in state courts.[13] In the 1834 case of Wheaton v. Peters, the Supreme Court of the United States enunciated the doctrine of common law copyright in America:[14]

> That an author at common law has a property right in his manuscript, and may obtain redress against any one who endeavors to realize a profit by its publication, cannot be doubted; but this is a very different right from that which asserts a perpetual and exclusive property in the future publication of the work, after the author shall have published it to the world.

Before launching into more detailed discussion of common law and statutory copyright, consider the following three principles:

1) *Facts or ideas cannot be copyrighted.*

Copyright applies only to the literary style of an article, news story, book, or other intellectual creation. It does *not* apply to the themes, ideas, or facts contained in the copyrighted material. Anyone may write about any subject. Copyright's protection extends only to the particular manner or style of expression. What is "copyrightable" in the print media, for example, is the order and selection of words, phrases, clauses, sentences, and the arrangement of paragraphs.[15]

2) *Copyright is both a protection for and a restriction of the communications media.*

Copyright protects the media by preventing the wholesale taking of the form of materials, without permission, from one person or unit of the media for publication by another person or unit of the media. Despite the guaranty of freedom of the press, newspapers and other communications media must acquire permission to publish material that is protected either by common law

---

[13] Wheaton v. Peters, 33 U.S. (8 Peters) 591, 8 L.Ed. 1055 (1834); W. W. Willoughby, Constitutional Law of the United States, p. 446.

[14] 8 Pet. 561, 657, 8 L.Ed. 1055 (1834); Hirsh v. Twentieth-Century Fox Films Corp., 207 Misc. 750, 144 N.Y.S.2d 38, 105 U.S.P.Q. 253 (1955).

[15] Kaeser & Blair, Inc. v. Merchants Ass'n, 64 F.2d 575, 577 (6th Cir.1933); Eisenshiml v. Fawcett, 246 F.2d 598 (7th Cir. 1957).

copyright or by provisions of federal copyright statutes.[16]

3) *As a form of literary property, copyright belongs to that class of personal property including patents, trade-marks, trade names, trade secrets, good will, unpublished lectures, musical compositions, and letters.*

a) Copyright, it must be emphasized, is quite different from a patent. Copyright covers purely composition, style of expression or rhetoric, while a patent is the right given to protect a novel ideal which may be expressed physically in a machine, a design, or a process.

b) Copyright may be distinguished from a trade-mark in that copyright protects a particular literary style while a trade-mark protects the sign or brand under which a particular product is made or distributed.

c) When someone sends you a letter, you do not have the right to publish that letter. You may keep the letter, or throw it away; indeed, you can do anything you wish with the letter but publish it. Although the recipient of a letter gets physical possession of it—of the paper it is written upon—the common law copyright ownership remains with the sender.[17]

SEC. 40. COMMON LAW COPYRIGHT

Common law copyright is a claim to literary or artistic property which is automatic and which lasts indefinitely until publication occurs.

Copyright is an exclusive, legally recognizable claim to literary or pictorial property. It is a right, extended by either the common law or by federal statute, to entitle the originator to ownership of the literary or artistic product of his mind. If the product remains unpublished, it receives protection of common law copyright. Common law copyright automatically belongs to the author or creator of an intellectual work, and exists completely apart from the federal copyright statutes. However, common law copyright has a number of major disadvantages for authors or creators.

First, common law copyright lasts only until the material involved is "published." When it is published and distributed to

---

[16] Cf. Chicago Record-Herald Co. v. Tribune Ass'n, 275 F. 797 (7th Cir. 1921).

[17] Baker v. Libbie, 97 N.E. 109, 210 Mass. 599 (1912); Ipswich Mills v. Dillon, 157 N.E. 604, 260 Mass. 453 (1927).

the general public, common law copyright lapses immediately and the work will become part of the public domain: available for use by anyone.

Second, common law copyright can be very difficult to prove. To make a claim of infringement of common law copyright stick, an author or creator must somehow be able to show that the work under common law copyright was first produced by him.

For example, the author of an unpublished novel may have shown copies of his manuscript to friends and perhaps to representatives of several publishing houses. But even if *his* novel then appears in published form under someone else's name, how can the actual author prove that it was *his* novel? Even the people who had seen the novel in manuscript would not be likely to remember much more than the general story line, and almost certainly would not be able to testify to the exact order of words, sentences, phrases and paragraphs. Such vague testimony doubtless would be insufficient to support a claim of "plagiarism" or "copyright infringement." Some authors try to lessen the problem by the simple expedient of sending to their own addresses—by registered mail—a copy of a manuscript. The author can hold the envelope unopened in case it becomes necessary to present proof of authorship.[18]

Two advantages which common law copyright has over statutory copyright are that it is automatic and it is perpetual as long as the manuscript or creation is not published. Suffice it to say, for now, that an author or creator may make some limited use of his own work without losing common law copyright. For instance, a play or a musical composition may be performed publicly without being considered to have been "published."

An author may circulate copies of a manuscript among friends or publishing houses without "publication" in the legal sense having occurred. A limited number of copies may even be printed and circulated to a specific group without constituting publication. Whenever a work is offered to the general public, however, common law copyright ends. The author or creator must then be protected by statutory copyright or lose his property rights completely.[19]

If an author is so careless as to authorize publication of his manuscript without complying with the provisions for statutory copyright, he loses his common law protection. However, if a manuscript is stolen from him and published, or if it is publish-

[18] Harriet F. Pilpel and Theodora Zavin, Rights and Writers (New York: E. P. Dutton & Co., 1960) pp. 115–116.

[19] Classic cases on this point are Donaldson v. Beckett, 4 Burr. 2408 (1709), and Wheaton v. Peters, 33 U.S. (8 Peters) 591, 8 L.Ed. 1055 (1834).

ed without his authority, his common law property right is not lost. He could either sue for damages or bring a suit in equity to prevent usurpation of his work.[20]

It has long been recognized that production of an artistic or literary work results in a property right which resides with the creator or author and which gives him the power to control what is done with his work. As an old and respected tome—aptly titled *Drone on Copyright*—asserts, "the creator is the first possessor of that which he creates." [21]

The laborer is entitled to the fruits of his labors, and so the writer or the author is entitled to whatever he produces, so long as what he writes or designs is not being produced for another person under an expressed or implied contract. The author's thoughts are his own and so long as these thoughts are not voluntarily given to the public, he possesses a right of common law copyright in his production. This common law right to a literary or artistic production is not abrogated by statutory copyright. The Copyright Act of 1909, which is still in force in this respect, states: [22]

> That nothing in this Act shall be construed to annul or limit the right of the author or proprietor of an unpublished work, at common law or in equity, to prevent the copying, publication, or use of such unpublished work without his consent, and to obtain damages therefor.

This statute thus makes it clear that the federal copyright law does not supersede common law copyright in an unpublished work. Compliance with the Copyright Act gives protection to the author when and if his work is published under its provisions.

Materials protected under common law copyright are a form of personal property. Such "property" may be created by the author for himself [23] or it may be developed by an individual as an employee of another person or of a business or corporation.

SEC. 41. STATUTORY COPYRIGHT

The Federal copyright statute protects manuscripts or other intellectual or artistic productions after publication.

As a practical matter, authors have little choice as to whether they will depend upon common law copyright or statutory copy-

---

[20] Rolland v. Henry Holt & Co., 152 F.Supp. 167, 113 U.S.P.Q. 253 (D.C.N.Y., 1957); 17 U.S.C.A. § 101.

[21] E. S. Drone, Law of Property in Intellectual Productions (Boston: Little, Brown, 1879) p. 3.

[22] Sec. 2, Act of March 4, 1909, 17 U.S.C.A. § 2 (1964).

[23] Wheaton v. Peters, 33 U.S. (8 Peters) 591, 8 L.Ed. 1055 (1834).

right.   Once a work such as a book or an article is published, only statutory copyright can apply.   Publication immediately destroys common law copyright.[24]   As Harriet F. Pilpel and Theodora Zavin have observed, however, there are some kinds of works which may receive the protection of statutory copyright before "publication."   In this category are such things as musical compositions or dramatic works, unpublished lectures, motion pictures, photographs, and works of art such as painting or sculpture.   In the print media, authors must wait until publication occurs before they can apply for statutory copyright.[25]

Statutory copyright provides some real advantages over common law protection.   Should an author wish to sue for infringement of copyright, the certificate of copyright—plus copies of his work which have been filed with the Register of Copyrights in Washington, D. C.—will be of great help in building his case.   Authorship is thus much easier to prove where statutory copyright is in force.[26]

In some cases, copyright statutes provide that minimum damages *must* be awarded to the copyright owner once he has proven copyright infringement in a lawsuit.   For example, should a newspaper *unknowingly* infringe copyright by reproducing a copyrighted photograph, minimum damages would be $50, with maximum possible damages to be $200.[27]   Or, if unknowing infringement occurs "of a copyrighted dramatic or dramatico-musical work by a maker of a motion picture and his agencies for distribution thereof to exhibitors," the copyright owner can receive damages not exceeding $5,000 and not less than $250.[28]

Although these statutorily set damages may not seem to be unduly large amounts, consider this passage from the federal copyright statute:[29]

> DAMAGES AND PROFITS; AMOUNTS; OTHER REMEDIES.—To pay to the copyright proprietor *such damages as the copyright proprietor may have suffered due to the infringement, as well as all the profits which the infringers shall have made from such infringement,* and in proving profits the plaintiff shall be required to prove sales only, and the defendant shall be required

[24] Leon H. Amdur, Copyright Law and Practice (New York: Clark Boardman Co., 1936) pp. 64–65.

[25] 17 U.S.C.A. §§ 202.6–202.15 (1964): Pilpel and Zavin, op. cit., p. 117.

[26] Pilpel and Zavin, loc. cit.

[27] 17 U.S.C.A. § 101(b) (1964).

[28] Ibid.

[29] Ibid.   Emphasis added.

> to prove every element of cost which he claims, or in
> lieu of actual damages and profits, *such damages as to
> the court shall appear just * * *.*

In translating this statutory language, pay special attention to
the italicized passage. In other words, if a copyright holder can
prove copyright infringement, he can collect—in effect—net
profits which have accrued to the infringer. In one case involving a movie script, this involved an award to a copyright holder
of well over $100,000.[30] Furthermore, the unsuccessful defend-
ant in a copyright infringement suit may wind up paying court
costs, including "a reasonable attorney's fee" for the plaintiff.[31]
In addition, if a work is protected by statutory copyright, the importation of unauthorized copies into the United States is prohibited.[32]

Although common law copyright lasts perpetually until a work
is published, statutory copyright exists for only a limited time.
Under existing federal statutes, the initial copyright period is 28
years. This copyright may be renewed once for another 28 years
if a "proper and timely" application for renewal is made. The
reason why two 28-year periods have been chosen is by no means
clear. As Pilpel and Zavin have written: [33]

> Some believe (and there is support for this position in
> some legislative records) that this device was for the
> benefit of authors in order to give them (or their fam-
> ilies in the event of their death) an opportunity to make
> better financial arrangements for the exploitation of
> their works during the renewal period than the author
> was able to make initially. Other, perhaps, more cynical,
> observers opine that the chief function served by the
> necessity to renew copyright is to create a set of cir-
> cumstances where it is likely that works will fall into
> the public domain.

It should be carefully noted that the copyright statute is very
explicit about the period for renewal of copyright. The statute
provides: [34]

> * * * the proprietor [owner] of such copyright shall
> be entitled to a renewal and extension of the copyright

[30] Sheldon v. Metro-Goldwyn Pictures Corp., 309 U.S. 390, 60 S.Ct. 681
(1940).

[31] 17 U.S.C.A. § 116.

[32] 17 U.S.C.A. §§ 106–107.

[33] Pilpel and Zavin, op. cit., p. 122. Copyright © 1955, 1956, 1957, 1958,
1959 by Harriet F. Pilpel. Copyright © 1960 by Harriet F. Pilpel and Theodora S. Zavin. All rights reserved. Printed in the U. S.

[34] 17 U.S.C.A. § 24.

in such work for the further term of twenty-eight years when application for such renewal and extension shall have been made to the copyright office and duly registered therein within one year prior to the expiration of the original term of copyright.

The crucial time for copyright renewal is the twelve-month period beginning 27 years from the date of the first publication. For example, if a book were published on June 1, 1970, the application to renew and extend copyright could be made with the Register of Copyrights on any day between June 1, 1997 and May 31, 1998. Otherwise, the material goes into the public domain, and rights to exclusive profit from it are lost to the author or his heirs as of June 1, 1998.

Renewal of copyright under the terms of the federal statute is noteworthy in the terms set forth for *who* can renew the protection. The statute says: [35]

> * * * the author of such work, if still living, or the widow, widower, or children of the author, if the author be not living, or the widow, widower, or children of the author, if the author be not living, or if such author, widow, widower, or children be not living, then the author's executors, or in the absence of a will, his next of kin shall be entitled to a renewal and extension of the copyright in such work for a further term of twenty-eight years when application for such renewal and extension shall have been made to the copyright office and duly registered therein within one year prior to the expiration of the original term of copyright * * *.

This is a remarkable piece of law, because it imposes restricttions upon the bequeathing or disposal of literary or artistic property which do not apply to other forms of personal property. With other kinds of personal property—be they houses, livestock, automobiles, or stocks and bonds—the owners can do as they please.

When a person is hired to produce a work of an artistic nature, copyright in whatever he produces will normally go to his employer. If the person hired does not wish this to happen, the author or creator must first arrange with the employer by means of a contract specifying who shall have the copyright. As a recent federal court decision has declared, "in the absence of an express contractual reservation of the copyright in the artist, the presumption arises that the mutual intent of the parties is

[35] Ibid.

that the title to the copyright shall be in the person at whose instance and expense the work is done." [36] Thus, whenever the intent to assign ownership cannot be determined, "the presumption of ownership runs in favor of the employer." [37] Obviously, however, when a writer, photographer, or artist "free lances" and produces a work on his own volition and at his own expense, he is the owner of that work.[38]

SEC. 42. SECURING A STATUTORY COPYRIGHT

Essentials in acquiring statutory copyright protection include notice of copyright, application, deposit of copies in the Library of Congress, and payment of the required fee.

Under present federal law, the protection of statutory copyright is gained *automatically* by placing a copyright notice at certain specified locations on every copy of a published work. This copyright notice must include three things:

1.   The symbol ©, the word "Copyright," or the abbreviation "Copr." [39]

2.   The name of the copyright proprietor(s).

3.   The year in which the copyright was secured by publication.[40]

A typical copyright notice might read: © Harold L. Nelson and Dwight L. Teeter, 1973. Such a notice should appear on the published material as provided by the statute: [41]

> The notice of copyright shall be applied, in the case of a book or other printed publications, upon its title page or the page immediately following, or if a periodical either upon the title page or upon the first page of text of each separate number or under the title heading, or if a musical work either upon its title page or the first page of music. One notice of copyright in each volume or in

[36] Lin-Brook Builders Hardware v. Gertler, 352 F.2d 300 (9th Cir. 1965), quoting Yardley v. Houghton-Mifflin Co., 108 F.2d 28 (2d Cir. 1939).

[37] Brattleboro Publishing Co. v. Winmill Publishing Co., 369 F.2d 565 (2d Cir. 1966).

[38] Lumiere v. Robertson-Cole Distributing Co., 280 F. 550 (2d Cir. 1922), 24 A.L.R. 1317, certiorari denied 259 U.S. 583, 42 S.Ct. 586 (1922).

[39] 17 U.S.C.A, § 19 (1964). The symbol © is to be preferred; it has the advantage of being accepted by the Universal Copyright Convention, signed at Geneva on Sept. 6, 1952, and which came into force in the United States on Sept. 16, 1955. See 17 U.S.C.A. § 9(c) (1964).

[40] 17 U.S.C.A. § 19.

[41] 17 U.S.C.A. § 20.

each number of a newspaper or periodical published shall suffice.

Once these things have been done, the claim for copyright has been made. However, to make this claim stand up in court, application must be made to the Register of Copyrights, Washington, District of Columbia. Two complete copies "of the best edition" of the work "shall be promptly deposited in the Copyright Office" or mailed to the Register of Copyrights.[42]

Additionally, fees specified by law must be paid.[43]

In actual practice, the mechanics of applying for copyright—including the filing of required copies and fees with the Register of Copyrights—often are not carried out until a considerable length of time after publication. Sometimes, it should be noted, use of the symbol © is a form of bluff because the author or creator has not gone through with the formalities of dealing with the Register of Copyrights. Under the present copyright law, registration of the material involved is not necessary to provide protection. Such protection is automatically assured by including the required copyright notice on each copy of a published work.[44]

If deposit of copies is not made promptly, however, the Register of Copyrights may give notice to the copyright proprietor,

[42] 17 U.S.C.A. § 13.

[43] 17 U.S.C.A. § 215. Fees. The Register of Copyrights shall receive, and the persons to whom the services designated are rendered shall pay, the following fees: For the registration of a claim to copyright in any work, including a print or label used for articles of merchandise, $6; for the registration of a claim to renewal of copyright, $4; which fees shall include a certificate for each registration: *Provided*, That only one registration fee shall be required in the case of several volumes of the same book published and deposited at the same time: *and provided further*, That with respect to works of foreign origin, in lieu of payment of the copyright fee of $6 together with one copy of the work and application, the foreign author or proprietor may at any time within six months from the date of first publication abroad deposit in the Copyright Office an application for registration and two copies of the work which shall be accompanied by a catalog card in form and content satisfactory to the Register of Copyrights. For every additional certificate of registration, $2. For certifying a copy of an application for registration of copyright, and for all other certifications, $3. For recording every assignment, agreement, power of attorney or other paper not exceeding six pages, $5; for each additional page or less, 50 cents; for each title over one in the paper recorded, 50 cents additional. For recording a notice of use, or notice of intention to use, $3, for each notice of not more than five titles; and 50 cents for each additional title. For any requested search of Copyright Office records, works deposited, or other available material or services rendered in connection therewith, $5, for each hour of time consumed. (As amended Oct. 27, 1965, Pub.L. 89–297, § 2, 79 Stat. 1072.)

[44] However, the accidental omission of a copyright notice from a particular copy (or some of the copies) will not invalidate copyright or prevent recovery for infringement. 17 U.S.C.A. § 21.

requiring the deposit.　If the deposit is not then made, the copyright proprietor is subject to a fine of $100 plus twice the retail price of the copyrighted work.　The copyright then becomes void.[45]　No action for infringement of copyright can succeed until the required deposit of copies is made.[46]　Any person who gives false notice of copyright (of an uncopyrighted article) *with intent to defraud*, or who removes or alters a copyright notice *with intent to defraud*, commits a misdemeanor and is subject to a fine of not less than $100 or more than $1000.[47]

SEC. 43.　ORIGINALITY

The concept of originality means that an author or artist has done his own work, and that his work is not copied or grossly imitative of another's literary or artistic property.

Originality is a fundamental principle of copyright; originality implies that the author or artist created the work through his own skill, labor, and judgment.[48]　The concept of originality means that the particular work must be firsthand, pristine, not copied or imitated.　Originality, however, does not mean that the work must be necessarily novel or clever, or that it have any value as literature or art.　What constitutes originality was explained in an old but frequently quoted case, Emerson v. Davies. The famous Justice Joseph Story of Massachusetts stated: [49]

> In truth, in literature, in science and in art, there are, and can be, few, if any, things, which, in an abstract sense, are strictly new and original throughout.　Every book in literature, science, and art, borrows, and must necessarily borrow, and use much which was well known and used before.　No man creates a new language for himself, at least if he be a wise man, in writing a book. He contents himself with the use of language already known and used and understood by others.　No man writes exclusively from his own thoughts, unaided and uninstructed by the thoughts of others.　The thoughts of every man are, more or less, a combination of what other men have thought and expressed, although they may be modified, exalted, or improved by his own genius or reflection.　If no book could be the subject of copy-

[45] 17 U.S.C.A. § 14.

[46] 17 U.S.C.A. § 13.

[47] 17 U.S.C.A. § 105.　Emphasis added.

[48] American Code Co. v. Bensinger, et al., 282 F. 829 (2d Cir. 1922).

[49] 8 Fed.Cas. 615, No. 4,436 (C.C.Mass.1845).

right which was not new and original in the elements of which it is composed, there could be no ground for any copyright in modern times, and we should be obliged to ascend very high, even in antiquity, to find a work entitled to such eminence. * * *

An author has as much right in his plan, and in his arrangements, and in the combination of his materials, as he has in his thoughts, sentiments, opinions, and in his modes of expressing them. The former as well as the latter may be more useful or less useful than those of another author; but that, although it may diminish or increase the relative values of their works in the market, is no ground to entitle either to appropriate to himself the labor or skill of the other, as embodied in his own work.

It is a great mistake to suppose, because all the materials of a work or some parts of its plan and arrangements and modes of illustration may be found separately, or in a different form, or in a different arrangement, in other distinct works, that therefore, if the plan or arrangement or combination of these materials in another work is new, or for the first time made, the author, or compiler, or framer of it (call him what you please), is not entitled to a copyright.

The question of originality seems clear in concept but this quality of composition is not always easy to separate and identify in particular cases, especially when different authors have conceived like expressions or based their compositions upon commonly accepted ideas, terms, or descriptions in sequence. It must be borne in mind that an idea as such cannot be the subject of copyright; to be eligible for copyright, ideas must have particular physical expressions, as signs, symbols, or words. As was stated in Kaeser & Blair, Inc. v. Merchants' Association, Inc., "copyright law does not afford protection against the use of an idea, but only as to the means by which the idea is expressed." [50]

Artistic treatment is one element in the consideration of copyright but not an absolutely necessary element. One might compile a directory of residents of a city, giving names, occupations, places of business and residence; the individual's name and information about him and his residence cannot be subject of copy-

[50] 64 F.2d 575, 577 (6th Cir. 1933). See also Holmes v. Hurst, 174 U.S. 82, 19 S.Ct. 606 (1899); Eisenshiml v. Fawcett Publications, Inc., 246 F.2d 598, 114 U.S.P.Q. 199 (7th Cir. 1957).

right, but when thousands of citizens' names are compiled, together with directory information about them, the whole forms a result that may be the subject of copyright. In Jewelers' Circular Pub. Co. v. Keystone Pub. Co., the court stated: [51]

> The right to copyright a book upon which one has expended labor in its preparation does not depend upon whether the materials which he has collected consist or not of matters which are *publici juris* [news of the day], or whether such materials show literary skill or originality, either in thought or language, or anything more than industrious collection. The man who goes through the streets of a town and puts down the names of each of the inhabitants, with their occupations and their street number, acquires material of which he is the author.

While such a compiler would have no right to copyright information on a mere listing of one man and his address and occupation, he would have a right to copyright a compilation of a large number of such names, their addresses, and occupations.

Copyrightable subject matter under the Act of March 4, 1909, as amended by the Act of August 24, 1912, includes the following: [52]

    (a) Books, including composite and cyclopaedic works, directories, gazetteers, and other compilations;

    (b) Periodicals, including newspapers;

    (c) Lectures, sermons, addresses (prepared for oral delivery);

    (d) Dramatic or dramatico-musical compositions;

    (e) Musical compositions;

    (f) Maps;

    (g) Works of art; models or designs for works of art;

    (h) Reproductions of a work of art;

    (i) Drawings or plastic works of a scientific or technical character;

    (j) Photographs;

    (k) Prints and pictorial illustrations;

---

[51] Jewelers' Circular Publishing Co. v. Keystone Publishing Co., 281 F. 83, 88, 26 A.L.R. 571 (2d Cir. 1922).

[52] 17 U.S.C.A. § 5, as amended by Public Law 92–140, 92nd Congress, S. 646, Oct. 15, 1971, 85 Stat. 391. The amendment added subsection (n) concerning sound recordings in an effort to combat the widespread practice of record piracy.

(*l*) Motion-picture photoplays;

(m) Motion pictures other than photoplays;

(n) Sound recordings.

In sum then, the best advice is this: do your own work. You may keep it in mind that the law does not copyright ideas or facts; only the manner in which these ideas or facts are expressed is protected by the law of literary property. As the Supreme Court of the United States said in 1899, "the right secured by copyright is not the right to forbid the use of certain words or facts or ideas by others; it is a right to that arrangement of words which the author has selected to express his ideas which the law protects." [53] Or, as a Circuit Court of Appeals said so aptly in 1951, " 'Original' in reference to a copyrighted work means that the particular work 'owes its origin' to the author. No large measure of novelty is necessary." [54] Thus, if care is taken to express ideas in one's own words—and to do one's own research or creative work—he is not likely to run afoul of copyright law.

SEC. 44. INFRINGEMENT

Violation of copyright includes such use or copying of an author's work that his possibility of profit is lessened.

In order to win a lawsuit for copyright infringement, a plaintiff must establish two separate facts, as the late Circuit Judge Jerome N. Frank wrote some years ago: "(a) that the alleged infringer copied from plaintiff's work, and (b) that, if copying is proved, it was so 'material' or substantial as to constitute unlawful appropriation." [55] Even so, the material copied need not be extensive or "lengthy" in order to be infringement. "In an appropriate case," Judge Frank noted, "copyright infringement might be demonstrated, with no proof or weak proof of access, by showing that a simple brief phrase, contained in both pieces, was so idiosyncratic in its treatment as to preclude coincidence.[56] Judge Frank also noted that even a great, famous author or artist might be found guilty of copyright infringement. He wrote,

[53] Holmes v. Hurst, 174 U.S. 82, 19 S.Ct. 606 (1899); Van Renssalaer v. General Motors, 324 F.2d 354 (6th Cir. 1963).

[54] Lin-Brook Builders Hardware v. Gertler, 352 F.2d 298, 301 (9th Cir. 1965) quoting Alfred Bell & Co., Ltd. v. Catalda Fine Arts, Inc., 191 F.2d 99, 102 (2d Cir. 1951).
    See also Runge v. Lee, 441 F.2d 579 (9th Cir. 1971), certiorari denied 404 U.S. 887, 92 S.Ct. 197 (1971).

[55] Heim v. Universal Pictures Co., 154 F.2d 480, 487 (2d Cir. 1946).

[56] Ibid., p. 488.

"we do not accept the aphorism, 'when a great composer steals, he is "influenced"; when an unknown steals, he is "infringing." ' " [57]

Copyright protection continues even though a usurper gives away the copyrighted material or obtains his profit on some associated activity. The old case of Herbert v. Shanley (1917) is relevant here. Shanley's restaurant employed musicians to play at mealtimes. Victor Herbert's song "Sweethearts," was performed, but no arrangement had been made with Herbert or his representatives to use the song. Defendant Shanley argued that he had not infringed upon Herbert's copyright because no profit came from music which was played merely to lend atmosphere to his restaurant. The Supreme Court of the United States, however, held that Shanley had benefited from the playing of the music.[58]

Federal copyright law imposes statutory limitations of damages which may be awarded: the minimum amount is $250 if infringement is found by a court, and the maximum amount is $5,000.[59] Damages are not the only thing which may be recovered. *Profits* made by a copyright infringer may also be awarded to the original author or creator by a court. Profits, then, are clearly distinct from damages, and if the original author or creator can prove large profits, he may be awarded them against the infringer.

In seeking to recover profits from a copyright infringer, the burden of proof falls upon the plaintiff to show the gross sales or profits arising from the infringement. The copyright infringer is permitted to deduct any legitimate costs or expenses which he can prove were incurred during publication of the stolen work. The winner of a suit to recover profits under copyright law can receive only the *net profits* resulting from an infringement. As the Supreme Court of the United States has declared, " 'The infringer is liable for actual, not for possible, gains.' " [60]

Net profits can run to a great deal of money, especially when the plagiarized work is a commercial success as a book or motion picture. Edward Sheldon sued Metro-Goldwyn Pictures Corp. and others for infringing on his play, "Dishonored Lady"

[57] Ibid.

[58] 242 U.S. 591, 37 S.Ct. 232 (1917).

[59] 17 U.S.C.A. § 101.

[60] Sheldon v. Metro-Goldwyn Pictures Corp., 309 U.S. 390, 400–401, 60 S.Ct. 681, 683 (1940); Golding v. R.K.O. Radio Pictures, Inc., 35 Cal.2d 690, 221 P. 2d 95 (1950).

through the production of the Metro-Goldwyn film, "Letty Lynton." A federal district court, after an accounting had been ordered, found that Metro-Goldwyn had received net profits of $585,604.37 from their exhibitions of the motion picture.[61]

Mr. Sheldon did not get *all* of Metro-Goldwyn's net profits from the movie, however. On appeal, it was held that Sheldon should not benefit from the profits that motion picture stars had made for the picture by their talent and box-office appeal. Sheldon, after his case had been heard by both a United States Court of Appeals and the Supreme Court of the United States, came out with "only" 20 per cent of the net profits, or roughly $117,700. It still would have been much cheaper for Metro-Goldwyn to simply buy Sheldon's script. Negotiations with Sheldon for his play had been started by Metro-Goldwyn, but were never completed. The price for movie rights to the Sheldon play was evidently to be about $30,000, or slightly more than one-fourth of the amount the courts awarded to the playwright.[62]

One line which appears at the end of some court decisions should have a chilling ring for a plagiarist: § 116. COSTS; ATTORNEY'S FEES.—"In all actions, suits, or proceedings under this title, except when brought by or against the United States or any officer thereof, full costs shall be allowed, and the court may award to the prevailing party a reasonable attorney's fee as part of the costs." [63]

That is, if you lose a copyright infringement lawsuit, you could wind up paying court costs and the opposing attorney's fees. Thus, even if you lost "only" $100 or $250 for copyright infringement, you could still incur considerable costs in the form of court costs and attorney's fees.

Copyright cases involving music have proved to be difficult. The evidence in such cases is largely circumstantial, resting upon similarities between songs. The issue in such a case, as one court expressed it, is whether "so much of what is pleasing to the ears of lay listeners, who comprise the audience for whom such popular music is composed, that defendant wrongfully appropriated something which belongs to the plaintiff." [64]

More than "lay listeners" often get involved in such cases, however. Expert witnesses sometimes testify in copyright in-

61 Sheldon v. Metro-Goldwyn Pictures Corp., 26 F.Supp. 134, 136 (D.C.N.Y. 1938), 81 F.2d 49 (2d Cir. 1936).

62 309 U.S. 390, 398, 407, 60 S.Ct. 681, 683, 687 (1940).

63 17 U.S.C.A. § 116.

64 Arnstein v. Porter, 154 F.2d 464, 473 (2d Cir. 1946).

fringement cases involving music. But it can happen that the plaintiff who feels that his musical composition has been stolen, and the defendant as well, will *both* bring their own expert witnesses into court, where these witnesses expertly disagree with each other.[65]

In proving a case of copyright infringement—and not just for those cases dealing with music—it is often useful if plaintiffs can show that the alleged plagiarizer had "access" to the original work from which the copy was supposed to have been made. Such "access" needs to be proved by the plaintiff, if only by the circumstantial evidence of similarity between two works.

During the 1940s, songwriter Ira B. Arnstein tried to show that the noted composer, Cole Porter, not only had access to his work, but that Porter had plagiarized freely from Arnstein. The courts declared that Porter had not infringed any common law or statutory copyrights held by Arnstein. Porter's victory in the courts was hard-won, however.

Arnstein began a copyright infringement lawsuit against Cole Porter in a federal district court. Arnstein charged that Porter's "Begin the Beguine" was a plagiarism from Arnstein's "The Lord is My Shepherd" and "A Mother's Prayer." He also claimed that Porter's "My Heart Belongs to Daddy" had been lifted from Arnstein's "A Mother's Prayer."

On the question of access, plaintiff Arnstein testified that 2,000 copies of "The Lord is My Shepherd" had been published, and sold, and that over one million copies of "A Mother's Prayer" had been published and sold. Furthermore, Arnstein complained that his apartment had been burglarized and accused Porter of receiving the stolen manuscripts from the burglars. Arnstein declared that Porter's "Night and Day" had been stolen from Arnstein's "I Love You Madly," which had never been published but which had been performed once over the radio. Technically, this meant that Arnstein's "I Love You Madly" had never been published.

In reply, Porter swore that he had never seen or heard any of Arnstein's compositions, and that he did not know the persons said to have stolen them. Even so, Arnstein's lawsuit asked for a judgment against Porter of "at least one million dollars out of the millions this defendant has earned and is earning out of all the plagiarism." [66]

At the original trial, the district court directed the jury to bring in a summary verdict in favor of Porter. Arnstein then

[65] Ibid.

[66] Ibid., 474.

appealed to the Circuit Court of Appeals, where Judge Jerome Frank explained what the appellate court had done.   The Circuit Court of Appeals had listened to phonograph records of Cole Porter's songs and compared them to records of Arnstein's songs.   As he sent the case back to a district court jury, Judge Frank wrote: [67]

> * * * we find similarities, but we hold that unquestionably, standing alone, they do not compel the conclusion, or permit the inference, that defendant copied.   The similarities, however, are sufficient so that, if there is enough evidence of access to permit the case to go to the jury, the jury may properly infer that the similarities did not result from coincidence.

The jury then found that Cole Porter's "Begin the Beguine" had indeed been written by Cole Porter.

SEC. 45.   COPYRIGHT AND THE NEWS

The news element of a story is not subject to copyright, although the style in which an individual story is written may be protected from infringement.   Reporters, in short, should do their own reporting.

Any unauthorized and unfair use of a copyrighted news story constitutes an infringement which will support either lawsuits for damages or an action in equity to get an injunction against further publication.   Although a news story—or even an entire issue of a newspaper—may be copyrighted, the *news element* in a newspaper story is not subject to copyright.   News is *publici juris*—the history of the day—as was well said by Justice Mahlon Pitney in the important 1918 case of International News Service v. Associated Press.   Justice Pitney wrote: [68]

> A News article, as a literary production, is the subject of copyright.   But the news element—the information respecting current events in the literary production, is not the creation of the writer, but is a report of matters that ordinarily are publici juris; it is the history of the day.   It is not to be supposed that the framers of the Constitution, when they empowered Congress to promote the progress of science and useful arts, by securing for limited times to authors and inventors the exclusive rights to their respective writings and discov-

[67] Ibid.

[68] 248 U.S. 215, 39 S.Ct. 68, 71 (1918).

eries (Const. Art. 1, § 8, par. 8), intended to confer upon one who might happen to be first to report an historic event the exclusive right for any period to spread the knowledge of it.

The Associated Press had complained of news pirating by a rival news-gathering agency, International News Service. The Supreme Court granted the Associated Press an injunction against the appropriation, by INS, or AP stories while the news was still fresh enough to be salable. "The peculiar value of news," Justice Pitney declared, "is in the spreading of it while it is fresh; and it is evident that a valuable property interest in the news, as news, cannot be maintained by keeping it secret."

Justice Pitney also denounced the taking, by INS, of AP stories, either by quoting or paraphrasing. Justice Pitney wrote that INS, "in appropriating * * * news and selling it as its own is endeavoring to reap where it has not sown, and by disposing of it to newspapers that are competitors * * * of AP members is appropriating to itself the harvest of those who have sown.[69]

What, then, can a newspaper or other communications medium do when it has been "beaten" to a story by its competition? It must be emphasized that the historic case of International News Service v. Associated Press did *not* say that the "beaten" news medium must sit idly by. "Pirating" news, of course, is to be avoided: pirating has been defined as "the bodily appropriation of a statement of fact or a news article, with or without rewriting, but without independent investigation or expense." [70] However, first-published news items may be used as "tips." When one newspaper discovers an event, such as the arrest of a kidnaper, its particular news presentation of the facts may be protected by copyright. Even so, such a first story may serve as a tip for other newspapers or press associations. After the first edition by the copyrighting news organization, other organizations may independently investigate and present their own stories about the arrest of the kidnaper. In such a case, the time element between the appearance of the first edition of the copyrighting newspaper and the appearance of a second or third edition by a competing newspaper might be negligible as far as the general public is concerned; only a few hours. If other newspapers or press associations make their own investigations and obtain their own stories, they do not violate copyright.

[69] 248 U.S. 215, 239–240, 39 S.Ct. 68, 71–72 (1918).

[70] 248 U.S. 215, 243, 39 S.Ct. 68, 74 (1918).

However, to copy a copyrighted news story—or to copy or paraphrase substantially from the original story—may bring about a successful court action for infringement, as was shown in the 1921 case of Chicago-Record-Herald Co. v. Tribune Association. The point of this case is clear: "lifting" or "stealing" of news items can lead to the courts. This case arose when the *New York Tribune* copyrighted a special news story on Germany's reliance upon submarines. This story, printed in the *New York Tribune* on Feb. 3, 1917, was offered for simultaneous publication in the *Chicago Herald*. The *Herald* declined this opportunity, and the *Chicago Daily News* then purchased the Chicago rights to the story.

With full knowledge that the *Tribune's* story on the German submarine campaign was fully copyrighted, the *Herald* nevertheless ran a condensed version or rewrite of the same story on the morning of Feb. 3.

A comparison of stories as reported in the official report of the case follows:

Chicago Herald

Germany Pins Hope of Fleet on

300 Fast Supersubmarines

New York, Feb. 3—3 a. m. (special).—The Tribune this morning in a copyrighted article of Louis Durant Edwards, a correspondent in Germany, says that Germany to make the final effort against Great Britain has plunged 300 or more submersibles into the North Sea. These, according to this writer, were mobilized from Kiel, Hamburg, Wilhemshaven, and Bremerhaven where for months picked crews were trained.

"They form the world's first diving battle fleet," he says, "a navy equally prepared to fight above or beneath the waves."

There are two types of these new boats now in commission, one of 2,400 tons and one of 5,000 tons displacement.

They dive beneath the water in a fraction of the time that it takes the older types to submerge. They mount powerful guns, are capable of great surface speeds, and are protected by a heavy armor of tough steel plate.

The motors develop 7,000 horsepower and drive the boats under the surface at 22 knots an hour. These smaller cruisers carry a crew of from 60 to 80 men.

The submersibles have a radius of action of 8,000 miles.

New York Tribune

**By Louis Durant Edwards. Copyright, 1917, by
The Tribune Association (New York Tribune).**

Germany plays her trumps. Three hundred or more submersibles have plunged into the waters of the North Sea to make the final effort against Great Britain. They mobilized from Kiel, Hamburg, Wilhemshaven, Bremerhaven, where, for months, picked crews have trained.

*   *   *   *   *   *   *   *   *

They form the world's first diving battle fleet, a navy equally prepared to fight above or beneath the waves.

*   *   *   *   *   *   *   *   *

There are two types of these new boats now in commission, one of 2,400 tons and one of 5,000 tons displacement.

*   *   *   *   *   *   *   *   *

They dive beneath the water in a fraction of the time that it took the older types to submerge. They mount powerful guns, are capable of great surface speeds, and are protected by a heavy armor of tough steel plate.

*   *   *   *   *   *   *   *   *

The motors develop 7,000 horsepower, and drive the boats over the surface at a speed of 22 knots an hour. These smaller cruisers carry a crew of from 60 to 80 men.

*   *   *   *   *   *   *   *   *

They have a radius of action of 8,000 miles.[71]

*   *   *   *   *   *   *   *   *

The *Chicago Daily News* then refused to publish the story or to pay the *New York Herald Tribune* for it. The *Daily News*, having agreed to purchase an exclusive story, had the right to refuse a story already published in its market. The publishers of the *New York Tribune* sued the *Chicago Daily News* for payment, but lost.[72]

[71] 275 F. 797 (7th Cir. 1921).

[72] Ibid.

In International News Service v. Associated Press (1918), the AP won its case despite the fact that the news stories it telegraphed to its members were not copyrighted. There, the Supreme Court of the United States held that the AP had a "quasi property" right in the news stories it produced, even after their publication. Once the Supreme Court found that such a "quasi property" right existed, it then declared that appropriation of such stories by INS amounted to unfair competition and could be stopped by a court-issued injunction against INS.[73]

Far more recently, a newspaper—the Pottstown, Pa., *Mercury* —won an unfair competition suit against a Pottstown radio station, WPAZ, getting an injunction which prevented WPAZ " 'from any further appropriation of the newspaper's local news without its permission or authorization.' " [74] The court noted that competition among radio, television, and newspapers were "competing with each other for advertising which has become a giant in our economy." This court viewed the Pottstown *Mercury's* news as "a commercial package of news items to service its advertising business." In the rather jaundiced view of the Pennsylvania Supreme Court, advertising has become virtually all-important, with "the presentation of news and entertainment almost a subsidiary function of newspapers, radio and television stations." Although copyright infringement was not the precise issue here, the Pennsylvania Supreme Court found itself able to punish the radio station for appropriating news stories under the area of law dealing with unfair competition. The court said: [75]

> * * * for the purpose of an action of unfair competition the specialized treatment of news items as a service the newspaper provides for advertisers gives the News Company [publishers of the Pottstown *Mercury*] a limited property right which the law will guard and protect against wrongful invasion by a competitor whereas, for the purpose of an action for the infringement of copyright, the specialized treatment of news is protected because "the law seeks to encourage creative minds."

The limited property right in news is to some extent waived by member organizations of the Associated Press. All A.P. members are entitled to all *spontaneous* news from areas served by

---

[73] The case of International News Service v. Associated Press was cited as important by the more recent case of Pottstown Daily News Publishing Co. v. Pottstown Broadcasting Co., 411 Pa. 383, 192 A.2d 657, 662 (1963).

[74] Ibid.

[75] 411 Pa. 383, 192 A.2d 657, 663–664 (1963).

other A.P. member newspapers or broadcasting stations. Membership in the Associated Press includes agreement to follow this condition as stated in Article VII of the A.P. bylaws: [76]

> Sec. 3. Each member shall promptly furnish to the [A.P.] Corporation all the news of such member's district, the area of which shall be determined by the Board of Directors. No news furnished to the Corporation by a member shall be furnished by the Corporation to any other member within such member's district.

> Sec. 4. The news which a member shall furnish to the Corporation shall be all news that is spontaneous in origin, but shall not include news that is not spontaneous in its origin, or which has originated through deliberate and individual enterprise on the part of such member.

A.P. member newspapers or broadcasting stations are expected to furnish spontaneous or "spot" news stories to the Associated Press for dissemination to other members throughout the nation. However, Section 3 of the A.P. By-Laws (above) will protect the news medium originating such a story within its district. If a newspaper copyrights a spot news story about the shooting of a deputy sheriff by a gambler, other A.P. members could use the story despite the copyright. By signing the A.P. By-Laws, the originating newspaper has given its consent in advance for all A.P. members to use news stories of *spontaneous* origin. On the other hand, if a newspaper copyrights an exposé of gambling in a city based on that newspaper's individual enterprise and initiative, the other A.P. members could not use the story without permission from the copyrighting newspaper.

We now turn to a discussion of a major defense against claims of copyright infringement: the judicial doctrine of "fair use."

SEC. 46. THE JUDICIAL DOCTRINE OF FAIR USE

To soften the impact of the terms of the Federal copyright statute, courts have developed the doctrine of fair use which allows "reasonable" use of another's literary property.

The United States Copyright Act gives each copyright holder an exclusive right to "print, reprint, publish, copy and vend the copyrighted work * * * ". As stated in the Act, this is an *absolute* right. As librarians are fond of pointing out, this statute is stated in terms so absolute that even "pencil-and-paper

---

[76] Charter and By-Laws of the Associated Press (30th ed., Nov. 1, 1963).

copying traditionally performed in libraries is a violation of the U. S. Copyright Act as written." [77] If the Copyright Law were enthusiastically enforced to the letter, it could prevent anyone except the copyright holder from making any copy of any part of a copyrighted work.

Because the federal Copyright Law's terms are so absolute and so unenforceable, courts have responded by developing the doctrine of "fair use." American courts have assumed—in creating a judge-made exception to the copyright statute—that "the law implies the consent of the copyright owner to a fair use of his publication for the advancement of science or art." [78] Courts and copyright authorities agree that there is such a principle as "fair use," but the concept is exceedingly hard to define. One expert has asserted that fair use of someone's copyrighted materials exists "somewhere in the hinterland between the broad avenue of an independent creation and the jungle of unmitigated plagiarism." [79]

No easy or automatic formula can be presented which will draw a safe line between fair use and plagiarism. Counting words cannot help. Fifty words taken from a magazine article might be fair use, while taking one line from a short poem might be held to be plagiarism. Generally speaking, courts have been quite lenient with quotations used in scholarly works or critical reviews. However, courts have sometimes been less friendly toward use of copyrighted materials for commercial or non-scholarly purposes, or in works which are competitive with the original copyrighted piece.[80]

The problems surrounding the meaning of the phrase "fair use" have often arisen in connection with scientific, legal, or scholarly materials. With such works, it is perhaps to be expected that there will be similar treatment given to similar subject matters.[81] A crucial question, obviously, is whether the writer

[77] 17 U.S.C.A. § 10 (1964); Lazowska, op. cit., p. 123; Verner W. Clapp, "Library Photocopying and Copyright: Recent Developments, Law Library Journal Vol. 55:1 (February, 1962) pp. 12–15, at p. 12.

[78] Wittenberg, op. cit., p. 148, offers a good non-technical explanation of fair use.

[79] Arthur N. Bishop, "Fair Use of Copyrighted Books," Houston Law Review Vol. 2:2 (Fall, 1964) pp. 206–221, at p. 207.

[80] Eisenshiml v. Fawcett Publications, Inc., 246 F.2d 598 (7th Cir. 1957); Benny v. Loew's, Inc., 239 F.2d 532 (9th Cir. 1956), affirmed 356 U.S. 43, 78 S.Ct. 667, rehearing denied 356 U.S. 934, 78 S.Ct. 770 (1958); Pilpel and Zavin, op. cit., pp. 160–161.

[81] Eisenshiml v. Fawcett Publications, Inc., 246 F.2d 598 (7th Cir. 1957), certiorari denied 355 U.S. 907, 78 S.Ct. 334 (1957).

availed himself of an earlier writer's work without doing substantial independent work himself. Wholesale copying is not regarded as fair use.[82] Even if a writer had no intention of making unfair use of someone else's copyrighted work, he still could be found liable for copyright infringement.[83] The idea of "independent investigation" is very important here. Copyrighted materials may be used as a guide for the purpose of gathering information, provided that the researcher or writer then makes an original investigation *on his own.*[84]

Although many cases have expressed a narrow, restrictive view of the doctrine of fair use, more recent decisions suggest that in the public interest, the privilege of making fair use of copyrighted materials will be of great importance to journalists and scholars. A key case here is the 1967 decision known as Rosemont Enterprises, Inc. v. Random House, Inc. and John Keats. This case arose because Howard Hughes, a giant in America's aviation, oil and motion picture industries has a passionate desire to remain anonymously out of the public eye. A brief chronology will illustrate how this copyright infringement action came about:

* January and February, 1954: *Look* magazine, owned by Cowles Communications, Inc., published a series of three articles by Stanley White, titled "The Howard Hughes Story."

* In 1962, Random House, Inc., hired Thomas Thompson, a journalist employed by *Life* magazine, to prepare a book-length biography of Hughes. Later, either Hughes or his attorneys learned of the forthcoming Random House book. An attorney employed by Hughes warned Random House that Hughes did not want this biography and "would make trouble if the book was published." Thompson resigned from the project, and Random House then hired John Keats to complete the biography.

* Rosemont Enterprises, Inc., was organized in September, 1965 by Hughes' attorney and by two officers of his wholly-owned Hughes Tool Company.

* On May 20, 1966, Rosemont Enterprises purchased copyrights to the *Look* articles, advised Random House of this, and five days later brought a copyright infringement suit in New York. Attorneys for Rosemont had somehow gained possession of Random House galley proofs of the Random House biography

[82] Benny v. Loew's Inc., 239 F.2d 532 (9th Cir. 1956), affirmed 356 U.S. 43, 78 S.Ct. 667, rehearing denied 356 U.S. 934, 78 S.Ct. 770 (1958).

[83] Wihtol v. Crow, 309 F.2d 777 (8th Cir. 1962).

[84] Jeweler's Circular Pub. Co. v. Keystone Pub. Co., 281 F. 83 (2d Cir. 1922), certiorari denied 259 U.S. 581, 42 S.Ct. 464 (1922).

of Hughes then being published: "Howard Hughes: a Biography by John Keats." [85]

Rosemont Enterprises sought an injunction to restrain Random House from selling, publishing, or distributing copies of its biography of Hughes because the book amounted to a prima facie case of copyright infringement. With his five-day-old ownership of the copyrights for the 1954 Look magazine articles, Hughes was indeed in a position to "cause trouble" for Random House.

The trial court agreed with the Rosemont Enterprises argument that infringement had occurred, and granted the injunction against Random House, holding up distribution of the book. The trial court rejected Random House's claims of fair use of the Look articles, saying that the privilege of fair use was confined to "materials used for purposes of criticism or comment or in scholarly works of scientific or educational value." This district court took the view that if something was published "for commercial purposes"—that is, if it was designed for the popular market—the doctrine of fair use could not be employed to lessen the severity of the copyright law.[86] The district court found that the Hughes biography by Keats was for the popular market and therefore the fair use privilege could not be invoked by Random House.[87]

Circuit Judge Leonard P. Moore, speaking for the Circuit Court of Appeals, took another view. First of all, he noted that the three *Look* articles, taken together, totalled only 13,500 words, or between 35 and 39 pages if published in book form. Keats' 1966 biography on the other hand, had 166,000 words, or 304 pages in book form. Furthermore, Judge Moore stated that the *Look* articles did not purport to be a biography, but were merely accounts of a number of interesting incidents in Hughes' life. Judge Moore declared: [88]

> * * * there can be little doubt that portions of the *Look* article were copied. Two direct quotations and one eight-line paraphrase are attributed to Stephen White, the author of the articles. A mere reading of the *Look* articles, however, indicates that there is considerable doubt as to whether the copied and paraphrased matter constitutes a material and substantial

[85] Rosemont Enterprises, Inc. v. Random House, Inc. and John Keats, 366 F.2d 303, 304–305 (2d Cir. 1966).

[86] Ibid., p. 304, citing the trial court, 256 F.Supp. 55 (D.C.N.Y.1966).

[87] Ibid.

[88] Ibid., pp. 306–307, certiorari denied 385 U.S. 1009, 87 S.Ct. 714 (1967).

portion of those articles * * *. Furthermore, while the mode of expression employed by White is entitled to copyright protection, he could not acquire by copyright a monopoly in the narration of historical events. Finally, in an affidavit submitted to the district court, Thompson asserted that he engaged in extensive research while preparing his manuscript, which included personal interviews with many people familiar with Hughes' activities (fifteen of whom he listed by name) and the employment of a Houston newspaperman to conduct additional interviews for him. There is no dispute that defendant Keats, named as author of the biography, was retained solely to revise Thompson's manuscript, which, as described in his contract with Random House, was to include rewriting and reorganization, rechecking facts against the sources used, and such additional research as was necessary to "update the work and fill in facts and events."

Circuit Judge Moore noted, however, that Thompson's research work remained the core of Keats' book. In any case, the Keats book should fall within the doctrine of fair use. Quoting a treatise on copyright, Judge Moore stated: "Fair use is a privilege in others than the owner of a copyright to use the copyrighted material in a reasonable manner without his consent, notwithstanding the monopoly granted to the owner * * *." [89]

Judge Moore demanded that public interest considerations— the public's interest in knowing about prominent and powerful men—be taken into account. He wrote that "public interest should prevail over possible damage to the copyright owner." He complained that the district court's preliminary injunction against Random House deprived the public of the opportunity to become acquainted with the life of a man of extraordinary talents in a number of fields: "A narration of Hughes' initiative, ingenuity, determination and tireless work to achieve his concept of perfection in whatever he did ought to be available to a reading public." [90]

A stunning event—the assassination of President John F. Kennedy—gave rise to a copyright case which added lustre to the defense of fair use in infringement actions. On November 22, 1963, dress manufacturer Abraham Zapruder of Dallas sta-

[89] Ibid., p. 306, quoting Ball, Copyright and Literary Property, p. 260 (1944).

[90] Ibid., p. 309. And, at p. 311, Judge Moore discussed Rosemont's claim that it was planning to publish a book: "One can only speculate when, if ever, Rosemont will produce Hughes' authorized biography."

tioned himself along the route of the President's motorcade, planning to take home movie pictures with his 8 millimeter camera. As the procession came into sight, Zapruder started his camera. Seconds later, the assassin's shots fatally wounded the President and Zapruder's color film caught the reactions of those in the President's car.

On that same day, Zapruder had his film developed and three color copies were made from the original film. He turned over two copies to the Secret Service, stipulating that these were strictly for governmental use and not to be shown to newspapers or magazines because Zapruder expected to sell the film. Three days later, Zapruder negotiated a written agreement with *Life* magazine, which bought the original and all three copies of the film (including the two in possession of the Secret Service). Under that agreeemnt, Zapruder was to be paid $150,000, in yearly installments of $25,000. *Life*, in its November 29, 1963, issue then featured thirty of Zapruder's frames. *Life* subsequently ran more of the Zapruder pictures. *Life* gave the Commission appointed by President Lyndon B. Johnson to investigate the killing of President Kennedy permission to use the Zapruder film and to reproduce it in the report.[91]

In May of 1967, *Life* registered the entire Zapruder film in the Copyright office as an unpublished "motion picture other than a photoplay." Three issues of *Life* magazine in which the Zapruder frames had been published had earlier been registered in the Copyright office as periodicals.[92] This meant that *Life* had a valid copyright in the Zapruder pictures when Bernard Geis Associates sought permission from *Life* magazine to publish the pictures in Thomas Thompson's book, Six Seconds in Dallas, a serious, thoughtful study of the assassination. The firm of Bernard Geis Associates offered to pay *Life* a royalty equal to the profits from publication of the book in return for permission to use specified Zapruder frames in the book. *Life* refused this offer.

Having failed to secure permission from *Life* to use the Zapruder pictures, author Thomas Thompson and his publisher decided to copy certain frames anyway. They did not reproduce the Zapruder frames photographically, but instead paid an artist $1,550 to make charcoal sketch copies. Thompson's book

[91] Time, Inc. v. Bernard Geis Associates, 293 F.Supp. 130, 131–134 (S.D. N.Y.1968). Although the Commission received permission from Time, Inc. to reproduce the photos, the Commission was told that it was expected to give the usual copyright notice. That proviso evidently was disregarded by the Commission.

[92] Ibid., p. 137.

was then published, relying heavily on the sketches, in mid-November of 1967. Significant parts of 22 copyrighted frames were reproduced in the book.[93]

The court ruled that *Life* had a valid copyright in the Zapruder film, and added that "the so-called 'sketches' in the Book are in fact copies of the copyrighted film. That they were done by an 'artist' is of no moment." The Court then quoted copyright expert Melville B. Nimmer: [94]

> "It is of course, fundamental, that copyright in a work protects against unauthorized copying not only in the original medium in which the work was produced, but also in any other medium as well. Thus copyright in a photograph will preclude unauthorized copying by drawing or in any other form, as well as by photographic reproduction."

The court then ruled that the use of the photos in Thompson's book was a copyright infringement, "unless the use of the copyrighted material in the Book is a 'fair use' outside the limits of copyright protection." [95] This led the court to a consideration of fair use, the issue which is " 'the most troublesome in the whole law of copyright.' " [96] The court then found in favor of Bernard Geis Associates and author Thompson, holding that the utilization of the Zapruder pictures was a "fair use." [97]

> There is an initial reluctance to find any fair use by defendants because of the conduct of Thompson in making his copies and because of the deliberate appropriation in the Book, in defiance of the copyright owner. Fair use presupposes "good faith and fair dealing." * * * On the other hand, it was not the nighttime activities of Thompson which enabled defendants to reproduce copies of Zapruder frames in the Book. They could have secured such frames from the National Archives, or they could have used the reproductions in the Warren Report [on the assassination of President Kennedy] or in the issues of *Life* itself. Moreover, while hope by a defendant for commercial gain is not a significant factor in this Circuit, there is a strong point for defendants in their offer to surrender to *Life* all

---

[93] Ibid., pp. 138–139.

[94] Ibid., p. 144, citing Nimmer on Copyright, p. 98.

[95] Ibid., p. 144.

[96] Ibid., quoting from Dellar v. Samuel Goldwyn, Inc., 104 F.2d 661 (2d Cir. 1939).

[97] Ibid., p. 146.

profits of Associates from the Book as royalty payment for a license to use the copyrighted Zapruder frames. It is also a fair inference from the facts that defendants acted with the advice of counsel.

In determining the issue of fair use, the balance seems to be in favor of defendants.

There is a public interest in having the fullest information available on the murder of President Kennedy. Thompson did serious work on the subject and has a theory entitled to public consideration. While doubtless the theory could be explained with sketches * * * [not copied from copyrighted pictures] * * * the explanation actually made in the Book with copies [of the Zapruder pictures] is easier to understand. The Book is not bought because it contained the Zapruder pictures; the Book is bought because of the theory of Thompson and its explanation, supported by the Zapruder pictures.

There seems little, if any, injury to plaintiff, the copyright owner. There is no competition between plaintiff and defendants. Plaintiff does not sell the Zapruder pictures as such and no market for the copyrighted work appears to be affected. Defendants do not publish a magazine. There are projects for use by plaintiff of the film in the future as a motion picture or in books, but the effect of the use of certain frames in the Book on such projects is speculative. It seems more reasonable to speculate that the Book would, if anything, enhance the value of the copyrighted work; it is difficult to see any decrease in its value.

SEC. 47. THE *FORTNIGHTLY* DECISION AND EFFORTS TO REVISE THE COPYRIGHT STATUTE

Technological advances typified by the computer-electronics-microform explosion complicate efforts to revise the Federal copyright statute.

The inadequacy of a federal copyright statute enacted in 1909 and only superficially amended since then becomes clear in cases involving some of the recent products of scientific and promotional genius. One such case is the 1968 decision of the Supreme Court of the United States in Fortnightly Corporation v. United Artists Television, Inc.,[98] involving community antenna television

---

[98] 392 U.S. 390, 88 S.Ct. 2084 (1968).

(CATV) systems proliferating in this country. Fortnightly Corporation owns and operates CATV systems in Clarksburg and Fairmont, West Virginia.

In 1960, when the *Fortnightly* case began, this CATV corporation was using its antennas on hills above Clarksburg and Fairmont to bring in a total of five television broadcasting signals from three Pittsburgh, Pennsylvania, stations, plus stations in Steubenville, Ohio and Wheeling, West Virginia. A cable carried the signals received to the home television sets of individual subscribers to the Fortnightly Corporation's CATV service.[99]

United Artists Television, Inc., which holds copyrights on a number of motion pictures, sued the Fortnightly Corporation for infringement of copyright because the CATV system had not received permission to carry these movies via CATV. In both a federal district court and a United States Circuit Court of Appeals, infringement of United Artists Television's movie copyrights was found.[100] The Supreme Court of the United States granted a writ of certiorari to consider the important questions this case raised under the Copyright Act of 1909.[1]

Speaking for a five-man majority (with Justices Douglas, Marshall, and Harlan taking no part in the decision), Mr. Justice Potter Stewart declared that no copyright infringements had occurred. Justice Stewart said:[2]

> The Copyright Act does not give a copyright holder control over all uses of his copyrighted work. Instead, § 1 of the Act enumerates several "rights" that are made "exclusive" to the holder of the copyright. * * * The respondent's CATV systems infringed the respondent's [United Artists Television, Inc.] * * * exclusive right to "perform * * * in public for profit" * * * and its * * * exclusive right to "perform publicly" (dramatic works). The petitioner [Fortnightly Corporation] maintains that its CATV systems did not "perform" the copyrighted works at all.

Justice Stewart, however, held that the CATV corporation did not "perform" copyrighted works "in any conventional sense of that term, or in any manner envisaged by the Congress that enacted the law in 1909. He stated that if CATV systems were

99 392 U.S. 390, 88 S.Ct. 2084, 2087–2089 (1968).

100 392 U.S. 390, 88 S.Ct. 2084, 2090 (1968).

1 389 U.S. 969, 88 S.Ct. 474 (1967).

2 392 U.S. 390, 88 S.Ct. 2084, 2087 (1968).

made liable for copyright infringement in such situations, even apartment house owners who erect antennas for their tenants— or even every television set manufacturer—might by that logic be held responsible for copyright infringement. Essentially, declared Justice Stewart,[3]

> a CATV system no more than enhances the viewer's capacity to receive the broadcaster's signals; it provides a well-located antenna with an efficient connection to the viewer's television. It is true that a CATV system plays an "active" role in making reception possible, but so do ordinary television sets and antennas.

CATV systems, the Court ruled, neither broadcast nor rebroadcast television programs. "We hold that CATV operators, like viewers and unlike broadcasters, do not perform the programs that they receive and carry." [4] Justice Stewart added for his brethren on the Supreme Court, "We take the Copyright Act of 1909 as we find it." Any declarations which would "accommodate various competing considerations of copyright, communications, and antitrust policy" were thus held to be a job for Congressional legislation.[5]

In a dissent from the Court's opinion, Justice Fortas wrote that the *Fortnightly* CATV case "calls not for the judgment of Solomon but for the dexterity of Houdini." He added that the Supreme Court was here asked [6]

> * * * to consider whether and how a technical, complex, and specific Act of Congress, the Copyright Law, which was drafted in 1909, applies to * * * CATV.
>
> *   *   *   *   *   *   *   *   *
>
> Applying the normal jurisprudential tools—the words of the Act, legislative history, and precedent—to the facts of the case is like trying to repair a television set with a mallet.

Justice Fortas noted the argument that, on the one hand, making CATV systems liable for copyright infringement could ruin that new and important instrument of mass communications. He also reiterated the conflicting assertion that a decision that CATV systems never infringe copyrights of the programs they carry might permit such systems "to overpower local broadcasting stations which must pay, directly or indirectly, for copyright

---

3 392 U.S. 390, 88 S.Ct. 2084, 2087–2088 (1968).

4 392 U.S. 390, 88 S.Ct. 2084, 2090 (1968).

5 Ibid.

6 392 U.S. 390, 88 S.Ct. 2084, 2091 (1968).

licenses and with which CATV is in increasing competition." [7]
Fortas then called for Congressional action: [8]

> Our [the Supreme Court's] major object, I suggest,
> should be to do as little damage as possible to tradition-
> al copyright principles and to business relationships,
> until the Congress legislates and relieves the embarrass-
> ment * * *.

Justice Fortas' pained dissenting opinion in the *Fortnightly
Corporation* case only hints at some of the chaos facing legislators who try to revise the copyright statute. Some of the questions dealt with in recent proposed revision bills are listed briefly
below:

Duration of Copyright: The author's life plus 50 years, instead of a term of 28 years plus another renewal term of 28 years
has been suggested.[9]

Fair Use: The revision bill, unlike the old 1909 Copyright
Statute and its amendments, includes the term "fair use." The
bill says, "Notwithstanding the provisions of section 106, fair
use of a copyrighted work * * * is not an infringement of
copyright." [10] Fair use is not exhaustively defined by that proposed revision, and definition of that term would be left largely
to existing precedent and future court decisions.

Computer Age Technology: The revision bill is broadly stated
so that numerical symbols or materials such as computer programs can be classed as literary works and protected by copyright statute.[11]

The impact of computers, electronics, and microform techniques
upon the copyright field, however, cannot be so easily solved with
a few words in a bill. Take just one example. One "input" of
a book into a nationwide system of computers could be made.
Then, all across the nation, the book's information could be
"printed out" on demand. Such a vast copyright network, of
course, would cut sharply into sales of and profits from books
published in traditional form. Should persons be allowed to feed
a book into a computer for the retail price of a single copy?
Many other similarly tough questions remain.[12]

[7] 392 U.S. 390, 88 S.Ct. 2084, 2091 (1968).

[8] 392 U.S. 390, 88 S.Ct. 2084, 2091–2092 (1968).

[9] See House Bill 2512, 90th Congress, 1st Session, Chapter 3, § 302.

[10] Ibid., Chapter 1, § 107.

[11] Ibid., Chapter 1, § 101.

[12] Arthur J. Greenbaum, "Copyright and the Computer: Why the Unauthorized Duplication of Copyrighted Materials for Use as Computer Input

Jukeboxes: Should jukebox operators continue to be exempt from paying royalties each time their machines played a record?

Photocopying Machines: Should photocopying of copyrighted materials be allowed for libraries or educational institutions? Could a copyright clearing house be devised to pay royalties to an author or publisher for photocopying his work? [13]

Such a brief list suggests only a few problems facing the field of copyright law. Community Antenna Television (CATV) systems are at this writing the cause of great additional problems in revising the copyright statute. The development of CATV has been so swift that the Federal Communications Commission is hard pressed to keep up with it. With its CATV rulings, the FCC has made orders which are sure to have an almost terrifying impact upon the copyright revision picture. For example, FCC reports and rulings issued Dec. 13, 1968, covered more than 200 pages concerning Subscription Television and CATV systems.[14]

Technological promises held out by CATV systems are staggering, and these promises contain many threats to successful revision of copyright statutes. Consider the copyright complications implicit in statements by the FCC. The Commission noted that CATV systems are not handicapped by limited channel capacity, having 12 channels in comparison to the one channel of an individual broadcaster. As a result, a CATV has the technical flexibility "to provide different types of programs or services on some channels without affecting the service simultaneously provided on other channels. Also, "the CATV industry generally is placing increased emphasis on program origination, both of a local public service nature and of the entertainment type." [15]

All of this means that there will be more channels, using more information, in forms difficult to envision today. This broadcasting revolution in CATV must be accounted for in any new

---

Should Constitute Infringement," in Lowell H. Hattery and George P. Bush, eds., Automated Information Systems and Copyright Law, A Symposium of American University, Congressional Record, Vol. 114; No. 102 (Washington, D. C., June 11–14, 1968), pp. 8–9; see also Charles H. Lieb's "Economics, Automation, and Copyright," in ibid., pp. 10–12, and Irwin Karp's "Author's Rights," in ibid., pp. 16–17.

13 Lazowska, op. cit., pp. 123, 127–128.

14 See New York Times, Dec. 14, 1968, p. 91, col. 1; FCC Proceedings numbered FCC 68–1174 (24193), FCC 68–1175 (24194), and FCC 68–1176 (24195), all adopted Dec. 12, 1968 and released Dec. 13, 1968.

15 Federal Communications Commission, Notice of Proposed Rule Making and Notice of Inquiry, Docket No. 18397, FCC 68–1176 (24195), Dec. 13, 1968, p. 3.

copyright statute which is passed. The FCC has considered some of the forms CATV broadcasting may take, noting: [16]

8. It has been suggested that the expanding multichannel capacity of cable systems could be utilized to provide a variety of new communications services to homes and businesses within a community, in addition to services now commonly offered such as time, weather, news, stock exchange ticker, etc. While we shall not attempt an all-inclusive listing, some of the predicted services include: facsimile reproduction of newspapers, magazines, documents, etc.; electronic mail delivery; merchandising; business concern links to branch offices, primary customers or suppliers; access to computers, e. g., man to computer communications in the nature of inquiry and response (credit checks, airlines reservations, branch banking, etc.), information retrieval (library and other reference material, etc.), and computer to computer communications; the furtherance of various governmental programs on a Federal, State and municipal level, e. g., employment services and manpower utilization, special communications systems to reach particular neighborhoods or ethnic groups within a community, and for municipal surveillance of public areas for protection against crime, fire detection, control of air pollution and traffic; various educational and training programs, e. g., job and literacy training, pre-school programs in the nature of "Project Headstart," and to enable professional groups such as doctors to keep abreast of developments in their fields; and the provision of a low cost outlet for political candidates, advertisers, amateur expression (e. g. community or university drama groups) and for other moderately funded organizations or persons desiring access to the community or a particular segment of the community.

9. It has been suggested further that there might be interconnection of local cable systems and the terminal facilities of high capacity terrestrial and/or satellite inter-city systems, to provide numerous communications

---

[16] Ibid., pp. 4–5. For views of some of the perplexities involving satellite telecommunication and the law, including copyright law, see Fred S. Siebert, "Property Rights in Materials Transmitted by Satellites, Journalism Quarterly 48:1 (Spring, 1971) pp. 17–25; note the bibliography at pp. 24–25, and D. D. Smith, "Legal Ordering of Satellite Telecommunications," Indiana Law Journal 44:3 (1969) p. 337ff.

services to the home, business and educational or other center on a regional or national basis. The advent of CATV program origination in such cities as New York and Los Angeles (where is also CATV activity) gives rise to the possibility of a CATV origination network or networks. The so-called "wired city" concept, embraces the possibility that television broadcasting might eventually be converted, in whole or in part, to cable transmission (coupled with the use of microwave or other intercity relay facilities), thereby freeing some broadcast spectrum for other uses and making it technically feasible to have a greater number of national and regional television networks and local outlets. More broadly in the area of general communications, the present and future development of intercity facilities with very high communications capacity (e. g., the L5 coaxial cable, millimeter wave guides, communications by laser beams), coupled with the potential of the computer and communications satellite technologies, may stimulate the provision of new nationwide or regional services of various kinds, which would require connection to high capacity communications facilities within the locality and from the street to the premises of the consumer. Another matter to be explored in this area is the expanding multi-channel capacity of CATV (together with its proposed auxiliary use of high capacity, local microwave links), including the question of whether it is technically and economically feasible for CATV to develop capability for two-way and switched services.

Competing interests and technological advances have thus combined to stymie, at this writing, passage of a copyright revision bill. Representative Robert W. Kastenmeier assessed chances for copyright revision early in 1969: [17]

The prospects for such a revision bill are somewhat clouded at this point by the continuing problems posed by the CATV issue and the onrushing problems of the new technologies. Senator [John L.] McClellan [D, Arkansas] has indicated that since the Senate did not pass the House-passed legislation in the 90th Congress, he feels responsible for initiating the effort on the Senate side this year, so as not to repeat the procedure of having the House pass the legislation which the Senate

[17] Representative Robert W. Kastenmeier, letter to Dwight L. Teeter, Jr., Jan. 14, 1969.

would not act upon. Accordingly, it would appear that the Senate will have first opportunity to resolve the question of CATV and computers and micro-form.

Any initiative by the House would probably unduly complicate the efforts being made by the Senate, and it is, therefore, difficult to make any clear assessment of the prospects for passage of this legislation in the 91st [1969–1970] Congress. Efforts will be made however to realize some legislative accomplishments out of all the extensive efforts that have been made in this area.

As Representative Kastenmeier said in 1973, " *   *   * problems of copyright revision seem largely unchanged. For some years now, it has been my position that our Copyright Subcommittee should await passage of a revision bill by the Senate before offering the House another revision like H.R. 2512 of the 90th Congress that passed the House in April, 1967." [18]

The democratic ideal of an individual's free access to ideas and information collides headlong with rights of authors or publishers to profit from their work. Advocates of each side are now contributing to difficulties in passing a new copyright statute. The issues are not clear-cut, and there are plausible arguments being advanced for both the free access to ideas and for the rights of authors, artists, or publishers. Technological revolutions have added new dimensions to the problems of making law in a tortured area. The only agreement, from both sides, is that something must be done.

[18] Rep. Kastenmeier to Teeter, March 20, 1973. For added information on recent and baffling copyright problems, see "Copyright Law—Legality of Photocopying Copyrighted Publications," William and Mary Law Review 13:4 (Summer, 1972) pp. 940–948, and J. Timothy Keane, "The Cable Compromise: Integration of Federal Copyright and Telecommunications Policies," Saint Louis University Law Journal 17:3 (Spring, 1973) pp. 340–354.

Chapter 8

FREE PRESS—FAIR TRIAL

SEC. 48. PARTIES IN THE CONTROVERSY

**Attorneys and members of the press are trying to settle long
standing issues in the "free press-fair trial" dispute. Guidelines for the release of information to the media—including
the American Bar Association's 1968 "Reardon Report"—
were symptoms of the controversy.**

"Trial by newspaper" or "trial by mass media" were phrases
often heard during the 1960s as a rancorous "free press-fair
trial" controversy accelerated between the press and the bar.
This controversy generated much noise, with some attorneys
blaming the mass media for many of the shortcomings of the
American court system.[1] In reply, many journalists went to
considerable lengths in attempting to justify the actions of the
mass media in covering criminal trials.[2]

Many of the lawyers' arguments contained the assertion that
the media were destroying the rights of defendants in criminal
trials by publicizing cases before they got to court. Such publicity, it was often contended, prejudiced potential jurors to such a
degree that a fair trial was impossible. The media, the argument ran, were too often operating—where sensational trials

[1] See, e. g., Advisory Committee on Fair Trial and Free Press, Standards
Relating to Fair Trial and Free Press (New York, 1966); see also draft
approved Feb. 19, 1968, by delegates to American Bar Association convention
as published in March, 1968.

[2] See, e. g., American Newspaper Publishers Association, Free Press and
Fair Trial (New York): American Newspaper Publishers Association, 1967,
p. 1 and passim.

276

were involved—to defeat the Constitutional right to a fair trial guaranteed by the Sixth Amendment.[3]

Editors and publishers—and some attorneys too—were quick with rejoinders that the media were not all *that* harmful, and that, in any case, the First Amendment's free press guarantees took precedence over any other Constitutional provisions, including the Sixth Amendment's.[4]

In the 1970s, press-bar relationships showed some improvement as journalists and lawyers and judges have made strenuous efforts to work out guidelines for covering criminal trials in order to protect both defendants' rights and the right of the public to know about the administration of justice.

The free press-fair trial controversy of the 1960s took place against a background including a number of sensational, nationally publicized trials and the assassinations of President John F. Kennedy in 1963 and Senator Robert Kennedy in 1968. This continuing dispute, which arrayed the media's right to report against defendants' rights to a fair trial, generated new law in the form of several important Supreme Court decisions, and also brought forth attempts to codify or regularize dealings between the media and law enforcement officials with a view toward protecting defendants' rights to a fair trial.[5]

Although the mass media became a favorite whipping boy of some attorneys and legal organizations, with all manner of violations of defendants' rights laid at the media's doorstep, this is most certainly the result of oversimplification. To the extent that the media, in some cases, *did* create an atmosphere in which it was difficult to select a jury which had not already made up its mind, law enforcement officials which made available such prejudicial information to the press also deserved a share of the blame. Statements by a public official—Los Angeles Mayor Samuel Yorty—during the aftermath of the assassination of Senator Robert Kennedy in 1968—provide a case in point.

When Robert Kennedy was fatally wounded in a kitchen corridor in Los Angeles' Ambassador Hotel in June, 1968, a suspect —Jordanian immigrant Sirhan Bishara Sirhan—was apprehended on the spot by Kennedy's bodyguards and onlookers. Sirhan

---

3 See footnote 1, above.

4 American Newspaper Publishers Association, op. cit., p. 1.

5 See Advisory Committee on Fair Trial and Free Press, op. cit., passim; see also, Irvin v. Dowd, 366 U.S. 717, 81 S.Ct. 1639 (1961); Rideau v. Louisiana, 373 U.S. 723, 83 S.Ct. 1417 (1963); Sheppard v. Maxwell, 384 U.S. 333, 86 S.Ct. 1507 (1966).

was placed under tight security guard, and newsmen and even Sirhan's attorney entering the courtroom for the arraignment were frisked for weapons. Los Angeles Police Chief Thomas Reddin was very careful as he answered newsmen's questions. He refused to speculate on anything of which he did not have first-hand knowledge. Chief Reddin told reporters that even if Sirhan confessed, that news would not be released in order to avoid prejudicing the case. Mayor Yorty, however, was not nearly so cautious in his utterances concerning the assassination of Robert Kennedy.

The day after the shooting, Yorty began holding press conferences. At one such conference, Yorty released the contents of two notebooks which he said had been found in Sirhan's home. Yorty reported that one of the notebooks said, "Kennedy has to be assassinated before June 5, 1968," the first anniversary of the start of an Arab-Israeli conflict in which the Arabs were ignominiously defeated. Yorty also commented vaguely about "Communist influences" in Sirhan's life, and asserted that a car belonging to Sirhan had been seen near a place where a leftist W.E.B. DuBois Club was meeting.[6]

California Attorney General Thomas Lynch phoned Yorty immediately after the mayor's first press conference, expressing concern about the mayor's remarks. Lynch later said Yorty's statements "referred to evidence that would have to be ruled upon by the court. He said he wasn't going to make any more statements like that." Even so, Yorty again released statements about Sirhan's diary on the following day, saying that it revealed "definite Communist leanings" by Sirhan.[7]

Except for Mayor Yorty's ill-considered eloquence, Los Angeles officials did an excellent job of protecting the assassination suspect and in refusing to make utterances which might prejudice potential jurors. It should be noted, however, that videotaped television coverage of a pistol being wrestled away from Sirhan as Senator Kennedy lay dying on the hotel floor were rerun repeatedly by all three major television networks, which would be likely to make finding "unprejudiced" jurors incalculably more difficult if not impossible.

Los Angeles officials, however, had learned their lesson well from the events which followed the assassination of President

6 San Francisco Chronicle, This World, June 16, 1968, p. 5, cols. 4–5. The W.E.B. DuBois Clubs promptly attacked Yorty's insinuation that Sirhan had been connected with those clubs, saying that Sirhan had no connection with them. San Francisco Chronicle, June 8, 1968, p. 9, cols. 1–2.

7 San Francisco Chronicle, This World, June 16, 1968, p. 5, cols. 4–5.

Kennedy in 1963. That assassination had brought the problems of "trial by mass media" dramatically to public consciousness, a fact which was underscored by the report of a Presidential Commission headed by Chief Justice Earl Warren. The Warren Commission was intensely critical of both the Dallas police and the news media for their reports of the news of that event. Oswald, of course, never lived to stand trial, because he was assassinated by Jack Ruby in a hallway of Dallas police headquarters which was a scene of confusion, clogged with reporters, cameramen, and the curious.[8] Los Angeles police simply would not permit such a circus to occur, and took great pains to isolate Sirhan Bishara Sirhan from such dangerous mob scenes.

The month after President Kennedy's assassination, the American Bar Association charged that "widespread publicizing of Oswald's alleged guilt, involving statements by officials and public disclosures of the details of 'evidence' would have made it extremely difficult to impanel an unprejudiced jury and afford the accused a fair trial." Indeed, it is likely that had Oswald lived to stand trial, he might not have been convicted of the murder of President Kennedy, even though the Warren Commission—after the fact—declared that Oswald was in all likelihood Kennedy's assassin. Under American judicial procedures, it seems probable that Oswald could not have received a fair and unprejudiced trial, and any conviction of Oswald might well have been upset on appeal.[9]

The Warren Commission placed first blame on police and prosecutors, but additionally criticized the media for their part in the events following the President's death. The Commission said that "part of the responsibility for the unfortunate circumstances following the President's death must be borne by the news media * * *." Newsmen were excoriated by Commission members for showing a lack of self-discipline, and a code of professional conduct was called for as evidence that the press was willing to support the Sixth Amendment right to a fair and impartial trial as well as the right of the public to be informed.[10]

If the reporters behaved badly in Dallas, so did the Dallas law enforcement officials, who displayed "evidence" in crowded corridors and released statements about other evidence. Conduct of police and other law enforcement officials, however, has by no

8 Report of the President's Commission on the Assassination of President John F. Kennedy (Washington: Government Printing Office, 1964) p. 241.

9 William A. Hachten, The Supreme Court on Freedom of the Press: Decisions and Dissents (Ames, Iowa: Iowa State University Press, 1968) p. 106.

10 Report of the President's Commission on the Assassination of President John F. Kennedy, p. 241.

means been the only source of prejudicial materials which later appeared in the press to the detriment of defendants' rights. All too often, both defense and prosecution attorneys have released statements to reporters which are clearly at odds with the American Bar Association's Canons of Professional Ethics. Canon 20, first adopted more than 50 years ago, provides: [11]

> Newspaper publications by a lawyer as to pending or anticipated litigation may interfere with a fair trial in the Courts and otherwise prejudice the due administration of justice. Generally they are to be condemned. If the extreme circumstances of a particular case justify a statement to the public, it is unprofessional to make it anonymously. An *ex parte* reference to the facts should not go beyond quotation from the records and papers on file in the court; but even in extreme cases it is better to avoid any *ex parte* statement.

Canon 20, in theory, could be used as a weapon to silence lawyers who release statements to the press which harm a defendant's chances for a fair trial. Although this Canon has been adopted by the bar associations of most states, there has rarely if ever been a case brought to disbar or discipline an attorney or judge who makes prejudicial remarks to the press.[12] In mid-1968, however, flamboyant defense attorney F. Lee Bailey was removed from a case by the New Jersey Supreme Court. That court ruled that Bailey's behavior was " 'so gross that we cannot risk more of it.' " A United States District Court Judge [Robert Shaw] upheld the New Jersey Supreme Court's ruling, refusing to reinstate Bailey as defense attorney in the Kavanaugh-DeFranco murder cases.[13]

Because Canon 20, however, has been used virtually not at all to discipline attorneys, it may be argued that during the Twentieth Century, the bar has done little to set its own house in order concerning free press-fair trial problems. A famed defense attorney, Edward Bennett Williams, has argued that Canon 20, if enforced, could have gone far to solve difficulties from releasing prejudicial information to the media. Williams has argued that if police and both prosecuting and defense attorneys would refrain from making troublesome statements to the press, free press-fair trial problems would be diminished greatly. Of

[11] Canons of Professional and Judicial Ethics of the American Bar Association, Canon 20.

[12] Donald M. Gillmor, Free Press and Fair Trial (Washington, D. C., Public Affairs Press, 1966) p. 110.

[13] Associated Press dispatch, published June 19, 1968 in the San Francisco Chronicle, p. 1.

course, as Williams pointed out, courts and the bar's disciplinary committees would have to take stern action to effectively enforce Canon 20.[14]

Newsmen, then, are not the only offenders in creating what are called "trials by newspaper" or, more recently, "trials by mass media." A quick skimming of the General Index of a legal encyclopedia, *American Jurisprudence*, adds more support for such a generalization. The General Index of "Amjur" contains nearly 600 categories under the topic, "New Trial." New trials may be granted because something went awry in the original trial, somehow depriving a defendant of his right to a fair trial under the Sixth Amendment. These categories include such things as persons fainting in the courtroom, hissing, technical mistakes by attorneys, prejudice of judges, and misconduct by jurors: jurors who read newspapers.[15]

Findings of social scientists lend some support assumptions about jurors' being prejudiced by the mass media.[16] Much more research, however, remains to be done before assertions can be made confidently that what a juror reads or learns from the mass media will affect the juror's subsequent behavior. On the other hand, it has been argued that lawyers, before casting aspersions at the press, might consider the question of whether their own legal house is in order. Consider what psychologists can tell lawyers about a fair trial. Consider the rules of procedure in a criminal trial as attorneys make their final arguments to a jury. First, the prosecution sums up its case. Then the defense attorney makes his final argument. And last, the prosecuting attorney makes his final statement to the jury. For years, psychologists have been arguing about order of presentation in persuasion. Some evidence has been found that having the first say is most persuasive; other evidence that having the last word might be best.[17] But who gets neither the first say nor the last word during the final arguments before a jury? The defendant.[18]

---

[14] Cited by Gillmor, loc. cit., from Edward Bennett Williams, "On Trial: Jimmy Hoffa and Adam Clayton Powell," Saturday Evening Post, June 16, 1962.

[15] 3 Am.Jur., Gen.Index, New Trial, pp. 1030–1045.

[16] See, e. g., Mary Dee Tans and Steven H. Chaffee, "Pretrial Publicity and Juror Prejudice," Journalism Quarterly Vol. 43:4 (Winter, 1966) pp. 647–654, and a list of juror prejudice studies on p. 647, notes 4, 5 and 6.

[17] See, e. g., Carl I. Hovland, et al., The Order of Presentation in Persuasion, (New Haven: Yale, 1957) passim.

[18] The authors are grateful to Professors Jack M. McLeod and Steven H. Chaffee, both of the University of Wisconsin Mass Communications Research Center, for this insight.

One set of guidelines—the "Statement of Policy Concerning the Release of Information by Personnel of the Department of Justice Relating to Criminal Proceedings"—attempts to take both First and Sixth Amendment rights into account. These guidelines, more commonly known as the Katzenbach Guidelines after former Attorney General Nicholas deB. Katzenbach, were first announced on April 16, 1965. Note that these guidelines, reproduced below, allow the release of information prejudicial to a defendant when such information is in the public interest: something the public needs to know to protect itself. They are addressed not to the mass media, but to law enforcement officers.

Office of the Attorney General
Washington, D. C.

Statement of Policy Concerning the Release of Information by Personnel of the Department of Justice Relating to Criminal Proceedings

[28 C.F.R. § 50.2 (1965)]

The availability to news media of information in criminal cases is a matter which has become increasingly a subject of concern in the administration of criminal justice. The purpose of this statement is to formulate specific guidelines for the release of such information by personnel of the Department of Justice.

1. These guidelines shall apply to the release of information to news media from the time a person is arrested or is charged with a criminal offense until the proceeding has been terminated by trial or otherwise.

2. At no time shall personnel of the Department of Justice furnish any statement or information for the purpose of influencing the outcome of a defendant's trial.

3. Personnel of the Department of Justice, subject to specific limitations imposed by law or court rule or order, may make public the following information:

(A) The defendant's name, age, residence, employment, marital status, and similar background information.

(B) The substance or text of the charge, such as a complaint, indictment, or information.

(C) The identity of the investigating and arresting agency and the length of the investigation.

(D) The circumstances immediately surrounding an arrest, including the time and place of arrest, resistance, pursuit, possession and use of weapons, and a description of items seized at the time of arrest.

Disclosures should include only incontrovertible, factual matters, and should not include subjective observations. In addition, where background information relating to the circumstances of an arrest would be highly prejudicial and where the release thereof would serve no law enforcement function, such information should not be made public.

4. Personnel of the Department shall not volunteer for publication any information concerning a defendant's prior criminal record. However, this is not intended to alter the Department's present policy that, since federal criminal conviction records are matters of public record permanently maintained in the Department, this information may be made available upon specific inquiry.

5. Because of the particular danger of prejudice resulting from statements in the period approaching and during trial, they ought strenuously to be avoided during that period. Any such statement or release shall be made only on the infrequent occasion when circumstances absolutely demand a disclosure of information and shall include only information which is clearly not prejudicial.

6. The release of certain types of information generally tends to create dangers of prejudice without serving a significant law enforcement function. Therefore, personnel of the Department should refrain from making available the following:

(A) Observations about a defendant's character.

(B) Statements, admissions, confession, or alibis attributable to a defendant.

(C) References to investigative procedures, such as fingerprints, polygraph examinations, ballistic tests, or laboratory tests.

(D) Statements concerning the identity, credibility, or testimony of prospective witnesses.

(E) Statements concerning evidence or argument in the case, whether or not it is anticipated that such evidence or argument will be used at trial.

7.   Personnel of the Department of Justice should take no action to encourage or assist news media in photographing or televising a defendant or accused person being held or transported in federal custody.   Departmental representatives should not make available photographs of a defendant unless a law enforcement function is served thereby.

8.   This statement of policy is not intended to restrict the release of information concerning a defendant who is a fugitive from justice.

9.   Since the purpose of this statement is to set forth generally applicable guidelines, there will, of course, be situations in which it will limit release of information which would not be prejudicial under the particular circumstances.   If a representative of the Department believes that in the interest of the fair administration of justice and the law enforcement process information beyond these guidelines should be released in a particular case, he shall request the permission of the Attorney General or the Deputy Attorney General to do so.[19]

Attorneys General come, and go, and Justice Department guidelines change as time passes.   Attorney General Katzenbach's guidelines were revised in November of 1971 by Attorney General John Mitchell, and the ruling was obviously intended to cut down the flow of potentially prejudicial information to the press.   Mitchell, the former law partner of President Richard M. Nixon, promulgated guidelines forbidding Justice Department employees from discussing with the press most aspects of civil as well as criminal trials.   Mitchell also narrowed the guidelines on the kind of information which can be released in criminal cases.   Under the Mitchell order, Justice Department officials were forbidden to talk to newsmen about criminal cases "from the time a person is the subject of a criminal investigation."

Previously, employees of the Justice Department were forbidden to give information to the press only after a person had been indicted or arrested.   The revisions were said to have been proposed to Mitchell by United States Circuit Court of Appeals Judge Irving Kaufman, head of a judicial committee in New York which adopted the guidelines.[20]

---

[19] 28 C.F.R. § 50.2 (1965).

[20] "Mitchell Limits Staff in Talks With Press," UPI story in Milwaukee Journal, November 21, 1971, p. 14.

Although the Katzenbach guidelines for federal courts and law enforcement officers met considerable approval, the American Bar Association's (ABA's) concern continued.　On February 21, 1968, the ABA Convention meeting in Chicago approved the "Standards Relating to Fair Trial and Free Press" recommended by the Advisory Committee headed by Massachusetts Supreme Court Justice Paul C. Reardon.[21]　The "Reardon Report," as this document is more commonly known, was greated with outraged concern by a large segment of the American media.[22]

The Reardon Report's recommendations fell into these four broad categories: [23]

1.　Recommendations Relating to the Conduct of Attorneys in Criminal Cases.

2.　Recommendations Relating to the Conduct of Law Enforcement Officers, Judges, and Judicial Employees in Criminal Cases.

3.　Recommendations Relating to the Conduct of Judicial Proceedings in Criminal Cases.

4.　Recommendations Relating to the Exercise of the Contempt Power.

Section One, "Revisions of the Canons of Professional Ethics," prohibits lawyers from releasing certain information, when there is a "reasonable likelihood that such dissemination will interfere with a fair trial or otherwise prejudice the due administration of justice."　Also, where investigations or grand jury proceedings are involved, lawyers are cautioned to "refrain from making any extrajudicial statement, for dissemination by any means of public communication, that goes beyond the public record or that is not necessary to inform the public that the investigation is underway, to describe the general scope of the investigation, to obtain assistance in the apprehension of a suspect, to warn the public of any dangers, or otherwise to aid in the investigation." [24]　These stipulations were also made: [25]

> From the time of arrest, issuance of an arrest warrant, or the filing of a complaint, information, or indictment in any criminal matter until the commencement of trial

[21] Approved Draft, Standards Relating to Fair Trial and Free Press, March, 1968.　Hereafter cited as Approved Draft.　The ABA Standards are printed in seventeen volumes.　They may be ordered from the ABA Circulation Department, 1155 East 60th Street, Chicago, Illinois 60637.　Cost is $3.25 for a single volume;　$38 for a set of seventeen volumes;　$2.25 each for bulk orders of 10–24 of the same title, or $1.75 each for 25 or more of the same title.　Reprinted by permission.

[22] See footnotes 32 and 33, this chapter.

[23] Approved Draft, p. 1.

[24] Ibid., p. 1.

[25] Ibid., pp. 2–3.

or disposition without trial, a lawyer associated with the prosecution or defense shall not release or authorize the release of any extrajudicial statement, for dissemination by any means of public communication, relating to that matter and concerning:

(1) The prior criminal record (including arrests, indictments, or other charges of crime), or the character or reputation of the accused, except that the lawyer may make a factual statement of the accused's name, age, residence, occupation, and family status, and if the accused has not been apprehended, a lawyer associated with the prosecution may release any information necessary to aid in his apprehension or to warn the public of any dangers he may present;

(2) The existence or contents of any confession, admission, or statement given by the accused, or the refusal or failure of the accused to make any statement;

(3) The performance of any examinations or tests or the accused's refusal or failure to submit to an examination or test;

(4) The identity, testimony, or credibility of prospective witnesses, except that the lawyer may announce the identity of the victim if the announcement is not otherwise prohibited by law;

(5) The possibility of a plea of guilty to the offense charged or a lesser offense;

(6) Any opinion as to the accused's guilt or innocence or as to the merits of the case or the evidence in the case.

The foregoing shall not be construed to preclude the lawyer during this period, in the proper discharge of his official or professional obligations, from announcing the fact and circumstances of arrest (including time and place of arrest, resistance, pursuit, and use of weapons), the identity of the investigating and arresting officer or agency, and the length of the investigation; from making an announcement, at the time of seizure of any physical evidence other than a confession, admission or statement, which is limited to a description of the evidence seized; from disclosing the nature, substance, or text of the charge, including a brief description of the offense charged; from quoting or referring without comment to public records of the court in the case; from announcing the scheduling or result of any stage in the judicial process; from requesting assistance in obtaining evidence; or from announcing without further comment that the accused denies the charges made against him.

During the trial of any criminal matter, including the period of selection of the jury, no lawyer associated with the prosecution or defense shall give or authorize any extrajudicial statement or interview, relating to the trial or the parties or issues in the trial, for dissemination by any means of public communication, except that the lawyer may quote from or refer without comment to public records of the court in the case.

After the completion of a trial or disposition without trial of any criminal matter, and prior to the imposition of sentence, a lawyer associated with the prosecution or defense shall refrain from making or authorizing any extrajudicial statement for dissemination by any means of public communication if there is a reasonable likelihood that such dissemination will affect the imposition of sentence.

Nothing in this Canon is intended to preclude the formulation or application of more restrictive rules relating to the release of information about juvenile or other offenders, to preclude the holding of hearings or the lawful issuance of reports by legislative, administrative, or investigative bodies, or to preclude any lawyer from replying to charges of misconduct that are publicly made against him.

1.2 Rule of court.

In any jurisdiction in which Canons of Professional Ethics have not been adopted by statute or court rule, it is recommended that the substance of the foregoing section be adopted as a rule of court governing the conduct of attorneys.

As Michael J. Petrick has pointed out, even newsmen who are the most offended by the ABA's adoption of the free press-fair trial standards offered by the Reardon Report should note one bit of "fallout" favorable to journalists. That is, wherever the standards are given the force of law by statute or court rule, the provisions just listed under (6) above would in effect make police blotters into public records.

Enforcement of the six standards or rules listed above is in the hands of judicial or bar associations. Punishment for violation of the standards could vary from a reprimand from a judicial or bar association to suspension from practice, and, in flagrant cases, to outright disbarment.[26]

Section One, it should be noted, deals only with attorneys. Section Two *recommends* (not commands) that law enforcement agencies adopt internal rules for the release of information to the media virtually identical to Section One's rules for attorneys, listed above.[27]

Section Three recommends that defendants be allowed to move that any "preliminary hearing, bail hearing, or other pretrial hearing in a criminal case, including a motion to suppress evidence" be held in the judge's chambers or otherwise closed to the public, including newsmen. The ground for such a motion would be that the hearing might produce evidence which would be inadmissible at trial, and which if published by the news media, could prejudice a defendant's right to a fair and impartial trial. If the jury is not sequestered, the defendant can move that the public—including the news media—be removed from the courtroom during presentation of any matters when the jury is not present. The argument here is that dissemination of arguments may otherwise reach the jurors and interfere with defendant's right to a fair trial. The free press-fair trial standards recommend that the defendant's motions to exclude press and public be granted unless the judge "determines that there is no substantial likelihood" of interfering with defendant's right to a fair trial before an impartial jury.[28]

On balance, the "Reardon Report" has had useful effects for lawyers, journalists and citizens, despite the report's early draft's suggestions that contempt penalties should be employed against the news media. In the aftermath of the Warren Commission report on the Kennedy assassination (which called for curtailment of pretrial news), the *Sheppard* case—discussed at length later in this chapter—came along to illustrate once again just how wretchedly prejudicial news coverage of a criminal trial could become. In that setting, the American Bar Associa-

26 Ibid., pp. 3–4. See Michael J. Petrick, "The Press, the Police Blotter, and Public Policy," Journalism Quarterly 46:3 (Autumn, 1969) pp. 475–481.

27 An earlier draft of the Reardon Report aroused great protest from the press because it would have *required* courts to make rules for the conduct of law enforcement officials. Persons opposed to such a step argued violently that while courts could regulate the conduct of judges and attorneys, they could not control the actions of members of the executive branch of government without violating separation of powers. Cf. 1966 Tentative Drafts, Standards Relating to Fair Trial and Free Press With The Approved Draft published March, 1968; see Marc A. Franklin, The Dynamics of American Law (Mineola, N. Y., Foundation Press, 1968) p. 736.

28 Approved Draft, pp. 7, 11.

tio (ABA) Advisory Committee on Fair Trial-Free Press (Reardon Committee) was formed. As Professor J. Edward Gerald of the University of Minnesota has written,[29]

> the American Newspaper Publishers Association responded defensively with its Committee on Free Press and Fair Trial. Other associations in law and journalism joined in, and a long dialogue ensued in which strong positions were taken. However, these positions masked a serious discussion between liberals, moderates, and conservatives inside both the bar and the press.

> The internal discussions caused attitudes to change. Criminal sanctions for lawyers, peace officers, or journalists, freely discussed at the outset, no longer seem tenable. Concurrently, pretrial use of prejudicial news has been substantially curtailed by the mass media.

In many places, a press-bar *rapprochement* occurred, leading to construction, by joint committees of press and bar, of guidelines for the coverage of criminal trials. In Wisconsin, for example, the following guidelines were adopted:[30]

STATEMENT OF PRINCIPLES OF THE WISCONSIN BAR AND NEWS MEDIA

The bar and news media of Wisconsin recognize that freedom of the news media and the right to a fair and swift trial are fundamental to the basic liberties guaranteed by the first and sixth amendments of the United States Constitution. The news media and the bar further recognize that these basic rights must be rigidly preserved and responsibly practiced according to highest professional standards.

The bar and the news media, and indeed all citizens, are obliged to preserve the principle that any person suspected or accused of a crime is innocent until found guilty in a court under competent evidence fairly presented and accurately reported.

---

[29] J. Edward Gerald, "Press-Bar Relationships: Progress Since *Sheppard* and Reardon," Jouralism Quarterly 47:2 (Summer, 1970) p. 223. See also the Report of the President's Commission on the Assassination of President John F. Kennedy (1964), and Judicial Conference of the United States Committee on the Jury System, Report of the Committee on the Operation of the Jury System on the Free Press-Fair Trial Issue 1–3 (1968).

[30] Reprinted from Wisconsin Bar Bulletin, February, 1969, pp. 7–9.

The bar and news media recognize that access to legitimate information involving the administration of justice is as vital to the public's concern in the commission of crimes against society as is guaranteeing the suspect and the state a fair trial free of prejudicial information and conduct. The same principles apply in all civil proceedings.

To promote understanding toward reconciling the constitutional guarantees of freedom of the press and the right to a fair, impartial trial, the following principles, mutually drawn and submitted for voluntary compliance, are recommended to all members of these professions in Wisconsin.

1. The news media have the right and responsibility to disseminate the news. Free and responsible news media enhance the administration of justice. Members of the bar should co-operate, within their canons of legal ethics, with the news media in the reporting of the administration of justice.

2. All parties to litigation, including the state, have the right to have their causes tried fairly by an impartial tribunal. Defendants in criminal cases are guaranteed this right by the Constitutions of the United States and Wisconsin.

3. No trial should be influenced by the pressure of publicity from news media or by the public. Lawyers and journalists share responsibility to prevent the creation of such pressures.

"Strive for Accuracy"

4. All news media should strive for accuracy and objectivity. The public has a right to be informed, the accused the right to be judged in an atmosphere free from undue prejudice.

5. The news media and bar recognize the responsibility of the judge to preserve order in the court and to seek the ends of justice by all appropriate legal means.

6. Decisions about handling news rest with editors. In the exercise of news judgment, the communicator should remember that:

(a) An accused person is presumed innocent until proved guilty.

(b) Readers, listeners and viewers are potential jurors.

(c) No person's reputation should be injured needlessly.

7. The public is entitled to know how justice is being administered. No lawyer should use publicity to promote his side of a pending case. The public prosecutor should not take unfair advantage of his position as an important source of news. These cautions shall not be construed to limit a lawyer's obligation to make available information to which the public is entitled.

Meaning of Rights

8. Journalistic and legal training should include instruction in the meaning of constitutional rights to a fair trial, freedom of press, and the role of both journalist and lawyer in guarding these rights.

9. A committee of representatives of the bar and the media, possibly aided by or including representatives of law enforcement agencies and other interested parties, should meet from time to time to promote understanding of these principles by the public and especially by all directly involved persons, agencies or organizations. Its purpose may include giving advisory opinions concerning the interpretation and application of these principles as specific problems arise.

GUIDELINES ON THE REPORTING OF CRIMINAL PROCEEDINGS

1. There should be no restraint on making public the following information concerning the defendant:

(a) The defendant's name, age, residence, employment, marital status and other factual background information.

(b) The substance or text of the charge, such as complaint, indictment, information or, where appropriate, the identity of the complaining party.

(c) The identity of the investigating and arresting agency, and the nature of the investigation where appropriate.

(d) The circumstances surrounding an arrest, including the time and place of arrest, resistance, pursuit, possession and use of weapons and a description of items seized at the time of arrest.

2.   The release to news media of certain types of information, or its publication, may create dangers of prejudice to the defense or prosecution without serving a significant law enforcement or public interest function. Therefore, all concerned should be aware of the dangers of prejudice in making pretrial public disclosures of the following:

(a) Opinions about a defendant's character, his guilt or innocence.

(b) Admissions, confessions or the contents of a statement or alibis attributable to a defendant.

(c) References to investigative procedures, such as fingerprints, polygraph examinations, ballistic tests or laboratory tests.

(d) Statements concerning the credibility or anticipated testimony of prospective witnesses.

(e) Opinions concerning evidence or argument in the case, whether or not it is anticipated that such evidence or argument will be used at trial.

Exceptions to these points may be in order if information to the public is essential to the apprehension of a suspect, or where other public interests will be served.

3.   Prior criminal charges and convictions are matters of public record, available through police agencies or court clerks. Law enforcement agencies should make such information available upon legitimate inquiry but the public disclosure of it may be highly prejudicial without benefit to the public's need to be informed. The news media and law enforcement agencies have a special duty to report the disposition or status of prior charges.

4.   Law enforcement and court personnel should not prevent the photographing of defendants, or suspects, when they are in public places outside the courtroom. They should not promote pictures or televising nor should they pose a defendant or suspect of a person in custody against his will. They may make available a suitable photograph of a defendant or a person in custody.

5.   Photographs of a suspect not in custody may be released by law enforcement personnel provided a valid

law enforcement function is served thereby. It is proper to disclose information necessary to enlist public assistance in apprehending fugitives. Disclosure may include photographs as well as records of prior arrests and convictions.

6. Freedom for news media to report proceedings in open court is generally recognized. The bench may utilize measures—such as cautionary instructions, sequestration of the jury and the holding of hearings on evidence in the absence of the jury—to insure that the jury's deliberations are based upon evidence presented to them in court. All concerned should co-operate toward that end.

7. Sensationalism should be avoided by all.

GUIDELINES FOR REPORTING JUVENILE OFFENSES

The news media and the bar recognize the distinction between juvenile and adult offenders established by law. We also recognize the right of the media to have free access to all matters concerning juvenile offenders and juvenile proceedings and to report the same, except as prohibited by law.

The bar and the media further recognize that they share, with the courts and other officials, responsibility for developing sound public interest in and understanding of juvenile problems as they relate to the community.

We therefore recommend:

1. In the handling of juvenile matters, basic principles of fairness and cooperation, as defined in the Statement of Principles of the bench-media committee of Wisconsin, shall apply. When a juvenile is regarded as an adult under criminal law, the bar-media guidelines for reporting crime and ordinance violations shall apply.

2. When news media attend sessions of the juvenile court, they may disclose names or identifying data of the participants, unless prohibited by law. News media should make every effort to fully observe and report such sessions, and the disposition thereof by the court, with regard for the juvenile's rights and the public interest.

SEC. 49. CONTEMPT

The Reardon Report's suggestion that judges use the contempt power to control pre-trial or during-trial reporting brought outraged rejoinders from the press.

Section Four of the Reardon Report recommended that "limited" use be made of the courts' contempt power to punish publications which judges see as violating a defendant's right to a fair trial: [31]

> It is recommended that the contempt power should be used only with considerable caution but should be exercised under the following circumstances:
>
> (a) Against a person who, knowing that a criminal trial by jury is in progress or that a jury is being selected for such a trial:
>
> (i) disseminates by any means of public communication an extrajudicial statement relating to the defendant or to the issues in the case that goes beyond the public record of the court in the case, that is wilfully designed by that person to affect the outcome of the trial, and that seriously threatens to have such an effect; or
>
> (ii) makes such a statement intending that it be disseminated by any means of public communication.
>
> (b) Against a person who knowingly violates a valid judicial order not to disseminate, until completion of the trial or disposition without trial, specified information referred to in the course of a judicial hearing * * * [which has been closed to the public, including the news media].

Replies from representatives of the news media were not long in coming after the ABA House of Delegates adopted the "Reardon Report" on February 19, 1968. J. Edward Murray, managing editor of *The Arizona Republic,* said: "Fortunately, neither the ABA nor the House of Delegates makes the law." Murray emphasized that the ABA action was merely advisory, and had no force of law unless adopted by statutes or as rules of courts at the state and local levels.[32] The Reardon Report touched off many press-bar meetings, seeking to reach voluntary guidelines on coverage of the criminal arrest, arraignment, hearing and trial

---

[31] Approved Draft, "Reardon Report," pp. 13–14.

[32] "Bar Votes to Strengthen Code on Crime Publicity," Editor & Publisher, Vol. 101, (Feb. 24, 1968) p. 9.

process. Some two dozen states, by 1973, had adopted voluntary agreements based on conferences among judges, lawyers, and members of the media.[33]   States with such guidelines include Colorado, Massachusetts, Minnesota, New York, Oregon, Washington, and Wisconsin.

Newspaper editorial writers attacked the ABA guidelines with considerably more vehemence than J. Edward Murray's statements displayed.   Editorials termed the ABA guidelines "loathsome censorship," an "arrogant, precipitous move," one which heralded "a sad day for freedom in America."   Meanwhile, Editor & Publisher magazine saw evidence that judges were going to follow "the spirit of the Reardon code" by restricting reporters' access to pretrial hearings.   Judges presiding in such cases, however, told the media that pretrial evidence would become public during the course of the trial itself, to be held in open court.[34]

Despite the Reardon Report and the recriminations it occasioned in the press, the right to comment freely upon pending cases is still quite solidly established in American law.[35]   The contempt power, however, as applied to reporters (See Section 50), is obviously still a threat to the news media.

SEC. 50.   RESTRICTIVE ORDERS AND REPORTING THE JUDICIAL PROCESS

"Gag orders" could severely inhibit reporting of the criminal justice process.

Such bar-press guidelines tried to honor and forward both the public's right to know about the judicial process and a defendant's right to a fair trial.   Not all was well, however, despite the various meetings-of-minds between press and bar.   A disturbing counter-current was perceived during the late 1960s, starting mainly in California and involving judges issuing "restrictive" or "gag" orders in some cases.[36]   In a Los Angeles County Superior Court in 1966, for example, a judge ordered the attorneys in a case, the defendants, the sheriff, chief of police, and members of the Board of Police Commissioners not to talk to the news

---

[33] Ibid.

[34] "ABA Code Attacked on the Home Front," Editor & Publisher, March 2, 1968, p. 12.

[35] Bridges v. California, 314 U.S. 252, 62 S.Ct. 190 (1941).

[36] Robert S. Warren and Jeffrey M. Abell, "Free Press-Fair Trial: The 'Gag Order,' A California Aberration," Southern California Law Review 45:1 (Winter, 1972) pp. 51–99, at pp. 52–53.

media about the case in question. The order forbade "[r]eleasing or authorizing the release of any extra-judicial statements for dissemination by any means of public communication relating to the alleged charge or the Accused" and concerning such matters as:

—the defendant's prior record or reputation,

—the existence or contents of any confession, admission, or statement given by the defendant,

—the defendant's performance or refusal of any examinations or tests,

—the identity, testimony, or credibility of prospective witnesses, or

—statements about the defendant's guilt or innocence, or the possibility of a plea of "guilty" to the offense charged or a lesser offense.

Thus, a single judge in a single community felt it appropriate to issue a blanket prohibition against speech by the District Attorney, the Sheriff, the Chief of Police, and indeed, the County and City themselves, and thereby assume the role of the Legislature, the Supreme Court, the executive head of local government, the promulgator of rules of professional conduct, and most importantly, a censor of speech. Although this effort fared ill on appeal, the text of the prohibitory order was not an individual judicial aberration but was modeled closely upon a rule proposed for universal application by a prestigious committee of the American Bar Association.

All that could be reported under such an order were the facts and circumstances of the arrest, the substance of the charge against the defendant, and the defendant's name, age, residence, occupation, and family status. If such an arrangement were to be worked out on a voluntary basis between press and bar, that might be one thing. However, the fact of a judge's *order*—a "gag rule"—worried some legal scholars.[37]

Such fears about the so-called gag rules appear to have substance, in light of a number of orders from judges that reporters curtail various aspects of their reporting of criminal trials. Although the line of decisions is by no means straight and unwavering, it seems that newsmen who appeal against such restrictive orders are more often than not winning their cases.[38]

---

[37] Ibid., p. 53.

[38] See, e. g., Phoenix Newspapers v. Jennings, 107 Ariz. 557, 490 P.2d 563 (1971); State ex rel. Superior Court of Snohomish County v. Sperry, 79 Wash.

One kind of "gag rule" deals with judges telling reporters that they should confine themselves to reporting only those events which take place in front of a jury, in open court. Judge Thomas D. McCrea of the Snohomish County, Washington, Superior Court issued such an order to reporters just before a jury trial for first-degree murder was about to begin in his courtroom. Reporters Sam Sperry and Dee Norton of the Seattle Times ignored the order, and wrote a story about an evidence hearing which occurred while the jury was outside of the courtroom.

After they were cited for contempt, reporters Sperry and Norton appealed to the Washington Supreme Court, claiming that the judge's order was prior restraint in violation of the First Amendment.

The Washington Supreme Court overturned the contempt citation, saying that the trial court's earnest efforts to provide a fair and impartial jury had taken away the reporters' constitutional right to report to the public what happened in the open trial.[39]

In a New York case during 1971, Manhattan Supreme Court Justice George Postel, concerned about possibly prejudicial news accounts, called reporters into his chambers and laid down what he called "Postel's Law." The trial involved Carmine J. Persico, who had been charged with extortion, coercion, criminal usury ("loan sharking") and conspiracy. Justice Postel admonished the reporters not to use Persico's nickname ("The Snake") in their accounts and not to mention Persico's supposed connections with Joseph A. Columbo, Sr., a person said to be a leader of organized crime. The reporters, irked by Postel's declarations, reported what the judge had told them, including references to "The Snake" and to Columbo.

Persico's defense attorney then asked that the trial be closed to the press and to the public, and Judge Postel so ordered. However, the prosecutor—Assistant District Attorney Samuel Yasgur—complained that the order would set an unfortunate and dangerous precedent. For one thing, Yasgur declared, the absence of press coverage might mean that possible witnesses who could become aware of the trial through the media would remain

2d 69, 483 P.2d 608 (1971); Oliver v. Postel, 30 N.Y.2d 171, 331 N.Y.S.2d 407, 282 N.E.2d 306 (1972), and People of the State of New York v. Holder, 70 Misc.2d 31, 332 N.Y.S.2d 933 (1972).

39 State ex rel. Superior Court of Snohomish County v. Sperry, 79 Wash. 2d 69, 483 P.2d 608, 613 (1971).

ignorant of the trial and thus could not come forward to testify: Prosecutor Yasgur added: [40]

> But most importantly, Your Honor, as the Court has noted, the purpose of having press and the public allowed and present during the trial of a criminal case is to insure that defendants do receive an honest and a fair trial.

Newsmen appealed Judge Postel's order closing the trial to New York's highest court, the Court of Appeals. Chief Judge Stanley H. Fuld then ruled that the trial should not have been closed.[41]

> "Because of the vital function served by the news media in guarding against the miscarriage of justice by subjecting the police, prosecutors, and the judicial processes to extensive public scrutiny and criticism," the Supreme Court has emphasized that it has been "unwilling to place any direct limitations on the freedom traditionally exercised by the news media for '[w]hat transpires in the court room is public property.'"
> * * * This, though, imposes a heavy responsibility on the press, not alone to the accused on trial but to the administration of justice as well, to weigh carefully the potential impact of material considered for publication relating to a pending criminal prosecution lest there be a mistrial or a reversal on appeal.

Chief Judge Fuld added that courts should meet problems of prejudicial publicity not by declaring mistrials, but by taking careful preventive steps to protect their courts from outside interferences. In most cases, Judge Fuld suggested, a judge's cautioning jurors to avoid exposure to prejudicial publicity, or to disregard prejudicial material they had already seen or heard, would be effective. In extreme situations, he said, a court might find it necessary to sequester ("lock up") a jury for the duration of a trial.[42]

In an Arizona case, the Supreme Court of that state suggested that the right to a public trial belongs not only to an accused person but to the public as well. Attorneys for John G. Freeman, who was to answer murder charges in a preliminary hear-

---

[40] *New York Times*, "Trial of Persico Closed to Public," pp. 1, 40, November 16, 1971.

[41] Oliver v. Postel, 30 N.Y.2d 171, 331 N.Y.S.2d 407, 282 N.E.2d 306, 311 (1972).

[42] Ibid. See also People of the State of New York v. Holder, 70 Misc.2d 31, 332 N.Y.S.2d 933 (1972).

ing, evidently believed that if the hearing were reported, it would imperil Freeman's right to a fair trial by an impartial jury. After locally published articles reporting that Freeman had earlier been accused of child molesting in Los Angeles were shown to the justice of the peace who was to conduct the preliminary hearing, that hearing was ordered closed. Defendant Freeman was involved in a clearly sensational case, one involving the homicide of seven persons.

Phoenix Newspapers, Inc. then appealed the closing of the case to the Arizona Supreme Court. Chief Justice Fred C. Struckmeyer, Jr. said, for a unanimous court, that the exclusionary order was not justified. He noted that Standard 3.1 of the Standards Relating to Fair Trial and Free Press as approved by the American Bar Association in 1968 recommended excluding the press from preliminary or other pre-trial hearings when such hearings might disclose evidence which would be inadmissible during the actual trial of a defendant. Nevertheless, the Arizona Supreme Court said that the "disclosure of evidentiary facts by which the public may form an opinion as to the guilt or innocence of a defendant does not pose a clear and present threat to a fair trial sufficient to support an order excluding the public from a preliminary hearing." [43]

Although reporters were ultimately vindicated in the *Postel, Sperry,* and *Phoenix Newspapers* cases, a Louisiana case has gone against the press and, at this writing, has been appealed to the Supreme Court of the United States. This case, United States v. Dickinson, arose when reporters Larry Dickinson and Gibbs Adams of the Baton Rouge *Star Times* and the *Morning Advocate* tried to report on a U.S. District Court hearing involving a VISTA worker who had been indicted by a Louisiana state grand jury on suspicion of conspiring to murder a state official. The District Court hearing was to ascertain whether the state's prosecution was legitimate. In the course of this hearing, District Court Judge E. Gordon West issued this order:

"And, at this time, I do want to enter an order in the case, and that is in accordance with this Court's rule in connection with Fair Trial—Free Press provisions, the Rules of this Court.

"It is ordered that no report of the testimony taken in this case today shall be made in any newspaper or by radio or television, or by any other news media."

---

[43] Phoenix Newspapers, Inc. v. Jennings, Justice of the Peace, 107 Ariz. 557, 490 P.2d 563, 566–567 (1971).

Reporters Dickinson and Adams ignored that order, and wrote articles for their newspapers summarizing the day's testimony in detail.   After a hearing, Dickinson and Adams were found guilty of criminal contempt and were sentenced to pay fines of $300 each.   Appealing to the Court of Appeals for the Fifth Circuit, the reporters were told that the District Court judge's gag order was unconstitutional.[44]   They were not in the clear, however.   The Court of Appeals sent their case back to the District Court so that the judge could reconsider the $300 fines. The judge again fined the reporters $300 apiece, and they again appealed to the Court of Appeals.   This time, the contempt fines were upheld.   The Fifth Circuit Court declared that the reporters could have asked for a rehearing or appealed against the judge's order not to publish.   Once the appeal was decided in their favor, the court evidently reasoned, *then* they could publish.[45]

New York Times Vice President James C. Goodale—an attorney himself—was indignant.

> It doesn't take much analysis to see that what the Court has sanctioned is the right of prior restraint subject to later appeal. * * * What this case means, in effect, is that when a judge is disposed to order a newspaper not to report matters that are transpiring in public he may do so, and a newsman's only remedy is to appeal or decide to pay the contempt penalty, be it a fine or imprisonment.

As this book goes to press in the fall of 1973, the Supreme Court refused to hear the reporters' appeal, thus allowing the contempt fines to stand and perhaps indicating tolerance for a form of prior restraint.

SEC. 51.   PRE–TRIAL PUBLICITY

Pre-trial publicity which makes it difficult—if not impossible— for a defendant to receive a fair trial was summed up in the Supreme Court cases of Irvin v. Dowd (1961) and Rideau v. Louisiana (1963).

Many lawyers and judges no doubt approve of the ABA's fair trial and free press guidelines, which include recommendations that contempt sanctions be used to punish pre-trial or during-

---

44 United States v. Dickinson, 465 F.2d 496, 514 (1972).

45 476 F.2d 373, 374 (1973) ;   349 FS 227 (1972).   See also James C. Goodale's "The Press 'Gag' Order Epidemic," Columbia Journalism Review, Sept./Oct. 1973, pp. 49–50.

trial publications which are believed to impair a defendant's rights. This kind of reliance on contempt sanctions, however, is not now the law. While contempt convictions of newspapers are possible in certain circumstances, the Supreme Court of the United States has never upheld the contempt conviction of any news medium in a situation directly involving defendants' rights. As discussed in Chapter 10, decisions in contempt cases during the 1940s, including Bridges v. California, Pennekamp v. Florida, and Craig v. Harney, upheld media freedom to report on judicial proceedings without ever really reaching questions of defendants' rights.[46]

Maryland v. Baltimore Radio Show

A 1950 decision of the Supreme Court of the United States in Maryland v. Baltimore Radio Show is in point here. The Baltimore Radio Show, Inc., WFBR, the Baltimore Radio Broadcasting Corporation, WCBM, and the Maryland Broadcasting Company had been found guilty of contempt by a trial court for broadcasting news items about a man suspected of killing a 10-year-old girl. The suspect was in police custody at the time of the broadcasts. The broadcasts asserted that the murder suspect had confessed, that he had a long criminal record, and that he had re-enacted the crime when police returned him to its scene. It was said that the suspect dug down into some leaves to recover the knife which he had used to kill the little girl.

The Maryland Court of Appeals, however, reversed the contempt conviction, leaning heavily upon the Supreme Court's reasoning in the *Bridges, Pennekamp,* and Craig v. Harney decisions. The State of Maryland then sought a writ of certiorari from the Supreme Court of the United States. The Supreme Court, however, denied the petition, which meant only that less than four justices believed that certiorari should be granted.[47] Justice Felix Frankfurter, however, filed an outraged opinion on the Court's denial of the petition for a writ of certiorari. Frankfurter believed that certiorari should have been granted and the contempt conviction of the trial court upheld. Justice Frankfurter quoted the trial court: [48]

> The question * * * before us is: Did that broadcast and others which were less damaging by the other

[46] See Bridges v. California, 314 U.S. 252, 62 S.Ct. 190 (1941); Pennekamp v. Florida, 328 U.S. 331, 66 S.Ct. 1029 (1946); Craig v. Harney, 331 U.S. 367, 67 S.Ct. 1249 (1947).

[47] 338 U.S. 912, 70 S.Ct. 252 (1950).

[48] 338 U.S. 912, 913–916, 70 S.Ct. 252, 253–254 (1950).

stations, have a clear and present effect upon the administration of justice? * * * Judges are supposed to be made of sterner stuff than to be influenced by irresponsible statements regarding pending cases. They are trained to put aside inadmissible evidence * * *.

Now, what about the jury?

* * * * * * * *

[T]he Court cannot help but feel that the broadcast referred to in these cases must have had an indelible effect upon the public mind and that that effect was one that was bound to follow the members of the panel into the jury room.

* * * * * * * *

Now, gentlemen, the Court must conclude that these broadcasts did constitute, not merely a clear and present danger to the administration of justice, but an actual obstruction of the administration of justice, in that they deprived the Defendant * * * of his right to have an impartial jury trial.

Justice Frankfurter then insisted: [49]

The issues considered by the Court of Appeals bear on some of the basic problems of a democratic society. Freedom of the press, properly conceived, is basic to our constitutional system. Safeguards for the fair administration of criminal justice are enshrined in our Bill of Rights. Respect for both of these indispensable elements of our constitutional system presents some of the most difficult and delicate problems for adjudication when they are before the Court for adjudication. It has taken centuries of struggle to evolve our system for bringing the guilty to book, protecting the innocent, and maintaining the interests of society consonant with our democratic professions. One of the demands of a democratic society is that the public should know what goes on in courts by being told by the press what happens there, to the end that the public may judge whether our system of criminal justice is fair and right. On the other hand our society has set apart court and jury as the tribunal for determining guilt or innocence on the basis of evidence adduced in court, so far as it is humanly possible. It would be the grossest perversion of all that Mr. Justice Holmes represents to

[49] 338 U.S. 912, 919–920, 70 S.Ct. 252, 255–256 (1950).

suggest that it is also true of the thought behind a
criminal charge " *   *   * that the best test of truth
is the power of the thought to get itself accepted in the
competition of the market."

Abrams v. United States, 250 U.S. 616, 630, 40 S.Ct.
17, 22, 63 L.Ed. 1173. Proceedings for the determination of guilt or innocence in open court before a jury
are not in competition with any other means for establishing the charge.

Contempt has still not been used by the Supreme Court in cases touching the free press-fair trial issue. More recently the Supreme Court has reflected great concern for the rights of defendants in criminal trials. The cases of Irvin D. Dowd,[50] Rideau v. Louisiana,[51] and Sheppard v. Maxwell[52] all involved excessive pre-trial publicity. All three of these cases resulted in
declarations by the Supreme Court that the publicity prevented
fair trials, and in the ordering of new trials for the defendants.

Irvin v. Dowd (1961)

The Irvin case represents the first time that the Supreme
Court overturned a state criminal conviction because publicity
before the trial had prevented a fair trial before an impartial
jury.[53]

The defendant in this murder case, Leslie Irvin, was subjected
to a barrage of prejudicial news items in the hysterical wake of
six murders which had been committed in the vicinity of Evansville, Indiana. Two of the murders were committed in December, 1954, and four in March, 1955. These crimes were covered
extensively by news media in the locality, and created great agi-
tation in Vanderburgh County, where Evansville is located, and
in adjoining Gibson County.[54]

Leslie Irvin, a parolee, was arrested on April 8, 1955, on suspicion of burglary and writing bad checks. Within a few days,
the Evansville police and the Vanderburgh County prosecutor issued press releases asserting that "Mad Dog Irvin" had confessed to all six murders, including three members of one family.
The news media had what can conservatively be described as a
field day with the Irvin case, and were aided and abetted in this

---

[50] 366 U.S. 717, 81 S.Ct. 1639 (1961).

[51] 373 U.S. 723, 83 S.Ct. 1417 (1963).

[52] 384 U.S. 333, 86 S.Ct. 1507 (1966).

[53] Gillmor, op. cit., pp. 116–117.

[54] 366 U.S. 717, 719, 81 S.Ct. 1639, 1641 (1961).

by law enforcement officials. Many of the accounts published or broadcast before Irvin's trial referred to him as the "confessed slayer of six." Irvin's court-appointed attorney was quoted as saying he had received much criticism for representing Irvin; the media, by way of excusing the attorney, noted that he faced disbarment if he refused to represent the suspect.[55]

Irvin was soon indicted by the Vanderburgh County Grand Jury for one of the six murders. Irvin's court-appointed counsel sought—and was granted—a change of venue. However, the venue change was made only from Vanderburgh County to adjoining Gibson County, which had received similar prejudicial accounts about "Mad Dog Irvin" from the news media in the Evansville vicinity. Irvin's attorney then sought to have the trial removed from Gibson County to a location which had not received such widespread and inflammatory publicity. This motion was denied on grounds that Indiana law allowed only one change of venue.[56]

The trial began November 14, 1955. Of 430 prospective jurors examined by the prosecution and defense attorneys, 370—nearly 90 per cent—had formed some opinion about Irvin's guilt. These opinions ranged from mere suspicion to absolute certainty.[57] Irvin's attorney had used up all of his 20 peremptory challenges. When 12 jurors were finally seated by the court, the attorney then unsuccessfully challenged all jurors on grounds that they were biased. He complained bitterly that four of the seated jurors had stated that Irvin was guilty.[58] Even so, the trial was held, Irvin was found guilty, and the jury sentenced him to death. Irvin's conviction was upheld by the Indiana Supreme Court, which denied his motions for a new trial.[59] Protracted appeals brought Irvin's case to the Supreme Court of the United States twice,[60] but his case was not decided on its merits by the nation's highest court until 1961.

---

55 366 U.S. 717, 725–726, 81 S.Ct. 1639, 1641, 1645 (1961); Gillmor, op. cit., p. 9.

56 366 U.S. 717, 720, 81 S.Ct. 1639, 1641 (1961).

57 366 U.S. 717, 727, 81 S.Ct. 1639, 1645 (1961).

58 359 U.S. 394, 398, 79 S.Ct. 825, 828 (1959).

59 236 Ind. 384, 139 N.E.2d 898 (1957).

60 Irvin's appeal for a writ of *habeas corpus* to a Federal District Court was denied on the basis that he had not exhausted his opportunities to appeal through the Indiana courts. 153 F.Supp. 531 (D.C.Ind.1957). A United States Court of Appeals affirmed the dismissal of the writ, 251 F.2d 548 (7th Cir. 1958). In a 5–4 decision in 1959, the Supreme Court of the United States sent Irvin's case back to the Federal Court of Appeals for reconsideration. 359 U.S. 394, 79 S.Ct. 825 (1959). The Court of Appeals again refused

Then, in 1961, all nine members of the Supreme Court ruled that Irvin had not received a fair trial. The upshot of this was that Irvin received a new trial, although he was ultimately convicted. This time, however, his sentence was set at life imprisonment.[61]

In his majority opinion, Justice Tom C. Clark—a former attorney general of the United States—concentrated on the effect of prejudicial publicity on a defendant's rights. Clark noted that courts do not require that jurors be totally ignorant of the facts and issues involved in a criminal trial. It is sufficient if a juror can render a verdict based on the evidence presented in court.[62]

Justice Clark then considered the publicity Irvin had received, and concluded: "Here the build-up of prejudice is clear and convincing." He noted that arguments for Irvin presented evidence that "a barrage of newspaper headlines, articles, cartoons and pictures was unleashed against him during the six or seven months before his trial" in Gibson County, Indiana. Furthermore, that evidence indicated that the newspapers in which the stories appeared were delivered regularly to 95 per cent of the residences in that county. Furthermore, "Evansville radio and TV stations, which likewise blanketed the county, also carried extensive newscasts covering the same incidents." Clark added: [63]

> These stories revealed the details of his background, including a reference to crimes committed when a juvenile, his convictions for arson almost 20 years previously, for burglary and by a courtmartial on AWOL charges during the war. He was accused of being a parole violator. The headlines announced his police line-up identification, that he faced a lie detector test, had been placed at the scene of the crime and that the six murders were solved but petitioner refused to confess. Finally, they announced his confession to the six murders and the fact of his indictment for four of them in Indiana. The reported petitioner's offer to plead guilty if promised a 99-year-sentence, but also the determination, on the other hand, of the prosecutor to secure the death penalty. * * * One story dramati-

to grant a writ of *habeas corpus* to Irvin, 271 F.2d 552 (7th Cir. 1959). Irvin's case was then appealed to the Supreme Court for the second time.

[61] Gillmor, op. cit., pp. 11–12.

[62] Irvin v. Dowd, 366 U.S. 717, 723, 81 S.Ct. 1639, 1642–1643 (1961).

[63] 366 U.S. 717, 725–726, 81 S.Ct. 1639, 1644 (1961).

cally related the promise of a sheriff to devote his life to securing petitioner's execution by the State of Kentucky, where petitioner is alleged to have committed one of his six murders, if Indiana failed to do so. Another characterized petitioner as remorseless and without conscience but also as having been found sane by a court-appointed panel of doctors. In many of the stories petitioner was described as the "confessed slayer of six * * *."

After noting the difficulty in finding impartial jurors, Justice Clark emphasized that eight of the 12 jurors finally placed in the jury box believed Irvin to be guilty. One juror announced that he " 'could not * * * give the defendant the benefit of the doubt that he is innocent.' " Another said that he had " 'somewhat' certain fixed opinions" about Irvin's guilt. Justice Clark concluded: [64]

> No doubt each juror was sincere when he said that he would be fair and impartial to petitioner, but psychological impact requiring such a declaration before one's fellows is often its father. Where so many, so many times, admitted prejudice, such a statement of impartiality can be given little weight. As one of the jurors put it, "You can't forget what you hear and see." With his life at stake, it is not requiring too much that petitioner be tried in an atmosphere undisturbed by so huge a wave of public passion and by a jury other than one in which two-thirds of the members admit, before hearing any testimony, to possessing a belief in his guilt.

In a concurring opinion, Justice Frankfurter unleashed a bitter denunciation of "trial by newspapers instead of trial in court before a jury." He stated that the Irvin case was not an isolated incident or an atypical miscarriage of justice. Frankfurter wrote: [65]

> Not a term passes without this Court being importuned to review convictions, had in States throughout the country, in which substantial claims are made that a jury trial has been distorted because of inflammatory newspaper accounts—too often, as in this case, with the prosecutor's collaboration—exerting pressures upon potential jurors before trial and even during the course of trial, thereby making it extremely difficult, if not

[64] 366 U.S. 717, 728, 81 S.Ct. 1639, 1645 (1961).

[65] 366 U.S. 717, 730, 81 S.Ct. 1639, 1646 (1961).

impossible, to secure a jury capable of taking in, free of prepossessions, evidence submitted in open court. Indeed such extraneous influences, in violation of the decencies guaranteed by our Constitution, are sometimes so powerful that an accused is forced, as a practical matter, to forego trial by jury.

Justice Frankfurter concluded his opinion with a thinly veiled threat that legal restrictions might be found which could halt pre-trial publicity: [66]

This Court has not yet decided that the fair administration of criminal justice must be subordinated to another safeguard of our constitutional system—freedom of the press, properly conceived. The Court has not yet decided that, while convictions must be reversed and miscarriages of justice result because the minds of jurors were poisoned, the poisoner is constitutionally protected in plying his trade.

Trial by Television: Rideau v. Louisiana (1963)

If Leslie Irvin was mistreated primarily by newspapers during the period before his trial, Wilbert Rideau found that television was the major offender in interfering with his right to a fair trial. Early in 1961, a Lake Charles, La., bank was robbed. The robber kidnaped three of the bank's employees and killed one of them. Several hours later, Wilbert Rideau was arrested by police and held in the Calcasieu Parish jail in Lake Charles. The next morning, a moving picture film—complete with a sound track—was made of a 20-minute "interview" between Rideau and the Sheriff of Calcasieu Parish. The Sheriff interrogated the prisoner and elicited admissions that Rideau had committed the bank robbery, the kidnaping, and the murder. Later in the day, this filmed interview was broadcast over television station KLPC in Lake Charles. Over three days' time, the film was televised on three occasions to an estimated total audience of 97,000 persons, as compared to the approximately 150,000 persons then living in Calcasieu Parish.[67]

Rideau's attorneys subsequently sought a change of venue away from Calcasieu Parish. It was argued that it would take away Rideau's right to a fair trial if he were tried there after the three television broadcasts of Rideau's "interview" with the sheriff. The motion for change of venue was denied, and Rideau was convicted and sentenced to death on the murder charge

[66] 366 U.S. 717, 730, 81 S.Ct. 1639, 1647 (1961).

[67] Rideau v. Louisiana, 373 U.S. 723, 724, 83 S.Ct. 1417, 1419 (1963).

in the Calcasieu Parish trial court. The conviction was affirmed by the Louisiana Supreme Court,[68] but the Supreme Court of the United States granted *certiorari*.[69]

Justice Potter Stewart's majority opinion noted that three of the 12 jurors had stated during *voir dire* examination before the trial that they had seen and heard Rideau's "interview" with the Sheriff. Also, two members of the jury were Calcasieu Parish deputy sheriffs. Although Rideau's attorney challenged the deputies, asking that they be removed "for cause," the trial judge denied this request. Since Rideau's lawyer had exhausted his "peremptory challenges"—those for which no reason need be given—the deputies remained on the jury.[70]

Justice Stewart then described the televised "interview" in withering fashion.[71]

> What the people of Calcasieu Parish saw on their television sets was Rideau, in jail flanked by the sheriff and two state troopers, admitting in detail the commission of the robbery, kidnaping, and murder, in response to leading questions by the sheriff. The record fails to show whose idea it was to make the sound film, and broadcast it over the local television station, but we know from the conceded circumstances that the plan was carried out with the active cooperation and participation of the local law enforcement officers. And certainly no one has suggested that it was Rideau's idea, or even that he was aware of what was going on when the sound film was being made.

Justice Stewart noted that the *Rideau* case did not involve physical brutality. However, he declared that the "kangaroo court proceedings in this case involved a more subtle but no less real deprivation of due process of law." Justice Stewart added:[72]

> Under our Constitution's guarantee of due process, a person accused of committing a crime is vouchsafed basic minimal rights. Among these are the right to counsel, the right to plead not guilty, and the right to be tried in a courtroom presided over by a judge. Yet in this case the people of Calcasieu Parish saw and heard,

---

[68] 242 La. 431, 137 So.2d 283 (1962).

[69] 371 U.S. 919, 83 S.Ct. 294 (1962).

[70] 373 U.S. 723, 725, 83 S.Ct. 1417, 1418 (1963).

[71] 373 U.S. 723, 725, 83 S.Ct. 1417, 1419 (1963).

[72] 373 U.S. 723, 727, 83 S.Ct. 1417, 1419 (1963).

not once but three times, a "trial" of Rideau in a jail, presided over by a sheriff, where there was no lawyer to advise Rideau of his right to stand mute.

Rideau's conviction was reversed, and a new trial was ordered by the Supreme Court.

SEC. 52.   PUBLICITY DURING TRIAL

The notorious kidnaping trial of Bruno Richard Hauptmann of the 1930s and the 1965 Supreme Court decision in the case of Billie Sol Estes are examples of excessive publicity while a case is underway.

"The Lindbergh Case" and "the trial of Bruno Hauptmann" are phrases heard whenever the free press—fair trial debate heats up. These phrases, of course, refer to the kidnaping in 1932 of the 19-month-old son of the aviator famed for the first solo crossing of the Atlantic. The child's kidnaping was front-page news for weeks, long after the child's body was found in a shallow grave not far from the Lindbergh home in New Jersey.

More than two years later, in September, 1934, Bruno Richard Hauptmann was arrested. His trial for the kidnap-murder of the Lindbergh child did not begin until January, 1935. The courtroom where Hauptmann was tried had a press section jammed with 150 reporters. During the Hauptmann trial, which lasted more than a month, there were sometimes more than 700 newsmen in Flemington, N. J., the site of the trial.[73]

Much of the publicity of the Hauptmann trial was prejudicial, and lawyers and newsmen authored statements which were clearly inflammatory. Hauptmann was described in the press, for example, as a "thing lacking in human characteristics."[74] After the trial—and after Hauptmann's execution—a Special Committee Between the Press, Radio, and Bar was established to search for "standards of publicity in judicial proceedings and methods of obtaining an observance of them." In a grim report issued in 1937, the 18-man committee—including lawyers, editors, and publishers—termed Hauptmann's trial "the most spectacular and depressing example of improper publicity and professional misconduct ever presented to the people of the United States in a criminal trial."[75]

[73] John Lofton, Justice and the Press (Boston: Beacon Press, 1966) pp. 103–104.

[74] Lofton, op. cit., p. 124.

[75] American Bar Association, "Report of Special Committee on Cooperation between Press, Radio and Bar," Annual Report, Volume 62, pp. 851–866 (1937),

One result of the committee's investigation of the Hauptmann trial was the American Bar Association's adoption in 1937 of Canon 35 of its Canons of Professional Ethics. Canon 35 as updated, now reads: [76]

> Proceedings in court should be conducted with fitting dignity and decorum. The taking of photographs in the courtroom, during sessions of the court or recesses between sessions, and the broadcasting or televising of court proceedings detract from the essential dignity of the proceedings, distract the participants and witnesses in giving testimony, and create misconceptions with respect thereto in the mind of the public and should not be permitted.
>
> Provided that this restriction shall not apply to the broadcasting or televising, under the supervision of the court, of such portions of naturalization proceedings (other than the interrogation of applicants) as are designed and carried out exclusively as a ceremony for the purpose of publicly demonstrating in an impressive manner the essential dignity and the serious nature of the naturalization.

Canon 35, in and of itself, does not have the force of law. However, it has been adopted by order of the highest courts of some 20 states and has for the most part been followed in all the rest of the states except for Colorado and Texas. Federal court rules forbid televising or photographing proceedings.[77] Television personnel and photographers have attacked Canon 35 with great vigor, making it a topic of continuing and strenuous debate. When newsmen demonstrated that modern photography could operate unobtrusively in the courtroom without noise or special lights, even some judges and attorneys recommended that courts be opened to photographers and to television. It was argued that the public could thereby be enlightened about the democratic process and the American judicial system.[78]

Estes v. Texas

Excesses in televising a trial in Texas during the 1960s, now seem to mean that most criminal trials may not be televised.

at p. 861. See also New Jersey v. Hauptmann, 115 N.J.L. 412, 180 Atl. 809 (Ct.Err. & App.1935), certiorari denied 296 U.S. 649, 56 S.Ct. 310 (1935).

76 American Bar Association, Annual Report, op. cit., p. 1134; as updated by Justice John Marshall Harlan in his concurring opinion in Estes v. Texas, 381 U.S. 532, 601n; 85 S.Ct. 1628, 1669n (1965).

77 Lofton, op. cit., p. 124.

78 Gillmor, op. cit., pp. 34–35.

The crucial case involved the swindling trial of flamboyant Texas financier, Billie Sol Estes. Estes was ultimately convicted, but not until he had received a new trial as a result of the manner in which a judge allowed Estes' original trial to be photographed and televised.

Estes came before a judicial hearing in Smith County, Texas, in September, 1962, after a change of venue from Reeves County, some 500 miles west. At a hearing which began on September 24, the courtroom was packed and about 30 persons stood in the aisles. A New York *Times* story described the setting for the trial in this way: [79]

> A television motor van, big as an intercontinental bus, was parked outside the courthouse and the second-floor courtroom was a forest of equipment. Two television cameras have been set up inside the bar and four more marked cameras were aligned just outside the gates.
>
> * * *

Cables and wires snaked over the floor.

With photographers roaming unchecked about the courtroom, Estes' attorney moved that all cameras be excluded from the courtroom. As the attorney spoke, a cameraman walked behind the judge's bench and took a picture.[80]

After the two-day hearing was completed on September 25, 1962, the judge granted a continuance (delay) to the defense, with the trial to begin on October 22. Meanwhile, the judge established ground rules for television and still photographers. Televising of the trial was allowed, with the exception of live coverage of the interrogation of prospective jurors or the testimony of witnesses. The major television networks, CBS, NBC, and ABC, plus local television station KLTV were each allowed to install one television camera (without sound recording equipment) and film was made available to other television stations on a pooled basis. In addition, through another pool arrangement, only still photographers for the Associated Press, United Press, and from the local newspaper would be permitted in the courtroom.

At its own expense, and with the permission of the court, KLTV built a booth at the back of the courtroom, painted the same color as the courtroom. An opening in the booth permit-

---

[79] Estes v. Texas, 381 U.S. 532, 553, 85 S.Ct. 1628, 1638 (1965). Quoted from the concurring opinion by Chief Justice Warren, with whom Justice Douglas and Goldberg concurred.

[80] 381 U.S. 532, 553, 85 S.Ct. 1628, 1638 (1965). From concurring opinion by Chief Justice Warren.

ted all four television cameras to view the proceedings. However, in this small courtroom, the cameras were visible to all.[81]

Despite these limitations the judge placed on television and still photographers, a majority of the Supreme Court held that Estes had been deprived of a fair trial in violation of the due process clause of the Fourteenth Amendment. Chief Justice Warren and Justices Douglas, Goldberg, and Clark asserted that a fair trial could not be had when television is allowed in any criminal trial. Justice Harlan, the fifth member of the majority in this 5–4 decision, voted to overturn Estes' conviction because the case was one of "great notoriety." Even so, it should be noted that Harlan reserved judgment on the televising of more routine cases.

In delivering the opinion of the Court, Mr. Justice Clark wrote: [82]

> We start with the proposition that it is a "public trial" that the Sixth Amendment guarantees to the "accused." The purpose of the requirement of a public trial was to guarantee that the accused would be fairly dealt with and not unjustly condemned. His story had proven that secret tribunals were effective instruments of oppression * * *.

> It is said, however, that the freedoms granted in the First Amendment extend a right to news media to televise from the courtroom, and that to refuse to honor this privilege is to discriminate between the newspapers and television. This is a misconception of the rights of the press.

> The free press has been a mighty catalyst in awakening public interest in governmental affairs, exposing corruption among public officers and employees and generally informing the citizenry of public events and occurrences, including court proceedings. While maximum freedom must be allowed the press in carrying on this important function in a democratic society its exercise must necessarily be subject to the maintenance of absolute fairness in the judicial process.

Justice Clark then attempted to dispose of one of the arguments often made by proponents of electronic journalism. He took aim on the assertion that if courts exclude television cameras or microphones, they are thus discriminating in favor of the

---

[81] 381 U.S. 532, 554–555, 85 S.Ct. 1628, 1638–1639 (1965), from Chief Justice Warren's concurring opinion.

[82] 381 U.S. 532, 538–539, 85 S.Ct. 1628, 1631 (1965).

print media. But Clark retorted, "[t]he news reporter is not permitted to bring his typewriter or printing press." Clark also suggested that technical advances might someday make television equipment and cameras quieter and less obtrusive.[83]

Justice Clark believed that televising and photographing criminal trials did not aid the courts' solemn purpose of endeavoring to ascertain the truth. Instead, he argued, television injects an irrelevant factor into court proceedings which might well increase the chance of prejudicing jurors. Jurors might not only be distracted by the presence of cameras, with their "telltale red lights," but by an awareness of the fact of televising felt by jurors throughout an entire trial. Also, if a new trial be ordered, prospective jurors for the second trial might be prejudiced by what they had seen over television of the first trial.[84]

Justice Clark maintained that televising a trial could impair the quality of witnesses' testimony.[85]

> The impact upon a witness of the knowledge that he is being viewed by a vast audience is simply incalculable. Some may be demoralized and frightened, some cocky and given to overstatement; memories may falter, as with anyone speaking publicly, and accuracy of statement may be severely undermined. Embarrassment may impede the search for truth, as may a natural tendency toward overdramatization.

In addition, televising a trial could simply make a judge's task of attempting to insure fairness in the proceedings that much more difficult. And finally, the presence of the television cameras in a courtroom was termed by Clark a form of mental if not physical harassment, "resembling a police line-up or the third degree." Clark added: [86]

> A defendant on trial for a specific crime is entitled to his day in court, not in a stadium, or a city or nationwide arena. The heightened public clamor resulting from radio and television coverage will inevitably result in prejudice. Trial by television is, therefore, foreign to our system. Furthermore, telecasting may also deprive an accused of effective counsel. The distractions, intrusions into confidential attorney-client relationships and the temptation offered by television to

83 381 U.S. 532, 540, 85 S.Ct. 1628, 1631 (1965).

84 381 U.S. 532, 544–547, 85 S.Ct. 1628, 1634–1636 (1965).

85 381 U.S. 532, 547, 85 S.Ct. 1628, 1635 (1965).

86 381 U.S. 532, 549, 85 S.Ct. 1628, 1636 (1965).

play to the public audience might often have a direct effect not only upon the lawyers, but the judge, the jury and the witnesses.

Chief Justice Warren was joined by Justices Douglas and Goldberg in his concurring opinion. Warren agreed with Clark that televising criminal trials is a denial of due process of law. Warren argued that televising diverts a trial from its proper purpose by having an inevitable impact on all the trial participants. Furthermore, a televised trial seemed to Warren to detract from the dignity of court proceedings and to lessen their reliability. Finally, the Chief Justice argued that some defendants—those whose trials are televised—are singled out for days in court under prejudicial conditions not experienced by other defendants.[87]

Chief Justice Warren rejected contentions that excluding cameras and microphones from court unfairly or unconstitutionally discriminated against the electronic media. Warren wrote: [88]

> So long as the television media, like the other communications media, is free to send representatives to trials and to report on those trials to its viewers, there is no abridgment of the freedom of the press. The right of the communications media to comment on court proceedings does not bring with it the right to inject themselves into the fabric of the trial process to alter the purpose of that process.
>
> *   *   *   *   *   *   *   *
>
> On entering that hallowed sanctuary, where the lives, liberty and property of people are in jeopardy, television representatives have only the rights of the general public, namely, to be present to observe the proceedings, and thereafter, if they choose, to report them.

In his concurring opinion, Justice John Marshall Harlan agreed that in the notorious *Estes* case, the use of television was made in such a way that the right to a fair trial assured by the Due Process Clause of the Fourteenth Amendment was infringed. But even so, Harlan suggested that [89]

> * * * the day may come when television will have become so commonplace an affair in the daily life of the average person as to dissipate all reasonable likelihood that its use in courtrooms may disparage the judi-

[87] 381 U.S. 532, 565, 85 S.Ct. 1628, 1644 (1965).

[88] 381 U.S. 532, 585–586, 85 S.Ct. 1628, 1654 (1965).

[89] 381 U.S. 532, 595–596, 85 S.Ct. 1628, 1662 (1965).

cial process. If and when that day arrives, the constitutional judgment called for now would of course be
subject to re-examination in accordance with the traditional workings of the Due Process Clause.

In a strongly worded dissent, Justices Stewart, Black, Brennan and White raised constitutional arguments in objecting to
the ban on television from courtrooms, at least at that stage of
television's development. Justice Stewart wrote: [90]

> I think that the introduction of television into a court-
> room is, at least in the present state of the art, an ex-
> tremely unwise policy. It invites many constitutional
> risks, and it detracts from the inherent dignity of a
> courtroom. But I am unable to escalate this personal
> view into a *per se* constitutional rule. And I am unable
> to find, on the specific record of this case, that the cir-
> cumstances attending the limited televising of the peti-
> tioner's trial resulted in the denial of any right guar-
> anteed to him by the United States Constitution.

Justice Stewart argued that the Court was not here dealing
with mob domination of a courtroom, with a kangaroo court atmosphere, or with a jury inflamed with bias. He argued that
the Court's limited grant of certiorari should have permitted his
brethren to consider only one thing: "the regulated presence of
television and still photography at the trial itself." Pre-trial
events, such as the circus-like two-day hearing in September,
1962, were not the problem. The only problem for the Supreme
Court's consideration, Stewart argued, should have been Estes'
trial, which officially began on Oct. 22, 1962.[91] Justice Stewart
wrote: [92]

> While no First Amendment claim is made in this case,
> there are intimations in the opinions filed by my Breth-
> ren in the majority which strike me as disturbingly al-
> ien to the First and Fourteenth Amendments' guaran-
> tees against federal or state interference with the free
> communication of information and ideas. The sugges-
> tion that there are limits upon the public's right to
> know what goes on in the courts causes me deep con-
> cern. The idea of imposing upon any medium of com-
> munications the burden of justifying its presence is
> contrary to where I had always thought the presump-
> tion must lie in the area of First Amendment freedoms.

[90] 381 U.S. 532, 601–602, 85 S.Ct. 1628, 1669 (1965).

[91] 381 U.S. 532, 611, 85 S.Ct. 1628, 1675 (1965).

[92] 381 U.S. 532, 613, 85 S.Ct. 1628, 1675–1676 (1965).

The constitutional question in *Estes*, to Mr. Justice Stewart, became one of whether the Fourteenth Amendment excludes television cameras from criminal trials in state courtrooms. Justices Stewart, White, Black, and Brennan simply did not believe that the case against televising trials had been sufficiently well proved. A flat ban against such televising, Justices White and Brennan said in a separate dissenting opinion, was premature.[93]

In a final separate dissenting opinion, Justice Brennan contended that the *Estes* decision was *"not* a blanket constitutional prohibition against the televising of state criminal trials." Television according to the opinions on the majority side of *Estes*, barred television only from "notorious trials." [94]   Nevertheless, judges are certainly apt to ask themselves whether allowing television into a courtroom, even under the most carefully regulated circumstances, might not in and of itself make a trial "notorious." As William A. Hachten has written, "[t]he *Estes* decision doesn't kill television in the courtroom, but it leaves it in a critical condition." [95]

SEC. 53.   PUBLICITY BEFORE AND DURING TRIAL

The long ordeal of Dr. Samuel Sheppard ended with the reversal of his murder conviction on grounds that pre-trial and during-trial publicity had impaired his ability to get a fair trial.

The Trial of Dr. Sam Sheppard

When the free press-fair trial controversy is raised, the case most likely to be mentioned is that *cause celebre* of American jurisprudence, Sheppard v. Maxwell.[96]   This case was one of the most notorious—and most sensationally reported—trials in American history. With perhaps the exception of the Lindbergh kidnaping case of the 1930s, the ordeal of Dr. Sam Sheppard may well have been the most notorious case of the Twentieth Century.

This case began in the early morning hours of July 4, 1954, when Dr. Sheppard's pregnant wife, Marilyn, was found dead in the upstairs bedroom of their home. She had been beaten to death. Dr. Sheppard, who told authorities he had found his

93 381 U.S. 532, 615, 85 S.Ct. 1628, 1677 (1965).

94 381 U.S. 532, 615–616, 85 S.Ct. 1628, 1677–1678 (1965).

95 Hachten, op. cit., p. 273.

96 384 U.S. 333, 86 S.Ct. 1507 (1966).

wife dead, called a neighbor, Bay Village Mayor Spence Houk. Dr. Sheppard appeared to have been injured, suffering from severe neck pains, a swollen eye, and shock.

Dr. Sheppard, a Bay Village, Ohio, osteopath, told a rambling and unconvincing story to officials: that he had dozed off on a downstairs couch after his wife had gone upstairs to bed. He said that he heard his wife cry out and ran upstairs. In the dim light from the hall, he saw a "form" which he later described as a bushy haired man standing next to his wife's bed. Sheppard said he grappled with the man and was knocked unconscious by a blow to the back of his neck.

He said he then went to his young son's room, and found him unharmed. Hearing a noise, Sheppard then ran downstairs. He saw a "form" leaving the house and chased it to the lake shore. Dr. Sheppard declared that he had grappled with the intruder on the beach, and had been again knocked unconscious.[97]

From the outset, Dr. Sheppard was treated as the prime suspect in the case. The coroner was reported to have told his men, " 'Well, it is evident the doctor did this, so let's go get the confession out of him.' " Sheppard, meanwhile, had been removed to a nearby clinic operated by his family. While under sedation, Sheppard was interrogated in his hospital room by the coroner. Later, on the afternoon of July 4, he was also questioned by Bay Village police, with one policeman telling Sheppard that lie detector tests were "infallible." This same policeman told Dr. Sheppard, " 'I think you killed your wife.' " Later that same afternoon, a physician sent by the coroner was permitted to make a careful examination of Sheppard.[98]

As early as July 7—the date of Marilyn Sheppard's funeral— a newspaper story appeared quoting a prosecuting attorney's criticism of the Sheppard family for refusing to permit his immediate questioning. On July 9, Sheppard re-enacted his recollection of the crime at his home at the request of the coroner. This re-enactment was covered by a group of newsmen which had apparently been invited by the coroner. Sheppard's performance was reported at length by the news media, including photographs. Front-page headlines also emphasized Sheppard's refusal to take a lie-detector test.[99]

On July 20, 1954, newspapers began a campaign of front-page editorials. One such editorial charged that someone was "get-

[97] 384 U.S. 333, 335–336, 86 S.Ct. 1507, 1508–1509 (1966).

[98] 384 U.S. 333, 337–338, 86 S.Ct. 1507, 1509–1510 (1966).

[99] 384 U.S. 333, 338, 86 S.Ct. 1507, 1510 (1966).

ting away with murder." The next day, another front-page editorial asked, "Why No Inquest?" A coroner's inquest was indeed held on that day in a school gymnasium. The inquest was attended by many newsmen and photographers, and was broadcast with live microphones stationed at the coroner's chair and at the witness stand. Sheppard had attorneys present during the three-day inquest, but they were not permitted to participate.[1]

The news media also quoted authorities' versions of the evidence before trial. Some of this "evidence"—such as a detective's assertion that " 'the killer washed off a trail of blood from the murder bedroom to the downstairs section' "—was never produced at the trial. Such a story, of course, contradicted Sheppard's version of what had happened in the early morning hours of July 4, 1954.[2]

The news media's activities also included playing up stories about Sheppard's extramarital love life, suggesting that these affairs were a motive for the murder of his wife. Although the news media repeatedly mentioned his relationship with a number of women, testimony taken at Sheppard's trial never showed that Sheppard had any affairs except the one with Susan Hayes.[3]

Late in July, newspaper editorials appeared bearing titles such as "Why Don't Police Quiz Top Suspect?" and "Why Isn't Sam Sheppard in Jail?" Another headline shrilled: "Quit Stalling—Bring Him In." The night that headline appeared—July 30—Sheppard was arrested at 10 p.m. at his father's home on a murder charge. He was then taken to the Bay Village City Hall where hundreds of spectators, including many reporters, photographers, and newscasters, awaited his arrival. The Supreme Court of the United States, in Justice Tom C. Clark's majority opinion in the Sheppard case in 1966, summed up the news accounts in this way: [4]

> The publicity then grew in intensity until his indictment on August 17. Typical of the coverage during this period is a front-page interview entitled: "Dr. Sam: 'I Wish There Was Something I Could Get Off My Chest—but There Isn't.' " Unfavorable publicity included items such as a cartoon of the body of a

1 384 U.S. 333, 339, 86 S.Ct. 1507, 1510 (1966).

2 384 U.S. 333, 340, 86 S.Ct. 1507, 1511 (1966).

3 384 U.S. 333, 340–341, 86 S.Ct. 1507, 1511 (1966).

4 384 U.S. 333, 341–342, 86 S.Ct. 1507, 1511–1512 (1966).

sphinx with Sheppard's head and the legend below: " 'I Will Do Everything In My Power to Help Solve This Terrible Murder.'—Dr. Sam Sheppard." Headlines announced, *inter alia* [among other things], that: "Doctor Evidence is Ready for Jury," "Corrigan Tactics Stall Quizzing." "Sheppard 'Gay Set' Is Revealed by [Bay Village Mayor Spence] Houk," "Blood Is Found in Garage," "New Murder Evidence Is Found, Police Claim," "Dr. Sam Faces Quiz At Jail on Marilyn's Fear Of Him."

Justice Clark indicated that there were many other newspaper articles which appeared before and during the trial: "five volumes filled with similar clippings from each of the three Cleveland newspapers covering the period from the murder until Sheppard's conviction in December, 1954." Although the record of Sheppard's trial included no excerpts from radio and television broadcasts, the Court assumed that coverage by the electronic media was equally extensive since space was reserved in the courtroom for representatives of those media.

Justice Clark also noted that the chief prosecutor of Sheppard was a candidate for common pleas judge and that the trial judge, Herbert Blythin, was a candidate to succeed himself. Furthermore, when 75 persons were called as prospective jurors, all three Cleveland newspapers published their names and addresses. All of the prospective jurors received anonymous letters and telephone calls, plus calls from friends, about the impending Sheppard trial.[5]

Even the physical arrangements made in the courtroom to accommodate the newsmen and photographers seemed to work to Dr. Sheppard's disadvantage. The courtroom where the trial was held measured only 26 by 48 feet. In back of the single counsel table, inside the bar, a long temporary table stretching the width of the courtroom was set up, accommodating about 20 reporters who were assigned seats for the duration of the trial. One end of this table was less than three feet from the jury box. Behind the bar railing were four rows of benches, with seats likewise assigned by the court for the entire trial. The first row behind the bar was assigned to representatives of the television and radio stations, with the second and third rows being occupied by reporters from out-of-town newspapers and magazines. Thus the great majority of the seats in the courtroom were occupied by reporters. Private telephone lines were installed in other rooms on the same floor with the courtroom, and

[5] 384 U.S. 333, 342, 86 S.Ct. 1507, 1512 (1966).

one radio station was allowed to make broadcasts from the room next to the jury room throughout the trial, and while the jury reached its verdict. Photographs could be taken in court during recesses. All of these arrangements, and the massive coverage by the media, continued during the nine weeks of the trial. Reporters moving in an out of the courtroom during times when the court was in session caused so much confusion that it was difficult for witnesses and lawyers to be heard despite a loudspeaker system.[6]

During the trial, pictures of the jury appeared more than 40 times in the Cleveland newspapers. And the day before the jury rendered its verdict of guilty against Dr. Sam Sheppard, while the jurors were at lunch in the company of two bailiffs, the jury was separated into two groups to pose for pictures which were published in the newspapers. The jurors, unlike those in the Estes case, were not sequestered ["locked up" under the close supervision of bailiffs]. Instead, the jurors were allowed to do what they pleased outside the courtroom while not taking part in the proceedings.[7]

The intense publicity given the Sheppard case in the news media continued unabated while the trial was actually in progress. Sheppard's attorneys took a "random poll" of persons on the streets asking their opinion about the osteopath's guilt or innocence in an effort to gain evidence for a change of venue. This poll was denounced in one newspaper editorial as smacking of "mass jury tampering" and stated that the bar association should do something about it.

A debate among newspaper reporters broadcast over radio station WHK in Cleveland contained assertions that Sheppard had admitted his guilt by hiring a prominent criminal lawyer. In another broadcast heard over WHK, columnst and radio-TV personality Robert Considine likened Sheppard to a perjurer. When Sheppard's attorneys asked Judge Blythin to question the jurors as to how many had heard the broadcast, Judge Blythin refused to do this. And when the trial was in its seventh week, a Walter Winchell broadcast available in Cleveland over both radio and television asserted that a woman under arrest in New York City for robbery had stated that she had been Sheppard's mistress and had borne him a child. Two jurors admitted in open court that they had heard the broadcast. However, Judge Blythin merely accepted the jurors' statements that the broad-

---

6 384 U.S. 333, 343–344, 86 S.Ct. 1507, 1512–1513 (1966).

7 384 U.S. 333, 345, 353, 86 S.Ct. 1507, 1513, 1517 (1966).

cast would have no effect on their judgment and the judge accepted the replies as sufficient.[8]

When the case was submitted to the jury, the jurors were sequestered for their deliberations, which took five days and four nights. But this "sequestration" was not complete. The jurors had been allowed to call their homes every day while they stayed at a hotel during their deliberations. Telephones had been removed from the jurors' hotel rooms, but they were allowed to use phones in the bailiffs' rooms. The calls were placed by the jurors themselves, and no record was kept of the jurors who made calls or of the telephone numbers or of the persons called. The bailiffs could hear only the jurors' end of the telephone conversations.[9]

When Sheppard's case was decided by the Supreme Court of the United States in 1966, Justice Tom C. Clark's majority opinion included this ringing statement of the importance of the news media to the administration of justice.[10]

> The principle that justice cannot survive behind walls of silence has long been reflected in the "Anglo-American distrust for secret trials." A responsible press has always been regarded as the handmaiden of effective judicial administration, especially in the criminal field. Its function in this regard is documented by an impressive record of service over several centuries. The press does not simply publish information about trials but guards against the miscarriage of justice by subjecting the police, prosecutors, and judicial processes to extensive public scrutiny and criticism.

Implicit in some of Justice Clark's other statements in his opinion was deep disapproval of the news media's conduct before and during the Sheppard trial. But the news media were by no means the only culprits who made it impossible for Sheppard to get a fair trial. There was more than enough blame to go around, and Justice Clark distributed that blame among the deserving: news media, police, the coroner, and the trial court. The trial judge, Herbert Blythin, had died in 1960, but Justice Clark nevertheless spelled out what Judge Blythin should have done to protect the defendant.

At the outset of Sheppard's trial, Judge Blythin stated that he did not have the power to control publicity about the trial. Jus-

---

8 384 U.S. 333, 346, 348, 86 S.Ct. 1507, 1514–1515 (1966).

9 384 U.S. 333, 349, 86 S.Ct. 1507, 1515 (1966).

10 384 U.S. 333, 349–350, 86 S.Ct. 1507, 1515–1516 (1966).

tice Clark declared that Judge Blythin's arrangements with the news media "caused Sheppard to be deprived of that 'judicial serenity and calm to which [he] was entitled.'" Justice Clark added that "bedlam reigned at the courthouse during the trial and newsmen took over practically the entire courtroom hounding most of the participants in the trial, especially Sheppard." [11] Justice Clark asserted: [12]

> The carnival atmosphere at trial could easily have been avoided since the courtroom and courthouse premises are subject to the control of the court. As we stressed in *Estes*, the presence of the press at judicial proceedings must be limited when it is apparent that the accused might otherwise be prejudiced or disadvantaged. Bearing in mind the massive pretrial publicity, the judge should have adopted stricter rules governing the use of the courtroom by newsmen, as Sheppard's counsel requested. The number of reporters in the courtroom itself could have been limited at the first sign that their presence would disrupt the trial. They certainly should have not been placed inside the bar. Furthermore, the judge should have more closely regulated the conduct of newsmen in the courtroom. For instance, the judge belatedly asked them not to handle and photograph trial exhibits lying on the counsel table during recesses.

In addition, the trial judge should have insulated the jurors and witnesses from the news media, and "should have made some effort to control the release of leads, information, and gossip to the press by police officers, witnesses, and the counsel for both sides." Justice Clark contended: [13]

> The fact that many of the prejudicial news items can be traced to the prosecution, as well as the defense aggravates the judge's failure to take any action. * * * More specifically, the trial court might well have proscribed extrajudicial statements by any lawyer, party, witness, or court official which divulged prejudicial matters, such as the refusal of Sheppard to submit to interrogation or take any lie detector tests; any statement made by Sheppard to officials; the identity of prospective witnesses or the probable testimony;

11 384 U.S. 333, 355, 86 S.Ct. 1507, 1518 (1966).

12 384 U.S. 333, 358, 86 S.Ct. 1507, 1520 (1966).

13 384 U.S. 333, 359, 361, 86 S.Ct. 1507, 1521–1522 (1966).

any belief in guilt or innocence; or like statements concerning the merits of the case. See State v. Van Duyne, 43 N.J. 369, 389, 204 A.2d 841, 852 (1964) in which the court interpreted Canon 20 of the American Bar Association's Canons of Professional Ethics to prohibit such statements.

Justice Clark appeared to emphasize the trial judge's duty—more than that of the press or of any participants in a trial—to protect the defendant's rights. He insisted that courts must take remedial measures which will prevent prejudice.[14]

> The courts must take such steps by rule and regulation that will protect their processes from prejudicial outside interferences. Neither prosecutors, counsel for defense, the accused, witnesses, court staff nor enforcement officers coming under the jurisdiction of the court should be permitted to frustrate its function.

> Collaboration between counsel and the press as to information affecting the fairness of a criminal trial is not only subject to regulation, but is highly censurable and worthy of disciplinary measures.

Because the trial judge had not protected Dr. Sheppard from prejudicial publicity, the Supreme Court granted a writ of habeas corpus. The Court ordered that Sheppard be released from prison unless the State of Ohio again pressed its charges against him "within a reasonable time." Justice Clark's opinion was handed down on June 6, 1966. The State of Ohio then tried Sheppard again, and he was acquitted on November 16, 1966, becoming a free man for the first time in 12 years.

SEC. 54. THE JUDGE'S ROLE

It is the judge's responsibility to see that each defendant receives a fair trial.

The decision in the Sheppard case left its mark in the recommendations of the American Bar Association's "Reardon Report" discussed earlier in this chapter. The cases discussed in this chapter—*Irvin, Rideau, Estes,* and *Sheppard*—generated new law and suggested strongly that American courts may insist more and more on tighter controls over the information released to the news media in criminal trials by police, prosecution and defense attorneys, and by other employees under the control of

---

[14] 384 U.S. 333, 363, 86 S.Ct. 1507, 1522–1523 (1966).

the courts. The primary responsibility, however, for seeing to it that a defendant receives a fair trial, rests with the courts. Judges are expected to remain in control of trials in their courts.

A judge who has great respect for the press, Frank W. Wilson of a U.S. District Court in Nashville, Tenn., has written: "Certain it is that the press coverage of crimes and criminal proceedings make more difficult the job that a judge has of assuring a fair trial. But no one has yet shown that it renders the job impossible. In fact, no one has yet shown, to the satisfaction of any court, an identifiable instance of miscarriage of justice due to press coverage of a trial where the error was not remedied." [15] Note that Judge Wilson says that it is the *judge's* job in assuring a fair trial. Judge Wilson has declared, "show me an unfair trial that goes uncorrected and I will show you a judge who has failed in his duty." [16]

Judge Wilson thus placed great—many would argue *too* great — [17] reliance upon the remedies which a judge can use to attempt to set things right for the defendant once he has received what the judge considers to be an undue amount of prejudicial publicity. Some of the most important of these trial-level "remedies" are outlined below:

> 1) *Change of venue,* moving the trial to another area in hopes that jurors not prejudiced by mass media publicity or outraged community sentiment can be found. This "remedy," however, requires that a defendant give up his Sixth Amendment right to a trial in the "State and *district* wherein the crime shall have been committed * * *." [18] Change of venue may have been a relatively effective remedy, say, in 1900, before radio and television blanketed the nation so effectively with instantaneous communications. Also, one locality's sensational trial, after it is moved, will become another locality's sensational trial, largely defeating the change of venue.

---

[15] Frank A. Wilson, "A Fair Trial and a Free Press," presented at 33rd Annual convention of the Ohio Newspaper Association, Columbus, Ohio, Feb. 11, 1966.

[16] Ibid.

[17] Don R. Pember, Pretrial Newspaper Publicity in Criminal Proceedings: A Case Study (unpublished M.A. thesis, Michigan State University, East Lansing, Mich.) pp. 12–16.

[18] Constitution, Sixth Amendment, emphasis added; Lawrence E. Edenhöfer, "The Impartial Jury—Twentieth Century Dilemma: Some Solutions to the Conflict Between Free Press and Fair Trial," Cornell Law Quarterly Vol. 51 (Winter, 1966) pp. 306, 314.

2) *Continuance or postponement.* This is simply a matter of postponing a trial until the publicity or public clamor abates. A problem with this "remedy" is that there is no guarantee that the publicity will not begin anew. It might be well to remember the axiom, "justice delayed is justice denied." A continuance in a case involving a major crime might mean that a defendant —even an innocent defendant—might thus be imprisoned for a lengthy time before his trial. A continuance means that a defendant gives up his Sixth Amendment right to a *speedy* trial.

3) *Voir dire* examination of potential jurors. This refers to the procedure by which each potential juror is questioned by opposing attorneys and may be dismissed "for cause" if the juror is shown to be prejudiced. (In addition, attorneys have a limited number of "peremptory challenges" which they can use to remove jurors whose prejudice cannot be sufficiently demonstrated but who may give hints that they favor the other side in the impending legal battle.) Professor Don R. Pember of the University of Washington says that the voir dire examination is an effective tool and one of the best available trial-level remedies.

4) *Sequestration,* or "locking up" the jury. Judges have the power to isolate a jury, to make sure that community prejudices—either published or broadcast in the mass media or of the person-to-person variety— do not infect a jury with information which might harm a defendant's chances for a fair trial by an impartial jury. This remedy, of course, could not halt the pre-trial publicity which jurors might have seen or heard before the trial. As Professor Pember has said, judges are reluctant to do this today because of the complexities in the life of the average person.[19]

5) *Contempt of Court.* This punitive "remedy" is discussed at length in Chapter 10. Courts have the power to cite for contempt those actions—either in court or out of court—which interfere with the orderly administration of justice. American courts have been very re-

[19] Another trial-level remedy which is more infrequently used is the blue-ribbon jury. When a case has received massive prejudicial publicity, a court may empower either the prosecution or the defense to empanel a special, so-called "blue ribbon" jury. Intelligent jurors are selected through the use of questionnaires and interviews, under the assumption that a more intelligent jury will be more likely to withstand pressures and remain impartial.

luctant, for the most part, to use the contempt remedy to punish pre-trial or during-trial publications. As a result, some critics of the American mass media wish to see the British system of using contempt of court citations as a weapon to control media coverage of criminal cases.

The British system of contempt citations to regulate media activities has worked well, according to some observers. The British press—knowing that the threat of a contempt citation hangs over it for a misstep—cannot quote from a confession (or even reveal its existence); nor can the British publish material—including previous criminal records—which would not be admissible evidence. One of the things about the British system which is most offensive to American journalists is the prohibition of a newspaper's making its own investigation and printing the results of it. After the trial is concluded, *then* British newspapers can cover the trial.[20]

As distinguished American journalists have pointed out, however, America is not Britain. The *New York Times'* Anthony Lewis has suggested that the British system of using contempt citations to preclude virtually all comment on criminal cases simply could not work in the United States. While some criminal trials in the United States drag on for years, even trials involving major crimes—including appeals—are usually completed in Britain in less than two months' time.[21] Anthony Lewis has also argued that Britain is a small, homogenous nation where police or judicial corruption is virtually unknown. America has not been so fortunate: occasionally corrupt policemen or judges are discovered, and perhaps the media's watchdog function is more needed in reporting on police and courts in this nation than it is in Britain.[22]

If American news media indulge themselves in orgies of sensationalism as detailed earlier in this chapter in the discussions of the *Irvin, Estes,* and *Sheppard* cases, the result may be a marked diminution of press freedom to report on criminal trials. And if the press does suffer such a diminution, it will have to accept a large share of the blame. Surely the press can share the Supreme Court's concern with the rights of defendants in criminal trials, as can defense lawyers, prosecutors and policemen.

[20] Harold W. Sullivan, Trial by Newspaper (Hyannis, Mass., Patriot Press, 1961).

[21] New York Times, June 20, 1965.

[22] Ibid.

B. FREE EXPRESSION AND THE RIGHTS OF THE STATE AND MORAL ORDER

Chapter 9

CRIMINAL WORDS: LIBEL

SEC. 55. CRIMINAL LIBEL UNDER COMMON LAW AND STATUTES

At common law, criminal libel included sedition, obscenity, blasphemy, and defamation, but state statutes ordinarily treat it as defamation.

Having seen one citizen suing another in civil actions for defamation, privacy, and copyright, we turn now to actions where the state brings charges that words are a crime against society and the public good. Various kinds of spoken and written statements have been viewed as harmful to the general public welfare, punishable by fine or imprisonment. The injured citizen bringing a civil suit for damages has his counterpart in the public prosecutor who places a criminal charge for harm to society.

The law of criminal words embraces many kinds of spoken and written statements. The spoken variety is called slander in some of its forms. Slander was generally not an indictable offense at common law, but various state statutes make it a misdemeanor, especially when it falsely imputes unchastity to a woman or questionable conditions to banks and other financial institutions. Obscenity, sedition, blasphemy, and contempt of court or legislative body have been charged on the basis of spoken as well as written words.

Words and statements that violate the criminal law, however, are more often printed or written than spoken. And under common law principles, the general term "criminal libel" includes several classes of offensive words: printing or writing which tends to cause a breach of the peace, disrupt by force the established public order, offend public morals, revile the Deity. In

327

Kennerly v. Hennessy, the court spoke about these classes of words:[1]

> At common law a criminal prosecution for libel is warranted only when the alleged libel affects the public, as when it corrupts the public morals or incites to violations of the criminal law or when the necessary or natural effect of the alleged publication is to cause an injury to a person or persons of such a nature and extent as to render a breach of the peace imminent or probable.

While civil libel deals largely with defamation of persons, criminal libel has recognized that defamation of religion, public morality, and the state could occur, as well as defamation of persons; and the term "libel" thus has an appropriate reference to blasphemy, obscenity, and sedition, respectively, where common law principles hold.[2]

> At the time of Revolution the English common law divided unlawful publications into four species of libel, viz.: defamatory libels, or publications defamatory of personal or professional reputations; seditious libels, or publications defamatory of existing public officers, government, institutions, and laws; blasphemous libels, or publications defamatory of the Christian religion; obscene and immoral libels, or publications defamatory of England's existing standard of public morality.

However, most states today define criminal libel in statutes separate from those defining blasphemy, sedition, and obscenity, each of which is likely to be the subject of a separate statute.[3]

This book treats each offense separately.

Certain minor aspects of the law of criminal words lie near the concerns of libel but will receive no detailed consideration here. For example, in some states it is a misdemeanor to communicate knowingly false information about any person to a newspaper with the intent that such information be published. In a few states, also, statutes declare that making threats to defame another, or offering to prevent a libel for valuable consideration is a misdemeanor. And libelous writings or writings of a threatening kind on any envelope or wrapper may not be sent through the mails. Anyone depositing such nonmailable matter

---

[1] 68 Fla. 138, 139, 66 So. 729, 19 A.L.R. 1470, 1471 (1914).

[2] Schofield, Henry, "Freedom of the Press in the United States," II Constitutional Law and Equity 510, 515 (Boston, 1921).

[3] 19 A.L.R. 1470, 1471.

for distribution is subject to a fine of not more than $1,000 or imprisonment for not more than one year, or both.[4]

As stated above, criminal libel is used here in general in the statutory sense of defamation of persons, excluding blasphemy, obscenity, sedition and other word offenses. A rather typical statute defines criminal libel thus: [5]

> A libel is a malicious defamation, expressed either by writing, printing, or by signs or pictures, or the like, tending to blacken the memory of one who is dead, or to impeach the honesty, integrity, virtue, or reputation or publish the natural or alleged defects of one who is alive, and thereby to expose him to public hatred, contempt, or ridicule.

As will be seen below, an occasional statute adds that among libelous words are those that "provoke one to wrath", or that "tend to cause a breach of the peace".

Criminal libel may best be read as history, perhaps, for little of it remains today. About 100 cases in all states per decade were reported after 1885 until a sharp decline set in soon after World War I. By 1935–45 the number had dropped to fewer than 15; [6] by 1970, the action had almost disappeared from compilations. The decline is related to the fact that, under most state statutes, there is little or no difference between libel under the criminal law and libel under the civil law—both concentrating upon protection of individual reputations—and that courts have increasingly taken the position that the civil remedy is much to be preferred to the criminal, which seems inappropriate to personal squabbles.[7] As for the defamed himself, he ordinarily has more to gain through a civil judgment for damages than through a criminal conviction that helps only in the sense that it is a "moral victory."

SEC. 56. CRIMINAL LIBEL AND BREACH OF THE PEACE

The tendency of words to cause a breach of the peace remains as an infrequently used justification for prosecuting publishers.

The central rationale justifying the criminal libel action existed at common law as far back as the early seventeenth century,

---

[4] Wis.Stat.1955, § 942.03; McKinney's N.Y.Penal Law, Consol.Laws, c. 40 § 926–a; 18 U.S.C.A. § 1718 (1951).

[5] West's Ann.Cal.Penal Code § 248.

[6] Stevens, J. D., et al., "Criminal Libel as Seditious Libel, 1916–65," 43 Journalism Quarterly 110, 111 (1966).

[7] Garrison v. La., 379 U.S. 64, 69, 85 S.Ct. 209, 213 (1964); State v. Browne, 206 A.2d 591, 596, 86 N.J.Super. 217 (1965); S.H.A. (Ill.) c. 38, § 27.

and has persisted in some states since the early national period. This was the reasoning which said that harsh words about another person tend to cause him to seek revenge through violence against the writer, and that such breach of the peace is a public evil to be guarded against. The Star Chamber decision of 1605, De Libellis Famosis, often is given credit for shaping the thought behind criminal libel and its sanctions: [8]

> If it be against a private man it deserves a severe punishment, for although the libel be made against one, yet it incites all those of the same family, kindred, or society to revenge, and so tends *per consequens* to quarrels and breaches of the peace, and may be the cause of shedding of blood, and of inconveniences: if it be against a magistrate or other public person, it is a greater offense; for it concerns not only the breach of peace, but also the scandal of government.

Furthermore, the reasoning went, if the offending words were true, the offense was aggravated, for true defamation would make revenge even more sought after than would a lie, which could be disproved. This was the rule known to the eighteenth century as "the greater the truth, the greater the libel."

Such ancient roots underlying today's few representatives of the common law view are now largely decayed. The evils of duelling as a way of avenging verbal insults were perhaps real enough to the seventeenth and eighteenth centuries, to justify laws for choking off inflaming talk that led to swordplay and pistols; but such breach of the peace became less and less likely as civil actions in courts of law displaced personal violence as an avenue for satisfying one's outrage at being defamed.[9]

Furthermore, the rule of "the greater the truth, the greater the libel" received a series of body blows in the American colonies and the new nation. The truth, it was argued in major cases and major legislation, ought to be a defense for the accused, not an exacerbation of a supposed crime. Heavily influenced by the action of New York in 1805, state after state passed statutes that ignored the old breach of peace rationale for the crime and provided for truth as a defense.[10]

By mid-twentieth century, relatively few states continued to rely upon breach of the peace as an element in criminal libel. It

[8] 5 Coke 125 (1605), 3 Coke's Reports (Fraser ed., 1826) 254, part 5–125a.

[9] Garrison v. La., 379 U.S. 64, 68, 85 S.Ct. 209, 212 (1964).

[10] Tannehaus, Joseph, "Group Libel," 35 Cornell L.Q. 261, 273 and fn. 67 (1950).

persisted in the statutes of Alabama, Connecticut, Illinois, and Virginia [11] and in a modified form (words that "provoke to wrath") in a handful of states.[12] In addition, those states without criminal libel statutes relied upon common law and thus presumably on breach of the peace.[13]

In the case of State v. Gardner, the latter published in the *Bridgeport* (Conn.) *Herald* an article about the police chief of New Britain, saying in part:

> Chief Hart is the owner of three autos * * *. I believed these were bought with bootleg money. Chief Hart and his wife are bootleggers. In fact the whole d_____ family are. They meet bootleggers at the town line and escort them in and many times the illicit liquor is transferred to the Chief's car, or his wife's auto, and delivered to the consumers.

In upholding Gardner's conviction for criminal libel, the Connecticut Supreme Court indicated its reliance on breach of the peace, saying "The gist of the crime is, not the injury to the reputation of the person libeled, but that the publication affects injuriously the peace and good order of society." [14]

In a subsequent case in the same state, it was made plain by the Supreme Court that the crime lies in the *tendency* of the words to create a breach of the peace, and that "it is immaterial that no one was incited to commit any act by reason of the libel * * *. The court correctly ruled that it was not incumbent upon the state to prove that a disturbance of the public peace actually resulted from the publications." [15]

Nor is it necessary that the person attacked in a criminal libel consider himself scandalized or disgraced by the words. In State v. Levand, the editor of the *Casper* (Wyo.) *Herald* printed a story attacking a jury for freeing Undersheriff Cantlin who had shot and killed a woman when she committed a minor traffic violation. Levand's attorneys presented in defense a Mr. Jackson, member of the jury that had been attacked; and Jackson testified that he had lost no friends or been disgraced by the

[11] Ala.Code, 1958, Tit. 14, § 347; C.G.S.A. (Conn.) § 53–174; Ill.Rev.Stat.1965, c. 38, § 27–1; Va.Code, 1950, § 18–133.

[12] I.C.A. (Iowa) § 737.1; Me.Rev.Stat.1944, c. 117, § 30; T.C.A. (Tenn.) § 39–2701; V.A.M.S. (Mo.) § 559.410.

[13] These states are Delaware, Kentucky, Maryland, Massachusetts, New Hampshire, Rhode Island, Vermont, and West Virginia: Beauharnais v. Ill., 343 U.S. 250, 255 fn. 5, 72 S.Ct. 725, 730 (1952).

[14] State v. Gardner, 112 Conn. 121, 124, 151 A. 349, 350 (1930).

[15] State v. Whiteside, 148 Conn. 208, 169 A.2d 260 (1961).

article in any way. The court held that Jackson's assessment of the effects of the article made no difference: [16]

> The basis for criminal liability for libel is its injurious effect on the public or its tendency to provoke breach of the peace. And it is generally held that a defendant may be held responsible in a criminal case if the defamatory words are of such a nature that they *tend* to disgrace and degrade the person libeled or hold him up to public hatred, contempt, or ridicule * * *. Mr. Jackson and any of the other jurors in the Cantlin case against whom the article in question was directed might be among those least able to judge as to the effect or tendency thereof.

In 1966, The Supreme Court of the United States focussed on breach of the peace in common law criminal libel, and found that it did not square with the First Amendment. Merely to say that words which tend to cause breach of the peace are criminal, is too indefinite to be understandable, the court said. The case, Ashton v. Kentucky,[17] involved a pamphlet in which Ashton charged a police chief with law-breaking during a strike of miners, a sheriff with attempts to buy off a prosecution, and a newspaper owner with diverting food and clothing collected for strikers, to anti-strike workers. Ashton was convicted under a definition of criminal libel given, in part, by the judge as "any writing calculated to create disturbances of the peace." The Supreme Court said that without specification that was too vague an offense to be constitutional: [18]

> We agree * * * that "since the English common law of criminal libel is inconsistent with constitutional provisions, and since no Kentucky case has redefined the crime in understandable terms, and since the law must be made on a case to case basis, the elements of the crime are so indefinite and uncertain that it should not be enforced as a penal offense in Kentucky."
>
> The case is close to Cantwell v. State of Connecticut * * *. In reversing we said: "The offense known as breach of the peace embraces a great variety of conduct destroying or menacing public order and tranquility. It includes not only violent acts but acts and words likely to produce violence in others * * *. Here we have a situation analogous to a conviction under a stat-

---

[16] State v. Levand et al., 262 P. 24, 29 (1927).

[17] 384 U.S. 195, 86 S.Ct. 1407 (1966).

[18] Ibid., 384 U.S. 195, 198, 86 S.Ct. 1407, 1409–1411.

ute sweeping in a great variety of conduct under a general and indefinite characterization, and leaving to the executive and judicial branches too wide a discretion in its application."

* * * * * * * *

* * * to make an offense of conduct which is "calculated to create disturbances of the peace" leaves wide open the standard of responsibility. It involves calculations as to the boiling point of a particular person or a particular group, not an appraisal of the comments *per se.* This kind of criminal libel "makes a man a criminal simply because his neighbors have no self-control and cannot refrain from violence." Chafee, Free Speech in the United States 151 (1954).

Here * * * we deal with First Amendment rights. Vague laws in any area suffer a constitutional infirmity. When First Amendment rights are involved, we look even more closely lest, under the guise of regulating conduct that is reachable by the police power, freedom of speech or of the press suffer. We said in Cantwell v. Connecticut, supra, that such a law must be "narrowly drawn to prevent the supposed evil," and that a conviction for an utterance "based on a common law concept of the most general nature," * * * could not stand.

All the infirmities of the conviction of the common-law crime of breach of the peace as defined by Connecticut judges are present in this conviction of the common-law crime of criminal libel as defined by Kentucky judges.

Reversed.

There are two special circumstances in which criminal libel is held to stem from the tendency of words to cause a breach of the peace. One, extremely rare, is libel of the dead, which is presumed to provoke relatives and friends of the deceased to violence.[19] The other, also infrequently charged, is libel of groups. The leading case of the latter in recent decades is Beauharnais v. Illinois, decided in 1952.[20] It involved a leaflet attack

---

[19] State v. Haffer, 94 Wash. 136, 162 P. 45 (1916).

[20] 343 U.S. 250, 72 S.Ct. 725 (1952). See also People v. Spielman, 318 Ill. 482, 149 N.E. 466 (1925). Also "Knights of Columbus" cases: People v. Turner, 28 Cal.App. 766, 154 Pac. 34 (1914); People v. Gordon, 63 Cal.App. 62, 219 P. 486 (1923); Crane v. State, 14 Okl.Crim. 30, 166 P. 1110 (1917); Alumbaugh v. State, 39 Ga.App. 599, 147 S.E. 714 (1929). And see Joseph Tannehaus, "Group Libel," 35 Cornell L.Q. 261 (1950).

on the Negro race in Chicago, at a time when the memory of Hitler Germany's proscription, ostracism, and mass killing of Jews was fresh in the minds of the nation. Migration of Negroes from the south into northern cities was swelling. Beauharnais, president of the White Circle League, had organized his group to distribute the leaflets, and they did so in downtown Chicago. Among other things, the leaflet called for city officials to stop "the further encroachment, harassment, and invasion of the white people * * * by the Negro * * *", and predicted that "rapes, robberies, knives, guns, and marijuana of the negro" surely would unite Chicago whites against blacks.

Beauharnais was prosecuted and convicted under an Illinois law making it unlawful to exhibit a publication which "portrays depravity, criminality, unchastity, or lack of virtue of a class of citizens, of any race, color, creed or religion which said publication * * * exposes the citizens of any race, color, creed or religion to contempt, derision, or obloquy or which is productive of breach of the peace or riots." [21]

In affirming the conviction, Justice Frankfurter's decision said that this statute did not suffer from vagueness, as had some laws declared unconstitutional in other cases involving punishment for words tending to cause breach of the peace. This feature of the Illinois statute was thus constitutional.

The charges against Negroes, said the Court, were unquestionably libelous; and the central question became whether the "liberty" of the Fourteenth Amendment prevents a state from punishing such libels when they are directed not at an individual, but at "designated collectivities." The Court said that only if the law were a "wilful and purposeless restriction unrelated to the peace and well-being of the State," could the Court deny a state power to punish utterances directed at a defined group.

Justice Frankfurter found that for more than a century, Illinois had been "the scene of exacerbated tension between races, often flaring into violence and destruction." He cited the murder of abolitionist Elijah Lovejoy in 1837, the "first northern race riot"—in Chicago in 1908—in which six persons were killed, and subsequent violence in the state of Illinois down to the Cicero, Ill. race riot of 1951. He concluded that "In the face of this history and its frequent obligato of extreme racial and religious propaganda, we would deny experience to say that the

21 Beauharnais v. Ill., 343 U.S. 250, 251, 72 S.Ct. 725, 728 (1952). The statute was not re-enacted when in 1961 Illinois revised its criminal law.

Illinois legislature was without reason in seeking ways to curb false or malicious defamation of racial and religious groups." [22]

Four members of the court delivered strong dissents to the majority opinion that sustained Beauharnais' conviction. Justice Hugo Black stated much of the case against the concept of group libel as an offense acceptable to American freedom. Calling the law a "state censorship" instrument, Black said that permitting states to experiment in curbing freedom of expression "is startling and frightening doctrine in a country dedicated to self-government by its people." He said that criminal libel as "constitutionally recognized" has provided for punishment of false, malicious, scurrilous charges against individuals, not against huge groups.[23]

> This limited scope of the law of criminal libel is of no small importance. It has confined state punishment of speech and expression to the narrowest of areas involving nothing more than private feuds. Every expansion of the law of criminal libel so as to punish discussions of matters of public concern means a corresponding invasion of the area dedicated to free expression by the First Amendment * * *.
>
> The Court's reliance on Chaplinsky v. New Hampshire, 315 U.S. 568, is also misplaced. New Hampshire had a state law making it an offense to direct insulting words at an *individual* on a public street. Chaplinsky had violated that law by calling a man vile names "face-to-face." We pointed out in that context that the use of such "fighting" words was not an essential part of exposition of ideas. Whether the words used in their context here are "fighting" words in the same sense is doubtful, but whether so or not they are not addressed to or about *individuals*. Moreover, the leaflet used here was also the means adopted by an assembled group to enlist interest in their efforts to have legislation enacted. And the fighting words were but a part of arguments on questions of wide public interest and importance. Freedom of petition, assembly, speech and press could be greatly abridged by a practice of meticulously scrutinizing every editorial, speech, sermon or other printed matter to extract two or three naughty words on which to hang charges of "group libel."

[22] Ibid., 343 U.S. 250, 258–261, 72 S.Ct. 725, 731–732.

[23] Ibid., 343 U.S. 250, 270, 272, 273, 72 S.Ct. 725, 737–738.

SEC. 57. CRIMINAL LIBEL AS DEFAMATION
OF INDIVIDUALS

Most state statutes treat criminal libel as defamation of individuals which warrants criminal prosecution and punishment.

As noted earlier, statutes in the nineteenth century replaced the common law rules of criminal libel in many states, and most of them ignored the tendency of harsh words to cause breach of the peace. The definition of criminal libel became almost indistinguishable from that of civil libel in the majority of states,[24] as the focus turned to defamation of individuals: printing, writing, signs, pictures that impeach the honesty, integrity, virtue, or reputation of an individual, or expose him to public hatred, contempt, ridicule, or financial injury, or deprive him of public confidence or social intercourse.[25] Vestiges of the breach of peace rationale remained even in some of these laws, however, where the special cases of libel of the dead or of groups still were credited with the power to arouse uncontrollable anger of surviving relatives or of members of interest groups,[26] and were made punishable.

In Garland v. State, for example, breach of peace was not at issue, but rather, said the Georgia Supreme Court, whether Garland's article in the *Monroe Advertiser* defamed the members of a jury. In speaking of a trial jury that had convicted one William Ogiltree, Garland had said "I know the jury composed of fine men, did not even deliberate on the case—the verdict was already made." The Georgia court ruled in reversing Garland's Conviction: [27]

> The controlling and decisive question is whether the published words * * * are words of defamation as applied to the members of the jury * * *. The words do not charge that the jurors had prejudged the case before they were sworn as jurors in the case. They do not charge that the jurors violated their oath * * *. Taking the words as they would be ordinarily understood, they meant that the jury, after retiring, did not deliberate * * * or consult with one anoth-

[24] "Constitutionality of the Law of Criminal Libel," 52 Col.L.R. 521, 525 (1952); Tannehaus, op. cit., 273.

[25] For common formulas, see Beauharnais v. Ill., 343 U.S. 250, 255 fn. 5, 72 S.Ct. 725, 730 (1952).

[26] E. g., I.C.A. (Iowa) § 737.1.

[27] Garland v. State, 211 Ga. 48, 84 S.E.2d 13, 14 (1954).

er to form an opinion as to the guilt or innocence of the prisoner, but that their individual and collective minds had arrived at a verdict of guilty when they reached the jury room. It is not a ground for granting a new trial that the jury in a capital-felony conviction case returned a verdict of guilty within fifteen minutes after receiving the case for consideration * * *. We know of no rule or law or code of juror's ethics that prevents a juror from rendering his conscientious judgment on the first ballot in the jury room.

In a New Jersey case, Reade was indicted for criminal libel in publishing an article charging Rediker with stealing, "political chicanery," and bribery of officials to promote his business enterprises. He appealed, saying the indictment did not state facts sufficient to constitute the crime of libel. The State Supreme Court, however, ruled against him. It said nothing about breach of the peace as part of libel, but that "printed words are libelous which impute to a person that he has been guilty of any crime, fraud, dishonesty, immorality, vice, or dishonorable conduct, or which have a tendency to injure him in his office, profession, calling, or trade." And Reade, it said, was completely and adequately apprised of the crime charged against him by this language in the indictment: [28]

> * * * libelous words and matters then and there were used by the said Walter Reade in a defamatory sense, to wit, in the sense that * * * Joe Rediker plundered, stole and employed political chicanery to gain his unlawful ends and to promote his business enterprises * * *; that he the said Joe Rediker had bribed and illegally influenced officials of the city of Asbury Park to award him contracts to operate bathing and dance hall concessions of the public property of the City of Asbury Park * * * to the great injury, scandal and disgrace of the said Joe Rediker * * *.

SEC. 58. CRIMINAL LIBEL AND PUBLIC OFFICIALS

The Supreme Court of the United States ruled in Garrison v. Louisiana that a criminal libel action against a public official could be maintained only if actual malice could be shown, thus drastically limiting the field for libel of officials.

Criminal libel actions have often been brought for criticism of public officials. One study found that 31, or about one-fifth of

---

[28] State v. Reade, 136 N.J.L. 432, 435, 56 A.2d 566, 567 (1948).

Nelson & Teeter Mass Com.2d Ed. F.P.—22

the 148 criminal libel cases reported in the half-century after World War I, grew out of charges made against officials.[29]

These actions have sometimes been viewed as a substitute for seditious libel prosecutions, or perhaps as seditious libel actions in disguise: government's punishment of those who dare to criticize its personnel.[30]

The Supreme Court's ruling in New York Times Co. v. Sullivan, however, has had its impact in the realm of criminal libel as well as civil libel: the new requirement that criticism of a public official must be characterized by actual malice to support a libel charge has found its way into criminal libel. The leading case is Garrison v. Louisiana.[31] Here Garrison, a prosecuting attorney for the State of Louisiana, gave out a statement at a press conference attacking several judges of his parish (county) for laziness and inattention to their official duties. He was convicted of criminal libel, and his case ultimately reached the Supreme Court of the United States.

The Court cited the famous *New York Times* rule defining malice—that a public official might recover damages as a remedy for civil libel only "if he establishes that the utterance was false and that it was made with knowledge of its falsity or in reckless disregard of whether it was false or true." [32]

> The reasons which led us so to hold * * * apply with no less force merely because the remedy is criminal. The constitutional guarantees of freedom of expression compel application of the same standard to the criminal remedy. Truth may not be the subject of either civil or criminal sanctions where discussion of public affairs is concerned. And since " * * * erroneous statement is inevitable in free debate * * *" only those false statements made with the high degree of awareness of their probable falsity demanded by New York Times may be the subject of either civil or criminal sanctions. For speech concerning public affairs is more than self-expression; it is the essence of self-government.

The Louisiana court's ruling that Garrison's criticism of the judges constituted an attack on the personal integrity of the judges, rather than on their official conduct, was not accepted

[29] Stevens, op. cit., at 110.

[30] Ibid.; Garrison v. Louisiana, 379 U.S. 64, 80, 85 S.Ct. 209, 218, 220 (1964).

[31] Ibid.

[32] Ibid., at 74, at 215.

by the United States Supreme Court. The state court had said
that Garrison had imputed fraud, deceit, and dishonesty to the
judges; violation of Louisiana's "deadhead" statute; and malfeasance in office.   But, said the United States Supreme
Court: [33]

> Of course, any criticism of the manner in which a pub-
> lic official performs his duties will tend to affect his
> private, as well as his public, reputation. The New
> York Times rule is not rendered inapplicable merely be-
> cause an official's private reputation, as well as his
> public reputation, is harmed. The public official rule
> protects the paramount public interest in a free flow of
> information to the people concerning public officials,
> their servants. To this end, anything which might
> touch on an official's fitness for office is relevant.
> Few personal attributes are more germane to fitness
> for office than dishonesty, malfeasance, or improper
> motivation * * *.

SEC. 59.   SPECIAL REQUIREMENTS IN CRIMINAL LIBEL

**Rules on publication, breach of the peace, and group libel distin-
guish the criminal libel action from the civil action.**

It is frequently said that malice must be present if criminal libel is to be found. This is true where public officials or persons
involved in matters of public or general interest are concerned;
otherwise, it is true in the sense of "malice in law" which means
only that the writer intended to publish the words that gave
offense.[34] For public officials, the actual malice that must be
proved is not the old "ill will" or "intent to harm"; since New
York Times Co. v. Sullivan, malice has been defined as knowing
falsehood or reckless disregard for truth on the part of the writer. The malice requirement, thus, is no different from that in
civil libel.

In the requirement as to publication of a criminal libel, states
differ. Some hold to the old rule that the words need to be published only to the defamed, and not (as in the tort of libel) to a
third party. It was enough under the breach of peace theory
that the insult reach the target, for no "third party" needed to
be aware of the insult to cause the injured person to make a
physical assault on the writer. But where the breach of peace

[33] Ibid., at 77, at 217.

[34] 19 A.L.R. 1470, 1485–1486; State v. Lambert, 188 La. 968, 178 So. 508 (1938).

rationale disappeared, and the injury was recognized as damage to the repute in which the defamed was held, the need for publication to a third party became apparent.[35]   One study has shown that no reported criminal libel case between 1920 and 1955 depended upon this difference.[36]

One might say, then, that major differences that distinguish the crime from the tort of libel are 1) the state's part as prosecutor and the possible criminal punishment, as distinct from the citizen's role as complainant and his possible recovery of damages; and 2) the breach of peace rationale under criminal libel, albeit much-restricted when compared to an earlier time.   The latter, in turn, underlies two special cases which are crimes but not torts—group libel and (hypothetically at least) libel of the dead.   It also underlies the requirement in some states that publication need reach only the defamed, not a third party, to support a criminal libel prosecution.

[35] Cf. Wis.Stat.1955, § 942.01, and Me.Rev.Stat.1949, § 559.430.

[36] Leflar, R.A., "Social Utility of the Criminal Law of Defamation," 34 Texas L.R. 984, 1012 (1956).

DIRECT → Constructive (INDIRECT)

Chapter 10

CRIMINAL WORDS: CONTEMPT

SEC. 60. CONTEMPT AS INHERENT POWER OF THE COURTS

Courts have power to cite and punish for contempt. Punishment for constructive contempt not well based in the common law.

Annette Buchanan wrote a story for her college newspaper, the University of Oregon *Daily Emerald*, about the use of marijuana among students at the University. She said that seven students, whom she did not name, gave her information. And when the district attorney asked her to name the sources of information to a grand jury that was investigating drug use, and subsequently a judge directed her to do so, she refused. A reporter should be privileged not to reveal his sources, she said, and not to break confidences. To betray a pledge of secrecy to a source, Miss Buchanan added, would be a signal to many sources to "dry up." The judge, and upon appeal the Oregon Supreme Court, found her in contempt of court for refusing to obey the judge's order.[1]

Miss Buchanan's was a case of "direct" contempt: it took place in the presence of the judge. Goss, a television personality, was not within shouting distance of the court or judge when on his program he attacked witnesses in a divorce case in which Goss was accused of adultery with the wife. For his attempt to prevent witnesses from giving testimony unfavorable to him by vilifying them, he was convicted of indirect ("constructive") contempt—that which takes place away from the court.[2]

[1] State v. Buchanan, 250 Or. 244, 436 P.2d 729 (1968), certiorari denied 392 U.S. 905, 88 S.Ct. 2055 (1968).

[2] People v. Goss, 10 Ill.2d 533, 141 N.E.2d 385, 390 (1957).

341

In the *Goss* case as in the *Buchanan* case, a reporter's acts interfered with the administration of justice. The acts were contemptuous of the court. And in both cases, the court used its inherent power to punish the interference. Without some means of enforcing their judgments, decrees, or orders courts would be powerless. Punishment for contempt as a weapon of the court is the basis of all legal procedure,[3] whether the contempt is civil contempt for disobedience to court orders or to the enforcement of process or criminal contempt for other acts which interfere with judicial procedure, including out-of-court contempt.

Use of summary punishment for criminal contempt of the Court of Chancery was made by the Star Chamber until that body was abolished by Parliament in 1641. Justification for contempt procedures today stems not from the discredited Star Chamber, however, but from Eighteenth and Nineteenth-Century practice. Thus the summary power of a judge to accuse and sit in judgment on his own case and to deprive the defendant of a trial by jury is often justified by reference to William Blackstone, who stated:[4]

> Some * * * contempts may arise in the face of the court; as by rude and contumelious behavior; by obstinacy, perverseness, or prevarication; by breach of the peace; or any wilful disturbance whatever; others, in the absence of the party; as by disobeying or treating with disrespect the king's writ, or the rules of process of the court; by perverting such writ or process to the purposes of private malice, extortion, or injustice; by speaking or writing contemptuously of the court or judges, acting in their judicial capacity; by printing false accounts (or even true ones, without proper permission) of causes then depending in judgment; and by any thing, in short, that demonstrates a gross want of that regard and respect, which, when once courts of justice are deprived of, their authority, (so necessary for the good order of the kingdom) is entirely lost among the people. * * *

The process of attachment for these and the like contempts must necessarily be as ancient as the laws themselves * * * A power therefore in the supreme courts of justice to suppress such contempts by an immediate attachment of the offender results from the

---

[3] Fox, Sir John C. History of Contempt of Court, p. 1.

[4] Blackstone 284, 285.

first principles of judicial establishments and must be an inseparable attendant upon every superior tribunal.

As for the United States, an act declaratory of the law of contempt in the federal courts, passed in 1831, is the basis of contempt proceedings before federal judges. It specifies that the power to issue attachments and inflict summary punishments for contempts of court does not extend to any cases "except the misbehaviour of any person or persons in the presence of said courts, or so near thereto as to obstruct the administration of justice." [5] State courts likewise possess the power to punish for contempt, under authority of inherent power or statute, or both.[6]

The proceedings for contempt may be either civil or criminal. A civil contempt infringes private rights while a criminal contempt is an offense against society. A civil contempt is one affecting the relationship of the parties themselves, as where one party is given certain rights in a court case and the other party disregards the rights thus established.[7] A criminal contempt action is applied, for example, to one who interferes with the administration of justice by disrespect to the decorum of the court, or by interference with the impartial conduct of a case through such means as prejudicing the jury.[8]

Indirect or constructive contempt arose with the growth of printing, journalism and out-of-court publication which might criticize or comment on cases pending in courts. The power to punish such publications in Anglo-American jurisprudence is founded on Almon's case,[9] in which because of a technicality no judgment was ever rendered. Sir John C. Fox, in his History of Contempt of Court, points out that the notes of Justice Wilmot in this case do not give adequate foundation for acceptance of constructive contempt for out-of-court publications as part of the common law.[10] There has been nevertheless practical acceptance of the Wilmot doctrine in both England and America.

The Act of 1831, that is the basis of contempt proceedings before federal judges specifies that the power to issue attachments

[5] Act of Mar. 2, 1831, c. 99, 4 Stat. 487.

[6] See Nelles, W., and C. W. King, Contempt by Publication in the United States, 28 Columbia Law Review 554, 1928.

[7] People v. Solomon, 150 Misc. 873, 271 N.Y.S. 136 (1934); Donato v. U. S., 48 F.2d 142 (3d Cir. 1931); Seaboard Air Line R. Co. v. Tampa Southern R. Co., 101 Fla. 468, 134 So. 529 (1931); Hendrix v. Consolidated Van Lines, Inc., 176 Kan. 101, 269 P.2d 435 (1954).

[8] In re Magen, 18 F.2d 288 (D.C.N.Y.1926); Wilson v. Prochnow, 359 Ill. 148, 194 N.E. 246 (1935).

[9] Fox, p. 5 and references there cited.

[10] Ibid., p. 15.

and inflict summary punishments for contempts of court does not extend to any cases "except the misbehavior of any person or persons in the presence of said courts, or so near thereto as to obstruct the administration of justice." [11] Under the authority of this act, newspaper comments on proceedings pending in a federal court were for some time held contemptuous, as in Toledo Newspaper Co. v. United States.[12] In the same case, however, the dissenting opinion of Justice Holmes reasoned that "so near thereto as to obstruct the administration of justice" means so near as actually to obstruct, and that misbehavior means more than unfavorable comment or even disrespect. And in 1941 the decision in Nye v. United States declared that "so near thereto" referred to physical proximity to the court, weakening the position in the Toledo decision.[13]

Courts have clung to the power of summary punishment for out-of-court contempt in the face of legislative action to limit such proceedings; State v. Morrill [14] and Toledo Newspaper Co. v. United States [15] are only two of many important cases testifying to the courts' determination. The *Morrill* case will illustrate. Here a charge published in a newspaper that an alleged murderer had bribed the state supreme court was the basis for summary contempt proceedings. The court was faced with a state statute limiting contempt proceedings to certain specified acts, which did not include an out-of-court publication.

The court, however, held that the statute was not binding, and said that the legislature meant merely that citation for contempt was unnecessary except in the specified cases, quoting the decision in Neel v. State.[16] It said that the power in courts to punish for contempt springs into existence upon the creation of the courts.[17]

Thus the attempt by Congress and the legislatures of the states to limit contempt to certain specific classifications has not been universally successful. The legislative and judicial branches of government are coordinate. While the legislative branch of any of our governmental units has the power to make the law, the judicial branch has inherent rights to enforce its orders,

[11] Act of Mar. 2, 1831, c. 99; 4 Stat. 487.

[12] 247 U.S. 402, 38 S.Ct. 560, 62 L.Ed. 1186 (1918).

[13] 313 U.S. 33, 61 S.Ct. 810, 85 L.Ed. 1172 (1941).

[14] 16 Ark. 384 (1855).

[15] 247 U.S. 402, 38 S.Ct. 560, 62 L.Ed. 1186 (1918); U. S. v. Sanders, 290 F. 428 (D.C.Tenn.1923).

[16] 9 Ark. 259, 50 Am.Dec. 209 (1849).

[17] State v. Morrill, 16 Ark. 384, 407 (1855).

rules, writs, or decrees. Even in states where there is a strict definition of what constitutes contempt, under special circumstances there is precedent for the courts' considering their inherent power above the legislative enactment.[18]

Some headway has been made by those who pose a more general challenge to the contempt power of courts, and who assert that jury trials should be substituted for a judge's summary proceeding. It is sometimes objected by these that American traditions are violated where a judge may sit as accuser, prosecutor, and judge in his own or a fellow judge's case: "It is abhorrent to Anglo-Saxon justice as applied in this country that one man, however lofty his station or venerated his vestments, should have the power of taking another man's liberty from him." [19] There are flaws in the Blackstonian position that summary procedure is an "immemorial power" of judges in constructive contempt cases; [20] and the United States Supreme Court in 1968 addressed itself to the problem and said that the old rule did not justify denying a jury trial in serious contempt cases. It ruled in Bloom v. Illinois [21] that "If the right to jury trial is a fundamental matter in other criminal cases, * * * it must also be extended to criminal contempt cases." The length of the sentence imposed was used by the Court as the test of "seriousness," and it decided that a two-year jail term for Bloom denoted seriousness.

SEC. 61. THE CONTEMPT POWER IN LEGISLATIVE AND ADMINISTRATIVE BODIES

Congress, state legislatures, and some administrative bodies have power to cite for contempt.

In addition to courts, legislative bodies are jealous of their power to cite for contempt. The press, especially in its investigational activities, encounters the danger of legislative contempt when either Congress or a legislature begins an investigation. Yet the citation of newsmen for contempt of the legislative branch is rare indeed. It has happened, however, when newsmen have refused to answer the questions of an investigating committee of Congress.

[18] Farr v. Superior Court, 22 Cal.App.3d 60, 99 Cal.Rptr. 342, 348 (1972).

[19] Ballantyne v. U. S., 237 F.2d 657, 667 (5th Cir. 1956); Gerald. J. Edward, The Press and the Constitution, pp. 30–31.

[20] Nelles and King, pp. 408, 409.

[21] 391 U.S. 194, 88 S.Ct. 1477, 1485 (1968).

The legislative power to cite for contempt derives its force from the power possessed by the English Parliament, on which both the legislatures and the Congress were modeled.[22]   No limitations are imposed upon Congress in its punishment for either disorderly conduct or contempt but in Marshall v. Gordon,[23] it was held that the punishment imposed could not be extended beyond the session in which the contempt occurs.

The Supreme Court has conceded to Congress the power to punish nonmembers for contempt when there occurs "either physical obstruction of the legislative body in the discharge of its duties, or physical assault upon its members, for action taken or words spoken in the body, or obstruction of its officers in the performance of their official duties, or the prevention of members from attending so that their duties might be performed, or finally, for refusing with contumacy to obey orders, to produce documents or to give testimony which there was a right to compel." [24]

Seldom has a newsman gone to jail for refusing to reveal to Congress the source of his information.   One of the rare cases involved Z. L. White and Hiram J. Ramsdell, Washington correspondents of the *New York Tribune*.   They published what they claimed was the "Treaty of Washington," a document being studied by the Senate in executive meeting.   They refused to say from whom they got the copy, were tried and convicted of contempt by the Senate, and were committed to the custody of the Sergeant at Arms until the end of the Session.[25]

Congress has not in many decades chosen to try and convict for contempt.   Instead, it has cited for contempt and certified the persons cited to the district attorney of the District of Columbia for prosecution under a law that gives the courts power to try such cases.[26]

It is uncertain how far the principles of freedom of the press protect a newsman from contempt charges if he refuses to answer the questions of a Congressional Committee.   Newsmen have argued that the First Amendment sharply limits Congress

---

[22] Radin, Max, Anglo American Legal History, pp. 63, 64.

[23] 243 U.S. 521, 37 S.Ct. 448, 61 L.Ed. 881, L.R.A.1917F, 279, Ann.Cas. 1918B, 371 (1917).

[24] Ibid., 243 U.S. 521, 37 S.Ct. 448, 61 L.Ed. 881, L.R.A.1917F, 279, Ann.Cas. 1918B, 371 (1917).

[25] U. S. Senate, Subcommittee on Administrative Practice and Procedure of Committee on the Judiciary, The Newsman's Privilege, 89 Cong. 2 Sess., Oct. 1966, pp. 57–61.

[26] 2 U.S.C.A. §§ 192, 194.

in questioning and investigating the press: Congress may investigate only the matters on which it may legislate, they point out, and the First Amendment says that "Congress shall make no law * * * abridging freedom of * * * the press."

In 1971, a prize-winning television documentary by CBS, "The Selling of the Pentagon," raised a storm of protest against alleged bias in the film's portrayal of the American military's public information programs. Selective editing for the documentary, the military charged, distorted the intent, management and messages of the military. The House of Representatives Commerce Committee, under its chairman Rep. Harley O. Staggers, undertook an investigation of the matter, and CBS's president Frank Stanton refused to furnish the committee parts of film edited out of the final version. In response to the subpoena ordering him to appear with the materials, he appeared but declared that furnishing materials would amount to a violation of freedom of the press. The Committee voted 25 to 13 to recommend to Congress a contempt citation. The House, however, turned down the recommendation, Rep. Emanuel Celler declaring that "The First Amendment towers over these proceedings like a colossus. No tenderness of one member for another should cause us to topple over this monument to our liberties." [27]

The courts have not decided contempt of Congress cases on First Amendment grounds, one of them saying "We shrink from this awesome task" of drawing lines between the investigative power of Congress and the First Amendment rights of a member of the press.[28] Instead, the courts have found other reasons for reversing convictions of newsmen who were found in contempt of Congress for refusing to answer questions. In 1956, William Price of the *New York Daily News* and Robert Shelton and Alden Whitman of the *New York Times* refused to answer certain questions put by committees of Congress that were investigating communism. All three were indicted for contempt and convicted. The Supreme Court overturned the convictions, not on press freedom grounds, but because the indictments that put the newsmen before the grand jury were faulty. They failed to state the subject of the investigation, the Court held, and without knowing that, Price, Shelton and Whitman could not know just what they were accused of. "Price was put to trial and convicted upon an indictment which did not even purport to inform him in any way of the identity of the topic under

[27] Quill, 59:8, Aug. 1971, p. 14.

[28] Shelton v. U. S., 117 U.S.App.D.C. 155, 327 F.2d 601 (1963); 89 Editor & Publisher 12, July 7, 1956.

subcommittee inquiry. * * * Far from informing Price of the nature of the accusation against him, the indictment instead left the prosecution free to roam at large—to shift its theory of criminality so as to take advantage of each passing vicissitude of the trial and appeal." [29]

Under certain circumstances there may be contempt of a semi-judicial administrative body like the Securities and Exchange Commission, the Interstate Commerce Commission, or the Federal Trade Commission. Certain state public utility, tax, and other commissions, which have power to subpoena witnesses to testify in hearings before such bodies, have statutory authority to cite and punish for contempt in some jurisdictions. Where there is no statutory authority to cite, these bodies in some instances may apply to the courts for an order directing a person who has refused to answer a commission's subpoena to appear before the commission or one of its examiners for examination. Refusal to comply with the court's order may then be cited as contempt of the court's order. Such essentially is the provision of the Securities Act of 1933, as amended in 1934.[30]

SEC. 62. DIRECT CONTEMPT AS A PRESS RESTRICTION

Interference with the orderly administration of justice in the presence of the court may subject the newspaper to contempt proceedings.

When the claim of freedom of the press comes into conflict with the contempt power, the former may emerge from the contest second best. The variety of journalistic activities other than publication that may collide with the contempt power is illuminated in considering four news procedures that may cause direct contempt citations:

1. Any disobedience of a court's order.

2. Any disturbance in the courtroom.

3. Attempts to influence decisions or participants in court cases.

4. Refusal to testify as to a news source by a reporter called on to reveal in a trial the source of news, unless such refusal is permitted under "newsman's privilege" statutes.

[29] Russell v. U. S., 369 U.S. 749, 82 S.Ct. 1038, 1049 (1962).

[30] Sec. 22(b), 15 U.S.C.A. § 77v(b). See R. John Tresolini, "The Use of Summary Contempt Powers by Administrative Agencies," 54 Dickinson Law Review 395, 1950.

(1) The first circumstance—disobedience of a court's order—appeared in the case of Ex parte Sturm et al.[31] Here the appellants were adjudged in contempt of trial court for violation of its orders about photographing Richard Whittemore, held on an indictment for murder. Shortly before the beginning of trial in the criminal court of Baltimore, a photographer took a flash picture of the prisoner as he entered the courthouse lockup. The noise of the flash was heard by the judge, who ordered the photographer to surrender the photographic plate. Unknown to the judge, the plate which the photographer surrendered was a blank.

Following the opening of court, the judge said that he felt it incompatible with judicial dignity to allow the courtroom or the precincts of the court to be used for taking pictures. He mentioned the confiscation of the picture taken that morning. The court declared that the prisoner, unable to protect himself, would be protected by the court. Nevertheless, photographer William Sturm of the *Baltimore News* took several pictures secretly with a small camera following an order of his city editor who had previously been informed of the court's ruling in regard to taking pictures. Two of the pictures taken by Sturm appeared in the *News* that day, and in the *Baltimore American* (published by the same owner) the next day.

Judge O'Dunne instituted contempt proceedings against the managing editors of both newspapers, the city editor of the *News*, and the two photographers. Upon appeal the contempt proceedings were upheld; the court stated: [32]

> The challenge in this case of the court's right to forbid the use of cameras in the courtroom during the progress of the trial presents an issue of vital importance. If such a right should yield to an asserted privilege of the press, the authority and dignity of the courts would be seriously impaired. It is essential to the integrity and independence of the judicial tribunals that they shall have the power to enforce their own judgment as to what conduct is incompatible with the proper and orderly course of their procedure.

Ex parte Sturm displays a court decision in the main historical stream of the use of the contempt power: the court has an inherent power to institute contempt proceedings that will back

[31] 152 Md. 114, 136 A. 312, 51 A.L.R. 356 (1927).

[32] 152 Md. 114, 121, 136 A. 312, 315, 51 A.L.R. 356 (1927). See also Seymour v. U. S., 373 F.2d 629 (5th Cir. 1967).

up its orders. Furthermore, in Maryland there was legislative authority for summary punishment for contempt.[33]

The order of a judge that no pictures would be taken in a courtroom did not extend, however, to a photographer who took a picture of the court in session through the window of a door leading to a corridor. A conviction for contempt for disobeying the court order was overruled, the appeals court saying that the order did not extend to taking pictures from the corridor.[34]

(2) We may see the courts and the press in conflict over disturbance to the court—the second cause listed above—in a Georgia case where a judge forbade photography in the near environs of a court house. Here Atlanta Newspapers brought a petition excepting to a court order that barred taking pictures of spectators and others not in the custody of the court, who were gathered on streets and sidewalks surrounding the court house. The newspapers argued that freedom of the press was limited by the order. The petition was denied and the Georgia Supreme Court upheld the denial. The circumstances of the case involved crowds of some 300 persons completely blocking traffic on the street and sidewalk around the court house; defense counsels' addresses from the steps of the court house to the crowds; and some 50 or 60 reporters and photographers who were covering the gathering for the news media. The Georgia code provides that "Every court has power * * * to preserve and enforce order in its immediate presence, and as near thereto as is necessary to prevent interruption, disturbance, or hindrance to its proceedings. * * *" The Supreme Court said that "the duty and disposition of a court to accord a justly ample scope to the liberty of the press should not be carried to the point of an undue abridgment of the court's own freedom," and ruled that the trial judge had not abused his discretionary powers in his order banning photography under these circumstances.[35]

(3) Influencing participants in a court case is illustrated by Ex parte Aldridge.[36] While a jury in a murder case was being chosen, several veniremen waited to be called in a corridor outside the courtroom, as instructed. The judge learned that 20 copies of a publication called *C.C.C. News* had been placed on a

---

[33] Acts 1853, Code 1951, art. 26, § 4, gives as one ground for contempt proceedings: The misbehaviour of any person or persons in the presence of said courts, or so near thereto as to obstruct the administration of justice.

[34] In re Greenfield, 163 N.E.2d 910, 82 Ohio Law Abstracts 120 (Ohio App. 1959).

[35] Atlanta Newspapers, Inc. v. Grimes, 216 Ga. 74, 114 S.E.2d 421 (1960).

[36] 169 Tex.Crim. 395, 334 S.W.2d 161 (1959).

chair near the veniremen, and that a story in it intimated that
the defense attorney claimed he had special influence with
the judge. The judge was convinced that circulation of the publication among the veniremen meant that a fair trial could not
be had and a jury could not be selected from this group of veniremen. He postponed the case. A charge of contempt was
placed against the editor and publisher of the publication, and
he was convicted. On appeal, the court held that circulation of
the publication interfered with the due administration of justice,
and that it was a case of direct contempt because the presence of
the court extended to the courtroom, jury, and veniremen.[37]

(4) Perhaps no aspect of contempt of court has so raised a
wall of protest from newsmen as that stemming from their refusal to testify before grand juries and courts about confidential
sources and about information obtained from such sources.
Subpoenas to appear and testify had for decades been only an
occasional problem for newsmen whose stories suggested to officialdom that the reporters had information of use to government; there are probably fewer than 40 reported contempt cases
for newsmen's refusal to testify when subpoenaed prior to 1970.
But in 1969 and 1970 the sometime problem of subpoenas
changed to a burst, and across the nation reporters faced demands that they appear and testify. No one was able to track
down every subpoena issued during these years and in 1971 and
1972. Vice President Richard W. Jencks of CBS testified that
in a 2½ year period during the upsurge, 121 subpoenas calling
for the production of news material were given CBS and NBC
alone.[38] More than 30 subpoenas were served on newspapers
published by Field Enterprises, Inc., in the three-year period,
two-thirds of them issued on behalf of the government.[39]

In particular demand were newsmen who had been reporting
widespread social and political turmoil. Grand juries wanted
these journalists to reveal their confidential sources as well as to
surrender their unpublished notes and records, unused photographs, tape recordings and television film "outtakes." To
much of this, newsmen responded "no" with intensity and
solidarity.[40] The unwritten code of ethics of newsmen stood in
the way of their breaking confidences, they said; but more im-

[37] Ibid., at 165.

[38] House of Rep. Committee on the Judiciary, Subcommittee No. 3, 92 Cong.,
2d Sess., "Newsmen's Privilege," Hearings, Oct. 4, 1972, p. 204.

[39] Ibid., Sept. 27 1972, p. 134.

[40] S.Res. 3552, 91 Cong., 2d Sess., 116 Cong.Rec. 4123–31, 1970; Noyes & Newbold, "The Subpoena Problem Today," Am. Soc. Newspaper Editors Bull., Sept.
1970, pp. 7–8; Editor & Publisher, Feb. 7, 1970, p. 12.

portant, if they broke confidences they would become known as untrustworthy and their sources would dry up, thereby harming or destroying their usefulness as news gatherers for the public. Moreover, they said, compelling them to disclose their news sources was tantamount to making them agents of government investigation.

As for turning over unused film, files, photos and notes, some media adopted the policy of early destruction of unpublished materials after *Time, Life, Newsweek,* the *Chicago Sun-Times,* CBS, NBC and others were called by subpoena, or in the name of cooperation with government, to deliver large quantities of news materials.[41] According to Attorney General John Mitchell, the newsmen's willingness to accept contempt convictions and jail terms rather than reveal confidences, along with their unyielding protests to government, made the controversy "one of the most difficult issues I have faced * * *."[42] The storm of objection to subpoenas issuing from the Department of Justice led Mitchell to issue "Guidelines for Subpoenas to the News Media"—a set of instructions to Justice Department attorneys over the nation—that sought to resolve testimonial questions with newsmen through negotiating rather than through subpoenas except in the last resort.[43]

The privilege not to break the confidence of sources has deep roots in the history of certain professional groups. The common law and some states by statute have long provided full or partial protection to the attorney in relation to his client, the physician to his patient, and the priest to his parishioner.[44] Here the private interest of the person seeking help is in some circumstances paramount to the needs of the state in obtaining evidence. But the common law never provided such a privilege for newsmen, and legal authority heavily opposed extending the privilege to new groups such as social workers and journalists.[45]

The first state statute to shield newsmen from being compelled to testify was passed by Maryland in 1896; other states

[41] Columbia Journalism Rev., Spring 1970, pp. 2–3.

[42] Editor & Publisher, Aug. 15, 1970, pp. 9–10.

[43] Department of Justice, Memo No. 692, Sept. 2, 1970.

[44] 8 J. Wigmore, Evidence §§ 2286, 2290, 2394 (J. McNaughton rev. ed. 1961).

[45] Ibid., § 2285. Major studies on newsmen's privilege include Blasi, Vince, Press Subpoenas: An Empirical and Legal Analysis, 1972, for Reporters' Committee on Freedom of the Press; Gordon, A.D., Protection of News Sources: the History and Legal Status of the Newsman's Privilege, Dec. 1970 (Ph.D. dissertation, Univ. of Wis.); Guest & Stanzler, The Constitutional Argument for Newsmen Concealing Their Sources, 64 N.W.U.L.Rev. 18, 1969.

followed, the list reaching more than 20 by 1973.[46] By then, newsmen had learned that if they were to have substantial protection, their shield would have to be such statutes.

The Constitutional Protection

Newsmen who have assumed or asserted that the First Amendment guarantee of freedom of the press once was a bulwark against compelling testimony have not reckoned with the history of court decisions. Privilege cases were adjudicated for most of a century under the common law or state statutes without the Constitution's even entering the picture. Not until 1958, in Garland v. Torre,[47] was the first claim to First Amendment protection an issue in the reported cases.

Here, Marie Torre, columnist for the *New York Herald Tribune*, attributed to an unnamed executive of a broadcasting company, certain statements which actress Judy Garland said libeled her. In the libel suit, Torre refused to name the executive, asserting privilege under the First Amendment. She was cited for contempt and convicted, and the appeals court upheld the conviction. "The concept that it is the duty of a witness to testify in a court of law," the decision said, "has roots fully as deep in our history as does the guarantee of a free press." It added that if freedom of the press was involved here, "we do not hesitate to conclude that it too must give place under the Constitution to a paramount public interest in the fair administration of justice."[48] Subsequent claims to constitutional protection were likewise denied in other cases.[49]

The United States Supreme Court in 1972 ruled for the first time on whether the First Amendment protects newsmen from testifying about their confidential sources and information. The cases of three reporters who had refused to testify before grand

---

[46] Ala.Code tit. 7, § 370 (1960); Alaska Stat. §§ 09.25.150–.220 (Supp.1970); Ariz.Rev.Stat.Ann. § 12–2237 (Supp.1970); Ark.Stat.Ann. § 43–917 (1964); West's Ann.Cal.Code Evid. § 1070 (1966); Ill.Legis.H.Bill 1756, 1971 Gen. Assembly; Ind.Ann.Stat. § 2–1733 (1968); Ky.Rev.Stat.Ann. § 421.100 (1969); La.Rev.Stat. Ann. §§ 45:1451–54 (Supp.1971); Md.Ann.Code art. 35, § 2 (1971); Mich.Stat. Ann. § 28.945(1) (1954); Mont.Rev.Codes Ann. §§ 93–601–1 to 2 (1964); Nev.Rev. Stat. § 48.087 (1968); N.J.Stat.Ann. § 2A:84A–21 (Supp.1970); N.M.Stat.Ann. § 20–1–12.1 (1970); McKinney's N.Y.Civ.Rights Law § 79–h (Supp.1971); Ohio Rev.Code Ann. § 2739.12 (Baldwin 1970); Pa.Stat.Ann. tit. 28, § 330 (Supp. 1971).

[47] 259 F.2d 545 (2d Cir. 1958), certiorari denied 358 U.S. 910, 79 S.Ct. 237.

[48] Ibid., at 548–549.

[49] In re Goodfader's Appeal, 45 Haw. 317, 367 P.2d 472 (1961); In re Taylor, 412 Pa. 32, 193 A.2d 181 (1963); State v. Buchanan, 250 Or. 244, 436 P.2d 729 (1968) certiorari denied 392 U.S. 905, 88 S.Ct. 2055 (1968); Murphy v. Colo., (Colo. Supreme Court), certiorari denied, 365 U.S. 843, 81 S.Ct. 802 (1961).

juries during 1970 and 1971 were decided together in Branzburg
v. Hayes.[50] Paul Branzburg, a reporter for the *Louisville Courier-Journal*, had observed two people synthesizing hashish from
marijuana and written about that and drug use, and had refused
to answer the grand jury's questions about the matters. Paul
Pappas, a television reporter of New Bedford, Mass., had visited
Black Panther headquarters during civil turmoil in July 1970,
and refused to tell a grand jury what he had seen there. Earl
Caldwell, a black reporter for the *New York Times* in San Francisco, who had covered Black Panther activities regularly for
some years, was called by a federal grand jury and had refused
to appear or testify.

Only Caldwell received protection from the lower courts. The
federal district court of California and the Ninth Circuit Court
of Appeals ruled that the First Amendment provided a qualified
privilege to newsmen and that it applied to Caldwell.[51] The
Kentucky Court of Appeals refused Branzburg protection under
either the Kentucky privilege statute, or the First Amendment
interpretation of the Caldwell case.[52] And the Supreme Judicial
Court of Massachusetts, where no privilege statute existed, rejected the idea of a First Amendment privilege.[53]

The Supreme Court of the United States found that none of
the three men warranted First Amendment protection. It reversed the Caldwell decisions of the lower federal courts and upheld the Kentucky and Massachusetts decisions, in a 5–4
decision.[54] It said that the First Amendment would protect a
newsman if grand jury investigations were not conducted in
good faith, or if there were harassment of the press by officials
who sought to disrupt a reporter's relationship with his news
sources.[55] But it found neither of these conditions present here.
The newsman's obligation is to respond to grand jury subpoenas
as other citizens do and to answer questions relevant to commission of crime, it said.

The Caldwell decisions in lower courts had focused on the
need of recognition for First Amendment protection for the
news gathering process; the Supreme Court said "It has gener-

[50] Branzburg v. Hayes, 408 U.S. 665, 92 S.Ct. 2646 (1972).

[51] Application of Caldwell, 311 F.Supp. 358 (N.D.Cal.1970); Caldwell v. U. S.,
434 F.2d 1081 (9th Cir. 1970).

[52] Branzburg v. Pound, 461 S.W.2d 345 (Ky.1971); Branzburg v. Hayes, 408
U.S. 665, 92 S.Ct. 2646 (1972).

[53] In re Pappas, 358 Mass. 604, 266 N.E.2d 297 (1971).

[54] Branzburg v. Hayes, 408 U.S. 665, 92 S.Ct. 2646 (1972).

[55] Ibid., at 2669–2670.

ally been held that the First Amendment does not guarantee the press a constitutional right of special access to information not available to the public generally * * *," and "Despite the fact that news gathering may be hampered, the press is regularly excluded from grand jury proceedings, our own conferences, the meetings of other official bodies gathered in executive session * * *." [56]

The newsmen had asserted that the First Amendment should take precedence over the grand jury's power of inquiry. The Supreme Court said that at common law, courts consistently refused to recognize a privilege in newsmen to refuse to reveal confidential information; and that the First Amendment claim to privilege had been turned down uniformly in earlier cases, the courts having concluded "that the First Amendment interest asserted by the newsman was outweighed by the general obligation of a citizen to appear before a grand jury or at trial, pursuant to a subpoena, and give what information he possesses." [57] It said that the only constitutional privilege for unofficial witnesses is the Fifth Amendment privilege against compelled self-incrimination, and the Court declined to create another.

The newsmen argued that the flow of news would be diminished by compelling testimony from them; the Supreme Court said it was unconvinced, and "the evidence fails to demonstrate that there would be a significant constriction of the flow of news to the public if the Court reaffirms the prior common law and constitutional rule regarding the testimonial obligations of newsmen." [58]

The newsmen said the freedom of the press would be undermined; the Court said this is not the lesson that history teaches, for the press had operated and thrived without common law or constitutional privilege since the beginning of the nation. [59]

The Supreme Court said that while the Constitution did not provide the privilege sought, Congress and the state legislatures were free to fashion standards and rules protecting newsmen from testifying by passing legislation.

Concurring, Justice Lewis F. Powell, Jr., expanded, in general terms, the possibilities for First Amendment protection for newsmen subpoenaed to testify. "The Court," he said, "does not hold that newsmen * * * are without constitutional rights with respect to the gathering of news or in safe-guarding their

[56] Ibid., at 2657, 2658.

[57] Ibid., at 2658, 2659.

[58] Ibid., at 2662.

[59] Ibid., at 2665.

sources. * * * the courts will be available to newsmen under circumstances where legitimate First Amendment interests require protection." [60]

The dissenting justices wrote two opinions. One was that of Justice William O. Douglas, who said that a reporter's immunity from testifying is "quite complete" under the First Amendment and a newsman "has an absolute right not to appear before a grand jury * * *." He grounded his opinion on two principles: One that an individual must have "absolute privacy over whatever information he may generate in the course of testing his opinions and beliefs" and that Caldwell had the status of one who pursued empirical research to enlarge his own intellectual viewpoint. The other principle was that the majority's decision would "impede the wide open and robust dissemination of ideas and counterthought which a free press both fosters and protects and which is essential to the success of intelligent self-government." [61]

Writing for himself and two others, Justice Potter Stewart argued for a qualified privilege. He called the majority's opinion a "crabbed view of the First Amendment" that reflected a disturbing insensitivity to the critical role of an independent press. And he said that in denying the protection, "The Court * * * invites state and federal authorities to undermine the historic independence of the press by attempting to annex the journalistic profession as an investigative arm of government." Justice Stewart said the protection was essential, not "for the purely private interests of the newsman or his informant, nor even, at bottom, for the First Amendment interests of either partner in the news-gathering relationship." [62]

> Rather it functions to insure nothing less than democratic decision-making through the free flow of information to the public, and it serves, thereby, to honor the "profound national commitment to the principle that debate on public issues should be uninhibited, robust, and wide-open."

Stewart indicated what he felt the government should be required to do in overriding a constitutional privilege for the reporter: [63]

> * * * "it is an essential prerequisite to the validity of an investigation which intrudes into the area of consti-

---

[60] Ibid., at 2670, 2671.

[61] U. S. v. Caldwell, 408 U.S. 665, 92 S.Ct. 2686, 2691 (1972).

[62] Branzburg v. Hayes, 408 U.S. 665, 92 S.Ct. 2646, 2678 (1972).

[63] Ibid., at 2679–2680.

tutionally protected rights of speech, press, association and petition that the State *show a substantial relation between the information sought and a subject of overriding and compelling state interest."*

*   *   *   *   *   *   *   *

Government officials must, therefore, demonstrate that the information sought is *clearly* relevant to a *precisely* defined subject of governmental inquiry. * * * They must demonstrate that it is reasonable to think the witness in question has that information. * * * And they must show that there is not any means of obtaining the information less destructive of First Amendment liberties.

These were essentially the requirements placed upon government by the lower courts in holding that Caldwell had been protected by the First Amendment, and Stewart endorsed that decision. He would have upheld the protection for Caldwell, and vacated and remanded the Branzburg and Pappas judgments.

Newsmen's Privilege under Statutes

The Supreme Court found little protection in the Constitution for the newsman called to testify, but it had made it plain that either Congress or the states might pass laws providing a shield against testifying. State statutes, in fact, dated back to that of Maryland in 1896. Of the two-score statutes that followed, some provided absolute protection and others qualified. The absolute or unqualified laws flatly prohibited compelling newsmen to testify, as Alabama's, passed in 1935 and amended in 1949: [64]

No person engaged in, connected with, or employed on any newspaper (or radio broadcasting station or television station) while engaged in a news gathering capacity shall be compelled to disclose, in any legal proceeding or trial, before any court or before a grand jury of any court, or before the presiding officer of any tribunal or his agent or agents, or before any committee of the legislature, or elsewhere, the sources of any information procured or obtained by him and published in the newspaper (or broadcast by any broadcasting station or televised by any television station) on which he is engaged, connected with, or employed.

Among states that hedged the privilege, Illinois, for example, said that a person seeking the reporter's information could apply for an order divesting the newsman of the privilege. The appli-

[64] Ala.Code, tit. 7, § 370, 1960.

cation would have to state the specific information sought, its relevancy to the proceedings, and a specific public interest which would be adversely affected if the information sought were not disclosed. And the court would have to find, before granting divestiture of the privilege, that all other available sources of information had been exhausted and that disclosure of the information was essential to the protection of the public interest involved.[65]

But absolute or qualified, every state law contained loopholes through which certain newsmen, under certain conditions, could lose the privilege. Branzburg, before seeking constitutional protection, had failed to receive protection under Kentucky's statute. The statute gave him a firm shield, as a newspaper employee, against disclosing before a court or grand jury, the source of information procured by him and published in a newspaper. But the Kentucky court held that he himself was the source of information for a story reporting his observation of the manufacture of hashish by others. He would have to give the identity of the manufacturers—to identify those whom he saw breaking the law. It was contempt for him to refuse to do so.[66]

Peter Bridge of the *Newark Evening News* wrote a story about the alleged offer of a bribe to Pearl Beatty, a member of the Newark Housing Authority. He quoted her as saying that an unknown man offered to pay her $10,000 to influence her vote for the appointment of an executive director of the authority. Subpoenaed to testify, he argued that the New Jersey statute—which preserved in his case its unbroken record of failing to protect New Jersey newsmen from testifying—should shield him. It said that one employed by a newspaper has a privilege to refuse to disclose the source, author, means, agency or person from or through whom any information published in his newspaper was procured.[67] He appeared before a grand jury but refused to answer questions about the matter, citing the statute. But the court held that, under another state evidence rule, he had waived his privilege through disclosure in the story of part of the privileged matter. Having in that way given some of the information—including the identity of the source—he would have to give other relevant information. He too was in contempt, and served 21 days in jail until the grand jury's term expired.[68]

65 Ill.Legis.H.Bill 1756, 1971 Gen. Assembly.

66 Branzburg v. Pound, 461 S.W.2d 345 (Ky.1970).

67 N.J.Stat.Ann. § 2A:84A–21 (Supp.1970).

68 In re Bridge, 120 N.J.Super. 460, 295 A.2d 3 (1972).

A third case widely publicized in 1972 and 1973 was that of William Farr, reporter for the *Los Angeles Herald Examiner*. Reporting the murder trial of Charles Manson, Farr learned that a Mrs. Virginia Graham had given a statement to a district attorney in the case, claiming that a Manson "family" member, Susan Atkins, had confessed taking part in the multiple crimes and told of the group's plans for other murders. The judge in the case had ordered attorneys, witnesses and court employees not to release for public dissemination, any content or nature of testimony that might be given at the trial; but Farr obtained copies of the Graham statement, according to him from two attorneys in the case. The court learned that he had the statement. Farr refused to tell the court the names of the sources, and published a story carrying sensational details. Later, he identified a group of six attorneys as including the two. The judge queried them, and all denied being the source. Once more the court asked Farr for his sources, and he continued to refuse under the California newsmen's privilege law.[69] The court denied him protection under the statute and he appealed.

The appeals court upheld the conviction for contempt. It said that courts' power of contempt is inherent in their constitutional status, and no legislative act could declare that certain acts do not constitute a contempt. If Farr were immunized from liability, it would violate the principle of separation of powers among the three branches of government; it would mean that the legislative branch could interfere with the judicial branch's power to control its own officers: [70]

> Without the ability to compel petitioner to reveal which of the six attorney officers of the court leaked the Graham statement to him, the court is without power to discipline the two attorneys who did so, both for their violations of the court order [concerning no publicity] and for their misstatement to the court that they were not the source of the leak.

Farr served 46 days in jail before he was released pending a further appeal, and in his uncertain freedom lived with the possibility of indeterminate, unlimited imprisonment if his appeal failed and he persisted in refusing to reveal his sources.

Though vulnerable under any law, newsmen occasionally got more protection from their states' courts than the statutes suggested might be available. One loophole in several "absolute"

---

[69] West's Ann.Cal.Evidence Code § 1070 (1966).

[70] Farr v. Superior Court of Calif., 22 Cal.App.3d 60, 99 Cal.Rptr. 342, 348 (1971).

statutes was their lack of provision protecting the newsman from revealing *information* that he had gathered, even though it protected him from revealing the *source* of that information. This was the case with Pennsylvania's law; but the state Supreme Court chose in deciding In re Taylor,[71] a 1963 case, to interpret the law broadly.

Robert L. Taylor, president and general manager, and Earl Selby, city editor of the *Philadelphia Bulletin*, were convicted of contempt of court for refusing to produce documents demanded by the district attorney in a grand jury investigation of possible corruption in city government. Both were fined $1000 and given five-day prison terms. They appealed, relying on the Pennsylvania statute stating that no newsman could be "required to disclose the source of any information" that he had obtained. "Source" they said, means "documents" as well as "personal informants." The Pennsylvania Supreme Court, reversing the conviction, agreed.

The court said that the legislature, in passing the act, declared the gathering of news and protection of the source of news as of greater importance to the public interest than the disclosure of the alleged crime or criminal. Lacking protection for news sources, newspapers would be unable to use tips and leads on official wrongdoing. "It is vitally important that this public shield against governmental inefficiency, corruption and crime be preserved against piercing and erosion," the court said.[72]

While there are very few other court decisions that endorse the privilege unequivocally, one California case of 1955 gave it broad support. Howard, a San Francisco reporter, would not tell in court who gave him a statement that he attributed to a labor leader. He appealed his conviction for contempt, and the California Supreme Court reversed the conviction.[73]

Courts have insisted that no "evidentiary privilege," as it is sometimes called, exists unless a statute has been enacted declaring it. Reporter Alan Goodfader of Honolulu refused to tell a court the name of the person who told him that the personnel director of a government commission was likely to be fired at a commission meeting. He said that to disclose the name would be a grievous breach of his professional ethics, and challenged the authority of the court to compel him to do so. The Supreme Court of Hawaii upheld the lower court's order. It said that the

---

[71] 412 Pa. 32, 193 A.2d 181 (1963).

[72] Ibid., at 185.

[73] In re Howard, 136 Cal.App.2d 816, 819, 289 P.2d 537, 538 (1955).

free press guarantee of the First Amendment is not sufficient to protect a reporter from the requirement to divulge his confidential sources in court. In the absence of a "statutory grant," it said, the privilege does not exist.[74]

The Drive for Laws

The *Branzburg* decision having barred the constitutional protection that the news world sought, the media turned to lobbying for statutes at the federal and state levels; and to strengthening the protection afforded in many of the 20 state laws in effect by 1973. The major news organizations turned their leaders and lawyers to work in appearances before congressional committees. There they found strong support from congressmen as well as strong opposition. It was estimated in early 1973 that more than 50 bills offering a shield of one sort or another had been introduced.[75] At the state level, bills were before a dozen legislatures at the same time.[76] Whatever the level of government considering the shield, the issues were similar.

(1) What are the competing social values in granting or denying newsmen an immunity from testifying? The newsman's ethic of not betraying sources, and his property right in not losing his effectiveness and value as a reporter through losing his sources, had long been asserted unsuccessfully in cases under the common law. Now he was grounding his claim in society's loss of his service if he lost his sources through betraying them.

Earl Caldwell was one of a corporal's guard of reporters who had gained the confidence of the Black Panthers at a time when society had a real need to know about this alienated group. The Ninth Circuit Court of Appeals accepted Caldwell's argument that he would lose the Panthers' confidence if he even entered the secret grand jury chambers, for this extremely sensitive group would not know what he might say under the compulsion of the legal agency.[77] And if Caldwell could not report the Panthers, society was the real loser. This situation illustrated the difference between the values served in the case of privilege for the journalist and that for the doctor, lawyer, or clergyman:

> " * * * the doctor-patient privilege is there to make it possible for patients to get better medical care. A journalist's privilege should be there not only to make

---

[74] In re Goodfader's Appeal, 45 Haw. 317, 367 P.2d 472 (1961).

[75] Collins, Thomas, "Congress Grapples With Press Bill," Milwaukee Journal, March 25, 1973, p. 16.

[76] FoI Digest, passim, Aug. 1972—July 1973 (Univ. of Mo.).

[77] Caldwell v. U. S., 434 F.2d 1081, 1088 (9th Cir. 1970).

it possible for a journalist to get better stories, but to contribute to the public's right to know. So in that sense it is a more critical privilege than some of these other privileges, which are based primarily on the relationship between two people." [78]

Asserting an equal service in the cause of the "public's right to know" was the position that in many circumstances, government-as-the-public sought information vital to the public weal, from newsmen. In State v. Knops,[79] an "underground" newspaper editor refused to tell a grand jury the names of people to whom he had talked about the bombing of a university building that killed a professor, and about alleged arson of another university building. "[T]he appellant's information could lead to the apprehension and conviction of the person or persons who committed a major criminal offense resulting in the death of an innocent person," said the Wisconsin Supreme Court in denying privilege to editor Mark Knops.[80] Here government was saying that the journalist was practicing secrecy similar to that which he so often criticized in government, and that government was trying to serve the public's right to know about a major crime.

A few newsmen, meanwhile, rejected the notion that the privilege was either needed by or appropriate to the journalist. They said that most journalists of the nation had done their work for decades without a shield. And they worried about unethical reporters' using a shield law to hide behind in dishonest reporting.[81]

(2) Can the news gathering function be protected by a qualified immunity, or must it be absolute? Hard positions for absolute shields were taken by many journalists and their organizations including the directors of the American Newspaper Publishers Association and those of the American Society of Newspaper Editors.[82] U.S. Sen. Alan Cranston of California, a former reporter, introduced a bill in Congress that was sweeping, simple and unconditional, saying that

> * * * a person connected with or employed by the news media or press cannot be required by a court, a legislature, or any administrative body to disclose be-

[78] House of Rep. Committee on the Judiciary, Subcommittee No. 3, 92 Cong., 2d Sess., "Newsmen's Privilege," Hearings, Testimony of Victor Navasky, Oct. 5, 1972, p. 236.

[79] State v. Knops, 49 Wis.2d 647, 183 N.W.2d 93 (1971).

[80] Ibid., at 99.

[81] Quill, 61:4, April 1973, p. 38.

[82] Ibid., 61:1, Jan. 1973, p. 29.

fore the Congress or any federal court or agency any information or the source of any information procured for publication or broadcast.[83]

Many taking the absolutist view argued from the position that government in the early 1970's—and especially the federal executive branch—was actively seeking ways to curb the press, trying to "prevent the press from performing its duties." [84] From this vantage point, qualifications in a shield bill often were seen as loopholes through which government could fire at the mass media. A qualified protection was no shield to these. They rejected the minority opinion in Branzburg v. Hayes that urged a shield unless the government could show a compelling and overriding interest in the information. The absolutists felt that courts would find "compelling and overriding interest" readily, although the federal trial and appeals courts had protected Earl Caldwell under that principle the first time that it had appeared in a newsman's privilege case.[85] Past protection afforded by qualified state shield laws under such circumstances, they held, was unlikely to be equal to the new challenge from government.

Yet the likelihood of achieving absolute protection from a federal shield bill seemed remote; in the climate of House and Senate hearings on the subject, Congressional leaders saw little chance for an unqualified bill.[86] In the states, the introduction of bills giving hard and sweeping protection without loophole or condition was widespread, but almost always the shield was weakened in the course of the legislative process.[87]

The qualifications were many: that the shield could be lowered if the government could show that all other sources of information had been exhausted and disclosure of the information was essential to the public interest; that disclosure could be required upon an order from a superior court; that privilege would not be granted where a reporter was testifying in a libel suit brought for words in his story; that disclosure was essential to prevent injustice; that the shield would protect a report-

---

[83] Editor & Publisher, Aug. 19, 1972, p. 9.

[84] Rosenthal, A.M., "Press-Government Conflict Escalates," Milwaukee Journal, Feb. 11, 1973, p. 1; Isaacs, N.E., "Beyond the 'Caldwell' Decision: 1," Columbia Journalism Rev., Sept./Oct. 1972, p. 18; Bridge, P.J., "Absolute Immunity, Absolutely," Quill 61:1, Jan. 1973, p. 8.

[85] Caldwell v. U. S., 434 F.2d 1081, 1089 (9th Cir. 1970).

[86] Collins, Thomas, "Congress Grapples With Press Bill," Milwaukee Journal, March 25, 1973, p. 16.

[87] Cook, Louise, Battle over News 'Shield' Shifted to Legislatures, Madison, Wis. Capital Times, April 26, 1973, p. 5.

er from testifying about material that had not been published or broadcast but not from testifying on what had been published or broadcast.

(3) Also at issue was the question of: Who deserves the shield? and following that: Would not defining "reporter" in effect be to license the newsman and thus bring him under state control? The United States Supreme Court in denying Paul Branzburg protection summarized the question and found that deciding it would bring practical and conceptual difficulties of a high order: [88]

> Sooner or later, it would be necessary to define those categories of newsmen who qualified for the privilege, a questionable procedure in light of the traditional doctrine that liberty of the press is the right of the lonely pamphleteer who uses carbon paper or a mimeograph just as much as of the large metropolitan publisher who utilizes the latest photocomposition methods * * *. Freedom of the press is a "fundamental personal right" which "is not confined to newspapers and periodicals. It necessarily embraces pamphlets and leaflets * * *. The press in its historic connotation comprehends every sort of publication which affords a vehicle of information and opinion * * *." The informative function asserted by representatives of the organized press in the present cases is also performed by lecturers, political pollsters, novelists, academic researchers, and dramatists. Almost any author may quite accurately assert that he is contributing to the flow of information to the public, that he relies on confidential sources of information, and that these sources will be silenced if he is forced to make disclosures before a grand jury.

Profound as the question was, it did not deter states as they adopted statutes from 1970 onward. New York's 1970 law defined "professional journalist" and "newscaster" in its law that protected only those agencies normally considered "mass media" —newspaper, magazine, news agency, press association, wire service, radio or television transmission station or network.[89] Illinois, in its 1971 statute, defined "reporter" as one who worked for similar media.[90] Neither included books among the

[88] Branzburg v. Hayes, 408 U.S. 665, 92 S.Ct. 2646, 2668 (1972).

[89] McKinney's N.Y.Civ.Rights Law § 79–h (Supp.1971).

[90] Ill.Legis.H. Bill 1756, 1971 Gen. Assembly.

media immunized; neither included scholars and researchers among the persons immunized.

SEC. 63. INDIRECT (CONSTRUCTIVE) CONTEMPT AS A PRESS RESTRICTION

When there is a danger that a news story will interfere with the orderly administration of justice, the news medium may be cited for contempt.

At what point may discussion in the media affect the attitude of possible veniremen drawn for jury duty in the very case being discussed, damage public confidence in the judicial system, or in some other way interfere with the orderly administration of justice and the rights of litigants or defendants?

The earliest American cases show judges convicting for publications that attacked courts or litigants while cases were pending, on the ground that the publications would prejudice the public mind and possible jurors. Two Pennsylvania convictions, and other actions in New York, led by 1830 to state statutes sharply limiting the scope of the out-of-court contempt power.[91]

But the Blackstonian position and the Wilmot theory of the inherent right of the court to cite for constructive contempt were beginning to make themselves felt in the United States. The theory was cited in the famous impeachment trial of Judge James H. Peck before the United States Senate in 1831. Judge Peck had convicted and jailed L. W. Lawless, an attorney, for contempt on the ground that Lawless had caused to be published a libel on the judge. Judge Peck was impeached for his action and although he was acquitted by a vote of 22 to 21, the Congressional reaction was to pass at once the statute of 1831 limiting the contempt power of judges. The power, said the statute, shall not extend "to any cases except the misbehaviour of any person or persons in the presence of said courts, or so near thereto as to obstruct the administration of justice * * * "[92]

For the next 30 years, conviction for contempt by out-of-court publication was a rarity in the United States. The thrust of the federal statute and public and legislative opinion checked the power. One conviction during this period, however, was to have

---

[91] Nelles and King, op. cit., pp. 409–422; Respublica v. Oswald, 1 U.S. (Dal.) 319, 1 L.Ed. 155, 1 Am.Dec. 246 (1788); Respublica v. Passmore, 3 Yeates 441, 2 Am.Dec. 388 (Pa.1802).

[92] Act of Mar. 2, 1831, C 98; 4 Stat. 487; Stansbury, Arthur J., Report of the Trial of James H. Peck.

great weight in later decades. This was State v. Morrill,[93] involving a newspaper account that suggested that the Arkansas Supreme Court had accepted bribery in a murder case. Rejecting the Arkansas statute that limited courts' power to cite for out-of-court contempt, the state Supreme Court upheld the conviction of the newspaperman.

It relied on the doctrine of its own inherent power, and said: [94]

> * * * every enlightened jurist in the United States, who has treated the subject, has held that the power to punish for contempts, is inherent in courts of justice, springing into existence upon their creation, as a necessary incident to the exercise of the powers conferred upon them.

> Had the Legislature never passed the act above quoted, or any act at all on the subject, could it be doubted that this court would possess the constitutional power to preserve order and decorum, enforce obedience to its process, and maintain respect for its judgments, orders and decrees, and as a necessary consequence, punish for contempts against its authority and dignity * * * ?

A drift toward the Arkansas court's position began after the Civil War, state after state adopting the position that the power to cite for contempt by publication was inherent in the courts, and that legislative enactments had little or no power to limit it. While a case was pending, a publication concerning it might be held in contempt if it had a tendency, or a "reasonable tendency," to interfere with the orderly administration of justice. The newspaper might do this in various ways, the chief ones being:

1. Any grossly false or inaccurate report of a court trial prejudicial to the court.

2. Any publication which might discredit the court, thus lowering the public's confidence in or respect for the integrity of the court, particularly during the pendency of a case.

3. Any publication of a news story, picture, article, or editorial whose object or tendency would be to affect the decision in a pending case.

In 1907, the United States Supreme Court gave weight to the power of citing for constructive contempt, holding that a publication which "would tend to obstruct the administration of justice" during a pending case was contemptuous. Pendency was

93 16 Ark. 384 (1855).

94 Ibid., at 390.

essential to the conviction, according to Justice Holmes who pointed out that "When a case is finished, courts are subject to the same criticism as other people, but the propriety and necessity of preventing interference with the course of justice by premature statement, argument or intimidation hardly can be denied.[95]

The ruling of the United States Supreme Court in Toledo Newspaper Co. v. United States[96] in 1918 was to become a leading authority for the "reasonable tendency" rule and the contempt power over publications. A Toledo street car company sought relief in the courts from a city council action regulating its fares and restricting its franchise. The *News-Bee* took the popular side in the controversy, commenting extensively on the case and ultimately drawing a contempt citation from the judge, and conviction. The Supreme Court upheld the conviction reasoning thus:[97]

> * * * however complete is the right of the press to state public things and discuss them, that right, as every other right enjoyed in human society, is subject to the restraints which separate right from wrong-doing. * * * Not the influence upon the mind of the particular judge is the criterion but the reasonable tendency of the acts done to influence or bring about the baleful result is the test.

Accompanying the pendency and reasonable tendency rules were other ramifications. Contempt must be toward the court engaged in a judicial duty rather than in a purely ministerial act.[98] The litigation must be such that it comes rightfully within the jurisdiction of the court in which it is pending, or be a case over which the court may assume jurisdiction.[99]

The newspaper having the contemptuous article may be published either in the city where the court is sitting, or in any other city within the jurisdiction of the court.[1] It is not necessary that the article alleged to be in contempt of the court come to

---

95 Patterson v. State of Colorado ex rel. Attorney General, 205 U.S. 454, 27 S.Ct. 556, 51 L.Ed. 879, 10 Ann.Cas. 689 (1907).

96 247 U.S. 402, 38 S.Ct. 560, 62 L.Ed. 1186 (1918).

97 Ibid., at 419–421.

98 Dunham v. State, 6 Iowa 245, 6 Clarke 245 (1858); Statter v. U. S., 66 F.2d 819 (9th Cir. 1933).

99 In re Pacific Tel. & Tel. Co., 38 F.2d 833 (D.C.Cal.1930).

1 U. S. v. Providence Tribune Co., 241 F. 524 (D.C.R.I.1917); Froelich v. U. S., 33 F.2d 660 (8th Cir. 1929); People v. Wilson, 64 Ill. 195, 16 Am.Rep. 528 (1872).

the attention of either the judge or the jury.[2] To be constructive contempt there must be no doubt of the harmful possibility of the publication on pending cases.[3] The publication must be explicit in its possible damaging effect.[4]

In the 1940s, the rule that assumed damage to the orderly administration of justice if comment was made while a case was pending, and the reasonable tendency rule, were attacked and underwent changes.

As for pendency, the question arose as to the length of time a case is pending. When the judge of a trial court gives his decision in a civil case, the end has not been reached for there may be granted a motion for a new trial, or the case may be appealed. Even when the highest court in a jurisdiction gives its decision, there may be a petition for a rehearing. Until the motion for a rehearing is denied by the highest court in the jurisdiction and the case is ordered returned to the trial court for execution of the decision, the case is still technically pending.[5]

Out of the prolonged court process that the foregoing suggests came questions as to whether the public interest was served by preventing the press from commenting on cases for months or years while the cases were moving through the courts. In 1941, the Supreme Court spoke of the problem in Bridges v. State of California.[6] Justice Frankfurter declared that "When a case is pending is not a technical, lawyer's problem, but it is to be determined by the substantial realities of the situation."[7] And the majority opinion, written by Justice Black, said that contempt judgments punishing utterances made during the pendency of a case "produce their restrictive results at the precise time when public interest in the matters discussed would naturally be at its height." He saw the danger of censorship: "An endless series of moratoria on public discussion, even if each were very short, could hardly be dismissed as an insignificant abridgement of freedom of expression. And to assume that each would be short

---

[2] U. S. v. Toledo Newspaper Co., 220 F. 458 (D.C.Ohio 1915), affirmed 237 F. 986 (6th Cir. 1916); Toledo Newspaper Co. v. U. S., 247 U.S. 402, 38 S.Ct. 560, 62 L.Ed. 1186 (1918); Lindsley v. Superior Court, 76 Cal.App. 419, 245 P. 212 (1926).

[3] Cheadle v. State, 110 Ind. 301, 11 N.E. 426, 59 Am.Rep. 199 (1887).

[4] Ex parte Spooner, 5 City Hall Recorder, 109 (N.Y.1820).

[5] McDougall v. Sheridan, 23 Idaho 191, 128 P. 954 (1913); Sullivan, H.W., Contempts by Publication, pp. 23, 24.

[6] 314 U.S. 252, 62 S.Ct. 190 (1941).

[7] 314 U.S. 252, 303, 304, 62 S.Ct. 190, 213 (1941).

is to overlook the fact that the 'pendency' of a case is frequently a matter of months or even years rather than days or weeks." [8]

Thus while ordinarily the case had to be pending if a contempt conviction were to be had for publication, the mere fact of pendency was not enough to permit assuming that comment would obstruct justice.

As for the rule that the publication, to be contempt, need present only a "reasonable tendency" to interfere with the orderly administration of justice, it gave way in a series of decisions of the United States Supreme Court to a requirement giving wider latitude to publications. The test that replaced it was whether the publication presented an immediate likelihood that justice would be thwarted—whether there were a clear and present danger that the publication would obstruct justice. The famous rule, expressed first in 1919 in Schenck v. United States [9] (a case involving seditious, rather than contemptuous expression), now was expanded to embrace alleged contempt of court, in Bridges v. California.[10] Neither an "inherent tendency" nor a "reasonable tendency" of words to interfere with the orderly administration of justice was sufficient to justify restriction of free expression, the court held. Instead, there must be a clear and present danger that the substantive evil would come about. The use of the test was continued in Pennekamp v. Florida [11] and in Craig v. Harney,[12] and courts since then have not relied on the term "reasonable tendency" as a criterion for what is contempt.

While the clear and present danger rule has persisted in contempt cases,[13] the fact is that the boundaries of "a clear and present danger to the orderly administration of justice" have not been defined sharply and, given the vagueness of the test, probably cannot be. Recognizing the test's imprecision, Justice Black said that what it amounts to in contempt cases is "a working principle that the substantive evil must be extremely serious and the degree of imminence extremely high before utterances can be punished." [14] That it is open to varying interpretations

---

[8] 314 U.S. 252, 268, 269, 62 S.Ct. 190, 196–197 (1941).

[9] 249 U.S. 47, 39 S.Ct. 247 (1919); Dennis v. U. S., 341 U.S. 494, 71 S.Ct. 857 (1951).

[10] 314 U.S. 252, 262, 273, 62 S.Ct. 190, 193–194, 198–199 (1941). In the same decision, the United States Supreme Court disposed of Times-Mirror Co. et al. v. Superior Court of California, also involving a contempt charge.

[11] 328 U.S. 331, 66 S.Ct. 1029, 90 L.Ed. 1295 (1946).

[12] 331 U.S. 367, 67 S.Ct. 1249, 91 L.Ed. 1546 (1947).

[13] Oliver v. Postel, 30 N.Y.2d 171, 331 N.Y.S.2d 407, 282 N.E.2d 306, 310 (1972).

[14] Bridges v. California, 314 U.S. 252, 263, 62 S.Ct. 190, 194 (1941).

by the courts is apparent in the cases that follow the decisions of the 1940's by the Supreme Court. They are arranged in subsequent sections under three major classes of newspaper publications involved in constructive contempt citations: attempts to influence decisions, discrediting the court, and false and inaccurate reports.

SEC. 64.   ATTEMPTS TO INFLUENCE DECISIONS

Los Angeles Times' conviction for constructive contempt reversed by United States Supreme Court, which found no clear and present danger to the administration of justice in the Times' advice to a judge.

The series of cases in the 1940's in which the U. S. Supreme Court restricted sharply the scope of the judiciary's power to find and punish for constructive contempt started in Los Angeles Superior Court. The Times-Mirror Co., publisher of the *Los Angeles Times*, was cited for contempt on affidavits brought by the Los Angeles Bar Association in 1938. The charges were based on seven editorials commenting on cases which had not been finally adjudicated. The *Times* was adjudged guilty of out-of-court contempt, the trial court holding that five of the seven editorials were contemptuous. One of the five, titled "Probation for Gorillas" and dated May 5, 1938, included this:

Probation for Gorillas?

Two members of Dave Beck's wrecking crew, entertainment committee, goon squad or gorillas, having been convicted in Superior Court of assaulting nonunion truck drivers, have asked for probation. Presumably they will say they are "first offenders," or plead that they were merely indulging a playful exuberance when, with slingshot, they fired steel missiles at men whose only offense was wishing to work for a living without paying tribute to the erstwhile boss of Seattle.

Sluggers for pay, like murderers for profit, are in a slightly different category from ordinary criminals. Men who commit mayhem for wages are not merely violators of the peace and dignity of the State; they are also conspirators against it. * * *

   *   *   *   *   *   *   *   *

Judge A. A. Scott will make a serious mistake if he grants probation to Matthew Shannon and Kennan Holmes. This community needs the example of their assignment to the jute mill.

The conviction was appealed and reached the Supreme Court of the United States. In a single decision, the court disposed of this case and another California contempt case, Bridges v. California, the latter being used as the title. Dividing in its decision, the United States Supreme Court reversed the conviction, holding that "we are all of the opinion that, upon any fair construction, their possible influence on the course of justice can be dismissed as negligible, and that the Constitution compels us to set aside the convictions as unpermissible exercises of the state's power." [15] It declared that the test of contempt should be whether the expression presents a clear and present danger to the orderly administration of justice, and rejected the old "reasonable tendency" test.

> In accordance with what we have said on the "clear and present danger" cases, neither "inherent tendency" nor "reasonable tendency" is enough to justify a restriction of free expression. But even if they were appropriate measures, we should find exaggeration in the use of those phrases to describe the facts here.
>
> From the indications in the record of the position taken by the Los Angeles Times on labor controversies in the past, there could have been little doubt of its attitude toward the probation of Shannon and Holmes. In view of the paper's long-continued militancy in this field, it is inconceivable that any judge in Los Angeles would expect anything but adverse criticism from it in the event probation were granted. Yet such criticism after final disposition of the proceedings would clearly have been privileged. Hence, this editorial, given the most intimidating construction it will bear, did no more than threaten future adverse criticism which was reasonably to be expected anyway in the event of a lenient disposition of the pending case. To regard it, therefore, as in itself of substantial influence upon the course of justice would be to impute to judges a lack of firmness, wisdom, or honor—which we cannot accept as a major premise.

A subsequent case involved a husband who sought a divorce and custody of his child. During the suit, Goss, a broadcaster who was on television five nights a week, was accused of adultery with the wife. In broadcasts that followed, Goss said he would do everything in his power "to prevent the legal kidnaping of her child," called a witness in the case a "professional

---

15 Bridges v. California, 314 U.S. 252, 62 S.Ct. 190, 200, 86 L.Ed. 192 (1941).

sneak and liar," and said that the husband had "hoodlum connections." A contempt conviction resulted and Goss brought a writ of error to reverse the judge's order. The Illinois Supreme Court ruled that Goss's freedom of expression was not infringed by the contempt charge. It interpreted the clear and present danger test as not requiring judicial proof of an actual interference with the judicial process, and said: [16]

> What is required, we think, is that the character of the publication and the circumstances in which it was made must be scrutinized with special caution and concern because of the potential threat to free speech which the contempt power obviously holds. Comment on pending cases, even if it is unfair and inaccurate, is not to be adjudged contemptuous unless it constitutes an "imminent peril" to the administration of justice * * *
> But where comment is systematically designed to serve the contrary aim of thwarting the judicial process, then, as the Supreme Court has acknowledged, such comment is not constitutionally protected. * * *
> The comments involved here were delivered by one who had a personal and professional interest in the decision in a pending action, and they were admittedly designed to affect that decision by a sustained and systematic attempt to prevent or impugn unfavorable testimony by vilifying any witness who should offer such testimony. * * *
>
> We have before us infractions that were repeated, bold and defiant, which had for their purpose an interference with an actually pending judicial determination. We hold therefore that the statements of the plaintiff in error constituted a clear and present danger to the administration of justice.

In a third case involving an attempt to influence a decision, a conviction for constructive contempt was upheld without reliance on the clear and present danger test. During the trial of one Holifield, a man approached the wife of a juror and asked that she hand her husband a note, and "see if they could help Mr. Holifield in the case." [17] She gave the note to her husband, who later reported the incident. He had not been influenced by the note, he said, and, indeed, voted for conviction of Holifield. Young, the note-passer, was convicted of contempt, and the Mississippi Supreme Court upheld the conviction, saying that mani-

[16] People v. Goss, 10 Ill.2d 533, 141 N.E.2d 385, 390, 391 (1957).

[17] T. A. Young v. State, 230 Miss. 525, 93 So.2d 452 (1957).

festly the evidence was sufficient to establish the guilt of the contemnor beyond a reasonable doubt.

The extent to which the clear and present danger test affects newspaper publications which might affect a jury is not entirely clear. Before the *Bridges* case, a newspaper story charging a defendant in a criminal trial as a felon impelled the court to discharge the jury, and the publication was held contemptuous.[18] In some jurisdictions, indeed, decisions held that it was not necessary that the jurors read the newspaper story; it was sufficient if the story was published and possessed the tendency to interfere with their duty as unprejudiced members of the jury.[19]

In a 1960 case, however, the fact that jurors saw a newspaper report did not sustain a conviction. Georgia newspapers identified a man charged with robbery as "formerly Georgia's number one wanted man," and upon receiving evidence that jurors during recess had read the articles, the court declared a mistrial, cited the newspapers for contempt, and fined them $20,000. On appeal, the judgment was reversed, because, the Supreme Court of Georgia held, the newspapers had a right to believe that the jurors would be kept together or instructed not to read news of the case during recess in accord with Georgia law.[20]

SEC. 65. DISCREDITING THE COURT

Miami Herald's editorials and cartoon imputing partisanship to circuit judges in favoring persons charged with crime held by United States Supreme Court not to be contempt. Corpus Christi newspapers' articles reflecting on the competence of a judge in handling cases held not to be contempt.

When a judge is defamed by a newspaper, he may sue for libel as any citizen may. Another course sometimes open to him is citing the publisher for contempt—for "scandalizing the court," as it has been called, or bringing the court into disrepute through criticism during a pending case. It is the use of the contempt power under this circumstance that sometimes has been likened to the seditious libel actions.[21]

[18] In re Independent Pub. Co., 228 F. 787 (D.C.Mont.1917), affirmed 240 F. 849 (9th Cir. 1917); State ex rel. Phelps v. Judge of Civil District Court, 45 La.Ann. 1250, 14 So. 310, 40 Am.St.Rep. 282 (1895); Field v. Thornell, 106 Iowa 7, 75 N.W. 685, 68 Am.St.Rep. 281 (1898).

[19] Lindsley v. Superior Court of Cal. for Humboldt County, 76 Cal.App. 419, 245 P. 212 (1926); Telegram Newspaper Co. v. Commonwealth, 172 Mass. 294, 52 N.E. 445, 44 L.R.A. 159, 70 Am.St.Rep. 280 (1899).

[20] Atlanta Newspapers, Inc. v. State of Georgia, 216 Ga. 399, 116 S.E.2d 580 (1960).

[21] Nelles and King, pp. 406, 407.

Constructive contempt convictions involving criticism of judges, however, have been overruled by the United States Supreme Court in two leading cases that followed the *Bridges* decision and employed the clear and present danger test.

John D. Pennekamp, associate editor of the *Miami Herald* and the Miami Herald Publishing Company were adjudged in contempt of court for the publication of two editorials and a cartoon imputing partisanship to circuit court judges of Dade County, Florida, and suggesting that they favored persons charged with crime. This judgment was affirmed by the Supreme Court of Florida,[22] but the United States Supreme Court reversed.[23]

The *Herald* had offended in an editorial of November 2, 1944, which read in part:

Courts are Established for the People

It is beyond question that American courts are of, by and for the people.

Every accused person has a right to his day in court. But when judicial instance and interpretative procedure recognize and accept, even go out to find, every possible technicality of the law to protect the defendant, to block, thwart, hinder, embarrass and nullify prosecution, then the people's rights are jeopardized and the basic reason for courts stultified.

The seeming ease and pat facility with which the criminally charged have been given technical safeguard have set people to wondering whether their courts are being subverted into refuges for lawbreakers.

This week the people, through their grand jury, brought into court eight indictments for rape. Judge Paul D. Barns agreed with the defense that the indictments were not properly drawn. Back they went to the grand jury for re-presentation to the court.

Only in the gravest emergency does a judge take over a case from another court of equal jurisdiction. A padlock action against the Brook Club was initiated last spring before Judge George E. Holt, who granted a temporary injunction.

After five months, the case appeared Tuesday out of the blue sky before Judge Marshall C. Wiseheart at the

22 156 Fla. 227, 22 So.2d 875 (1945).

23 Pennekamp v. Florida, 328 U.S. 331, 66 S.Ct. 1029, 90 L.Ed. 1295 (1946).

time State Attorney Stanley Milledge was engaged with the grand jury.

Speedy decision was asked by defense counsel despite months of stalling. The State Attorney had to choose between the grand jury and Judge Wiseheart's court.

The judge dismissed the injunction against the club and its operators. The defense got delay when it wanted and prompt decision from the court when it profited it.

On Oct. 10 Judge Holt had before him a suit by the state to abate a nuisance (bookmaking) at the Tepee Club.

Five affidavits of persons who allegedly visited the premises for the purpose of placing bets were introduced by the state over the objection of the defendants.

Judge Holt ruled them out, explaining in denying the injunction against the Tepee Club:

"The defendant cannot cross-examine an affidavit. The court cannot determine who is testifying and whether belief can be placed upon such testimony * * *. The fact that such affidavits were taken before the State Attorney does not give them any additional weight or value."

If technicalities are to be the order and the way for the criminally charged either to avoid justice altogether or so to delay prosecution as to cripple it, then it behooves our courts and the legal profession to cut away the deadwood and the entanglements.

Accompanying the first editorial in the *Herald* was a caricature—a robed, compliant figure of a judge on the bench tossing aside formal charges and handing to a powerful figure of an intentionally designed criminal type, a document labeled "Defendant dismissed." At the right of the bench stood a figure labeled "Public Interest" vainly protesting.

In the court's citation for contempt, it was charged that associate editor Pennekamp and the Herald reflected adversely on the court in reference to the right indictments for rape, and further that the judges had not fairly and impartially heard these cases. Pennekamp was fined $250 and the corporation $1,000.

The United States Supreme Court in reversing the judgment of the Florida Supreme Court stated: [24]

24 328 U.S. 331, 348, 66 S.Ct. 1029, 1038 (1946).

The comments were made about judges of courts of general jurisdiction—judges selected by the people of a populous and educated community. They concerned the attitude of the judges toward those who were charged with crime, not comments on evidence or rulings during a jury trial. Their effect on juries that might eventually try the alleged offenders against the criminal laws of Florida is too remote for discussion. Comment on pending cases may affect judges differently. It may influence some judges more than others. Some are of a more sensitive fiber than their colleagues. The law deals in generalities and external standards and cannot depend on the varying degrees of moral courage or stability in the face of criticism which individual judges may possess any more than it generally can depend on the personal equations or individual idiosyncrasies of the tort-feasor. * * * We are not willing to say under the circumstances of this case that these editorials are a clear and present danger to the fair administration of justice in Florida.

What is meant by clear and present danger to a fair administration of justice? No definition could give an answer. Certainly this criticism of the judge's inclinations or actions in these pending non-jury proceedings could not directly affect such administration. This criticism of his actions could not affect his ability to decide the issues. Here there is only criticism of judicial action already taken, although the cases were still pending on other points or might be revived by rehearings. For such injuries, when the statements amount to defamation, a judge has such remedy in damages for libel as do other public servants.

The following year brought a second major case involving criticism of the courts, Craig v. Harney.[25] Three Texas newspapermen, in 1945, were cited for contempt and the Court of Criminal Appeals of Texas denied their application for a review of judgment. The United States Supreme Court reversed the judgment of the Texas court, holding that the publications in question did not interfere legally with the administration of justice.

The petitioners were publisher, editorial writer, and reporter for newspapers published in Corpus Christi, Texas. The bases for the contempt proceedings were an editorial and news stories published in May 1945. The articles concerned a forcible detain-

[25] 331 U.S. 367, 67 S.Ct. 1249 (1947).

er case. Jackson v. Mayes, in which Jackson sought to regain from Mayes possession of a business building in Corpus Christi which Mayes, a war veteran, claimed under a lease. The question in the case was whether Mayes' lease was forfeited because of nonpayment of rent. At the trial, Judge Joe D. Browning instructed the jury to return a verdict for Jackson, but the jury returned its verdict for Mayes. The court refused to accept the verdict for Mayes, and the jury a second time, contrary to the judge's instruction, returned a verdict for Mayes. Again the court refused to accept the verdict. The jury finally complied, with an added statement that it had acted under coercion of the court and against its own conscience.

On June 4 an officer of the county court filed a complaint charging the men with contempt by publication, referring specifically to the editorial and news articles which had appeared in their publications on and after May 26.

Over several days, the *Corpus Christi Caller-Times* made statements such as these:

> At 7 p.m., Browning, without listening to argument, from counsel for either side on a plaintiff's motion, presented by Dudley Tarlton for Jackson, and without giving the six-man jury opportunity to weigh the evidence, instructed the jury to find against Mayes.

> Walter M. Lewright, Mayes' attorney, protested that the court's arbitrary action had ruled that Tarlton's "one-page motion" did not need supporting argument and citation of authorities.

> *   *   *   *   *   *   *   *   *

> Browning accepted Tarlton's one-page motion and, without permitting argument or citation of authorities to support the motion, ruled that it be granted. The effect of this ruling was that Browning took the matter from the jury.

> *   *   *   *   *   *   *   *   *

> Browning's behavior and attitude has brought down the wrath of public opinion upon his head, properly so. Emotions have been aggravated. American people simply don't like the idea of such goings on, especially when a man in the service of his country seems to be getting a raw deal. * * * Then the plaintiff's counsel offered a motion for an instructed verdict for his client. It was granted immediately, without having him cite his authority or without giving the defendant's attorney a chance to argue against it.

That was the travesty on justice, the judge's refusal to hear both sides. That's where a legal background would have served him in good stead. It is difficult to believe that any lawyer, even a hack, would have followed such high handed procedure in instructing a jury. It's no wonder that the jury balked and public opinion is out-raged.

In its reversal of the conviction, the Supreme Court of the United States said: [26]

> But there was here no threat or menace to the integrity of the trial. The editorial challenged the propriety of the court's procedure, not the merits of its ruling. Any such challenge, whether made prior or subsequent to the final disposition of a case, would likely reflect on the competence of the judge in handling cases. But as we have said, the power to punish for contempt depends on a more substantial showing. Giving the editorial all of the vehemence which the court below found in it we fail to see how it could in any realistic sense create an imminent and serious threat to the ability of the court to give fair consideration to the motion for rehearing.

The thrust of the United States Supreme Court's decisions of the 1940's may be seen in a subsequent Colorado case. An editorial in the *Englewood Herald* suggested that possibly the Colorado Supreme Court, in releasing an announcement of a decision in advance of the full, 32-page decision itself, was still looking for reasons for its decision, or was merely sending up a trial balloon. The editor was directed to show cause why he should not be punished for contempt. The court said, in its decision, that the editor had "accused this court and every judge thereof of conduct abhorrent to every esteemed tradition of the judiciary. * * *" [27] Nevertheless, it said, there was no clear and present danger to an impartial decision by the court of issues involved in the case pending before it, and the editor thus was not guilty of contempt.

That the test is open to varying interpretations, however, is plain from an examination of a case in which a man seeking admission to the Wyoming bar assailed the state supreme court. Stone, after being denied admission, used letters (with copies to news agencies), legal motions, and advertisements in his prolonged attack. He accused the court of "having fomented a con-

[26] 331 U.S. 367, 67 S.Ct. 1249, 1255 (1947).

[27] In re Jameson, 139 Colo. 171, 340 P.2d 423 (1959).

spiracy" to "deprive me of my livelihood, willfully, knowingly, maliciously," and characterized the court as "unfair, prejudiced, partial and biased." [28]

The court held Stone in contempt, interpreting the clear and present danger test thus: [29]

> In no case in which the United States Supreme Court has discussed the clear and present danger doctrine has there been an instance similar to that now being considered, where there has been a sustained, continuous, and planned attack by a person professing to be learned in the law * * * against a court and its members with the apparent intention of vilifying and degrading the judiciary of a state by false, vicious, and malicious propaganda calculated to besmirch and destroy in the mind of the public the honor, integrity, and reputation of the state's judicial officers through direct charges, innuendoes, sly suggestions and perversions of truth.
>
> * * * We hold that these writings filed by the defendant with this court * * * are contemptuous and constitute a clear and present danger to the administration of justice in the supreme court and in the district courts of the State of Wyoming.

SEC. 66. FALSE AND INACCURATE REPORTS

Grossly misleading reports of court cases may be held contemptuous if they endanger the orderly administration of justice

False and inaccurate newspaper reports of court proceedings have been held contemptuous. The *San Francisco Chronicle* reported that the California Supreme Court had voted to reverse a decision of a lower court. It based its story on "confidential and authoritative sources," and included the statement that the accused had won a new trial for the murder charge of which he had been convicted. Contempt proceedings were brought by the chief justice, who said that the newspaper statements were grossly inaccurate, that the case was not yet even assigned to a justice for writing the opinion, and the case was pending and not decided.[30] The *Chronicle* was convicted under the state penal code providing that publishing a false report of a court proceeding was contempt.

[28] Application of Stone, 77 Wyo. 1, 305 P.2d 777 (1957).

[29] Ibid., at 787, 788.

[30] In re San Francisco Chronicle, 1 Cal.2d 630, 36 P.2d 369 (1934).

But here, as with contempt citations for attempts to influence decisions and for discrediting the courts, the clear and present danger doctrine has had an impact. The editor of the *Englewood Herald* printed the following editorial after the Colorado Supreme Court published a brief announcement of its decision in a case, in advance of the full, 32-page decision: [31]

A Colorado Supreme Court ruling Thursday in the Arapahoe county valuation case deserves a close looking at and some questions on behalf of the taxpayers of Arapahoe County.

*   *   *   *   *   *   *   *   *

In view of these circumstaces enumerated, it seems to me that a number of questions develop in the minds of the taxpayers concerning the Colorado Supreme Court decision.

One of these is: "Is the supreme court still hunting for justification of its ruling and that is the reason that an opinion explaining the ruling was not filed with the ruling?"

Could this be something like a judge who might say to a man: "You're guilty. Come back next week and by then I'll have the reasons why." ·

Or could this ruling—without an opinion—have been a sort of a feeler, or a trial balloon as the politicians say —to find out how the public might feel?

Could it have been that if the populace should rise up in wrath that the opinion could temper down the ruling, or, if it went almost unnoticed, the court could breathe easier and file an opinion backing up its ruling to the hilt?

Or could it have been that the justices—they are elected state-wide, too—felt that the problem of getting politically powerful school teachers paid on time justifies the means used of issuing a quick ruling without legal opinion in its support?

I don't know the answers, but I do know that unless the opinion within a week or softens the broad terms of the sketchy ruling the court has chiseled away more of our vanishing local governmental rights.

The court, which had published the announcement instead of waiting for the full decision in order to prevent delay that would

---

[31] In re Jameson, 139 Colo. 171, 340 P.2d 423, 424 (1959).

have hampered county officials in their duties, ordered the editor to show cause why he should not be cited for contempt. After hearing him, the court said that "Without the slightest investigation of the facts, and in total disregard of the truth * * * respondent * * * accused this court and every judge thereof of conduct abhorrent to every esteemed tradition of the judiciary. * * *" It said that while the editor "professed a 'sacred trust' to keep his readers informed, he actually betrayed that trust by giving them only untruths. * * *"[32] In spite of such inaccuracy, however, the court held that the editor was not in contempt because the inaccuracy presented no clear and present danger to an impartial decision by the court.

SEC. 67.   DEFENSE FOR CONTEMPT

Though decisions are not in agreement, the general rules are that neither truth nor absence of intent necessarily absolves contempt charge.

Defense to a citation for constructive contempt may be a challenge to the constitutionality of the charge, a denial of the facts, absence of intent, and the truth of the charge published. The decisions are not always in agreement on principle of law, and specific facts of course may alter the application of general principles. It has been held that any publication to constitute contempt must have been an intended disrespect for the authority of the court;[33] however, there is a line of cases which holds that if the intent is uncertain and any intended disrespect of the court is disavowed under oath, there would thereby be a purge of the contempt. In State ex rel. Haskell v. Faulds,[34] the respondent was discharged on the ground that no contempt of the court was intended in the publication of the following story:

> The Supreme Court of Montana, the highest tribunal of justice in the state, was the first to throw down the bars and deal out injustice to the people of Ravalli county. The dirty deal is made the more obnoxious through the action of Governor Rickards in his reasons for granting the pardon.

[32] Ibid., at 427.   See also People of the State of New York v. Post Standard Co., where the court held that "mere errors in reporting, where no willfulness is alleged, are not usually considered a sound basis for contempt proceedings." 13 N.Y.2d 185, 245 N.Y.S.2d 377, 195 N.E.2d 48 (1963); In re Look Magazine, 109 N.J.Super. 548, 264 A.2d 95 (1970), where a biased account was insufficient to support contempt in view of sequestering of jury.

[33] Fishback v. State, 131 Ind. 304, 30 N.E. 1088 (1891).

[34] 17 Mont. 140, 42 P. 285 (1895).

It is not necessarily a defense that the contemptuous statement was true, particularly if the statement is made while the case is pending in court.[35] The fact that the contemnor is contrite and apologizes does not absolve him, although it may ameliorate the offense.[36] However, the fact that a communication is privileged has been held a defense to contempt proceedings.[37] In proceedings to punish for contempt because of failure to obey a court order, the fact that the order was indefinite or uncertain has been held a good defense.[38] And in People v. Stapleton, it was stated that a newspaper publisher could not exonerate himself by denying that he had any previous knowledge of the article in question, though this fact could be used in mitigation.[39]

[35] Patterson v. Colo., 205 U.S. 454, 27 S.Ct. 556, 558 (1906); Dale v. State, 198 Ind. 110, 150 N.E. 781 (1926); s.c., 273 U.S. 776, 47 S.Ct. 332 (1927).

[36] Brannon v. State, 202 Miss. 571, 29 So.2d 916 (1947).

[37] Froelich v. U. S., 33 F.2d 660 (8th Cir. 1929).

[38] Brody v. Dist. Ct. of Pottawattamie Co., 250 Iowa 1217, 98 N.W.2d 726 (1959).

[39] 18 Colo. 568, 33 P. 167 (1893).

Chapter 11

CRIMINAL WORDS: OBSCENITY AND BLASPHEMY

SEC. 68. OBSCENITY: THE FREEDOM TO READ VERSUS CONCEPTS OF CONTROL

American courts and legislatures have long been searching for a "dim and uncertain line" which separates obscenity from constitutionally protected expression.

Legislative enactments and court decisions on obscenity have shown remarkable ability in creating chaos out of mere disorder. In 1973, just as this book was going to press, the Supreme Court of the United States unburdened itself of five decisions on obscenity. Study of these decisions, which are discussed at length in Sec. 74 of this chapter, will show that the Court has not yet succeeded in devising a formula which will define obscenity with sufficient precision to protect free discussion of sex while punishing what *Time* magazine might call "sexploiters." [1]

The 1973 decisions on obscenity are the latest links in a chain of court actions and statute-making which has a long, if unpleasant, history in this nation. In recent years, the dilemma of the "dirty" book—or magazine or movie—has taken up more and more time in American courts. Back in 1948, Justice Robert H. Jackson voiced the fear that the Supreme Court would become the High Court of Obscenity.[2] Since his words were spoken, the task

[1] See Miller v. California, —— U.S. ——, 93 S.Ct. 2607 (1973); Paris Adult Theatre I v. Slaton, —— U.S. ——, 93 S.Ct. 2628 (1973); United States v. Orito, —— U.S. ——, 93 S.Ct. 2674 (1973); Kaplan v. California, —— U.S. ——, 93 S.Ct. 2680 (1973), and United States v. 12 200-Ft. Reels of Super 8 mm Film, —— U.S. ——, 93 S.Ct. 2665 (1973).

[2] Quoted by Anthony Lewis, "Sex and the Supreme Court," Esquire, Vol. 59 (June, 1963) p. 82.

of attempting to define obscenity has increasingly become that of the Supreme Court. The Court's aging, dignified members have been forced to undertake the industrious study of works including John Cleland's *Memoirs of a Woman of Pleasure* and even more explicit—and raunchier-depictions of sexual activities on print and film.

The wording of the Justices' opinions about obscenity reflects profound discomfiture. The Justices have complained that they are judges, not literary historians or philosophers; one problem is that one person's obscenity may be another's art. As Justice Potter Stewart has noted, the Court persists in "trying to define what may be indefinable." [3] Even if he couldn't define obscenity, Justice Stewart added that he knows it when he sees it. In trying to define the obscene, the Supreme Court has had to try to perceive a dim and uncertain line which separates obscenity from constitutionally protected expression.

In search for such a dim and uncertain line, American courts have been left floundering by a society which makes enormous financial successes of literature, motion pictures and art which celebrate all manner of sexual exploits and bodily functions. Some observers called America of the 1960's and early 1970's "the permissive society;" it was said that "anything goes" in art and literature.

Yet this greater freedom—which many view as license—is not unopposed. Earnest, if censorious, individuals strive mightily to clean up bookstores, news-stands, and movies. And if selling obscenity is profitable business, opposing obscenity is often smart politics. So-called dirty books and dirty politics often go hand-in-hand. Decent literature drives by district attorneys or attorneys general often crop up before election time. Too many candidates wrap themselves in the Flag and declare themselves against obscenity and in favor of God, Motherhood, and Mom's Apple Pie.

The 1960's and 1970's brought greater judicial activity in the law of obscenity. The years which endured "beatniks," "hippies," and "swingers" saw "floods of paperback and comic book violence, and scabrous periodicals and girlie magazines were in evidence as never before; under-the counter, hard-core pornography (perhaps as undefinable as 'the obscene') flourished." [4]

---

3 Concurring opinion in Jacobellis v. Ohio, 378 U.S. 184, 197, 84 S.Ct. 1676, 1683 (1964).

4 Harold L. Nelson, Freedom of the Press from Hamilton to the Warren Court (New York, Bobbs Merrill, 1967) p. xiv.

During the 1960's, paperback books, in particular, attracted the attention of the censorious: flashy covers on books, depicting scantily clad exemplars of femininity, excited outrage even when the books in question were classics which had never been challenged when published in hard-cover.   In the 1970's, materials which many persons would term hard-core pornography came out from under the counter and showed up on movie screens. Some motion pictures, such as Bernardo Bertolucci's "Last Tango in Paris" starring Marlon Brando, might be termed erotic realism;   indeed, some reputable critics gave "Tango" high marks.   If simulated sex was permissible in "Tango," what then about the goings-on in "Deep Throat?" [5]

So the battle lines have been drawn, and so the fight continues.   The courts are faced with cases which call upon choices between countervailing interests: protecting the public from noxious literature or films, and protecting the freedom to read or see.[6]

The Freedom to Read

The freedom to read is implicit in the First and Fourteenth Amendments to the Constitution.[7]   But the freedom to read, as part of our freedoms of speech and press, is not absolute.[8]   For the most part, however, we are free to read what we want.   It may not occur to most Americans that many books they enjoy reading today might have been banned as obscene and held out of circulation in another time or place.

The late Jake Ehrlich, one of America's leading criminal lawyers, said that "every book that is worthwhile was condemned somewhere by someone."[9]   Ehrlich's statement is disquietingly credible, for such works as Keats' *Endymion,* Shelley's *Queen Mab,* Whitman's *Leaves of Grass,* Defoe's *Moll Flanders,* Dreiser's *An American Tragedy* and various editions of the *Bible* have at some time been condemned as obscene.[10]

[5] *Time,* Jan. 22, 1973, pp. 51ff.

[6] Zechariah Chafee, Jr., Government and Mass Communications, 2 vols. (Chicago, University of Chicago Press, 1947) Vol. I, pp. 210–211.

[7] See, e. g., Near v. Minnesota, 283 U.S. 697, 713–717, 51 S.Ct. 625, 630–631 (1931); Ex parte Jackson, 96 U.S. 727, 733 (1897).

[8] See, e. g., Near v. Minnesota, 283 U.S. 697, 51 S.Ct. 625 (1931); Schenck v. United States, 249 U.S. 47, 39 S.Ct. 247 (1919).

[9] David Perlman, " 'Howl' Not Obscene, Judge Rules," San Francisco Chronicle, Oct. 4, 1957, p. 1.   See also People of the State of California v. Lawrence Ferlinghetti (Municipal Court, Dept. 10, San Francisco, Oct. 3, 1957).

[10] Stanley Fleishman et al., Brief for Appellant in the Supreme Court of the United States (in the case of David S. Alberts v. State of California, No. 61, Oct. Term 1956) p. 78.

This list of banned titles—classics all—indicates that the freedom to read cannot be safely taken for granted. Laws which make it a criminal offense to distribute or possess obscene literature are one way in which that freedom may be diminished if the laws are overzealously applied. Such laws, which will be discussed later in this chapter, draw no lines between literary obscenity and art. Obscenity is never really defined; only various synonyms are presented. The laws say only that writings, pictures, statues, or substances which are obscene, lewd, immoral, lascivious, licentious, and so forth, may not be circulated in or imported into this country.[11]

The roots of the freedom to read may be traced to what has been called the Democratic Creed, which has been expressed in the writings of John Milton, John Stuart Mill, Thomas Jefferson and many others. As Milton wrote in his *Areopagitica*: [12]

> Since * * * the knowledge and survey of vice is in this world so necessary to the constituting of human virtue, and the scanning of error to the confirmation of truth, how can we more safely, and with less danger, scout into the regions of sin and falsity than by reading all manner of tractates and hearing all manner of reason?

The idea that knowledge, knowledge of any kind, will make man better able to cope with life is thus basic to the freedom to read.

Concepts of Control

Concepts of control, to the contrary, often have as their premise the notion that Man is inherently weak and can be further weakened or even destroyed by reading improper literature. Attempts to censor literature regarded as obscene—or to legislate against it—are grounded on the assumption that if persons read such material, antisocial thoughts or actions will be induced.

The roots of the various concepts of control may be traced to such varying personalities as Plato, St. Thomas Acquinas, and Anthony Comstock. This wildly differing trio had at least one

---

11 See, e. g., Roth v. United States, 354 U.S. 476, 493–494, 77 S.Ct. 1304, 1314 (1957); United States v. Bennett, 24 Fed.Cas. 1093, 1104, No. 14,571 (S.D.N.Y., 1879); United States v. Levine, 83 F.2d 156, 158 (2d Cir. 1936); United States v. One Book Entitled "Ulysses," 5 F.Supp. 182, 184 (S.D.N.Y., 1933); Besig v. United States, 208 F.2d 142, 146 (9th Cir. 1953); William B. Lockhart and Robert C. McClure, "Literature, the Law of Obscenity, and the Constitution," Minnesota Law Review Vol. 38: 4 (March, 1954) p. 324.

12 John Milton, The Student's Milton, ed. by Frank Allen Patterson, (Rev. ed., Appleton-Century Crofts, Inc., New York, 1933), p. 738.

thing in common: all approved state control of moral virtue. Plato asserted that poets should be censored lest their subtleties corrupt children. St. Thomas believed that the aim of laws should be to make men good, and it followed that the control of the arts as part of education was within the sphere of man's laws.[13]

Anthony Comstock was a Victorian American who played a major and sexually preoccupied part in the passage of federal and state obscenity statutes in the United States. These statutes were calculated to protect the young and the weak from being defiled by impure literature. Comstock was not without legal precedents to trot out in his attacks on literature, although the extent to which "obscenity" was a crime under English Common Law is by no means clear.[14]

An early case in the Anglo-American legal tradition which involved obscene conduct was that of The King v. Sir Charles Sedley. In 1663, Sir Charles, nude, drunk, and garrulous, appeared on a London Balcony and delivered a lengthy harangue to the crowd gathered below. He hurled bottles filled with an "offensive liquor" upon the crowd.[15]

Hurling flasks, however, was not the same as publishing. Perhaps the first *recorded* prosecution for publication of obscene literature was Curll's case, circa 1727. Mr. Curll had published a nastily anti-Catholic writing called "Venus in the Cloister or the Nun in Her Smock," which was held to be a threat to morals and suppressed.[16] This decision apparently had little effect on the flourishing sale of lusty literature, and by the 19th century, England had entered what has been called its pornographic period. In America, meanwhile the Tariff Act of 1842 proscribed the "importation of all indecent and obscene prints, paintings, lithographs, engravings, and transparencies." [17] In 1865, in response to complaints about the reading materials mailed to many soldiers who served in the Civil War (including Cleland's notorious *Memoirs of a Woman of Pleasure*), Congress for the first time outlawed mailing obscene matter.[18]

[13] Mortimer Adler, Art & Prudence (1st ed., New York, Longmans Green & Co., 1937), p. 103.

[14] H. Montgomery Hyde, A History of Pornography (New York, Farrar, Straus and Giroux, 1965) pp. 165, 174.

[15] Concurring opinion of Mr. Justice Douglas in the "Fanny Hill" case, 383 U.S. 413, 428n, 86 S.Ct. 975, 983n (1966).

[16] Hyde, op. cit. 165; 2 Strange 788, 93 Eng.Rep. 849 (N.B. 1727).

[17] U. S. Public Statutes at Large, Vol. 5, Ch. 270, Sec. 28, pp. 566–567.

[18] James C. N. Paul and Murray L. Schwartz, Federal Censorship: Obscenity in the Mail (New York: Free Press of Glencoe, 1961) p. 255, citing Congressional Globe, 38th Congress, 2nd Sess. pp. 660–662 (1865).

The Comstock Law

Anthony Comstock began his decency campaign shortly after the Civil War, and fervently denounced anyone who spoke up against him as lechers and defilers of American Womanhood.

"MORALS, not Art or Literature!" was the Comstockian battle cry.[19] In 1873, censorious pressure groups who favored what has come to be called "Comstockery" helped to force an obscenity bill through both houses of Congress. This law provided a maximum criminal punishment of a $5,000 fine or a five-year penitentiary term, or both for anyone who sent obscene matter through the mail.[20] Although amended several times to broaden the definition of "obscene matter," the law is still on the books. The law now provides, in part, that: [21]

> Every obscene, lewd, lascivious, indecent, filthy or vile article, matter, thing, device or substance; and
> * * *
>
> *   *   *   *   *   *   *   *   *
>
> Every written or printed card, letter, circular, book, pamphlet, advertisement, or notice of any kind giving information, directly or indirectly, where, or how, or from whom, or by what means such mentioned matters * * * may be obtained * * *
>
> *   *   *   *   *   *   *   *   *
>
> Is declared to be nonmailable matter and shall not be conveyed in the mails or delivered from any post office or by any letter carrier.

The 1873 Comstock Law was the forerunner of many other obscenity laws and ordinances which were soon thereafter enacted at the federal, state and local government levels. In California, for example, an obscenity law was put on the books within a year after the passage of the first Comstock law.[22]

Framework of Control

Obscenity statutes, however, are by no means government's only weapons against allegedly obscene literature or material. One of the most important methods of suppression has been administrative censorship: the customs power and the Post Of-

[19] Alpert, loc. cit.

[20] 18 U.S.C.A. § 1461 (1966), See Historical and Revision Notes, p. 491.

[21] Ibid.

[22] See West's Ann.Cal.Penal Code, §§ 311–314.

fice's control of the mails.[23]   Court battles started because publications were declared non-mailable or non-importable on grounds of obscenity have played, as will be shown, a major part in attempts to judicially define just what is and what is not "obscene."   Additionally, state statutes and local ordinances forbidding the sale or possession of obscene literature or materials have also generated many court actions which have added to judge-made law on obscenity.

A statutory weapon frequently used against literature thought to be obscene is the old Comstock law as amended, now known as 18 United States Code § 1461, which makes it a crime to mail obscene material.   Enforcement of this law has been decidedly uneven and inconsistent over the years.   Often, however, the Post Office Department would start an administrative action to declare a book non-mailable instead of bringing criminal proceedings against a publisher or book-seller.   Then, if the publisher or book-seller wished to fight out the question of a book's obscenity, the courts heard appeals from the Postmaster General's actions.   This way, there was no risk of a jail sentence. The worst penalty that could befall the publisher or bookseller under the administrative procedure was exclusion of a book or magazine from the mails.[24]

But after the Supreme Court handed down its landmark obscenity decision in Roth v. United States,[25] administrative proceedings against supposedly obscene materials were largely ignored.   Instead, more and more full-scale criminal proceedings became the rule, with defendants getting sentenced to as much as twenty-five years in jail.   During the three years from 1955 through 1957, a total of 625 arrests were made under 18 U.S.C. A. § 1461.   But after the Roth decision of 1957, the next three years brought 997 arrests under that statute.   And in 1965 alone, there were 874 arrests under 18 U.S.C.A. § 1461.[26]

While federal obscenity prosecutions accelerated, there was also an increase in the number of state criminal prosecutions. It has been noted that the threat of criminal prosecution is much more likely to make merchants think twice before handling any questionable books or magazines, even those which are legally mailable and not obscene.   It is embarrassing to be charged with

23 See Paul and Schwartz, op. cit.

24 Leon Friedman, "The Ginzburg Decision and the Law," The American Scholar, Vol. 36:1 (Winter 1966–1967) p. 80.

25 Ibid., 82; See U. S. v. West Coast News Co., 357 F.2d 855, 864 (6th Cir. 1966); see Friedman, p. 82.

26 Friedman, op. cit., p. 80.

the crime of selling obscene literature, and defending against criminal prosecutions is expensive, exhausting and terrifying.[27]

The Hicklin Rule

Once the laws were passed, it was up to the American courts to decide how the laws should be applied. When obscenity cases reached the American courts, there was little American precedent to follow. So, American courts found a decision which was to lay a chilling hand on the circulation of literature for years to come: the 1868 decision, in England, in the case of Regina v. Hicklin.

In *Hicklin*, Lord Chief Justice Cockburn ruled that an anti-Catholic pamphlet, The Confessional Unmasked, was obscene. Lord Cockburn set down this test for obscenity: [28]

> whether the tendency of the matter charged as obscene is to deprave and corrupt those whose minds are open to such immoral influences and into whose hands a publication of this sort might fall.

This "Hicklin rule" was readily accepted by American courts.[29] It can be seen that this test of obscenity echoed the concepts of control voiced by Plato and St. Thomas Acquinas and seconded, with more fervor and far less intellect, by America's own Anthony Comstock. Under such a test, a book did not have to offend or harm a normal adult. If it could be assumed that a book might have a bad effect on children or abnormal adults— "those whose minds are open to such immoral influences"—such a book could be suppressed.

American law added the so-called "partly obscene" test to the *Hicklin* rule. This was the practice of judging a book by passages pulled out of context. If a book had any obscenity in it, the entire book was obscene.[30] Perhaps the most troublesome portion of the *Hicklin* rule, for Americans who tried to defend their freedom to read, was the statement that a book was obscene if it suggested "thoughts of a most impure and libidinous character." [31] This judicial preoccupation with *thoughts* induced by the reading of literature—with no requirement that

---

[27] Ibid., p. 81.

[28] L.R. 3 Q.B. 360, 370 (1868).

[29] See United States v. Bennett, 24 Fed.Cas. 1093, 1103–1104, No. 14,571 (S.D.N.Y.1879); Commonwealth v. Friede, 271 Mass. 318, 320, 171 N.E. 472, 473 (1930).

[30] Lockhart & McClure, op. cit., p. 343.

[31] Ibid., p. 339.

antisocial actions be tied to the reading matter—has continued to this time. In the law of obscenity, no harm or even likelihood of harm to readers need be shown in order to suppress a book as obscene.[32]

In 1913, Judge Learned Hand wrote an often quoted protest against the *Hicklin* rule, which he termed "mid-Victorian precedent." Although Judge Hand felt compelled to uphold the condemnation as obscene of Daniel Goodman's novel *Hagar Revelley*, the judge wrote:[33]

> I question whether in the end men will regard that as obscene which is honestly relevant to the adequate expression of innocent ideas, and whether they will not believe that truth and beauty are too precious to be mutilated in the interests of those most likely to pervert them to base uses. Indeed, it seems hardly likely that even today we are so lukewarm in our interest in letters or serious discussion to be content to reduce our treatment of sex to the standard of a child's library in the supposed interest of a salacious few, or that shame will long prevent us from adequate portrayal of some of the most serious and beautiful sides of human nature * * *.

Despite such moving protests, the *Hicklin* rule remained the leading test of obscenity in America until the 1930s.[34]

The Ulysses Decision

About this time, however, other American courts began to relax enforcement of the *Hicklin* rule to some extent. A mother who wrote a book to help her children learn about sex—and who later published the book at the suggestion of friends—successfully defended herself against charges that the book (*Sex Side of Life*) was obscene.[35] And in 1933, James Joyce's famed stream-of-consciousness novel *Ulysses*, now an acknowledged classic, was the target of an obscenity prosecution under the Tariff Act of 1930.[36]

[32] See Roth v. United States, 354 U.S. 476, 490, 77 S.Ct. 1304, 1312 (1957); see also dictum by Mr. Justice Frankfurter, Beauharnais v. Illinois, 343 U.S. 250, 266, 72 S.Ct. 725, 735 (1952).

[33] United States v. Kennerley, 209 F. 119 (S.D.N.Y.1913).

[34] See, e. g., Commonwealth v. Friede, 271 Mass. 318, 320, 171 N.E. 472, 473 (1930).

[35] United States v. Dennett, 39 F.2d 564, 76 American Law Reports 1092 (2d Cir. 1931).

[36] United States v. One Book Called "Ulysses," 5 F.Supp. 182 (S.D.N.Y. 1933); Paul and Schwartz, op. cit., p. 66.

Customs officers had prevented an actress from bringing *Ulysses* into this country. An American publishing firm, Random House, Inc., learned of the seizure of the book, intervened in the case, and pleaded that the court read the book in its entirety to see whether it was truly obscene. When *Ulysses* reached trial, Judge John Woolsey—a literate man acquainted with far more than law books—did read the entire book. He attacked the *Hicklin* test head-on and ruled that *Ulysses* was art, not obscenity. His decision has become one of the most noted in the law of criminal words, even though it by no means brought the end of the *Hicklin* rule, which continued to appear, in varying degrees of virulence, in the decisions of some other courts.[37] Overrated or not, the *Ulysses* decision represents an often cited step toward nullifying some of the most obnoxious aspects of the old *Hicklin* yardstick.

The *Ulysses* decision provided a new definition of obscenity for other courts to consider: that a book is obscene if it [38]

> tends to stir the sex impulses or to lead to sexually impure and lustful thoughts. Whether a particular book would tend to excite such impulses must be the test by the court's opinion as to its effect (when judged as a whole) on a person with average sex instincts.

Four principles of law came from the *Ulysses* decision which had not then been accepted by most other courts:

1) The purpose of the author in writing his book was taken into account. This was one way of giving a book a kind of judicial benefit of the doubt, because a court could disregard "impure" words if purity of purpose was found.

2) The opinion rejected the isolated passages ("partly obscene") standard for judging whether a book was obscene. Instead, a book was considered as a whole, by its dominant effect.

3) A book was judged by its effect on reasonable persons, not children or abnormal adults.

4) Finally, literary or artistic merit was weighed against any incidental obscenity in the book.[39]

Only one portion of the old *Hicklin* rule appeared in Judge Woolsey's *Ulysses* opinion: the emphasis on thoughts produced by a book as an indicator of a book's obscene effect on a reader. This judicial preoccupation with thoughts—and the tests out-

[37] See e. g., United States v. Two Obscene Books, 99 F.Supp. 760 (N.D.Cal. 1951), affirmed as Besig v. United States, 208 F.2d 142 (9th Cir. 1953).

[38] 5 F.Supp. 182, 184 (S.D.N.Y.1933).

[39] Ibid., pp. 182–184.

lined by Judge Woolsey in 1933—are markedly similar to rules for judging obscenity laid down in the Supreme Court's landmark decision in the 1957 case of Roth v. United States.[40]

SEC. 69.   POSTAL CENSORSHIP

For many years, the Post Office Department attempted to control obscenity through administrative censorship.

After the *Ulysses* decision, the Bureau of Customs changed its procedures. No longer would customs collectors have decision-making powers to judge the purity or impurity of a book or work of art. The Bureau of Customs hired Huntington Cairns, a literate Baltimore attorney, to serve in an advisory role as a kind of super-censor. Cairns' advice helped bring an end to confiscation of accepted though ribald literature such as Voltaire's *Candide* or books by Rabelais unless the illustrations in such books were shockingly gamy.[41]

Although the Bureau of Customs "got the message" from the *Ulysses* decision, the Post Office Department did not. Over the years, the Post Office had slowly developed a method of administrative censorship, denying the mails to publications suspected of obscenity even if prosecution was not actually intended. Postal censors thus became something of a law unto themselves. A publisher who wanted to fight the Post Office would have to hire an attorney and sue to enjoin the censors' activities.[42]

The Post Office did not hire an expert, but instead used various attorneys in the office of its Solicitor to rule whether certain publications were "obscene" and should thus be denied the mails. Among books excluded from the mails in the 1930s and early 1940s were Erskine Caldwell's *Tobacco Road* and *God's Little Acre;* and John O'Hara's *Appointment in Samarra* and Ernest Hemingway's *For Whom the Bell Tolls* were confiscated when found in the mails even though they were sold freely in bookstores. John Steinbeck's *Grapes of Wrath* was cleared for mailing, although a Post Office lawyer complained that it contained obscene passages.[43]

During World War II, however, the Post Office Department over-reached itself in trying to discipline *Esquire* magazine. In 1943, the Department attempted to withdraw second-class mail-

---

[40] 354 U.S. 476, 77 S.Ct. 1304 (1957).

[41] Paul and Schwartz, op. cit. pp. 68–69.

[42] Ibid., pp. 72–73.

[43] Ibid., pp. 69–70.

ing rates in order to punish *Esquire* for its "smoking car" humor. Post Office officials cited the "fourth qualification" for obtaining second-class rates, which said that a magazine must be "published for the dissemination of information of a public character, or devoted to literature, the sciences, arts, or some special industry * * *." [44] This qualification was interpreted by the Department to mean that a magazine had to be published for the "public good." [45] *Esquire's* publishers, fully realizing that higher mailing rates would cost them an additional $500,000 a year and might well put them out of business, went to court. [46]

Speaking for a unanimous Court, Justice William O. Douglas demolished the Post Office's contentions. Justice Douglas recognized the second-class mailing privilege as a subsidy to the press, and declared that the laws which set up the subsidy gave officials no power to set themselves up as censors by withdrawing the subsidy. Congress had not intended, Justice Douglas added, that each applicant for the second-class rate must convince the Postmaster General that his publication "positively contributes to the public good or public welfare." He added: [47]

> What is good literature, what has educational value, what is refined public information, what is good art, varies with individuals as it does from one generation to another. There doubtless would be a contrariety of views concerning Cervantes' Don Quixote, Shakespeare's Venus and Adonis, or Zola's Nana. But a requirement that literature or art conform to some norm prescribed by an official smacks of an ideology foreign to our system. The basic values implicit in the Fourth Condition [for receiving a second-class mailing permit] can be served only by uncensored distribution of literature.

Despite the *Esquire* decision, the Post Office department still has the power to withdraw the second-class privilege if a publisher mails a series of "non-mailable" issues. But in practice, this decision has meant that the Post Office department has largely given up the practice of revoking second-class permits to suppress materials which an administrator deems obscene. [48]

44 Hannegan v. Esquire, 327 U.S. 146, 148–149, 66 S.Ct. 456, 457–458 (1946).

45 327 U.S. 146, 150, 66 S.Ct. 456, 458 (1946).

46 327 U.S. 146, 151n, 66 S.Ct. 456, 459n (1946).

47 327 U.S. 146, 157–158, 66 S.Ct. 456, 462 (1946).

48 Paul and Schwartz, op. cit., pp. 76–77.

For additional information about the Post Office department concerning obscenity, see Section 75 of this chapter.

Standards of Guilt

Although the Post Office, since the *Esquire* decision, has been more cautious in its attempts to use the mailing privileges to sanitize Americans' reading matter, far thornier thickets remain in the law of obscenity. One of the most perplexing problems involves what lawyers call the question of *scienter* or "guilty knowledge:" if the obscenity statutes are so vague, how—and when—does a bookseller or distributor know when he has done something wrong? As will be shown this question has remained through the 1960s.[49]

An important case here—and one which may yet play a crucial role in the development of obscenity law—is that of Winters v. New York.[50] The *Winters* case involved a publication which allegedly provided incentive to commit the crime of indecent exposure. This decision is of interest because it held that a law restricting freedom of expression must draw standards of guilt in such a way that a person will know whether he is violating the law. The *Winters* case arose under a statute which provided that:[51]

> A person * * * who prints, publishes, sells, distributes * * * any publication * * * devoted to news, accounts of bloodshed, lust, crime * * * is guilty of a misdemeanor.

Although this statute did not deal directly with obscenity, the Supreme Court's decision in the *Winters* case seems broad enough to include at least some of the obscenity statutes within its language. Writing for a six-to-three majority, Mr. Justice Stanley J. Reed's opinion recognized that the New York law, if enforced to the letter, could punish newspapers for a routine story describing a robbery or burglary. The gist of Justice Reed's comments relating to standards of guilt may be seen in this sentence:[52]

> A failure of a statute limiting freedom of expression to give fair notice of what acts will be punished and such

---

[49] Scienter questions were raised in such cases as Ginzburg v. United States, 383 U.S. 463, 86 S.Ct. 942 (1966), and Ginsberg v. New York, 390 U.S. 629, 88 S.Ct. 1274 (1968).

[50] 333 U.S. 507, 68 S.Ct. 665 (1948).

[51] 333 U.S. 507, 508, 68 S.Ct. 665, 666 (1948).

[52] 333 U.S. 507, 509–510, 68 S.Ct. 665, 667 (1948).

statute's inclusion of prohibitions of the First Amendment, violates an accused's rights under procedural due process and freedom of speech and press.

Since *Winters,* the Supreme Court has held that for an obscenity conviction to stand, the person accused of the crime must have been shown to have had "guilty knowledge" that he was violating a law.

In the leading case discussing the element of *scienter* in obscenity prosecutions, Smith v. California, the Supreme Court declared a Los Angeles ordinance unconstitutional because it made a bookseller liable to punishment even when he did not know the contents of a book. Justice Brennan, speaking for a unanimous court, concluded that the city ordinance's " * * * elimination of the scienter requirement * * * [was] an elimination which may tend to work a substantial restriction on the freedom of speech and press." Brennan added: [53]

> For if the bookseller is criminally liable without knowledge of the contents and the ordinance fulfills its purpose, he will tend to restrict the books he sells to those he has inspected; and thus the State will have imposed a restriction upon the distribution of constitutionally protected as well as obscene literature. * * * And the bookseller's burden would become the public's burden, for by restricting him the public's access to reading matter would be restricted. If the contents of bookshops and periodical stands were restricted to material of which their proprietors had made an inspection they might be depleted indeed.

SEC. 70. THE *ROTH* LANDMARK

In Roth v. United States, the Supreme Court held that obscenity is not constitutionally protected expression and set down its most influential standard for judging what is—or is not—obscene.

Even though efforts to control obscenity have a long history in this nation, it was not until the reasonably recent date of 1957—in the case of Roth v. United States—that the Supreme Court directly upheld the constitutionality of obscenity statutes.[54]

---

[53] Smith v. California, 361 U.S. 147, 149, 153, 80 S.Ct. 215, 216 (1959). For more recent Supreme Court decisions involving questions of *scienter*, see, e. g., Ginsberg v. State of New York, 390 U.S. 629, 88 S.Ct. 1274, 1282–1283 (1968), and Miller v. California, —— U.S. ——, 93 S.Ct. 2607 (1973).

[54] 354 U.S. 476, 77 S.Ct. 1304 (1957).

This decision remains the most influential case in the law of obscenity because it declared that both state and federal anti-obscenity laws are valid exercises of government's police power.

Although this decision is customarily called "the Roth case," it embraced two cases. The Court simultaneously decided cases involving New York book dealer Samuel Roth and Los Angeles book merchant David S. Alberts.[55] Roth was indicted on 26 counts on suspicion of violating the federal obscenity statute by mailing various circulars plus a book, *American Aphrodite*. A United States district court jury convicted Roth on four of the 26 counts, and Judge John M. Cashin imposed the maximum sentence: a $5,000 fine *plus* a five-year penitentiary term. The conviction was affirmed by the United States Circuit Court of Appeals for the Second Circuit, although the great Judge Jerome Frank questioned the constitutionality of obscenity laws in a powerful concurring opinion. In words which have been called the beginning of the modern law of obscenity, Judge Frank declared that obscenity laws are unconstitutionally vague.[56] Writing with great force and humor, Judge Frank noted that Benjamin Franklin, named Postmaster General by the First Continental Congress, had written books, including *The Speech of Polly Baker*, which a 20th Century jury might find obscene. He added,[57]

> The troublesome aspect of the federal obscenity statute * * * is that (a) no one can now show that with any reasonable probability obscene publications tend to have any effects on the behavior of normal, average adults, and (b) that under the [federal] statute * * * punishment is apparently inflicted for provoking, in such adults, undesirable sexual thoughts, feelings, or desire—not overt dangerous or anti-social conduct, either actual or probable.

Despite Judge Frank's denunciation of the "exquisite vagueness" of obscenity laws, Chief Judge Clark's opinion for the Court of Appeals carried the day against Roth. Judge Clark refused to consider the contention that obscenity statutes are unconstitutionally vague curbs on speech and press. The judge held that such an argument of unconstitutionality could be considered only by the Supreme Court of the United States because

[55] United States v. Roth, 237 F.2d 796 (2d Cir 1956) ; People v. Alberts, 138 Cal.App.2d Supp. 909, 911, 292 P.2d 90, 91–92 (1956).

[56] 237 F.2d 796, 826–827 (2d Cir. 1956).

[57] Ibid., pp. 802, 806. Stanley Fleishman, "Witchcraft and Obscenity: Twin Superstitions," Wilson Library Bulletin, April, 1965, p. 4.

that Court had previously held the federal obscenity statutes to be constitutional. The Supreme Court of the United States then granted certiorari.[58]

Alberts v. California

While Roth came to grief under a federal statute, David S. Alberts had been charged with violating a state law. The California statute involved provided that anyone who "writes, composes, stereotypes, prints, publishes, sells, distributes, keeps for sale, or exhibits an obscene or indecent writing * * * is guilty of a misdemeanor." Another clause of this section forbids the advertising of obscene or indecent writings.[59]

Alberts ran a mail-order book business in Los Angeles, Calif. In 1955, he was served with a warrant and his business office, warehouse, and residence were all searched. Police seized hundreds possibly thousands—of pictures and books.[60] At the trial in Beverly Hills Municipal Court, the district attorney selected from among the items seized 31 books, a large number of pictures, and 10 magazines. These items, along with three different mail order advertising circulars, were divided into 22 exhibits. The judge found the books in two exhibits to be obscene:[61]

> Exhibit 9: [titles of books] "To Beg I Am Ashamed," "Witch on Wheels," "The Pleasures of the Torture Chamber," and "She Made It Pay."
>
> Exhibit 11. "Sword of Desire."

Although the books in these two exhibits were found obscene, the trial judge did not read them in their entirety, showing that the *Ulysses* decision's 1933 holding that a book should be judged as a whole was not always followed.[62] In discussing "Sword of Desire," the judge wrote:

> This book is about a psychiatrist who is using his ability in the touching of certain nerve centers, and so forth, to develop a sexual desire in any woman. Up to where I read he had used it twice. I did not go beyond p. 49.

[58] 352 U.S. 964, 77 S.Ct. 361 (1957).

[59] West's Ann.Cal.Pen.Code, § 311.

[60] Fleishman, op. cit., p. 10.

[61] Ibid., Alberts was tried by a judge sitting alone since Alberts had waived jury trial.

[62] United States v. One Book Entitled "Ulysses," 5 F.Supp. 182 (S.D.N.Y. 1933).

The judge added about "Snow Job," "And I suppose that I could read through the rest of the book and continue to find references to sex, because that definitely seems to be what it is for." [63]

Alberts' conviction was upheld by the Appellate Department of the Superior Court for the State of California in Los Angeles County. This court concluded that the words "obscene" and "indecent" were not unconstitutionally vague. The Supreme Court of the United States then noted probable jurisdiction over the Alberts case.[64]

In jointly considering the *Roth* and *Alberts* cases, the Court did not rule on whether the books sold by the two men were in fact obscene. The only issue reviewed in each case was the validity of an obscenity law on its face. Mr. Justice William J. Brennan wrote for a majority of the Court: [65]

> The dispositive question is whether obscenity is utterance within the area of protected speech and press. Although this is the first time this question has been squarely presented to this court, either under the First Amendment or the Fourteenth Amendment, expressions found in numerous opinions indicate that this Court has always assumed that obscenity is not protected by the freedoms of speech and press.

Alberts argued that this mail-order business could not be punished under California law because a state cannot regulate an area pre-empted by the federal obscenity laws. The majority opinion replied that the federal statute deals only with actual mailing and does not prevent a state from punishing the advertising or keeping for sale of obscene literature.[66]

Roth contended, on the other hand, that the power to punish speech and press offensive to morality belongs to the states alone under the powers of the First, Ninth, and Tenth Amendments to the Constitution. The majority opinion discarded this argument by returning to its earlier pronouncement that obscenity is not speech or expression protected by the First Amendment.[67] Justice Brennan added, in language which was to greatly affect later decisions in the law of obscenity: [68]

> All ideas having even the slightest redeeming social importance—unorthodox ideas, controversial ideas, even

[63] Justice Brennan quoting judge's charge to the jury in the original trial 911 (1956).

[64] Alberts v. California, 352 U.S. 962, 77 S.Ct. 349 (1956).

[65] 354 U.S. 476, 77 S.Ct. 1304, 1307 (1957).

[66] 354 U.S. 476, 493–494, 77 S.Ct. 1304, 1314 (1957).

[67] 354 U.S. 476, 492, 77 S.Ct. 1304, 1313 (1957).

[68] 354 U.S. 476, 484, 77 S.Ct. 1304, 1309 (1957).

ideas hateful to the prevailing climate of opinion—have
the full protection of the guaranties [of free speech
and press], unless excludable because they encroach
upon the limited area of more important interests. But
implicit in the history of the First Amendment is the
rejection of obscenity as utterly without redeeming social importance.

This passage, as will be seen in subsequent court decisions relying upon *Roth*, had within it elements of freeing literature; later cases would make much of the phrase "slightest redeeming social importance" as a lever to protect the freedom to read.[69]

Thoughts versus Actions

Both Roth and Alberts argued that obscenity laws are unconstitutional because they punish the incitation of sexual thoughts
which are not shown to be related to overt sexual conduct. In
Alberts' original trial, the judge used this test for obscenity:
whether the material has " 'a substantial tendency to deprave or
corrupt its readers by inciting lustful thoughts or arousing lustful desires.' "[70] In *Roth*, the trial judge instructed the jury:
" 'The words "obscene, lewd and lascivious" as used in the law,
signify that form of immorality which has relation to sexual impurity and has a tendency to excite lustful thoughts.' "[71]

Alberts and Roth argued that under these tests, convictions
could be had without proof that the supposedly obscene material
created a clear and present danger that antisocial acts would be
performed by readers of the material. Justice Brennan answered this contention by quoting Mr. Justice Frankfurter's dictum
in Beauharnais v. Illinois:[72]

> "Libelous utterances not being within the area of con-
> stitutionally protected speech, it is unnecessary either
> for us or for the State courts, to consider the issues be-
> hind the phrase 'clear and present danger.' Certainly,
> no one would contend that obscene speech, for example,
> may be punished only upon a showing of such circum-
> stances."

69 See, e. g., A Book Named John Cleland's "Memoirs of a Woman of Pleasure" v. Massachusetts, 383 U.S. 415, 419–420, 86 S.Ct. 975, 977–978 (1966).

70 People v. Wepplo, 78 Cal.App.2d Supp. 959, 178 P.2d 853, 855 (1947).

71 Justice Brennan quoting judge's charge to the jury in the original trial
of Samuel Roth, 354 U.S. 476, 486, 77 S.Ct. 1304, 1309 (1957).

72 343 U.S. 250, 266, 72 S.Ct. 725, 735 (1952), quoted at 354 U.S. 476, 486–487,
77 S.Ct. 1304, 1310 (1957).

Although the majority opinion approved the tests which the lower courts had used in convicting Alberts and Roth, the Supreme Court added a third definition: "Obscene material is material which deals with sex in a manner appealing to prurient interest." [73]

The Roth Test

Then Justice Brennan set down the crucial words of the *Roth* decision: words which have become the key to judicial attempts to define the obscene. Brennan implied that the proper standard for judging obscenity should focus on thoughts, not actions: [74]

> * * * whether to the average person, applying contemporary community standards, the dominant theme of the material taken as a whole appeals to prurient interest.

Subsequent decisions have returned to these words again and again for guidance. This *"Roth* test" rejected some features of the American rendition of the *Hicklin* rule. The practice of judging books by the presumed effect of isolated passages upon the most susceptible persons was rejected because it "might well encompass material legitimately dealing with sex." [75]

Although the language of the *Roth* test, as will be shown, was used in later decisions to uphold the freedom to read, Mr. Justice Brennan's words were not wholly libertarian. The *Roth* test, instead, is a "deprave and corrupt" test. Under *Roth,* a book could be declared obscene if it could be assumed that it might induce obscene thoughts in an hypothetical average person.[76] There is no need for the prosecution to prove that there is a "clear and present danger" [77] or even a "clear and possible danger" [78] that a book will lead to antisocial conduct. Even so,

[73] 354 U.S. 476, 487, 77 S.Ct. 1304, 1310 (1957). The terms used in the three "tests" approved in Roth—"lustful desire," "lustful thoughts," and "appeal to prurient interest"—all imply that if a book can be assumed to cause or induce "improper" sexual thoughts, that book can be "banned." The "appeal to prurient interest" test was drawn from the American Law Institute's Model Penal Code, Tentative Draft No. 6 (Philadelphia, American Law Institute, May 6, 1957).

[74] 354 U.S. 476, 77 S.Ct. 1304, 1311 (1957).

[75] 354 U.S. 476, 489, 77 S.Ct. 1304, 1311 (1957).

[76] 354 U.S. 476, 486, 77 S.Ct. 1304, 1310 (1957).

[77] 354 U.S. 476, 486, 77 S.Ct. 1304, 1310 (1957).

[78] 354 U.S. 476, 77 S.Ct. 1304, 1310 (1957), citing Dennis v. United States, 341 U.S. 494, 71 S.Ct. 857 (1952).

Justice Brennan's *Roth* test has had, for the most part, a freeing effect on literature.[79]

Roth: Concurrences and Dissents

Chief Justice Earl Warren was evidently bemused by the idea that *books* rather than men, were defendants in obscenity prosecutions. His brief concurring opinion in *Roth* has proved to be remarkably influential since 1957. Chief Justice Warren stated that in an obscenity trial, the conduct of the defendant rather than the obscenity of a book should be the central issue:[80]

> The nature of the materials is, of course, relevant as an attribute of the defendant's conduct, but the materials are thus placed in context from which they draw their color and character. A wholly different result might be reached in a different setting * * *.

The Chief Justice concluded that both Roth and Alberts had engaged in "the commercial exploitation of the morbid and shameful craving for materials with prurient effect" and said that the state and federal governments could constitutionally punish such conduct.[81] Justice Brennan's majority opinion in *Roth* has influenced the course of the law of obscenity. So, in an increasing degree in recent years, has Chief Justice Warren's concurring opinion, which insisted that the behavior of the defendant, rather than the nature of the book itself, was the "central issue" in an obscenity case.[82] The impact of the legal formulations in *Roth* by Justice Brennan and Chief Justice Warren will be discussed later in this chapter.

The cases of Samuel Roth and David S. Alberts were decided jointly by the Supreme Court, but Justice John Marshall Harlan distinguished between the two contests. Justice Harlan wrote an opinion which concurred in the *Alberts* case and which dissented in *Roth*. This meant that Harlan would have upheld the California conviction of Alberts, while freeing Roth. The basis of Justice Harlan's opinion was his conviction that the states, not Congress, have the power to protect sexual morality. He contended that it is not dangerous if one state, through its legislature, decides that a book such as *Lady Chatterly's Lover* is so offensive that it should be banned. Other states, however, would be free to make their own decisions about the book.

[79] See footnote 93 in Section 74 later in this chapter.

[80] 354 U.S. 476, 495, 77 S.Ct. 1304, 1315 (1957).

[81] 354 U.S. 476, 496, 77 S.Ct. 1304, 1315 (1957).

[82] 354 U.S. 476, 495, 77 S.Ct. 1304, 1314–1315 (1957).

Justice Harlan also disagreed with the majority opinion's conclusion that obscenity laws are constitutional because an earlier Supreme Court had found that obscenity is "utterly without redeeming social importance": [83]

> This sweeping formula appears to me to beg the very question before us. The Court seems to assume that "obscenity" is a particular *genus* of speech and press, which is as distinct, recognizable and classifiable as poison ivy is among plants. On this basis, the *constitutional* question before us becomes, as the Court says, whether "obscenity," as an abstraction, is protected by the First and Fourteenth Amendments, and the question whether a *particular* book may be suppressed becomes a mere matter of classification, of "fact" to be entrusted to a fact-finder and insulated from independent judgment.

Justice Harlan thus told his fellow justices that the vital question was "what is obscenity?" not "is obscenity good or bad?"

While Harlan asked this challenging question of his brethren on the Court, Justice William O. Douglas was joined by Justice Hugo L. Black in a scathing attack on obscenity laws and obscenity prosecutions. This dissent foreshadowed arguments these Justices would advance in obscenity cases which subsequently followed *Roth* to the Supreme Court: [84]

> When we sustain these convictions, we make the legality of a publication turn on the purity of thought which a book or tract instills in the mind of the reader. I do not think we can approve that standard and be faithful to the command of the First Amendment which by its terms is a restraint on Congress and which by the Fourteenth Amendment is a restraint on the States.

Douglas wrote that Roth and Alberts were punished "for thoughts provoked, not for overt acts nor antisocial conduct." He was unimpressed by the possibility that the books involved might produce sexual thoughts: "The arousing of sexual thoughts and desires happens every day in normal life in dozens of ways." [85] Justice Douglas added: [86]

> The absence of dependable information on the effect of obscene literature should make us wary. It should put

[83] 354 U.S. 476, 497, 77 S.Ct. 1304, 1315 (1957).

[84] 354 U.S. 476, 508, 77 S.Ct. 1304, 1321 (1957).

[85] 354 U.S. 476, 509, 77 S.Ct. 1304, 1322 (1957).

[86] 354 U.S. 476, 511, 77 S.Ct. 1304, 1323 (1957).

us on the side of protecting society's interest in literature, except and unless it can be said that the particular publication has an impact on action that the government can control.

Problems involving freedom of speech and press, it was
argued, must not be solved by "weighing against the values of
free expression, the judgment of a court that a particular form
of expression has 'no redeeming social importance.'" Justice
Douglas warned: [87]

> For the test that suppresses a cheap tract today can
> suppress a literary gem tomorrow. All it need do is in-
> cite a lascivious thought or arouse a lustful desire.
> The list of books that judges or juries can place in that
> category is endless.

SEC. 71. PATENT OFFENSIVENESS

**In the Manual Enterprises case, the Supreme Court added a new
element—"patent offensiveness"—to its attempts to define
obscenity.**

Although *Roth* remains the leading decision on obscenity and
said much, subsequent court decisions showed that it had settled
little. Five years after *Roth* the Supreme Court attempted to
refine its definition of obscenity in Manual Enterprises, Inc. v.
J. Edward Day, Postmaster General of the United States. In
writing for the Court, Justice Harlan termed *MANual* [sic],
Trim, and *Grecian Pictorial* "dismally unpleasant, uncouth and
tawdry" magazines which were published "primarily, if not exclusively, for homosexuals." [88]

Despite this, a majority of the Supreme Court held that these
magazines which presented pictures of nude males were not obscene and unmailable because they were not "patently offensive."
Harlan wrote: [89]

> These magazines cannot be deemed so offensive on their
> face as to affront current community standards of
> decency—a quality that we shall hereafter refer to as
> "patent offensiveness" or "indecency." Lacking that
> quality, the magazines cannot be deemed legally ob-
> scene * * *.

*   *   *   *   *   *   *   *

[87] 354 U.S. 476, 514, 77 S.Ct. 1304, 1324 (1957).

[88] 370 U.S. 478, 481, 82 S.Ct. 1432, 1434 (1962).

[89] 370 U.S. 478, 482–486, 82 S.Ct. 1432, 1434–1436 (1962).

> Obscenity under the federal statute * * * requires proof of two distinct elements: (1) patent offensiveness; and (2) "prurient interest" appeal. Both must conjoin before challenged material can be found obscene under § 1461. In most obscenity cases to be sure, the two elements tend to coalesce, for that which is patently offensive will also usually carry the requisite "prurient interest" appeal. It is only in the unusual instance where, as here, the "prurient interest" appeal of the material is limited to a particular class of persons that occasion arises for a truly independent inquiry into the question of whether or not the material is patently offensive.

Harlan reaffirmed the Supreme Court's long-held position that mere nudity was not enough to support a conviction for obscenity.[90]

> Divorced from their "prurient interest" appeal to the unfortunate persons whose patronage they were aimed at capturing (a separate issue), these portrayals of the male nude cannot fairly be regarded as more objectionable than many portrayals of the female nude that society tolerates. Of course every portrayal of male or female nudity is not obscene.

After adding the "patent offensiveness" qualification to its definition of obscenity, the Court then turned to the tricky problem of giving meaning to the "contemporary community standards" phrase used in *Roth*. This time, a movie—the French film called *"Les Amants"* ("The Lovers") was the vehicle of expression which confronted the Court. Nico Jacobellis, manager of a Cleveland, Ohio, motion picture theater, had been convicted under Ohio law on two counts of possessing and exhibiting an obscene film. Jacobellis had been fined a total of $2,500 and his conviction was upheld by the Ohio Supreme Court.[91]

Writing for the Supreme Court in reversing Jacobellis' conviction, Mr. Justice Brennan ruled that the film was not obscene. He rejected the argument that the "contemporary community standards" aspect of the *Roth* test implied "a determination of the constitutional question of obscenity in each case by the standards of the particular local community from which the case arises." Brennan held that no " 'local' definition of the 'commu-

---

[90] 370 U.S. 478, 490, 82 S.Ct. 1432, 1438 (1962).

[91] 378 U.S. 184, 84 S.Ct. 1676 (1964).

nity' could properly be employed in delineating the area of expression that is protected by the Federal Constitution." [92]

> The Court has explicitly refused to tolerate a result whereby "the constitutional limits of free expression in the Nation would vary with state lines. * * * we see even less justification for allowing such limits to vary with town or county lines. We thus reaffirm the position taken in *Roth* to the effect that the constitutional status of an allegedly obscene work must be determined on the basis of a national standard. It is, after all, a national Constitution we are expounding.[93]

Despite these brave words, a majority of the Court failed to agree with Brennan that there should be a national standard for judging obscenity. On March 21, 1966, the Supreme Court again tackled the tough problem of defining obscenity as decisions were announced in three cases, the *"Fanny Hill"* case,[94] Mishkin v. State of New York,[95] and Ginzburg v. United States.[96]

SEC. 72.   FROM CONTENT TO CONDUCT: *FANNY HILL* TO *GINSBERG v. NEW YORK*

> From 1966 into 1968, the Supreme Court shifted its emphasis from attempting to judge the *content* of a publication to trying to gauge the character of a bookseller's or distributor's actions or *conduct*.

First announced was the decision in the *Fanny Hill* case, in which the Supreme Court had to deal with one of the most durable wenches in Anglo-American literary history. *Fanny Hill,* or, as the book is sometimes known, *Memoirs of a Woman of Pleasure,* was written in England about 1749 by John Cleland. The book came to be well known in the American colonies, and was first published in America sometime around 1800 by Isaiah Thomas, of Worcester, Massachusetts, of the foremost printers of the American Revolution.[97]   *Fanny Hill,* it should be noted, was also the first book in America to be the subject of an obscenity trial: in Massachusetts in 1821.[98]   More than 140 years

---

[92] 378 U.S. 184, 84 S.Ct. 1676, 1677 (1964).

[93] 378 U.S. 184, 194–195, 84 S.Ct. 1676, 1682 (1964).

[94] 383 U.S. 413, 86 S.Ct. 975 (1966).

[95] 383 U.S. 502, 86 S.Ct. 958 (1966).

[96] 383 U.S. 463, 86 S.Ct. 942 (1966).

[97] Peter Quennell, introduction to John Cleland's Memoirs of a Woman of Pleasure (New York: Putnam, 1963) p. xv.

[98] Commonwealth v. Peter Holmes, 17 Mass. 336 (1821).

later, *Fanny Hill* was back in the courts of Massachusetts, as well as in New York, New Jersey and Illinois.[99]

Fanny Hill, in one respect, was an oddity among books which are involved in obscenity cases. There is not one of the "four letter words" which have so often put more modern literature than *Fanny Hill* before the courts. But although the language of *Fanny Hill* was quite sanitary, author Cleland's descriptions of Fanny's bedroom performances left little to the imagination. Even so, some experts—including poet and critic Louis Untermeyer—testified that *Fanny Hill* was a work of art and was not pornographic. The experts, however, were asked by a cross-examining prosecuting attorney if they realized that the book contained "20 acts of sexual intercourse, four of them in the presence of others; four acts of lesbianism, two acts of male homosexuality, two acts of flagellation and one of female masturbation." [1]

Fanny Hill, then, is a frankly erotic novel. In the best constructed decision of the three the Court handed down on March 21, 1966, Justice Brennan summed up the tests for obscenity which the highest court had approved: [2]

> We defined obscenity in *Roth* in the following terms: "[W]hether to the average person, applying contemporary community standards, the dominant theme of the material taken as a whole appeals to prurient interest." 354 U.S. at 489; 77 S.Ct. at 1311. Under this definition, as elaborated in subsequent cases, three elements must coalesce: it must be established that (a) the dominant theme of the materials taken as a whole appeals to a prurient interest in sex; (b) the material is patently offensive because it affronts contemporary community standards relating to the description or representation of sexual matters; and (c) the material is utterly without redeeming social value.

In considering *Fanny Hill*, the Massachusetts trial court held the book to be "obscene, indecent and impure," and "utterly without redeeming social importance." By a 4–3 vote, the Supreme Judicial Court, Massachusetts' highest court, upheld the ruling that *Fanny Hill* was obscene.

[99] These prosecutions, as Justice Douglas pointed out, seemed a bit ironic in view of the fact that the Library of Congress had asked permission to translate the book into braille. 383 U.S. 413, 425–426, 86 S.Ct. 975, 981 (1966).

[1] Cf. the outraged dissent by Justice Tom C. Clark, 383 U.S. 413, 445–446, 86 S.Ct. 975, 990–991 (1966).

[2] 383 U.S. 413, 418, 86 S.Ct. 975, 977 (1966).

The Supreme Court of the United States, however, held that the Massachusetts courts had erred in finding that a book didn't have to be "unqualifiedly worthless" before it could be deemed obscene. Justice Brennan, writing for the Court, stated that a book "can not be proscribed unless it is found to be *utterly* without redeeming social value." [3]

Next, Mr. Justice Brennan announced the Court's decision in the *Mishkin* case. Edward Mishkin, who operated a bookstore near New York City's Times Square, was appealing a sentence of three years and $12,500 in fines. Mishkin's publishing specialty was sadism and masochism, and he had been found guilty by New York courts of producing and selling more than 50 different paperbacks. Titles involved included *Dance With the Dominant Whip, Cult of the Spankers, Swish Bottom, Mrs. Tyrant's Finishing School* and *Stud Broad.* [4]

Mishkin had instructed one author working for him that the books should be " 'full of sex scenes and lesbian scenes * * *. [T]he sex had to be very strong, it had to be rough, it had to be clearly spelled out.' " [5] Mishkin's defense, however, was based on the notion that the books he published and sold did not appeal to the prurient interest of an average person. The average person, it was argued, would be disgusted and sickened by such books.[6]

Justice Brennan's majority opinion, however, dismissed Mishkin's argument.[7]

> Where the material is designed primarily for and primarily disseminated to a clearly defined deviant sexual group, rather than the public at large, the prurient-appeal requirement of the *Roth* test is satisfied if the dominant theme of the material taken as a whole appeals to the prurient interest of the members of that group.
>
> *   *   *   *   *   *   *   *   *
>
> In regard to the prurient-appeal requirement, the concept of the "average" or "normal" person was employed in *Roth* to serve the essentially negative purpose of expressing our rejection of that aspect of the *Hicklin* test * * * that made the impact on the most

---

[3] 383 U.S. 413, 419, 86 S.Ct. 975, 978 (1966).

[4] 383 U.S. 502, 514–515, 86 S.Ct. 975, 978 (1966).

[5] 383 U.S. 502, 505, 86 S.Ct. 958, 961 (1966).

[6] 383 U.S. 502, 508, 86 S.Ct. 958, 963 (1966).

[7] 383 U.S. 502, 508–509, 86 S.Ct. 958, 963–964 (1966).

susceptible person determinative. We adjust the prurient-appeal requirement to social realities by permitting the appeal of this type of material to be assessed in terms of sexual interests of its intended and probable recipient group.

After upholding Mishkin's conviction, Mr. Justice Brennan then turned to the *Ginzburg* case. With this opinion, the Supreme Court brought another element to the adjudication of obscenity disputes: the manner in which the matter charged with obscenity was sold. Justice Brennan wrote:

> * * * the question of obscenity may include consideration of the setting in which the publications were presented as an aid to determining the question of obscenity, and [we] assume without deciding that the prosecution could not have succeeded otherwise.[8]

The *Ginzburg* case involved three publications: "EROS, a hard-cover magazine of expensive format; Liaison, a bi-weekly newsletter; and The Housewife's Handbook on Selective Promiscuity, * * * a short book." Justice Brennan took notice of "abundant evidence" from Ralph Ginzburg's federal district court trial "that each of the accused publications was originated or sold as stock in trade of the sordid business of pandering— 'the business of purveying textual or graphic matter openly advertised to appeal to the erotic interest of their customers.' "[9]

Included as evidence of this "pandering" were EROS magazine's attempts to get mailing privileges from the whimsically named hamlets of Intercourse and Blue Ball, Pa. Mailing privileges were finally obtained in Middlesex, N. J.[10]

Also, Justice Brennan found " 'the leer of the sensualist' " permeating the advertising for the three publications. *Liaison,* for example, was extolled as "Cupid's Chronicle," and the advertising circulars asked, "Are you a member of the sexual elite?"[11] It is likely, however, that publisher Ginzburg believed that the *Roth* test had left him on safe ground, for his advertising proclaimed:[12]

> "EROS handles the subjects of Love and Sex with complete candor. The publication of this magazine—which is frankly and avowedly concerned with erotica—has

[8] 383 U.S. 463, 465–466, 86 S.Ct. 942, 944–945 (1966).

[9] 383 U.S. 463, 467, 86 S.Ct. 942, 945 (1966).

[10] 383 U.S. 463, 467, 86 S.Ct. 942, 945 (1966).

[11] 383 U.S. 463, 469n, 86 S.Ct. 942, 946n (1966).

[12] Ibid.

been enabled by recent court decisions ruling that a literary piece or painting, though explicitly sexual in content, has a right to be published if it is a genuine work of art."

"EROS is genuine work of art."

The Court was severely split over the *Ginzburg* case, however, with Justices Black, Douglas, Harlan and Stewart all registering bitter dissents. Justice Black set the tone for his dissenting brethren, declaring: [13]

> Only one stark fact emerges with clarity out of the confusing welter of opinions and thousands of words written in this and two other cases today. * * * That fact is that Ginzburg, petitioner here, is now finally and authoritatively condemned to serve five years in prison for distributing printed matter about sex which neither Ginzburg nor anyone else could possibly have known to be criminal.

Justice Harlan accused the Court's majority of rewriting the federal obscenity statute in order to convict Ginzburg, and called the new "pandering" test unconstitutionally vague.[14] And Justice Stewart asserted in his dissent that Ginzburg "was not charged with 'commercial exploitation'; he was not charged with 'pandering'; he was not charged with 'titillation.'" Convicting Ginzburg on such grounds, Stewart added, was to deny him due process of law.[15]

Justice Douglas added his denunciation of the condemnation of materials as obscene not because of their content, but because of the way they were advertised.[16]

> The advertisements of our best magazines are chockfull of thighs, ankles, calves, bosoms, eyes, and hair, to draw the potential buyers' attention to lotions, tires, food, liquor, clothing, autos, and even insurance policies. * * * And I do not see how it adds or detracts from the legality of the book being distributed. A book should stand on its own, irrespective of the reasons why it was written or the wiles used in selling it. I cannot imagine any promotional effort that would make chapters 7 and 8 of the Song of Solomon any the less or any more worthy of First Amendment protec-

[13] 383 U.S. 463, 476, 86 S.Ct. 942, 954 (1966).

[14] 383 U.S. 463, 476, 86 S.Ct. 942, 954 (1966).

[15] 383 U.S. 463, 494, 86 S.Ct. 942, 954 (1966).

[16] 383 U.S. 463, 494, 497, 86 S.Ct. 942, 954, 956 (1966).

tion than does   its unostentatious inclusion in the average edition of the Bible.

Protecting the Young: The Ginsberg Case and the "Variable Obscenity" Concept

As if to confound careless spellers, it has happened that one of the most important cases after the Ralph *Ginzburg* case involved a man named *Ginsberg*: Sam Ginsberg.   In the 1968 *Ginsberg* case, the Supreme Court held by a 6–3 vote that a New York statute which defined obscenity on the basis of its appeal to minors under 17 was not unconstitutionally vague.

Sam Ginsberg and his wife operated "Sam's Stationery and Luncheonette" in Bellmore, Long Island.   In 1965, a mother sent her 16-year-old son to the luncheonette to buy some "girlie" magazines.   The boy purchased two magazines—apparently *Sir* and *Gent* or similar publications—and walked out of the luncheonette.   On the basis of this sale, Sam Ginsberg was convicted of violation of a New York law making it a misdemeanor "knowingly to sell * * * to a minor" under 17 "any picture * * * which depicts nudity * * * and which is harmful to minors" and "any * * * magazine * * * which contains * * * [such pictures] and which, taken as a whole, is harmful to minors." [17]

It should be noted that magazines such as the 16-year-old boy purchased from Sam Ginsberg's luncheonette had recently been held *not* obscene for adults by the Supreme Court.[18]   However, the judge at Sam Ginsberg's obscenity trial found pictures in the two magazines which depicted nudity in a manner that was in violation of the New York statute which forbids [19]

> "the showing of * * * female * * * buttocks with less than a full opaque covering, or the showing of the female breast with less than a fully opaque covering of any portion thereof below the top of the nipple * * * "

Additionally, the trial judge found that the pictures were "harmful to minors," because they had, under the terms of the New York law,[20]

[17] Ginsberg v. New York, 390 U.S. 629, 634, 88 S.Ct. 1274, 1277 (1968).   The statute is Article 484–H of the New York Penal Law, McKinney's Consol. Laws c. 40.

[18] Redrup v. New York, 386 U.S. 767, 87 S.Ct. 1414 (1967).

[19] Ginsberg v. New York, 390 U.S. 629, 632, 88 S.Ct. 1274, 1276 (1968), quoting New York Penal Law Article 484–h as enacted by L.1965, c. 327, subsections (b) and (f).

[20] 390 U.S. 629, 633, 88 S.Ct. 1274, 1276 (1968).

that quality of * * * representation * * * of
nudity * * * [which] * * * (i) predominant-
ly appeals to the prurient, shameful or morbid interest
of minors, and (ii) is patently offensive to prevailing
standards in the adult community as a whole with respect to what is suitable material for minors, and (iii)
is utterly without redeeming social importance for minors.

In affirming Ginsberg's conviction, Justice Brennan approved
the concept of "variable obscenity." In a footnote, he recognized that this concept had been developed by two University of
Minnesota law professors, William B. Lockhart and Robert C.
McClure, who wrote: [21]

Variable obscenity * * * furnishes a useful tool
for dealing with the problem of denying adolescents access to material aimed at a primary audience of sexually mature adults. For variable obscenity focuses attention upon the make-up of primary and peripheral
audiences in varying circumstances, and provides a reasonably satisfactory means for delineating the obscene
in each circumstance.

Brennan noted that the magazines involved in the *Ginsberg* case
were not obscene for sale to adults. However, the New York
statute forbidding their sale to minors "does not bar the appellant from stocking the magazines and selling them to persons 17
years of age or older." Brennan also reiterated the holding that
obscenity is not within the area of protected speech or press.[22]
He added that it was permissible for the state of New York to
"accord to minors under 17 a more restricted right than that assured to adults to judge and determine for themselves what sex
material they may read or see." Justice Brennan concluded that
the Court could not say that the New York statute invades the
"area of freedom of expression constitutionally secured to
minors." [23]

Finally, Justice Brennan disposed of arguments for Ginsberg
that the New York law's *scienter* requirements were such that
an honest distributor of publications might violate the law by

[21] 390 U.S. 629, 635n, 88 S.Ct. 1274, 1278n (1968), quoting Lockhart and Mc-
Clure, "Censorship of Obscenity: The Developing Constitutional Standards,"
45 Minnesota Law Review 5, 85 (1960).

[22] 390 U.S. 629, 635, 88 S.Ct. 1274, 1277–1278 (1968); see Butler v. Michigan,
352 U.S. 380, 77 S.Ct. 524 (1957); Roth v. United States, 354 U.S. 476, 485, 77
S.Ct. 1304, 1309 (1957).

[23] 390 U.S. 629, 637, 88 S.Ct. 1274, 1279 (1968).

mistake.   But Brennan replied: "As is required by Smith v. People of State of California   *   *   *   [the New York law] prohibits only those sales made 'knowingly.' " [24]   Brennan expressed satisfaction that Ginsberg had received adequate warning that he was committing a crime: under Section 484–h of the New York law prohibiting sales to minors, he should have had a "reason to know" or a "belief or ground for belief which warrants further inspection" before making the sale of the girlie magazines to a youth.[25]   It would seem that this definition of *scienter* requirement regarding an obscenity statute is a marked narrowing of *scienter* requirements set down in Smith v. California.[26]

Thus the Supreme Court, by late 1968, appeared to be taking a tougher stand on the distribution of literature.   In the case which resulted in the fining and jailing of *Eros* publisher Ralph Ginzburg, the Supreme Court served notice that not only *what* was sold but *how* it was sold would be taken into account.[27]   The *how* of selling or distributing literature can include a legitimate public concern over the materials which minor children see. That is the lesson of the case of Ginsberg v. New York, and that lesson is wrapped up in the concept of "variable obscenity." That is, some materials are not obscene for adults but are obscene when children are involved.[28]   Difficulties in the concept of "variable obscenity" are readily apparent: will this now mean that adolescents will have to show an ID card—or a note demonstrating parental consent—to check out books at a public library?   And which books and authors would be placed in this troublesome category of being "variably obscene?"   Rabelais? Twain?   Hemingway?   Steinbeck?   Or merely Ralph Ginzburg?

SEC. 73.   INDECISIVENESS ON OBSCENITY: *REDRUP* AND *STANLEY*

From 1967 until 1973, many convictions were reversed by the Supreme Court of the United States because a majority could not agree upon a definition of obscenity.

In the spring of 1967, the Supreme Court of the United States openly admitted its confusion over problems in the law of ob-

---

[24] 390 U.S. 629, 643, 88 S.Ct. 1274, 1283 (1968).

[25] Ibid.

[26] 361 U.S. 147, 80 S.Ct. 215, 216, 218–219 (1959).

[27] Ginzburg v. United States, 383 U.S. 463, 86 S.Ct. 942 (1966).

[28] Ginsberg v. New York, 390 U.S. 629, 88 S.Ct. 1274 (1968).

scenity, in the case known as Redrup v. New York.[29] This decision did not *look* important: it took up only six pages in *United States Reports* and only about four pages were devoted to its *per curiam* [unsigned "by the court"] majority opinion. The other two pages were given over to a dissent by the late Justice John Marshall Harlan, with whom the now-retired Justice Tom C. Clark joined.[30] Redrup was an important case, not because of what the Court said in defining obscenity, but because the Court was unable to agree on a standard which could declare "girlie magazines" and similar publications to be obscene.

Redrup seemed for a time to be the most important obscenity case since Roth v. United States because it was used by both state and federal courts for several years to avoid many of the complexities of judging whether works of art or literature are obscene. On June 12, 1967, the date the Court's term ended that year and less than two months after Redrup was decided, the Court reversed 11 obscenity convictions by merely referring to Redrup v. New York.[31] Another dozen state or federal obscenity convictions were reversed during the next year, with Redrup being listed as an important factor in each reversal.[32]

Redrup's unsigned majority opinion was merely a sketchy review of the varying—and sometimes contradictory—attempts made by the Court to define obscenity. After reviewing the justices' differing views on the subject, the *Redrup* majority opinion took a new tack. The Court ruled that no matter what test was applied to the sexy paperback novels (*Lust Pool* and *Shame Agent*) or girlie magazines (*Gent, High Heels, Spree*) before the Court, the convictions for obscenity reviewed in *Redrup* simply could not be upheld. The unsigned majority opinion concluded, "Whichever of these constitutional views [definitions of obscenity listed sketchily in the *Redrup* opinion] are brought to bear upon the cases before us, it is clear that the judgments [obscenity convictions in the lower courts] before us cannot stand.[33]

The *Redrup* case, as later applied by the Supreme Court, appeared to have at least one of two meanings. Either a majority of the justices did not believe the publications coming before it were obscene,[34] or the publications were not sold in such a "pan-

---

[29] 386 U.S. 767, 87 S.Ct. 1414 (1967).

[30] 386 U.S. 767, 771, 87 S.Ct. 1414, 1416 (1967).

[31] Dwight L. Teeter, Jr., and Don R. Pember, "The Retreat from Obscenity: Redrup v. New York," Hastings Law Journal Vol. 21 (Nov., 1969) pp. 175–189.

[32] 386 U.S. 767, 771–772, 87 S.Ct. 1414, 1416–1417 (1967).

[33] 386 U.S. 767, 87 S.Ct. 1414, 1416 (1967).

[34] Cf. Memoirs v. Massachusetts, 383 U.S. 413, 418–419, 86 S.Ct. 975, 977 (1966); Roth v. United States, 354 U.S. 476, 489, 77 S.Ct. 1304, 1311 (1957).

dering" fashion as to make them legitimate targets for obscenity prosecutions.[35]

The majority opinion in *Redrup*, although it is by no means a clear statement of the Court's intent, appeared to place significant reliance upon its 1966 decision in Ginzburg v. United States. In *Ginzburg,* discussed earlier in this chapter, it will be recalled that the Court took special notice of the *manner* in which magazines or books were sold.[36] *Redrup* echoed this concern, but also took into account the *recipients* of materials charged with obscenity. The Court suggested that convictions for selling or mailing obscenity should be upheld in three kinds of situations:

1) Where there is evidence of "pandering" sales as in Ginzburg v. United States.

2) Where there is a statute reflecting "a specific and limited state concern for juveniles." [37]

3) Where there is "an assault upon individual privacy by publication in a manner so obtrusive as to make it impossible for the unwilling individual to avoid exposure to it.[38]

Beyond these kinds of forbidden conduct—"pandering," selling to minors which violates a carefully, narrowly drawn statute, or somehow invading privacy with a publication—*Redrup* gives little guidance. Perhaps, however, it may be hazarded that Redrup meant this: If the *conduct* of the seller did not offend the three kinds of prohibited actions listed above, and if the *contents* were not so wretched that they would be held to be "hardcore pornography," [39] then the materials involved are con-

[35] Cf. Ginzburg v. United States, 383 U.S. 463, 86 S.Ct. 942 (1966).

[36] 383 U.S. 463, 86 S.Ct. 942 (1966).

[37] Redrup v. New York, 386 U.S. 767, 769, 87 S.Ct. 1414, 1415 (1967). Note that (2) above, announced in Redrup on May 8, 1967, forecasts with considerable precision the Court's decision in Ginsberg v. New York, 390 U.S. 629, 88 S.Ct. 1274 (1968).

[38] Ibid., citing Breard v. Alexandria, 341 U.S. 622, 71 S.Ct. 920 (1951), and Public Utilities Commission v. Pollak, 343 U.S. 415, 72 S.Ct. 813 (1952).

[39] 386 U.S. 767, 771n, 87 S.Ct. 1414, 1416n, referring to Justice Potter Stewart's quotation, in his dissent in Ginzburg v. United States, of this definition of hardcore pornography, including writings and "photographs, both still and motion picture, with no pretense of artistic value, graphically depicting acts of sexual intercourse, including various acts of sodomy and sadism, and sometimes involving several participants in scenes of orgy-like character. * * * verbally describing such activities in a bizarre manner with no attempt whatsoever to afford portrayals of character or situation and with no pretense to literary value." See Ginzburg v. United States, 383 U.S. 463, 499n, 86 S.Ct. 942, 956n (1966).

stitutionally protected. As the Court said in *Redrup*, the publications involved in that case are "protected by the First and Fourteenth Amendments from governmental suppression." [40]

Even though the words of *Redrup* are unclear, the impact of that decision was sharp and distinct: *Redrup* was used repeatedly as controlling precedent in reversing obscenity convictions.

In the summer of 1969, there seemed to be hope that the Supreme Court of the United States—obviously out-of-sorts with its role as the "High Court of Obscenity"—would bring a modicum of order to that troublesome area of law. Indeed, the Supreme Court's wish to retreat from writing such frequent obscenity decisions had become apparent in Redrup v. New York [41] and in Stanley v. Georgia. [42]

Since, significant changes have occurred in the law, and those changes seem to be bad news for defendants in obscenity cases. Two themes may be discerned:

1) The Supreme Court, in three cases decided on February 23, 1971, tied the hands of federal courts, making it far more difficult for them to squelch obscenity prosecutions at the state and local level.

2) In two cases decided May 3, 1971, the Supreme Court explicitly returned to that 1957 "landmark," Roth v. United States. [43] In so doing, the Court reiterated the notion that obscenity can be defined, and that once defined, can be prohibited.

Revitalizing State Power Over Obscenity

In the wake of the Redrup and Stanley cases, state power in obscenity prosecutions was waning. The Stanley case arose in 1966 when a Georgia state investigator and three federal agents, operating under a federal search warrant, searched the home of Robert E. Stanley, looking for bookmaking records. Evidence of bookmaking was not found, but the searchers found three reels of 8 millimeter film and—handily—a projector. They treated themselves to a showing and decided that the films were obscene. When Stanley's appeal reached the Supreme Court,

40 386 U.S. 767, 770, 87 S.Ct. 1414, 1416 (1967).

41 386 U.S. 767, 87 S.Ct. 1414 (1967).

42 394 U.S. 557, 89 S.Ct. 1243 (1969).

43 354 U.S. 476, 77 S.Ct. 1304 (1957).

Mr. Justice Thurgood Marshall—writing for a unanimous court [44] named two constitutional rights:

1) A right growing out of the First Amendment, a "right to receive information and ideas, regardless of their social worth." [45]

2) A constitutional right to privacy tied to the right to receive information and ideas: [46]

> * * * [F]undamental is the right to be free, except in very limited circumstances, from unwanted governmental intrusions into one's privacy. * * * These are the rights that appellant [Stanley] is asserting. * * * the right to satisfy his intellectual and emotional needs in the privacy of his own home.

Because Stanley v. Georgia involved no dangers of either injuring minors or invading the privacy of the general public, the Supreme Court concluded: [47]

> We hold that the First and Fourteenth Amendments prohibit making mere private possession of obscene material a crime. Roth and the cases following that decision are not impaired by today's holding. As we have said, the States retain broad power to regulate obscenity; that power simply does not extend to mere possession by the individual in the privacy of his own home.

As 1971 decisions of the Supreme Court have shown, by way of hindsight, the last two sentences quoted above should have received closer attention from a number of courts which instead jumped at the phrase "right to receive information and ideas, regardless of their social worth." The Stanley case, it should be emphasized, is now regarded by the Supreme Court as more of a privacy decision than an obscenity decision. The High Court has now rebuffed efforts to read a great liberalization of obscenity doctrine into the Stanley case.

On February 23, 1971, the Supreme Court upheld three state obscenity prosecutions in Perez v. Ledesma,[48] Dyson v. Stein,[49]

---

[44] Black, J., concurred in the opinion of the Court.

[45] 394 U.S. 557, 89 S.Ct. 1243 (1969), citing Winters v. New York, 333 U.S. 507, 510, 68 S.Ct. 665 (1948).

[46] 394 U.S. 557, 564–565, 89 S.Ct. 1243, 1247–1248 (1969).

[47] 394 U.S. 557, 568–569, 89 S.Ct. 1243, 1249–1250 (1969).

[48] 401 U.S. 82, 91 S.Ct. 674 (1971).

[49] 401 U.S. 200, 91 S.Ct. 769 (1971).

and Byrne v. Karalexis.[50] Ironically, these three cases which re-
vitalized obscenity prosecutions at the state level were largely
the handiwork of the late Justice Hugo Black, a longtime ex-
ponent of the idea that there is no such thing as obscene literature
and that the First Amendment is an absolute command: hands
off expression! But Black, who made explicit his anger at the
time and energy which the Court is forced to spend on obscenity
cases, found an over-riding concept in the principle of federalism. To decide Perez v. Ledesma, Justice Black relied on the
"doctrine of abstention" which he had explicated in two other
cases decided that same day. To see the implications of abstention doctrine for the law of obscenity, consider Perez v. Ledesma.

August M. Ledesma and several co-defendants were operating
a newsstand in Louisiana, selling allegedly obscene books, magazines, and playing cards. After they were charged, among other
things, with violating the Louisiana obscenity statute, the co-defendants sought a ruling from a three-judge federal court that
the statute be declared unconstitutional. The three-judge court,
however, ruled the statute constitutional. But because no adversary hearing had been held to determine the nature of the materials which had been taken from the newsstand by authorities,
the court issued an order suppressing evidence and returning materials which had been seized.[51]

Writing for the Supreme Court, Mr. Justice Black said at the
outset that other decisions of the Court announced that same
day contained the formula for deciding Perez v. Ledesma.
Those cases, Younger v. Harris [52] and Samuels v. Mackell,[53]
meant this to Justice Black: "[in those cases] we have determined when it is appropriate for a federal court to intervene in
the administration of a state's criminal laws. * * *" [54] In
Younger v. Harris, Justice Black declared that even if the California Criminal Syndicalism Statute [55] were unconstitutional on
its face, a federal court could not intervene in a prosecution under the law unless the defendant could show harassment or that

50 401 U.S. 216, 91 S.Ct. 777 (1971).

51 Delta Book Dist., Inc. v. Cronvich, 304 F.Supp. 662, 667–670 (D.C.La.1969).

52 401 U.S. 37, 91 S.Ct. 746 (1971).

53 401 U.S. 66, 91 S.Ct. 764 (1971).

54 401 U.S. 82, 91 S.Ct. 674, 676 (1971).

55 West's Ann.Cal.Penal Code, §§ 11400 and 11401.

the prosecution was undertaken in bad faith, with no hope of success.[56] Black wrote in the *Ledesma* case: [57]

> Here Ledesma was free to present his federal constitutional claims concerning arrest and seizure of materials or other matters to the Louisiana courts in the manner permitted in that State. Only in cases of proven harassment or prosecutions undertaken by state officials in bad faith without hope of obtaining a valid conviction and perhaps in other extraordinary circumstances where irreparable injury can be shown is federal injunctive relief against pending state prosecutions appropriate.

Black added that the record held no indication that Louisiana officials were making "other than a good-faith attempt" at enforcing state criminal laws. Concluding that the three-judge federal court had improperly intruded into the state's criminal process, the Supreme Court reversed the orders suppressing evidence in the pending state prosecutions.[58]

Then, emphasizing the "abstention doctrine" and its role in obscenity prosecutions, the Supreme Court issued brief *per curiam* (unsigned "by the court") decisions in Dyson v. Stein and Byrne v. Karalexis. Brent Stein, publisher of an underground newspaper in Dallas, Texas, had earlier been victorious when a three-judge federal court declared the Texas obscenity statute [59] to be unconstitutional because of "overbreadth." "Overbreadth" is a term used to describe a situation where a statute proscribes not only what may be constitutionally proscribed, but also forbids conduct which is protected.[60] The three-judge court in the Stein case said that Stanley v. Georgia meant that obscenity was deprived of First Amendment protection only in the context of "public actions taken or intended to be taken with obscene matter." Therefore, the three-judge court reasoned that the Texas statute was overbroad because it prohibited private possession of obscene materials as well as public distribution of them.[61]

[56] 401 U.S. 37, 91 S.Ct. 746 (1971).

[57] 401 U.S. 82, 91 S.Ct. 674 (1971).

[58] 401 U.S. 82, 91 S.Ct. 674, 676–677 (1971).

[59] Article 527, Texas Penal Code.

[60] See Overstock Book Co. v. Barry, 305 F.Supp. 842 (D.C.N.Y.1969). See also U. S. v. Articles of "Obscene" Merchandise, 315 F.Supp. 191 (S.D.N.Y.1970). An influential decision in which federal courts refused to declare an obscenity statute unconstitutional, thereby turning aside "overbreadth" considerations, was Gable v. Jenkins, 309 F.Supp. 998 (N.D.Ga.1969) (three judge court), affirmed 397 U.S. 592, 90 S.Ct. 1351 (1970).

[61] Stein v. Batchelor, 300 F.Supp. 602 (D.C.Tex.1969).

But again, the Supreme Court of the United States used the doctrine of abstention, ruling that the prosecution of Stein could continue.[62]

> * * * [F]ederal intervention affecting pending state criminal prosecutions, either by injunction or by declaratory judgment, is proper only where irreparable injury * * * therefore * * * the case is remanded for reconsideration in the light of Younger v. Harris, 401 U.S. 37, 91 S.Ct. 746 * * * and Samuels v. Mackell, 401 U.S. 66, 91 S.Ct. 764 * * *.

Mr. Justice Douglas dissented vigorously in both Perez v. Ledesma and Dyson v. Stein. In the latter case, Douglas described incursions into Stein's newspaper office as "search and destroy missions in the Vietnamese sense of the phrase." Douglas added that if such a technique could be used against an underground newspaper in Dallas, it could just as well be used against the *New York Times*, the *Washington Post*, the *Seattle Post Intelligencer*, or the *Sacramento Bee*.[63]

> Government certainly has no power to close down newspapers. Even censorship—whether for obscenity, for irresponsible reporting or editorials, or otherwise —is taboo.

Douglas, however, had no voice at all in the third decision announced that day by the Court, Byrne v. Karalexis, which involved "I Am Curious (Yellow)", a film distributed by Grove Press. Douglas had allowed *Evergreen Review*, a Grove Press publication, to print a lengthy segment from his book, *Points of Rebellion*.

In Byrne v. Karalexis, the owners and operators of a theater sued in United States District Court for a declaration that a Massachusetts obscenity statute[64] was unconstitutional and to enjoin further state prosecutions for exhibiting the film.[65] The three-judge court, with one judge dissenting, granted a preliminary injunction forbidding execution of sentence in the state prosecution or the starting of any future prosecutions.[66]

Ruling for the theater, Circuit Judge Bailey Aldrich wondered whether Stanley v. Georgia should be limited to "mere private possession of obscene material." He asked whether the *Stanley*

---

[62] Dyson v. Stein, 401 U.S. 200, 91 S.Ct. 769, 777 (1971).

[63] 401 U.S. 200, 91 S.Ct. 769, 773 (1971).

[64] Mass. Annotated Laws, Ch. 272, § 28a.

[65] 306 F.Supp. 1363 (D.C.Mass.1969).

[66] Ibid.; prob. juris. noted 397 U.S. 985, 90 S.Ct. 1123 (1970).

case should be read as "the high water mark of a past flood, or is it the precursor of a new one?" Judge Aldrich then decided that the Stanley decision overturned the Roth v. United States ruling that "obscenity is not within the area of constitutionally protected speech or press. Instead, he argued that [67]

> * * * Roth remains intact only with respect to public distribution in the full sense * * * restricted distribution, adequately controlled, is no longer to be condemned. It is difficult to think that if Stanley has a constitutional right to view obscene films, the Court would intend its exercise to be only at the expense of a criminal act on behalf of the only logical source, the professional supplier. A constitutional right to receive a communication would seem meaningless if there were not a coextensive right to make it * * *. If a rich Stanley can view a film, or read a book, a poorer Stanley should be free to visit a protected theatre or library. We see no reason for saying he must go alone.

But in a *per curiam* decision, the Supreme Court of the United States showed that it was not impressed by the logic of Circuit Judge Aldrich's arguments. The Supreme Court erased the injunction and remanded the case for further prosecution at the state level. The Supreme Court ruled that because the three-judge district court had been without the guidance provided by Younger v. Harris and Samuels v. Mackell, that the lower court's judgment in favor of the theater should be vacated.[68]

In sum, the Supreme Court's decisions in Perez v. Ledesma, Dyson v. Stein, and Byrne v. Karalexis suggest that defendants in state obscenity prosecutions should not expect intervention from federal courts. Unless a defendant can show that he is suffering from a harassing or bad-faith prosecution, he will have to exhaust his remedies in state courts before being able to appeal to a federal court.

The Return to Roth

After giving state prosecutions renewed vigor, the Supreme Court, on May 3, 1971, rejuvenated federal obscenity prosecutions. On that date, Justice Byron R. White—writing for the Court in both United States v. Thirty-Seven Photographs [69] and

---

[67] Ibid., 1366–1367 (citations omitted).

[68] 401 U.S. 200, 216, 91 S.Ct. 769, 777 (1971).

[69] 402 U.S. 363, 91 S.Ct. 1400 (1971).

United States v. Reidel [70]—declared that federal obscenity statutes are constitutional. The key case here involved Norman Reidel, who was charged with mailing a single copy of "The True Facts About Imported Pornography" to a postal inspector (who was more than 21 years old) who had responded to a newspaper advertisement.

The federal trial court—with the judge assuming for purposes of the trial that the book was obscene—granted Reidel's motion to dismiss. The trial court ruled that Reidel, under the reasoning of Stanley v. Georgia, had made a constitutionally protected delivery.

The Supreme Court of the United States, however, flatly rejected that manner of reading the Stanley case, and explicitly returned to the approach to obscenity used in Roth v. United States (1957). Justice White's opinion in the Reidel case reiterated the Roth v. United States holding that "obscenity is not within the area of constitutionally protected speech or press * * *." [71] Justice White added: [72]

> The District Court ignored both *Roth* and the express limitations on the reach of the *Stanley* decision. Relying on the statement in *Stanley* that "the Constitution protects the right to receive information and ideas * * * regardless of their social worth," 394 U.S. at 564, 89 S.Ct. at 1247, the trial judge reasoned that "if a person has the right to receive and possess this material, then someone must have the right to deliver it to him." He concluded that 6,1461 could not be validly applied "where obscene material is not directed at an unwilling public, where the material such as in this case is solicited by adults. * * * "
>
> *   *   *   *   *   *   *   *   *
>
> Whatever the scope of the "right to receive" referred to in Stanley, it is not so broad as to immunize the dealings in obscenity in which Reidel engaged here—dealings which *Roth* held unprotected by the First Amendment.

Thus the Supreme Court of the United States returned to a "definitional" approach to obscenity, saying that what was defined as obscene might therefore be prohibited because obscenity

[70] 402 U.S. 351, 91 S.Ct. 1410 (1971).

[71] 402 U.S. 351, 91 S.Ct. 1410, 1411 (1971), quoting Roth v. United States, 354 U.S. 476, 485, 77 S.Ct. 1304, 1309 (1957).

[72] 402 U.S. 351, 91 S.Ct. 1410, 1412 (1971).

is not constitutionally protected expression. By returning to such an attempt to judge the "content" of publications, pictures, or films, the Court inevitably turned its back on the emphasis on punishing *conduct* (sales to minors, pandering sales, invading privacy of unwilling adults) suggested by its decisions in the Redrup and Stanley cases.

A cartoonist has probably done better than most (if not all) judges in making sense of the law of obscenity. The cartoon (by Lichty) showed one judge saying to another: "I know it's obscenity if it makes my Adam's apple bobble." What sense can be made of this area of law? It now seems that the Court's decisions in *Reidel* and *Thirty Seven Photographs* were attempts to clean up some of the judicial flotsam left behind in the wake of the *Redrup* and *Stanley* cases: [73]

> the Court suggested in *Redrup* and *Stanley* that in the absence of antisocial conduct such as selling sexy reading materials to juveniles or advertising in a pandering or privacy-invading manner, obscenity prosecutions could not succeed. Such interpretations of *Redrup* and *Stanley*, however, are now out of the question thanks to the Supreme Court's decisions of the spring of 1971.
>
> *   *   *   *   *   *   *   *   *
>
> *Redrup* and *Stanley*, however, needed even more clarification than did *Roth*. *Redrup*, for example, suggested that there are two kinds of obscenity, but only defined one: hard core pornography. *Redrup* appears to have envisioned a kind of Utopian society in which people who deal in obscenity would nicely follow the rules laid down in the decision. *   *   *
>
> The confusion of *Redrup* was carried over to *Stanley*. Justice Marshall and the majority of the Court apparently did not consider the problems which would arise by granting to man the right to read whatever he pleases in his own home. How would this material get into the home if it were not purchased? And if there were a purchaser, then obviously there must be a seller and a publisher. Their activities, to continue the line of such reasoning, must also be condoned. That a number of lower courts made such an extrapolation from Stanley was natural. Many scholars did so as well. An additional lack of precision has been generated by

[73] Dwight L. Teeter, Jr. and Don R. Pember, "Obscenity, 1971: The Rejuvenation of State Power and the Return to *Roth*," Villanova Law Review 17:2 (December, 1971) pp. 211–245, at pp. 242–243.

unanswered questions lurking within *Stanley*. For example, what kind of obscenity *is* insulated by the First Amendment?

Even after Redrup v. New York, Stanley v. Georgia and following cases, Roth v. United States remained the most important case in the law of obscenity.

SEC. 74. *MILLER v. CALIFORNIA,* ET AL: FREEING THE CENSORS?

In 1973, a new majority emerged on the Supreme Court in obscenity cases, and ruled that "community standards" used in judging literature or films need not be national.

Just as its term ended in the summer of 1973, the Supreme Court of the United States reworked its obscenity standards. The altered rules are by no means clear; the Court added even more complexities to the already tangled law of obscenity. Although the new standards are scattered through five decisions delivered by the Court on June 21, 1973,[74] their main thrust may be discerned. These decisions indicate, among other things:

—That the Court will not demand a national standard for judging obscenity. Instead, a jury may measure the factual questions of "prurient interest" and "patent offensiveness" by the standard that prevails in the jury's community.[75]

—That obscenity may not be transported across state lines via common carrier [76] or imported into the country, even for an individual's own personal use.[77]

—That although an individual may possess and view obscene materials and films in the privacy of his own home,[78] a person's right of privacy or First Amendment rights do not protect exhibition of obscene films in an "adult theatre" setting. Such films may be forbidden, even though the exhibitors admit no minors, do not advertise in a pandering fash-

---

[74] Miller v. California, —— U.S. ——, ——, 93 S.Ct. 2607 (1973); Paris Adult Theatre I v. Slaton, —— U.S. ——, 93 S.Ct. 2628 (1973); United States v. Orito, —— U.S. ——, 93 S.Ct. 2674 (1973); Kaplan v. California, —— U.S. ——, 93 S.Ct. 2680 (1973), and United States v. Twelve 200–ft. Reels of Super 8 mm Film, —— U.S. ——, 93 S.Ct. 2665 (1973).

[75] Miller v. California, —— U.S. ——, 93 S.Ct. 2607, 2618–2620 (1973).

[76] United States v. Orito, —— U.S. ——, 93 S.Ct. 2674 (1973).

[77] United States v. Twelve 200–ft. Reels of Super 8 mm Film, —— U.S. ——, 93 S.Ct. 2665 (1973).

[78] Stanley v. Georgia, 394 U.S. 557, 89 S.Ct. 1243 (1969).

ion, and thus restrict viewing of such films to "consenting adults" who have been forewarned of their content.[79]

Although the ramifications of the 1973 obscenity decisions are by no means fully predictable, there was virtually instantaneous reaction: censors said, in effect, "Hooray!" Censorship boards began forming in numerous locales across the nation, and many adult movie houses and book stores shut down or "cleaned up." [80] Writing a month after the five decisions, critic Charles Champlin warned of the perils of misguided state or local censorship, which he argued will surely follow the 1973 Court rulings. He declared that the movie "Carnal Knowledge," although too gloomy an indictment of man-woman relationships in middle-class America, was certainly a serious work of art. Champlin wrote: "To find it obscene, as the Georgia Supreme Court just did, is itself equally obscene." He added:[81]

> Equally, to attempt to censor the movie "Paper Moon" on grounds that Tatum O'Neal was too young to smoke or swear, as a Dallas jury recently did, is a kind of malevolent foolishness. But they are where community standards are—or rather, where the attempts to invent community standards are.

Miller v. California

The most important and far-ranging of the five obscenity cases decided June 21, 1973, was Miller v. State of California. In this case, as in the four others of that date, the Court split 5–4, thereby revealing a new coalition among the Justices concerning obscenity and pornography. The coalition consisted of Justice Byron R. White (appointed by President John F. Kennedy), and four Justices appointed by President Richard M. Nixon (Chief Justice Warren Burger, and Justices Harry Blackmun, William Rehnquist, and Lewis Powell). Dissenting on all five obscenity cases were Justices Thurgood Marshall, Potter Stewart, William O. Douglas, and the author of the *Roth* test of 1957 and of most of the Court's subsequent obscenity decisions, Justice William J. Brennan, Jr.

Miller v. California arose when Marvin Miller mailed five unsolicited brochures in an envelope addressed to a restaurant in

---

[79] Paris Adult Theatre I v. Slaton, —— U.S. ——, 93 S.Ct. 2628 (1973).

[80] "Smut Peddlers Closing Doors—Or Cleaning Up," Associated Press dispatch in St. Louis Globe-Democrat, June 23, 1973, Section A, pp. 1, 12.

[81] Charles Champlin, "Obscenity Decision May Bring Misguided Local Censorship," Los Angeles Times—Washington Post Service story in Louisville Courier-Journal, July 21, 1973, p. A–6.

Newport Beach. The envelope was opened by the restaurant's manager, with his mother looking on, and they complained to police. The brochures advertised four books, *Intercourse, Man-Woman, Sex Orgies Illustrated,* and *An Illustrated History of Pornography,* plus a film titled *Marital Intercourse.* The brochures were mostly pictures and drawings of men and women in groups of two or more engaging in a variety of sexual activities, with genitals often prominently displayed.[82]

After a jury trial, Miller was convicted of a misdemeanor under the California Penal Code.[83]

Writing for the majority in *Miller,* Chief Justice Burger ruled that California could punish such conduct. He noted that the case involved "a situation in which sexually explicit materials have been thrust by aggressive sales action upon unwilling recipients who had in no way indicated any desire to receive such materials. He added: [84]

> This Court has recognized that the States have a legitimate interest in prohibiting dissemination of obscene material when the mode of dissemination carries with it a significant danger of offending the sensibilities of unwilling recipients or of exposure to juveniles. * * * It is in this context that we are called on to define the standards which must be used to identify obscene material that a State may regulate without infringing on the First Amendment as applicable to the States through the Fourteenth Amendment.

Endeavoring to formulate a new standard, Chief Justice Burger first returned to *Roth's* assurance that obscene materials were not protected by the First Amendment.[85] Then, he denounced the test of obscenity suggested in the Fanny Hill (*Memoirs of a Woman of Pleasure*) case nine years after *Roth,* in 1966. In that case, three justices, in a plurality opinion, held

---

[82] —— U.S. ——, 93 S.Ct. 2607, 2611–2612 (1973).

[83] West's Ann. California Penal Code, § 312.2(a) makes it a misdemeanor to knowingly distribute obscene matter. After the jury trial, the Appellate Department, Superior Court of California, Orange County, summarily affirmed the conviction without offering an opinion.

[84] Miller v. State of California, —— U.S. ——, 93 S.Ct. 2607, 2612 (1973). Relevant cases cited included Stanley v. Georgia, 394 U.S. 557, 89 S.Ct. 1243 (1969); Ginsberg v. New York, 390 U.S. 629, 88 S.Ct. 1274 (1968); Interstate Circuit, Inc. v. Dallas, 390 U.S. 676, 88 S.Ct. 1298 (1968); Redrup v. New York, 386 U.S. 767, 87 S.Ct. 1414 (1967); Jacobellis v. Ohio, 378 U.S. 184, 84 S.Ct. 1676 (1964), and Rabe v. Washington, 405 U.S. 313, 92 S.Ct. 993 (1972).

[85] —— U.S. ——, 93 S.Ct. 2607, 2613 (1973), citing Roth v. United States, 354 U.S. 476, 77 S.Ct. 1304 (1957).

that material could not be judged obscene unless it were proven
to be "utterly without redeeming social importance." Burger
added: [86]

> While *Roth* presumed "obscenity" to be "utterly with-
> out redeeming social value," *Memoirs* required that to
> prove obscenity it must be affirmatively established
> that the material is *"utterly* without redeeming social
> value." Thus, even as they repeated the words of *Roth,*
> the *Memoirs* plurality produced a drastically altered
> test that called on the prosecution to prove a negative,
> *i. e.,* that the material was *"utterly* without redeeming
> social value"—a burden virtually impossible to discharge
> under our criminal standards of proof.

The Chief Justice said that since the 1957 decision in *Roth,*
the Court had not been able to muster a majority to agree to a
standard of what constitutes "obscene, pornographic material
subject to regulation under the States' police power." [87] In
1973, however, Burger found himself in substantial agreement
with four other Justices. He made the most of it, setting out
general rules on what States could regulate ("hard-core pornography") and re-wording the *Roth* and *Memoirs* tests into a standard more congenial to convicting persons for distribution or possession of sexually explicit materials.[88]

> . . . [W]e now confine the permissible scope of
> such regulation to works which depict or describe sex-
> ual conduct. That conduct must be specifically defined
> by the applicable state law, as written or authoritative-
> ly construed. A state offense must also be limited to
> works which, taken as a whole, appeal to the prurient
> interest in sex, which portray sexual conduct in a pat-
> ently offensive way, and which, taken as a whole, do

[86] — U.S. —, 93 S.Ct. 2607, 2613–2614 (1973), citing Memoirs of a Woman of
Pleasure v. Massachusetts, 383 U.S. 413, 86 S.Ct. 975 (1966). Emphasis the
Court's.

[87] — U.S. —, 93 S.Ct. 2607, 2614 (1973).

[88] — U.S. —, 93 S.Ct. 2607, 2615 (1973). Emphasis the Court's. Chief
Justice Burger wrote that a State could, through statute, forbid:
"(a) Patently offensive representations or descriptions of ultimate sexual
acts, normal or perverted, actual or simulated.
"(b) Patently offensive representations or descriptions of masturbation,
excretory functions, and lewd exhibition of the genitals.
"Sex and nudity may not be exploited without limit by films or pictures
exhibited or sold in places of public accommodation any more than live sex and
nudity can be exhibited or sold without limit in such public places. At a
minimum, prurient, patently offensive depiction or description of sexual conduct must have serious literary, artistic, political or scientific value to merit
First Amendment protection."

not have serious literary, artistic, political, or scientific value.

> The basic guidelines for the trier of fact must be: (a) whether "the average person, applying contemporary community standards" would find that the work, taken as a whole, appeals to the prurient interest * * * (b) whether the work depicts or describes, in a patently offensive way, sexual conduct specifically defined by the applicable state law, and (c) whether the work, taken as a whole, lacks serious literary, artistic, political or scientific value. We do not adopt as a constitutional standard the *"utterly* without redeeming social value" test of Memoirs v. Massachusetts . . .: that concept has never commanded the adherence of more than three Justices at one time.

The Chief Justice dared to believe that sense can be made out of the law of obscenity; he boldly stated that the *Miller* Court ". . . undertakes to formulate standards more concrete than in the past . . .." [89] The majority opinion then declared that there can be no uniform national standard for judging obscenity or what appeals to "prurient interest" or what is "patently offensive." "[O]ur nation is simply too big and diverse for this Court to reasonably expect that such standards could be articulated for all 50 States in a single formulation . . .." [90] Asserting that a requirement that a State conform its obscenity proceedings around a national standard would be an exercise in futility, the Chief Justice added: [91]

> It is neither realistic nor constitutionally sound to read the First Amendment as requiring that the people of Maine or Mississippi accept public depiction of conduct found tolerable in Las Vegas or New York City. * * * People in different States vary in their tastes and attitudes, and this diversity is not to be strangled by the absolutism of imposed uniformity. * * * We hold the requirement that the jury evaluate the materials with reference to "contemporary standards of the State of California" serves this protective purpose and is constitutionally adequate.

Chief Justice Burger conceded that the "sexual revolution" may have been useful in striking away layers of prudery. Nev-

89 —— U.S. ——, 93 S.Ct. 2607, 2615 (1973).

90 —— U.S. ——, 93 S.Ct. 2607, 2618 (1973).

91 —— U.S. ——, 93 S.Ct. 2607, 2619–2620 (1973).

ertheless, he concluded with an angry, if tortured, analogy: "But it does not follow that no regulation of patently offensive 'hard core' materials is needed or permissible; civilized people do not allow unregulated access to heroin because it is a derivative of medicinal morphine." [92]

Deep disagreement with Justice Brennan sounded throughout the Chief Justice's opinion, providing a rather shrill counterpoint to Burger's main arguments. Brennan, the author of the majority opinion in Roth, and long considered the Court's obscenity specialist, drew Burger's fire because Brennan had experienced a profound change of mind about obscenity. Because of Justice Brennan's long study of this area of law, he will be quoted at some length. [93]

> I am convinced that the approach initiated 15 years ago in Roth v. United States * * * culminating in the Court's decision today, cannot bring stability to this area of the law without jeopardizing First Amendment values, and I have concluded that the time has come to make a significant departure from that approach.
>
> *   *   *   *   *   *   *   *
>
> Our experience with the Roth approach has certainly taught us that the outright suppression of obscenity cannot be reconciled with the fundamental principles of the First and Fourteenth Amendments. For we have failed to formulate a standard that sharply distinguishes protected from unprotected speech, and out of necessity we have resorted to the Redrup approach, which resolves cases as between parties, but offers only the most obscure guidance to legislation, adjudication by other courts, and primary conduct.
>
> *   *   *   *   *   *   *   *
>
> It comes as no surprise that judicial attempts to follow our lead conscientiously have often ended in hopeless confusion.

[92] —— U.S. ——, 93 S.Ct. 2607, 2621–2622 (1973).

[93] Brennan, in company with Marshall and Stewart, dissented in all five of the obscenity decisions of the Court on June 21, 1973. Douglas dissented separately in all five cases. Brennan's dissent in Miller was brief, and referred to the major statement of his views in his dissent in the accompanying case of Paris Adult Theatre I v. Slaton, —— U.S. ——, 93 S.Ct. 2607, 2627–2628 (1973), at pp. 2642–2663. Justice Brennan wrote opinions of the Court (or plurality opinions of the Court) in Roth v. United States, 354 U.S. 476, 77 S.Ct. 1304 (1957); Jacobellis v. Ohio, 378 U.S. 184, 84 S.Ct. 1676 (1964); Ginzburg v. United States, 383 U.S. 463, 86 S.Ct. 942 (1966); Mishkin v. New York, 383 U.S. 502, 86 S.Ct. 958 (1966), and Memoirs v. Massachusetts, 383 U.S. 413, 86 S.Ct. 975 (1966).

Of course, the vagueness problem would be largely of our own creation if it stemmed primarily from our failure to reach a consensus on any one standard. But after 15 years of experimentation and debate, I am reluctantly forced to the conclusion that none of the available formulas, including the one announced today, can reduce the vagueness to a tolerable level while at the same time striking an acceptable balance between the protections of the First and Fourteenth Amendments, on the one hand, and on the other the asserted state interest in regulating the dissemination of certain sexually oriented materials. Any effort to draw a constitutionally acceptable boundary on state power must resort to such indefinite concepts as "prurient interest," "patent offensiveness," "serious literary value," and the like. The meaning of these concepts necessarily varies with the experience, outlook, and even idiosyncracies of the person defining them. Although we have assumed that obscenity does exist and that we "know it when [we] see it . . . we are manifestly unable to describe it in advance except by reference to concepts so elusive that they fail to distinguish clearly between protected and unprotected speech.

We have more than once previously acknowledged that "constitutionally protected expression . . . is often separated from obscenity only by a dim and uncertain line." Bantam Books, Inc. v. Sullivan, 372 U.S. 58, 66, 83 S.Ct. 631, 637 (1963). * * * I need hardly point out that the factors which must be taken into account are judgmental and can only be applied on a "case-by-case, sight-by-sight" basis. * * * These considerations suggest that no one definition, no matter how precisely or narrowly drawn, can positively suffice for all situations, or carve out fully suppressible expression for all media without also creating a substantial risk of encroachment upon the guarantees of the Due Process Clause and the First Amendment.

Brennan's final rejection of the *Roth* test—and its modifications as expressed in *Memoirs* [94] and in Miller v. California [95]—was based in large measure upon his growing belief that obscen-

---

[94] Memoirs of a Woman of Pleasure v. Massachusetts, 383 U.S. 413, 86 S.Ct. 975 (1966).

[95] Miller v. State of California, —— U.S. ——, 93 S.Ct. 2607 (1973).

ity statutes are unconstitutionally vague. That is, there are
"scienter" problems: obscenity laws are so formless that defendants often do not have fair notice as to whether publications or
films they distribute or exhibit are obscene. Without fair notice,
there may occur a "chilling effect" upon protected speech.[96]

In addition, the vagueness of obscenity statutes creates another, although more subtle, set of problems. "These problems,"
Brennan wrote, "concern the institutional stress that inevitably
results where the line separating protected from unprotected
speech is excessively vague. In *Roth*, the Court had noted that
marginal cases might occur, in which it would be difficult to ascertain whether a particular expression was obscene or not obscene and therefore protected by the First Amendment. However, he declared, virtually every obscenity case turned out to be
marginal, on the boundary line between protected and unprotected speech.[97]

Brennan found Chief Justice Burger's reformulation of the
Roth test—and of the *Memoirs* test derived from *Roth*—to be
highly troublesome. The differences between Burger's attempt
to define obscenity and the *Memoirs* test seemed "for the most
part academic" to Brennan.[98]

> In my view, the restatement leaves unresolved the very
> difficulties that compel our rejection of the underlying
> *Roth* approach, while at the same time contributing
> substantial difficulties of its own. The modification of
> the *Memoirs* test may prove sufficient to jeopardize the
> analytic underpinnings of the entire scheme. And to-
> day's restatement will likely have the effect, whether
> or not intended, of permitting far more sweeping sup-
> pression of sexually oriented expression, including ex-
> pression that would almost surely be held protected un-
> der our current formulation.

Brennan argued that the Court's new modification of the
Roth-Memoirs test assumes that some works will be deemed obscene, even though they clearly have *some* social value. Under
the Burger variation of the test, convictions can be had whenever a State is able to prove that the value, "measured by some
unspecified standard, was not sufficiently 'serious' to warrant

---

[96] Brennan dissent in Paris Adult Theatre I v. Slaton, —— U.S. ——, 93 S.Ct.
2628, 2651 (1973).

[97] —— U.S. ——, 93 S.Ct. 2628, 2651 (1973).

[98] —— U.S. ——, 93 S.Ct. 2628, 2653–2654 (1973).

constitutional protection." [99]   He contended that the Court's new approach added no clarity, and that it did nothing about the problem of providing fairer notice to booksellers, theatre owners, and to the reading and viewing public.   Brennan was also dissatisfied with the Court's definition of obscenity as being limited to depictions of explicit sexual acts and physical conduct. The "physical conduct" formulation, he said, would be difficult to apply to pictorial matter, and virtually impossible to apply to determine which descriptions of sexual conduct are protected and which are not.[1]   Brennan urged that the Court withdraw from judging so many individual obscenity cases.[2]

> Our experience since *Roth* requires us not only to abandon the effort to pick out obscene materials on a case-by-case basis, but also to reconsider a fundamental postulate of *Roth*: that there exists a definable class of sexually oriented expression that may be totally suppressed by the Federal and State governments.   Assuming that such a class of expression does in fact exist, I am forced to conclude that the concept of "obscenity" cannot be defined with sufficient specificity and clarity to provide fair notice to persons who create and distribute sexually oriented materials, to prevent substantial erosion of protected speech as a by-product of the attempt to suppress unprotected speech, and to avoid very costly institutional harms.   Given these inevitable side-effects of state efforts to suppress what is assumed to be *unprotected* speech, we must scrutinize with care the state interest that is asserted to justify the suppression.   For in the absence of some very substantial interest in suppressing such speech, we can hardly condone the ill effects that seem to flow inevitably from the effort.

*   *   *   *   *   *   *   *

> The opinions in *Redrup* and Stanley v. Georgia reflected our emerging view that the state interests in protecting children and in protecting unconsenting adults may stand on a different footing from the other asserted state interests.   It may well be, as one commentator has argued, that "exposure to [erotic material] is for some an intense emotional experience.   A

---

[99] — U.S. —, 93 S.Ct. 2628, 2654 (1973).

[1] — U.S. —, 93 S.Ct. 2628, 2656 (1973).

[2] — U.S. —, 93 S.Ct. 2628, 2657, 2658, 2659, 2660 (1973).

communication of this nature, imposed upon a person contrary to his wishes, has all the characteristics of a physical assault. . . . [and it] constitutes an invasion of his privacy . . . .[3]

*   *   *   *   *   *   *   *

But the State's interest in regulating morality by suppressing obscenity, while often asserted, remains essentially unfocused and ill-defined. And, since the attempt to curtail unprotected speech necessarily spills over into the area of protected speech, the effort to serve this speculative interest through the suppression of obscene material must tread heavily on rights protected by the First Amendment.

*   *   *   *   *   *   *   *

In short, while I cannot say that the interests of the State—apart from the question of juveniles and unconsenting adults—are trivial or nonexistent, I am compelled to conclude that these interests cannot justify the substantial damage to constitutional rights and to this Nation's judicial machinery that inevitably results from state efforts to bar the distribution even of unprotected material to consenting adults.

*   *   *   *   *   *   *   *

I would hold, therefore, that at least in the absence of distribution to juveniles or obtrusive exposure to unconsenting adults, the First and Fourteenth Amendments prohibit the state and federal governments from attempting wholly to suppress sexually oriented materials on the basis of their allegedly "obscene" contents. Nothing in this approach precludes those governments from taking action to serve what may be strong and legitimate interests through regulation of the manner of distribution of sexually oriented material.[4]

Brennan's dissenting opinions, of course, are not the law at this writing; they were quoted at such length because they show where the law of obscenity has gone over the past 15 years and what it is likely to become under the Court's new formulation. Justices Stewart and Marshall joined in Brennan's dissents, but

---

[3] Brennan quoted Thomas I. Emerson, The System of Freedom of Expression (1970), at p. 496.

[4] —— U.S. ——, 93 S.Ct. 2628, 2662 (1973).

Nelson & Teeter Mass Com.2d Ed. F.P.—28

Justice Douglas filed separate dissents. Douglas said, in Miller
v. California: [5]

> Today, we leave open the way for California to send a
> man to prison for distributing brochures that advertise
> books and a movie under freshly written standards de-
> fining obscenity which until today's decision were
> never part of any law. * * * [T]here are no con-
> stitutional guidelines for deciding what is and what is
> not "obscene." The Court is at large because we deal
> with tastes and standards of literature. What shocks
> me may be sustenance for my neighbor. What causes
> one person to boil up in rage over one pamphlet or
> movie may reflect only his neurosis, not shared by
> others. We deal here with problems of censorship
> which, if adopted, should be done by constitutional
> amendment after full debate by the people.

Douglas, of course, is well known for his long expressed "absolutist" position that the First Amendment forbids censorship
of literature or films. But in his dissent in *Miller,* Douglas
suggested a scheme of pre-judging with a view to protecting publishers. He proposed that a constitutional amendment
could set up an administrative agency which would rule whether
individual works were obscene. Then, if and when publishers defied the censor and sold their literature, they could be subject to
criminal prosecution. Under such a regime, Douglas said, a
publisher would at least know when he was on dangerous
ground. He added: [6]

> Under the present regime—whether the old standards
> or the new ones are used—the criminal law becomes a
> trap. A brand new test would put a publisher behind
> bars under a new law improvised by the courts after
> the publication. That was done in *Ginzburg* and has
> all the evils of an *ex post facto* law.
>
> My contention is that until a civil proceeding has
> placed a tract beyond the pale, no criminal prosecution
> should be sustained. For no more vivid illustration of
> vague and uncertain laws could be designed than those
> we have fashioned.
>
> *   *   *   *   *   *   *   *
>
> No such protective procedure has been designed by
> California in this case. Obscenity—which even we

---

[5] Miller v. State of California, —— U.S. ——, 93 S.Ct. 2607, 2622, 2623–2624
(1973).

[6] —— U.S. ——, 93 S.Ct. 2607, 2624–2625, 2627 (1973).

cannot define with precision—is a hodge-podge. To
send men to jail for violating standards they cannot
understand, construe, and apply is a monstrous thing
to do in a Nation dedicated to fair trials and due
process.

*　　*　　*　　*　　*　　*　　*　　*

Perhaps the people will decide that the path toward
a mature, integrated society requires that all ideas
competing for acceptance must have no censor. Perhaps they will decide otherwise. Whatever the choice,
the courts will have some guidelines. Now we have
none except our own predilections.

Paris Adult Theatre I v. Slaton (1973)

The most important things the Supreme Court said about obscenity during 1973 were in Chief Justice Burger's majority
opinion in Miller v. California and in the answering dissents by
Justice Brennan in *Miller* and in *Paris Adult Theatre I*. Burger
also wrote the majority opinion in *Paris Adult Theatre I*, declaring that state regulation of access by consenting adults to obscene material does not violate the constitutionally protected
right to privacy of the movie house's customers.[7]

The case involved two commercial cinemas in Atlanta, Georgia. These theatres were festooned with prominent signs warning, "Adults Only," "You Must Be 21 and Able to Prove It," and
"If the Nude Body Offends You, Don't Enter." No pictures
were displayed outside the theatres to draw the attention of pas-
sers-by, and the theaters enforced a systematic policy of screening out minors.[8]

The State of Georgia brought a civil action to enjoin the
showing of two films, "It All Comes Out in the End" and "Magic Mirror," alleging that the films were obscene under a Georgia
statute.[9] The Georgia Supreme Court ruled that showing of the
films could be enjoined, and characterized them as "hard core
pornography" which left little to the imagination. Chief Justice
Burger's majority opinion agreed, declaring: "We categorically
disapprove the theory . . . that obscene, pornographic
films acquire constitutional immunity from state regulation sim-

[7] — U.S. —, 93 S.Ct. 2628, 2639–2640 (1973).

[8] — U.S. —, 93 S.Ct. 2628, 2632 (1973).

[9] — U.S. —, 93 S.Ct. 2628, 2632 (1973).

ply because they are exhibited for consenting adults only." [10]
He wrote:

> Even assuming that petitioners have vicarious standing
> to assert potential customers' rights, it is unavailing to
> compare a theatre, open to the public for a fee, with the
> private home of Stanley v. Georgia . . . and the
> marital bedroom of Griswold v. Connecticut . . .
>
> *   *   *   *   *   *   *   *
>
> Nothing in this Court's decisions intimates that there
> is any "fundamental" privacy right "implicit in the
> concept of ordered liberty" to watch obscene movies in
> places of public accommodation.
>
> If obscene material unprotected by the First Amend-
> ment in itself carried with it a "penumbra" of constitu-
> tionally protected privacy, this Court would not have
> found it necessary to decide *Stanley* on the narrow basis
> of the "privacy of the home," which was hardly more
> than a reaffirmation that "a man's home is his castle."
> * * * Moreover, we have declined to equate privacy
> of the home in *Stanley* with a "zone" of privacy that
> follows a distributor or a consumer of obscene ma-
> terials wherever he goes.[11] * * * The idea of a
> "privacy" right and a place of public accommodation
> are, in this context, mutually exclusive. Conduct or de-
> pictions of conduct that the state police power can pro-
> hibit on a public street does not become automatically
> protected by the Constitution merely because the conduct
> is moved to a bar or a "live" theatre stage, any more
> than a "live" performance of a man and woman locked
> in sexual embrace at high noon in Times Square is pro-
> tected by the Constitution because they simultaneously
> engage in a valid political dialogue.

The majority opinion then added that nothing in the Court's
holdings precludes the State of Georgia from regulating the exhibition of allegedly obscene materials. The State need only
provide applicable law which, "as written or authoritatively interpreted by the Georgia courts, meets the First Amendment
standards set forth in Miller v. California. . . ." The

---

10 —— U.S. ——, 93 S.Ct. 2628, 2635 (1973). Burger cited the Hill-Link
Minority Report of the Commission on Obscenity and Pornography (1970 ed.),
pp. 390–412.

11 Citing United States v. Orito, —— U.S. ——, 93 S.Ct. 2674, 2676–2678 (1973),
and United States v. Twelve 200-Ft. Reels, —— U.S. ——, 93 S.Ct. 2665, 2667–
2669 (1973).

Court then remanded the case to Georgia so the state's obscenity law could be re-evaluated in light of Miller v. California.[12]

Obscenity, 1973: A Summing Up

Chief Justice Burger also wrote the Court's majority opinions in three other obscenity cases which were decided on June 21, 1973. Briefly, here is the main thrust of those cases:

> * * * United States v. Orito: Federal statutes, if construed in line with Miller v. California, can prohibit interstate transportation of obscene material on a common carrier. George Orito had flown from San Francisco to Milwaukee on Trans World Airlines and North Central Airlines planes, carrying 83 reels of film (with as many as 10 copies of some of the allegedly obscene films).[13] The majority opinion declared that any constitutionally protected zone of privacy which might allow possession of obscene materials in one's home does not extend to transporting such materials by common carrier.[14]

> * * * United States v. Twelve 200-ft. Reels of Super 8 mm Film: The Court's five-man majority ruled that because obscene material is not protected by the First Amendment, an attempt by a Mr. Paladini to import movie films, color slides, and other sexually explicit printed and graphic matter from Mexico could be halted by customs officers.[15] The Court rejected Paladini's claim that under Stanley v. Georgia,[16] "the right to possess obscene material in the privacy of the home creates a right to acquire it or import it from another country." The Court held that the materials could be confiscated even if Paladini intended them solely for his own private use.[17]

> * * * Kaplan v. California: Murray Kaplan, who ran an "adult" business—the Peek-A-Boo Bookstore in Los Angeles, was convicted under California's obscenity

---

[12] —— U.S. ——, 93 S.Ct. 2628, 2642 (1973).

[13] —— U.S. ——, 93 S.Ct. 2674 (1973).

[14] —— U.S. ——, 93 S.Ct. 2674, 2676 (1973). This case was vacated and remanded for further proceedings in line with Miller v. California, —— U.S. ——, 93 S.Ct. 2607 (1973).

[15] —— U.S. ——, 93 S.Ct. 2665, 2667–2668 (1973). See 19 U.S.C.A. § 1305(a).

[16] 394 U.S. 557, 89 S.Ct. 1243 (1969).

[17] —— U.S. ——, 93 S.Ct. at 2667 (1973). Vacated and remanded for further proceedings in line with Miller v. California.

statute after selling an undercover police officer a book named *Suite 69*.[18] There were no pictures in the book, and this case presented the issue of whether a book can be legally obscene because of expression by words alone. The Court's majority ruled:[19] Obscenity can, of course, manifest itself in conduct, in the pictorial representation of conduct, or in the written and oral description of conduct. The Court has applied similarly conceived First Amendment standards to moving pictures, to photographs, and to words in books.

After the Court's 1973 decisions on obscenity, there is some handwriting on the wall and the word is censorship. Although the net effect of Miller v. California et al. will not emerge for some time, the Court has modified tests for obscenity in a way that encourages prosecutors and discourages booksellers and theatre owners. Government *can* regulate expression with obscenity laws *if* certain rules are followed. As Chief Justice Burger summarized the Court's opinion in *Miller*,[20]

> In sum, we (a) reaffirm the *Roth* holding that obscene material is not protected by the First Amendment, (b) hold that such material can be regulated by the States, subject to the specific safeguards enunciated above, without a showing that the material is *utterly* without redeeming social value," and (c) hold that obscenity is to be determined by applying "contemporary community standards" . . . not "national standards."

Thus the Court's five-man majority followed the essence of *Roth*, assuming that obscenity is recognizable and can be isolated and defined, and that (however defined) obscenity is not entitled to First Amendment protection.[21] But how to define the "obscene," or, for that matter, "hard-core pornography"? The law of obscenity continues to be a multi-faced enigma wrapped inside the dilemma of whether or not there shall be freedom of expression. No persons have emerged as sufficiently clever verbalizers—on the Court or elsewhere—to devise a formula which will define obscenity or pornography with sufficient precision to protect free discussion of sex.

At this writing, there is great confusion about what the phrase "contemporary community standards" means or can be

---

18 — U.S. —, 93 S.Ct. 2680, 2682 (1973).

19 — U.S. —, 93 S.Ct. 2680, 2683–2684 (1973). Vacated and remanded for further proceedings in line with Miller v. California.

20 — U.S. —, 93 S.Ct. 2607, 2627 (1973).

21 354 U.S. 476, 77 S.Ct. 1304 (1957).

made to mean. The Court declared, in *Miller* and its companion cases, that there should not be a national standard for judging obscenity, and that state standards will suffice. Many questions arise. Will any jury ever accurately reflect state standards? (Or even local standards?) Are there *really* any state standards or local standards? Is Northern California like Southern California? Is San Francisco's North Beach area like its Pacific Heights District? Would Eastern South Dakota agree with Western South Dakota? Would upstate New York have the same outlook as Manhattan?

Will the Court ultimately settle on *local* (as opposed to state) standards? If so, how small—or how large—is the community in the phrase "contemporary community standards?" Is each county a community? If so, for example, Kentucky could then have 120 community standards, one for each of its 120 counties.

Beyond such questions, there is the suspicion that obscenity prosecutions are not always started with an even, unbiased hand. It is hard to shake the impression that more obscenity prosecutions begin in those years when prosecuting attorneys are up for re-election. In some degree, "community standards" turn out to be dependent upon the whim of individual prosecutors.

Unfortunately, it seems that there is no such thing as a little censorship. The same legal jargon which closes "Deep Throat" or "Lash of Lust" in New York City may be used to ban Boccaccio's *De Cameron* in Dubuque or Salinger's *Catcher in the Rye* in Council Bluffs. As Justice Douglas wrote,[22]

> The idea that the First Amendment permits government to ban publications that are "offensive" to some people puts an ominous gloss on freedom of the press. That test would make it possible to ban any paper or any journal or magazine in some benighted place. The First Amendment was designed "to invite dispute" * * *. The idea that the First Amendment permits punishment for ideas that are "offensive" to the particular judge or jury sitting in judgment is astounding. No greater leveler of speech has ever been designed. To give the power to the censor, as we do today, is to make a sharp and radical break with the traditions of a free society. The First Amendment was not fashioned as a vehicle for dispensing tranquilizers to the people. Its prime function was to keep debate open to "offensive" as well as to "staid" people. The tendency throughout history has been to subdue the individual and to exalt the power of government. The use of the standard

[22] — U.S. —, 93 S.Ct. 2607, (1973).

"offensive" gives authority to government that cuts the very vitals out of the First Amendment.

SEC. 75. THE POST OFFICE: AWAY FROM CENSORSHIP?

A 1968 "antipandering" statute appears to be supplanting "administrative stop orders" and federal prosecutions by providing a weapon against the mailing of material which the Post Office Department believes to be pornographic.

The 1946 Supreme Court decision in Hannegan v. Esquire, discussed earlier, has meant that the Postmaster Generals are not using his mail classification powers as a subterfuge to keep materials which he considers obscene out of the mails.[23] The basic federal anti-obscenity statute, however, forbids mailing obscene literature or materials, and this has kept the Post Office Department very much involved with efforts to control obscene literature.[24] During the 1950s, the Post Office Department often made use of the Postmaster General's administrative powers to stop mailings of questionable materials. This "administrative stop order" procedure works in this way: an administrative decision by the Post Office Department would declare a book nonmailable. However, the person seeking to mail the book had the right to appeal from Post Office's administrative order (issued in the name of the Postmaster General). The administrative order could be appealed to a United States District Court and there, in court, the issue of whether or not the book was obscene could be decided. If the court ruled that the book was obscene, it was excluded from the mails. If the book was declared not obscene, it could be freely mailed. And the person mailing the book, under such a procedure, did not have to fear heavy criminal penalties. The only issue was the mailability of the book; the only penalty for losing such a case would be that the distributor could not mail his book.[25]

J. Edward Day, Postmaster General of the United States from 1961 to 1963, has explained the frustrations of the Post Office Department with the administrative stop-order procedure: [26]

> Prior to 1961, this type of administrative stop order had been used many times. However, it had often

[23] Paul and Schwartz, op. cit., pp. 76–77.

[24] 18 U.S.C.A. § 1461.

[25] Friedman, op. cit., p. 80; J. Edward Day, "Mailing Lists and Pornography," American Bar Association Journal Vol. 52 (Dec. 1966) p. 1104.

[26] Day, loc. cit.

proved relatively easy for the mailer to get a court to issue a temporary restraining order suspending the ban. Then the mailings would go on during an extended period of court proceedings. In the meantime, publicity about the attempted ban provided priceless advertising for the questionable publication. If the court eventually sustained the ban it was then no trick for the offender to start business again with a new corporate name or with slightly revised merchandise. The stop order procedure involved no penalty.

*   *   *   *   *   *   *   *   *

I concluded that grand juries and petit juries—representing community standards—are more appropriate bodies for deciding whether or not mail is obscene than are administrative officials at the Post Office * * *. In early 1961, when we [the Post Office Department] dropped the administrative stop-order approach, we announced a crackdown on obscenity in the mails.

In 1968, however, there were indications that the Post Office Department was decreasing its requests that the Justice Department prosecute under the federal obscenity laws. Under a new "antipandering" statute which went into effect in 1968, the Post Office Department can concentrate upon dealers who mail questionable material to persons who complain. This statute says, in part: [27]

Whoever for himself, or by his agents or assigns, mails or causes to be mailed any pandering advertisement which offers for sale matter which the *addressee in his sole discretion believes to be erotically arousing or sexually provocative* shall be subject to an order of the Postmaster General to refrain from further mailings of such materials to designated addresses * * *

The wording of this statute places considerable discretion in the hands of the recipient of the materials. If a person receives mail which offends him, he can complain to his Post Office. If the recipient requests that no more materials be sent to him by a specific sender, the Post Office Department can order the sender to discontinue all mailings to the recipient. Also, the Postmaster General can order that the recipient's name be removed from all mailing lists which the sender owns or controls. If the mailings continue, another complaint from the recipient can result in

---

[27] P.L. 90–206, Title 3, § 301; 81 Stat. 645; 39 § 4009 (1968). Emphasis added. See also §§ 4006–4007 (now §§ 3006–3007).

the Post Office Department's requesting the Justice Department to get a court order to halt such mailings. If a court order is ignored, the court will punish violations as contempt of court.[28]

Late in 1968, Chief Postal Inspector Harry B. Montague told the Associated Press that the "antipandering" law was proving to be of great assistance to him and to the 1,080 postal inspectors across the nation. Montague said that the Post Office—because of limitations promulgated by court decisions or administrative orders—is "no longer in the censorship business—postal inspectors now 'channel all their efforts [against obscenity] into dealer cases.' " From April until October, 1968, the Post Office Department received nearly 75,000 complaints about materials which recipients had found in their mail boxes and which they objected to as "erotically arousing or sexually provocative." [29] In 1970, however, the Supreme Court squelched a postal censorship operation on grounds that the procedures involved were so cumbersome that First Amendment rights were not protected. The case of Blount v. Rizzi called into question a section of the United States Code which said that the Postmaster General, after administrative hearings, could halt use of the mails and of postal money orders for commerce in allegedly obscene materials. Also, the legislation allowed the Postmaster General to obtain a court order permitting him to detain incoming mail pending the outcome of proceedings against the person suspected in trafficking in obscene materials. Writing for the Court, Justice Brennan quoted Justice Oliver Wendell Holmes: " 'The United States may give up the Post Office when it sees fit, but while it carries it on the use of the mails is almost as much a part of free speech as the right to use our tongues.' " Justice Brennan and the Court held that the censorship procedures were constitutionally deficient because they did not require that the Postmaster General seek a prompt judicial determination of the obscenity of the materials involved.[30]

---

[28] Ibid.

[29] Associated Press story, "U. S. Changes Course in Pornography War," from Wisconsin State Journal, Madison, Section 1, p. 20, Oct. 13, 1968.

[30] Blount v. Rizzi, 400 U.S. 410, 91 S.Ct. 423 (1970). See 39 U.S.C. § 3006 and § 3007.

SEC. 76. MOTION PICTURE CENSORSHIP

Not until 1952, in Burstyn v. Wilson, did the Supreme Court extend First Amendment protection to the motion picture industry.

While problems arising out of attempts to censor allegedly obscene printed materials have presented an apparently insoluble dilemma for American courts and legislatures, censorship of motion pictures has proved to be equally puzzling. With motion picture censorship, the assumption is the same as in attempts to censor the printed word: the depiction of sexual scenes—if the sex is sufficiently blatant or explicit—is socially harmful and should be suppressed.

Motion pictures, however, have had some problems with censors which are their very own. For one thing, the motion pictures are a relatively new medium, one which is scarcely more than 60 years old in the public commercial sense. In recent years, the movies have been granted some of the protections of the First and Fourteenth Amendments, yet they have also been subjected to censorship. And, in some cases the courts have upheld systems of prior censorship over motion pictures.

Perhaps the shining of human images on a screen made motion pictures, in the eyes of the censorious, is even more likely to "deprave and corrupt" than words on a printed page. In any case, pressures for movie censorship have long been apparent. As early as 1907 a film censorship ordinance was enacted in Chicago.[31]

It was soon established that movies were not protected by the Bill of Rights. In 1915, a distributor of motion pictures in Ohio tried to get that state's motion picture censorship law enjoined as an unconstitutional interference with freedom of speech and press. A federal district court, however, rejected the film distributor's complaint, holding that the Constitution's first eight amendments were not a bar to state action for the protection of morals. An appeal to the Supreme Court of the United States netted the distributor only more frustration, and suggested that the movies would be subject to the vagaries of censors for many years to come. The Supreme Court approved state censorship of motion pictures, with Justice Joseph McKenna ruling:[32]

> It cannot be put out of view that the exhibition of moving pictures is a business, pure and simple, originated

[31] Block v. Chicago, 239 Ill. 251, 87 N.E. 1011 (1909).

[32] Mutual Film Corp. v. Industrial Commission of Ohio, 236 U.S. 230, 244, 35 S.Ct. 387, 391 (1915).

and conducted for profit, like other spectacles, not to be regarded, nor intended to be regarded by the Ohio Constitution, we think, as part of the press of the country, or as organs of public opinion.

It should be noted that this decision was made early in the history of films, before talking motion pictures appeared and before newsreels. Movies, in that setting, were seen as entertainment of the "magic lantern" variety and little else. In fairness to the justices of the Supreme Court, perhaps they could not have been expected to look into the future and see a time when motion pictures would be an important medium for social comment. But in their failure to see how motion pictures might develop, the justices put their stamp of approval on a form of prior censorship which later they were to disapprove.[33]

In response to public and legal pressures, the American motion picture industry decided that it must regulate the content of its own pictures, lest the states and cities do it by laws and censorship boards. In 1922, the Motion Picture Producers and Distributors of America (MPPDA) was formed, and former postmaster general Will Hays was hired to apply a code to preserve decency on the screen. Even so, self-censorship did not remove pressures exerted by persons who believed that motion pictures were still insufficiently moral in tone. The years 1920 to 1927 saw many bills proposing motion picture censorship filed in state legislatures. In 1923, a proposal was made to Congress that a Federal Motion Picture Commission be added to the Department of the Interior. This bill failed to pass.[34]

During the 1930s, in an effort to silence advocates of censorship, the movie industry tried self-regulation in the form of the Motion Picture Code. This code listed categories which were to be handled with care: crime, costumes, dances, religion, bedroom scenes, national feelings, titles and repellent subjects. Other categories were to be forbidden altogether: explicit sexual scenes, vulgarity, obscenity and profanity. This code also made it mandatory that each motion picture company submit its films to a committee of the MPPDA before public showings. If the committee found violations of the code, a producer could not release the picture until its offending scenes had been snipped out.[35]

[33] See, e. g., Burstyn v. Wilson, 343 U.S. 495, 502, 72 S.Ct. 777, 781 (1952).

[34] Raymond Moley, The Hays Office, (New York: Bobbs Merrill, 1945); Morris L. Ernst and Alexander Lindey, The Censor Marches On, (New York: Doubleday, Doran, 1940), p. 80.

[35] Howard T. Lewis, The Motion Picture Industry (New York: Van Nostrand, 1933), p. 376.

The Motion Picture Code, although it underwent minor amendments, continued in force well into the 1960s.[36] This code, despite its drawbacks, apparently played a role in reducing the number of state and local censorship groups and may have helped to avoid the creation of a federal movie censorship organization. Self-regulation by the motion picture industry continues, and is responsive to decisions by the courts which indicate kinds of censorship activities which the courts view as legally permissible. For example, in the wake of the Supreme Court's decision in Interstate Circuit, Inc. v. Dallas [37] a case which is discussed near the end of this chapter—the motion picture industry adopted a film rating system reflecting the Court's renewed interest in protecting minors.

This rating system, which went into effect November 1, 1968, was sanctioned by American film producers, exhibitors, and distributors.[38] The Motion Picture Association of America's (MPAA's) code established a Production Code and Rating Administration will rate films according to these classifications: [39]

G—Suggested for GENERAL audiences

GP—Suggested for MATURE audiences: adults and mature young people. Parental discretion advised.

R—RESTRICTED. *Persons under 16 not admitted,* unless accompanied by parent or adult guardian.

X—*Persons under 16 not admitted.* This age restriction may be higher in certain areas. Check theater or advertising.

In supporting this code, president of the National Association of Theatre Owners, Julian Rifkin said theater owners in America have agreed to support the rating system at the box office, where they will enforce the age restrictions which accompany certain ratings.[40] These ratings were praised by the prestigious New York *Times* for warning the public—and parents—that

[36] Two of the code's chief critics have charged that it created a "viciously false picture of life" and that its mandates are too general. See Morris L. Ernst and Alexander Lindey, The Censor Marches On p. 89. The code was amended in 1956, in order that movies could deal with narcotics after a critically praised film, The Man With the Golden Arm, had been denied an MPPDA seal for depicting a narcotic addict's problems. In 1961, the code was altered to "permit restrained, discreet treatment of sexual aberration in movies."

[37] 390 U.S. 676, 88 S.Ct. 1298 (1968).

[38] Vincent Canby, "Movie Ratings for Children Grown Up," New York Times Oct. 8, 1968, p. 1 ff.

[39] Ibid., at p. 41.

[40] Ibid.

some movies may be "offensive." The *Times* said that the rating system avoided falling into "the pit of censorship" while offering "some protection to children from the more lurid screen projections * * * [without interfering] with the freedom neither of legitimate movie producers nor of adult audiences." [41]

Burstyn v. Wilson

The motion picture industry's efforts at self regulation to forestall external controls—and relevant state laws and local ordinances setting up controls over content—all started because movies had been declared to be outside the protection of the First Amendment. [42]

In 1952, a case involving film distributor Joseph Burstyn of New York was the first since 1915 to raise before the Supreme Court the issue of whether movies were protected under the First Amendment. The film involved was Roberto Rossellini's Italian production of "The Miracle." This film was accused not of obscenity but of "sacrilege." "The Miracle" was a story of a simple-minded girl goatherd who had been raped by a bearded stranger. She believed the stranger to be St. Joseph. But when she went to her village, pregnant, the villagers made fun of her. The goatherd was forced to live alone in a cave. [43]

Burstyn's film distributing company had brought suit to test a New York statute which made it unlawful:

> to exhibit, or to sell, lease or lend for exhibition at any place of amusement for pay or in connection with any business in the state of New York, any motion picture film or reel unless there is at the time in full force and effect a valid license or permit.

The New York Education Department had issued a license to allow showing of "The Miracle," but the Education Department's governing body, the New York Regents, ordered the license withdrawn after the regents had received protests that the film was "sacrilegious." [44] Burstyn appealed the license's withdrawal to the New York Courts, claiming that the state's licensing statute was unconstitutional. New York's courts, however, rejected the argument that the New York law abridged freedom of speech and press and approved the Regents' ruling that the film was "sacrilegious."

---

41 New York Times editorial, "Rating the Movies," Oct. 9, 1968, p. 46.

42 See Mutual Film Corp. v. Industrial Commission of Ohio, 236 U.S. 230, 35 S.Ct. 387 (1915).

43 Joseph Burstyn, Inc. v. Wilson, 343 U.S. 495, 72 S.Ct. 777 (1952).

44 Ibid. Wilson was chairman of the New York Board of Regents.

The Supreme Court of the United States, however, ruled unanimously that the New York statute and the term "sacrilegious" were so vague that they abridged freedom of expression. Speaking for the court, Mr. Justice Clark ruled that motion pictures are "a significant medium for the communication of ideas," important for the expression of political or social views and thus an important organ of public opinion. Justice Clark added: [45]

> [W]e conclude that expression by means of motion pictures is included within the free speech and free press guaranty of the First and Fourteenth Amendments. To the extent that language in the opinion of Mutual Film Corp. v. Industrial Comm. is out of harmony with the views here set forth, we no longer adhere to it.

Clark declared that the fact that motion pictures are produced by a large, profitable industry does not remove the protection of Constitutional guarantees. Although the Court said in *dicta* that a clearly drawn obscenity statute to regulate motion pictures might be upheld, the main thrust of the *Burstyn* decision was toward greater freedom. Not only were films given protection under the First and Fourteenth Amendments, movies which offended a particular religious group need not, for that reason alone, be banned. Thus "sacrilege" can no longer be a ground for censoring movies.[46]

Seven years after the *Burstyn* decision, the Supreme Court—in Kingsley International Pictures Corp. v. New York—again upheld the idea that films are within the protection of the First Amendment. The *Kingsley* decision, however, had within it the possibilities for once again expanding controls over films. The Court specifically refused to decide whether "the controls which a State may impose upon this medium of expression are precisely co-extensive with those allowable for newspapers, books, or individual speech.[47]

Times Film Corp. v. City of Chicago

Despite the veiled warning in the *Kingsley* opinion that the Supreme Court might once again strengthen controls over motion pictures, a bold attempt was made to get a prior censorship ordinance declared unconstitutional. This was the 1961 case of Times Film Corp. v. City of Chicago, which involved a film with

[45] 343 U.S. 495, 502, 72 S.Ct. 777, 781 (1952).

[46] The Burstyn holding that films are within the protection of the First Amendment was supported in Kingsley International Pictures Corp. v. Regents of New York, 360 U.S. 684, 79 S.Ct. 1362 (1959).

[47] 360 U.S. 684, 689–690, 79 S.Ct. 1362, 1366 (1959).

a spicy name: "Don Juan." However, this film was merely a motion picture version of Mozart's opera, "Don Giovanni," obviously not obscene.

The Times Film Corporation paid the license fee for "Don Juan," but refused to submit the film to Chicago's Board of Censors for a license. Although the film was quite sedate, the company never argued that "Don Juan" was not obscene. Instead, the only question presented by the film company's lawyers was whether the Chicago ordinance which provided for pre-screening and licensing of motion pictures *before* public exhibition was constitutional. Thus the constitutionality of *prior restraint* was the sole issue in this film censorship case. Perhaps officials of the Times Film Corporation were irked by the Big-Brotherish overtones of Chicago's film censorship ordinance, which said:[48]

> It shall be unlawful for any person to show or exhibit in a public place * * * any * * * motion picture * * * without first having secured a permit therefore from the superintendent of police.

A person who exhibited a picture without a permit could be fined from $50 to $100 each day that the motion picture was shown without a permit.[49] A permit is denied to a film if it is "obscene, or portrays depravity, criminality, or lack of virtue of a class of citizens of any race, color, creed, or religion and exposes them to contempt, derision, or obloquy * * *." In addition, if

> * * * the picture, considered as a whole, has the dominant effect of substantially arousing sexual desires in any person less than seventeen years of age, or if the picture is indecent, or is contrary to contemporary community standards in the description or representation of nudity and sex.

the film is given a special permit limiting its showing to persons over the age of sixteen years.[50] After a Federal District Court had dismissed the Times Film Corporation's complaint—and after a Court of Appeals had affirmed that decision—the Supreme Court of the United States granted certiorari.[51]

[48] Municipal Code of Chicago, Chapter 155, Section 1. However, Section 2 provided that newsreels do not have to be previewed. Films were to be approved before public showing by either the superintendent of police or by the "Film Review Section," six persons appointed by the superintendent of police.

[49] Ibid.

[50] Ibid. Chapter 155, Section 4. On the age-17 requirement, see Ginsberg v. New York, 390 U.S. 629, 88 S.Ct. 1274 (1968).

[51] 362 U.S. 917, 80 S.Ct. 672 (1960).

The Supreme Court, by a 5–4 decision, held that Chicago's censorship ordinance was constitutional. Mr. Justice Clark, writing for the majority, said the question presented by this case was whether a film exhibitor has "complete and absolute freedom to exhibit, at least once, any and every kind of motion picture." Clark replied, however, "It has never been held that liberty of speech is absolute. Nor has it been suggested that all previous restraints on speech are invalid." [52]

Clark noted that the content of the motion picture had not been raised as an issue. Instead, the Times Film Corporation challenged the censor's basic authority. By raising such a challenge to prior restraint, Times Film Corporation simply aimed too high. It might have helped the corporation's case had its attorneys shown that the film involved was not objectionable. But this was not done. As a result, a majority of the Supreme Court upheld the Chicago ordinance, drawing on language first used in the Burstyn case and echoed in the Kingsley Films decision. Motion pictures are not "necessarily subject to the precise rules governing any other particular method of expression." [53]

The Supreme Court's Times Film Corporation decision evoked strenuous dissents. Chief Justice Warren charged that the decision came "perilously close to holding that not only may motion pictures be censored but that a licensing scheme may also be applied to newspapers, books and periodicals, radio, television, public speeches and every other medium of expression." [54] And Justice Douglas declared that the Chicago ordinance instituted a "guilty until proven innocent" system of dealing with films. He argued that the presumption of innocence, the right to a jury trial, and proof of guilt beyond a reasonable doubt are barriers which should be placed "in the path of officials who want to impose their standard of morality on the author or producer." [55]

---

[52] Times Film Corp. v. Chicago, 365 U.S. 43, 47, 81 S.Ct. 391, 393 (1961), citing Near v. Minnesota, 283 U.S. 697, 51 S.Ct. 625 (1931).

[53] 365 U.S. 43, 46, 49, 81 S.Ct. 391, 393–394 (1961); Burstyn v. Wilson 343 U.S. 493, 72 S.Ct. 777 (1952); Kingsley International Pictures v. Board of Regents, 360 U.S. 684, 79 S.Ct. 1362 (1959).

[54] 365 U.S. 43, 75, 81 S.Ct. 391, 408 (1961).

[55] 365 U.S. 43, 83–84, 81 S.Ct. 391, 413 (1961). The American Society of Newspaper Editors, seeing the addition of a precedent upholding prior restraint, filed an *amicus curiae* brief trying to help the Times Film Corp. to get a rehearing before the Supreme Court, as did the HMH Publishing Co., the Authors' League of America, Inc., the American Book Publishers' Council, Inc., Motion Picture Association of America, Inc., National Association of Broadcasters, American Society of Magazine Photographers, and the Society of Magazine Writers. Despite these briefs, the Supreme Court refused to reconsider its decision.

A later decision—this one squarely pegged on the question of whether or not a film was obscene—resulted in the Court's saying, once again: "Motion pictures are within the ambit of the constitutional guarantees of freedom of speech and press." This case involved the conviction—and $2,500 in fines—assessed against Nico Jacobellis, manager of a Cleveland motion picture theater.[56]

In his majority opinion, Mr. Justice Brennan took pains to explain the Supreme Court's role in deciding obscenity cases. He wrote that the determination of whether a particular book, motion picture, or other work of expression is obscene can not be treated as a purely factual judgment in which a jury's verdict or the decision of a lower state or federal court is allowed to stand as conclusive. He added:[57]

> Since it is only "obscenity" that is excluded from the constitutional protection, the question whether a particular work is obscene necessarily implicates an issue of constitutional law. * * * "Our duty admits of no substitute for facing up to the tough individual problems of constitutional judgment involved in every obscenity case."

In 1965, the Supreme Court moved to take a bit of the sting out of its 1961 holding in Times Film Corporation v. City of Chicago.[58] The *Times Film* decision had upheld Chicago's movie censorship ordinance, and the 1955 case of Freedman v. Maryland presented a challenge to the constitutionality of a similar law. Freedman had shown the film "Revenge at Daybreak" in his Baltimore theater without first submitting the picture to the State Board of Censors as required by Maryland law.[59]

However, Freedman's challenge to the Maryland film censorship statute was much more focused and precise than the Times Film Corporation's attack on the Chicago censorship ordinance. Writing for the Court, Mr. Justice Brennan noted that[60]

> [u]nlike the petitioner in Times Film, appellant does not argue that Article 2 [of the Maryland statute] is unconstitutional simply because it may prevent even

56 Jacobellis v. Ohio, 378 U.S. 184, 84 S.Ct. 1676, 1677 (1964), citing Burstyn v. Wilson, 343 U.S. 495, 72 S.Ct. 777 (1952).

57 378 U.S. 184, 188, 84 S.Ct. 1676, 1678 (1964).

58 365 U.S. 43, 81 S.Ct. 391 (1961).

59 Article 66A of the 1957 Maryland Statutes made it unlawful to sell, lease, lend or exhibit a motion picture unless the film had first been submitted to and approved by the Maryland State Board of Censors.

60 Freedman v. Maryland, 380 U.S. 51, 54, 85 S.Ct. 734, 737 (1965).

the first showing of a film whose exhibition may legitimately be the subject of an obscenity prosecution. He
presents a question quite distinct from that passed on
in Times Film; accepting the rule in Times Film, he
argues that Article 2 constitutes an invalid prior restraint because, in the context of the remainder of the
statute, it presents a danger of unduly suppressing protected expression.

Brennan added that the Maryland law made it possible for the
state's Censorship Board to halt the showing of any film it disapproved, unless and until the film exhibitor started a time-con-
suming appeal procedure through Maryland Courts and got the
Censorship Board's ruling overturned. So in the Freedman
case, prior restraint of movies was disallowed because of insufficient procedural safeguards in the Maryland law for the protection of the film exhibitor.

Nevertheless, the Court maintained that the "requirement of
prior submission to a censor sustained in Times Film is consistent with our recognition that films differ from other forms of
expression." Justice Brennan suggested that an orderly, speedy
procedure for pre-screening films could be constitutional. He
proposed, as a model, standards laid down in the 1957 case of
Kingsley Books, Inc. v. Brown.[61] The Supreme Court there upheld a New York injunctive procedure to prevent the sale of obscene books. The Court said: [62]

> That procedure postpones any restraint against sale
> until a judicial determination of obscenity following no-
> tice and an adversary hearing. The statute provides
> for a hearing one day after joinder of the issue; the
> judge must hand down his decision within two days
> after termination of the hearing. * * * [T]he
> chilling effect of a censorship order, even one which re-
> quires judicial action for its enforcement, suggests all
> the more reason for expeditious determination of the
> question whether a particular film is constitutionally
> protected.

Early in 1968, the Supreme Court struck down a Dallas ordinance which made it possible for an appointed, nine-member Motion Picture Classification Board to declare certain films "not
suitable for young persons." Under this ordinance, young persons were defined as children who had not yet reached their six-

---

[61] 354 U.S. 436, 77 S.Ct. 1325 (1957).

[62] 380 U.S. 51, 60, 85 S.Ct. 734, 740 (1965), citing Kingsley Books, Inc. v.
Brown, 354 U.S. 436, 77 S.Ct. 1325 (1957).

teenth birthday.   In holding this ordinance unconstitutional,
however, the Supreme Court emphasized that "a State may regulate the dissemination to juveniles of, and their access to, material which a State clearly could not regulate as to adults."[63]

Despite approval of State efforts to protect juveniles from
gamy films and literature, the Court concluded that the Dallas
ordinance setting up the Motion Picture Classification Board
was unconstitutionally vague.   In announcing the judgment of
the Court, Mr. Justice Thurgood Marshall said, "we conclude
only that 'the absence of narrowly drawn, reasonable and definite standards for officials to follow * * * is fatal.' "[64]
The Dallas ordinance thus became an example of the kind of
prior censorship which, because of the lack of definite standards
and a failure to set up speedy adjudicative procedures, the Court
will not tolerate.

The Dallas ordinance set up complicated procedures for exhibitors to follow in order to get Motion Picture Classification
Board approval of films for public showing.   In sticky instances,
the wording of the ordinance made it entirely possible that three
weeks or more could pass before an exhibitor could get a defini-
tive ruling from a judge.[65]

The *Interstate Circuit* case arose after the Dallas Motion Picture Classification Board voted to classify the film *Viva Maria*
as "not suitable for young persons."   Only five members of the
Board had actually viewed the film, although eight of the nine
Board members—with the ninth person abstaining—had voted
to label the film "not suitable."   The Board gave no reason for
its finding at the time, although it later argued that the film
portrayed " 'sexual promiscuity in such a manner as to encourage delinquency or sexual promiscuity on the part of young persons or to appeal to their prurient interests.' "[66]

Speedy judicial determination was of little help to the Interstate Circuit Corporation.   As Interstate Circuit appealed the
Board's classification order, the film was shown to a Dallas
judge, who said offhandedly:

> Oh, I realize you gentlemen [of the Classification
> Board] may be right.   There are two or three features

[63] 390 U.S. 676, 690, 88 S.Ct. 1298, 1306 (1968), citing Ginsberg v. New York,
390 U.S. 629, 88 S.Ct. 1274 (1968).

[64] Ibid., citing Niemotko v. Maryland, 340 U.S. 268, 271, 71 S.Ct. 325, 327
(1951).

[65] 390 U.S. 676, 694–700, 88 S.Ct. 1298, 1308–1312 (1968).

[66] 390 U.S. 676, 685–686, 88 S.Ct. 1298, 1304 (1968).

in the picture that look to me would be unsuitable to young people. * * * So I enjoin the exhibitor * * * from exhibiting it.[67]

The Supreme Court, however, directed its scrutiny at the wording of the ordinance. Under the ordinance, the Board could declare a film "not suitable for young people"

> if, in the judgment of the Board, there is a substantial probability that * * * [the film] will create the impression on young persons that * * * [crime, delinquency or sexual promiscuity] is profitable, desirable, acceptable, respectable, praiseworthy, or commonly accepted.[68]

Justice Marshall's majority opinion ruled that this wording in the ordinance was so nebulous that the film industry might be intimidated into showing only totally inane films. Marshall declared: [69]

> Appellants [including the Interstate Circuit Corp.] attack these standards as unconstitutionally vague. We agree. Motion pictures are, of course, protected by the First Amendment, Joseph Burstyn, Inc. v. Wilson, 343 U.S. 495, 72 S.Ct. 777 (1952), and thus we start with the premise that "[p]recision of regulation must be the touchstone." NAACP v. Button, 371 U.S. 415, 438, 83 S.Ct. 328, 340 (1963). And while it is true that this Court refused to strike down, against a broad and generalized attack, a prior restraint requirement that motion pictures be submitted to censors in advance of exhibition, Times Film Corp. v. City of Chicago, 365 U.S. 43, 81 S.Ct. 391 (1961), there has been no retreat in this area from rigorous insistence upon procedural safeguards and judicial superintendence of the censor's action. See Freedman v. Maryland, 380 U.S. 51, 85 S. Ct. 734 (1965).

In conclusion, problems of defining and controlling obscenity —whether in the electronic or print media or in motion pictures —are among the most tangled in all of American law. Not seldom, efforts to control obscenity have within them elements of high comedy. Consider this comment from a 1968 issue of *The Saturday Review*: "The Fort Lauderdale (Florida) City Com-

---

[67] Interstate Circuit, Inc. v. City of Dallas, 390 U.S. 676, 686, 88 S.Ct. 1298, 1305 (1968).

[68] 390 U.S. 676, 688, 88 S.Ct. 1298, 1305 (1968).

[69] 390 U.S. 676, 682, 88 S.Ct. 1298, 1302 (1968).

mission just passed an ordinance banning obscenity in books, magazines, and records. The law is so specific that it is obscene in itself and cannot be made public." [70]

SEC. 77. BLASPHEMY

Publications which defile the Deity were long held to be blasphemous; in 20th Century America, the crime has all but disappeared.

The law of blasphemy, as it remains in the United States, is little more than an historical artifact. But blasphemy statutes —although never invoked today in America—are still on the books of some 15 states. The ancient crime of blasphemy (technically, a form of criminal libel) was first a common-law offense, although the crime was later codified into statutory form in both England and America. Blackstone defined blasphemy as "denying [God's] being, or providence; or by contumelious reproaches of our Saviour Christ." [71] Black's Law Dictionary defines blasphemy as "[a]ny oral or written reproach maliciously cast upon God, His name, attributes, or religion." [72]

Blasphemy should be distinguished from several other allied offenses:

Sacrilege: "The crime of breaking a church or chapel, and stealing therein. * * * The desecration of anything considered holy * * *".[73]

Heresy: "An offense against religion, consisting not in a total denial of Christianity, but of some of its essential doctrines [such as the Trinity], publicly and obstinately avowed." [74]

Apostacy: "The total renunciation of Christianity, by embracing either a false religion or no religion at all." [75]

Profanity: "Irreverence toward sacred things; particularly, an irreverent or blasphemous use of the name of God." [76] Public swearing and cursing—variously defined—seems to be treated

[70] Jerome Beatty, Jr., "Trade Winds," Saturday Review, November 23, 1968, p. 23.

[71] William Blackstone, Commentaries on the Laws of England, Vol. IV, adapted by Robert Malcolm Kerr (Boston: Beacon Press, 1952) p. 55.

[72] Henry Campbell Black, Black's Law Dictionary, 4th ed. (St. Paul, Minn., West Publishing Co., 1951) p. 216.

[73] Ibid., 1501.

[74] Ibid., 859.

[75] Ibid., 122.

[76] Ibid., 1375.

as "disturbing the peace" or a related offense in many jurisdictions today.

Witchcraft: This old and nearly forgotten crime doubtless has
the bloodiest history of any offense listed in this brief catalog.
Witchcraft—sometimes called sorcery, enchantment, or conjura-
tion—has been called supposed communication with evil spirits.
This offense was punishable by death, on the theory, evidently,
that witches (female) and warlocks (male) revered the Devil
more than God.   Once people rejected the picturesque theology
of the supernatural power of evil, prosecutions for witchcraft
ceased.   But in Salem Village, Massachusetts, in 1692, belief in
witches and warlocks was in full flower.   Twenty persons were
killed for witchcraft in that enlightened village.[77]

Note that the early beginnings of the Anglo-American law of
blasphemy were shot through with perfervid, right-minded attachment to the idea that there was only one true religion:
Christianity.   Violent advocates of such a view, in the 17th Century, were all too ready to kill, maim, or imprison nonconfor-
mists who questioned their views.   Over time, however, severity
of punishment for blasphemy and related offenses in the United
States decreased enormously.   It should be noted, nevertheless,
that as recently as 1937, a man was convicted in Connecticut for
violating that state's blasphemy statute.[78]   But there is now
grave doubt whether any statute serving as the basis for a conviction for blasphemy could be upheld as constitutional.[79]

[77] Ibid., 1776.

[78] "Fined as Blasphemer," New York Times, Oct. 14, 1937, p. 29, col. 1.

[79] See, e. g., Burstyn v. Wilson, 343 U.S. 495, 72 S.Ct. 777 (1952).

Part III

FOR THE GREATEST GOOD: COMMUNICATIONS LAW AND THE PUBLIC INTEREST

Chapter 12

ACCESS TO GOVERNMENT INFORMATION

SEC. 78. THE PROBLEM OF SECRECY IN GOVERNMENT

Following World War II, access to information at various levels of government became an acute problem to many newsmen.

A self-governing people needs to know what its public officials are up to. The proposition seems plain to newsmen who work from day to day in the offices and chambers of government, as they gather information for publication to the people of a democracy. If officials in any branch of government, at any level, may do their work in secret, they may shield themselves from accountability. Ancient words like "tyranny" and "oppression" take on reality for modern man where secrecy pervades government; unfairness, unchecked power, unconcern for human rights and needs, and inefficiency and corruption can thrive in seclusion. The democratic public has every reason to assume that the great bulk of the work of government will be open and available for inspection.

The assumption has honorable origins. Colonial courts had been generally open, following Britain's practice since the mid-Seventeenth Century, and the new America accepted the practice as a matter of course. The Revolutionary Continental Congresses had, indeed, been highly secret bodies, as the colonial legislatures before them had generally been. But with the 1780s and 1790s, first the House of Representatives and then the Senate had opened its doors to the public and press. Granting access had been hard for some congressmen to concede; both Houses wrote rules under which they might operate behind closed doors if the need arose.[1] But the policy was plain and was to be rarely breached during the decades to come: Legislative debates and halls were the domain of people and press as they were of the elected representatives.

No segment of the American public has been more concerned about tendencies to secrecy in government than newsmen. Some feel that it is the central threat to freedom of expression in mid-Twentieth Century America. Accepting, during World War II, the need for extensive secrecy for an enormous war machine in a government bureaucracy grown gigantic, newsmen after the war soon detected a broad pattern of continued secrecy in government operations. Access to meetings was denied; reports, papers, documents at all levels of government seemed less available than before officialdom's habits of secrecy developed in the passion for security during World War II. An intense, insistent campaign for access to government information was launched in the 1950's by editors, publishers, reporters, and news organizations. It went under a banner labeled "Freedom of Information," and under the claim that the press was fighting for the "people's right to know." [2]

To combat what they viewed as a severe increase in denial of access to the public's business, journalists took organized action. "Freedom of Information" committees were established by the American Society of Newspaper Editors (ASNE) and by the professional newsmen's fraternity, Sigma Delta Chi. The ASNE commissioned newspaper attorney Harold L. Cross to perform a major study on the law of access to government activity. His book, *The People's Right to Know*, was published in 1953 and served as a central source of information. Annual reports on the condition of access to government were issued by Sigma Delta Chi. State and local chapters of professional groups worked for the adoption of state access laws. In 1958, a Freedom of Information Center was opened at the University of Missouri School of Journalism, as a clearing house and research facility for those concerned with the subject. Meanwhile, an ally was found in the House Subcommittee on Government Information under Rep. John E. Moss of California, created to in-

[1] Secret Journal of Congress, 1775–1788, Introduction; Deschler, Lewis, Constitution, Jefferson's Manual, and Rules of the House of Representatives, 82 Cong. 2d. Sess., House Doc. 564 (1953), Rule 29.

[2] See Annual Reports, Sigma Delta Chi Advancement of Freedom of Information Committee (Chicago, Sigma Delta Chi).

vestigate charges of excessive secrecy in the Executive branch of government.[3]

Newsmen had powerful allies also in the scientific community. It found that the advance of knowledge in vast areas of government-sponsored science was being slowed, sometimes crippled for years, in the blockage of the flow of research information between and even within agencies of the federal government. Fear of "leakage" of secrets important to defense in the Cold War with the Soviet Union brought administrative orders that were contrary to the tenets of scientists and researchers. A snarl of regulations, rules, and red tape, besides official policy that fostered sequestering, prevented scientists from sharing their findings with others. Their concern about the damage to the advance of knowledge in science paralleled the news fraternity's alarm about damage to the democratic assumption that free institutions rest on an informed public.[4]

SEC. 79.   ACCESS AND THE CONSTITUTION

Courts have given little support to the position that the First Amendment includes a right of access to government information.

In many newsmen's view, freedom of speech and press and the First Amendment encompass a right to gather government information as much as they encompass the right to publish and distribute it. Constitutional protection against denial of access seems to them only reasonable. Madison said that "A popular government without popular information or the means of acquiring it, is but a prologue to a farce or a tragedy, or perhaps both."[5] For their own time, the legal scholar Harold Cross argued that "Freedom of information is the very foundation for all those freedoms that the First Amendment of our Constitution was intended to guarantee."[6]

Jacob Scher, attorney, teacher of journalism, and counsel to the Moss subcommittee, worked to develop a rationale for a Con-

---

[3] Moss, Rep. John E., Preface to Replies from Federal Agencies to Questionnaire Submitted by the Special Subcommittee on Government Information of the Committee on Government Operations, 84 Cong. 1 Sess. (Nov. 1, 1955), p. iii.

[4] Science, Education and Communication, 12 Bulletin of Atomic Scientists 333 (Nov. 1956).

[5] James Madison to W. T. Barry, 1822, quoted in Padover, Saul, ed., The Complete Madison (New York: Harper & Brothers, 1953), p. 337.

[6] Cross, Harold L., The People's Right to Know (Morningside Heights: Columbia Univ. Press, 1953), pp. xiii-xiv.

stitutional right of access. He said that the existence of an access factor in the First Amendment [7]

> * * * is part of the great body of residual rights left to the people in the Ninth and Tenth Amendments, based on the experiences of the colonists as free-born Englishmen and their panoply of "natural rights" one of which was the right to report and comment on government. Article 4, Section 4 of the Constitution provides that "each House" shall keep and publish a Journal. The Sixth Amendment, which protects the rights of accused from arbitrary exercise of power, provides for a public trial, because publicity was considered a restraint upon such exercise of power * * *.

> The fact that a right has lain inchoate or dormant for a long time in no way is in derogation of that right. It may be brought to life by statutory enactment or by judicial construction.

Yet newsmen's arguments for a constitutionally provided right of access find little support in the courts, except where the Sixth Amendment provides it for judicial proceedings (Sec. 79 below). The federal Constitution has provided scant acknowledgement of a "right of access" under the First Amendment in cases that have argued for it. Reporter William Worthy of the *Baltimore Afro-American* in 1956 ignored an order of Secretary of State John Foster Dulles which barred American newsmen from going to Red China to report. When Worthy returned to the United States, the State Department revoked his passport and refused to give him another. Worthy went to court to attempt to regain his passport. Part of his attorneys' argument was that Secretary Dulles, "By preventing this man * * * from traveling to certain countries * * * has effectively curtailed the freedom of the press." The trial court held, without elaborating, that Dulles' refusal to issue the passport did not violate Worthy's rights under the First Amendment. Worthy appealed, but his argument for First Amendment protection failed, the Court of Appeals holding: [8]

> * * * the right here involved is not a right to think or speak; it is a right to be physically present in a certain place * * *.

[7] Scher, Jacob, Access to Information: Recent Legal Problems, 37 Journalism Quarterly 41 (1960).

[8] Worthy v. Herter, 106 U.S.App.D.C. 153, 270 F.2d 905 (1959).

The right to travel is a part of the right to liberty, and
a newspaperman's right to travel is a part of freedom
of the press. But these valid generalizations do not
support unrestrained conclusions. For the maintenance and preservation of liberty, individual rights
must be restricted for various reasons from time to
time.

Freedom of the press bears restrictions * * *.
Merely because a newsman has a right to travel does
not mean he can go anywhere he wishes. He cannot
attend conferences of the Supreme Court, or meetings
of the President's Cabinet or executive sessions of the
Committees of Congress. He cannot come into my
house without permission or enter a ball park without a
ticket of admission from the management, or even
cross a public street downtown between cross-walks
* * *. A newsman's freedom to travel about is a restricted thing, subject to myriad limitations.

The Supreme Court denied certiorari in that case brought by
a newsman. In a later case, it granted review. Here Zemel was
denied a passport to go to Cuba—after the United States had
broken diplomatic relations with that nation—to satisfy his curiosity and to make himself a better informed citizen. Zemel
argued that the travel ban by the State Department was a direct
interference with the First Amendment rights of citizens to inform themselves at first hand of events abroad. The Court
agreed that the Secretary's denial rendered "less than wholly
free the flow of information concerning that country," but denied that a First Amendment right was involved. "The right to
speak and publish does not carry with it the unrestrained right
to gather information," [9] the Court said. It drew parallels with
other situations where access is restricted, such as the prohibition of unauthorized entry to the White House.

A rare state case has held that freedom of speech and press
protects a right of access. The Pawtucket, R.I., city council allowed one newspaper to examine tax cancellation and abatement
records, but refused access to the *Providence Journal*. The
Journal brought court action, alleging that the other paper was
granted access because it supported the political party which
controlled the council, while the Journal had opposed the party.

---

[9] Zemel v. Rusk, 381 U.S. 1, 17–18, 85 S.Ct. 1271, 1281 (1965). See also
Trimble v. Johnston, 173 F.Supp. 651 (D.C.D.C.1953); In re Mack, 386 Pa.
251, 126 A.2d 679 (1956).

The federal district court ruled that the denial had abridged freedom of the press: [10]

> Where such records as these are public records and where there is no reasonable basis for restricting their examination and publication, the attempt here to prohibit their publication is an abridgement of speech and of the press. They seek to place in the discretion of the city council the granting or denial of a constitutional right.

Seemingly, then, if the materials had not been "public records," or if there had been some "reasonable basis" for denying access to them, the constitutional protection would not have held.

Besides the unusual holding such as the foregoing, there has been an occasional dissenting opinion by a judge that argues for constitutional protection for a right of access. Pennsylvania Justice Musmanno, dissenting in In re Mack, said: [11]

> *   *   * freedom of the press is the right of the people to be informed through the press and other media of communication *   *   *. Freedom of the press is not restricted to the operation of linotype machines and printing presses. *   *   * A print shop without material to print would be as meaningless as a vineyard without grapes, an orchard without trees or a lawn without verdure. Freedom of the press means freedom to gather news, write it, publish it and circulate it. When any one of these integral operations is interdicted, freedom of the press becomes a river without water.

News media have had to find arguments other than the First Amendment to press their case for access to non-judicial proceedings. Many reporters have testified that the best pry on government is their own relentless hammering and pressure, ceaseless vigilance, and the nourishing of many sources of information. Others have found that an effective offense is the use of laws at the various government levels—laws which state that public policy demands maximum access for the public and press to the affairs of government. These laws are the main basis of the following discussion.

[10] Providence Journal Co. et al. v. McCoy et al., 94 F.Supp. 186 (D.C.R.I. 1950).

[11] 386 Pa. 251, 126 A.2d 679, 689 (1956). See also Lyles v. Oklahoma, 330 P.2d 734 (Okl.Cr.1958).

SEC. 80.   THE FEDERAL PUBLIC RECORDS LAW

Access to federal executive and administrative records is provided under a law of July 4, 1966, which bespeaks a broad policy of disclosure and provides nine exceptions to open access.

On July 4, 1966, President Lyndon B. Johnson signed the Federal Public Records Law,[12] providing for the availability to the public of the records of executive and administrative agencies of the federal government.   It replaced section 3 of the Administrative Procedure Act of 1946.   In the words of Attorney General Ramsey Clark: [13]

> * * * this statute imposes on the executive branch an affirmative obligation to adopt new standards and practices for publication and availability of information.   It leaves no doubt that disclosure is a transcendent goal, yielding only to such compelling considerations as those provided for in the exemptions of the act.

President Johnson said in signing the law that it sprang "from one of our most essential principles: a democracy works best when the people have all the information that the security of the Nation permits."   He expressed a "deep sense of pride that the United States is an open society in which the people's right to know is cherished and guarded." [14]

Both the President and the Attorney General stressed the fact that the law did not open every record to the public.   But whatever records might have a claim to secrecy under it, the new law was issued in an atmosphere that stressed openness and disclosure.   Its predecessor permitted secrecy if it was required in the public interest, or for "good cause." [15]   The earlier law also required disclosure only to "persons properly and directly concerned" with the subject at hand.   The new law expressed neither of these limitations, and had indeed been passed by Congress in the plain purpose that records would become far more accessible.   It has come to be called the Freedom of Information (FoI) Act.

For the "guidance of the public" under the law, each agency is to publish in the Federal Register its organization plan, and the agency personnel and methods through which the public can get

[12] 5 U.S.C.A. § 552 (1970).

[13] Foreword, Attorney General's Memorandum on the Public Information Section of the Administrative Procedure Act (1967).

[14] Public Papers of the Presidents, Lyndon B. Johnson, 1966 II, p. 699.

[15] 5 U.S.C.A. § 1002 (1946).

information.   The agency's procedural rules and general policies are to be published.   Final opinions given by agencies in the adjudication of cases, staff manuals and instructions to staff that affect the public, and final votes of agency members in its proceedings are to be available.   If records are improperly withheld, the United States district court can enjoin the agency from withholding the records and can order disclosure.   The burden of proof is on the agency to show that the record should be withheld.   And if agency officials fail to comply with the court order, they may be punished for contempt.

There are nine exceptions to that which must be made public. The "open records" provisions are not applicable to matters that are:

1.   specifically required by Executive order to be kept secret in the interest of national defense or foreign policy;

2.   related solely to the internal personnel rules and practices of any agency;

3.   specifically exempted from disclosure by statute;

4.   trade secrets and commercial or financial information obtained from any person and privileged or confidential;

5.   inter-agency or intra-agency memorandums or letters which would not be available by law to a private party in litigation with the agency;

6.   personnel and medical files and similar files the disclosure of which would constitute a clearly unwarranted invasion of personal privacy;

7.   investigatory files compiled for law enforcement purposes except to the extent available by law to a private party;

8.   contained in or related to examination, operating, or condition reports prepared by, on behalf of, or for the use of any agency responsible for the regulation or supervision of financial institutions;

9.   geological and geophysical information and data (including maps) concerning wells.

It is in these exceptions ("exemptions") to disclosure, and the interpretation of their scope by the courts, that the degree of access to information in federal government agencies will be considerably defined.   Newsmen noted early that the nine exceptions to disclosure were more in number than the earlier law had provided.[16]

---

[16] Editor & Publisher, 99:46, p. 11 (Nov. 12, 1966).

While the bill that would become the new law was still unsigned one newspaper assessed it this way: [17]

> The escape clauses that bother most newsmen are those covering manuals outlining investigative techniques, originally meant to protect the FBI, and the President's power to protect "sensitive matters" by executive order.

During the first years of the law's life, news media made little use of its provision for court action to compel disclosure. The cases that were brought to court got there on complaint of persons and firms other than newspapers, magazines, and television.

A study of the first four years of the FoI Act by Samuel J. Archibald [18] showed that 112 cases had been filed under it. Analyzing major court decisions under the act—about one-third of the total, digested by the American Law Division of the Library of Congress—Archibald said some of the nine exceptions to disclosure had had too little litigation to reveal trends. With respect to others, however, "it is possible to conclude that the courts are rejecting government arguments that public records may be withheld if they contain privileged or confidential financial or commercial information. And they are rejecting government arguments that inter-agency memoranda are exempt from the disclosure requirements * * *."

As for exemption number 7 listed above, however, "The courts * * * are generally agreeing with the government's contention that investigatory files compiled for law enforcement purposes need not be made public."

Under the new act, Archibald added, the courts are imposing "their judgments upon the bureaucracy and the court judgment leans toward the people's right to know." Further, the act has made available countless documents by requiring all agencies of the executive branch of the federal government to index and make public the details of day-to-day operations. Agency rules were required to be established by the act, and most include an appeal process to the agency head if lower levels of an agency refuse public access.

[17] Wall Street Journal, May 10, 1966, digested in Kruger, Helen N., "The Access to Federal Records Law," Freedom of Information Center Report No. 186, Sept. 1967 (Columbia: Univ. of Mo. School of Journalism).

[18] The FOI Act Goes to Court, Freedom of Information Center Report No. 280, April 1972 (Columbia: Univ. of Mo. School of Journalism). Quoted parts below are from pages 1 and 2 of the study.

Environmental Protection Agency v. Mink [19] reached the Supreme Court and was decided in 1973.   In it, Rep. Patsy Mink and 32 others of the House of Representatives brought an action for disclosure of reports to the President about the advisability of nuclear tests scheduled in Alaska.   Recommendations in the reports included those of an inter-departmental committee named to investigate the matter.

Exemptions 1 and 5 (above) of the FoI Act were at issue. The Environmental Protection Agency (EPA) said that exemption 1—protecting from disclosure matters required by executive order to be kept secret in the interest of national defense or foreign policy—was operative: at least six documents were classified secret or top secret under Executive Order No. 10501.   The Supreme Court said that that was enough: The history of the act in Congress showed that the test for secrecy "was to be simply whether the President has determined by Executive Order that particular documents are to be kept secret." [20]   It was not appropriate, the Court said, to subject the documents to review by a judge *in camera* to enable the court to separate the secret parts of documents from the supposedly nonsecret parts and order disclosure of the latter.   Justice Stewart, concurring with displeasure, said that the law was plain: Congress had built into the FoI Act "an exemption that provides no means to question an Executive decision to stamp a document 'secret,' however cynical, myopic, or even corrupt that decision might have been." In enacting the law, Stewart said, "Congress chose * * * to decree blind acceptance of Executive fiat." [21]

As for exemption 5—permitting secrecy for inter or intra-agency memoranda and letters—the Court said Congress here intended to incorporate in the law a recognized rule that "confidential intra-agency advisory opinions * * * are privileged from inspection."   While factual matter—as distinct from policy or legal recommendations—might be appropriate for disclosure, if the former were intertwined inextricably with the latter, any disclosure might compromise parts legally secret.   The Court said that on remand of the case to the lower courts, the EPA should have a chance to demonstrate to the trial court, without displaying the documents *in camera* to the judge, that they were not properly subject to disclosure.   It might be, the Court said, that *in camera* inspection would be appropriate, "But it need not

[19] 410 U.S. 73, 93 S.Ct. 827, 35 L.Ed.2d 119 (1973).

[20] Ibid., 129.

[21] Ibid., 136.

be automatic * * *" so far as intra-agency memoranda were concerned.[22]

Thus the United States Supreme Court has strengthened the sequestering power of exception 1 above, which Archibald found had been reflected in earlier lower courts' decisions. Defense and foreign policy matters, secret under Executive Order 10501, seem to be compelling reasons for the courts to endorse secrecy under the FoI Act.

As for exemption 7—investigatory files compiled for law enforcement purposes—Archibald found court endorsement of secrecy strong there also. One of the few actions brought by a news medium under the FoI Act demonstrated this. Cowles Communications, Inc., which published the late *Look* magazine, sought records in the Immigration and Naturalization Service concerning Salvatore Marino. The government refused. Bringing an action under the FoI Act, Cowles argued that exemption 7 was not applicable, as no proceedings were pending against Marino. But the federal district court said that the confidentiality of the informant who gives material for investigatory files should be kept secret, lest he refuse to inform; and more importantly, citizens' right of privacy should not be jeopardized by making investigatory files available to private persons.[23] The fact that there was no enforcement proceeding after compiling the file did not make the file any less one compiled for law enforcement purposes.

The nine exceptions to public inspection that Congress provided in the Federal Public Records Law are statutory additions to a power of withholding that has always been asserted by the President and his Executive Department heads. This is the power exercised under the doctrine of "executive privilege." President George Washington was asked by Congress to make available documents relating to General St. Clair's defeat by Indians. He responded that "the Executive ought to communicate such papers as the public good would permit, and ought to refuse those, the disclosure of which would injure the public * * *."[24] In this case the records were made available to Congress, but many presidents since have refused to yield records, as have the heads of Executive departments. Their power to do so was upheld early in the nation's history by the

---

22 Ibid., 135.

23 Cowles Communications, Inc. v. Department of Justice, 325 F.Supp. 726 (N.D.Cal.1971).

24 Rourke, Francis E., Secrecy and Publicity (Baltimore: Johns Hopkins Press, 1961), p. 65. And see Ibid., pp. 64–69, for general discussion of executive privilege.

United States Supreme Court. The famous decision written by
Chief Justice John Marshall was delivered in 1803 in Marbury v.
Madison, where Marshall said that the Attorney General (a
presidential appointee) did not have to reveal matters which had
been communicated to him in confidence:[25]

> By the Constitution of the United States, the president
> is invested with certain important political powers, in
> the exercise of which he is to use his own discretion,
> and is accountable only to the country in his political
> character and to his own conscience.

Justice Marshall elaborated the principle in the trial of Aaron
Burr, accused of treason, saying that "The propriety of withholding * * * must be decided by [the President] himself,
not by another for him. Of the weight of the reasons for and
against producing it he himself is the judge." [26]

Executive privilege came to be asserted and used much more
often than before during the government's efforts to maintain
security in the cold war with the U.S.S.R. following World War
II. Presidents Truman and Eisenhower used the power to issue
orders detailing what might and might not be released from the
executive departments. President Truman's Executive Order
10–290, of Sept. 24, 1951, set up a system of classifying "official
information which requires safeguarding in the interest of the
security of the United States." Subsequently, President Eisenhower's Order 10–501, of Nov. 6, 1953, modified the classification system and deleted many departments authorized to classify. Both came under heavy attack from Congress and the news
media.[27] Further modification came under President Nixon's
Executive Order No. 11–652 of March 8, 1972, replacing that of
President Eisenhower.

One of the most far-reaching directives of this period was issued by President Eisenhower in 1954. A senate subcommittee
was engaged in the investigation of a controversy between the
Army and the late Senator Joseph McCarthy of Wisconsin.
President Eisenhower sent to Secretary of the Army Robert Stevens a message telling him that his departmental employees
were to say nothing about internal communications of the
Department:[28]

[25] U.S. (1 Cranch.) 137 (1803).

[26] 1 Burr's Trial 182.

[27] Rourke, pp. 75–83.

[28] House Report, No. 2947, 84 Cong., 2 Sess., July 27, 1956. Availability of
Information from Federal Departments and Agencies. Dwight D. Eisenhower
to Sec. of Defense, May 17, 1954, pp. 64–65.

> Because it is essential to efficient and effective administration that employees of the executive branch be in a position to be completely candid in advising with each other on official matters, and because it is not in the public interest that any of their conversations or communications, or any documents or reproductions, concerning such advice be disclosed, you will instruct employees of your Department that in all of their appearances before the subcommittee of the Senate Committee on Government Operations regarding the inquiry now before it they are not to testify to any such conversations or communications or to produce any such documents or reproductions.

While the directive was aimed at a single situation and a single Executive Department, it soon became used by many other executive and administrative agencies as justification for their own withholding of records concerning internal affairs.[29] While newsmen protested the spread of the practice, and while Congressional allies joined them, there was not much legal recourse then apparent.

Two decades later, a head-on confrontation emerged in the Watergate investigations, as President Richard M. Nixon refused to turn over to a grand jury, tape recordings of conversations with his White House aides. Federal Judge John J. Sirica ruled Aug. 29, 1973, that the tapes must be submitted to him for private scrutiny and possible forwarding to the grand jury. The President, in an unsuccessful appeal to the U. S. Court of Appeals, District of Columbia, said he was protecting "the right of himself and his successors to preserve the confidentiality of discussions in which they participate in the course of their constitutional duties." Special prosecutor Archibald Cox argued it was intolerable that "the President would invoke executive privilege to keep the tape recordings from the grand jury but permit his aides to testify fully as to their recollections of the same conversations." The President fired Cox, and the Attorney General resigned and his Deputy was fired before the President yielded the tapes amid a public cry for his impeachment.[29a] The Court of Appeals finding, not yet delivered at this writing, was expected to be appealed to the United States Supreme Court.

[29] Rourke, p. 74.

[29a] New York Times, Sept. 11, 1973, p. 36; Oct. 24, 1973, p. 1.

SEC. 81.   RECORDS AND MEETINGS IN THE STATES

The extent of access in the states varies under statutes providing what shall be open and what closed in the meetings and records of executive and administrative agencies.

Many states have laws declaring that public policy demands maximum disclosure of official business, both meetings and records.   Nowhere, however, it is conceded that every act or every document of officialdom be open to public scrutiny; every branch of government within the states performs some of its work and maintains some of its records in secret.   There are situations here as in the federal government's domain which favor secrecy as protection for the individual's private rights and for government's carrying out its work.   But the principle of disclosure and openness is as central to the democratic spirit at the state and local level as it is at the federal.   A study by the University of Missouri Freedom of Information Center in mid-1968 found that 38 states had laws providing for open meetings of public agencies, and that 42 had open records laws.[30]   Some are more "open" than others.

The diversity among these statutes is far too great to treat in detail here.   Every newsman who reports government needs to know the peculiarities and special provisions of his own state's access laws.   Even among those newspapers or broadcast stations that rely more on their own power than on access laws to penetrate the offices and meetings of government, ignorance of the law's provisions leaves the newsman at the mercy of officials leery of disclosure.   What can be done in this chapter is to illustrate some types of access laws and detail some courts' holdings.

To start with records kept by government offices, the fact that many may be termed "public" records does not necessarily mean that they are open to inspection by the public or the press.   The common law definition of "public records" referred to the need of government to preserve the documents that gave evidence of the activities of its officers.   Thus the definition of public record under the common law is that it is a written memorial by an authorized public officer in discharge of a legal duty to make such a memorial to serve as evidence of something written, said, or done.[31]   For those relatively few states which have no statutes defining public records, the common law defini-

[30] Anon., State Access Statutes, Freedom of Information Center Report No. 202, June 1968 (School of Journalism, University of Missouri).

[31] Amos v. Gunn, 84 Fla. 285, 287, 94 So. 615, 616 (1922).

tion may persist. Its connotations do not go to the "right to inspect," although a qualified right to inspect public records unquestionably exists under the common law. Generally, the common law right of inspection depends on the citizen's having a proper purpose in seeing or copying the record, or an interest that the law would recognize as legitimate.[32]

Most of the states have statutes defining public records. They may define records in extensive lists, or they may do so in brief but general terms. Ordinarily they acknowledge and approve the fact that some of the state's laws specifically provide for secrecy, for example income tax laws that include clauses protecting the individual's income tax returns from disclosure. Laws concerning health department records, motor vehicle accident reports, and public assistance records are other typical examples. In cases like these, lawmakers have determined that injury to individuals concerned may result from disclosure of the records. An "open records" law commonly sanctions such secrecy.

North Dakota's law, admirably brief, states a broad exception at the outset, and goes on to state in general terms what shall be open:[33]

> Except as otherwise specifically provided by law, all records of public or government bodies, boards, bureaus, commissions or agencies of the state or any political subdivision of the state, or organizations or agencies supported in whole or in part by state funds, or expending public funds, shall be public records, open and accessible for inspection during reasonable office hours.

Where state "open records" laws enumerate exceptions to the accessible records, the enumeration seldom is a guarantee that every exception provided by other statutes is included in the list. Virginia's enumerated exceptions, perhaps unusually sweeping, are these:[34]

1. Memoranda, correspondence, evidence and complaints related to criminal investigations and reports submitted to the State Police in confidence.

2. Applications for licenses to the Alcoholic Beverage Control Board and records of investigations connected therewith.

---

[32] Cross, pp. 55–56.

[33] N.D.Stats. § 44–04–18 (1957).

[34] Va.Acts of 1968, Chap. 479.

3. State income tax returns, medical and mental records, scholastic records, welfare records, adoption records, illegitimate births and personnel records.

4. Memoranda, working papers and correspondence held by the Office of the Governor or the Mayor or other chief executive officer of any political subdivision of the state.

5. Memoranda, working papers and records compiled specifically for use in litigation and material furnished in confidence to said offices.

Occasionally, the records law will provide penalties for an official who refuses to disclose materials that the statute declares open. Thus in New Mexico, an officer who has custody of state, county, school, city or town records and refuses a citizen of the state the right to inspect public records [35]

> * * * shall be guilty of a misdemeanor and shall, upon conviction thereof, be fined not less than $250 nor more than $500, or be sentenced to not less than 60 days nor more than six months in jail, or both * * * for each separate violation.

In most states, however, the only enforcement provided for is getting a court order to compel disclosure.

The sequestering tendencies of public officials reach to limitless kinds of records. Actions to compel disclosure indicate some of the range, but there is little use in cataloguing these here, for often that which may be seen in some states may not be seen in others. A "representative" list would be hard to compile. Here are a few records that courts have held to be open for inspection: Maps of county or city subdivisions; [36] audit of records of the sheriff and collector in connection with tax money; [37] records of the state auditor general; [38] books of a municipal corporation; [39] records of a municipal electric plant,[40] city operated docks and terminals,[41] water supply commission,[42] de-

[35] N.M.Stats. § 5–6–17 (1959).

[36] Miller v. Murphy, 78 Cal.App. 751, 248 P. 934 (1926).

[37] Collins v. State, 200 Ark. 1027, 143 S.W.2d 1 (1941).

[38] Nowack v. Fuller, 243 Mich. 200, 219 N.W. 749 (1928).

[39] North v. Foley, 238 App.Div. 731, 265 N.Y.S. 780 (1933).

[40] Mushet v. Dep't of Public Service of Los Angeles, 35 Cal.App. 630, 170 P. 653 (1918).

[41] State ex rel. Cummer v. Pace, 118 Fla. 496, 159 So. 679 (1935).

[42] Egan v. Board of Water Supply of New York, 205 N.Y. 147, 98 N.E. 467 (1912).

partment of conservation;[43] records of licenses of many kinds including automobile licenses;[44] poll books and final results in elections;[45] a school census;[46] records of the clerk of county and circuit court.[47]

On the side of non-disclosure, courts have refused access to the jury roll;[48] police records of various kinds;[49] records of the state fire marshal concerning his investigations;[50] letters to a state board supervising prison terms and paroles;[51] pawnbroker license renewals.[52] Again, the list is only suggestive.

News media seldom take secrecy cases to court. Often they are able to "pry open" records to which they are at first refused access without resort to a legal action. It is more common for a case of this kind to reach the courts through the initiative of a citizen not connected with a news organization than through that of the newspaper or broadcaster.

In Wisconsin, city officials refused to release to the *Waukesha Freeman* a report that concerned alleged mistreatment of citizens by police. In the first reported case brought by a newspaper to force access to Wisconsin government records, the Freeman obtained a court order requiring the release of the report, under the state records law, and the city appealed to the State Supreme Court. The high court, in a preliminary decision, ordered the Circuit Court to read the secret document before deciding whether it should be made public. The Circuit Judge read it and again ordered that it be made public. Once more the city appealed, and the State Supreme Court in 1965 upheld the Circuit Court's order.[53]

[43] State ex rel. Wogan v. Clements, 192 So. 126 (La.App.1940).

[44] Direct Mail Service, Inc. v. Registrar of Motor Vehicles, 296 Mass. 353, 5 N.E.2d 545 (1937).

[45] State ex rel. Thomas v. Hoblitzelle, 85 Mo. 620 (1885).

[46] Harrison v. Powers, 19 Cal.App. 762, 127 P. 818 (1912).

[47] Bend Pub. Co. v. Haner, 118 Or. 105, 244 P. 868 (1926).

[48] State ex rel. Denson v. Miller, 204 Ala. 234, 85 So. 700 (1920).

[49] In re Zeigler, 122 Misc. 351, 203 N.Y.S.2d 19 (1924); Hale v. City of New York, 251 App.Div. 826, 296 N.Y.S. 443 (1937).

[50] State v. Freedy, 198 Wis. 388, 223 N.W. 861 (1929).

[51] Runyon v. Board of Prison Terms and Paroles, 26 Cal.App.2d 183, 79 P.2d 101 (1938).

[52] Round v. Police Com'r for City of Boston, 197 Mass. 218, 83 N.E. 412 (1908).

[53] State ex rel. Youmans v. Owens, 28 Wis.2d 672, 137 N.W.2d 470 (1965).

The Supreme Court of Wisconsin placed real responsibility upon the officer withholding documents, in determining whether a request to disclose would be proper: [54]

> The duty of first determining that the harmful effect upon the public interest of permitting inspection outweighs the benefit to be gained by granting inspection rests upon the public officer having custody of the record or document sought to be inspected. If he determines that permitting inspection would result in harm to the public interest which outweighs any benefit that would result from granting inspection, it is incumbent upon him to refuse the demand for inspection and state specifically the reasons for this refusal.

And once the officer states the reasons for the refusal, if the person seeking inspection takes the action to court, then the trial court has responsibilities: [55]

> * * * the proper procedure is for the trial judge to examine *in camera* the record or document sought to be inspected. Upon making such *in camera* examination, the trial judge should then make his determination of whether or not the harm likely to result to the public interest by permitting the inspection outweighs the benefit to be gained by granting inspection.

> In reaching a determination so based upon a balancing of the interests involved, the trial judge must ever bear in mind that public policy favors the right of inspection of public records and documents, and, it is only in the exceptional case that inspection should be denied.

In another case in the same state, a private citizen brought an action to force the police chief of Madison to release traffic citation records. Here also the Supreme Court of Wisconsin held that the documents were public records, saying that custodians of public records " * * * must bear in mind that public policy, and hence the public interest, favors the right of inspection of documents and public records." [56]

A village clerk of Cornwall, New York, refused to produce the village books for the *Times Herald Record,* claiming that the paper was not a resident or taxpayer of the village. The newspaper brought action, and the village argued that the newspaper had no standing to sue for production of the records. But the

[54] Ibid., 682.

[55] Ibid., 682–683.

[56] Beckon v. Emery, 36 Wis.2d 510, 153 N.W.2d 501 (1967).

New York court said that it was not necessary that a person asking to see the records be a resident or taxpayer. Further, it ruled, news media do have standing in such cases; they can, and do, competently and effectively accomplish purposes underlying "right to know" statutes.[57]

In another New York case, the *New York Post* sought to inspect some of the files, records, and minutes of the Triborough Bridge and Tunnel Authority. A lower court dismissed its petition, saying that the Post had no special interest or clear legal right entitling it to access. But on appeal, the denial was reversed, the appeals court saying that legislative policy in New York is to make available for public inspection all records, papers and documents kept in a public office unless there is a specific law prohibiting access. There was no such law here. The court added that any citizen or taxpayer has the right of inspection under the open records laws.[58]

There was no news medium involved in yet another New York case in which a court stressed the legislative intent to provide access. A woman who had been accidentally shot was refused her request to see police department records of the shooting, on grounds that a Nassau County law forbade disclosure of police records. She applied for a subpoena of the records, and was granted it. The court said that "There is strong legislative policy to make records kept in a public office available for inspection by a person having a legitimate interest in them which overrides the limitation" of the county law.[59]

The rules of states and municipalities about disclosure of police records vary so widely that generalizing about them is almost fruitless. The foregoing cases concerning police records come down on the side of disclosure, but the situation from state to state, and within some states, can leave no doubt that discretion is wide for city councils that make ordinances on the matter, and for police officers who are the custodians of the records. The most exhaustive study of the general picture of access—that by the late Harold L. Cross—finds that press and public have no enforceable legal right to inspect police records, "using that term broadly, as such, as a whole, or without exceptions."[60] Developing friendships and good working relations with police is

57 Orange County Pubs. Division of Ottaway News-Radio, Inc. v. White, 55 Misc.2d 42, 284 N.Y.S.2d 293 (1967).

58 New York Post Corp. v. Moses, 12 A.D.2d 243, 210 N.Y.S.2d 88 (1961).

59 Kruger v. Nassau County, 53 Misc.2d 166, 278 N.Y.S.2d 28 (1967).

60 Cross, Chap. 8 and p. 118.

probably as valuable an avenue to their records, for newsmen, as relying on statutes about access.

The power of state law to overrule local ordinances is illustrated in State v. Mayo.[61] Here the city of Hartford, Conn., had exercised its local option powers to pass its own building code, instead of adopting the state code. Part of the Hartford code provided that documents in support of applications for building permits were not public records. Two state agencies dealing with engineering and architecture wanted to review the documents, but Glendon R. Mayo, Hartford's Director of Licenses and Inspections, refused to disclose them on the basis of the city code. The state petitioned for a disclosure order, and won it. The court held that the Connecticut "right to know" statute should be construed broadly. The "exception" clauses of the statute did not cover the documents in question, it said, and no city ordinance in conflict with a state statute can stand, since the city's powers to legislate are conferred by the state.

A North Dakota statute provides that court records are open for inspection only to "persons having business therewith." It also has an open records law, and under this the *Grand Forks Herald* sought to compel the county court to permit it to inspect court records dealing with wills admitted to probate, marriage license records, and other documents. County Judge Lyons refused to disclose the records on grounds that the open records law has an "exceptions" clause that says records shall be open "except as otherwise specifically provided by law." The Supreme Court of North Dakota upheld Judge Lyons in her refusal. It said that the open records law does not cover county court records. And the law permitting inspection of court records to "persons having business therewith," it said, does not mean the newspaper. The word "business" in the statute, it held, implies some activity involving a direct or personal interest, and the Herald did not have that interest.[62]

Limiting access to records to persons who have such an interest in them goes far back in the common law. Some people need official records to show their claim to property. Some need them for purposes in litigation.[63] Ultimately, people who wanted to make copies of records for profit showed that they, too, had an "interest." The newspaper's special interest in access to

---

[61] 4 Conn.Cir. 511, 236 A.2d 342 (1967).

[62] Grand Forks Herald, Inc. v. Lyons, 101 N.W.2d 543 (N.D.1960).

[63] Cross, pp. 27–29.

records is recognized in some states; gathering news of government is an essential part of its business.[64]

Along with "interest" in some states, are rules which say that the purpose of the person seeking access must be proper or legitimate. This, too, is part of the common law rule.[65] In some states it has been held that "idle curiosity" on the part of the applicant is definitely not a sufficient purpose.[66] Yet the reverse holds in other states, where the motive of the applicant is said not to matter.[67]

To shift now from laws on government records to those on meetings of executive and administrative bodies, states again display great differences in the degree of access permitted. The State of New Mexico demonstrates a highly open approach with few exceptions, so far as final decision-making by agencies and boards is concerned. The law reads: [68]

> (A) The governing bodies of all municipalities, boards of county commissioners, boards of public instruction and all other government boards and commissions of the state or its subdivisions, supported by public funds, shall make all final decisions at meetings open to the public, provided, however, meetings of grand juries shall not be included as public meetings within the meaning of this statute.

> (B) Any person violating any of the provisions of this section is guilty of a misdemeanor and upon conviction shall be punished by a fine not exceeding one hundred dollars * * * for each offense.

As with its open records law, New Mexico is unusual in providing a specific penalty for officials who violate the act.

Virginia, on the other hand, details a long list of exceptions to open meetings.[69] Its law permits closed meetings for discussion of employment, discipline, and other action on state personnel; discussion on the condition and use of property that the state owns or may want; protection of privacy of individuals; discus-

---

[64] Holcombe v. State ex rel. Chandler, 240 Ala. 590, 200 So. 739 (1941); Nowack v. Fuller, 342 Mich. 200, 219 N.W. 749 (1928).

[65] Cross, p. 36.

[66] Bend Pub. Co. v. Haner, 118 Or. 105, 244 P. 868 (1926); Hardman v. Collector of Taxes of North Adams, 317 Mass. 439, 58 N.E.2d 845 (1945).

[67] State ex rel. Halloron v. McGrath, 104 Mont. 490, 67 P.2d 838 (1937).

[68] N.M.Stats. § 5–6–17 (1959).

[69] Va.Acts of 1968, §§ 1.4, 1.5.

sions on locating new businesses; investing of funds; and other matters. It covers meetings of its General Assembly and legislative committees and commissions, stating conditions for closed meetings.

Wisconsin's meetings law is fairly typical in stating the kinds of topics considered by the state as appropriate for closed meetings. Leading off with the statement that broad access to meetings of public agencies is necessary, for "a representative government of the American type is dependent upon an informed electorate * * *", it goes on to state the exceptions: [70]

> Nothing herein contained shall prevent executive or closed sessions for the purpose of:
>
> (a) Deliberating after judicial or quasi-judicial trial or hearing;
>
> (b) Considering employment, dismissal, promotion, demotion, compensation, licensing or discipline of any public employee or person licensed by a state board or commission or the investigation of charges against such person, unless an open meeting is requested by the employee or person charged, investigated or otherwise under discussion;
>
> (c) Probation, parole, crime detection and prevention;
>
> (d) Deliberating or negotiating on the purchasing of public property, the investing of public funds, or conducting other public business which for competitive or bargaining reasons require closed sessions;
>
> (e) Financial, medical, social or personal histories and disciplinary data which may unduly damage reputations;
>
> (f) Conferences between any local government or committee thereof, or administrative body, and its attorney concerning the legal rights and duties of such agency with regard to matters within its jurisdiction.

Like many other states' statutes, Wisconsin's provides no penalty for violation of the law. It is ordinarily impossible to take an alleged violation to court to have the law enforced on the spot; to get a directive from the Attorney General stating whether the meeting should be open is somewhat more feasible. Either course, however, illustrates the problem with many "open meeting" laws: before a court order or an Attorney General's statement can be gotten, the meeting has been held and ad-

---

[70] Wis.Stats. § 14.90 (1959).

journed. News media, partly because of this problem, very seldom go to court with an alleged violation of an open meetings law.[71] Moreover, some reporters and editors assert that the laws are harmful to the public's "right to know": knowledgeable municipal or state officials, these newsmen's argument runs, can turn the law to their own advantage and engage in secret session within the letter, but outside the spirit, of anti-secrecy laws. Other newsmen, however, find the laws to be effective background support—real door-openers when used by a reporter who is faced with the prospect of a closed meeting. Some newsmen carry a copy of their state law at all times.

To pursue the Wisconsin situation as an example, no cases are reported in which state news media have gone to court over the secret meeting of a state government agency. Since the passage of the first open meetings law in 1959, however, news media have frequently turned to the Attorney General for an "informal opinion" as to secrecy in specific meetings (only public officials and bodies receive "formal" opinions). Two of three Attorneys General between 1958 and 1969 expressed strong support for the open meetings law. While their statements and opinions did not, of course, carry the force of court decisions, they had the weight of legal authority. Not every opinion by any means was favorable to open sessions; under the exceptions to open meetings listed in the statute, at times they found that closed sessions were proper.

Taking office as Attorney General in 1965, Bronson C. LaFollette early made a statement to the press, describing his support for open meetings and saying: [72]

> *   *   *   all meetings of all public agencies must be conducted in public unless the subject matter clearly falls within one of the exceptions to the statute *   *   *. I call upon all State Departments, boards, commissions and committees to implement the requirement of the statute. Any doubt whether a matter falls within one of the exceptions should be resolved in favor of open public meetings.

He took up two situations illustrated by news stories of the previous few weeks. One involved a closed meeting of the University of Wisconsin Human Rights Committee made up of students and faculty. It had met secretly in March, 1965, upon unani-

[71] Cross, p. 194.

[72] LaFollette, Attorney General Bronson C., Statement to Continuing Seminar for Jouralists, Oshkosh (Wis.) State University, May 20, 1965, p. 2.

mous vote of the members, to consider the case of a fraternity that had allegedly practiced discrimination in membership.[73] The other situation involved a Board of Economic Development, made up of non-government businessmen appointed by Governor Warren Knowles as an advisory body. It also had met in March in closed session. To the press' objections, Knowles had responded that the Board was not, in his opinion, subject to the meetings law which called for open sessions of "all state and local governing and administrative bodies, boards, commissions, committees and agencies * * *." He defended secrecy for the Board, on grounds that it was not a statutory body, that it did not have an appropriation of public funds, and that it had no power to act for the state government.[74]

Though he did not specifically refer to these incidents, La-Follette raised the general points and gave his opinion. As for University committee meetings, he noted that the "Anti-Secrecy Law has been held to apply to meetings of the University of Wisconsin faculty * * *. It is my opinion that the law also applies to meetings of duly constituted committees of the faculty, unless such meetings are concerned with matters which clearly fall within one of the state exceptions provided by the statute." [75]

Also, he said, in his opinion the law "is applicable to meetings of advisory boards and committees when governmental affairs and governmental business are discussed or considered. Advisory committees and groups dealing with governmental affairs and the transaction of governmental business must comply with the requirements of the statute." [76] This, of course, went to the matter of the Knowles Board of Economic Development.

Two months later, LaFollette delivered an informal opinion in a letter to the director of the Citizens' Governmental Research Bureau, a privately supported organization for improving government in the Milwaukee area. Director Norman N. Gill had asked whether a village board might meet in secret to consider the appointment of a person to fill a vacant elective position on the board.

LaFollette replied that such a closed meeting would violate the law on open meetings. He said that the provision in the law's exceptions which refers to employment, dismissal, promotion

[73] Milwaukee Journal, March 30, 1965, Part 1, p. 12.

[74] (Madison) Wisconsin State Journal, March 30, 1965, p. 4.

[75] LaFollette, Statement to Continuing Seminar for Journalists, p. 4.

[76] Ibid.

and other matters concerning personnel applies to public employees, not to public officers. "A person who seeks appointment to public office must necessarily submit his qualifications to public scrutiny," LaFollette said. "He should not expect privacy in this respect." [77]

Another informal opinion from the Wisconsin Attorney General was given after it was announced that newsmen would be barred from a state government committee meeting that was to select a site for a new university. The newsmen appealed to LaFollette, and in response he clarified the meaning of the rule permitting closed meetings for deliberating on the purchase of public property where competitive or bargaining considerations were involved. He said that the committee might meet in secret for discussions on land not already acquired. But for discussing two other categories of land, he said, the committee should meet in public session: and already held by government agencies, and land on which the government agencies already had options to buy.[78] In the latter two, competitive factors would not affect discussions in open sessions.

He added that to comply with the spirit of the anti-secrecy law, the committee should have a court reporter transcribe all the proceedings of the secret part of the meeting, and make the transcription available to the public when the final decision about the land was made.[79]

Other opinions delivered by the Attorney General in 1965 and 1966 included one on "preliminary negotiations" between a government body and a labor union, which he said might be closed; [80] and one on a Republican party convention's closed meeting on the draft of a platform for the party, which he said should be open. "The Republican Party Platform Convention is created by the statutes of the State of Wisconsin," he ruled. "It is, therefore, a public agency *   *   *." [81]

The news medium that wants legal action on an agency's proposal to close a government meeting, or on one in session, may find a court order far too slow to meet the needs of the moment. As an alternative, it may wish to consider getting an attorney

---

[77] LaFollette letter to Gill, July 15, 1965.

[78] Statement of Attorney General Bronson C. LaFollette on the Proposed Meeting of the Site Selection Committee, Feb. 23, 1966.

[79] Ibid.

[80] LaFollette letter to Milwaukee Corporation Counsel Robert P. Russell, Aug. 19, 1965.

[81] LaFollette letter to State Sen. Frank E. Panzer, Oct. 4, 1966.

general's opinion, which may or may not come down on the side of opening the meeting but which in any event should give guidance for the future.

SEC. 82.   ACCESS TO JUDICIAL PROCEEDINGS

Under the Sixth Amendment to the United States Constitution and under state constitutions, criminal trials are seldom closed to the press, but trials of several kinds of civil cases are closed, and broadcasting and photography are seldom permitted.

Criminal cases in American courts are open under the Sixth Amendment of the Constitution and under state constitutions. The former reads that "In all criminal prosecutions, the accused shall enjoy the right to a speedy and public trial * * *." The rule arose out of abhorrence to the practice in European nations of arbitrary tribunals' ordering severe punishments in secret trials.   The Spanish Inquisition, the reputation of the English Star Chamber, and the use of the *lettre de cachet* by the French all, perhaps, contributed to the revulsion which caused the Founders to assert the principle of open trials.

There is no guarantee that every person who wishes to attend a trial may do so.   Cross has pointed out that the law does not require a courtroom to be so large that all who line up at the courtroom door must be provided room, nor that disruptive persons may not be removed from the court.[82]   But beyond these plain matters of orderly handling of court business lie decisions and principles that limit access of the printed and broadcast media.

Courts have sometimes discussed whether the right to a public trial is primarily for the benefit of the accused, or of the public which needs to know how its servants are handling official business.   An old case held that "The law does not indeed authorize any court to act arbitrarily and unreasonably exclude persons, but the right to have the courts open is the right of the public and not of the individual."[83]   Yet such a thorough going assertion that the public's right is paramount has not received wide judicial endorsement.   Another view is that the public trial provision "Primarily * * * is for the benefit of the accused— to afford him the means of proving a fact with reference to some question of procedure * * * and to see that he is not unjustly condemned * * *"; but that it also "involves ques-

---

[82] Cross, p. 157.

[83] State v. Copp, 15 N.H. 212 (1844).

Nelson & Teeter Mass Com.2d Ed. F.P.—31

tions of public interest and concern   *   *   *" because people have the right to know what is done in their courts.[84]

A decision of 1954 ruled squarely that the public trial principle may be asserted only by the accused: the interest of the individual is paramount.   In this case millionaire Minot Jelke was accused of pandering, and as sensational sexual details emerged at trial and more were in prospect, Judge Valente closed the court to the public and the press on grounds of public decency. Jelke was convicted.   He appealed his conviction on grounds that he was denied a public trial by the court order, and the New York Court of Appeals upheld his claim.[85]

Meanwhile, United Press, the wire service, was bringing a separate action against Judge Valente for excluding the press and the public.   It argued that the public had a right to be at all criminal trials: the value to be protected was the public's right to know what its courts do, as much as the accused's right not to be tried in secrecy.   But the Court of Appeals denied United Press' claim.   It said that the right to a public trial is particularly a right of the individual accused, safeguarding him against unjust prosecution and abuse of judicial authority.   It said that on some occasions the accused might ask for a private trial, perhaps when the crime had aroused intense public emotions and he felt that a public trial would be to his disadvantage.   In such circumstances, the Court held, allowing press and public a right of access to the trial could be "in hostility to" the rights of the accused.   The public's right to know, it said, is adequately protected so long as the accused may claim his right to public trial.[86]

Yet where a justice, angered at newsmen for printing the previous criminal record of Carmine Persico who was on trial for extortion and conspiracy, first threatened contempt actions against them and later closed the trial, the New York Court of Appeals said the issues were different and ruled that the trial should not have been closed.   In contrast to *United Press*, the Court said, the trial justice's order "was aimed specifically at the news media and was intended as a punishment for what the [justice]   characterized   as   their   'contumacious   conduct   *   *   *'." [87]   The newsmen had a personal stake in the outcome of the controversy, as the justice's action was aimed at them and would limit their ability to act as newsmen, and that stake gave

---

84 State v. Keeler, 52 Mont. 205, 156 P. 1080 (1916).

85 People v. Jelke, 284 App.Div. 211, 130 N.Y.S.2d 662 (1954).

86 United Press Ass'n v. Valente, 308 N.Y. 71, 123 N.E.2d 777 (1954).

87 Oliver v. Postel, 30 N.Y.2d 171, 331 N.Y.S.2d 407, 282 N.E.2d 306, 309 (1972).

them the standing to challenge the validity of his order. The articles that the justice objected to had not reached the jury and there was no basis for the threatened contempt citation. The justice's order was an unwarranted effort to punish and censor the press.

In an Ohio case in which a judge excluded newspaper reporters from the courtroom during a pandering trial, a newspaper successfully challenged the trial court's action. Reporters had been excluded at the request of the defendant during cross-examination of a state witness, counsel saying to the judge that he would be "better able to compel the witness to tell the truth" if she could be cross-examined in private. The Ohio Supreme Court held that the exclusion order violated the constitutional guarantee of a public trial in a criminal case. The Supreme Court said that sometimes a defendant can waive his right to a public trial, but can not waive the right of the people to insist that court proceedings, "insofar as practicable and in the interest of the public health and public morals, be open to public view." There is no right, the Court said, to a private trial.[88]

One kind of judicial activity that is universally closed is the grand jury proceeding which of course is not a trial. The grand jury investigates and deliberates the question whether persons must stand trial. In these proceedings, public policy calls for secrecy because early investigation may implicate persons who later turn out to be blameless, and publicity could injure them needlessly. Also, publicity during early stages of a grand jury investigation could serve as a warning for the guilty, not yet in custody, to escape.[89]

There are a few classes of civil cases that are closed in some states to public and press. These generally have to do with family relations, divorce, and juvenile proceedings. Considerations about "public morals" lie behind the seclusion of divorce proceedings and domestic relations, which may involve heavy sexual content. As for juvenile proceedings, they are commonly held in secret on grounds of the welfare of the child, whose present or future, it is thought, may be damaged by publicity of his delinquency or neglect.

Colorado's statute on divorce provides that the court exclude all except court officers or persons connected with the case, while in West Virginia, divorce trials are to be held in the judge's chambers.[90] Wisconsin's law on juveniles provides that

[88] E. W. Scripps et al. v. Fulton, 100 Ohio App. 157, 125 N.E.2d 896 (1955).

[89] Cross, pp. 173–174.

[90] Comp.L.1921, C.C.P., § 463; St.1935, Mar. 9, c. 35, § 23, respectively.

the media may not publish the names of offenders under 18 that emerge in juvenile court proceedings.[91] This does not prohibit news media from publishing names of juveniles obtained in some way outside the proceedings of the courts, however.

Although the pencil-wielding reporter is seldom excluded from a criminal trial, his fellow reporter who carries a still camera, television camera, or microphone faces an entirely different situation. Many courts bar the photographer and broadcaster from taking the tools of their trade into the courts. A long and vigorous campaign has been waged against the ban, by individuals and organizations of newsmen who use the camera and microphone. They have argued that the barrier prevents the public from getting the fullest, most direct knowledge of its courts' work. They have declared that a great opportunity for public education in government, offered by the television medium, is wasted by preventing television coverage. They have insisted that barring their instruments, while permitting the paper-and-pad newsman to report, discriminates against visual and audio media. They have demonstrated to courts that they can operate the cameras of the 1970s without lights, with unobtrusive accessories, and without disrupting the "decorum of the court." They have not widely won their case.[92]

A variety of court rules and decisions stops the broadcaster and cameraman at the courtroom door or further away. Rule 53 of the Federal Rules of Criminal Procedure, long barring phototaking and radio broadcasting of federal judicial proceedings, since 1962 has applied to the "environs" of the court, not only to the courtroom itself; and to any judicial proceeding, not only to criminal proceedings as formerly.[93] Precisely what the "environs" of the court are may be open to interpretation. In 1964, Los Angeles federal judges ordered photographers and broadcasters to stay away from the courtroom floor of the Federal Building, and from a hearing room on another floor. The federal courts go unphotographed and unbroadcast.[94]

Number 35 of the American Bar Association (ABA) Canons of Judicial Ethics is a source for denial of access to state courts. The Canons are voluntarily adopted or not in the states, according to the judicial rulemaking authorities of each state. They

[91] Wis.Stat. 48.26 (1955).

[92] Am.Bar Ass'n., Special Committee on Proposed Revision of Canon 35, Report, Feb. 5, 1963, pp. 4–6.

[93] Am.Bar Ass'n., Special Committee on Proposed Revision of Judicial Canon 35, Interim Report and Recommendations, July 23, 1962, pp. 95–96.

[94] 97 Editor & Publisher 52 (Feb. 1, 1964).

may be incorporated into state laws or adopted as a rule of the courts. Many states have adopted Canon 35, which reads as follows: [95]

> Proceedings in court should be conducted with fitting dignity and decorum. The taking of photographs in the courtroom, during sessions of the court or recesses between sessions, and the broadcasting or televising of court proceedings, distract participants and witnesses in giving testimony, and create misconceptions with respect thereto in the mind of the public and should not be permitted.

The Canon makes an exception for televising or broadcasting naturalization proceedings carried out by courts, where the proceedings are "a ceremony for the purpose of publicly demonstrating in an impressive manner the essential dignity and the serious nature of naturalization." [96]

Two states, Colorado and Texas, did not bar television and photographers from the courtroom. They did not adopt Canon 35, but left televising up to the discretion of the judge in the individual case, Colorado adding that televising should not take place over the objection of a witness or juror and Texas not over the objection of a witness.[97] In Colorado, about 95 trials were broadcast between 1956 and 1962. Important trials arose in both states. One occurred in Colorado in 1958, when John G. Graham was charged with placing a bomb on an airplane, with the result that 45 persons were killed, including his mother. Although he objected to being televised, Judge Joseph H. McDonald permitted cameras to operate. He was quoted as saying that he felt that the defendant (not a witness or juror, whose objections would have been honored) "has no rights in the premises," and that as judge, he felt Graham's rights were not being violated by the presence of television.[98]

In Texas, the trial of Billie Sol Estes on a state charge of swindling farmers by selling them non-existent fertilizer tanks and equipment, was televised (see Chap. 8 herein). The famous

[95] American Bar Association Special Committee on Proposed Revision of Judicial Canon 35, Report, p. 3. The canon was revised and adopted by the ABA House of Delegates Feb. 5, 1963.

[96] Ibid. Canon 35 has been replaced by Canon 3A7 of the Code of Judicial Conduct, adopted by the ABA House of Delegates 8/16/72. Its provisions are similar to those of Canon 35. See ABA Law Student Division, Code of Professional Responsibility and Code of Judicial Conduct, p. 47, 1972.

[97] Ibid., pp. 9–10.

[98] Special Committee on Proposed Revision of Judicial Canon 35, Report, p. 10.

Estes, a man with close connections in the White House, objected to the televising of the pre-trial proceedings, but his motion
was denied. Heavy coverage resulted, with at least 12 cameramen taking motion and still pictures. Cables and wires
stretched over the courtroom floor, and three microphones were
on the judge's bench. At trial, coverage was far less intense
and obtrusive. Estes was convicted, and appealed on the ground
that he was deprived of his rights to due process of law under
the Fourteenth Amendment by the televising and broadcasting
of the trial. The United States Supreme Court, by a 5–4 vote,
reversed his conviction.[99] Mr. Justice Tom Clark rested his argument heavily on the possible adverse psychological effect of
being "on television" for witnesses, jurors, judge, and defendant, rather than on television's possible tendencies to disrupt order and decorum in the courtroom. These possible effects, he
said, "are real enough to have convinced the Judicial Conference
of the United States, this Court and the Congress that television
should be barred in federal trials * * *; in addition they
have persuaded all but two of our States to prohibit television in
the courtroom."[1]

Following the Estes decision, Colorado revised its court rules
to prohibit broadcasting and photography at the objection of the
defendant, as well as of witness or juror.[2]

[99] Estes v. Texas, 381 U.S. 532, 85 S.Ct. 1628 (1965).

[1] Ibid., 1634–1636.

[2] 98 Editor & Publisher 59 (July 10, 1965).

Chapter 13

PUBLIC ACCESS TO MASS MEDIA

SEC. 83. REGULATION OF BROADCASTING AND FREE EXPRESSION

Government regulates broadcasting in ways that it does not regulate printed media because the air waves are of the nature of a public resource that can carry only a limited number of voices.

Voice broadcasting emerged in the 1920's under law that permitted anyone who applied for a broadcast license to get one. By 1926, the limited number of frequencies available for broadcasting was unable to carry the traffic without intolerable interference among stations. A dial-twirler's excursion across his radio set frequencies was a tour of Babel. At broadcasters' request and with full agreement from officials, Congress passed the Radio Act of 1927, establishing a Federal Radio Commission (FRC) as an administrative agency to regulate and control traffic and to see that broadcasting was carried out according to the "public interest, convenience, or necessity." The FRC was to choose among applicants for access to the air waves, and license the chosen. In 1934, Congress passed the Communications Act establishing the Federal Communications Commission (FCC), under which radio and television have been regulated since, and telephone and telegraph as well.[1]

The nature of the physical universe had dictated that broadcasting somehow be controlled; there were not enough frequencies to permit everyone who wished to do so to broadcast. And

[1] Head, Sydney W., Broadcasting in America (Boston: Houghton Mifflin Company, 1972) 2d ed., Chap. 8. The Act of 1927 is 44 Stats. 1162; of 1934, 48 Stat. 1064.

the fact that individuals and corporations could scarcely lay claim to ownership of the air waves, which existed much more in the context of a public resource than of a private one, argued for government's controlling access to the air waves in the name of the public.

Yet this situation plainly raised questions about government's relation to free speech and press. No agency of government regulated newspapers, books and magazines. The government's choosing among applicants and subsequent licensing of the chosen was a process that was not tolerable under free press principles for the print media. The FCC was indeed barred by the Communications Act from censorship of the content of broadcasting, but the choosing and licensing process was upheld by the courts as constitutional. It was held in National Broadcasting Co. v. U. S.: [2]

> Freedom of utterance is abridged to many who wish to use the limited facilities of radio. Unlike other media of expression, radio inherently is not available to all. That is its unique characteristic; and that is why, unlike other modes of expression, it is subject to governmental regulation. Because it cannot be used by all, some who wish to use it must be denied * * *. The standard provided for the licensing of stations by the Communications Act of 1934 was the "public interest, convenience, or necessity." Denial of a station license on that ground, if valid under the Act, is not a denial of free speech.

Principles of free speech, then, did not stand in the way of denying a person a license. Furthermore, there were positive obligations upon the holder of a license to operate in the public interest, obligations which were not imposed upon the printed media. In a case involving complaints against a station for programming public affairs shows that had overtones of racial and religious discrimination, the Federal Court of Appeals spoke of the differences between newspapers and broadcasters: [3]

> A broadcaster has much in common with a newspaper publisher, but he is not in the same category in terms of public obligations imposed by law. A broadcaster seeks and is granted the free and exclusive use of a limited and valuable part of the public domain; when he accepts that franchise, it is burdened by enforceable

2 319 U.S. 190, 63 S.Ct. 997, 1014 (1943).

3 Office of Communication of United Church of Christ v. FCC, 123 U.S. App.D.C. 328, 359 F.2d 994, 1003 (1966).

obligations. A newspaper can be operated at the whim
or caprice of its owners; a broadcasting station cannot.
After nearly five decades of operation, the broadcasting industry does not seem to have grasped the simple
fact that a broadcast license is a public trust subject to
termination for breach of duty.

A striking example of expression that might result in the legal
foreclosure of continued broadcasting, but not of newspaper
publishing, appeared in a pair of court decisions in 1931 and
1932. The first was Near v. Minnesota; the second was Trinity
Methodist Church, South v. FRC. In the first case, the United
States Supreme Court ruled that government could not forbid a
newspaper to publish because it had made scurrilous attacks on
police and law enforcement officials, and on Jews. In the second, the Federal Appeals Court ruled that the Federal Radio
Commission could deny a radio broadcaster a new license and
thus access to the air waves because it had previously made
scurrilous attacks on judges and the administration of justice
and on Roman Catholics.

Near v. Minnesota [4] involved a scandal sheet published in Minneapolis by J. M. Near and a partner who ran afoul of an extraordinary Minnesota law. The famous "Gag law" provided
that it was a public nuisance to engage in the regular, persistent
publication of a "malicious, scandalous and defamatory" periodical. The state could step in, stop, and permanently suppress
such a publication. If a publisher disobeyed an injunction
against his publishing, and resumed it, he could be punished for
contempt of court. Under the law, Near was enjoined from continuing to publish his *Saturday Press*. He challenged the constitutionality of the law, and the United States Supreme Court reversed his conviction.

Chief Justice Charles Evans Hughes said the question was
whether a law authorizing such government action to restrain
publication squared with freedom of the press as historically
conceived and guaranteed. What was done to Near was to restrain him in advance of publication—the "prior restraint" that
was the licensing and censorship of old. Tracing the history of
the guarantee of free press, he said that previous restraint is
unconstitutional except in "exceptional cases" such as publication of troop movements in war time and incitements to acts of
violence endangering the community. He said it was unavailing
to the state to insist [5]

---

[4] 283 U.S. 697, 51 S.Ct. 625 (1931).

[5] Ibid., 283 U.S. 697, 722, 51 S.Ct. 625, 633 (1931).

* * * that the statute is designed to prevent the circulation of scandal which tends to disturb the public peace and to provoke assaults and the commission of crime. Charges of reprehensible conduct, and in particular of official malfeasance, unquestionably create a public scandal, but the theory of the constitutional guaranty is that even a more serious public evil would be caused by authority to prevent publication.

Hughes said that "reckless assaults upon public men * * * exert a baleful influence" and deserve condemnation by public opinion. But, he said, the growth of complexity in government, the opportunities for corruption in government, the rise in crime and the danger of its protection by unfaithful officials and official neglect, emphasize "the primary need of a vigilant and courageous press." He added: [6]

The fact that the liberty of the press may be abused by miscreant purveyors of scandal does not make any the less necessary the immunity of the press from previous restraint in dealing with official misconduct.

Prosecutions and law suits for libel, said Justice Hughes, are the proper remedy for false and defamatory statements, not prohibition of publishing which is "the essence of censorship." The law was unconstitutional, and Near was free to publish.

But not so the Reverend Doctor Schuler, lessee and operator of radio station KGEF in Los Angeles. He filed for the renewal of his broadcast license in 1930, and numerous citizens protested to the FRC. It denied Schuler's request for re-licensing on grounds that his broadcasts attacked the Roman Catholic Church, were sensational rather than instructive, and obstructed the orderly administration of public justice (he had been convicted of contempt for attacking judges). The Reverend Schuler's church, Trinity Methodist South, took the decision to court on grounds that it violated free speech and due process. The Federal Appeals Court denied its appeal and upheld the denial of a license.[7] It said that Congress has the right to establish agencies to regulate the airwaves, and such agencies can refuse to renew licenses to one who has abused a license to broadcast defamatory and untrue matter. This denial of a permit, the Court held, is different from taking away property. Then it spoke of

6 Ibid., 720.

7 Trinity Methodist Church, South v. FRC, 61 U.S.App.D.C. 311, 62 F.2d 850 (1932), certiorari denied 284 U.S. 685, 52 S.Ct. 204 (1932), 288 U.S. 599, 53 S.Ct. 317 (1933).

the kinds of materials and attacks that KGEF had broadcast, and gave its view as to their effect: [8]

> If it be considered that one in possession of a permit to broadcast in interstate commerce may, without let or hindrance from any source, use these facilities, reaching out, as they do, from one corner of the country to the other, to obstruct the administration of justice, offend the religious susceptibilities of thousands, inspire political distrust and civic discord, or offend youth and innocence by the use of words suggestive of sexual immorality, and be answerable for slander only at the instance of the one offended, then this great science, instead of a boon, will become a scourge, and the nation a theatre for the display of individual passions and collision of personal interests. This is neither censorship nor previous restraint, nor is it a whittling away of the rights guaranteed by the First Amendment, or an impairment of their free exercise * * *.

Taken together, the two decisions made it clear that a newspaper owner could not be stopped from publishing because of his attacks on officials and religious groups, but that a radio broadcaster could be stopped for similar attacks. Denying a license is not a violation of freedom of speech, but the application of the regulatory power of Congress.[9]

SEC. 84. THE EQUAL OPPORTUNITY REQUIREMENT

If a broadcaster furnishes air time to one candidate for public office, he must offer equal opportunity to opposing candidates.

The Communications Act of 1934 under which the FCC holds its powers to regulate broadcasting carries a specific provision that shows Congress' concern over possible damage to the political process that unregulated broadcasting could cause. This is Section 315 of the Act, known to every radio and television newsman as the "equal time" or "equal opportunities" provision. It says, broadly, that if a station provides time for one political candidate, it must do so for his opponents. From the start of regulation in 1927, this principle has been part of the law, writ-

---

[8] Ibid., 61 U.S.App.D.C. 311, 62 F.2d 850, 852–853 (1932).

[9] Red Lion Broadcasting Co. v. FCC, 395 U.S. 367, 389, 89 S.Ct. 1794, 1806 (1969).

ten to prevent the development of unequal treatment among candidates by partisan broadcasters. Its first part reads: [10]

> If any licensee shall permit any person who is a legally qualified candidate for any public office to use a broadcasting station, he shall afford equal opportunities to all other such candidates for that office in the use of such broadcasting station: *provided*, that such licensee shall have no power of censorship over the material broadcast under the provisions of this section. No obligation is imposed upon any licensee to allow the use of its station by any such candidate.

This said to a broadcaster: Refuse time to all qualified candidates for a political position, or accept all. While refusing access was thus legal, it hardly squared with the great potentialities of the medium for contributing to public information about candidates. Both politicians and citizens had legitimate questions to put to broadcasters who did not make air time available during campaign periods. Yet for the broadcaster, it could cause real problems, especially in contests where a great many candidates were running. Who could furnish "equal opportunities"—either on a free basis or on a "paid time" basis—to every candidate if 15 were running for mayor? Many broadcasters found the requirement a perilous one, and some were willing to accept the opprobrium that might go with refusing all candidates.

Within the terms of Section 315, the FCC had power to make rules as to what could constitute "equal opportunities." Through rules, letters, hearings, opinions and decisions of the FCC on various practices, as well as through stations' appeals to the courts, the details of "equal opportunities" were gradually described.[11]

The term "equal time" does not cover the entire consideration that must be given a candidate whose opponent has preceded him. The candidate must receive not only as much time, but also just as desirable a time of day or week as his opponent; a half hour on Sunday morning at 9 o'clock is not an "equal opportunity" for a candidate if his opponent has had prime evening time.[12] This does not mean, however, that all candidates must

---

[10] 48 Stat. 1064, 1088, 47 U.S.C.A. §§ 151, 315, 1934.

[11] Barrow, Roscoe L., The Equal Opportunities and Fairness Doctrines in Broadcasting: Pillars in the Forum of Democracy, 37 Cincinnati L.Rev. 447, 452–459, 1969.

[12] 31 Fed.Reg. 6660, 6661, 6669, 1966.

be given exactly the same opportunity, such as appearance on a regularly scheduled discussion program.

Equal opportunities do not extend to campaign managers or other spokesmen for candidates; Section 315 refers only to the candidates themselves.   In Felix v. Westinghouse Radio Stations,[13] the court ruled that political parties, as such, did not have claim to "equal opportunities"; the law extends the claim only to candidates.   This case also held that the "no-censorship" provision of Section 315 applies only to the candidates themselves, and not to their spokesmen.

Problems have arisen in the definition of the "legally qualified candidate" specified by Section 315.   The FCC has stated [14] a rule specifying at length just what is meant, and the law of each state must be taken into account as well.   Generally, one who has announced that he is running for nomination or election, who can be voted for, and who is eligible to serve if elected, is qualified.   "Equal opportunities" rules apply after a qualified candidate has announced his candidacy.

In nominating or primary elections, equal opportunities must be afforded the candidates for an office within a single party. But the fact that all Democrats running for nomination as sheriff are given equal opportunities does not mean that equal time must be made available to all Republicans seeking nomination for the same post.[15]

Section 315 talks of equal opportunities for candidates in the "use" of broadcasting stations.   The word "use" has caused many problems of interpretation.   It has been held by the FCC that "use" includes air time employed by a candidate who did not speak directly to his candidacy; a station was not to evaluate whether the original user was furthering his campaign in his talk.[16]   Also, the FCC held that a candidate who went on the air to broadcast in a capacity other than as a candidate, gave the basis for his opponent to claim equal opportunity.   A Congressman's weekly broadcast to his constituents, made after he became a candidate for re-election, might have no content dealing with his campaign, but it would furnish the ground for his opponent to claim equal time.[17]

The kinds of news broadcasts in which candidates' appearances might be considered as "use" of stations were limited by

13 186 F.2d 1 (3d Cir. 1950).

14 47 C.F.R. 73.120, 73.290, 73.657 (1965).

15 KWFT, Inc., 4 R.R. 885 (1948).

16 WMCA, Inc., 7 R.R. 1132 (1952).

17 KNGS, 7 R.R. 1130 (1952).

Congress in 1959, following a Chicago mayoralty primary election featuring Democratic incumbent Richard J. Daley, Republican Timothy Sheehan, and one Lar Daly, running for nomination on both tickets. Daly complained to the FCC that during the primary race both of his opponents had been shown in film clips by Chicago television stations which had subsequently refused him equal opportunity. The film clips included interviews with one of the candidates, shots of Daley and Sheehan filing petitions, and sections of the acceptance speeches of the latter two. The Commission held unanimously on Feb. 19 that most of the film clips were indeed a "use" under Section 315, and that Daly should have been granted equal opportunity.[18] Despite prolonged and heavy objection from broadcasters and others, the Commission reaffirmed its decision with a statement of June 15, 1959.[19]

Viewing the decision as a major threat to political coverage, newsmen took their case to the public and to Congress. The latter held hearings and determined to amend Section 315. In September, 1959, it passed an amendment which says that "use" of a broadcasting station by a candidate does not include appearance on a bona fide newscast, bona fide news interview, or bona fide news documentary, or in on-the-spot coverage of news events.[20] In effect today, this provision permits wide coverage of political affairs in campaign time.

Much remains subject, however, to the equal opportunities restriction. The problem of multiple candidacies for the Presidency continues to limit broadcasters' willingness to air appearances of the major-party Presidential candidates. Debates and discussions of issues by those seeking the highest office of the nation have been effectively forestalled in all but one election, that of 1960. In this case, Congress passed a resolution suspending the equal opportunities restriction as it applied to the Presidential and Vice-Presidential candidates. Candidates John F. Kennedy and Richard M. Nixon engaged in a series of four "debates," viewed by huge audiences.[21]

The problems of interpretation by the station continue to be real despite the amendment of 1959 to Section 315. The FCC continues to hold the effective interpretative power, of course,

[18] Columbia Broadcasting System, Inc., 26 F.C.C. 715 (1959).

[19] Emery, Walter B., Broadcasting and Government (Michigan State Univ. Press, 1961), pp. 221–224.

[20] Ibid., 224; 73 Stat. 557.

[21] Barrow, pp. 480–482.

and has issued a compilation of its rulings on the section.[22]
Such guidance is important. Broadcasters cannot necessarily divine, without it, some rather nice distinctions: for example, that
a president's press conference is not exempt from Section 315,
because he rather than the media controls the format of the
event and it cannot be considered a bona fide newscast; but that
telecasting his report on an international crisis escapes the strictures because it is on-the-spot coverage of a bona fide news
event.[23]

SEC. 85.   THE FAIRNESS DOCTRINE: CONTROVERSIAL ISSUES OF PUBLIC IMPORTANCE

**Broadcasters are charged by the Federal Communications Com-
mission with the affirmative duty to seek out and broadcast
contrasting viewpoints on controversial issues of public importance.**

Recognition of the public interest in wide ventilation of important public issues by broadcasting does not stop with the law
requiring equal opportunities for political candidates. The principle has been recognized by FCC decisions and documents for
decades in respect to the general airing of viewpoints on significant public issues. Under its "fairness doctrine" the Commission has taken and held the position that "public interest requires ample play for the free and fair competition of opposing
views * * *" and it considers "strict adherence to the fairness doctrine as the single most important requirement of operation in the public interest—the "sine qua non" for grant of a renewal of license."[24] The doctrine applies, the Commission holds,
in any case in which broadcast facilities are used for the discussion of a controversial issue of public importance. Its position
is laid out in fullest form in an FCC Report of 1949, Editorializing by Broadcast Licensees.[25] The station's part and the FCC's
part in applying the doctrine are described thus :[26]

> [T]he licensee, in applying the fairness doctrine, is
> called upon to make reasonable judgments in good faith

[22] Public Notice of April 27, 1966, Use of Broadcast Facilities by Candidates
for Public Office, 31 Fed.Reg. 6660, 1966.

[23] Columbia Broadcasting System, Inc., 3 R.R.2d 623 (1964); Republican
National Committee, 3 R.R.2d 647 (1964).

[24] Great Lakes Broadcasting Company, 3 F.R.C. 32 (1929); Committee for
the Fair Broadcasting of Controversial Issues, 25 F.C.C.2d 283, 292 (1970).

[25] 13 F.C.C. 1246 (1949).

[26] FCC Public Notice of July 1, 1964, Applicability of the Fairness Doctrine in the Handling of Controversial Issues of Public Importance, 29 Fed.
Reg. 10415, 10416 (1964).

on the facts of each situation—as to whether a controversial issue of public importance is involved, as to what viewpoints have been or should be presented, as to the format and spokesmen to present the viewpoints, and all the other facets of such programming *   *   *.

In passing on any complaint in this area, the Commission's role is not to substitute its judgment for that of the licensee as to any of the above programming decisions, but rather to determine whether the licensee can be said to have acted reasonably and in good faith. There is thus room for considerably more discretion on the part of the licensee under the fairness doctrine than under the "equal opportunities" requirement.

The doctrine applies broadly to both news and comment. The Commission has not stated specific rules for its interpretation. Broadcasters receive guidance through such means as compilations of important FCC rulings of the past, occasional statements elaborating or expanding its stance and the scope of the doctrine,[27] and court decisions.

Repeatedly, the Commission has returned to its 1949 Report Editorializing by Broadcast Licensees, for explaining what is called for in the fairness doctrine. In the case of John J. Dempsey,[28] it held that the broadcaster's obligations in the public interest are not met simply by a general policy of not refusing to broadcast opposing views where a demand is made upon it for air time. More positive attention to the public interest in hearing various positions is needed from broadcasters; the FCC 1949 Report said that [29]

*   *   * broadcast licensees have an affirmative duty generally to encourage and implement the broadcast of all sides of controversial public issues over their facilities, over and beyond their obligation to make available on demand opportunities for the expression of opposing views. It is clear that any approximation of fairness in the presentation of any controversy will be difficult if not impossible of achievement unless the licensee

---

[27] Ibid., for the former; for the latter, "In the Matter of the Handling of Public Issues Under the Fairness Doctrine and the Public Interest Standards of the Communications Act," 30 F.C.C.2d 26 (1971), is a Notice of Inquiry, announced by the F.C.C. as "a broad-ranging inquiry into the efficacy of the fairness doctrine and other Commission public interest policies in the light of current demands for access to the broadcast media *   *   *."

[28] 6 R.R. 615 (1950).

[29] 13 F.C.C. 1246 (1949).

> plays a conscious and positive role in bringing about
> balanced presentation of the opposing viewpoints.

This is sometimes referred to as the "seek out" rule, in that the
broadcaster is told it is his duty to take the initiative in encouraging those with varying viewpoints on an issue to broadcast.
The "seek-out" process is not finished if no opponent of an aired
view shows up in response to an over-the-air invitation to do so;
the licensee as a community expert on controversy should notify
persons with contrasting viewpoints of their opportunity to be
heard.

No aspect of broadcast regulation has come under heavier fire
from broadcasters, perhaps, than the fairness doctrine. Government's compelling "fairness", with failure to be "fair" a possible
ground for losing a license, flies in the face of the First Amendment, the argument runs, and demonstrates that freedom of expression is a weak freedom as applied to broadcasting. For the
print media, of course, "freedom to be unfair" is broadly protected under the First Amendment.

Determining what is a "controversial issue of public importance" is a matter of judgment, not defined by the Commission.
It is considerably up to the broadcaster; he is to "make reasonable judgments in good faith on the facts of each situation—as
to whether a controversial issue of public importance is involved,
as to what viewpoints have been or should be presented, as to
the format and spokesmen to present the viewpoints * * *." [30]
The New Broadcasting Company, WLIB, broadcast editorial
programs in support of a National Fair Employment Practices Commission. It did not take "affirmative steps" to encourage opposing viewpoints. The Commission ruled that its failure
to do so was "not in accord with the principles" of the 1949 Report. It said flatly that the establishment of an NFEPC is a
controversial issue of the kind anticipated by its Report, calling
it a "subject that has been actively controverted by members of
the public and by members of the Congress * * * and that
in the course of that controversy numerous differing views have
been espoused." [31] While the establishment of an NFEPC may
on its face present an important public issue, other topics require finer distinctions. An early ruling went to the questions
of whether a Governor's "Report to the People of New York
State" by radio contained controversial statements that should
have caused CBS to seek out and encourage others to broadcast
different points of view. The FCC said that labeling a program

---

[30] 29 Fed.Reg. 10415, 10416 (1964).

[31] New Broadcasting Co. (WLIB), 6 R.R. 258, 259 (1950).

"as a report to the people does not necessarily establish such a program as non-controversial in nature so as to avoid the requirement of affording time for the expression of opposing views." No formula can cover all cases, it said. The licensee is supposed to use his judgment and good sense in determining what subjects should be considered. It is up to him to make time available for opposing views "where the facts and circumstances in each case indicate an area of controversy and differences of opinion where the subject matter is of public importance." In this case, said the Commission, CBS did not show an abuse of judgment that would warrant holding a hearing on its application for license renewal.[32]

Not only politics and government are included in the realm of public controversial issues. A program called "Living Should Be Fun" featured a nutritionist who discussed such subjects as the fluoridation of water, the value of a substance called krebiozen in the treatment of cancer, and the use of high potency vitamins without medical advice. The nutritionist said, in his broadcast, that his views were opposed by many authorities. Several stations contended, in answer to complaints about the program, that a program on health and diet does not belong in the category of controversial public issues. But the FCC disagreed: the fairness doctrine applied in the broadcasting of such subjects.[33]

Besides exercising judgment and "good sense" in deciding what constitutes a public controversial issue, the licensee must gauge what is "reasonable opportunity" for an opposing viewpoint to be heard. A candidate for Attorney General of North Dakota complained to the FCC that he deserved more air time on a group of stations that carried a controversy about a state hospital and a state training school. The stations had carried three programs: A half-hour documentary on the hospital, the last five minutes of which had been given to two state officials to discuss the candidate's earlier charges about the hospital; a half-hour program about a week later, and at about the same time of day, in which the complainant aired his allegations about the hospital and school; and a half-hour documentary the following day on the state training school, with five minutes again devoted to the two officials' discussion of the complainant's charges.

Although the complainant asked for "equal time," the FCC said that that did not apply; no opposing candidate for Attorney

32 Paul E. Fitzpatrick, 6 R.R. 543 (1949).

33 Report on "Living Should Be Fun" Inquiry, 33 F.C.C. 101, 107, 23 R.R. 1599, 1606 (1962).

General was involved. Rather, it was a case which would have to be settled under the fairness doctrine. The FCC ruled for the broadcaster and his treatment of the issue: [34]

> Unlike the "equal opportunities" requirement of Section 315, the fairness doctrine requires that where a licensee affords time over his facilities for an expression of one opinion on a controversial issue of public importance, he is under obligation to insure that proponents of opposing viewpoints are afforded a reasonable opportunity for the presentation of such views. The Commission concludes that on the facts before it, the licensee's actions were not inconsistent with the principles enunciated in the Editorializing Report [i. e., the 1949 Report].

The discretion that the FCC gives to the broadcaster for the airing of controversial issues of public importance, includes that to choose a spokesman for the contrasting views. Again, the Commission relies on its 1949 Report as the basis for this position. Along with discretion to designate the techniques or formats of the program for contrasting views, the broadcaster's discretion in choosing spokesmen is wide; there is "no single group or person entitled as a matter of right to present a viewpoint differing from that previously expressed on the station." [35] This is different, of course, from the rule of the equal opportunities provision applying to political candidates, where the broadcaster does not have discretion to choose a spokesman for the reply.

The foregoing case also illustrates another difference between the equal opportunities rule regarding political candidates and the fairness doctrine applying to controversial issues. Under the former, the broadcaster who has charged the first candidate for air time, does not have to grant equal opportunity to an opponent who is not willing or able to pay. But under the fairness doctrine, the broadcaster who has aired one view on a controversial issue supported by a sponsor, may not refuse to air another view on the issue on grounds that a sponsor for the second view cannot be found. The FCC held in this case that "the public's paramount right to hear opposing views on controversial issues * * * cannot be nullified by * * * the inability of the licensee to obtain paid sponsorship of the broadcast time." [36]

---

[34] Hon. Charles L. Murphy, 23 R.R. 953 (1962).

[35] Letter to Cullman Broadcasting Co., Inc., F.C.C. 63–849, Sept. 18, 1963.

[36] Ibid.

It is also worth pointing out that the "affirmative duty" of the broadcaster to encourage various viewpoints on issues, differs from his more passive role where political candidates are concerned. In the latter, the burden is placed upon the candidate who wishes to reply; unless he requests time, the station does not have to furnish it.

The Commission relies almost entirely on the warning force of its opinions and rulings to get stations to change their ways under the fairness doctrine. It has power to deny re-licensing, to issue cease and desist orders, to give "short-term" license renewals (e. g., one year instead of the customary three), or even to revoke a license in mid-term. It has often come under heavy attack for not using these powers, its critics arguing that it is a "captive" of the industry it supposedly regulates. One study found that the FCC had used a sanction of this kind in only one fairness doctrine case to 1965.[37]

In this case, Lamar Life Broadcasting Co. was granted a conditional one-year renewal of its license for WLBT in Jackson, Miss. The United Church of Christ objected to any renewal, on grounds that the station's news and public affairs programming displayed racial and religious discrimination. The Church asked that it be granted the license instead. The FCC granted a one-year renewal of Lamar's license (instead of the usual three), provided that it comply strictly with the fairness doctrine and cease discriminatory programming patterns. It held no hearing in the matter.

The United Church of Christ took the case to federal court. There the FCC was told that renewal of the WLBT license was erroneous, for hearings should have been held and segments of WLBT's listening public allowed to intervene and participate. The church had standing to be heard as public intervenors.[38]

The FCC conducted the hearings, the church giving testimony about racial slurs, the cutting off of a network program and the results of its monitoring of the station for a week. The Commission then reconsidered the probationary license of one year, and decided it was in the public interest to remove the probationary status and grant WLBT a three-year renewal. Again the church appealed; the federal appeals court found for the church, and ordered the FCC to vacate its renewal of the license. The court said that the FCC examiner and the Commission itself incorrectly treated the intervenors like plaintiffs who must carry

37 Barrow, p. 469.

38 Office of Communication of United Church of Christ v. F.C.C., 123 U.S. App.D.C. 328, 359 F.2d 994 (1966).

the burden of proof. They exhibited, in the hearing and in their opinions and rulings: [39]

> * * * at best a reluctant tolerance of this court's mandate [in the earlier decision granting the church standing to intervene] and at worst a profound hostility to the participation of the Public Intervenors and their efforts.

The court said the hearing and the decision to renew were so faulty that "it will serve no useful purpose to ask the Commission to reconsider the Examiner's actions and its own Decision and Order * * *. The administrative conduct in this record is beyond repair." [40] It directed the Commission to invite applications to be filed for the license held by WLBT.

SEC. 86. THE FAIRNESS DOCTRINE: PERSONAL ATTACKS AND POLITICAL EDITORIALS

When a broadcast attacks the integrity or character of a person or group, or an editorial supports or opposes a political candidate, the station must promptly notify the person attacked or opposed, furnish him with the content of the attack, and offer him air time to respond.

An attack on the character, honesty, or integrity of a person or group during a broadcast of a controversial issue of public importance, calls for the application of special rules under the fairness doctrine. So does a station's editorial support for or opposition to a political candidate. In both cases, the FCC reasons that the public interest in full debate and airing of issues, rather than the interest of the one attacked, is the factor of first concern.

The Commission's policies developed in cases over the years were formalized in rules in 1967 and 1968. One is that the broadcaster must notify the target of the attack promptly, and furnish him with a transcript, tape, or summary of the attack. Also, an offer of time to reply must be given. Where the licensee has broadcast an editorial endorsing or opposing a political candidate, the opposing candidates are supposed to be notified within 24 hours after the attack, and furnished with the transcript and an offer of time.[41]

[39] Office of Communications of United Church of Christ v. F.C.C., 138 U.S. App.D.C. 112, 425 F.2d 543, 550 (1969).

[40] Ibid.

[41] Barrow, pp. 472–476.

A second rule refers to the kinds of programs that are exempt from the special provisions. A bona fide newscast, a broadcast of a bona fide news event, and news interviews and commentaries are not within the requirements. This leaves editorials and documentaries among the kinds of programs that remain under the special requirements.[42] The Commission recognizes, in the exceptions to the requirements, the broadcasters' strongly argued point that the rules calling for notice, transcript, and offer of time may have the effect of discouraging stations from airing important controversial issues.

One case involved the complaint of the general manager of a rural electric cooperative association. For five days, a station broadcast a series of editorials attacking him in connection with a public controversial issue. He learned of the attacks upon his arrival in town the fourth day. On the fifth day, he tried to get copies of the editorials, and on the same day, the station offered him a broadcast interview to answer the attacks. His total stay in town was for only two days, and he rejected the offer because he would not have time to prepare an adequate reply. In ruling that the station "had not fully met the requirements of the Commission's fairness doctrine," the FCC said that [43]

> [T]he fairness doctrine requires that a copy of the specific editorial or editorials shall be communicated to the person attacked either prior to or at the time of the broadcast * * * so that a reasonable opportunity is afforded that person to reply. This duty on the part of the station is greater where, as here, interest in the editorials was consciously built up over a period of days and the time within which the person attacked would have an opportunity to reply was known to be so limited.

Another case involved attacks on county and state officials, accusing them of using their offices for personal gain and charging that their administration employed procedures similar to political methods of dictators. The persons attacked were invited several times to use the station to discuss the matter. At license-renewal time, those attacked in the broadcasts said that the station was used for selfish purposes, and to vent personal spite. But the Commission renewed the license, saying that although the broadcast attacks were highly personal and impugned the character and honesty of named individuals, those

---

[42] Ibid.

[43] Billings Bctg. Co., 23 R.R. 951 (1962).

attacked were told of the attacks and were aware of the opportunities afforded them to reply.[44]

Another case involving repeated attacks by a commentator on California's Governor Brown, a candidate for reelection, illustrates a further rule in personal attack on political candidates under the fairness doctrine. This rule is that in affording the opportunity for response, the station may insist that an appropriate spokesman for the attacked candidate deliver the response rather than the candidate himself. If the candidate were permitted to respond, this would bring into operation the "equal opportunities" provision of Section 315 of the Communications Act, and the candidate's opponents could then insist on equal time. In the case involving Governor Brown, the FCC held that while the station could require that a spokesman rather than Brown make the response, "The candidate should * * * be given a substantial voice in the selection of the spokesman * * *." [45]

The strength and reach of the fairness doctrine are great. Broadcasters' attacks upon it as burdensome and unconstitutional have been rejected by the Supreme Court. And the application of the principle has been expanded, in decisions since 1969, to certain kinds of advertising.

Red Lion Broadcasting Co. v. FCC [46] produced a unanimous endorsement of the doctrine's personal attack rule by the court, and the flat declaration that the central First Amendment interest in free speech by broadcasting is the public's, not the broadcaster's. The case rose in Red Lion, Pa., after the company refused Fred J. Cook free time to answer attacks on him by the Rev. Billy James Hargis, a program moderator for its station, who associated Cook with left-wing activities. Cook took the case to the FCC which directed Red Lion to provide free time for Cook to reply, and Red Lion went to the courts, claiming the fairness doctrine unconstitutional. Meanwhile, Radio-Television News Directors Ass'n. (RTNDA), Columbia Broadcasting System and National Broadcasting Co. were bringing a separate action on constitutional grounds, claiming that the notification process of the personal attack—political editorial rules was expensive and burdensome, discouraging broadcasters from airing controversial issues.[47] The Supreme Court decided the two cases together in a decision since known as Red Lion.

[44] Clayton W. Mapoles, 23 R.R. 586 (1962).

[45] Times-Mirror Bctg. Co., 24 R.R. 404, 406 (1962).

[46] 395 U.S. 367, 89 S.Ct. 1794 (1969).

[47] Ibid.

Congress had ratified the long-standing fairness requirement of the FCC in positive legislation of 1959, when in amending Sec. 315 it said specifically that stations must "operate in the public interest and * * * afford reasonable opportunity for the discussion of conflicting views on issues of public importance." While Congress had not spoken precisely to the personal attack—political editorial rules, the Court found no reason to consider that these rules were out of joint with the "controversial issues of public importance" rule. As implementation of the statutory "public interest, convenience or necessity" provision, the fairness doctrine was within the FCC's function and not an unconstitutional exercise of power delegated by Congress.[48]

Then the Supreme Court considered the broadcasters' contention that the First Amendment protects their wish to use their allotted frequencies to broadcast whatever they choose and to exclude from the frequency whomever they choose. As other "new media," it said, broadcasting had to live with certain special standards under the First Amendment: Not everyone who wanted to could broadcast, or each would drown the other out because of the limited number of frequencies. "[I]t is idle to posit an unabridgeable First Amendment right to broadcast comparable to the right of every individual to speak, write or publish." [49]

The Court laid out its interpretation of whose First Amendment right is primarily at stake in free speech by broadcasting: the public's, not the licensee's.[50]

> But the people as a whole retain their interest in free speech by radio and their collective right to have the medium function consistently with the ends and purposes of the First Amendment. It is the right of the viewers and listeners, not the right of the broadcasters, which is paramount. * * * It is the purpose of the First Amendment to preserve an uninhibited marketplace of ideas in which truth will ultimately prevail, rather than to countenance monopolization of that market, whether it be by the Government itself or a private licensee. * * * It is the right of the public to receive suitable access to social, political, esthetic, moral, and other ideas and experiences which is crucial here.

Yet in spite of *Red Lion*, the Commission lives an uneasy life with the fairness doctrine. The FCC's "Notice of Inquiry in the

48 Ibid., 385.

49 Ibid., 388.

50 Ibid., 390.

Matter of the Handling of Public Issues under the Fairness Doctrine and the Public Interest Standards of the Communications Act" [51] of 1971 launched a re-examination of the doctrine's assumptions and application that was still underway almost two years later. Meanwhile, the FCC's reliance on it in refusing to renew a radio license has been bypassed by the District of Columbia Court of Appeals. The Court upheld, 2 to 1, the FCC's refusal to renew, but on grounds that the company—Brandywine-Main Line Radio, Inc., of Media, Pa.—had misrepresented itself in applying for transfer of the licenses of WXUR. [52]

The case involved Faith Theological Seminary of Elkins Park, Pa., and the Rev. Carl McIntire, one of its directors. The Seminary was approved for transfer of WXUR licenses after the FCC had carefully stressed to it the requirements of balance under the fairness doctrine; many groups had opposed the transfer on grounds that McIntire's previous record as radio commentator was evidence that he could not bring about a fair and balanced presentation of controversial public issues. Less than a year after the transfer, WXUR's licenses came up for renewal. The FCC found that the company had plunged into controversial-issue programming immediately after the transfer, had not provided opposing views a reasonable chance, and had engaged in much personal attack without observing the notification rules. All this was violation of the fairness doctrine so flagrant that license renewal was not warranted, the Commission ruled; and furthermore, the licensee had misrepresented its real programming intent when it had applied for the transfer of license.

Brandywine appealed to the courts. Of three judges at the Court of Appeals, one favored refusal to renew on grounds of both misrepresentation and violating the fairness doctrine, and one joined him only on the ground of misrepresentation. The third judge dissented, finding the misrepresentation grounds infected with aspects and overtones of the fairness doctrine, which, he said, while unquestioned for 50 years, now needed its values, purposes and effects re-examined. In silencing WXUR, Bazelon said, the Commission had dealt a death blow to the licensee's freedom of speech and press, and also denied the public access to many controversial issues. Judge Bazelon said that licensing and regulating radio and television come down in the end to an assumption of technical scarcity—limited frequencies to which all cannot have access; but the viewer now has the prospect in a few years of 400 television channels, and the enor-

[51] 30 FCC 2d 26 (1971).

[52] Brandywine-Main Line Radio, Inc. v. FCC, 25 R.R.2d 2010 (D.C.Cir. 1972).

mous capacity of cable television to carry communication is now a technical reality. "I fear that ancient assumptions and crystallized rules have blinded all of us to the depth of the First Amendment issues involved here," [53] he said. Does silencing WXUR in the name of the fairness doctrine violate the First Amendment? he asked.

SEC. 87.   THE FAIRNESS DOCTRINE: ADVERTISING

Under some circumstances, advertising that raises controversial issues of public importance may trigger the application of the fairness doctrine.

While the fairness doctrine was receiving its test in *Red Lion* and *RTNDA,* a new application of its reach was being asserted —to advertising. It is treated in detail herein in Chapter 14. Here, the central importance to be noted is that where a product advertised was hazardous to health, the fairness doctrine required that time be made available to counter the messages propounding it.[54] Applied in *Banzhaf* to cigarets specifically, the doctrine later was extended by FCC orders,[55] and court decision [56] to other products, particularly those alleged to be damaging to the environment. In the *Wilderness* ruling, the FCC held that commercials urging the early development of Alaskan oil deposits raised a controversial issue of public importance and extolled the benefits of "one side" of the issue. The fairness doctrine applied.

"Editorial advertisements," however, have been found by the Supreme Court to be outside the reach of the fairness doctrine. Business Executives' Move for Vietnam Peace (BEM), a nationwide group of 2,700 owners and executives, prepared radio spot ads urging immediate withdrawal of American forces from overseas military installations. WTOP, Washington, refused to sell time to BEM. The station said its long-established policy was not to sell time for spot announcements to groups or individuals who wished to set forth their views on controversial issues. The FCC upheld WTOP's policy of rejecting all editorial advertisements, saying that stations have wide leeway in the format they choose for airing controversial issues.[57] The Supreme Court, in

---

[53] Ibid., 2076.

[54] Banzhaf v. FCC, 132 U.S.App.D.C. 14, 405 F.2d 1082 (1968), certiorari denied 396 U.S. 842, 90 S.Ct. 50 (1969).

[55] In re Neckritz, 29 FCC2d 807, 1971; In re Wilderness Society, 30 F.C.C.2d 643, 1971.

[56] Friends of the Earth v. F.C.C., 146 U.S.App.D.C. 88, 449 F.2d 1164 (1971).

[57] Business Executives Move for Vietnam Peace, 25 F.C.C.2d 242 (1971).

a decision joining BEM to Columbia Broadcasting System, Inc., v. Democratic National Committee,[58] upheld the FCC.

SEC. 88.   "PROVOCATIVE" PROGRAMMING

Listeners offended by "provocative" programming do not have the right to insist that such programming be ruled off the airwaves through Federal Communications Commission denial of licenses.

The FCC's policy of encouraging the broadcasting of a wide spectrum of viewpoints is occasionally illustrated by a ruling that has no direct relation to Section 315 of the Communications Act of 1934, or to the fairness doctrine.   In a case decided in 1964 involving the three stations of the Pacifica Foundation, the Commission gave strong support to the airing of programs that some listeners found offensive.

Pacifica's FM stations—KPFA, San Francisco, WBAI, New York, and KPFK, Los Angeles—were subscription-supported stations heavily given to broadcasting controversial issues.   The American Civil Liberties Union had described the content of their programs as "daily application of the First Amendment's purpose, to expose the public to different political, economic, and social thought." [59]   Complaints were registered with the FCC that the stations had run "filthy" programs and aired Communist philosophy.   Programs attacked were a broadcast of Edward Albee's play, "The Zoo Story," a discussion by eight homosexuals of their problems, and readings of poetry by Lawrence Ferlinghetti and Robert Creeley.   The Senate Internal Security subcommittee held hearings on the complaints.

Holding up the renewal of Pacifica's licenses during its own investigation, the FCC at length issued its finding.   It renewed the licenses.   It said that there was no sustained "pattern of operation inconsistent with the public interest," and that it could have renewed the licenses on that basis alone.   But it added further reasoning as guidance to other broadcasters, who had taken almost no part in urging re-licensing for Pacifica.   The decision said of the programs: [60]

> We recognize that, as shown by the complaints here, such provocative programming as here involved may offend some listeners.   But this does not mean that

[58] 93 S.Ct. 2080, 36 L.Ed.2d 772 (1973).

[59] ACLU Denounces Investigation of Pacifica Fund's FM Radio Stations, Civil Liberties, No. 204, Feb. 1963, p. 1.

[60] Pacifica Foundation, 1 R.R.2d 747 (1964).

those offended have the right, through the commission's licensing power, to rule such programming off the airwaves. Were this the case, only the wholly inoffensive, the bland, could gain access to the radio microphone or TV camera. No such drastic curtailment can be countenanced under the Constitution, the Communications Act or the commission's policy.

We do not mean to indicate that those who have complained about the foregoing programs are in the wrong as to their worth and should listen to them. This is a matter solely for determination by the individual listener. Our function, we stress, is not to pass on the merits of the program * * *.

Pacifica had very great discretion to exercise its own judgment on the programs it carried, the FCC said, and there was not even a "close question" involved in the re-licensing.

SEC. 89. CABLE TELEVISION

The FCC has general authority over cable television, but leaves much control to municipalities and states under its rules of February 1972.

A new technology burst from its small-town environment in the late 1950's and swept the Federal Communications Commission into an unmapped sphere of regulation of communications systems. Known as CATV (Community Antenna Television), the system picked up distant and near-by television stations' signals with a powerful antenna, and fed them by cable into the sets of people in towns where television reception was weak or absent. It could be done for a $20 installation fee and $5.00 a month or less; and "the cable" as delighted set owners called it, had the capacity to carry multiple channels—five in early years, then 12, 20 and many more in prospect. Systems spread in the 1950's through small-town America, and then in the 1960's began moving into major cities with programs from afar to supplement the several television channels already operating. It was plain that CATV was in direct competition with existing television stations, and was entering FCC ground. Moreover, CATV's capacity to carry a vast variety of non-broadcasting communication suggested that its reach would transcend television considerations in the future.

The potential for profit spurred businessmen, financiers and investors, many of them innocent of experience with television. The concept of the "wired nation" in which the cable would be strung in city after city to scores of millions of households, and service sold, frequently in situations without competition, was as awesome to the beholder as exciting to the entrepreneuer.

And the potential for a new public service that would link people, groups and communities in new ways was equally challenging. It spurred the public-spirited to the possibilities of moving information in quantities never dreamed of by television; of two-way communication that would some day bring the traditional "receiver" of media messages into an interchange with the traditional "source"; of establishing some of the many available channels as "common carrier" services by which anyone who had the money and some who did not could claim time on a channel to say his say, speak his piece, reach his group.

As always with communication by wire or airwaves, the FCC was in the position of mediating agency. While the cable was neither telegraph nor telephone wire, neither radio nor television, its relationship to the facilities traditionally regulated by the FCC was plain. The Commission moved by steps to assert its authority over cable television and by 1966 had done so successfully,[61] the Supreme Court of the United States confirming its power by 1968 in U. S. v. Southwestern Cable Co.[62]

By early 1972 the contending commercial and organizational forces of broadcasting and cable, copyright owners, public interest groups, congressional inquirers, the President's Office of Telecommunications Policy, state and municipal representatives, and concerned individuals had been heard and taken into account. The courts had ruled on a few phases of cable. The FCC in early February 1972 issued its long-awaited general and basic rules for cable in 500 pages, Cable Television Service, Part 76, Rules and Regulations.[63] They describe the framework within which cable is to operate, and they reflect the Commission's resolution of competing demands: growth for cable, protection for television and copyright holders, and service for the public.

"The law" of cable as it stands is a product of extended, agitated debate lasting for years. The Commission itself was far from unanimous in adopting the 1972 Rules and Regulations [64] to say nothing of the commercial, congressional and public

---

[61] Federal Communications Commission, Second Report and Order, Docket Nos. 14895, 15233, 15971, 6 R.R.2d 1717 (1966).

[62] 392 U.S. 157, 88 S.Ct. 1994 (1968).

[63] Federal Communications Commission, CATV Rules (Docket 18397 et al.), 24 R.R.2d 1501, 1579–1615 (1972).

[64] Ibid., 1579–1615.

spokesmen and groups.[65]   But the debate over what the federal rules should be [66] or should have been stands outside the scope of the present treatment, which describes in digest major aspects of the law as the Commission states it.

Running through the 1972 document is the plain implication that cable must operate without destroying or severely damaging television—a service available to the public without charge, and to all set owners within range of its signal rather than only to those who obtain a paid-for cable connection.   This position had been taken in the FCC's First Report and Order on cable in 1965 in the context of preventing unfair competition,[67] and its rules at intervals since have assumed this.   Also taken for granted was the fact that large regulatory scope would be left for states and municipalities, which would issue franchises to cable systems as they had from the early years.   (Appendix E is a summary of a much longer analysis, by a specialist, of the ordinance for CATV of the City of Madison, Wis., in which a range of problems and public policy issues in cable is illustrated.)

The Supreme Court had furnished one "given" for FCC rules, in the decision in Fortnightly Corp. v. United Artists Television, Inc.[68]   This went to copyright law: Might CATV, which paid nothing and got no one's permission in receiving signals of television stations and transmitting them by wire, be violating copyright?   If, indeed, copyright law applied to CATV and required permission and payment for carrying others' copyrighted programs, its threat particularly to ultra high frequency television (largely, the independent stations served little by the networks) might be reduced.   Congress was mired in the complexities of revising the 50-year-old copyright law when in 1968 the *Fortnightly* decision came down.

The Court ruled that CATV is not a "performer" and is thus not subject to the copyright act's provisions: copyright to mov-

---

65 For industry reaction, see Nays Have Their Say on Cable, Broadcasting, March 20, 1972, pp. 23–24.

66 For major treatments of values and issues involved, see, e. g., Smith, R.L., The Wired Nation, Nation, May 18, 1970; LeDuc, D.R., The Cable Question: Evolution or Revolution in Electronic Mass Communications, The Annals of the American Academy of Political and Social Science, Vol. 400, March 1972; On the Cable: the Television of Abundance, Report of Sloan Commission on Cable Communications (New York: McGraw-Hill Book Co., 1972); Cable Communications in Wisconsin, Report of Governor's Cable Commission, Madison, Wis., Aug. 28, 1972. The Commission's rationale and explanation is at 24 R.R. 2d 1501–79, also given at 37 Fed.Reg. 3252, 2/12/72.

67 Federal Communications Commission, Docket Nos. 14895 and 15233, 4 R.R.2d 1725 (1965).

68 392 U.S. 390, 88 S.Ct. 2084 (1968).

ies held by United Artists was not infringed by Fortnightly CATV's receiving and transmitting these movies. The Court said: [69]

> * * * a CATV system no more than enhances the viewer's capacity to receive the broadcaster's signals; it provides a well-located antenna with an efficient connection to the viewer's television. It is true that a CATV system plays an "active" role in making reception possible, but do so ordinary television sets and antennas.

Five years later, Congress still had not revised the copyright law, although its laborious process continued and the FCC and television interests considered a revised law essential, in the long run, to the success of the 1972 Rules and Regulations.[70]

Digesting important elements of the FCC product of 1972 may be done under several headings: [71]

Federal-State/Local Regulatory Relationships. Almost all regulation of radio and television has been in the authority of the FCC, but not so cable. Franchises by local and state authority would be the givers of specific rules, within the framework of general FCC policy. Cable systems—natural monopolies within localities—would face questions of quality of service and repair, rates, technical standards. Local authorities would need to exercise "public interest judgment" about such matters as legal, financial, character and technical qualifications of the franchise applicants. They would need to deal with the area served, plans and arrangements for attachments with a public utility, details of channels for public or municipal use.

The new rules said that a "reasonable" fee would be charged the franchisee by the local authority, and named three to five per cent of gross subscriber revenue per year as reasonable. The franchising authority would grant the franchise only upon determination of capability based on public proceedings; it would approve initial rates charged subscribers for installation and service, and permit rate changes only after appropriate public proceedings. The franchise would be granted for a period of "reasonable duration" (15 years' maximum has been mentioned). The franchise would specify procedures for investigating and resolving complaints about quality of service.

[69] Ibid., 2089.

[70] The FCC Delivers on Cable, Broadcasting, Feb. 7, 1972, p. 18.

[71] Federal Communications Commission, CATV Rules (Docket 18397 et al.), 24 R.R.2d 1501, 1579–1615; 37 Fed.Reg. 3252, 2/12/72.

While the local franchising authority would be the municipality, there was nothing in the 1972 Rules and Regulations that forbid state governments from establishing statutes or rules within which franchises would be shaped.

Origination Cablecasting. This is programming provided by and subject to the exclusive control of the cable operator; it does not include television signals received and transmitted by the cable. Every cable system having 3,500 or more subscribers is required to operate "to a significant extent" as a local outlet by origination cablecasting. If it does not do so, it may carry no television station's broadcasts. In addition, these cable systems must have facilities for local production and presentation of programs. The rule was contested in an earlier version, and reached the Supreme Court of the United States as U. S. v. Midwest Video Corp.[72] Cable owners had objected to compulsory cablecasting, arguing that it put them into an endeavor wholly different from the transmission of signals. Producing programs and providing facilities for others to do so, they said, would be a highly expensive operation, drastically different from providing carriage of signals. But the Court, in a 5–4 decision, ruled that the Commission's program-origination rule was "reasonably ancillary to the effective performance of [its] various responsibilities for the regulation of television broadcasting." [73]

Origination cablecasting, furthermore, must be conducted within the terms of various other rules. The fairness doctrine of radio and television applies to this programming. So do the provisions of the equal opportunities rule for public office. Information about lotteries is barred from origination cablecasting. Material that is "obscene or indecent" may not be cablecast. Advertisements in origination cablecasting are permitted at the beginning and conclusion of each program "and at natural intermissions or breaks within a cablecast." Natural breaks in cablecasts are defined as intermissions beyond the control of the cable operator, such as time-outs in sporting events, intermissions in a play or recesses in a city council meeting.

Carriage of Television Broadcasts. CATV systems in the "top-50" markets may carry three networks and three independent stations, while the next-50 may carry three network and two independent stations. In addition, the systems in these 100 markets are permitted to carry two distant signals. Cable systems

---

[72] 406 U.S. 649, 92 S.Ct. 1860 (1972).

[73] Ibid., 662–663.

in markets below the top-100 may carry three network signals and one independent.   All must carry all local educational stations.

Program Exclusivity.   Television broadcasting is protected through rules that require cable systems to refrain for varying periods of time from carrying syndicated programming—generally, programs sold or distributed to television stations in more than one market for non-network television use.   Cable systems in the top-50 markets may not carry syndicated programming for one year after its first appearance in any market, and not during the life of the contract under which a local station buys it.   In the next-50 markets, periods of time up to two years provide exclusivity for television stations in carrying syndicated programming.

Diversification of Control.   No cable system that carries television broadcast signals may own, operate, control, or have an interest in a national television network, or a television station whose Grade B contour signal reaches into the service area of the cable system.

Channel Capacity and Access Channels.   Each cable system operating in a community in a major television market is required to have the equivalent of 20 broadcast channels ("120 MHz of bandwidth"), available for immediate or potential use. And, in language terse and spare, perhaps the most extraordinary capability of cable is required to be built into each system: "Each * * * system shall maintain a plant having technical capacity for nonvoice return communications * * * " [74]—the two-way communication capacity by which audiences of a mass communication medium will some day participate in the process instead of acting as receivers only.

Every cable system in a major market must also provide at least one channel to which the public has access without cost—a specially designated, noncommercial public access channel available on a first-come, nondiscriminatory basis.

In addition, it must have available for public use, at least minimal program-production equipment and facilities; production costs for live studio presentations more than 5 minutes long may be charged for.   Each system must have one channel designated for use of local educational authorities, and one for local government uses.   Other portions of the system's bandwidth, including unused parts of the specially designated channels, shall be of-

[74] Federal Communications Commission, CATV Rules (Docket 18397 et al.), 24 R.R.2d 1501, #76.251(3).

fered for leased access services.   Advertising is not permitted on the public-access and education-access channels.

Through these rules and others in the 500-page 1972 document of the FCC ran the underlying basic theme of access to a communication technology: Who would have access to franchises for public communication, and under what conditions would he retain it?   Who would have access to the channels of the franchisee?   Much was provided for industry, bitted and bridled though it was by the rules; something was provided for the public in the letter of the rules—more than had been provided where radio and television had been concerned.

SEC. 90.   ACCESS TO PRINT MEDIA

The Florida Supreme Court has held that newspapers which criticize political candidates in news or editorials are required to print the candidates' replies, under a Florida statute.

A decision by the Supreme Court of Florida in mid-1973 told newspapers that a right of public access to their columns exists under a Florida statute.   In Tornillo v. Miami Herald,[75] the Florida Court declared the statute constitutional in requiring newspapers which criticized political candidates, in news or editorial columns, to print the candidates' replies.   The Herald had refused to print a reply by Pat L. Tornillo, Jr., to an editorial critical of him in his unsuccessful race for the Florida Legislature in 1972.   Thus a state supreme court upheld a right of reply in print media similar to that granted under the equal opportunities and fairness doctrines to persons attacked by broadcast media and cable.

The first substantial legal ruling that public access to mass media includes access to printed media, the decision was in accord with a position brought to widespread attention in media and legal circles by an article in the May 1967 *Harvard Law Review* by Jerome A. Barron.[76]   Barron's position was that the First Amendment was meant for the public and the public weal, not for the media; and in an age of mass communication, people must have access to mass media if their voices are to be heard. The author said that for many decades the high cost of ownership of media had barred countless voices from a part in the "marketplace of ideas."   The media—giant in size and cost; relatively few in number and owned by largely like-minded entre-

---

[75] 287 So.2d 78 (1973), rev'd, —— U.S. ——, 94 S.Ct. 2831 (1974).

[76] "Access to the Press—a New First Amendment Right," 80 Harv.Law Rev. 1641 (1967).

preneuers devoted to the economic and political *status quo*; and possessed of the power to deny the citizen the right to have his message communicated widely—are themselves, in this view, a crucial barrier to diversity of opinion and fact in the marketplace. And diversity is the *sine qua non* of the liberal view of freedom of expression. "At the very minimum," Barron wrote, "the creation of two remedies is essential—(1) a nondiscriminatory right to purchase editorial advertisements in daily newspapers, and (2) a right of reply for public figures and public officers defamed in newspapers." [77]

Newspapers declared the logical extension of this view a practical impossibility. The *New York Times*, for example, said that almost half its issues would have to be devoted entirely to letters to the editor if all it received were printed. Newsmen argued also that freedom of the press includes freedom *not* to publish as much as freedom to publish. But in the words of the Florida Court, the First Amendment "is not for the benefit of the press so much as for the benefit of us all," and it added: [78]

> The right of the public to know all sides of a controversy and from such information to be able to make an enlightened choice is being jeopardized by the growing concentration of the ownership of the mass media into fewer and fewer hands, resulting ultimately in a form of private censorship.

The *Miami Herald* promised that it would appeal the decision to the Supreme Court of the United States. [79] Whether the high court's ruling in Red Lion Broadcasting Co. Inc. v. F. C. C. [80] would be extended to the print media remained to be seen.

[77] Jerome A. Barron, Freedom of the Press for Whom? (Bloomington, Ind., 1973), p. 6.

[78] Tornillo v. Miami Herald, 287 So.2d 78 (1973).

[79] New York Times, July 22, 1973, p. 28.

[80] 395 U.S. 367, 89 S.Ct. 1794 (1969).

Chapter 14

REGULATION OF ADVERTISING

SEC. 91. FROM *CAVEAT EMPTOR* TO CONSUMER PROTECTION

The history of advertising in the United States has seen a gradual change away from the motto of *caveat emptor* ("let the buyer beware").

It is hardly news that advertising is both a necessity and a nuisance in American society. It encourages and advances the nation's economy by providing information to the public about goods and services. Although its economic rule in supporting the news media has been criticized, advertising has footed the bill for most of the news and vicarious entertainment which we receive. Historically, we owe advertising another debt. The rise of advertising in the 19th Century did much to free the press from excessive reliance on political parties or government printing contracts which tended to color news columns with their bias.

Despite advertising's undeniably worthwhile contributions, this chapter unavoidably must emphasize the seamy side of American salesmanship. We will concentrate to a great extent upon issues raised by cheats and rascals. There can be little question that all too much advertising has been—and is—inexact, if not spurious and deceitful. Better units of the communications media now operate their advertising as a business with a definite obligation to the public. The realization evidently is

516

dawning that unless advertising is both truthful and useful, the
public may react unfavorably.

Advertising in the United States has a colorful if sometimes
sordid past. From the first days of the nation throughout the
Nineteenth Century, the philosophy motivating advertising was
largely *laissez faire*. Too much advertising, in spirit if not to
the letter, resembled this 1777 plug for "Dr. RYAN'S *incompara-
ble* WORM *destroying* SUGAR PLUMBS, *Necessary to be kept
in all* FAMILIES:" [1]

> The plumb is a great diuretic, cleaning the veins of
> slime; it expels wind, and is a sovereign medicine in
> the cholic and griping of the guts. It allays and car-
> ries off vapours which occasion many disorders of the
> head. It opens all obstructions in the stomach, lungs,
> liver, veins, and bladder; causes a good appetite, and
> helps digestion.

About two years later, some new advertising copy made
claims for Dr. Ryan's Sugar Plumbs which were even more
graphic. The plumbs were said to be a remedy for [2]

> PALENESS of the Face, Itching of the Nose, Höllow-
> ness of the Eyes, Grating of the teeth when asleep,
> Dullness, Pains, and Heaviness in the Head, a dry
> Cough, an Itching in the Fundament, white and thick
> Urine, unquiet Sleep, often starting, lost appetite,
> swell'd Belly, Gnawing and Biting about the Stomach,
> frightful Dreams, extreme Thirsts, the Body decay'd
> lean, Fits, often Vomiting, stinking Breath.

Such exploitation of the *laissez faire* philosophy went unpun-
ished for more than a century of this nation's existence. There
was little or no regulation; what would be termed unreliable or
even fraudulent advertising was published by some of the most
respectable newspapers and periodicals. The general principle
seemed to be that advertising columns were an open business forum with space for sale to all who applied.

Before 1900, advertising had little established ethical basis.
The liar and the cheat capitalized on glorious claims for dishonest, shoddy merchandise. The faker lured the ill and suffering
to build hopes on pills and tonics of questionable composition.
Cures were promised by the bottle. Fortunes were painted for
those who invested in mining companies of dubious reliability.
Foods were frequently adulterated. Fifteen dollar suits were of-

[1] Pennsylvania Gazette, March 12, 1777.

[2] Ibid., March 31, 1779.

fered as being worth $25. Faked testimonials praised dishonest or unproved wares. Manufacturers of these products were able to buy advertising space in reputable journals.

Earl W. Kintner,[3] chairman of the Federal Trade Commission from 1959 to 1961, has given this striking review of early advertising:

> The early proponents of *laissez faire* practiced the belief that a seller had a natural right to describe the attractions of his goods in any manner he saw fit. One of the famous early English cases on which most first year law students cut their teeth involves the sale of a Bezor stone.[4] From what I can gather Bezor stones were thought to have curative powers some 400 years ago. The seller told the buyer: "This is a Bezor stone." After the sale had been consummated the buyer was rudely awakened to the fact that the item he has purchased was not a Bezor stone. He then sued the seller. The court denied him recovery, saying that the buyer had a remedy only if the seller had said "I *warrant* this stone to be a Bezor stone." The court went on to say that the seller's simple declaration that the stone was a Bezor stone was mere legitimate puffing of the article for sale.

> This case represents the high noon of the doctrine of *caveat emptor* ["let the buyer beware"]. For the next 300 years some protection was afforded to buyers by the gradually enlarged law of warranty, but in the main the buyer was left to develop his own armor against false and misleading claims, and certainly most sellers felt no ethical compunction against describing their goods in the most wildly extravagant terms. This legal and ethical climate prevailed almost to the birth of the twentieth century. Indeed, as the industrial revolution progressed conditions grew worse. As education spread, publishing media mushroomed. As the railroad net spread and improved, the means for the widespread distribution of goods was now at hand. These two conditions fostered the development of a new technique in marketing. It was now feasible to market a branded consumer product on a nationwide basis. It was now easy to distribute the product from a central

---

[3] Member of the Bar of the District of Columbia, Chairman of the Federal Trade Commission from June 11, 1959 to March 20, 1961.

[4] Chancellor v. Lopus, Exchequer Chamber, Cro.Jac. 4 (1603).

location, and the tremendous growth of publishing media, coinciding with the ability of a large portion of the citizenry to read, meant that it was now possible to create a widespread consciousness of a brand name through advertising. Unfortunately, among the first to recognize and exploit the new marketing technique were a horde of quacks. Stewart Holbrook in his delightful book *The Golden Age of Quackery* [5] describes some of the vastly popular patent medicines, nostrums, and healing devices, and the extravagant claims that were made for them. Let there be no mistake: some of these early patent medicines did have a powerful effect. Mr. Holbrook presents this analysis of one of the most popular of these sovereign remedies, Hostetter's Celebrated Stomach Bitters. At the time of the Civil War, Mr. Holbrook writes, " *   *   * the Bitters contained modest amounts of cinchona bark, gentian root, orange peel, anise, and a less than modest dose of alcohol. Whether or not the alcoholic content was increased during the war is not clear, but for many years it ran to approximately 47 per cent by volume." [6] This 94 proof compound undoubtedly warmed many a prim and temperate soul. The patent medicine king reigned supreme from the end of the Civil War to the early 20th century. The magazines, newspapers, posters and brochures of this period are loaded with announcements of miraculous cures of persons afflicted with every disease known to man. The advertisements were replete with testimonials from Congressmen, admirals, actresses and, most often, from clergymen.

It was not long before the manufacturers of other branded consumer products grasped the possibilities of the new marketing technique. Soon soaps and cereals, cough drops and canned milk all joined the parade to nationwide advertising and distribution. However, we would do well to center our attention on the patent medicines and healing devices for it was in this area that the drive for ethical standards in advertising began.

Courageous journalists, medical societies, aroused public-spirited citizens and advertising men concerned with the future of advertising, all contributed to the expo-

[5] Stewart Holbrook, The Golden Age of Quackery (New York, MacMillan, 1959).

[6] Ibid., p. 158.

sure and condemnation of the untruthful claims of the
quacks. The late Samuel Hopkins Adams made a monumental contribution through his famed series on patent medicines that appeared in *Collier's* in 1906. Many
historians credit the Adams series for tipping the balance in favor of passage of the Pure Food and Drug
Act of 1906.[7] In 1911 the first volume of the American Medical Association series entitled *Nostrums and
Quackery* appeared. And 1911 is a signal year in the
history of advertising for another reason, for it was in
that year that the advertising industry itself made the
first major effort directed at all forms of deceptive advertising in general.

Exposés of frauds and fraud promoters who were using advertising to ensnare new prospects were important early in the
Twentieth Century. (Mark Sullivan exposed medical fakes and
frauds in the *Ladies Home Journal* in 1904.) Upton Sinclair's
novel, *The Jungle*, revolted readers with its description of filthy
conditions in meat-packing plants. Spurred by such exposés,
Congress passed the Pure Food and Drug Act in 1906. Despite
being a truth-in-labeling measure the 1906 statute did nothing
to insure truth in advertising.[8]

Campaigning against advertising and promotional chicanery,
many magazines and newspapers exposed fraudulent practices.[9]
Some newspapers of this period, including the Cleveland Press
and other Scripps-McRae League papers, monitored advertisements, refusing those which appeared to be fraudulent or misleading. A Scripps-McRae official asserted that the newspaper
group turned away approximately $500,000 in advertising reve-
nue in one year by rejecting advertisements.

SEC. 92.   FEDERAL ADMINISTRATIVE CONTROLS: THE FEDERAL TRADE COMMISSION

**The most important governmental controls over advertising are
exercised by the Federal Trade Commission.**

FEDERAL TRADE COMMISSION ACT

The Federal Trade Commission is perhaps more important
than all other official controls over advertising combined. The

---

[7] 34 Stat. 768 (1906).

[8] Ibid.

[9] H. J. Kenner, The Fight for Truth in Advertising (1936) pp. 13–14; Alfred
McClung Lee, The Daily Newspaper in America (1937) p. 328.

FTC Act was passed in 1914 to supplement sanctions over unfair competition which had been provided by the Sherman Anti-Trust Act of 1890 and by the Clayton Act of 1914.[10] Gradually, the FTC law has thrown an important light upon the business picture of the country. While the FTC Act was conceived to prevent monopoly and restraint of trade, checking of the burgeoning menace of dishonest advertising has become a principal activity of the Commission.

This change of emphasis, created partly by criticisms of advertising, has not been without major opposition on the part of American business. There was fear that the government would so shackle advertising and sales efforts that business enterprise and even freedom of the press would be hampered.

The Federal Trade Commission is a major example of administrative rule and law-making authority delegated by Congress. Five Federal Trade Commissioners are appointed by the President and confirmed by the Senate. No more than three of the five commissioners may be from the same political party.

The Federal Trade Commission has come under increasing attack in recent years as the tides of "consumerism" mounted; the FTC's critics, to borrow adman Stan Freberg's phrase, could be counted on the fingers of the Mormon Tabernacle Choir. One of the persons leading the charge against the FTC is Consumer advocate Ralph Nader; such critics have not only denigrated its effectiveness; they have even questioned its right to continue to exist.[11] In addition to such "self-appointed" critics, the American Bar Association weighed in in 1969 with a harshly critical evaluation of FTC performance. The ABA study concluded that FTC activity had been declining while FTC staff and budget increased. The report contended that the FTC had mismanaged its resources, and that it had failed to set goals and provide necessary guidance for its staff.[12]

[10] Sherman Act, 26 Stat. 209 (1890), 15 U.S.C.A. § 1 (1964); Clayton Act, 38 Stat. 730 (1914); 15 U.S.C.A. § 12.

[11] See Report of "Nader's Raiders," The Consumer and the Federal Trade Commission—A Critique of the Consumer Protection Record of the FTC, published in 115 Congressional Record 1539 (1969); William F. Lemke, Jr., "Souped Up Affirmative Disclosure Orders of the Federal Trade Commission, 4 University of Michigan Journal of Law Reform (Winter, 1970), p. 193. See also Charles McCarry, Citizen Nader (New York: Saturday Review Press, 1972).

[12] American Bar Association, Report of the ABA Commission to Study the Federal Trade Commission, reprinted as Appendix II, pp. 123–244, "Federal Trade Commission Procedures," Hearings Before the Subcommittee on Administrative Practice and Procedures of the Committee on the Judiciary, United States Senate, First Session, Ninety-First Congress, Part I (Washington, D. C.: Government Printing Office, 1970).

Through an inadequate system of recruitment and promotion, it has acquired and elevated to important positions a number of staff members of insufficient competence. The failure of the FTC to establish and adhere to established and adhere to a system of priorities has caused a misallocation of funds and personnel to trivial matters rather than to matters of pressing public concern.

The primary responsibility for these failures must rest with the leadership of the Commission. In recent years, bitter public displays of dissension have confused and demoralized the FTC staff, and the failure to provide leadership has left enforcement activity largely aimless.

Turning to specific areas of FTC efforts, we find, first, that in the field of consumer protection, the agency has been preoccupied with technical labeling and advertising practices of the most inconsequential sort. This failing derives in large part from a detection technique which relies almost exclusively on the receipt of outside complaints.

At the same time, the FTC has exercised little leadership in the prevention of retail marketing frauds. * * * Unjustified doubts within the FTC as to its power or effectiveness in dealing with local frauds have caused it to remain largely passive in this area of enforcement

We recommend a new and vigorous approach to consumer fraud. The FTC should establish task forces in major cities to concentrate exclusively on this problem.

After the ABA study, a far-reaching reorganization of the FTC was carried out under Chairman Caspar W. Weinberger, and went into effect on July 1, 1970. Until that time, major responsibility for inhibiting delusory advertising rested with the FTC's Bureau of Deceptive Practices, which had five units:

1) Food and Drug Advertising.

2) General Practices—restrained deceptive selling practices concerning products other than foods and drugs.

3) Scientific Opinions—investigated through scientific analysis truth or falsity of the increasingly complicated claims made for products.

4) Special projects—did research in special consumer protection areas.

5) Division of compliance—was responsible for enforcement when violations of laws or FTC rules were found.[13]

Under the 1970 reorganization, all FTC consumer-oriented activities were brought under the new Bureau of Consumer Protection. This Bureau's responsibility extends not only to the enforcement of consumer protection statutes but also to the development of trade regulation rules and industry guidelines and to consumer education programs.

The Bureau of Consumer Protection has seven divisions, including:

1) Industry Guidance—This division is charged with attacking deceptive practices, not only those existing in one or in a few industries, but also those existing throughout an entire industry or across industry lines. This FTC division issues Industry Guides, which are interpretations of the laws it administers by the FTC. One goal of such guidelines is to provide statements of FTC policy in advance of problems in order to head off litigation. These are advisory interpretations, and do not constitute advance findings of fact by the FTC. The Industry Guidance division also issues Trade Regulation Rules, which are announced after hearings open to all interested parties. Trade Regulation Rules are legally binding upon all companies which fall within their scope.[14]

2) Food & Drug Advertising—This division is responsible for regulating national advertising practices. Innovative regulatory approaches suggested by this FTC division includes "corrective advertising" and the affirmative disclosure doctrine both of which are discussed in Section 95 of this chapter. The FTC also began an "Advertising Substantiation Program," announcing plans to select certain industries each year and require substantiation of advertising claims about safety, quality, performance, and comparative pricing.[15]

3) Special Projects—This FTC unit pays special attention to the enforcement of the Truth in Lending Act and the Fair Credit Reporting Act.[16]

[13] See Federal Trade Commission, "Here is Your Federal Trade Commission," Washington: Government Printing Office, 1964.

[14] Federal Trade Commission, Annual Report, 1971 (Washington, D.C. Government Printing Office, 1971) pp. 7–8.

[15] Ibid., pp. 9–13.

[16] Ibid., pp. 13–14.

4) Textile and Furs—This division enforces the Flammable Fabrics Act, Wool Products Labeling Act, Textile Fiber Products Identification Act and the Fur Products Labeling Act in order to prevent flammable fabrics, improperly branded textiles or misbrand furs out of the marketplace.[17]

5) Consumer Education—This organization attempts "to increase consumer competence" by making services of the FTC more readily available to consumers, disseminating information about FTC programs.[18]

6) Scientific Opinions—This division provides scientific facts and opinions to all other divisions or bureaus of the FTC, and also operates the FTC's Tobacco Testing and Research Laboratory. This division maintains an information exchange with the National Bureau of Standards, the Bureau of Radiological Health of the Department of Health, Education and Welfare, the U. S. Department of Agriculture, and the Naval Research Laboratory.[19]

7) Compliance—This division enforces some 8,000 Commission cease and desist orders issued over the years to prevent false or deceptive trade practices, including those involved in advertising.[20]

This complicated bureaucratic structure is just part of the FTC machinery which attempts to enforce Section 5 of the Federal Trade Commission Act, says: "Unfair methods of competition in commerce, and unfair or deceptive practices in commerce, are declared unlawful." [21]

Early FTC cases which came before the courts cast doubt on the Commission's powers over advertising.[22] However, in 1921, something as mundane as partly wool underwear masquerading as real woolies gave the FTC the case it needed to establish its authority. For many years the Winsted Hosiery Company had been selling its underwear in cartons branded with labels such as "Natural Merino," "Natural Wool," or "Australian Wool." In fact, none of this company's underwear was all wool, and, some of its products had as little as 10 per cent wool.

[17] Ibid., pp. 14–16.

[18] Ibid., pp. 17–18.

[19] Ibid., pp. 18–19.

[20] Ibid., pp. 19–20.

[21] 15 U.S.C.A. § 45(a)(1).

[22] Federal Trade Commission v. Gratz, 253 U.S. 421, 40 S.Ct. 572 (1920); L. B. Silver Co. v. Federal Trade Commission, 289 F. 985 (6th Cir. 1923).

The FTC complaint against Winsted Hosiery asked the company to show cause why the use of its brands and labels which seemed deceptive should not be discontinued. After hearings, the FTC issued a cease and desist order against the company. On appeal, the FTC lost, with a United States Circuit Court saying: "Conscientious manufacturers may prefer not to use a label which is capable of misleading, and it may be that it will be desirable to prevent the use of the particular labels, but it is in our opinion not within the province of the Federal Trade Commission to do so." [23]

In 1922, the Supreme Court of the United States upheld the FTC in language broad enough to support the Commission's power to control false labeling and advertising as unfair methods of competition. Speaking for the Court, Justice Brandeis declared that the Commission was justified in its conclusions that the hosiery company's practices were unfair methods of competition. He authorized the Commission to halt such practices. Brandeis said, "when misbranded goods attract customers by means of the fraud which they perpetrate, trade is diverted from the producer of truthfully marked goods." [24]

Despite the efforts of the Federal Trade Commission, the idea of consumer protection had little support from the Courts during the early 1930s. In 1931, the *Raladam* case, for example, cut sharply into the FTC's attempts to defeat the ancient, amoral doctrine of *caveat emptor*, "let the buyer beware." The Raladam Company manufactured an "obesity cure" containing "dessicated thyroid." This preparation, sold under the name of "Marmola," was advertised in newspapers and on printed labels as being the result of scientific research. It was claimed that "Marmola" was "safe and effective and may be used without discomfort, inconvenience, or danger of harmful results to health."

The FTC complained that the ingredient known as " 'dessicated thyroid' could not be presumed to act with reasonable uniformity upon the bodies of all users, or without impairing the health of a substantial portion of them * * * or with safety * * * " without continued competent medical advice. [25]

The FTC complaint focused upon the likelihood of actual physical harm to consumers who used Marmola believing it safe

[23] Winsted Hosiery Co. v. Federal Trade Commission, 272 F. 957, 961 (2d Cir. 1921).

[24] Federal Trade Commission v. Winstead Hosiery Co., 258 U.S. 483, 493–494, 42 S.Ct. 384, 385–386 (1922).

[25] Federal Trade Commission v. Raladam Co., 283 U.S. 643, 51 S.Ct. 587, 589 (1931).

as claimed. The Supreme Court, however, disallowed the FTC's order that the Raladam Corporation cease such advertising. Speaking for the Court, Justice George Sutherland ruled that Section 5 of the FTC Act did not forbid the deception of consumers unless the advertising injured competing businesses in some way. Section 5 of the FTC Act, the Court said, provided the Commission only with authority to halt "unfair methods of competition in commerce." [26] Accordingly, the FTC was not allowed to work directly for consumer protection.[27]

The FTC's authority over advertising had a slow and tortuous growth. As late as 1936—when the FTC had been in operation for some 22 years—the famed Judge Learned Hand of a U. S. Circuit Court decided a case against the FTC and in favor of an advertising scheme for encyclopedias which involved false representation. The publisher of the encyclopedias tried to lure customers into believing that the company gave them a set of encyclopedias "free," and that the customer's payment of $69.50 was only for a loose leaf supplement to the encyclopedia. The $69.50 was actually the combined regular price for *both* books and supplements.[28] Despite this, Judge Hand could declare: [29]

> We cannot take too seriously the suggestion that a man who is buying a set of books and a ten years' 'extension service' will be fatuous enough to be misled by the mere statement that the first are given away, and that he is paying only for the second. * * * Such trivial niceties are too impalpable for practical affairs, they are will-o'-the-wisps, which divert attention from substantial evils.

When this case reached the Supreme Court, Justice Hugo L. Black reacted indignantly, noting that the sales method used to peddle the encyclopedia "successfully deceived and deluded its victims." [30] In overturning Judge Hand's "let the buyer beware" ruling in the lower court, Justice Black added: [31]

> The fact that a false statement may be obviously false to those who are trained and experienced does not change its character, nor take away its power to de-

---

[26] 283 U.S. 643, 51 S.Ct. 587, 589 (1931).

[27] 283 U.S. 643, 51 S.Ct. 587, 589 (1931).

[28] 52 Stat. 111 (1938).

[29] 302 U.S. 112, 116, 58 S.Ct. 113, 115 (1937), quoting Judge Hand's opinion in the same case in the Circuit Court, 86 F.2d 692, 695 (2d Cir. 1936).

[30] 302 U.S. 112, 117, 58 S.Ct. 113, 115 (1937).

[31] 302 U.S. 112, 116, 58 S.Ct. 113, 115 (1937).

ceive others less experienced.   There is no duty resting upon a citizen to suspect the honesty of those with whom he transacts business.   Laws are made to protect the trusting as well as the suspicious.   The best element of business has long since decided that honesty should govern competitive enterprises, and that the rule of caveat emptor [let the buyer beware] should not be relied upon to reward fraud and deception.

In 1938, the year after the Supreme Court endorsed the concept of consumer protection from advertising excesses, Congress acted to give the FTC greater authority over deceptive advertising.   The 1938 Wheeler-Lea Amendment changed Section 5 of the Federal Trade Commission Act to read: "Unfair methods of competition in commerce, *and unfair or deceptive acts or practices in commerce*, are hereby declared unlawful.[32]   Note the italicized phrase.   These words were added by the Wheeler-Lea Amendment, and this seemingly minor change in phrasing proved to be of great importance.   The italicized words removed the limits on FTC authority imposed by the *Raladam* decision.   No longer would the FTC have to prove that a misleading advertisement harmed a competing business.   Now, if an advertisement deceived *consumers*, the FTC's enforcement powers could be put into effect.[33]

Aiming at false advertising, the Wheeler-Lea Amendment also inserted Sections 12 and 15(a) into the Federal Trade Commission Act.   Section 12 provides: [34]

It shall be unlawful for any person, partnership, or corporation to disseminate, or cause to be disseminated, any false advertisement—(1) by United States mails, or in [interstate] commerce by any means, for the purpose of inducing, or which is likely to induce, directly or indirectly, the purchase in commerce of food, drugs, devices or cosmetics.

Section 15(a) of the FTC Act says:

The term 'false advertising' means an advertisement, other than labeling, which is misleading in a material respect; and in determining whether any advertisement is misleading, there shall be taken into account

---

[32] 52 Stat. 111 (1938); 15 U.S.C.A. § 45 (1964).   Italics added.

[33] Ibid.;   Earl W. Kintner, "Federal Trade Commission Regulation of Advertising," Michigan Law Review Vol. 64:7 (May, 1966) pp. 1269–1284, at pp. 1275–1276, 1276n.

[34] Section 12, 52 Stat. 114 (1938), 15 U.S.C.A. § 52 (1964);   Section 15(a), 52 Stat. 114 (1938), 15 U.S.C.A. § 55(a) (1964).

(among other things) not only representations made or suggested by statement, word, design, device, sound, or any combination thereof, but also the extent to which the advertisement fails to reveal facts material in the light of such representations or material with respect to consequences which may result from the use of the commodity to which the advertisement relates under the conditions prescribed in said advertisement, or under such conditions as are customary or usual.

Such interpretations by the courts have given the FTC the power it sought to protect consumers. As FTC Commissioners Everette MacIntyre and Paul Rand Dixon once wrote, the Wheeler-Lea "amendment put the consumer on a par with the businessman from the standpoint of deceptive practices." [35] With the tremendous volume of interstate commerce in this nation, the FTC has a well-nigh impossible task in attempting to regulate advertising. The FTC's budget of nearly $15 million in 1967, while appearing sizable, has simply not provided enough personnel to handle the Commission's enormous workload. Nevertheless, many persons contend that the FTC has compiled an impressive record. Professor Glenn E. Weston wrote in 1964, on the 50th anniversary of the establishment of the FTC, that the Commission's accomplishments "probably dwarf that of any other administrative agency, state or federal." Up to 1964 the FTC had accepted over 12,000 stipulations from advertisers to halt certain practices, and had also obtained "countless" promises to discontinue false advertising claims. At a more formal level of enforcement, the FTC has issued "several thousand" complaints and cease-and-desist orders against advertisers. Finally, the FTC has inspected millions of advertisements in looking for false or deceptive statements.[36]

Not everyone, as might be expected, has such a friendly view of the Federal Trade Commission. The delays which have attended FTC enforcement procedures—especially those involved in lengthy court battles—have become almost legendary. An often cited example of this is the famed "Carter's Little Liver Pills" case. In 1943, the FTC decided that the word "liver" was misleading, and a classic and lengthy battle was on. Carter's Little Liver Pills, had been a well-known laxative product for three-quarters of a century. It took the FTC a total of 16 years

---

[35] Everette MacIntyre and Paul Rand Dixon, "The Federal Trade Commission After 50 Years," Federal Bar Journal Vol. 24:4 (Fall, 1964) pp. 377–424, at p. 416.

[36] Glenn E. Weston, "Deceptive Advertising and the Federal Trade Commission," Federal Bar Journal 24:4 (Fall, 1964) pp. 548–578, at p. 548.

—from 1943 to 1959—to win its point before the courts and get "liver" deleted.[37]

The FTC has five weapons to use against misleading advertising:

1) *Letters of Compliance*—The FTC may be satisfied with an informal promise that the advertiser will cease certain practices. Such a procedure can often be effective from an FTC standpoint, and is less costly in both time and money than would be a more formal procedure.

2) *Stipulations*—The advertiser agrees in writing to cease and desist from practices which the FTC has investigated and found misleading. With both letters of compliance and the more formal stipulation agreements, the FTC reserves the right to prosecute the advertiser at a later date should it then appear that the advertising practices involved have done real harm.[38]

3) *Consent Orders*—These may be handed down by the FTC after a formal complaint has been issued by the Commission. As is also true with the Letter of Compliance and Stipulation procedures, Consent Orders do not mean that advertisers are admitting guilt for engaging in an illegal, fraudulent advertising practice. The advertiser is merely agreeing not to continue a certain practice.[39]

4) *Cease and Desist Orders*—These are findings of "guilty" by the Commission after formal hearings have been held. Such orders may be appealed through the Federal Courts. Unless a cease and desist order of the FTC is appealed within 60 days after it is issued, the order becomes self-executing.[40]

The Federal statutes ruling this procedure have a built-in 60-day delay. If an advertiser decides not

[37] See Carter Products Co. v. Federal Trade Commission, 268 F.2d 461 (9th Cir. 1959), certiorari denied 361 U.S. 884, 80 S.Ct. 155 (1959).

[38] See Rock v. Federal Trade Commission, 117 F.2d 680 (7th Cir. 1941); Note, "The Regulation of Advertising," Columbia Law Review Vol. 56:7 (Nov. 1956) pp. 1019–1111, at p. 1034.

[39] Note, "Developments in the Law—Deceptive Advertising," Harvard Law Review Vol. 80:5 (March, 1967), pp. 1005–1163, at p. 1072. For a list of federal and state statutes on advertising, see Note, "The Regulation of Advertising," op. cit., pp. 1097–1111.

[40] 38 Stat. 719 (1914), as amended, 15 U.S.C.A. § 45(c) (1964).

to appeal a cease-and-desist order of the FTC, he may continue to use the advertisement for 60 days, or until the cease-and-desist order goes into effect with the force of law. However, if the advertiser does appeal during the 60-day period, courts may then issue an injunction to prohibit further use of the advertising until the Federal courts have completed adjudicating the advertiser's appeal.[41]

5) *Publicity*—The FTC publicizes the complaints and cease-and-desist orders which it promulgates. News releases on such subjects are regularly issued to the press, and publicity has proven to be a strong weapon at the Commission's disposal.

It can be seen from the foregoing list of FTC activities that it is not solely dependent on harsh actions such as cease-and-desist orders or court procedures. The Commission also takes positive steps to attempt to clarify its view of fair advertising practices. The Commission has four major programs which attempt to secure voluntary compliance. These are:

1. TRADE PRACTICE CONFERENCES. Since 1926, the FTC has held conferences tailored to the needs of specific industries to attempt to formulate clear rules for the application of federal laws regulating advertising. Following conferences with interested persons, public hearings are held on proposed rules. After the Commission adopts the rules, they are published in the Federal Register and members of the industry are invited to become signatories to the rules.

2. INDUSTRY GUIDES. This program involves issuing interpretations of the rules of the Commission to its staff. These guides are made available to the public, and are aimed at certain significant practices of a particular industry, especially those involved in advertising and labeling. The guides can be issued by the Commission as its interpretation of the law without a conference or hearings, and, therefore, in a minimum of time.

3. ADVISORY OPINIONS. In 1962, the FTC began giving advisory opinions in response to industry questions about the legality of a proposed industry action. Advisory opinions generally predict the FTC's response, although the Commission reserves the right to reconsider its advice if the public interest so requires.

4. TRADE REGULATION RULES. The FTC publishes a notice before issuing a Trade Regulation Rule on a specific prac-

---

[41] 38 Stat. 719 (1914), as amended, 15 U.S.C.A. Article 45(c) (1964).

tice. Industry representatives may then comment on the proposed Trade Regulation before the rule is adopted and put into effect.[42]

Unfortunately, voluntary compliance with laws and FTC rules is not always forthcoming. The FTC is frequently compelled to begin a case against an advertiser. Cases most often open after a complaint from an aggrieved citizen or a competitor who has suffered a loss because of what he believes to be illegal activity. The FTC also screens advertisements, looking for false or misleading statements. When a suspicious advertisement is found, a questionnaire is sent to the advertiser. The FTC may also request samples of the product advertised, if practicable. If the product is a compound, its formula may be requested. Copies of all advertisements published or broadcast during a specified period are requested, together with copies of supplementary information such as booklets, folders, or form letters.

Product samples are referred to the Commission's Scientific Opinions division or to another appropriate government agency for scientific analysis. If false or misleading advertising claims are indicated by such an examination, the advertiser is advised of the scientific opinions of the Commission's experts. The advertiser is allowed to submit evidence in support of his advertisement.

If the advertising is found truthful, the case is closed. However, if the Commission feels that the advertisement is false or misleading, a complaint may be issued. At this point it is also possible for the Commission to negotiate a stipulation in which the advertiser agrees to "cease and desist" from practices which the FTC finds legally objectionable. Thus the FTC's Bureau of Stipulations gives businessmen an opportunity to settle without the necessity of formal adversary proceedings.

If the advertiser ignores a cease and desist order, he is subject to a civil penalty of $5,000 for each violation. If there is a violation of the Wheeler-Lea provisions of the Federal Trade Commission Act involving false or misleading advertising of "food, drugs, devices, or cosmetics," the Commission may sue in U. S. District Court to enjoin temporarily the dissemination of the advertising. If such an injunction is granted, it will remain in force during court consideration of the FTC's complaint. Continued circulation of the advertising of a commodity which may be harmful to health or which is intended to defraud constitutes a misdemeanor. Convicted offenders may be fined up to $5,000, sentenced to up to six months in jail, or both. Succeeding viola-

---

[42] Federal Trade Commission, "Here is Your Federal Trade Commission," (Washington: Government Printing Office, 1964) pp. 17–21.

tions call for a fine of up to $10,000, imprisonment for up to a year, or both.

The six "basic ground rules" described a few years ago by former FTC Chairman Earl Kintner are useful in understanding just how the Commission approaches problems of controlling advertising.

1. *Tendency to deceive.* The Commission is empowered to act when representations have only a *tendency* to mislead or deceive. Proof of *actual* deception is not essential, although evidence of actual deception is apparently conclusive as to the deceptive quality of the advertisement in question.

2. *Immateriality of knowledge of falsity.* Since the purpose of the FTC act is consumer protection, the Government does not have to prove knowledge of falsity on the part of the advertiser; the businessman acts at his own peril.

3. *Immateriality of intent.* The intent of the advertiser is also entirely immaterial. An advertiser may have a wholly innocent intent and still violate the law.

4. *General public's understanding controls.* Since the purpose of the act is to protect the consumers, and since some consumers are "ignorant, unthinking and credulous," nothing less than "the most literal truthfulness" is tolerated. As the Supreme Court has stated, "laws are made to protect the trusting as well as the suspicious." Thus it is immaterial that an expert reader might be able to decipher the advertisement in question so as to avoid being misled.

5. *Literal truth sometimes insufficient.* Advertisements are not intended to be carefully dissected with a dictionary at hand, but rather are intended to produce an overall impression on the ordinary purchaser. An advertiser cannot present one overall impression and yet protect himself by pointing to a contrary impression which appears in a small and inconspicuous portion of the advertisement. Even though every sentence considered separately is true, the advertisement as a whole may be misleading because the message is composed in such a way as to mislead.

6. *Ambiguous advertisements interpreted to effect purposes of the law.* Since the purpose of the FTC Act is the prohibition of advertising which has a tendency and capacity to mislead, an advertisement which can be

read to have two meanings is illegal if one of them is false or misleading.[43]

SEC. 93.   LITERAL TRUTH IS NOT ENOUGH

Even literally true statements may cause an advertiser difficulty if those statements are part of a misleading advertisement.

Sometimes even the *literal truth* can be misleading. When truth misleads in an advertisement, the FTC is able to issue a "cease and desist" order and make it stick. A photo album sales scheme offers a case in point. Door-to-door salesmen told customers that for $39.95, they could take advantage of a "once in a lifetime combination offer" and receive a "free" album by purchasing 10 photographic portraits at the "regular price" of the photographs alone.

The FTC ordered the company selling the photo albums to stop suggesting that its albums were given away free, when in fact the albums were part of a $39.95 package deal. The company was also ordered to stop claiming that it sold only to "selected persons" and that a special price was involved. The photo album company retorted that its sales pitch was the literal truth, and that the FTC's cease and desist order should, therefore, be set aside by the courts.[44] The company argued that its customers actually were "selected;" that the word "few" is a relative term which is very elastic, and that the $39.95 price was in fact "promotional" because it tended to support the sale of the albums.

A U. S. Court of Appeals, upheld the FTC's cease and desist order. The Circuit Court announced that there should be a presumption of validity when courts reviewed FTC orders involving advertising. Tendencies of advertisements to mislead or deceive were held to be factual questions which would be determined by the FTC. Finally, the Circuit Court vigorously upheld the idea that even literal truthfulness of statement cannot protect an advertisement if it is misleading. A statement may be deceptive even if the constituent words may be literally or technically construed so as not to constitute a misrepresentation.[45]

Other courts' decisions have supported FTC contentions that literal truth of an advertisement is not enough to prevent it from being misleading, as illustrated in the case of P. Lorillard

---

[43] Earl W. Kintner, Michigan Law Review, Vol. 64:7 (May, 1966), pp. 1269–1284, at pp. 1280–1281. Reprinted by permission.

[44] Kalwajtys v. Federal Trade Commission, 237 F.2d 654, 655–656 (7th Cir. 1957).

[45] 237 F.2d 654, 656 (7th Cir. 1957).

Co. v. Federal Trade Commission (1950). An advertisement for Old Gold cigarettes during the late 1940s urged readers to see an issue of *Reader's Digest* magazine which reported tests on the tar and nicotine content of various brands of cigarettes. True, Old Golds, among six leading cigarette brands, had been found by scientific tests to have less—infinitesimally less—nicotine and tar than the other brands. This led to advertising blurbs that Old Golds were "lowest in throat-irritating tars and resins."

The FTC issued a cease and desist order, saying that it was false and misleading advertising. In upholding the FTC order, a United States Court of Appeals quoted from the *Reader's Digest* article: " 'The laboratory's general conclusion will be bad news for the advertising copy writers but good news for the smoker, who need no longer worry as to which cigarette can most effectively nail down his coffin. For one nail is just about as good as another.' " [46] The court denounced the advertisement saying: [47]

> An examination of the advertisements * * * shows a perversion of the meaning of the *Readers Digest* article which does little credit to the company's advertising department,—a perversion which results in the use of the truth in such a way as to cause the reader to believe the exact opposite of what was intended by the writer of the article * * *.

A more recent case involved the seemingly endless advertising battles among manufacturers of aspirin and competing analgesic products. An FTC attempt to get a temporary injunction against advertising by the makers of Bayer Aspirin failed in 1963 after a strenuous court battle. Bayer Aspirin's tribulations with the FTC in this case originated from an article published late in 1962 in the *Journal of the American Medical Association*. Two medical doctors had studied pain-relieving effectiveness of five leading analgesics: Bayer Aspirin, St. Joseph's Aspirin, Bufferin, Anacin, and Excedrin. The doctor's study "failed to show any statistically significant difference among the drugs" as far as pain-relieving capabilities were concerned. However, the doctors' study did have some findings which advertising copywriters for Bayer Aspirin seized upon:

> Excedrin and Anacin form a group for which the incidence of upset stomach is significantly greater than is

[46] P. Lorillard Co. v. Federal Trade Commission, 186 F.2d 52, 57 (4th Cir. 1950).

[47] Ibid.

the incidence after [taking] Bayer Aspirin, St. Joseph's Aspirin, [or] Bufferin * * *.

This study was supported by a grant from the Federal Trade Commission, Washington, D. C.

The U. S. Court of Appeals was sympathetic to Sterling Drug, makers of Bayer, noting that one of its competitors had boasted that its product "works twice as fast as aspirin" and "protects you against stomach distress you can get from aspirin alone." [48] The court commented on the Bayer advertising:

Believing that the Judgment Day has finally arrived and seeking to counteract the many years of hard sell by what it now believed to be the hard facts, Sterling and its co-defendants prepared and disseminated advertising of which the following, appearing in Life magazine and numerous newspapers throughout the country, is representative:

"GOVERNMENT-SUPPORTED MEDICAL TEAM COMPARES BAYER ASPIRIN AND FOUR OTHER POPULAR PAIN RELIEVERS."

"FINDINGS REPORTED IN THE HIGHLY AUTHORITATIVE JOURNAL OF THE AMERICAN MEDICAL ASSOCIATION REVEAL THAT THE HIGHER PRICED COMBINATION-OF-INGREDIENTS PAIN RELIEVERS UPSET THE STOMACH WITH SIGNIFICANTLY GREATER FREQUENCY THAN ANY OF THE OTHER PRODUCTS TESTED, WHILE BAYER ASPIRIN BRINGS RELIEF THAT IS AS FAST, AS STRONG, AND AS GENTLE TO THE STOMACH AS YOU CAN GET."

The court denied the FTC's application for a temporary injunction against the advertising. The Commission had objected that the Bayer Aspirin advertisements had "falsely represented, directly and by implication," the findings of the medical researchers who were endorsed by the United States Government and also by the American Medical Association and by the medical profession. This injunction the FTC had argued to be in the public interest, "since the consuming public would otherwise un-

[48] Federal Trade Commission v. Sterling Drug Co., 317 F.2d 669, 672 (2d Cir. 1963).

warrantedly rely upon the advertising to their [sic] 'irreparable injury' * * * ".49

The court, however, stated that the Commission had not shown grounds for a reasonable belief that the public would be misled by the Sterling Drug Company's advertisements. The court added:

> Our affirmance of the order of the District Court [refusing the FTC's application for a temporary injunction to halt use of the Bayer advertisement] should not, however, be thought to render fruitless the Commission's activities in its pending administrative proceeding against Sterling Drug, Inc. Should further evidence be adduced, a cease and desist order may well be had * * *.50

A famous case in which the FTC—supported by the courts— held an advertiser responsible for the *literal* meaning of his words is the 1944 decision in Charles of the Ritz Distributors Corporation v. Federal Trade Commission.51 A cosmetics firm was using the trademark "Rejuvenescence" for a face cream. This trademark, in the view of the FTC, was utilized in such a manner that the cream promised a youthful complexion to the user regardless of her age. In upholding the FTC's cease and desist order against the Charles of the Ritz Corporation, a United States Circuit Court of Appeals said that "[t]he important criterion is the impression which the advertisement is likely to make upon the general populace * * *," although experts or knowledgeable persons would not be deceived by such a statement. The court defended the right of the FTC to protect the gullible: 52

> And, while the wise and the worldly may well realize the falsity of any representations that the present product can roll back the years, there remains "that vast multitude" of others who, like Ponce de Leon, still seek a perpetual fountain of youth. As the Commission's expert further testified, the average woman, conditioned by talk in magazines and over the radio of "vitamins, hormones, and God knows what," might take "rejuvenescence" to mean that this "is one of the mod-

49 Ibid., pp. 673–674.

50 Ibid., p. 678.

51 143 F.2d 676 (2d Cir. 1944).

52 Ibid., p. 680; see also Gelb v. Federal Trade Commission, 144 F.2d 580 (2d Cir. 1944), where a claim that a compound could color hair "permanently" was taken literally by the FTC and the courts and held to be misleading.

ern miracles" and is "something which would actually cause her youth to be restored." It is for this reason that the Commission may "insist upon the most literal truthfulness," in advertisements * * * and should have the discretion, undisturbed by the courts, to insist if it chooses "upon a form of advertising clear enough so that, in the words of the prophet Isaiah, 'wayfaring men, though fools, shall not err therein'."

SEC. 94. THE FEDERAL TRADE COMMISSION AND THE "SANDPAPER SHAVE" CASE

In the famed 1965 decision in Federal Trade Commission v. Colgate Palmolive Company, the Supreme Court attempted to define which kinds of "mock-up" demonstrations were permissible in television commercials.

Advertising—especially television advertising—can be frivolous even if not amusing. There were some entertaining features behind a 1965 decision of the U.S. Supreme Court sometimes termed "The Great Sandpaper Shave" case.[53] Kyle Rote and Frank Gifford—both professional football players, more recently well known as sports commentators—figured prominently in this story. In 1959 Rote and Gifford, both rugged males with heavy "sandpaper beards," appeared in advertisements for a Colgate-Palmolive Co. product, Rapid Shave aerosol shaving cream.

The televised commercials showed both Rote and Gifford shaving easily and unconcernedly with Rapid Shave.[54] The advertising firm of Ted Bates & Company, Inc. prepared commercials to demonstrate that "Rapid Shave out-shaves them all." The commercials showed that Rapid Shave not only worked well on heavy beards, but could soften even coarse sandpaper. An announcer smoothly told the audience that, " 'To prove RAPID SHAVE'S super-moisturizing power, we put it right from the can onto this tough, dry sandpaper. It was apply * * * soak * * * and off in a stroke.' " As the announcer spoke, Rapid Shave was applied to a substance that appeared to be sandpaper, and immediately thereafter a razor was shown shav-

---

[53] Federal Trade Commission v. Colgate-Palmolive Co., 380 U.S. 374, 85 S.Ct. 1035 (1965). For an amusing account of this case, see Daniel Seligman, "The Great Sandpaper Shave: A Real-Life Story of Truth in Advertising," Fortune (Dec.1964) pp. 131–133ff.

[54] Seligman, ibid., p. 131.

ing the substance clean, removing every abrasive grain in its path.[55]

By the time the Federal Trade Commission issued a complaint against Colgate and Bates, the "sandpaper shave" commercial was old-hat to television viewers.   An FTC hearing examiner took testimony after the FTC's complaint that the commercial was deceptive.   Evidence showed that sandpaper of the kind used in the commercial could not be "shaved" immediately after the Rapid Shave had been applied, but needed a lengthy soaking period of about 80 minutes.   The FTC examiner also found that the substance shaved in the Ted Bates-produced commercial was in fact a simulated prop or "mock-up" made of plexiglas to which sand had been applied.   The examiner *did* find, however, that Rapid Shave could shave sandpaper, even if a much longer time was needed than represented by the commercials.   As a result, the examiner dismissed the FTC complaint, because in his opinion there had been no material deception that would mislead the public.[56]

The Federal Trade Commission was of a different mind and overturned the ruling of the hearing examiner late in 1961.   The Commission reasoned that the undisclosed use of plexiglas as a substitute for sandpaper—plus the fact that Rapid Shave could not shave sandpaper within the time depicted in commercials—amounted to materially deceptive acts.   Furthermore, even if sandpaper could be shaved just as the commercials showed, the Commission decided that viewers had been tricked into believing that they had seen, with their own eyes, the actual shaving being done.   The Commission issued a cease-and-desist order against Colgate and Bates, forbidding them from taking these actions: [57]

> Representing, directly or by implication, *in describing, explaining,* or purporting to prove the quality or merits of any products, that pictures, depictions, or demonstrations * * * *are genuine or accurate representations* * * * *of,* or prove the *quality or merits of, any product,* when such pictures, depictions, or demonstrations are *not in fact genuine or accurate representations* * * * *of,* or do not prove the quality or merits of, *any such product.*

This inclusive Federal Trade Commission order of December 29, 1961, set off protracted litigation.   When a Court of Appeals considered the FTC order, it expressed concern that the flexible

---

[55] 380 U.S. 374, 376, 85 S.Ct. 1035, 1038 (1965).

[56] 380 U.S. 374, 376–377, 85 S.Ct. 1035, 1038 (1965).

[57] 380 U.S. 374, 380, 85 S.Ct. 1035, 1040 (1965), quoting 59 F.T.C. 1452, 1477–1478. Emphasis the Court's.

Article 5 of the FTC Act was being used in a hitherto unexplored area. Article 5 provides:

> Unfair methods of competition in commerce, and unfair or deceptive acts or practices in commerce, are declared unlawful.[58]

The Supreme Court of the United States noted: [59]

> The breadth of the Commission's order was potentially limitless, apparently establishing a per se rule prohibiting the use of simulated props in all television commercials since commercials by definition describe "the qualities or merits" of products. The court's impression that the order was "quite ambiguous" was not alleviated when in oral argument counsel for the Commission stated that if a prominent person appeared on television saying "I love Lipsom's ice tea," while drinking something that appeared to be tea but in fact was not the commercial would be a deceptive practice.

The Circuit Court of Appeals concluded that the FTC was going too far in declaring all mock-ups illegal. The court declared, "where the only untruth is that the substance [the viewer] sees on the screen is artificial, and the visual appearance is otherwise a correct and accurate representation of the product itself, he is not injured." [60]

Following this ruling by the Circuit Court, the FTC entered a new "proposed final order" on February 18, 1963, attempting to answer the court's criticisms of its earlier order to Colgate and Bates. The Commission explained that it did not intend to prohibit all undisclosed simulated props in commercials, but merely wanted to prohibit Colgate and Bates from misrepresenting to the public that it was actually seeing for itself a test, experiment or demonstration which purportedly proved a product claim. The Commission argued that the "sandpaper shave" commercial's demonstration left a misleading impression that a demonstration or experiment had actually been performed. On May 7, 1963, the Commission issued its final order that Colgate and Bates cease and desist from: [61]

> Unfairly or deceptively advertising any * * * product by presenting a test, experiment or demonstra-

---

[58] 380 U.S. 374, 376n, 85 S.Ct. 1035, 1038n, quoting 38 stat. 719, as amended, 52 Stat. 111, 15 U.S.C.A. § 45(a)(1) (1958 ed.).

[59] 380 U.S. 374, 380, 85 S.Ct. 1035, 1040 (1965).

[60] 380 U.S. 374, 381, 85 S.Ct. 1035, 1040 (1968), quoting 310 F.2d 89, 94 (1st Cir. 1962).

[61] 380 U.S. 374, 382, 85 S.Ct. 1035, 1041 (1965), quoting Colgate Palmolive Co., No. 7736, FTC, May 7, 1963. This clause was added by the FTC for the

tion that (1) is represented to the public as actual proof of a claim made for the product which is material to inducing a sale, and (2) is not in fact a genuine test, experiment or demonstration being conducted as represented and does not in fact constitute actual proof of the claim, because of the undisclosed use and substitution of a mock-up or prop instead of the product, article, or substance represented to be used therein.

Although Colgate and Bates also challenged the 1963 FTC order, the Supreme Court of the United States made the order stick. Note that the use of *all* mock-ups in televised commercials was not forbidden as deceptive. The Court found that "the undisclosed use of plexiglas" in the Rapid Shave commercials was "a material deceptive practice." [62] But there is a fine line between the forbidden kind of "demonstration" in the Rapid Shave commercial and an acceptable "commercial which extolled the goodness of ice cream while giving viewers a picture of a scoop of mashed potatoes appearing to be ice cream." The Court was able to draw such a distinction, stating: [63]

> In the ice cream case the mashed potato prop is not being used for additional proof of the product claim, while the purpose of the Rapid Shave commercial is to give the viewer objective proof of the claims made. If in the ice cream hypothetical the focus of the commercial becomes the undisclosed potato prop and the viewer is invited, explicitly or by implication, to see for himself the truth of the claims about the ice cream's rich texture and full color, and perhaps compare it to a "rival product," then the commercial has become similar * * * [to the Rapid Shave commercial.] Clearly, however, a commercial which depicts happy actors delightedly eating ice cream that is in fact mashed potatoes or drinking a product appearing to be coffee but which is in fact some other substance is not covered by the present order.

benefit of Ted Bates & Co., because advertising agencies do not always have all the information about a product that a manufacturer has. The clause said, " 'provided, however, that respondent [Bates] neither knew nor had reason to know that the product, article or substance used in the test, experiment, or demonstration was a mock-up or a prop.' "

[62] 380 U.S. 374, 390, 85 S.Ct. 1035, 1045 (1965).

[63] 380 U.S. 374, 390, 85 S.Ct. 1035, 1047 (1965). See also Campbell Soup Co., 3 Trade Reg.Rep. Para. 19,261 (FTC, 1970); the Campbell Soup Co. conscented to stop the practice of putting marbles in soup bowls to force solid chunks of meat and vegetables up to the surface of the soup so as to be visible to viewers of television ads.

SEC. 95. CORRECTIVE ADVERTISING
ORDERS OF THE FTC

The Federal Trade Commission has attempted to enforce truth in advertising by requiring some advertisers to correct past misstatements.

After being roughly handled by critics ranging from Ralph Nader to the American Bar Association during the late 1960's, the Federal Trade Commission of the 1970's became much more active than in previous years. Symptomatic of this increased activity was an FTC complaint against Standard Oil Company of California. The company's advertising had been claiming that its Chevron gasoline, thanks to an additive called F–310, could significantly decrease harmful substances in auto exhaust emissions, thus helping to reduce air pollution. This sort of corporate "we're good for the environment" advertising has been termed "Eco-Porn" (ecological pornography) by some cynical critics of advertising.

In any event, the FTC proposed a cease and desist order to put a halt to allegedly misleading F–310 advertising claims, but the matter did not end there. The FTC also demanded that Standard Oil Company run "corrective" ads for a year, disclosing that its earlier advertising campaign had included false and deceptive statements. The FTC proposed that 25 per cent of the advertising for Chevron—either published space or broadcast time—be devoted to making "affirmative disclosure" about the earlier, misleading advertising.[64]

At this writing, FTC Administrative Judge Eldon P. Shrup has dismissed charges that the F–310 advertising claims were false "for failure of proof." This, however, is not a final decision of the Commission, and may be appealed or reviewed.[65]

Other corporate defendants in cases where the FTC has sought to obtain corrective advertising include Coca Cola, for claims made about nutrient and vitamin content of its Hi-C fruit drinks,[66] and ITT Continental Baking Company, for ads imply-

---

[64] 3 Trade Reg.Rep. Para. 19,428 (FTC Complaint issued, Dec. 29, 1970). See also William F. Lemke, Jr., "Souped Up Affirmative Disclosure Orders of the Federal Trade Commission," 4 University of Michigan Journal of Law Reform (Winter, 1970) pp. 180–181; Note, "'Corrective Advertising' Orders of the Federal Trade Commission," 85 Harvard Law Review (December, 1971) pp. 477–478.

[65] Federal Trade Commission News, "FTC Administrative Law Judge Dismisses 'Chevron' Complaint," release date May 9, 1973.

[66] 3 Trade Reg.Rep. Para. 19,351 (FTC, 1970).

ing that eating Profile Bread could help people to lose weight. The FTC charged that Profile was different from other bread only in being more thinly sliced, meaning that there were seven fewer calories per slice. ITT Continental Baking Company consented to a cease and desist order which does two things: first, it prohibits all further claims of weight-reducing attributes for Profile Bread, and second, the company has to devote 25 per cent of its Profile advertising for one year to disclosing that the bread is not effective for weight reduction.[67] Television commercials indeed appeared, with an actress saying sweetly: [68]

> I'd like to clear up any misunderstandings you may have about Profile bread from its advertising or even its name. Does Profile have fewer calories than other breads? No, Profile has about the same per ounce as other breads. To be exact Profile has 7 fewer calories per slice. That's because it's sliced thinner. But eating Profile will not cause you to lose weight. A reduction of 7 calories is insignificant. * * *

Law Professor William F. Lemke, Jr. contends that such "affirmative disclosure" orders as part of cease and desist orders mean that the FTC is exceeding its authority. He has suggested that courts reviewing the appropriateness of such orders may regard them as punitive rather than regulatory.[69] Other legal scholars, however, regard "corrective advertising" orders of the FTC as legitimate and potentially useful additions to the regulation of advertising.[70]

Such orders, however, are mere palliatives, and do nothing to solve the FTC's great problems with delays. Delays of from three to five years between issuance of an FTC complaint and final issuance of a cease and desist order are commonplace. Meanwhile, the advertiser is free to continue his advertising campaign: "By the time the order has become final, the particular campaign has probably been squeezed dry, if not already discarded in favor of a fresh one." [71]

One solution to the delay problem has often been suggested by the FTC: that Congress provide the Commission with power to

---

[67] 3 Trade Reg.Rep. Para. 19,780 (FTC, Aug. 17, 1971); Note, " 'Corrective Advertising' Orders of the Federal Trade Commission," 85 Harvard Law Review (December, 1971), p. 478.

[68] *Newsweek*, Sept. 27, 1971, p. 98.

[69] Lemke, op. cit., pp. 180, 191.

[70] Note, " 'Corrective Advertising' Orders of the Federal Trade Commission," 85 Harvard Law Review (December, 1971) p. 506.

[71] Ibid., pp. 482–483.

enjoin—without delay—advertising which the FTC has reasonable cause to believe is deceptive. The FTC now has such power only in cases dealing with medical devices, foods, drugs, and cosmetics—products, in other words, which could pose an immediate health threat to consumers.[72]

SEC. 96. OTHER FEDERAL ADMINISTRATIVE CONTROLS

In addition to the Federal Trade Commission, many other federal agencies—including the Food and Drug Administration, the Federal Communications Commission, and the Post Office Department—exert controls over advertising in interstate commerce.

Although of paramount importance as a control over advertising, the FTC does not stand alone among federal agencies in its fight against suspect advertising. Federal agencies which have powers over advertising include:

1) The Food and Drug Administration
2) The Federal Communications Commission
3) The Post Office Department
4) The Securities and Exchange Commission
5) The Alcohol and Tobacco Tax Division of the Internal Revenue Service

Such a list by no means exhausts the number of federal agencies which, tangentially at least, can exert some form of control over advertising. Bodies such as the Federal Aeronautics Authority and perhaps the Interstate Commerce Commission and the Federal Power Commission have power to curtail advertising abuses connected with matters under each agency's jurisdiction.[73]

1. Food and Drug Administration

The Food and Drug Administration's (FDA) activities in controlling labelling and misbranding overlap the powers of the FTC to a considerable degree. The Pure Food and Drug Act gives the FDA jurisdiction over misbranding and mislabelling of foods, drugs, and cosmetics.[74] The FTC, however, was likewise

---

[72] Ibid., pp. 485–486.

[73] See Note, "The Regulation of Advertising," Columbia Law Review Vol. 56:7 (Nov.1956) pp. 1019–1111, at p. 1054, citing 24 Stat. 378 (1887), 49 U.S.C.A. § 1 (1952) (ICC); 41 Stat. 1063 (1920), 16 U.S.C.A. § 791(a) (1952) (FTC); 52 Stat. 1003 (1938), as amended, 49 U.S.C.A. § 491 (1952).

[74] 52 Stat. 1040 (1938), 21 U.S.C.A. § 301 (1964).

given jurisdiction over foods, drugs, and cosmetics by the Wheeler-Lea Amendment.[75] The FTC and the FDA have agreed upon a division of labor whereby FTC concentrates on false advertising and the FDA focuses attention on false labelling.[76] However, this division of labor is quite inexact. Pamphlets or literature distributed with a product have been held to be "labels" for purposes of FDA enforcement.[77]

2. The Federal Communications Commission

The Federal Communications Commission has been endowed by Congress with licensing and regulatory powers over broadcasting.[78] Although prohibited from exercising censorship over broadcasting stations, the FCC does have the power to judge overall performance when considering renewal of a station's license every three years. According to the Communications Act of 1934, broadcast licenses are granted or renewed if it is judged that a station operating in "the public interest, convenience, and necessity." [79] Occasionally, the FCC has looked at the merits and demerits of advertising broadcast by a station as it considered license renewal.[80]

FCC powers over advertising, however, were long regarded as potential and indirect rather than actual and direct.[81]

The FCC became more directly concerned with advertising in the mid-1960s. The Commission was drawn more heavily into this area by the troubled interrelationship between advertising and the issues which surfaced during the controversy over cigarette smoking and its harmful effects. The FCC's involvement began, with a letter in 1966 from John F. Banzhaf III, a young New York lawyer. Banzhaf complained that a network-owned station in New York, WCBS-TV had broadcast many cigarette

[75] See "The Wheeler Lea Amendment" to the Federal Trade Commission Act, 52 Stat. 111 (1938), as amended, 15 U.S.C.A. § 45(a)(1) (1964).

[76] See, for example, 2 CCH Trade Reg.Rep. (10th ed.), Paragraph 8540, p. 17,081 (1954).

[77] See U. S. v. Kordel, 164 F.2d 913 (7th Cir. 1947); U. S. v. Article of Device Labeled in Part "110 V Vapozone," 194 F.Supp. 332 (D.C.Cal.1961).

[78] Communications Act of 1934, 48 Stat. 1064, 47 U.S.C.A. § 151 (1964). See Appendix E, The Federal Communications Commission and Cigarette Advertising.

[79] 48 Stat. 1083, 1091 (1934), 47 U.S.C.A. §§ 307, 326 (1964).

[80] See, e. g., a case involving advertisements by a physician, Farmers & Bankers Life Insurance Co., 2 F.C.C. 455 (1936); for a case involving a lottery, WRBL Radio Station, Inc., 2 F.C.C. 687 (1936).

[81] See Note, "The Regulation of Advertising," Columbia Law Review Vol. 56 (1956) pp. 1019–1111, at pp. 1045–1046.

commercials without allowing time for spokemen to rebut the ads with information about smoking's harmful effects. WCBS-TV replied that it had telecast numerous programs, from 1962 to 1966, about the hazards cigarettes present to health.[82]

In his letter, Banzhaf urged that the FCC's long-standing "Fairness Doctrine" be invoked to allow replies to the many cigarette advertisements broadcast every day.[83] The Fairness Doctrine, in the past, had dealt primarily with the presentation of news or editorial matter. As articulated by the FCC in its 1949 report, *Editorializing by Broadcast Licensees,* the Fairness Doctrine—before Banzhaf—meant this: Issues of public significance should be broadcast in such a manner that the public will hear important—if not all—sides of such matters.[84] This FCC doctrine became a United States statute in a 1959 amendment to the Communications Act.[85] The 1959 amendment said:[86]

> Nothing in the foregoing sentence shall be as relieving broadcasters, in connection with the presentation of newscasts, news interviews, news documentaries, and on-the-spot coverage of news events, from the obligation imposed upon them under this chapter to operate in the public interest and to afford a reasonable opportunity for the discussion of conflicting views on issues of public importance.

On June 2, 1967, the FCC sent a letter to WCBS-TV, holding that the Fairness Doctrine was applicable to cigarette advertising, and that a station broadcasting cigarette advertising must give responsible voices opposing smoking an opportunity to be heard.[87]

That decision of the FCC—and the viability of the entire Fairness Doctrine as well—were in doubt for some time: the Fairness Doctrine was under attack in a case in the federal

[82] "Fairness, Freedom, and Cigarette Advertising, A Defense of the Federal Communications Commission," Columbia Law Review Vol. 67 (1967) pp. 1470–1489; Norman P. Leventhal, "Caution: Cigarette Commercials May Be Hazardous to Your License—The New Aspect of Fairness," Federal Communications Bar Journal Vol. 22:1 (1968) pp. 55–124, at pp. 92–93.

[83] Ibid.

[84] 13 F.C.C. 1246 (1949), also published in 25 Pike & Fischer Radio Regulations 1901 (1963).

[85] 48 Stat. 1088 (1934), as amended, 47 U.S.C.A. § 315(a) (1964); see also Note, "Administrative Law—FCC Fairness Doctrine—Applicability to Advertising," Iowa Law Review Vol. 53:2 (Oct.1967) pp. 480–491, at pp. 481–482.

[86] 47 U.S.C.A. § 315(a).

[87] WCBS-TV Case, 9 Pike & Fischer Radio Regulations 2d 1423 (1967); Leventhal, op. cit., p. 92.

court system.[88] In the spring of 1969, however, the Supreme Court, in deciding two cases which did not involve advertising, upheld the Fairness Doctrine. The Court's language was broad enough to include not only the right to answer personal attacks and political editorializing but also seemed to have enough scope to provide opportunity for answers to be broadcast to advertising which dealt with controversial political or social issues.[89]

The Court declared:[90]

> Because of the scarcity of radio frequencies, the Government is permitted to put restraints on licensees in favor of others whose views should be expressed on this unique medium. But the people as a whole retain their interest in free speech by radio and their collective right to have the medium function consistently with the ends and purposes of the First Amendment. It is the right of the viewers and listeners, not the right of the broadcasters, which is paramount. * * * "It is the purpose of the First Amendment to preserve an uninhibited marketplace of ideas in which truth will ultimately prevail, rather than to countenance monopolization of that market, whether it be by the Government itself or a private license. * * * [S]peech concerning public affairs is more than self-expression, it is the essence of self government. * * * It is the right of the public to receive suitable access to social, political, esthetic, moral, and other ideas and experiences which is crucial here. That right may not constitutionally be abridged either by Congress or by the FCC.
>
> *   *   *   *   *   *   *   *   *
>
> In view of the scarcity of broadcast frequencies, the Government's role in allocating those frequencies, and the legitimate claims of those unable without governmental assistance to gain access to those frequencies for expression of their views, we hold the regulations and ruling at issue are both authorized by statute and constitutional.

[88] See Red Lion Broadcasting Co. v. FCC, 127 U.S.App.D.C. 129, 381 F.2d 908 (1967), which upheld the Fairness Doctrine as 1) a constitutional delegation of Congress' legislative power; 2) sufficiently explicit to avoid being unconstitutionally vague; 3) not in violation of the 9th and 10th amendments to the Constitution, and 4) not an abrogation of broadcasting station licensees' rights under the 1st and 5th amendments.

[89] See Red Lion Broadcasting Co. v. FCC, 395 U.S. 367, 89 S.Ct. 1794 (1969), discussed Chapter 13.

[90] 395 U.S. 367, 390, 89 S.Ct. 1794, 1806, 1812 (1969).

For further discussion of the FCC and the Fairness Doctrine in relation to advertising, see Section 101 later in this chapter.

3. The Post Office Department

Postal controls over advertising can be very severe. Congress was provided with lawmaking power to operate the postal system under Article I, Section 8 of the Constitution. This power has been delegated by Congress to a Postmaster General and his Post Office Department. It has long been established that the mails could not be used to carry things which, in the judgment of Congress, were socially harmful.[91] The Postmaster General has the power to exclude articles or substances which Congress has proscribed as non-mailable. With non-advertising written or pictorial matter, however, Post Office Department actions limiting freedom of expression have been kept in careful check by the courts. If it appears that the Postmaster General's denial of the mails to a publication has been arbitrary, the courts have not allowed such decisions to stand.[92]

Perhaps the Post Office's greatest deterrent to false advertising is contained in the Postmaster General's administrative power to issue "fraud orders." Suppose that postal inspectors find that the Zilch Merchandising Corporation of Chillblain Falls, Minnesota, has been engaged in a mail fraud scheme based upon dishonest advertising promises. The Post Office Department, by issuing a fraud order, will halt all mail addressed to Zilch Merchandising in Chillblain Falls. Such mail will be labeled "FRAUDULENT," and returned to its senders. Therefore, the person or company sending false advertising through the mail cannot profit from it once the administrative fraud order has been issued.[93]

Such cases are heard by Hearings Examiners, who can recommend issuance of a fraud order. This decision may be appealed to the Post Office Department's judicial officer, who issues decisions under authority of the Postmaster General. The Judicial Officer's decision may be appealed to a United States District Court.[94]

[91] See, for example, early federal laws on obscenity discussed in Chapter 11, or see Public Clearing House v. Coyne, 194 U.S. 497, 24 S.Ct. 789 (1904).

[92] Hannegan v. Esquire, 327 U.S. 146, 66 S.Ct. 456 (1946).

[93] Or, if a lottery is involved, the mail will be stamped "lottery mail" and returned to its senders. See the discussion of lotteries later in this chapter. 74 Stat. 654 (1960), 39 U.S.C.A. § 4005 (1965).

[94] See Robert M. Ague, Jr., "Intent to Defraud in Postal Fraud Order Cases," Temple Law Quarterly Vol. 38:1 (Fall, 1964) at p. 62.

The administrative fraud order is not the only kind of mail fraud action available to the Post Office Department. Instead of administrative procedure through the Department, a *criminal* mail fraud case may be started. Criminal cases are prosecuted by a U. S. attorney in a United States District Court. Conviction under the federal mail fraud statute can result in a fine of up to $1,000, imprisonment for up to 5 years, or both.[95] Criminal fraud orders are used when the Post Office Department wishes to operate in a punitive fashion. The administrative fraud orders, on the other hand, are more preventive in nature.

4. The Securities and Exchange Commission

Securities markets are attractive to fast-buck artists, so the sale and publicizing of securities are kept under a watchful governmental eye. Most states have "Blue Sky" laws which enable a state agency to halt the circulation of false or misleading information about the sale of stocks, bonds or the like.[96] The work of the Securities and Exchange Commission, however, is far more important in protecting the public.

After the stock market debacle of 1929, strong regulations were instituted at the federal level to prevent deceptive statements about securities. Taken together, the Securities Act of 1933 [97] and the Securities Exchange Act of 1934 [98] gave the S.E.C. great power over the sale and issuance of securities.

Sale of securities to investors cannot proceed until complete and accurate information has been given, registering the certificates with the S.E.C.[99] A briefer version of the registration statement is used in the "prospectus" circulated among prospective investors before the stock or bond can be offered for sale.[1] If misleading statements have been made about a security "in any material respect" in either registration documents or in the prospectus, the Commission may issue a "stop order" which removes the right to sell the security.[2] Furthermore, unless a security is properly registered and its prospectus accurate, it is a

95 18 U.S.C.A. § 1341 (1964); Ague, ibid., p. 61.

96 See Note, "The Regulation of Advertising," Columbia Law Review op. cit. p. 1065.

97 48 Stat. 74 (1933), 15 U.S.C.A. § 77 (1964).

98 48 Stat. 881 (1934), as amended, 15 U.S.C.A. §§ 78(a)–78jj (1964).

99 48 Stat. 77 (1933), as amended, 15 U.S.C.A. § 77(f) (1964).

1 48 Stat. 78 (1933), 15 U.S.C.A. § 77(j) (1964).

2 48 Stat. 79 (1933), as amended, 15 U.S.C.A. § 77(h)(b) and (d) (1964).

criminal offense to use the mails to sell it or to advertise it for sale.[3]

An unscrupulous seller of securities has more to fear than just the S.E.C.   Under a provision of the United States Code, a person who has lost money because he was tricked by a misleading prospectus may sue a number of individuals, including persons who signed the S.E.C. registration statement and every director, officer, or partner in the firm issuing the security.[4]

5.   The Alcohol and Tobacco Tax Division, Internal Revenue Service

Ever since this nation's unsuccessful experiment with prohibition, the federal government has kept a close eye on liquor advertising.   The responsible agency is the Alcohol and Tobacco Tax Division of the Internal Revenue Service.[5]   Liquor advertising may not include false or misleading statements, and may not disparage competing products.   False statements may include misrepresenting the age of a liquor, or claiming that its alcoholic content is higher than it is in reality.[6]

The Alcohol and Tobacco Tax Division has harsh sanctions at its disposal.   If an advertiser violates a regulation of the Division, he is subject to a fine, and could even be put out of business if his federal liquor license is revoked.[7]

Jurisdiction of the Federal Trade Commission, the Food and Drug Administration, the Post Office Department, and other federal agencies is generally limited to advertising in *interstate* commerce.   In 1941, the Supreme Court held that an Illinois company which limited its sales to wholesalers located only in Illinois was not "in [interstate] commerce," [8] and thus was outside FTC control.   A leading authority on the Federal Trade Commission has pointed out, however, that because of the interdependence of modern business enterprises most firms which answer FTC complaints are found to be engaged in interstate commerce.[9]

[3] 48 Stat. 84 (1933), as amended, 15 U.S.C.A. § 77(e) (1964).

[4] 48 Stat. 82 (1933), 15 U.S.C.A. § 77(k) (1964).

[5] 49 Stat. 981 (1936), as amended, 27 U.S.C.A. § 205 (1965).

[6] Ibid.

[7] Ibid.

[8] Federal Trade Commission v. Bunte Bros., 312 U.S. 349, 61 S.Ct. 580 (1941).

[9] Ira M. Millstein, "The Federal Trade Commission and False Advertising," Columbia Law Review Vol. 64:3 (March, 1964) pp. 439–499, at p. 455.

The FTC and other federal agencies by no means provide the whole picture of controls over advertising. There are many state regulations affecting political advertising and legal advertising by government bodies, but they cannot be treated here. States also regulate the size and location of billboards, but space does not permit discussion of these statutes. We now turn to consideration of some of the ways in which states have commercial advertising in the mass media.

SEC. 97. THE PRINTERS' INK STATUTE

Most states have adopted some version of the model statute which makes fraudulent and misleading advertising a misdemeanor.

One of the best known restraints upon advertising exists at the state level in the various forms of the Printers' Ink statute adopted in 45 states. *Printers' Ink* magazine, in 1911, advocated that states adopt a model statute which would make false advertising a misdemeanor. Leaders in the advertising and publishing world realized the difficulty in securing prosecutions for false advertising under the usual state fraud statutes. Considerable initiative in gaining state enactment of Printers' Ink statutes was generated through the Better Business Bureau and through various advertising clubs and associations.

The model statute, as revised in 1945 and approved by the National Association of Better Business Bureaus, says:[10]

> Any person, firm, corporation or association or agent or employee thereof, who, with intent to sell, purchase or in any wise dispose of, or to contract with reference to merchandise, real estate, service, employment, or anything offered by such person, firm, corporation or association, or agent or employee thereof, directly or indirectly, to the public for sale, purchase, distribution, or the hire of personal services, or with intent to increase the consumption of or to contract with reference to any merchandise, real estate, securities, service, or employment, or to induce the public in any manner to enter into any obligation relating thereto, or to acquire title thereto, or an interest therein, or to make any loan, makes, publishes, disseminates, circulates, or places before the public, or causes, directly or indirectly, to be made, published, disseminated, circulated, or

---

10 "Basis for State Laws on Truth in Publishing—The Printers' Ink Model Statute," Reprint, Printers' Ink Publishing Corp., 1959.

placed before the public, in this state, in a newspaper, magazine or other publication, or in the form of a book, notice, circular, pamphlet, letter, handbill, poster, bill, sign, placard, card, label, or over any radio or television station or other medium of wireless communication, or in any other way similar or dissimilar to the foregoing, an advertisement, announcement, or statement of any sort regarding merchandise, securities, service, employment, or anything so offered for use, purchase or sale, or the interest, terms or conditions upon which such loan will be made to the public, which advertisement contains any assertion, representation or statement of fact which is untrue, deceptive, or misleading, shall be guilty of a misdemeanor.

All but three states—Arkansas, Delaware, and New Mexico— have some version of the Printers' Ink statute on their books.[11] Although the Printers' Ink statute is famous, its fame is perhaps greater than its present-day usefulness as a control over advertising. Relatively few relevant cases exist which indicate that the statute has seen little use in bringing cheating advertisers to court. The Printers' Ink statute may still be useful as a guideline, or in providing a sanction which local Better Business Bureaus may threaten to invoke even if they seldom do so.[12]

The Printers' Ink statute is aimed and enforced primarily against advertisers rather than against units of the mass media which may have no knowledge that an ad is false or misleading.[13] This statute was widely adopted, apparently because the common law simply did not provide adequate remedies against false advertising, especially in an economy which has grown so explosively.

The model statute is more flexible than common law prosecutions or fraud statutes. It does not make *scienter*, guilty knowledge or intent to publish false advertisements, an element of the offense. A number of states, however, have variants of the Printers' Ink statute which are not as comprehensive as the model law in that some element of *scienter* must be shown for conviction. Seventeen such states with less rigorous versions of the model statute are Arizona, California, Connecticut, Florida, Maine, Maryland, Massachusetts, Montana, New Hampshire,

---

[11] Note, "Developments in the Law—Deceptive Advertising," Harvard Law Review, op. cit., p. 1122.

[12] Note, "The Regulation of Advertising," op. cit., p. 1057.

[13] Ibid., pp. 1059–1060; State v. Beacon Publishing Co., 141 Kan. 734, 42 P. 2d 960 (1935).

North Carolina, Pennsylvania, South Carolina, South Dakota, Tennessee, Texas, Utah, and Vermont.[14]

A major and obvious difficulty with the Printers' Ink statute —and with all attempts to control advertising—is that concepts of "truth" and "falsity" tend to elude definition. What is misleading, deceptive, or untrue is not defined in the model statute.

The problem of making such a determination is left up to the jury. A state of Washington case in 1917 is in point. J. J. Massey had published this advertisement:

Pre-opening sale of Used Pianos

These pianos must be closed out to make room for carload of new pianos coming from the east. Every piano fully guaranteed two years; exchange privilege; unheard of easy terms. All look like new.

Smith & Barnes, oak case, was $400; now $200.

Schilling & Sons, beautiful case, was $375; now $167.

Brinkerhoff, art case, was $400; now $218.

Free delivery and stool.

J. J. Massey.

It was charged that the Smith & Barnes and the Schilling pianos never had market values of $400 and $375. In the trial, the defendant was convicted of fraudulent advertising. A higher court reversed the conviction, saying that the advertisement referred to the retail selling price, not to the true market value of the pianos.[15]

SEC. 98.   LOTTERIES

Advertising or publicizing of lotteries is prohibited by both federal and state laws.

Many journalists, be they newsmen or admen, pay little attention to federal and state statutes which forbid publicizing of lotteries. The theory of such laws is that the public needs to be protected from gambling. In practice, many cities have church bingo socials or merchants' promotional lottery schemes which are rarely if ever prosecuted. As a result, journalists often ignore lottery laws because they are ignored by law enforcement officials at the state or local level.

[14] Note, "Developments in the Law of Deceptive Advertising," Harvard Law Review loc. cit.

[15] State v. Massey, 95 Wash. 1, 163 P. 7 (1917).

When interstate commerce or use of the United States mails is involved, however, journalists should be especially careful to heed the laws forbidding lotteries. Advertising a lottery, for example, could result in having a publication's second-class mailing privilege lifted. Also, the persons responsible for publicizing or advertising the lottery could be prosecuted for committing a crime punishable by a fine of up to $1,000, imprisonment of up to two years, or both.

Often, journalists have difficulty in recognizing a lottery. There are three elements in a lottery:

1) *Consideration*: Commonly, consideration means money paid to purchase a lottery ticket or a chance on a sewing machine or automobile which some service organization, for example, is "giving away" in a fund-raising effort. However, one should know the laws of his individual state concerning "consideration." In some states, the consideration need not be money paid. Instead, the effort required to enter a contest, such as having to go to a certain store to get an entry blank or having to mail a product's label, might be deemed to be "consideration." [16]

2) *Prize*—A prize in a lottery is something of value, generally of greater value or worth than the consideration invested.[17]

3) *Chance*—The element of chance—the gambling element—is what led Victorian-era Congressmen to pass the first federal statutes against lotteries in 1890.[18] There can, however, be an element of certainty accompanying the element of chance in a lottery. For example, if a person buys a newspaper subscription he is certain to receive the newspaper which includes a chance in a prize contest, this kind of promotion has been held to be a lottery.[19]

Similarly, a scheme for the sale of bonds in which the purchaser gets investments, and also participates in a prize drawing, is a lottery.[20]

[16] Brooklyn Daily Eagle v. Voorhies, 181 F. 579 (D.C.N.Y.1910).

[17] U. S. v. Wallis, 58 F. 942, 943 (D.C.Idaho 1893).

[18] State ex inf. McKittrick v. Globe-Democrat Co., 341 Mo. 862, 110 S.W.2d 705 (1937).

[19] Stevens v. Cincinnati Times-Star, 72 Ohio St. 112, 73 N.E. 1058 (1905).

[20] Horner v. U. S., 147 U.S. 449, 13 S.Ct. 409 (1893).

A well known federal court decision from 1893, United States v. Wallis, portrays a kind of situation sometimes found in American newspapers. This advertisement resulted in a lottery charge against James H. Wallis: [21]

FIVE MORE DAYS

Arrangements Completed for Thursday's Event

The Participants of the Drawing

LIST OF SUBSCRIBERS ENTITLED TO PARTICIPATE

Five More Days Left for Delinquents to Pay Up

Next Thursday the grand drawing for the elegant Eldridge sewing machine to be given away to subscribers to the Post will take place at noon that day at this office. The play upon which the drawing will be conducted will be as follows: Tickets, upon which will be printed numbers corresponding with the numbers on the coupons held by the paid-up subscribers, will be placed in a covered box. The fifteenth number drawn from the box will be the lucky number, the subscriber holding which will be entitled to the machine. The person drawing the numbers from the box will be blindfolded, so as not to permit of any partiality, were such a thing possible. As the numbers are drawn from the box they will be called out, and then recorded. To make the drawing more interesting, the subscribers holding the last fifteen numbers taken from the box will each receive a copy of the World's Almanac. People indebted to the Post can receive a chance to the drawing any time between now and noon next Thursday by paying up their indebtedness.

The object of this contest, was to increase the circulation of the newspaper. Each participant paid the announced price for the subscription and was given a numbered ticket. The inducement was the chance that a subscriber's numbered ticket might be the lucky one. The court held that all the elements of a lottery were present: tickets, prizes, and a drawing. The chance of winning a prize was the inducement rather than the appeal of the publication alone.[22]

---

[21] U. S. v. Wallis, 58 F. 942, 943 (D.C.Idaho 1893).

[22] Ibid.

Lotteries are forbidden in the electronic media as well as in the print media. Sections 1301 through 1305 of Title 18 of the United States Code all use identical terminology. Section 1301 forbids the importing or transporting of lottery tickets; Section 1302 forbids the mailing of lottery tickets or related materials; Section 1303 prohibits participation in lottery schemes by postmasters and postal employees, and Section 1304 forbids the broadcasting of lottery information. All four sections contain the same phrase forbidding " 'any lottery, gift enterprise, or similar scheme, offering prizes dependent in whole or in part upon lot or chance.' " [23]

SEC. 99.   SELF-REGULATION BY PUBLISHERS

Leading newspapers have developed tough standards to govern their acceptance or rejection of advertising.

Publishers must know the legal status of advertising. If it can be proved that they know that an advertisement is fraudulent, they may be held responsible for that ad along with the person or company who placed it in the publication. Advertising departments on many newspapers, moreover, often serve as a kind of advertising agency. In this capacity, the advertising staff must be able to give knowledgeable counsel and technical advice to advertisers.

Publishers are not liable to the individual consumer for advertising which causes financial loss or other damage unless the publisher or his employees knew that such advertising was fraudulent or misleading. The absence of liability for damage, however, does not mean that there is an absence of responsibility to the public generally and to individual readers of a publication.

The newspaper which permits dishonest or fraudulent advertising hurts its standing with both its readers and its advertisers. Publishers, who perceive psychological and economic advantages in refusing dishonest advertising, also appear to be becoming more cognizant that they have a moral duty to protect the public.

Responsible publishers go to great lengths to ensure that advertising which they print is honest. An excellent example of this is the *New York Times'* pamphlet, *Standards of Advertising Acceptability*, which is reprinted below.

[23] Federal Communications Commission v. American Broadcasting Co., 347 U.S. 284, 292n, 74 S.Ct. 593, 598n (1954).

STANDARDS OF ADVERTISING ACCEPTABILITY [24]
FROM THE NEW YORK TIMES

The success of advertising depends upon its credibility. No matter how technically brilliant or compelling an advertisement may be, unless readers believe it, it fails in its purpose.

Likewise, the confidence of readers in a newspaper, its news and editorial columns as well as its advertising columns, depends upon the integrity of those columns.

This is why it is the policy of the New York Times to protect its readers as well as its advertisers by barring from its columns advertising that is misleading, inaccurate and fraudulent; that makes unfair competitive statements; or that fails to comply with its widely accepted high standards of decency and dignity.

The Times maintains a Department of Advertising Acceptibility whose function is to examine advertisements before they are published. All advertising submitted to The Times is carefully read to see whether it meets the standards of acceptability The Times has developed throughout the years.

If the advertising contains statements or illustrations which are not acceptable, and which The Times thinks should be changed or eliminated, the advertiser or his advertising agency is notified.

Frequently the Advertising Acceptability Department will conduct an active investigation to get further information about statements in an advertisement and thus help determine their accuracy. Recognized agencies of investigation, such as the Better Business Bureaus, are consulted. Sometimes they are asked to "shop" advertisements. Reports of commercial fact-finding organizations are used to get background information.

In some classifications, advertisers are required to fill out questionnaires before their advertising is considered. These include Financial, Book Exchange, Business Opportunities, Camps, Education, Gardens, Mail Order, Mortgages, Stamps and Coins.

---

[24] Standards of Advertising Acceptability of The New York Times, pamphlet dated June, 1967. Reprinted by permission.

In the case of new financial advertisers, questionnaires and advertising copy are reviewed by a special committee of Times executives which advises the Advertising Acceptability Department. Reports from government agencies are used to help in deciding upon the acceptability of these advertisers.

If an advertiser makes inaccurate or misleading statements and refuses to correct them, his advertising is declined.

The Advertising Acceptability Department investigates all complaints from readers about advertising in The Times. If investigation proves the complaints to be valid and shows that the business practices of the advertiser are unfair or questionable, The Times declines further advertising from that advertiser.

The Times refers all legal questions relating to advertising to its counsel. Advertising must sometimes be changed or even declined because of the applicability of laws dealing with such matters as libel, copyright and trademark, the right of privacy, the sale of securities, the sale of real estate (particularly subdivided vacant lands, cooperative apartments and condominiums), and political advertising.

The following describes some of the kinds of advertising which The Times will not accept:

1. *Generally*

Advertisements which contain fraudulent, deceptive, or misleading statements or illustrations.

Attacks of a personal character.

Matrimonial offers.

Unwarranted promises of employment in school advertising.

Advertisements that are overly competitive or that refer abusively to the goods or services of others.

2. *Investments*

Advertisements holding out the prospect of large guaranteed dividends or excessive profits, or which solicit investments in non-producing mining or oil royalties.

3. *Fortune Telling*

Advertisements of fortune telling, dream interpretations and individual horoscopes.

4. *Foreign Languages*

Advertisements in a foreign language (unless an English translation is included).

5. *Salesmen*

Advertisements for salesmen stating that specific sales volume or income will be achieved within a given period of time.   Advertisements which do not include the type of compensation to be paid to salesmen, such as salary, commission, etc., or which do not describe the articles and services to be sold.

6. *Discrimination*

Advertisements which discriminate on racial or religious grounds.

7. *Offensive to Good Taste*

Indecent, vulgar, suggestive or other advertising that may be offensive to good taste.

This list is not intended to include all the types of advertisements unacceptable to The Times.   Generally speaking, any other advertising that may cause financial loss to the reader, or injury to his health or morals, or loss of his confidence in reputable advertising and ethical business practices is likewise unacceptable.

RETAIL ADVERTISING

1. *Generally*

Untrue, deceptive or misleading statements or illustrations are not acceptable.

2. *Competitive Claims Which Refer to Quality or Price*

A.   Statements or representations which refer to the goods, price, service or advertising of any competitor are not acceptable.

B.   Statements which claim to undersell competitors are not acceptable.

3. *Competitive Claims on Policy or Business Methods*

A.   Statements which make or imply comparisons must confine those comparisons to the individual advertiser's own merchandise, services, prices or business methods.

B.   Statements of fact, if generally known and susceptible of definite proof are acceptable.

4. *"Bait" Offers*

"Bait" offers of merchandise wherein the customer is denied a fair opportunity to purchase are not acceptable.

Some examples follow of expressions in advertisements which are not acceptable and the changes required to make them acceptable:

NOT ACCEPTABLE	*ACCEPTABLE AS REVISED*
The lowest price ever offered	The lowest price we ever offered
The best buy in town	One of the best buys in town
Will surpass anything you could possibly find	Will surpass anything we could possibly offer
Unrivaled in fine quality	Unexcelled in fine quality
Unprecedented value (or quality)	Exceptional value (or quality)
Unheard of prices	Amazingly low prices
The finest coat we have ever seen	The finest coat we have ever sold
We give you the most for your dollar	We give you exceptional value for your dollar
Superior to any you've seen at this price	Superior to what you'd expect to find at this price
The outstanding value in men's footwear	An outstanding value in men's footwear
We believe you will find these values greater than elsewhere	We believe you will find these values unsurpassed

OPINION ADVERTISING

The policy of The Times on advertisements of political and social views is to keep its columns open to those who wish to express a particular point of view, no matter how widely divergent it may be from that of The Times * * *.

The New York Times general policy with respect to the acceptability of advertising of a political or propaganda nature was contained in an editorial, THE FREEDOM

OF ADVERTISING, printed December 28, 1961. The editorial dealt with an advertisement for a book about Latin America, but the principles are applicable to all types of advertising in which opinion is expressed. The editorial said in part: [25]

* * * should The Times accept * * * an advertisement containing political propaganda with which it strongly disagrees? When reduced to such fundamentals the answer is not difficult. The Times believes that, in furtherance of the objectives of the First Amendment of the Constitution, it should keep its advertising columns open to all points of view, no matter how strongly it disapproves of them.

Subject of course to the laws of libel and good taste and the requirements of factual accuracy, we think the principles of freedom of the press not only requires us to report events and occurrences of which we disapprove—such as the degeneration of the Cuban revolution under Fidel Castro—but also imposes on us the obligation to accept advertising of books whose contents we reject and of political parties and movements whose goals we despise.

The guarantees of the publishers' right to publish. They are, more importantly, guarantees of the public's right to know. We consider that that is what a free press truly means: the maintenance of open communication in the realm of ideas.

The political and other opinions of The New York Times—that is, our editorial policies—are expressed daily and exclusively in the editorial columns on this page. Our policy on "Letters to the Editor" is to print communications from our readers of general interest and of all shades of opinion. Our news policy is "to give the news impartially, without fear or favor, regardless of any party, sect, or interest involved," as Adolph S. Ochs put it sixty-three years ago. Our policy with respect to political advertising is to keep our columns open to those who wish to express a particular point of view, no matter how widely divergent it may be from our own.

[25] Excerpts from the New York Times editorial of December 28, 1961, are reproduced out of order for purposes of this chapter. In the Standards of Advertising Acceptability of The New York Times, the editorial's excerpts are published at the end, after the section titled "Medical Advertising."

These policies, as we see them, comprise the essence of the freedom and responsibility of the press.[26]

*   *   *   *   *   *   *   *   *

Full identification of the sponsors of an opinion advertisement is required. In general, the names of two or more of the officers of the organization must appear in the advertisement as well as the address of the advertiser.

If the names or pictures of other persons are to appear in the advertisement, the advertiser must furnish evidence that all such persons have given permission for use of their names or pictures.

MEDICAL ADVERTISING

All medical advertising even of acceptable preparations, is carefully scrutinized.

Before accepting the advertising of any preparation, medication or treatment, The Times seeks the opinion of medical authorities. These include members of its own Medical Department and the recognized local and national medical information bureaus.

These medical consultants do not exercise censorship over The Times columns. The Times applies its own judgment to their information and advice and makes its own decisions.

The Times does not accept the advertising of any preparations which might be habit-forming or contain dangerous drugs or which might lead to self-diagnosis or self-medication of any serious condition or illness.

The Times does not accept medical advertising which contains testimonials, questionable "before and after" illustrations, or any copy which goes too far in indicating that doctors "prescribe" or recommend any preparation for a stated illness or condition.

In addition, offers of free medical treatment or exaggerated remedial, relief or curative claims are not accepted. An example is the claim that any cosmetic will banish freckles or wrinkles.

The Times does not accept the advertising of preparations which may be harmless in themselves but which make grossly exaggerated claims in their advertising or on their labels or in their descriptive pamphlets.

[26] Ibid., end of Dec. 28, 1961, editorial from The New York Times.

Another major American newspaper which carefully polices its own advertising columns is *The Milwaukee Journal.* The Journal's basic rules for accepting advertising are reprinted below.

GUIDES FOR ADVERTISING ACCEPTANCE [27]

NEWSPAPERS, INC.

The Milwaukee Journal   *The Milwaukee Sentinel*

The basic advertising standard for Newspapers, Inc., is: "advertising published in our newspapers is accepted on the premise that merchandise and services offered are properly described and willingly sold to customers at the advertised price."

Advertisers are made aware of these conditions. Advertising not conforming to such a requirement, or that is deceptive, misleading, or does not comply with existing laws, is never knowingly accepted.

Advertising which violates local ordinances, state statutes or federal laws is also never knowingly accepted.

The following standards relating to advertising acceptance are based on matters of experience or judgment, or both. These standards are reviewed regularly. Revisions are made for the development of new products and services, new sales and marketing practices; but are always reviewed with the thought of what is in the best interest of the readers of The Milwaukee Journal and The Milwaukee Sentinel.

Some types of advertising Not Acceptable for Publication Are:
BAIT OFFERS—advertising of merchandise or service not willingly sold.

CURRENCY ILLUSTRATIONS—the use of U.S. or foreign currency in any advertisement is in violation of Section 474 of Title 18 of the United States Code.

DEROGATORY ADVERTISING—advertising which contains attacks of a personal, racial or religious nature, or reflects on competitive organizations, institutions, merchandise or services.

DISCRIMINATION—advertising which contains restrictive phrases as to race, color, religion, national origin and sex (as defined in the Civil Rights Act of 1964).

EXCESSIVE CLAIMS—advertising which makes grossly unwarranted claims.

---

[27] Milwaukee Journal—Milwaukee Sentinel Guides for Advertising Acceptance, May 1, 1973. Reprinted by permission.

EXAGGERATIONS—statements which cannot readily be established as a fact, such as "Lowest Prices In Town", "The Largest Selection Anywhere", etc.

EYE (VISUAL AID) GLASS PRICE ADVERTISING—is prohibited by Wisconsin State Statute.

FLAG OF THE UNITED STATES—it is a violation of Wisconsin law (Statute 946.06) to illustrate the U.S. flag in a commercial advertisement. The Statute also prohibits illustrating the United States flag in any advertisement offering the flag for sale.

FORTUNE TELLING, ETC.—advertising for fortune tellers, psychics, palmists, numerologists, clairvoyants, astrologists, phrenologists, E.S.P., hypnotists, etc.

GUNS—illustrations of hand guns or any other type of concealed weapon; advertisements for automatic weapons (machine guns, etc.).

ILLUSTRATIONS—pictures or artwork which do not properly depict the merchandise or service being offered.

IDENTIFICATION—advertising which does not carry the signature of a responsible firm or other means by which any necessary checking or follow-up can be made.

INTRODUCTION SERVICES—advertising that seeks introduction to members of the opposite sex; as well as computer dating services.

MAILING LISTS—advertising offering mailing lists for sale.

MATRIMONIAL OFFERS—advertisements proposing marriage.

MEDICAL ADVERTISING—advertising which makes curative claims not justified by facts or general experience. Advertising of medicines, toiletries or appliances which in themselves may be harmless but whose continued use may encourage the sufferer to delay medical treatment when needed. Advertising of products which are obviously narcotic, habit-forming or contraceptive.

MISREPRESENTATION—advertising that is ambiguous in wording or improper illustrations which may mislead.

MONEY REQUESTED—money directed to a U.S. Post Office box without permanent address of the advertiser prominently shown in the advertisement. Under no circumstances may money be directed to the business reply boxes of The Journal and The Sentinel.

MULTI-LEVEL MARKETING—violates Chapter Ag 122, Department of Agriculture, State of Wisconsin.

PERSONAL WELL-BEING—advertising which in the judgment of Newspapers, Inc., appears likely to cause injury to health or to cause financial loss.

PRESCRIPTION DRUGS PRICE ADVERTISING—is prohibited by Wisconsin State Statute.

PUBLICITY CONNECTED—advertising submitted with the condition of news material appearing in conjunction with it.

SPECULATIVE ADVERTISING—financial or business investment advertising which in the opinion of Newspapers, Inc., is fraudulent or highly speculative or promises prospects of unreasonably large profits. This category includes questionable oil fields, land developments, vending machines and other "on location" type businesses, chinchilla raising, etc.

READER STYLING ADVERTISING—editorial type advertising which does not carry the word "advertisement" above it.

TASTE—advertising which is indecent, repulsive, suggestive, or offensive in text or illustration.

ALSO INCLUDED is advertising for which special printing, positioning or payment requirements are specified; advertising with excessive black areas or in nonstandard shapes and sizes or which in any way requires difficulty in reading under normal conditions.

Other Types of Advertising For Which Guides
Have Been Established, or Laws Prevail, Are:

AUCTIONS—must be licensed by the municipality in which they are being conducted, and also fully comply with Newspapers, Inc., standards of acceptance.

AUTOMOTIVE—advertising is subject to Motor Vehicle Trade Practices, Department of Transportation, State of Wisconsin, MVD 24.02, "Advertising and Sales Representations".

COMPARATIVE PRICING—comparative prices and savings claims must meet the regulations of State of Wisconsin.

CORRESPONDENCE SCHOOLS—advertising for privately operated schools offering training at home requires complete information concerning the school before accepting. Copy containing promises or inferring job placement is not acceptable.

CONTESTS, LOTTERIES, SWEEPSTAKES—all contest advertising is subject to approval before publication. "Come-on" and "easy-win" contests are not acceptable. Lotteries and Sweepstakes must comply with Section 945.01, Wisconsin Statutes.

CREDIT TERMS—must conform with Federal Reserve Regulation Z—"Truth In Lending".

DISTRESS SALES (Going Out of Business, Fire, Liquidation, Removal, etc.)—must be licensed by the municipality in which the sale is being held, and fully comply with Newspapers, Inc., standards of acceptance.

EMPLOYMENT—advertising must conform to state and federal regulations concerning employment, as well as standards established by Newspapers, Inc.

FINANCIAL—business opportunity advertising is required to provide full information before an acceptance determination can be made. The sale of securities requires a license in the State of Wisconsin. Franchise advertising must be registered with the Commissioner of Securities, State of Wisconsin, before submitting advertising for review.

FOOD FREEZER PLANS—all advertising must conform with the provisions of Chapter Ag 109, "Freezer Meat and Food Service Plan Trade Practices", Department of Agriculture, State of Wisconsin.

FUND RAISING—complete information must be provided before an advertising acceptance determination can be made.

FREE GIVEAWAYS (requiring purchase)—the advertisement must clearly state that total price or unit price and minimum number of units required so that the purchaser may readily ascertain the total amount which must be paid. It must also clearly disclose any other requirement the customer must meet. Services as well as merchandise are included.

HOME IMPROVEMENT—acceptance procedures largely follow "Standards for the Advertising and Selling of Home Improvements", Home Improvement Council of Greater Milwaukee.

INSURANCE, DIRECT RESPONSE ADVERTISING—subject to licensing by the Commissioner of Insurance, State of Wisconsin; a thorough background check is made by Newspapers, Inc., and full disclosure of premiums and coverage is required in the copy.

MAIL ORDER—a Mail Order Questionnaire plus sample of the merchandise offered for sale in mail order advertising must be submitted for evaluation. All mail order advertising must carry a money back guarantee.

LOSS LEADER ADVERTISING—pricing is subject to the Unfair Sales Act, Section 100.30, Wisconsin Statutes.

MOTION PICTURES—the following regulations apply to "X", "R" and "Adults Only" display motion picture ads:

1) a box containing the full MPAA rating, or words "Adults Only" if the picture is not rated, is to be carried at the top of each ad. This box is to be a minimum of 1 column wide on 1 column ads, approximately ½ the width of the ad on 2, 3 or 4 column ads and in relative proportions on larger size ads. In the event more than one picture is included in the ad, and the picture carries a different rating, a full MPAA rating or "Adults Only" box prominent in size must be carried directly above the title of the film;

2) illustrations depicting suggestive poses, sensuous facial expressions, undue flesh exposure and scenes of violence are not acceptable;

3) text with *any* provocative sexual connotation or emphasis of violence is not acceptable;

4) titles of films are reviewed on an individual basis—those deemed to be objectionable are not accepted.

5) other general standards of advertising acceptance for Newspapers, Inc., are to be observed.

Copy for "GP" and "G" rated films in display advertising is accepted on the basis of the above regulations and reviewed on an individual basis. Cooperation in submitting correct copy in these two classifications is mandatory.

The Motion Picture Guide requires that all pictures carry the appropriate rating, or "Adults Only" immediately preceding the title of the film. The Same restrictions cited in point three for display ads "X", "R" and "Adults Only" display ads apply to guide copy. Guide copy not conforming to these requirements will be omitted from the insertion for which it is scheduled.

NEWS MATTER REPRODUCTION—all editorial material of Newspapers, Inc., is copyrighted and any reproduction requires the permission of the editors. Quotes out of context are not permissible.

POLITICAL ADVERTISING—disclaimers are required by Wisconsin State Law. The disclaimer must appear at the top of the ad with the words "Authorized and Paid For" followed by the name, given and surname, and address of the person placing the advertisement.

TELEPHONE NUMBERS, MOTEL AND HOTEL—the use of a motel or hotel telephone number in advertising is only acceptable with the approval of the management of the motel or hotel.

REFERRAL SELLING—advertising of this nature must comply with Chapter Ag 121, Department of Agriculture, State of Wisconsin.

WHOLESALE—this term is not acceptable in retail, consumer service or specified display rate advertising copy.

—May 1, 1973.

SEC. 100.   THE RIGHT TO REFUSE SERVICE

A newspaper or magazine is not a public utility and therefore may choose those with whom it cares to do business.

A newspaper or magazine is a private enterprise and as such may carry on business transactions with whom it pleases. If its managers so desire they may refuse to sell newspapers to individuals or news agents, or to publish news stories about any particular event or on any opinion. By weight of legal authority, a newspaper is not a public utility.

There is growing pressure to create a "right of access" to news and advertising columns of the media. Arguments heard with increasing frequency run something like this: [28]

> The free marketplace of ideas is not working at all well during the latter third of the 20th Century. Competition among newspapers, magazines, and the electronic media is so diminished that only ideas acceptable to the nation's establishment can gain a hearing. Laissez faire in the media has come to mean, as John P. Roche once said in another context, "Every man for himself —as the elephant said, dancing among the chickens." Government has an affirmative obligation to stop the discriminatory refusal of advertisements and notices in publications.

Such arguments, at this writing, are on the frontier of communications law and herald developments which may or may not be translated into viable law through court decisions or statutes. If a change does come which affects the right to refuse advertising, it would seem that advertising with a political or otherwise socially significant message might first be forced upon publishers before the right to refuse ordinary commercial advertising

[28] See, e. g., Jerome A. Barron, "Access to the Press—A New First Amendment Right," Harvard Law Review Vol. 80 (1967) p. 1641; Willard H. Pedrick, "Freedom of the Press and the Law of Libel," Cornell Law Quarterly Vol. 49 (1964) p. 581; Report of the 1968 Biennial Conference of the American Civil Liberties Union, New York, Sept., 1968; Gilbert Cranberg, "New Look at the First Amendment," Saturday Review, Sept. 14, 1968, pp. 136–137; Simon Lazarus, "The Right of Reply," New Republic, Oct. 5, 1968, p. 17.

would be affected. An old but important case decided in 1931 arose when a man sought a mandatory injunction, declaring:[29]

> The newspaper business is an ordinary business. It is a business essentially private in nature—as private as that of the baker, grocer, or milkman, all of whom perform a service on which, to a greater or less extent, the communities depend, but which bears no such relation to the public as to warrant its inclusion in the category of businesses charged with the public use. If a newspaper were required to accept an advertisement, it could be compelled to publish a news item. If some good lady gave a tea, and submitted to the newspaper a proper account of the tea, and the editor of the newspaper, believing that it had no news value, refused to publish it, she, it seems to us, would have as much right to compel the newspaper to publish the account as would a person engaged in business to compel a newspaper to publish an advertisement of the business that the person is conducting.

> Thus, as a newspaper is strictly a private enterprise, the publishers thereof have a right to publish whatever advertisements they desire and to refuse to publish whatever advertisements they do not desire to publish.

Non-private entities, however—such as transit authorities or state-owned publications—can not refuse advertising with impunity. Consider the 1967 case, Kissinger v. New York City Transit Authority, which originated from actions of members of Students for a Democratic Society (SDS). SDS attempted to buy space on subway walls and in subway trains for posters protesting the Vietnam War. The posters showed a little girl who was reported to have been burned by napalm. The SDS request was refused by an advertising agency which sold space for posters for the Transit Authority. Arguing that the poster copy was protected by the First and Fourteenth Amendments, and saying that the Transit Authority had to accept all advertisements submitted to it, SDS brought suit in a United States District Court. SDS sought a declaratory judgment which would force the Transit Authority to accept its posters.[30]

The U. S. District Court was sympathetic up to a point, ruling that the First and Fourteenth Amendments extended to the post-

[29] Shuck v. Carroll Daily Herald, 215 Iowa 1276, 1281, 247 N.W. 813, 815, 87 A.L.R. 975 (1933). See also Friedenberg v. Times Publishing Co., 170 La. 3, 127 So. 345 (1930); In re Wohl, Inc., 50 F.2d 254 (D.C.Mich.1931).

[30] Kissinger v. New York City Transit Authority, 274 F.Supp. 438, 441 (D.C.N.Y.1967).

ers.   Additionally, the advertising agency could not arbitrarily accept some posters and reject others.   The posters were neither obscene nor profane, and expressed political opinions.   The court said that the Transit Authority could not "refuse to accept the posters for display because they are 'entirely too controversial' and would be objectionable to large segments of our population." [31]

Although the court gave the above language to SDS, it gave the decision to the Transit Authority and its advertising agency. The court held that questions of whether the posters could be refused because they presented a "clear and present danger" or posed a "threat to public safety" could be determined only by a jury trial.   Thus the court denied the SDS motion for a summary judgment which would have required the Transit Authority to accept the posters.[32]

A California case involved a group called Women for Peace. In 1964, Women for Peace sought to place advertising placards in buses owned by the Alameda-Contra Costa Transit District. The placards said:

"Mankind must put an end to war or war will put an end to mankind."   President John F. Kennedy.

Write to President Johnson: Negotiate Vietnam. Women for Peace, P. O. Box 944, Berkeley.[33]

The private advertising agency which managed advertising for the transit district rejected the placards.   It was declared that "political advertising and advertising on controversial subjects are not acceptable unless approved by the [transit] district, and that advertising objectionable to the district shall be removed   *   *   *."[34]

The Women for Peace replied that the refusal of the advertising placards was an "unconstitutional abridgement of their right of free speech and that the exclusion of advertisements not connected with a political campaign constituted a denial of equal protection of the laws."[35]

After a trial and two appeals, the Women for Peace finally won their case in 1967 before the California Supreme Court. The court said that the ad was protected by the First Amend-

---

[31] Ibid., p. 443.

[32] Ibid.

[33] Wirta v. Alameda-Contra Costa Transit District, 64 Cal.Rptr. 430, 434 P.2d 982, 984 (1967).

[34] Ibid.

[35] Ibid.

ment and that once a public facility is opened for use of the general public, arbitrary conditions cannot be imposed upon the use of that facility.[36]

The California Supreme Court declared:[37]

> We conclude that defendants, having opened a forum for the expression of ideas by providing facilities for advertisements on its buses, cannot for reasons of administrative convenience decline to accept advertising expressing opinions and beliefs within the ambit of First Amendment protection.

In 1969, a college newspaper was told it could not refuse political advertising. A number of non-students wished to place political ads in the *Royal Purple*, the official campus newspaper at Wisconsin State University-Whitewater. Their requests for advertising space were denied on the ground that the newspaper had a policy against accepting "editorial advertisements"—those advertisements expressing political views. Refusal of the advertisements led to suits charging that the plaintiffs' First and Fourteenth Amendment rights had been violated by Wisconsin, acting through the regents of the state colleges, and by the university itself. This refusal, it was claimed, amounted to "state action" because the board of regents—a state agency—had delegated policy-setting powers to the president of the university and to the student publications board.[38]

The defendant regents and university contended that they had no knowledge of the newspaper's advertising policy, and that the newspaper itself was not even a real newspaper; it was, they said, a mere "journalistic experiment" or an "educational exercise."[39] In addition, it was argued that persons who were refused advertising space could ventilate their views in other ways through the *Royal Purple,* such as in letters to the editor.

U. S. District Judge James Doyle ruled that the *Royal Purple* should have accepted the advertisements:[40]

> Defendant's acceptance of commercial advertisements and of those public service advertisements that do not "attack an institution, group, person or product" and

[36] 64 Cal.Rptr, 430, 434 P.2d 982, 985 (1967), citing Danskin v. San Diego Unified School District, 28 Cal.2d 536, 171 P.2d 885 (1946).

[37] 64 Cal.Rptr. 430, 432, 434 P.2d 982, 984 (1967).

[38] Lee v. Board of Regents of State Colleges, 306 F.Supp. 1097 (D.C.Wis. 1969).

[39] Ibid., 1100.

[40] Ibid., 1101, affirmed 441 F.2d 1257 (7th Cir. 1971).

their rejection of editorial advertisements constitutes an impermissible form of censorship.

There can be no doubt that defendants' restrictive advertising policy—a policy enforced under color of state law—is a denial of free speech and expression.

En route to that holding Judge Doyle found that the *Royal Purple* was indeed a newspaper, and that letters to the editor— even if accepted for publication—would not be a proper substitute for a paid advertisement. Advertisements offered certain advantages in presentation, including options for large type, photographic display, and repeated publication as "some of the modes of expression available in an editorial advertisement that might not be available in a letter to the editor."[41]

Note that the theme of state action runs through all of the cases in which courts have listened with sympathy to demands that advertisements be accepted. That is, the agency refusing to accept an advertisement was either a transit authority funded by public moneys [42] or an official campus newspaper on a tax-supported campus which had advertising acceptance rules set up under delegated state authority.[43] In the absence of a strong showing of state action, however, the general rule is that advertisements may be refused by the print media.

The *Resident Participation* Case

One of the most eloquent pleas for forced access to advertising space can be found in an air pollution dispute in Denver, Colorado. The setting in Denver should be idyllic—a city ringed by the magnificent Rocky Mountains, close to some of the American continent's most spectacular scenery. But not all was well in Denver during the late 1960's: on some days, Denver residents suffered from an eyeburning smog which would seem more at home in Los Angeles, California, roughly 950 miles away.

When word got out that Pepcol, Inc.—a subsidiary of the giant conglomerate Beatrice Foods, Inc.—was going to build a rendering plant within the city limits of Denver, a protest resulted. A citizens group calling itself Resident Participation of Denver, spurred by visions of a malodorous plant processing "dead animals, guts, and blood" and producing "disgusting"

41 Ibid., p. 1101.

42 Cf. Kissinger v. New York City Transit Authority, 274 F.Supp. 438, 441 (D.C.N.Y.1967); Wirta v. Alameda-Contra Costa Transit District, 68 Cal.2d 51, 64 Cal.Rptr. 430, 434 P.2d 982, 984 (1967).

43 Lee v. Board of Regents, 441 F.2d 1257 (1971), affirming 306 F.Supp. 1097 (D.C.Wis.1969).

garbage,[44] attempted to place advertisements in Denver's two competing daily newspapers, the *Denver Post* and the *Rocky Mountain News*. The newspapers rejected the ads on the ground that the proposed wording called for a boycott of Beatrice Foods products, and boycott advertising is forbidden by Colorado statute.[45]

Undaunted, the Resident Participation group re-worded its advertising copy to avoid any reference to boycott, but listed such Beatrice Foods products as Meadow Gold milk, cheese, and ice cream, and Zooper Dooper fruit drinks and ice cream. The advertisement, as re-written, included suggested letters: readers were to be asked to clip out, sign, and mail the letters, thereby protesting the rendering plant project to city and state officials. Both newspapers again refused to print the advertisements.[46]

Resident Participation then sought a court order under the First Amendment to force the newspapers to publish the advertisements. The newspapers countered with arguments that the First Amendment forbids only official abridgments of free speech and press, not merely private ones, and this was an argument the ecology group was unable to overcome. Nevertheless, Resident Participation argued strenuously to have the court consider the newspapers refusals to publish the advertisements as a kind of official or state action. The citizens' group argued:[47]

> * * * state action is present in this case because defendant newspapers enjoy a special relationship with the State of Colorado and City of Denver which involves those governments in the newspaper business and because the papers "enjoy monopoly control in an area of vital public concern."

Resident Participation also contended that the state and city are involved in the newspaper business because of sections of the Colorado Revised Statutes which require that legal notices be published in newspapers of general circulation.[48] Other provisions which were said to make newspapers a public business included a statute which exempts editors and reporters from jury

---

[44] Plaintiffs Exhibit "A," Resident Participation, Inc. newsletter quoted in brief in Resident Participation of Denver, Inc. v. Love, 322 F.Supp. 1100 (D.C. Colo.1971). The authors wish to thank Thomas A. Stacey, graduate student in journalism at the University of Wisconsin-Madison, for his assistance.

[45] Colo.Rev.Stat.Ann. § 80–11–12.

[46] Resident Participation of Denver, Inc. v. Love, 322 F.Supp. 1100, 1101 (D.C.Colo.1971).

[47] Ibid., 1102.

[48] Colorado Rev.Stat.Ann. §§ 49–10–3, 49–8–1, 49–22–5, 49–22–11 (1963).

service,[49] and a Denver ordinance which allows newspaper vending machines on public property, including sidewalks.[50]

A three-judge federal district court rejected these arguments with dispatch, saying it could find nothing "remotely suggesting that these measures are sufficient to justify labeling the newspapers conduct state action." [51]   Chief Circuit Judge Alfred A. Arraj said that where private conduct is concerned, there has to be great justification for concluding that the private party serves as an alter ego for government, either because officialdom has in some important way become involved with the private party, or because the private party performs a function of a governmental nature.   Circuit Judge Arraj discussed some problems of access to the media for advertisers, and how the law should be applied to such problems.[52]

> Plaintiffs have made no allegations which would suggest a marriage among these parties, and the historic function of newspapers, like the pamphlets of a prior day, has been to oppose government, to be its critic not its accomplice.   While few newspapers may live up to that idea, plaintiffs do not allege that either the Rocky Mountain News or Denver Post is the lackey of a city or state administration or in any other way in the grip of official power.

> We are aware that lack of access to those media which reach large audiences has, some believe, given birth to a frustration which compels otherwise peaceful citizens to engage in violence to get their views to the nation. A cause of this frustration, one critic maintains, is that, although the courts have been vigorous in protecting free speech, they have been indifferent to creating opportunities for expression.   Barron, Access to the Press—A New First Amendment Right, 80 Harv.L.R. 1641 (1967).   We note, however, that while Professor Barron spends considerable space exploring a statutory solution to this problem, he devotes much less attention to constitutional arguments and but one paragraph to the problem of state action, which we find insurmountable.   Professor Barron simply concludes, without noticeable explanation, that newspapers can be subjected to the "constitutional restrictions which quasi-public

[49] Colo.Rev.Stat.Ann., § 7801–3 (1963).

[50] Denver Municipal Code, §§ 339G, 334.1–2.

[51] 322 F.Supp. 1100, 1103 (D.C.Colo.1971).

[52] 322 F.Supp. 1100, 1105 (D.C.Colo.1971).

status invites." Id. at 1169. As desirable as this result might be, we are unable in good faith to reach it.

Our conclusion that newspapers' conduct cannot be considered state action agrees with the conclusion arrived at by the Seventh Circuit Court of Appeals in Chicago Joint Board, Amalgamated Clothing Workers of America, AFL-CIO v. Chicago Tribune Co., 435 F.2d 470 (7th Cir. 1970), the only other case we have discovered which raises issues identical to those presented in this litigation.

As the Resident Participation case showed, general circulation newspapers cannot be compelled to accept and publish controversial advertisements. Some newspapers, however, publish controversial political advertisements as a matter of responsibility to the public. In the spring of 1972, for example, the New York Times published two advertisements which drew considerable protest from readers. The first advertisement, signed by a group of citizens calling themselves "The National Committee for Impeachment," demanded the removal from office of President Richard M. Nixon, alleging violations of law and the Constitution in his prosecution of the Vietnam war. A second advertisement, an open letter to President Nixon signed by Norman F. Dacey, inveighed against the President for a Middle East policy termed "blind support" for Israel.[53]

Readers responded to these advertisements with hundreds of letters, and many of these letters criticized *The Times* for publishing such emotionally loaded and politically heated ads, opinions with which neither *The Times*—nor a large part of its readership agreed. That criticism of *The Times* was expressed so frequently and with such obvious sincerity that *The Times* published an editorial, "Freedom to Advertise," stating the principles which guide The Times in accepting controversial advertising on topics of political or social importance. The editorial declared:[54]

*   *   *   *   *   *   *   *   *

As we see it, the issue goes to the very heart of the freedom and responsibility of the press. *The Times* believes it has an obligation to afford maximum reasonable opportunity to the public to express its views, however much opposed to our own, through various outlets in this newspaper including the advertising columns.

[53] See New York Times, May 31 and June 6, 1972.

[54] New York Times, June 16, 1972. © 1972 by The New York Times Company. Reprinted by Permission.

The Times does, of course, make every attempt to insure that the advertisements it carries are truthful and in good taste. Such standards are relatively easy to enforce in respect to commercial products—though even here sharp differences of opinion frequently arise over the precise applicability of our rules. But political advertising—the presentation of a point of view of an individual or a group through a paid announcement in our columns—presents a more difficult problem than the advertising of a commercial product. Here we feel that the widest possible latitude must be given the public to express what from our point of view may be even the most objectionable of opinions. There are indeed limits; we would not knowingly publish an advertisement containing a direct incitement to violence or other illegal action, or a clear misstatement of fact or a distorted quotation.

While *The Times* makes every effort to detect such violations and to eliminate them from the political advertising that it does accept, our screening process does fail us on occasion when, usually due to the pressures of time and deadlines, human error manages to nullify even the most carefully conceived administrative controls. Just such a regrettable lapse occurred in connection with the Dacey advertisement; in any event, it was the general tenor of this diatribe, rather than any of its specific charges, that gave offense to so many of our readers.

Times policy in this important question is not new. On this page nearly three years ago (Aug. 29, 1969) we stated:

"We at *The New York Times* have always felt an obligation to keep our advertising columns open to all comers, refusing ads only on the grounds of fraud or deception, vulgarity or obscenity and incitement to lawbreaking or to racial or religious hatred. In pursuit of that policy, *The Times* has printed many advertisements setting forth ideas we abhor but feel no right to censor."

It has long been held by American courts that a newspaper or magazine is a private enterprise, and that it may choose to omit certain news items or to refuse certain advertising. In recent years, and in part because of the thrust given to a "new right of access" by Professor Jerome Barron, the old "right to refuse ads" has undergone considerable challenge. Nevertheless, this generalization may still be made: unless the publication or agency which is to carry an advertisement is clearly some sort of a public entity because of some kind of "state action," an advertisement lawfully may be refused.

Take the case of a film exhibitor who was angered because the *Los Angeles Times* altered advertising copy for a movie, The Killing of Sister George, slightly changing a drawing of a female figure and omitting a reference to "deviate sexual conduct". *The Times*, by virtue of its enormous advertising revenues, was said by the film distributor to have attained a "substantial monopoly in Southern California." It was further argued that the *Times's* "semi-monopoly and quasi-public position" amounted to state action. The United States Court of Appeals for the 9th Circuit rejected the film distributors arguments, saying: "Unlike broadcasting, the publication of a newspaper is not a government conferred privilege. As we have said, the press and the government have had a history of disassociation."[55]

SEC. 101.   BROADCAST ADVERTISING AND THE FAIRNESS DOCTRINE

In 1973, the Supreme Court limited the sweep of the Fairness Doctrine, confirming in broadcasters a right to refuse editorial advertising on public issues such as war and politics.

Late in May of 1973, the Supreme Court ruled that broadcasters are not obligated to accept paid advertisements dealing with controversial political or social issues. Thus, by a 7–2 vote, the Court constructed a right to refuse advertisements for broadcasters which is analogous at some points with the print media's "right to refuse service." [56] The case, known as Columbia Broadcasting System, Inc. v. Democratic National Committee,[57] dealt with efforts of a political party and an anti-war group to get air time for their respective viewpoints. This decision is important, for it seems to have effectively blunted a number of efforts to have courts construct a "right of access" under the First Amendment and the Federal Communications Commission's "Fairness Doctrine."[58] Under such a right of access, broadcast-

---

55 Associates & Aldrich Co., Inc. v. Times Mirror Co., 440 F.2d 133, 136 (9th Cir. 1971), 39 U.S. Law Week 2583.

56 See Section 99 of this chapter, "The Right to Refuse Service.

57 —— U.S. ——, 93 S.Ct. 2080 (1973).

58 The Fairness Doctrine is discussed in Chief Justice Burger's opinion, —— U.S. ——, 93 S.Ct. 2080, 2086–2092 (1973), and is written of at greater length in Red Lion Broadcasting v. FCC, 395 U.S. at 375–386, 89 S.Ct. at 1798–1805 (1969).

ers could have been forced to accept paid commercials dealing with public issues.

This section will discuss Columbia Broadcasting System v. Democratic National Committee at some length, but will first provide some background, briefly describing cases which intermixed broadcast advertising and the Fairness Doctrine.

The Fairness Doctrine stems from a Federal Communications Commission (FCC) decision in 1949, saying that broadcasters could editorialize over their licensed facilities so long as they also provided a fair opportunity for differing views to be heard.[59] Until 1967, the Fairness Doctrine was applied only to the airing of major social and political issues.[60] John Banzhaf, III, then appeared on the scene. Banzhaf, then an unknown young New York lawyer, wrote a letter to the FCC urging extension of the Fairness Doctrine to cigarette commercials.[61] Banzhaf jarred the relationship between the FCC and broadcast advertising with that letter. In response, the FCC ruled in 1967 that the Fairness Doctrine did apply, which meant that licensees who broadcast cigarette commercials were thereafter forced to make available free time for messages warning viewers not to smoke.[62] The FCC declared that after U.S. government reports spelled out dangers of cigarette smoking, a controversial issue allowing reply under the Fairness Doctrine was raised when commercials portrayed cigarette puffing as "socially acceptable and desirable, manly, and a necessary part of a rich, full life."[63]

Initially, a majority of the FCC wished to treat cigarettes as a distinct or unique product, raising unique issues, not stretching the Fairness Doctrine to the point where it would open other commercial advertising channels. As Ira Mark Ellman has not-

---

[59] —— U.S. ——, 93 S.Ct. 2080, at 2090 (1973).

[60] Lee Loevinger, "The Politics of Advertising," address given before the International Radio and Television Society, Waldorf-Astoria Hotel, New York City, January 4, 1973. Speech copy courtesy of Television Information Office, 745 Fifth Avenue, New York, N.Y. 10022.

[61] "Fairness Freedom, and Cigarette Advertising, A Defense of the Federal Trade Commission," Columbia Law Review (1967) pp. 1470–1489; Norman P. Leventhal, "Caution: Cigarette Commercials May Be Hazardous to Your License—the New Aspect of Fairness," Federal Communications Bar Journal 22:1 (1968) pp. 55–124, at pp. 92–93.

[62] "CBS–TV Case, 9 Pike & Fischer Radio Regulations 2d 1423 (1967). Cigarette advertising was banned from television by Congress, effective January 2, 1971. See 15 U.S.C.A. Section 1335.

[63] Ira Mark Ellman, "And Now a Word Against Our Sponsor: Extending the Fairness Doctrine to Advertising," 60 California Law Review No. 4 (June, 1972), p. 1423.

ed, the "unique product" distinction did not last long, although the FCC tried hard to prevent extending the Fairness Doctrine's reach into commercial advertising beyond cigarette spots.[64]

A test case came when an environmental protection organization—Friends of the Earth—asked the FCC for time under the Fairness Doctrine to respond to commercials for cars with large engines, cars which created sizable air pollution problems. The FCC had wanted to ban cigarette advertising, but it was not similarly committed to curtailing advertising for large-engined automobiles, nor did it want "answers" being broadcast to such ads. A majority of the FCC ruled that the Fairness Doctrine did not apply to such auto advertising, but Friends of the Earth appealed. The Circuit Court of Appeals for the District of Columbia agreed with the environmentalists, finding an exact parallel between the dangers of cigarette advertising and the dangers of advertising big autos:[65]

> Commercials which continue to insinuate that the human personality finds greater fulfillment in the large car with the quick getaway * * * ventilate a point of view which not only has become controversial but involves an issue of public importance. When there is undisputed evidence, as there is here, that the hazards to health implicit in air pollution are enlarged and aggravated by such products, then the parallel with cigarette advertising is exact and the relevance of *Banzhaf* is inescapable.

Both the *Banzhaf* and *Friends of the Earth* cases involved health claims established by scientists. Although war is even unhealthier than cigarette smoke or polluted air, the Vietnam conflict was an enormously political issue. Two antiwar organizations, a servicemen's group and a Quaker group, had been refused their requests that broadcasting stations in Washington, D.C. and San Francisco donate time to allow these groups to broadcast messages opposing military service or informing the public of alternatives to military service.

The Circuit Court of Appeals for the District of Columbia ruled that the antiwar groups had not successfully shown that

---

[64] Ibid., p. 1424.

[65] Friends of the Earth v. FCC, 146 U.S.App.D.C. 88, 449 F.2d 1164, 1169 (1971), reversing and remanding 24 F.C.C.2d 743 (1970). See also a case involving environmentalists' efforts to answer Standard Oil of New Jersey ads pushing construction of a pipeline across the Alaskan wilderness; In re Wilderness Society, 30 F.C.C.2d 643, 729 (1971). The FCC ruled that licensees must insure that such advertisements were countered or "balanced" by material opposing construction of the pipeline.

the broadcast licensees' refusals to provide air time was an unreasonable exercise of judgment under the Fairness Doctrine. The Court of Appeals reached this judgment even though the stations had broadcast recruiting announcements in behalf of the armed services. These messages were treated as public service announcements by the stations and air time for them had been donated.[66]

As Ira Mark Ellman has suggested, the political sensitivity of this issue may well have affected the decisions of both the FCC and the Court of Appeals. "The outcome in *Green*," Ellman wrote, "may perhaps be best explained as the result of reluctance of both the Commission and the Court to take any action that could be characterized as challenging the government's ability to effectively wage war."[67]

In another kind of issue—a labor dispute—a labor union in 1970 won access for its advertising messages. Local 880 of the Retail Store Employees Union challenged the FCC's renewal of the license of Radio Station WREO, Ashtabula, Ohio. The union complained that the station's license was renewed without a hearing despite the union's protest. The issue involved here was the contention that the radio station could not carry advertising for Hill's Department Store of Ashtabula without allowing the union to buy ads to tell its side of the labor dispute.[68] In 1973, however, the Supreme Court of the United States denied access for controversial political advertising announcements.

CBS vs. Democratic National Committee

This case started when Business Executives' Move for a Vietnam Peace (BEM) filed a complaint with the Federal Communications Commission in January, 1970, contending that radio station WTOP in Washington, D.C., had refused to sell time to broadcast a series of one-minute spot announcements against the Vietnam War. WTOP refused, saying it had already presented full and fair coverage on important public issues, including the Vietnam War and the viewpoints of critics of U.S. policy.[69]

---

[66] Green v. FCC; G. I. Association v. FCC, 144 U.S.App.D.C. 353, 447 F.2d 323 (1971).

[67] Ellman, op. cit., p. 1433.

[68] Retail Store Employees Union, Local 880, Retail Clerks International Association, AFL–CIO v. FCC, 141 U.S.App.D.C. 94, 436 F.2d 248 (1970).

[69] Columbia Broadcasting System v. Democratic National Committee, —— U.S. ——, 93 S.Ct. 2080, 2084 (1973).

Four months later, in May, 1970, the Democratic National Committee (DNC) sought a declaratory ruling on this statement:[70]

"That under the First Amendment to the Constitution and the Communications Act, a broadcaster may not, as a general policy, refuse to sell time to responsible entities, such as DNC, for the solicitation of funds and for comment on public issues."

DNC, unlike BEM, did not object to policies of any particular broadcasters but claimed that its prior experiences made it clear that it would encounter great difficulty—if not total frustration —in purchasing time to present views of the Democratic party and to solicit funds. After reviewing the history of the Fairness Doctrine, and of the Communications Act of 1934—as well as the problems inherent in administering a right of access—the Commission rejected the demands of both DNC and BEM.[71] By a 2–1 vote, however, the Circuit Court of Appeals for the District of Columbia reversed the FCC. Writing the Court's decision, Judge J. Skelly Wright declared:[72]

The principle at stake here is one of fundamental importance: it concerns the people's right to engage in and to hear vigorous public debate on the broadcast media. More specifically, it concerns the application of that right to the substantial portion of the broadcast day which is sold to advertising. For too long advertising has been considered a virtual free fire zone, largely ungoverned by regulatory guidelines. As a result, a cloying blandness and commercialism—sometimes said to be characteristic of radio and television as a whole— have found an especially effective outlet. We are convinced that the time has come for the Commission to cease abdicating responsibility over the uses of advertising time. Indeed, we are convinced that broadcast advertising has great potential for enlivening and enriching debate on public issues, rather than drugging it with an overdose of non-ideas and non-issues as is now the case.

*   *   *   *   *   *   *   *   *

---

[70] — U.S. —, 93 S.Ct. 2080, 2084 (1973).

[71] — U.S. —, 93 S.Ct. 2080, 2085 (1973).

[72] Business Executives' Move for Vietnam Peace v. FCC, Democratic National Committee v. FCC, 146 U.S.App.D.C. 181, 450 F.2d 642 (1971), overturning Business Executives 25 F.C.C.2d 242 (1970), and Democratic National Committee, 25 F.C.C.2d 216 (1970).

We hold specifically that a flat ban on paid public issue announcements is in violation of the First Amendment, at least when other sorts of paid announcements are accepted. We do not hold, however, that the planned announcements of the petitioners—or, for that matter, of any other particular applicant for air time—must necessarily be accepted by broadcast licensees. Rather, we confine ourselves to invalidating the flat ban alone, leaving it up to the licensees and the Commission to develop and administer reasonable procedures and regulations determining which and how many "editorial advertisements" will be put on the air.

* * * * * * * * *

Even if broadcasters were to succeed in presenting a full spectrum of viewpoints and partisan spokesmen on nonadvertising time, their retention of *total* initiative and editorial control is inimical to the First Amendment.

* * * * * * * * *

We come now to the aspect of the broadcasters' policy which, petitioners say, trenches on the First Amendment interest in editorial advertising. The constitutional defect of that policy is somewhat ironic. The *New York Times* Court [New York Times v. Sullivan, 376 U.S. 254, 84 S.Ct. 710 (1964)] made clear that the fact distinguishing fully protected editorial advertising from less fully protected commercial advertising is that the former deals with controversial public issues. Indeed, the political nature of editorial advertising places it near the core of the First Amendment.

The Circuit Court then remanded the DNC and BEM matters to the Commission, with directions that the FCC develop "reasonable procedures and regulations determining which and how many 'editorial advertisements' will be put on the air." Judge Wright's vigorous opinion did not win over the Supreme Court, which voted against the DNC and BEM positions by a margin of 7 to 2.

Writing for the Court, Chief Justice Warren Burger quoted approvingly from Judge McGowan, who had dissented to Judge Wright's Circuit Court opinion. Judge McGowan had said: [73]

"It is presently the obligation of a licensee to advance the public's right to know by devoting a substantial amount of time to the presentation of controversial

[73] —— U.S. ——, 93 S.Ct. 2080, at 2085 (1973), quoting 450 F.2d at 666 (1971).

views on issues of public importance, striking a balance
which is always subject to redress by reference to the
fairness doctrine. Failure to do so puts continuation of
the license at risk—a sanction of tremendous potency,
and one which the Commission is under increasing
pressure to employ.

"This is the system which Congress has, wisely or
not, provided as the alternative to public ownership
and operation of radio and television communications
facilities. This approach has never been thought to be
other than within the permissible limits of constitutional choice."

Chief Justice Burger noted Judge McGowan's conclusion that
remanding the DNC and BEM matters to the Commission for
development of a constitutional right of access put the Commission in a "constitutional strait jacket" on a highly complex and
far-reaching issue. Burger covered some familiar ground, saying that because the broadcast media use a valuable and limited
public resource, there is present "an unusual order of First
Amendment values." [74]   The Chief Justice declared that the
Court must give great weight to the decisions of Congress and to
the experience of the FCC:[75]

Balancing the various First Amendment interests involved in the broadcast media and determining what
best serves the public's right to be informed is a task
of great delicacy and difficulty. The process must
necessarily be undertaken within the framework of the
regulatory scheme that has evolved over the course of
the past half-century. * * * The problems of regulation are rendered more difficult because the broadcast industry is dynamic in terms of technological
change; solutions adequate a decade ago are not necessarily so now, and those acceptable today may well be
outmoded 10 years hence.

Chief Justice Burger then turned to the legislative history of
the Radio Act of 1927 and the Communications Act of 1934, and
declared that the intent of Congress was to leave "broad journalistic discretion with the licensee." [76]   Further, Congress rejected
a proposal which would have placed a limited obligation on persons wishing to speak out on certain public issues. Instead,
Congress enacted a section of the Communications Act of 1934
which specifically provides that " 'a person engaged in radio
broadcasting shall not, insofar as such person is so engaged, be

[74] — U.S. —, 93 S.Ct. 2080, 2086 (1973).

[75] — U.S. —, 93 S.Ct. 2080, 2086 (1973).

[76] — U.S. —, 93 S.Ct. 2080, 2088 (1973).

deemed a common carrier.' " [77]   Burger also noted that although broadcasters were to receive renewable three-year licenses from the FCC, which would make rules for broadcasters consistent with "public interest, convenience and necessity," Section 326 of the Act specifically provides that:[78]

> Nothing in this chapter shall be understood or construed to give the Commission the power of censorship over radio communications or signals transmitted by any radio station, and no regulation or condition shall be promulgated or fixed by the Commission which shall interfere with the right of free speech by means of radio communication.

Burger paid particular attention, in light of Congress' refusal to make broadcasting stations into common carriers for all who wished to speak on public issues, to the Commission's development of its Fairness Doctrine.   Under this doctrine, broadcasters are responsible for providing the public with access to balanced presentation of information on issues of public importance.[79]   He added:[80]

> The basic principle underlying that responsibility is "the right of the public to be informed, rather than any right on the part of the government, any broadcast licensee or any individual member of the public to broadcast his own particular views on any matter. * * * Consistent with that philosophy, the Commission on several occasions has ruled that no private individual or group has a right to command the use of broadcast facilities. * * * Congress has not seen fit yet to alter that policy.

The Court compared a newspaper's freedom to that of a broadcast licensee, finding that a broadcaster has a large measure of freedom, but not as much as that exercised by a newspaper. Broadcasters are supervised—and periodically licensed—by the FCC, which must "oversee without censoring."   Yet the government control over broadcasting licensees is not sufficiently close to make "common carriers" or "public utilities" of broadcasting station.[81]   Common carrier status could allow virtually unlimited

[77]— U.S. —, 93 S.Ct. 2080, 2089 (1973).   See also Section 3(h), Communications Act of 1934, 48 Stat. 1065, as amended, 47 U.S.C.A. § 153(h).

[78] 47 U.S.C.A. § 326 quoted at — U.S. —, 93 S.Ct. 2080, 2090 (1973).

[79]— U.S. —, 93 S.Ct. 2080, 2090, citing Red Lion Broadcasting Co. v. FCC, 395 U.S. at 378, 89 S.Ct. at 1800 (1969).

[80]— U.S. —, 93 S.Ct. 2080, 2091–2092 (1973).

[81]— U.S. —, 93 S.Ct. 2080, 2094 (1973).

access to the broadcast media, and the Court chose another path.[82]

> Thus, it cannot be said that the government is a "partner" to the action of broadcast licensee complained of here, nor is it engaged in a "symbiotic relationship" with the licensee, profiting from the individious discrimination of its proxy. * * * The First Amendment does not reach acts of private parties in every instance where the Congress or the Commission has merely permitted or failed to permit such acts.

> *   *   *   *   *   *   *   *

> The concept of private, independent broadcast journalism, regulated by government to assure protection of the public interest, has evolved slowly and has been nurtured by processes of adjudication. That concept of journalistic independence could not co-exist with a reading of the challenged conduct of the licensee as governmental action. Nor could it exist without administrative flexibility to meet changing needs and the swift technological developments. We therefore conclude that the policies do not constitute government action violative of the First Amendment.

The Court turned to the question whether the "public interest" standard of the Communications Act requires broadcasters to accept editorial advertisements. Saying he was considering both the Fairness Doctrine and the First Amendment, Chief Justice Burger found no error on the part of the FCC in turning down the DNC and BEM demands that they be sold time for their editorial advertisements.[83]

> The Commission was justified in concluding that the public interest in providing access to the marketplace of "ideas and experiences" would scarcely be served by a system so heavily weighted in favor of the financially affluent . . . * * * Moreover, there is the substantial danger . . . that the time allotted for editorial advertising could be monopolized by those of one political persuasion.

> *   *   *   *   *   *   *

> If the Fairness Doctrine were applied to editorial advertising, there is also the substantial danger that

82 —— U.S. ——, 93 S.Ct. 2080, 2094–2095, 2096 (1973). Justice Stewart and Justice Rehnquist joined with Chief Justice Burger in writing Section III of the Court's opinion; the quoted excerpts here are taken from that section.

83 —— U.S. ——, 93 S.Ct. 2080, 2096–2097 (1973).

the effective operation of that doctrine would be jeopardized. To minimize financial hardship and to comply fully with its public responsibilities a broadcaster might well be forced to make regular programming time available to those holding a view different from that expressed in an editorial advertisement . . .. The result would be a further erosion of the journalistic discretion of broadcasters in the coverage of public issues, and a transfer of control over the treatment of public issues from the licensees who are accountable for broadcast performance to private individuals who are not. The public interest would no longer be "paramount," but rather subordinate to private whim . . ..

*   *   *   *   *   *   *   *

For better or worse, editing is what editors are for; and editing is selection and choice of material. That editors—newspaper or broadcast—can and do abuse this power is beyond doubt, but that is not reason to deny the discretion Congress provided. Calculated risks of abuse are taken in order to preserve higher values.

The Court expressed concern that a "right of access" as sought by DNC and BEM would cause too much supervision by the Federal Communications Commission. Chief Justice Burger said that the Commission would have to oversee much more of the day-to-day operation of broadcasters' conduct, "deciding such questions as whether a particular group has had sufficient opportunity to present its viewpoint . . .." He added: "Regimenting broadcasters is too radical a therapy for the ailment respondents complain of." [84]

Justice William O. Douglas concurred with the Court, but for quite different reasons. He declared that TV and radio stand in the same protected position under the First Amendment as do newspapers and magazines. [85]

The philosophy of the First Amendment requires that result, for the fear that Madison and Jefferson had of government intrusion is perhaps even more relevant to TV and radio than it is to newspapers and other

[84] — U.S. —, 93 S.Ct. 2080, 2098. Chief Justice Burger noted that study of the Fairness Doctrine was underway, in hearings by the FCC. He added: "Conceivably, at some future date Congress or the Commission—or the broadcasters—may devise some kind of limited right of access that is both practicable and desirable." — U.S. —, 93 S.Ct. 2080, 2100 (1973).

[85] — U.S. —, 93 S.Ct. 2080, 2109 (1973).

publications. That fear was founded not only on the spectre of a lawless government but of government under the control of a faction that desired to foist its views of the common good on the people.

Both Justice Douglas and Justice Potter Stewart, who also concurred separately in the judgment of the Court, had scathing things to say about the "right of access" as applied to the media. Douglas wrote: [86]

We have allowed ominous inroads to be made on the historic freedom of the newspapers. The effort to suppress the publication of the Pentagon Papers failed only by a narrow margin and actually succeeded for a brief spell in imposing prior restraint on our press for the first time in our history.

*   *   *   *   *   *   *   *

These growing restraints on newspapers have the same ominous message that the overtones of the present opinion has on TV and radio licenses.

The growing spectre of governmental control and surveillance over all activities of people makes ominous the threat to liberty by those who hold the executive power. Over and again attempts have been made to use the Commission as a political weapon against the opposition, whether to the left or to the right.

Justice Stewart concurred similarly.[87]

The First Amendment prohibits the Government from imposing controls upon the press. Private broadcasters are surely part of the press. * * * Yet here the Court of Appeals held, and the dissenters today agree, that the First Amendment *requires* the Government to impose controls upon private broadcasters—in order to preserve First Amendment "values." The appellate court accomplished this strange convolution by holding that private broadcasters *are* Government. This is a step along a path that could eventually lead to the proposition that private *newspapers* "are" Government. Freedom of the press would then be gone. In its place we would have such governmental controls upon the press as a majority of this Court at any particular moment might consider First Amendment "values" to require. It is a frightening spectre.

86 —— U.S. ——, 93 S.Ct. 2080, 2117, 2118 (1973).

87 —— U.S. ——, 93 S.Ct. 2080, 2101 (1973).

Justice Brennan, joined by Justice Marshall, dissented. He complained that the cases of DNC and BEM, as decided by the Court's majority, meant that broadcasters, in effect, can get away with airing nothing more than bland non-controversial mediocrities.[88]

> These cases require us to consider whether radio and television broadcast licensees may, with the approval of the Federal Communications Commission, refuse *absolutely* to sell any part of their advertising time to groups or individuals wishing to speak out on controversial issues of public importance. In practical effect, the broadcaster policy here under attack permits airing of only those paid presentations which advertise products or deal with "non-controversial" matters, while relegating the discussion of controversial public issues to formats such as documentaries, the news, or panel shows, which are tightly controlled and edited by the broadcaster.

> *   *   *   *   *   *   *   *

> . . . I can only conclude that the exclusionary policy upheld today can serve only to inhibit, rather than to further, "our profound national commitment to the principle that debate on public issues should be uninhibited, robust, and wide open. * * * I would therefore affirm the determination of the Court of Appeals that the challenged broadcaster policy is violative of the First Amendment.

Furthermore, Justice Brennan found much greater government action involved in broadcasting than did the Court's majority. Both radio and television use a natural resource—the electromagnetic spectrum—that is part of the public domain. He termed public ownership of the spectrum "an important and established indicium of 'government involvement.'" In addition, he argued, broadcasters are dependent upon government for licenses, for their "right to operate broadcasting frequencies, and they are also regulated by the FCC.[89] Such government action meant, to Justice Brennan, that broadcasting is essentially a government activity, and that citizens and groups should have greater access to the media. Access under the Fairness Doctrine, Brennan contended, is inadequate.[90]

---

[88] —— U.S. ——, 93 S.Ct. 2080, 2120, 2121 (1973).

[89] —— U.S. ——, 93 S.Ct. 2080, 2122, 2123–2124 (1973).

[90] —— U.S. ——, 93 S.Ct. 2080, 2130 (1973).

> Under the Fairness Doctrine, the broadcaster is required to present only *"representative* community views and voices on controversial issues" of public importance. Thus, by definition, the Fairness Doctrine tends to perpetuate coverage of those "views and voices" that are already established, while failing to provide for exposure of the public to those "views and voices" that are novel, unorthodox or unrepresentative of prevailing opinion.

Justice Brennan had scant patience with his brethren who raised "the spectre of administrative apocalypse" in projecting difficulties that the FCC would have in administering a right of access. Quoting Judge J. Skelly Wright's opinion in the court below, Justice Brennon's dissent concluded: [91]

> For the present, however, and until such time as these assertedly "overriding" administrative difficulties actually materialize, if ever, I must agree with the conclusion of the Court of Appeals that although "it may unsettle some of us to see an antiwar message or a political party message in the accustomed place of a soap or beer commercial—we must not equate what is habitual with what is right—or what is constitutional. A society already so saturated with commercialism can well afford another outlet for speech on public issues. All that we may lose is some of our apathy."

SEC. 102. ADVERTISING AND THE CONSTITUTION

Standard commercial advertising is not protected by the freedom of speech and press provisions of the First Amendment.

Commercial advertising customarily has been denied the First Amendment freedom of speech and press which the courts have accorded to unconventional religious minorities,[92] to men accused of blasphemy,[93] to free-love advocates,[94] and to persons sued for defaming a public official or figure.[95] The leading case in deny-

[91] —— U.S. ——, 93 S.Ct. 2080, 2138 (1973).

[92] Minersville School District v. Gobits, 310 U.S. 586, 60 S.Ct. 1010 (1940).

[93] Burstyn v. Wilson, 343 U.S. 495, 72 S.Ct. 777 (1952).

[94] Kingsley Pictures Corp. v. Regents, 360 U.S. 684, 688–689, 79 S.Ct. 1362, 1365 (1959).

[95] See New York Times v. Sullivan and subsequent cases, including Rosenblatt v. Baer, 383 U.S. 75, 86 S.Ct. 669 (1966); Curtis Publishing Co. v. Butts, Associated Press v. Edwin A. Walker, 388 U.S. 130, 87 S.Ct. 1975 (1967); St. Amant v. Thompson, 390 U.S. 727, 88 S.Ct. 1323 (1968).

ing First Amendment protection to advertising is the 1942 Supreme Court decision in Valentine v. Chrestensen.[96]

F. J. Chrestensen became incensed when New York City officials refused to allow him to exhibit, for profit, a former United States submarine which he owned. Chrestensen was told by Police Commissioner Lewis J. Valentine that he could not distribute handbills soliciting persons to visit the submarine for a fee. Meanwhile, Chrestensen's submarine was moored at a pier in the East River. No matter, said Police Commissioner Valentine. New York City's Sanitary Code forbade distribution of commercial and business advertising matter in the streets.

Chrestensen then altered his handbill. One side consisted of commercial advertising (with the deletion of the statement about the admission fee). The other side was a protest against an action of the City Dock Department refusing Chrestensen wharfage for his submarine. Police officials told Chrestensen that he could distribute a handbill criticizing the City Dock Department, but that the commercial advertising would have to go. Two years later, in 1942, Mr. Justice Owen J. Roberts spoke for a unanimous Supreme Court in saying that Chrestensen's advertising was not entitled to Constitutional protection.[97]

> This court has unequivocally held that the streets are proper places for the exercises of the freedom of communicating information and disseminating opinion and that, though the states and municipalities may appropriately regulate the privilege in the public interest, they may not unduly burden or proscribe its employment in these public thoroughfares. We are equally clear that the Constitution imposes no such restraint on government as respects purely commercial advertising.

The Court's decision in Valentine v. Chrestensen was brief, amounting to only five pages in the official *United States Reports*. Mr. Justice Roberts' statement that commercial advertising is not entitled to Constitutional protections was slipped into the opinion unsupported by a number of relevant cases which he might have cited.[98]

[96] 316 U.S. 52, 62 S.Ct. 920 (1942).

[97] 316 U.S. 52, 54, 62 S.Ct. 920, 921 (1942).

[98] See Mr. Justice William O. Douglas's concurring opinion in Cammarano v. United States, 358 U.S. 498, 513–515, 79 S.Ct. 524, 533–535 (1959), which listed two cases prior to the Chrestensen case which approved broad control over commercial advertising: Fifth Avenue Coach Co. v. New York, 221 U.S. 467, 31 S.Ct. 709 (1911), and Packer Corp. v. Utah, 285 U.S. 105, 52 S.Ct. 273 (1932). In the latter case, Justice Douglas noted, the First Amendment problem was never raised.

In 1959, Mr. Justice Douglas authored a concurring opinion in Cammarano v. United States in which he expressed concern over the rule laid down in Valentine v. Chrestensen. William R. Cammarano and his wife owned an interest in a beer distributorship in Washington state. They had paid nearly $900 into a trust fund which with other contributions, ultimately added up to over $50,000. This trust fund was being collected by persons opposed to a 1948 ballot measure which would have placed all wine and beer sales in Washington exclusively in the hands of the State. The trust fund was used for advertising which urged, and may well have helped secure, defeat of the ballot measure.

The Cammaranos sued the Department of Internal Revenue because they were not allowed to deduct their contribution to the trust fund as a "business expense." Writing for the Supreme Court, Justice John Marshall Harlan upheld a finding against the Cammaranos' contentions. He wrote:[99]

> Nondiscriminatory denial of deduction from gross income to sums expended to promote or defeat legislation is plainly not " 'aimed at the suppression of dangerous ideas.' " Rather, it appears to us that since purchased publicity can influence the fate of legislation which will affect, directly or indirectly, all in the community, everyone in the community should stand on the same footing as regards its purchase so far as the Treasury of the United States is concerned.

Although Mr. Justice Douglas concurred in the Court's decision, he expressed grave worries about the rule of Valentine v. Chrestensen that business advertisements and commercial matters do not enjoy the protection of the First Amendment as made applicable to the States by the Fourteenth. Douglas wrote:[1]

> The ruling [in Valentine v. Chrestensen] was casual, almost offhand. And it has not survived reflection. That "freedom of speech or of the press," directly guaranteed against encroachment by the Federal Government and safeguarded against state action by the Due Process Clause of the Fourteenth Amendment, is not in terms or by implication confined to discourse of a particular kind and nature. It has often been stressed as essential to the exposition and exchange of political ideas, to the expression of philosophical atti-

99 358 U.S. 498, 79 S.Ct. 524, 533 (1959).

1 358 U.S. 498, 513–515, 79 S.Ct. 524, 533–535 (1959).

tudes, to the flowering of the letters. Important as the
First Amendment is to all those cultural ends, it has
not been restricted to them. Individual or group protests against action which results in monetary injuries
are certainly not beyond the reach of the First Amendment * * *. A protest against government action
that affects a business occupies as high a place. The
profit motive should make no difference, for that is an
element inherent in the very conception of a press under our system of free enterprise. Those who make
their living through exercise of First Amendment
rights are no less entitled to its protection than those
whose advocacy or promotion is not hitched to a profit
motive.

*   *   *   *   *   *   *   .*   *

* * * I find it impossible to say that the owners of
the present business who were fighting for their lives
in opposing these initiative measures were not exercising First Amendment rights.

*   *   *   *   *   *   *   *   *

Deductions are a matter of grace, not of right.
* * * To hold that this item of expense must be allowed as a deduction would be to give impetus to the
view favored in some quarters that First Amendment
rights must be protected by tax exemptions. But that
proposition savors of the notion that First Amendment
rights are somehow not fully realized unless they are
subsidized by the State. Such a notion runs counter to
our decisions * * * and may indeed conflict with
the underlying premise that a complete hands-off policy
on the part of government is at times the only course
consistent with First Amendment rights.

The landmark 1964 libel decision of the Supreme Court of the
United States in New York Times v. Sullivan did not completely
endorse Justice Douglas's demand for a governmental policy of
"hands off" where expression is concerned. Nevertheless, the
Court did grant constitutional protection for advertisements
which deal with important or social matters. The *Sullivan* case,
discussed fully in libel chapters earlier in this book, carefully
distinguished the kind of advertising involved in the Valentine
v. Chrestensen case from the advertising involved in New York
Times v. Sullivan. It had been contended in the *Sullivan* case
that "the constitutional guarantees of freedom of speech and of
the press are inapplicable * * * at least so far as the Times

is concerned, because the allegedly libelous statements were published as part of a paid, 'commercial' advertisement." The Court rejected this argument, saying:[2]

> The argument relies on Valentine v. Chrestensen * * * where the Court held that a city ordinance forbidding street distribution of commercial and business advertising matter did not abridge the First Amendment freedoms, even as applied to a handbill having a commercial message on one side but a protest against certain official action on the other. The reliance is wholly misplaced. The Court in Chrestensen reaffirmed the constitutional protection for "the freedom of communicating information and disseminating opinion;" its holding was based upon the factual conclusions that the handbill was 'purely commercial advertising' and that the protest against official action had been added only to evade the ordinance.
>
> The publication here [in New York Times v. Sullivan] was not a 'commercial' advertisement in the sense in which the word was used in *Chrestensen*. It communicated information, expressed opinion, recited grievances, protested claimed abuses, and sought financial support on behalf of a [civil rights] movement whose existence and objectives are matters of the highest public interest and concern. * * * That the Times was paid for publishing the advertisement is as immaterial in this connection as is the fact that newspapers and books are sold. * * * Any other conclusion would discourage newspapers from carrying 'editorial advertisements' of this type, and so might shut off an important outlet for the promulgation of information and ideas by persons who do not themselves have access to publishing facilities—who wish to exercise their freedom of speech even though they are not members of the press. * * * The effect would be to shackle the First Amendment in its attempt to secure 'the widest possible dissemination of information from diverse and antagonistic sources.' To avoid placing such a handicap upon the freedoms of expression, we hold that if the allegedly libelous statements would otherwise be constitutionally protected * * * they do not forfeit that protection because they were published in the form of a paid advertisement.

2 New York Times v. Sullivan, 376 U.S. 254, 265–266, 84 S.Ct. 710, 718 (1964).

With these words, the Supreme Court showed that it is concerned with freedom of advertising as well as with the control of its abuses. A notable eighteenth-century Englishman, Dr. Samuel Johnson, directed his attention to advertising and turned this neat phrase: "Promise, large promise, is the soul of an advertisement."[3] To keep advertising's promises within socially manageable bounds is the task, worthy of Sisyphus, which falls upon the Federal Trade Commission and other federal and state agencies, as well as upon the profession of advertising and the mass media. It is a fearfully complex job. As Attorney Ira M. Millstein has written about the FTC, "most complicated, from the Commission's standpoint, are questions raised by critics as to the false social value of advertising. The line between false value and actionable false promise may sometimes be hard to draw."[4] The drawing of such a line is the continuing job of the advertising profession, of the media, and of various government agencies, including legislatures, courts, and commissions. This elusive line is still being sought as more law is made dealing with the control of advertising and the freedom of the marketplace.

[3] Statement attributed to Dr. Johnson quoted by Ira M. Millstein, "The Federal Trade Commission and False Advertising," Columbia Law Review Vol. 64:3 (March, 1964) pp. 439–499, at p. 439, from David Ogilvy, Confessions of an Advertising Man (New York: Dell Publishing, 1963 p. 116.

[4] Millstein, op. cit., at 447.

Chapter 15

ANTITRUST LAW AND THE MASS MEDIA

SEC. 103.   CONCENTRATION OR DIVERSITY?

The media of mass communications are subject to antitrust laws which affect other businesses.

"Concentration of newspaper ownership" * * * "problems of bigness and fewness" * * * "fewer voices in the marketplace of ideas:" these are some of the phrases which typify relationships between the mass media and the area of law known as "antitrust and restraint of trade." Because they are businesses, units of the mass media come under antitrust laws with which government seeks to discourage monopolization and unreasonable restraint of trade.

Back in 1947, the premier scholar of the law of mass communications asked to what extent antitrust laws should be used to prevent the concentration of media units from hindering the free interchange of news and ideas. This scholar, the late Professor Zechariah Chafee, Jr. of Harvard Law School, declared antitrust law problems to be the most important facing the press and also the most difficult.[1]

Professor Chafee's concern with antitrust law was prophetic. Antitrust law is a field which from time to time causes considerable fright among many publishers and broadcasters. In 1970, for example, the Federal Communications Commission proposed a rule to force separation of newspaper, radio and television ownership: this was called the FCC's "one to a customer" policy. This proposed rule suggested that within a five-year period, broadcast station owners would be forced to cut their mass me-

---

[1] Zechariah Chafee, Jr., Government and Mass Communications, 2 vols. (Chicago: University of Chicago Press, 1947) I, p. 537.

594

dia operations in any one community to just one outlet: either a newspaper, an AM-FM radio operation, or one television station. It was then estimated that should such a rule be adopted, 127 TV stations in the largest 50 metropolitan areas worth $3 billion and 526 radio stations valued at almost $500 million would have their ownership patterns affected.[2]   Mass media ownership patterns are now so concentrated that the "media barons" or corporate conglomerates who own newspaper, radio and television properties may well have legitimate worry about what the FCC or the Antitrust Division of the U.S. Department of Justice may turn up next.

Consider the following facts and figures, which sum up many years of concentration of ownership and declining competition among various parts of America's mass media:

—In 1914, there were 2,580 dailies published in the United States.

—In 1973, there were 1,749 dailies published in the United States.[3]

—One 1966 study showed that of 1,751 dailies then published, 786 (44.8%) were owned by 158 newspaper groups. But these groups produced 57% of the nation's weekday newspaper circulation and 62% of its Sunday circulation.[4]

Ben H. Bagdikian noted in 1973 that since 1968, chains have been buying up independent newspapers at a rate of 62 a year, leaving 1,015 dailies in chain ownership with only 734 independent dailies.   Bagdikian added: "At this rate (allowing for leap years), the last independent will disappear at 10:48 p.m. on June 7 eleven years hence—appropriately, a Thursday, a fat advertising day, and also appropriately, in the year 1984." [5]

The Commission on Freedom of the Press complained during the 1940's that "monopolies of fact and opinion are infinitely more mischievous" than other business monopolies.   If so, newspaper monopolies are only a part of a highly "mischievous" situation.   As Robert L. Bishop pointed out in 1972, cross-media owners—holders of print and broadcast media—control 36 per

[2] Charles R. Fowler, "Antitrust Policy and the FCC: The Evolution of Newspaper-Broadcast Ownership Regulation," unpublished paper presented at Mass Communications and Society Division, Association for Education in Journalism, Washington, D. C., August, 1970.

[3] Ben H. Bagdikian, "The Myth of Newspaper Poverty," Columbia Journalism Review, March/April 1973, p. 20.

[4] Arnold B. Barach, "Newspaper Mergers," Mergers and Acquisitions Vol. 1 (Summer, 1966) p. 20.

[5] Bagdikian, op. cit., p. 23.

cent of the daily newspapers, 25 per cent of all television stations, 8.6 per cent of AM radio, and 9.5 per cent of FM radio. Further, "the combined holdings of groups, cross-media owners, conglomerates, and firms related to the mass media encompass 58 per cent of daily newspapers, 77 per cent of TV stations, 27 per cent of AM and 29 percent of FM stations.[6] Earlier, FCC Commissioner Nicholas Johnson wrote about how mass media units—print, electronic, and film—overlap in ownership and control.[7]

> Most American communities have far less "dissemination of information from diverse and antagonistic sources" (to quote a famous description by the Supreme Court of the basic aim of the First Amendment) than is available nationally. Of the 1500 cities with daily newspapers, 96 percent are served by single-owner monopolies. Outside the top 50 to 200 markets there is a substantial dropping off in the number of competing radio and television signals. The FCC prohibits a single owner from controling two AM radio, or two television, stations with overlapping signals. But it has only recently expressed any concern over common ownership of an AM radio station and an FM radio station and a television station in the same market. Indeed, such ownership is the rule rather than the exception and probably exists in your community. Most stations are today acquired by purchase. And the FCC has, in part because of congressional pressure, rarely disapproved a purchase of a station by a newspaper.

> There are few statewide or regional "monopolies"—although some situations come close. But in a majority of our states—the least populous—there are few enough newspapers and television stations to begin with, and they are usually under the control of a small group. And most politicians find today, as Congress warned in 1926, "woe be to those who dare to differ with them." Most of our politics is still state and local in scope. And increasingly, in many states and local

[6] Robert L. Bishop, "The Rush to Chain Ownership," Columbia Journalism Review, November/December, 1972, p. 10.

[7] Nicholas Johnson, "The Media Barons and the Public Interest," from his How to Talk Back to Your Television Set (Boston: Atlantic-Little Brown; New York: Bantam, 1970) pp. 52–55. See also Mr. Johnson's Test Pattern for Living (New York: Bantam, 1972), and Christopher H. Sterling, "Newspaper Ownership of Broadcast Stations, 1920–1968," Journalism Quarterly 46:2 (Summer, 1969) pp. 227–236.

communities, congressmen and state and local officials are compelled to regard that handful of media owners (many of whom are out-of-state), rather than the electorate itself, as their effective constituency. Moreover, many mass media owners have a significant impact in more than one state. One case that came before the FCC, for example, involved an owner with AM-FM-TV combinations in Las Vegas and Reno, Nevada, along with four newspapers in that state, seven newspapers in Oklahoma, and two stations and two newspapers in Arkansas. Another involved ownership of ten stations in North Carolina and adjoining southern Virginia. You may never have heard of these owners, but I imagine the elected officials of their states return their phone calls promptly.

The principal national sources of news are the wire services, AP and UPI, and the broadcast networks. Each of the wire services serves on the order of 1200 newspapers and 2000 radio and television stations. Most local newspapers and radio stations offer little more than wire service copy as far as national and international news is concerned. To that extent one can take little heart for "diversity" from the oft-proffered statistics on proliferating radio stations (now over 6000) and the remaining daily newspapers (1700). The networks, though themselves heavily reliant upon the wire services to find out what's worth filming, are another potent force.

The weekly newsmagazine field is dominated by *Time*, *Newsweek*, and *U. S. News*. (The first two also control substantial broadcast, newspaper, and book or publishing outlets. *Time* is also in movies [MGM] and is hungry for three or four newspapers.) Thus, even though there are thousands of general and specialized periodicals and program sources with significant national or regional impact, and certainly no "monopoly" exists, it is still possible for a single individual or corporation to have vast national influence.

What we sometimes fail to realize, moreover, is the political significance of the fact that we have become a nation of cities. Nearly half of the American people live in the six largest states: California, New York, Illinois, Pennsylvania, Texas, and Ohio. Those states, in turn, are substantially influenced (if not politically dominated) by their major population-industrial-financial-media centers, such as Los Angeles, New York City, Chicago, and Philadelphia—the nation's four largest metropolitan areas. Thus, to have a major newspaper or television station influence in *one* of these cities is to have significant national power. And the number of interests with influence in *more* than one of these markets is startling.

Most of the top fifty television markets (which serve approximately 75 percent of the nation's television homes) have three competing commercial VHF television stations. There are about 150 such VHF commercial stations in these markets. Less than 10 percent are today owned by entities that do not own other media interests. In 30 of the 50 markets at least one of The stations is owned by a major newspaper published in that market—a total of one third of these 150 stations. (In Dallas-Fort Worth *each* of the network affiliates is owned by a local newspaper, and the fourth, an unaffiliated station, is owned by Oklahoma newspapers.) Moreover, half of the newspaper-owned stations are controlled by seven groups—groups that also publish magazines as popular and diverse as *Time, Newsweek, Look, Parade, Harper's, TV Guide, Family Circle, Vogue, Good Housekeeping,* and *Popular Mechanics.* Twelve parties own more than one third of all the major-market stations.

The communications media are businesses, and as such, are ringed about by federal and state laws which regulate businesses. Congress has enacted several statutes—most commonly called antitrust laws—which attempt to preserve competition. The most important statements of national antitrust policy are found in the Sherman [8] and Clayton [9] Acts.

The Sherman Act of 1890 begins: "Every contract, combination in the form of a trust or otherwise, or conspiracy, in restraint of trade or commerce among the several states, or with foreign nations, is hereby declared to be illegal." [10] Every person who acts to restrain trade, as mentioned generally above, is guilty of a crime. The Sherman Act prohibits "contracts, combinations * * * or conspiracies in restraint of trade or commerce" and makes it illegal to "monopolize, or attempt to mo-

[8] 26 Stat. 209; 15 U.S.C.A. §§ 1–7; P.L. No. 190, 51st Congress (1890).

[9] 38 Stat. 730, 15 U.S.C.A. §§ 12ff (1964); P.L. No. 201, 63rd Congress (1914).

[10] 15 U.S.C.A. § 1 (1964).

nopolize, or combine or conspire * * * to monopolize
* * * trade or commerce."

Criminal prosecution—with penalties of fines, imprisonment, or both—is provided for in the Sherman Act. The Act also enables the government to bring suits in equity to get injunctions against violations of the statute. As Chafee observed in 1947, suits in equity are "preferred because it is not always easy for businessmen to know in advance whether their transactions are illegal or not." [11] Also, a person (or business) who has suffered damages because a competitor has violated the Sherman Act may sue the competitor for *treble damages*.

Treble damage lawsuits work in this way: suppose that the Fluke Manufacturing Company has violated the Sherman Act. The United States Department of Justice takes Fluke Manufacturing to court and gets an order to make it stop certain monopolistic or trade-restraining practices. An interested spectator, meanwhile, is Fluke's competitor, whom we shall call the Flimsy Manufacturing Company. Flimsy Manufacturing then begins a treble damage antitrust suit, and is able to prove in court that Fluke Manufacturing's illegal business practices cost Flimsy $100,000 in business. However, since this would be a *treble damage* lawsuit, Flimsy Manufacturing would actually collect $300,000 from the competing Fluke company.

The Clayton Act of 1914 added to the government's antitrust enforcement powers, enumerating many acts as illegal when "they tend to lessen competition or to create a monopoly in any line of commerce." [12] Section 7 of the Clayton Act—more commonly called the Celler-Kefauver Act of 1950—is the most important section of the Clayton Act where newspapers are concerned.[13] The "Celler-Kefauver Act" forbids corporations to acquire stock or assets of a competing corporation "where * * * the effect * * * may be substantially to lessen competition, or tend to create a monopoly."

Upon such vaguely worded provisions of the Sherman and Clayton Acts is built federal antitrust policy. As Professor Lorry Rytting of the University of Utah has declared, the vagueness of the statutory provisions make antitrust one of the most perplexing branches of public law, especially where newspapers and other units of the communications media are involved.

---

11 Chafee, op. cit., p. 538.

12 15 U.S.C.A. § 18 (1964 ed.)

13 64 Stat. 1125, 15 U.S.C.A. § 18 (1964), P.L. 899, 81st Congress (1950).

Although decided just after the end of World War II, the Supreme Court's ruling in Associated Press v. United States [14] still ranks as a leading case in antitrust law affecting the media. The Justice Department had brought suit under the Sherman Act to get an injunction which would prevent the AP from continuing to operate under some of its by-laws. These by-laws prevented AP members from selling news to non-members. Other by-law provisions also gave a newspaper which had an AP membership virtual veto power over competing newspapers' attempts to get AP membership. [15]

One of several cases combined under the decision with the general heading Associated Press v. United States involved publisher Marshall Field's attempt to get an AP membership for his Chicago *Sun,* a new newspaper in competition with the redoubtable Col. Robert R. McCormick's powerful Chicago *Tribune.*

SEC. 104. ASSOCIATED PRESS v. UNITED STATES (1945)

Antitrust statutes, as applied to the press, are not in violation of the First Amendment guarantee of freedom of the press.

When a newspaper applied for AP membership and an existing member protested the application—as the *Tribune* protested the *Sun's* application—the AP by-laws then required a majority vote of all AP members before the new applicant could be admitted to the club. [16] Thus Marshall Field's Chicago *Sun* could not become an AP member without Col. McCormick's consent, unless the government intervened—in the public interest—to use antitrust laws to force an amendment of the AP bylaws.

In 1943, the Justice Department charged that the conduct of the AP, of the Chicago *Tribune,* and other defendants constituted "(1) a combination and conspiracy in restraint of trade and commerce in news among the states, and (2) an attempt to monopolize a part of that trade." [17] In finding that the AP by-laws

[14] 326 U.S. 1, 65 S.Ct. 1416 (1945).

[15] Chafee, op. cit., pp. 542–543; Associated Press v. United States, 326 U.S. 1, 9–10, 65 S.Ct. 1416, 1419 (1945).

[16] Chafee, p. 543; Associated Press v. United States, loc. cit. Another newspaper which like the Chicago Sun had applied for AP membership and had been turned down by a 2–1 vote of AP members, was the Washington Times-Herald.

[17] 326 U.S. 1, 4, 65 S.Ct. 1416, 1417 (1945).

did in fact violate the Sherman Act, Justice Hugo L. Black described the effect of exclusion from the AP: [18]

> These By-Laws, for a violation of which members may be * * * fined, suspended, or expelled, require that each newspaper member publish the AP news regularly in whole or in part, and that each shall "promptly furnish to the corporation, through its agents or employees, all the news of such member's district, the area of which shall be determined by the Board of Directors." All members are prohibited from selling or furnishing their spontaneous news to any agency or publisher except to AP. Other By-Laws require each newspaper member to conduct his or its business in such manner that the news furnished by the corporations shall not be made available to any non-member in advance of publication. The joint effect of these By-Laws is to block all newspaper non-members from any opportunity to buy news from AP or any of its publisher members. Admission to membership in AP thereby becomes a prerequisite to obtaining AP news or buying news from any one of its more than twelve hundred publishers. The erection of obstacles to the acquisition of membership consequently can make it difficult, if not impossible, for non-members to get any of the news furnished by AP or any of the individual members of this combination of American newspaper publishers.

> The By-Laws provide a very simple and non-burdensome road for admission of a non-competing applicant. The Board of Directors in such case can elect the applicant without payment of money or the imposition of other onerous terms. In striking contrast are the By-Laws which govern admission of new members who do compete. [Applicants in a competing field could be admitted only on payment of 10 per cent of the total assessments of that AP in that field since Oct. 1, 1900.] Historically, as well as presently, applicants who would offer competition to old members have a hard road to travel.

The Associated Press and the Chicago Tribune and other media defendants argued that the application of the Sherman Act in this case would be a violation of freedom of the press as guaranteed by the First Amendment. A majority of the Supreme

[18] 326 U.S. 1, 8–10, 65 S.Ct. 1416, 1419 (1945).

Court was not impressed by this argument. Justice Black replied,[19]

> Member publishers of AP are engaged in business for profit exactly as are other businessmen who sell food, steel, aluminum, or anything else people need or want * * *. All are alike covered by the Sherman Act. The fact that the publisher handles news while others handle goods does not, as we shall later point out, afford the publisher a peculiar constitutional sanctuary in which he can with impunity violate laws regulating his business practices.
>
> Nor is a publisher who engages in business practices made unlawful by the Sherman Act entitled to a partial immunity by reason of the "clear and present danger" doctrine which courts have used to protect freedom to speak, to print, and to worship. That doctrine, as related to this case, provides protection for utterances themselves so the printed or spoken word may not be the subject of previous restraint or punishment, unless their expression creates a clear and present danger of bringing about a substantial evil which the government has power to prohibit * * *. Formulated as it was to protect liberty of thought and expression, it would degrade the clear and present danger doctrine to fashion from it a shield for business publishers who engage in business practices condemned by the Sherman Act.

Finally, Justice Black answered the assertion that the Sherman Act's application to the Associated Press abridged the AP's First Amendment freedom. Black declared that it would be strange if the concern for press freedom underlying the First Amendment should be read "as a command that the government was without power to protect that freedom." Black continued,[20]

> The First Amendment, far from providing an argument against application of the Sherman Act, here provides powerful reasons to the contrary. That Amendment rests on the assumption that the widest possible dissemination of information from diverse and antagonistic sources is essential to the welfare of the public, that a free press is a condition of a free society. Surely a command that the government itself shall not impede the free flow of ideas does not afford non-governmental combinations as a refuge if they impose restraints on that constitutionally guaranteed freedom.

19 326 U.S. 1, 7, 65 S.Ct. 1416, 1418 (1945).

20 326 U.S. 1, 20, 65 S.Ct. 1416, 1424–1425 (1945).

Freedom to publish means freedom for all and not for some. Freedom to publish is guaranteed by the Constitution, but freedom to combine to keep others from publishing is not. Freedom of the press from governmental interference under the First Amendment does not sanction repression of that freedom by private interests. The First Amendment affords not the slightest support for the contention that a combination to restrain trade in news and views has any constitutional immunity.

Justice Frankfurter added other arguments in favor of government action under the Sherman Act to attempt to control media activities which tended to restrain trade. To Frankfurter, the press was a business, but it was also much more: "in addition to being a commercial enterprise, it [the press] has a relation to the public interest unlike that of any other enterprise pursued for profit." Following this premise, Justice Frankfurter then quoted words written by America's most famous United States Court of Appeals judge. The oft-quoted words below came from Judge Learned Hand's opinion at the Court of Appeals level in this same case of Associated Press v. United States.[21]

* * * that [the newspaper] industry serves one of the most vital of all general interests: the dissemination of news from as many different sources, and with as many different facets and colors as is possible. That interest is closely akin to, if indeed it is not the same as, the interest protected by the First Amendment; it presupposes that right conclusions are more likely to be gathered out of a multitude of tongues than through any kind of authoritative selection. To many this is, and always will be, folly; but we have staked upon it our all.

To Frankfurter, the By-Laws of the Associated Press were a clear restriction of commerce. Such a restriction was unreasonable because it subverted the function of a constitutionally guaranteed free press.

Dissents from Justices Owen J. Roberts and Frank Murphy took a traditional libertarian view: in general, government should leave the press alone. Justice Murphy wrote: [22]

Today is * * * the first time that the Sherman Act has been used as a vehicle for affirmative interven-

---

[21] 326 U.S. 1, 28, 65 S.Ct. 1416, 1428 (1945), quoting Judge Hand, Associated Press v. United States, 52 F.Supp. 362, 372 (D.C.N.Y.1943).

[22] 326 U.S. 1, 51–52, 65 S.Ct. 1416, 1439 (1945).

tion by the Government in the realm of dissemination of information. As the Government states, this is an attempt to remove "barriers erected by private combination against access to reports of world news." That newspapers and news agencies are engaged in business for profit is beyond dispute. And it is undeniable that the Associated Press and other associations can claim no immunity from the application of the general laws or of the Sherman Act in particular * * *. [The press associations] are engaged in collecting and distributing news and information rather than in manufacturing automobiles, aluminum or gasoline. We cannot avoid that fact. Nor can we escape the fact that governmental action directly aimed at the methods or conditions of such collection or distribution is an interference with the press, however differing in degree it may be from governmental restraints on written or spoken utterances themselves * * *. We should therefore be particularly vigilant in reviewing a case of this nature, a vigilance that apparently is not shared by the Court today.

SEC. 105. LORAIN JOURNAL COMPANY v. UNITED STATES (1951)

Restraint of trade by discriminatory refusal of advertising is forbidden.

The 1951 case of Lorain Journal Co. et al. v. United States [23] dealt with a straightforward instance of a newspaper's attempting to restrain trade by cutting into a radio station's advertising revenues. It seems safe to say that the newspaper company involved here placed its competitive practices in an even more unfavorable light before the courts because it previously had tried —and failed—to get a license to operate a radio station in Lorain.[24]

From 1933 until 1948, the publisher of the *Lorain Journal* in Lorain, Ohio, had enjoyed a "substantial monopoly in Lorain of the mass dissemination of news and advertising, both of a local and national character." This idyllic situation ended in 1948, however, when the Elyira-Lorain Broadcasting Company, a corporation independent of the newspaper publisher, was licensed

---

[23] 342 U.S. 143, 72 S.Ct. 181 (1951).

[24] See 92 F.Supp. 794, 796 (D.C.Ohio 1950). See also Lorain Journal Co. v. Federal Communications Commission, 86 U.S.App.D.C. 102, 180 F.2d 28 (1950).

by the Federal Communications Commission. The radio station —WEOL—was located in Elyria, just eight miles from Lorain, and also opened a branch studio in Lorain.[25]

The publishers of the *Lorain Journal* did not welcome this new competitor for advertising dollars, and set about trying to drive the radio station out of business. The newspaper refused to accept local advertising from Lorain merchants who also bought advertising time from the radio station. Because of the *Lorain Journal's* coverage of 99 per cent of Lorain's families, this forced many advertisers to avoid buying time from WEOL.

The United States government brought a civil antitrust suit against the Lorain Journal Company, charging an attempt to monopolize commerce under the Sherman Antitrust Act. The government sought an injunction against the publisher's business practices. In reply, the newspaper company argued that it had the right to select its customers and to refuse or accept advertising from whomever it pleases. Furthermore, the Journal Company declared that an injunction which would prevent the newspaper from refusing to print advertisements of persons or businesses who advertised over WEOL would restrict freedom of the press. That is, the newspaper publisher argued that such an injunction would amount to a prior restraint on what a newspaper may publish.[26]

In a trial in a United States district court, the Lorain Journal Company was found to be attempting to monopolize commerce. The court issued an injunction to prevent the newspaper's continuing the attempt.[27] The Lorain Journal Company appealed to the Supreme Court of the United States, but to no avail. By a 7–0 vote, the Court held that the District Court's injunction was justified.[28]

The Supreme Court, in fact, was quite unkind in its description of the Lorain Journal Company's business practices. It quoted the District Court's statement that the newspaper was guilty of " 'bold, relentless, and predatory commercial behavior.' " [29] The Court, through Mr. Justice Harold H. Burton's opinion, turned aside the newspaper's defense arguments one by one.

[25] 342 U.S. 143, 147, 72 S.Ct. 181, 183 (1951).

[26] 342 U.S. 143, 148–156, 72 S.Ct. 181, 184–187 (1951).

[27] 342 U.S. 143, 145, 72 S.Ct. 181, 182 (1951).

[28] 342 U.S. 143, 144, 72 S.Ct. 181, 182 (1951).

[29] 92 F.Supp. 794, 796 (1950), quoted at 342 U.S. 143, 72 S.Ct. 181, 184 (1951).

First, on the newspaper's right to do business with whomever it wished, Justice Burton wrote: [30]

> The right claimed by the publisher is neither absolute nor exempt from regulation. [The refusal to accept advertising] * * * as a purposeful means of monopolizing interstate commerce is prohibited by the Sherman Act. The operator of the radio station, equally with the publisher of the newspaper, is entitled to the protection of that Act. *"In the absence of any purpose to create or maintain a monopoly,* the act does not restrict the long recognized right of trader or manufacturer engaged in an entirely private business, freely to exercise his own independent discretion as to parties with whom he will deal."

Second, the court rejected the argument that the injunction to force the newspaper to cease its policy of discriminatory refusal of advertising to merchants who bought time from WEOL was an infringement of the newspaper's First Amendment rights.[31]

> We find [the injunction] * * * no restriction upon any guaranteed freedom of the press. The injunction applies to a publisher what the law applies to others. The publisher may not accept or deny advertisements in an "attempt to monopolize * * * any part of the trade or commerce among the several States * * *." Injunctive relief under § 4 of the Sherman Act is as appropriate a means of enforcing the Act against newspapers as it is against others.

With this decision, the Supreme Court forced the Lorain Journal Company to conform its business policies with the rugged conditions set forth by the injunction issued in the case by the United States District Court. These conditions in the injunction were not only onerous, they were downright embarrassing. The injunction ordered the *Lorain Journal* not to discriminatorily refuse advertisements—or to attach discriminatory conditions in accepting advertisements—against persons or businesses who advertised in other media.[32]

---

30 342 U.S. 143, 155, 72 S.Ct. 181, 187 (1951), quoting United States v. Colgate & Co., 250 U.S. 300, 307, 39 S.Ct. 465, 468 (1919). Emphasis the Court's.

31 342 U.S. 143, 156–157, 72 S.Ct. 181, 187–188 (1951).

32 "Final Judgment," quoted at 342 U.S. 143, 157–159, 72 S.Ct. 181, 188–189 (1951). The newspaper was forbidden to discriminate as to acceptance for publication, plus "price, space, arrangement, location, commencement or period of insertion or any other terms or conditions of publication of advertisement or advertisements where the reason for such refusal or discrimination is in whole or in part, express or implied, that the person, firm or corporation

The District Court retained jurisdiction over the case so that any of the parties to the judgment could ask for further orders or directions. In this way, the pressure was kept on the newspaper, because the District Court left itself in a position to step in quickly to clarify or amend the injunction, to enforce compliance, or to punish violations of the order.

All of this was doubtless bad enough, from the newspaper's point of view. But the injunction also forced the newspaper to publish notices admitting its violation of the Sherman Act for 26 consecutive weeks. The court's order said: [33]

> Commencing fifteen (15) days after the entry of this judgment and at least once a week for a period of twenty-five weeks thereafter the corporate defendant shall insert in the newspaper published by it a notice which shall fairly and fully apprise the readers thereof of the substantive terms of this judgment and which notice shall be placed in a conspicuous location.

The Lorain Journal Company's troubles were not finished, however. In antitrust law, the findings of fact in a civil or criminal suit brought by the government may be used as a springboard for a private *treble damage* lawsuit. In 1961 came the decision in the case of Elyria Lorain Broadcasting v. Lorain Journal. There it was held that the newspaper was liable to treble damages for lost revenue caused the radio station by the newspaper's illegal business practices.[34]

SEC. 106.   TIMES–PICAYUNE v. UNITED STATES (1953)

Where business practices do not produce a demonstrably harmful effect, the antitrust laws will not be enforced.

Although the United States government won its antitrust case against the Lorain Journal in 1950, it was not successful in proving violation of the Sherman Act in Times-Picayune v. United States in 1953. From the outset, the government side of this case must have looked like a sure victory for the antitrust lawyers employed by the United States. It appeared simply that two New Orleans newspapers owned by one publisher were ganging up on an independent, competing newspaper, trying to drive it out of business through illegal advertising contracts. However, for reasons which will be described below, the Su-

submitting the advertisement or advertisments has advertised, advertises, has proposed or proposes to advertise in or through another medium."

[33] Quoted at 342 U.S. 143, 158, 72 S.Ct. 181, 189 (1951).

[34] 298 F.2d 356 (6th Cir. 1961).

preme Court held that the government had presented insufficient evidence to show a violation of the Sherman Act.

At issue was the legality under the Sherman Act of the Times-Picayune Company's contracts for the sale of newspaper classified and general display (national) advertising. The company owned and published two New Orleans newspapers: the morning Times-Picayune (188,402 daily average circulation in 1950) and the evening States (105,235 daily average circulation in 1950). The Times-Picayune Company's two newspapers were competing with the evening New Orleans Item (114,660 daily average circulation in 1950).

The United States government filed a civil antitrust suit against the Times-Picayune Company because of the company's "unit" or "forced combination" contracts with its advertisers. That is, anyone wishing to buy classified advertising or local display advertising in either the morning Times Picayune or the evening States had to purchase space in *both* the morning and afternoon newspapers. The United States challenged these "forced combination" contracts with advertisers as unreasonable restraints of interstate trade and as part of an attempt to monopolize a segment of interstate commerce.[35] A United States District Court in Louisiana found violations of the Sherman Antitrust Act and issued an injunction against further use of the Times-Picayune Company's advertising contracts. Involved here was the complicated notion of "illegal tying" under the antitrust laws. "Tying" is unlawful when a business with a dominant position in its industry coerces its customers to buy an unwanted product along with the desired product.[36] The United States government case rested upon the belief that the morning Times-Picayune, with its circulation of 188,402, was such a "desired product" for advertisers. However, to be able to buy space in the Times-Picayune, the advertisers were forced to also buy space in its sister newspaper, the evening States, which had a circulation of only 105,235. This, of course, must have operated to take some advertising revenue away from the States' competitor, the afternoon Item, which had a circulation of 114,660. The government even contended that the Times-Picayune Company had deliberately operated its afternoon newspaper at a loss—with low advertising rates—in order to attract revenue away from the competing afternoon Item and drive it out of business.[37]

---

35 345 U.S. 594, 597, 73 S.Ct. 872, 874 (1953). See the Sherman Act, 15 U.S. C.A. §§ 1 and 2.

36 105 F.Supp. 670 (D.C.La.1952).

37 345 U.S. 594, 627, 73 S.Ct. 872, 890 (1953).

A majority of the Supreme Court of the United States, however, found that there had been no unlawful "tying." The Times-Picayune was not regarded as the "dominant" product, nor was the States seen as an "inferior" product. Instead, Justice Tom C. Clark's majority opinion held that the two newspapers—owned by one publisher—were selling identical products: advertising space in a newspaper.[38]

Although the Supreme Court's decision left the Times-Picayune Company's combined unit advertising contracts in operation, the Court may well have had some real misgivings. Many actions of the Times-Picayune Company which were charged by the government to be unlawful restraints of trade or monopolistic practices seemed to the Supreme Court to be defensible as legitimate business practices. The government's evidence was simply not strong enough, according to a majority of the Court, to support a finding that the Sherman Act had been violated. Justice Clark's majority opinion concluded with these words of caution: [39]

> We conclude, therefore, that this record does not establish the charged violations of § 1 and § 2 of the Sherman Act. We do not determine that unit advertising arrangements are lawful in other circumstances or in other proceedings. Our decision adjudicates solely that this record cannot substantiate the Government's view of this case. Accordingly, the District Court's judgment must be reversed.

An important part of Justice Tom C. Clark's majority opinion was his discussion of the relationship between freedom of expression and the economics of the newspaper business in the middle of the 20th century: [40]

> The daily newspaper, though essential to the effective functioning of our political system, has in recent years suffered drastic economic decline. A vigorous and dauntless press is a chief source feeding the flow of democratic expression and controversy which maintains the institutions of a free society. * * * By interpreting to the citizen the policies of his government and vigilantly scrutinizing the official conduct of those who administer the state, an independent press stimulates free discussion and focuses public opinion on issues and officials as a potent check on arbitrary ac-

---

[38] 345 U.S. 594, 614, 73 S.Ct. 872, 883 (1953).

[39] 345 U.S. 594, 627–628, 73 S.Ct. 872, 890–891 (1953).

[40] 345 U.S. 594, 602–604, 73 S.Ct. 872, 877–878 (1953).

tion or abuse. * * * Yet today, despite the vital task that in our society the press performs, the number of daily newspapers in the United States is at its lowest point since the century's turn: in 1951, 1,773 daily newspapers served 1,443 American cities, compared with 2,600 dailies published in 1,207 cities in the year 1909. Moreover, while 598 new dailies braved the field between 1929 and 1950, 373 of these suspended publication during that period—less than half of the new entrants survived. Concurrently, daily newspaper competition within individual cities has grown nearly extinct: in 1951, 81% of all daily newspaper cities had only one daily paper; 11% more had two or more publications, but a single publisher controlled both or all. In that year, therefore, only 8% of daily newspaper cities enjoyed the clash of opinion which competition among publishers of their daily press could provide.

Despite this statement by the Justice Clark, he later declared in his decision that the New Orleans Item—the newspaper in competition with the *Times-Picayune* and its sister paper, the States —was flourishing. He noted that between 1946 and 1950, the Item had increased its general display advertising volume by nearly 25 per cent. This local display linage, he added, was twice the equivalent linage in the States. Clark asserted: "The record in this case thus does not disclose evidence from which demonstrably deleterious effects on competition may be inferred." [41] One ironic footnote should be added: the only afternoon newspaper now published in New Orleans is published by the Times-Picayune Company. The name of this afternoon newspaper, thanks to a 1958 merger, is the *New Orleans States Item*.

SEC. 107. UNITED STATES v. KANSAS CITY STAR (1957)

Restraining the circulation of news and views has no constitutional immunity under the First Amendment

After the setback in the *Times-Picayune* case, the government turned to a *criminal* antitrust prosecution against the powerful *Kansas City Star*. The criminal prosecution, however, was by no means the whole story in the *Kansas City Star* case. The justice department also brought a concurrent *civil* antitrust action against the Star, which was later dropped when the Star signed a consent decree agreeing to cease and desist from cer-

41 345 U.S. 594, 620, 73 S.Ct. 872, 887 (1953).

tain business practices.[42]   Thus the case of United States v. Kansas City Star runs the gamut of antitrust activity, including a criminal prosecution, a civil antitrust action brought by the government, the signing of a consent decree, and finally, a welter of treble damage antitrust lawsuits brought against the Star by persons, publications, and firms who claimed that they had been injured by the Star's tough competitive practices.[43]

The Federal government brought a criminal antitrust action against the *Kansas City Star* and its advertising manager, Emil Sees, under the section of the Sherman Anti-Trust Act providing that every person who shall monopolize or attempt to monopolize interstate commerce shall be deemed guilty of a misdemeanor.[44] The Kansas City Star Company had been making the best of a favorable competitive situation.   The corporation was in an essentially monopolistic situation, owning the *Kansas City Times,* a morning newspaper with more than 350,000 circulation, and the *Kansas City Star,* an afternoon paper with more than 360,000 circulation.   The circulation of the *Sunday Star* amounted to more than 378,000.   In addition, the Kansas City Star Corporation owned WDAF radio and WDAF-TV.

The *Times* and *Star* were delivered to 96 per cent of all homes in Kansas City each day.   In order to get one of the Star Company's three newspapers, residents of Kansas City had to subscribe to all three.   Classified advertisers and general advertisers were required to run their advertisements in both the Star and the Times, regardless of the desire of some advertisers to use only one of the papers.

The facts of the *Kansas City Star* operation differed markedly from that which faced Federal antitrust attorneys in the Times-Picayune case.   First, unlike the New Orleans situation, the morning, afternoon, and Sunday newspapers were *forced* upon readers.   Persons who wished to place general or classified advertising were forced to buy space in all three newspapers as a condition of having their advertising accepted.   Second, and also unlike New Orleans, the *Star*'s daily competition, the Journal-Post, was bankrupt and had ceased publication.   Third, the Kansas City Star Corporation, thanks to its newspaper-radio-television enterprises, accounted for nearly 85 per cent of all mass

---

[42] Editor & Publisher, Nov. 23, 1957, p. 9.

[43] Consent decrees, discussed later in this chapter, are negotiated settlements reached between the Antitrust Division of the Justice Department and a defendant.   In such a decree the defendant agrees to stop certain business or to divest himself of certain holdings, but without admitting violation of any law.

[44] United States v. Kansas City Star, 240 F.2d 643 (8th Cir. 1957); 15 U.S.C.A. § 2 (1964 ed.).

media income in the Kansas City area in 1952. On facts such as these, the government built a strong antitrust case.[45]

In prosecuting its case, the government showed that the Star's dominant position in the Kansas City area gave it the power to exclude competition. The government also assembled evidence that the power had been used in rather ruthless fashion. For example, the manager of three Kansas City theatres testified that he had been told, several years earlier, to take his advertising out of the then-competing newspaper, the Kansas City Journal-Post. If not, he said, he was told that his advertisements would be left out of the *Kansas City Star* and *Times*.[46] Other evidence was found of threats and coercion by the Star Corporation to attempt to hamper competition. It was even charged that the dissemination of news was used to control advertising. Consider the instance of a big league baseball player who was a partner in a florist's shop in Kansas City.[47]

> The florist shop also advertised in the [competing newspaper, the] *Journal-Post*. A *Star* solicitor informed one of the partners that The *Star* would discontinue publicizing the baseball player if the florist shop continued using the *Journal-Post* for advertising, Sees [the *Star*'s advertising manager] instructing a *Star* solicitor to tell them," * * * to get out of the *Journal-Post* or he wouldn't get any sports, that he wouldn't get any cooperation from the sports desk on anything that he did in organized baseball."

Evidence was also presented that television and radio advertising on the stations owned by the Star Company went only to advertisers who were favored. In 1952, the *Star* refused time on its WDAF-TV station to a furniture company. A *Star* advertising salesman then called the furniture company's attention to the fact that the company did not advertise in the *Star* Company's newspapers. When the salesman was told that the furniture company had no need for newspaper advertising, the salesman replied that if that were the case, the furniture company likewise had no need for television.[48]

Also involved was the issue whether the *Kansas City Star* and the *Kansas City Times* were one and the same newspaper since they were published by the same firm. The Star corporation

---

[45] United States v. Kansas City Star, 240 F.2d 643, 648 (8th Cir. 1957).

[46] Ibid., p. 654.

[47] Ibid., p. 655.

[48] Ibid., p. 656.

argued that the *Star* and *Times* were one newspaper, published in 13 different editions each week. The government retorted that the *Times* and *Star* were in fact two separate and distinct newspapers owned by the *Star* company, and that this was a "forced combination" perpetrated upon subscribers and advertisers to exclude competition. The District Court trial jury found the Times and the Star to be separate newspapers, illegally tied together to restrain trade.[49]

Finally the courts were faced with the argument by the *Star* corporation that the government's anti-monopoly prosecution endangered freedom of the press as guaranteed by the First Amendment. It was argued that " ' *   *   * A newspaper is intimidated if it is subject at any moment to prosecution under the Sherman Act whenever it opposes or antagonizes those public officials in power.' " [50] The United States Court of Appeals, however, disposed of this argument by quoting Mr. Justice Hugo L. Black's majority opinion in Associated Press v. United States: [51]

> Freedom to publish means freedom for all and not for some. Freedom to publish is guaranteed by the Constitution, but freedom to combine to keep others from publishing is not. Freedom of the press from governmental interference under the First Amendment does not sanction repression of that freedom by private interests. The First Amendment affords not the slightest support for the contention that a combination to restrain trade in news and views has any constitutional immunity.

The United States Court of Appeals concluded: [52]

> Publishers of newspapers must answer for their actions in the same manner as anyone else. A monopolistic press could attain in tremendous measure the evils sought to be prevented by the Sherman Anti-Trust Act. Freedom to print does not mean freedom to destroy. To use the freedom of the press guaranteed by the First Amendment to destroy competition would defeat its own ends, for freedom to print news and express opinions as one chooses is not tantamount to having freedom to monopolize. To monopolize freedom is to destroy it.

[49] Ibid., pp. 656–657.

[50] Ibid., p. 665.

[51] Ibid., p. 666, quoting 326 U.S. 1, 20, 65 S.Ct. 1416, 1424 (1945).

[52] 240 F.2d 643, 666 (8th Cir. 1957).

By upholding the District Court conviction of the Kansas City
Star and its advertising manager, Emil Sees, the Circuit Court
approved fines of $5,000 against the newspaper corporation and
of $2,500 against Sees. But the Kansas City Star's tribulations,
even after the lengthy trial and the criminal antitrust conviction, were just beginning. While the *criminal* antitrust prosecution was underway, the government had also brought a *civil* antitrust action against the Star company. On November 15,
1957, ten months after the Circuit Court affirmed the criminal
conviction and fines, the Kansas City Star Corporation settled
the civil suit by agreeing to the terms of a consent decree.[53]

This decree, like other consent decrees between an antitrust
defendant and the government, was a negotiated settlement. In
return for getting government agreement to drop the action, the
Kansas City Star Company agreed to a tough settlement. The
Star agreed to sell its television and radio stations, and was forever prohibited from buying any Kansas City broadcasting or
publishing operation without first receiving government approval. Government approval of such a purchase could be secured
only upon a showing that it would not tend to restrain competition. The consent decree also forbade forcing advertisers to buy
advertising space in both the Star and the Times in order to get
an ad published. Furthermore, the Star was forbidden to discriminate among advertisers.[54]

Even the consent decree did not end the Star's problems. The
criminal antitrust conviction was used repeatedly as *prima facie*
evidence by would be competitors who brought treble-damage
antitrust suits. Defending against such lawsuits is an expensive
proposition, and a number of such actions were apparently settled out of court.[55]

SEC. 108.   UNITED STATES v. TIMES MIRROR CORPORATION (1967)

**Mergers which eliminate actual or potential competition in a
newspaper market area were forbidden.**

Mergers between newspapers which lessen competition in a
region were forbidden by the 1967 decision in United States v.

---

[53] See Editor and Publisher, Nov. 23, 1957, p. 9.

[54] Ibid.

[55] See, e. g., M. Robert Goodfriend and J. S. Levinson v. Kansas City Star
Co., 158 F.Supp. 531 (D.C.Mo.1958); Ernie M. Duff v. Kansas City Star Co.,
299 F.2d 320 (8th Cir. 1962), and Craig Siegfried v. Kansas City Star Co.,
193 F.Supp. 427 (D.C.Mo.1961).

Times-Mirror Corporation. That decision rescinded the $15 million purchase of The San Bernardino [California] Sun by the Times-Mirror Corporation of Los Angeles, California. The San Bernardino *Sun* is a profitable daily located about 40 miles from Los Angeles. In 1964, the Pulitzer Corporation of St. Louis offered $15 million to buy the *Sun*. Instead of accepting Pulitzer's offer, *Sun* publisher James A. Guthrie offered to sell to a long-time friend, Norman Chandler, chief executive of the Times-Mirror Corporation, for the same amount.

Mr. Guthrie evidently believed that the Times-Mirror Corporation had a greater interest in the development of the West than would a Missouri-based company such as the Pulitzer Corporation. Mr. Chandler, it has been noted, was on the board of directors of three of the largest corporations in San Bernardino County, Kaiser Steel Corporation, The Atchison, Topeka and Santa Fe Railroad, and Safeway Stores, Inc. In any event, the Chandler family accepted Guthrie's offer and purchased the Sun in 1964.[56]

Acquisition of the *Sun* by the Times-Mirror Corporation was challenged by the Antitrust Division of the Justice Department in 1965. The government complained that the merger meant that the publisher of California's largest daily newspaper, The Los Angeles *Times*, had gained control of the largest independent daily publisher in Southern California. The government contended: [57]

> Times-Mirror's acquisition and ownership of the stock of the Sun Company constitutes an unlawful control and combination which unreasonably restrains interstate trade and commerce in violation of Section 1 of the Sherman Act, 15 U.S.C.A. § 1, and that the effect of the acquisition may be to substantially lessen competition in violation of Section 7 of the Clayton Act, 15 U.S.C.A. § 18.

[56] United States v. Times-Mirror Corp., 274 F.Supp. 606, 609–611 (D.C.Cal. 1967), affirmed by the Supreme Court of the United States without opinion, 390 U.S. 712, 88 S.Ct. 1411 (1968).

[57] 274 F.Supp. 606, 609 (D.C.Cal.1967), Section 1 of the Sherman Act, 15 U.S.C.A. § 1, provides in pertinent part: "Every contract, combination in the form of trust or otherwise, or conspiracy, in restraint of [interstate] trade or commerce among the several states, or with foreign nations, is declared to be illegal * * *." Section 7 of the Clayton Act, 15 U.S.C.A. § 18, provides in pertinent part: "No corporation engaged in [interstate] commerce shall acquire, directly or indirectly, the whole or any part of the stock or other share capital * * * of another corporation engaged in [interstate] commerce in any section of the country the effect of such acquisition may be substantially to lessen competition, or to tend to create a monopoly."

The Times-Mirror Corporation, indeed, is a financial power-house. Between 1960 and 1964, its total assets including news-paper publishing, book publishing, and commercial printing as well as other holdings—more than doubled, rising from $81 million to $165 million. Times-Mirror's principal enterprise, *The Los Angeles Times*, in 1964 had daily circulation figures of 790,255 and Sunday circulation of 1,122,143. Since 1955, the Times has led all of the nation's newspapers in total annual daily and Sunday advertising lineage, and in total annual editorial and feature matter lineage since 1951. The Times also operates the Los Angeles Times Syndicate, which sells approximately 35 newspaper features to more than 1,000 publications throughout the world. Through the Los Angeles Times—Washington Post News Service, news material is provided to about 90 newspapers. Moreover, the Times-Mirror Corporation also published, through a wholly owned subsidiary located near San Bernardino, an evening daily newspaper, *The Orange Coast Daily Pilot*.[58]

The Sun Company of San Bernardino, less than one-twentieth as large as the Times-Mirror Corporation, was likewise in excellent financial condition at the time of its sale in 1964. Then, it had assets of roughly $4.5 million, with the net income for newspaper operations in 1964 exceeding $1 million. With its three newspapers the morning Sun (1964 daily circulation 53,-802), evening Telegram, and the Sunday Sun-Telegram (1964 circulation of 70,664). These newspapers were the only ones, other than the Los Angeles papers, which offered home delivery throughout San Bernardino County.[59]

After hearing the Federal government's complaint against the merger, U. S. District Court Judge Warren J. Ferguson traced diminishing patterns of newspaper competition in San Bernardino County in particular and in Southern California in general.[60]

> There has been a steady decline of independent owner-ship of newspapers in Southern California. A newspaper is independently owned when its owners do not publish another newspaper at another locality. In San Bernardino County as of January 1, 1962, six of the seven daily newspapers were independently owned. On December 31, 1966, only three of the eight dailies published there remained independent.
>
> In the Greater Los Angeles five-county market (Los Angeles and four surrounding counties) from January

---

58 274 F.Supp. 606, 609 (D.C.Cal.1967).

59 Ibid., p. 610.

60 Ibid., p. 621.

1, 1952, through December 31, 1966, while the number of daily newspapers increased from 52 to 64, the number of independent dailies decreased from 33 to 14. In 1952, 63% of all daily newspapers in this five-county area were independent; in 1966, only 22% were independent.

In the ten-county area of Southern California in the same period of time, the number of daily newspapers increased from 66 to 82, but the number independently owned decreased from 39 to 20. In 1952, 59% of Southern California dailies were independent; in 1966, only 24% were independent.

Judge Ferguson declared the acquisition of The Sun Company to be particularly "anticompetitive." The merger, he said, eliminated one of the few independent newspapers which had been able to operate successfully in the morning and Sunday fields in Southern California in the face of strong Los Angeles Times circulation.[61] In addition, Judge Ferguson found that the San Bernardino newspapers were in direct competition with the Times for advertising. The Sun's largest competitor for national advertising was the Times. The Times even ran promotional ads to convince national advertisers that advertisements placed in the Los Angeles Times were " 'a better buy than a carefully selected group of Southern California dailies.' " The "carefully selected group" included the Sun papers of San Bernardino.[62]

The impact of the merger may have been considerable upon a number of smaller Southern California dailies. Judge Ferguson noted: [63]

In San Bernardino County the following events have taken place since the acquisition:

1.   On March 31, 1965, the Richardson Newspapers, publishers of the Pomona Progress Bulletin purchased the Ontario-Upland Report.

2.   On October 1, 1965, the Colton [adjacent to San Bernardino] Courier ceased daily publication.

3.   On April 1, 1966, the Rialto Record-News quit the daily newspaper field.

4.   On May 9, 1967, the Lake Union Publishing Company, partially owned by the Scripps League, acquired the Fontana Herald-News, theretofore an independent

61 Ibid., p. 622.

62 Ibid., p. 618.

63 Ibid., p. 622.

daily. The Fontana and Ontario-Upland newspapers were the next two largest independent dailies after the Sun.

The acquisition has raised a barrier to entry of newspapers in the San Bernardino County market that is almost impossible to overcome. The evidence discloses the market has now been closed tight and no publisher will risk the expense of unilaterally starting a new daily newspaper there.

Judge Ferguson ruled that the purchase of The Sun Company by Times-Mirror violated the anti-merger provisions of Section 7 of the Clayton Act. As a result, the Times-Mirror Company was directed to divest itself of the stock of The Sun Company. The judge ordered that the Times-Mirror had only 60 days in which to present to the court "a plan for divestiture which shall provide for the continuation of The Sun Company as a strong and viable company." To make sure that its orders were carried out, the court retained jurisdiction over the case, and also ruled that the Times-Mirror Corporation would have to pay the government's costs in bringing the anti-trust suit.[64]

The Antitrust Division of the Department of Justice regarded its victory in the Times-Mirror case as greatly significant. One of the government's leading antitrust lawyers, Charles D. Mahaffie, Jr., wrote that the Antitrust Division is "and will continue to be particularly concerned with mergers which may eliminate the actual and potential competition afforded by the suburban, small city and community papers." [65]

Underlying such a statement, of course, is the basic philosophy of antitrust law as applied to the communications media. The idea is that many voices in the marketplace of information and opinion—"diversified, quarrelsome, and competitive"—are in the public interest.[66]

The San Bernardino Sun newspapers have since been acquired by the Gannett Corporation, a newspaper group headquartered in Rochester, New York. If the Times-Mirror Corporation's purchase had been allowed, the absentee ownership of the Sun pa-

---

[64] Ibid., p. 624.

[65] Charles D. Mahaffie, Jr., "Mergers and Diversification in the Newspaper, Broadcasting and Information Industries," The Antitrust Bulletin Vol. 13 (Fall, 1968) pp. 927–935, at p. 928.

[66] See the classic statement by Judge Learned Hand in Associated Press v. United States, 52 F.Supp. 362, 372 (D.C.N.Y.1943), quoted at 326 U.S. 1, 28, 65 S.Ct. 1416, 1428 (1945), and printed in the text to footnote 21 in this chapter. See also Keith Roberts, "Antitrust Problems in the Newspaper Industry," Harvard Law Review Vol. 82:2 (December, 1968) pp. 319–366, at p. 322.

pers would have been only about 40 miles from San Bernardino, as compared to the Gannett headquarters some two thousand miles away. Under Gannett ownership, will the San Bernardino newspapers be of as high quality as they would under ownership of the Times-Mirror Corporation? This is an unanswerable but nevertheless important question.

SEC. 109.   UNITED STATES v. CITIZEN PUBLISHING COMPANY (1968)

The government challenged as an antitrust violation a "joint operating agreement" which merged two newspapers' printing, circulation, and advertising operations.

In 1969, the Supreme Court of the United States decided a case of great importance to the daily newspaper industry: "The Tucson case." That decision declared "joint operating agreements" to be illegal, and such agreements are important to the profit margins if not to the survival of competing newspapers in some 22 communities.[67] The Court-declared stigma of illegality of joint operations, however, did not last long: The Supreme Court's ruling brought a wave of protests from publishers whose newspapers are involved in joint operating agreements. On March 12, 1969—just two days after the Tucson decision—a number of bills were offered in both the House of Representatives and the Senate to legalize joint operating agreements between two newspapers. Those bills tied in with lengthy hearings held by the preceding Congress on the so-called "Failing Newspaper Act." [68] The "Failing Newspaper Act" was given the more euphemistic label, "Newspaper Preservation Act," and was passed by both houses of Congress.[69] President Nixon signed the bill—called the Crybaby Publishers Bill by some—into law on July 24, 1970. This legislation is discussed in detail in Section 110 of this chapter.[70]

Joint operating agreements work in this fashion: two competing newspapers in one town combine their printing, advertising, circulation and business operations. The news and editorial op-

---

[67] Editor & Publisher, Jan. 18, 1969, p. 9. Such communities include Tucson, San Francisco, Madison, Wis., El Paso, Tex., and Honolulu.

[68] See Subcommittee on Antitrust and Monopoly of the Committee on the Judiciary, United States Senate, 90th Congress, First Session, on S. 1312, The Failing Newspaper Act, Part 1, July 12–14, 18–19, 25–26, 1967, at p. 2.

[69] 15 U.S.C.A. §§ 1801–1804.

[70] For a judicial interpretation of the Newspaper Preservation Act, see Bay Guardian Co. v. Chronicle Publishing Co., 344 F.Supp. 1155 (D.C.Cal., 1972).

erations of the two newspapers retain their identities. Then, the two newspapers—one appearing in the morning and the other published in the afternoon—can use the same publishing and business facilities, resulting in marked economies in operation. To say that the Tucson case caused a number of publishers concern would be a grave understatement. Arguments before the U. S. Supreme Court in the Tucson case early in 1969 included an *amicus curiae* brief filed on behalf of publishers of newspapers in 16 cities. In this brief, Chicago attorney Robert L. Stern asserted that " 'a joint operating plant is the only feasible way to preserve competition in cities which cannot support two completely separate newspapers.' "[71]

However, the Antitrust Division of the Department of Justice disagreed, and so did a Federal district court in Arizona in the Tucson case, more fomally known as United States v. Citizen Publishing Co.[72] The Tucson case included this rather complicated list of parties:[73]

 *The Citizen Publishing Company, publishers of *The Tucson Daily Citizen*, the city's only evening daily newspaper of general circulation. William A. Small, Jr., is the Citizen's publisher.

*The Star Publishing Company, publishers of *The Arizona Daily Star*, the only general circulation morning daily and the only general circulation Sunday newspaper in Tucson.

*Tucson Newspaper, Inc., the acting agent for advertising, printing, and circulation of the Tucson Citizen and the Arizona Star. Tucson Newspapers, Inc., was wholly owned by the Star Publishing Co. and the Citizen Publishing Co.

* Arden Publishing Company, with William A. Small, Jr., as the sole stockholder. This company was incorporated on December 21, 1964, by the stockholders of the Citizen Publishing Company to acquire the stock of the Star Publishing Company. On January 5, 1965, Arden Publishing Company purchased Star Publishing's stock, for $9,999,790, and on March 31, 1966, Star Publishing Company was liquidated.

This cast of characters had quite a history in Tucson. In March, 1940, the Citizen Publishing Company owed debts of more than $109,000. But on July 1, 1940, Citizen Publishing en-

 71 Editor & Publisher, Dec. 21, 1968, p. 9.

 72 United States v. Citizen Publishing Company, Tucson Newspapers, Inc., Arden Publishing Company, and William A. Small, Jr., 280 F.Supp. 978 (D.C.Ariz.1968), U. S. appeal pending, see 89 S.Ct. 234 (1968); case decided, 394 U.S. 131, 89 S.Ct. 927 (1969).

 73 280 F.Supp. 978, 979 (D.C.Ariz.1968).

tered into a joint operating agreement with Star Publishing.[74]
This agreement provided that the news and editorial departments of the Tucson Citizen and the Arizona Star would remain
separate, but that all other operating departments would be
merged. The joint operating agreement also provided for the
formation of Tucson Newspapers, Inc., an agency designed to reduce costs and to distribute the profits for the two newspapers.

The joint operating agreement was started because the publishers of the two newspapers believed that there could not be
successful operation of two competing dailies in a city with a
population of less than 100,000.[75] The agreement, by the mid-
1960s, had proved itself financially successful, as these figures
show:

	1940	1964
Combined Revenues, Star and Citizen	$519,168	$8,654,127 [76]
Before-tax profits, combined	27,531	1,727,217

In bringing the antitrust action against the Tucson Citizen
and the Arizona Star, the government raised two issues:

1) Whether the joint operating agreement between the Tucson Daily Citizen and the Arizona Daily Star was a conspiracy
to suppress competition in violation of the Sherman Act.

2) Whether the acquisition of the Arizona Star by the Arden
Publishing Company, whose sole stockholder is William A.
Small, Jr., publisher of the Tucson Citizen, is an anticompeti-
tive merger in violation of the Clayton Act.

The second issue added problems over and above those connected with the joint operating agreement. The Arizona Star
received an offer of approximately $10 million to sell to the
Brush-Moore Newspaper Group of Ohio. In order to prevent
Brush-Moore from buying the Star, members of The Citizen
Publishing Company then organized the Arden Publishing Company and purchased the Star. In Chief Judge James A. Walsh's
words, "As a result of the acquisition of the Star Publishing
Company by Arden, the news department of the Star, previously
independent, is now controlled by owners of [the] Citizen."
This purchase was held to be in violation of the anti-merger pro-

[74] Despite the indebtedness of the Citizen Publishing Company in 1940, U.
S. District Court Judge James A. Walsh ruled that there was no serious likelihood that the company would go out of business at the time it entered the
joint operating agreement. 280 F.Supp. 978, 980 (D.C.Ariz.1968).

[75] Ibid., 981.

[76] Ibid., 982.

visions of Section 7 of the Clayton Act. Defendants were directed by the court to divest themselves of The Arizona Star.[77]

Even without the purchase, which placed both of Tucson's newspapers' news departments under one ownership, the joint operation problem would remain. After lengthy findings of fact, Chief Judge Walsh declared Tucson's joint operating agreement to be illegal under the Sherman Act because it provided for "price fixing, profit pooling, and market allocations by the parties to the agreement."[78]

At the District Court level, arguments for the Tucson newspapers that their joint operating agreement was not anticompetitive were not sufficiently persuasive to avoid defeat. In arguments to the Supreme Court, the Tucson newspapers then insisted that joint operating agreements are necessary in a number of cities to allow newspapers to survive and maintain competing news and editorial voices in such communities. There are 22 cities with a total of 44 newspapers involved in joint operating agreements similar to the situation in Tucson before the 1964 purchase of The Arizona Star by the Arden Publishing Company. It was feared that the Justice Department, should it win the Tucson case, would begin antitrust actions against other newspapers' joint operating agreements.

The District Court's judgment, it should be noted, did not destroy all of the joint operating agreement. However, it could be seen that if the Supreme Court upheld Chief Judge Walsh's order against the Tucson papers, it would mean that "price fixing and profit pooling" arrangements between the Star and the Citizen would be broken up. This would mean that Tucson Newspapers, Inc., could no longer operate single advertising and circulation departments serving both newspapers.[79]

On March 10, 1969, the decision of the Supreme Court in the Tucson case did indeed find the joint operating agreement between the Citizen and the Star to be illegal. Writing for the Court, Mr. Justice Douglas ruled that the agreement was for the purpose of ending competition between the two newspapers. In order to implement that purpose, Douglas declared, three controls were exerted by Tucson Newspapers, Inc., the advertising-circulation-business facility set up by the joint operating agreement. He listed these three controls as price fixing, profit pool-

---

[77] 280 F.Supp. 978, 983–984, 994 (D.C.Ariz.1968).

[78] Ibid., 993–994.

[79] See Editor & Publisher, Jan. 18, 1969, p. 9; 280 F.Supp. 978, 993–994 (D.C.Ariz.1968); Editor & Publisher, loc. cit.

ing, and market control: all illegal under the Sherman Antitrust Act.

The Supreme Court thus affirmed the orders issued by the U. S. District Court in the Tucson case. This meant that the Tucson newspapers must "submit a plan for divestiture and re-establishment of the Star as an independent competitor and for modification of the joint operating agreement so as to eliminate the price-fixing, market control, and profit pooling provisions."

It should be noted that Mr. Justice Douglas emphasized the "failing company doctrine" as he wrote the majority opinion in the Tucson case. Douglas declared the "only real defense of appellants [the Citizen Publishing Company and its co-defendants] was the failing company defense—a judicially created doctrine." The failing company doctrine means that acquisition of a company by a competitor does not illegally lessen competition if the firm which has been purchased is in grave danger of business failure. Justice Douglas, however, found that the Citizen had not been a failing newspaper in 1940 when it entered the joint operating agreement with the Star, despite the fact that the Citizen was then losing money.[80]

The Supreme Court, as Justice Douglas put it, found that "beyond peradventure of doubt" the joint operating agreement between Tucson's two daily newspapers violated antitrust laws. Douglas said that the only real defense for the *Arizona Daily Star* and the *Tucson Daily Citizen* was the failing company defense. However, "the requirements of the failing company doctrine were not met." As noted in Section 101 of Chapter 15, the failing company doctrine can be a defense against antitrust charges under some circumstances. In general, the doctrine means that acquisition of a company by a competitor does not illegally lessen competition if the firm which has been purchased is in grave danger of business failure.

However, Douglas cited International Shoe Co. v. Federal Trade Commission,[81] where the failing company doctrine had operated to make an otherwise illegal merger legal. In that case, "the resources of one company were so depleted and the prospect of rehabilitation so remote that 'it faced the grave probability of a business failure.' "[82]

[80] 394 U.S. 131, 89 S.Ct. 927 (1969); United States Law Week, Vol. 37, pp. 4208–4212 (March 11, 1969); Barry Schweid, "Newspapers Want Congress to Legalize Joint Operations," Associated Press dispatch in Madison, Wis., Capital Times, March 11, 1969; "Publishers seek relief in Congress," Editor & Publisher, March 15, 1969, p. 9ff.

[81] 280 U.S. 291, 50 S.Ct. 89, 74 L.Ed. 431 (1930).

[82] Citizen Publishing Co. v. United States, 394 U.S. 131, 89 S.Ct. 927, 930 (1969); United States Law Week, Vol. 37, at p. 4209 (1969); Editor & Publish-

Douglas added that in the International Shoe Company case there had been " 'no other prospective purchaser.' " In that setting, the acquisition of one shoe company by another was held by the Court to be legal because it "did not substantially lessen competition within the meaning of § 7 [of the Clayton Act]."[83] Douglas then wrote:

In the present case the District Court found:

> "At the time Star Publishing and Citizen Publishing entered into the operating agreement, and at the time the agreement became effective, Citizen Publishing was not then on the verge of going out of business, nor was there a serious probability at that time that Citizen Publishing would terminate its business and liquidate its assets unless Star Publishing and Citizen Publishing entered into the operating agreement."

> The evidence sustains that finding. There is no indication that the owers of Citizen were contemplating a liquidation. They never sought to sell the Citizen and there is no evidence that the joint operating agreement was the last straw at which Citizen grasped. Indeed, the Citizen continued to be a significant threat to the Star. How otherwise is one to explain Star's willingness to enter into an agreement to share its profits with Citizen? Would that be true if as now claimed the Citizen was on the brink of collapse?

> The failing company doctrine plainly cannot be applied in a merger or in any other case unless it is established that the company that acquired it or brings it under dominion is the only available purchaser. For if another person or group could be interested, a unit in the competitive system would be preserved and not lost to monopoly power. So even if we assume *arguendo* that in 1940 the then owners of Citizen could not long keep the enterprise afloat, no effort was made to sell the Citizen; its properties and franchise were not put in the hands of a broker; and the record is silent on what the market, if any, for Citizen might have been.[84]

er, March 15, 1969, pp. 10–11, quoting International Shoe Co. v. Federal Trade Commission, 280 U.S. 291, 302, 50 S.Ct. 89, 93, 74 L.Ed. 431 (1930).

[83] Citizen Publishing Co. v. United States, 394 U.S. 131, 89 S.Ct. 927, 930 (1969); United States Law Week, loc. cit.; Editor & Publisher, op. cit., p. 11.

[84] Citizen Publishing Co. v. United States, United States Law Week, op. cit., pp. 4209–4210; Editor & Publisher, March 15, 1969, p. 11. Justices John

SEC. 110. THE NEWSPAPER PRESERVATION ACT

Congressional legislation created exemption to antitrust laws for newspapers which are tied together by "joint operating agreements" in more than twenty cities.

The Supreme Court's Tucson ruling [85] brought a wave of protests from publishers whose newspapers are involved in joint operating agreements. On March 12, 1969, only two days after the Tucson decision, eight bills were introduced into Congress with the aim of pulling the teeth from the Supreme Court's condemnation of joint operating agreements. Loud howls arose from publishers, who saw that as *Editor & Publisher* magazine reported, "[u]nless Congress acts to nullify the Supreme Court's Tucson ruling, the Justice Department's antitrust division will be free to proceed under the antitrust laws against the other [21] newspapers who are parties to joint agreements." [86]

The bills were filed so rapidly after the Supreme Court's decision because they were largely identical to an earlier version of "The Failing Newspaper Act" which was the subject of protracted hearings before the Senate Judiciary Subcommittee in 1967 and 1968.[87] If the judgment of the Court in the Tucson case were allowed to stand, it would mean that two separately owned newspapers in one city could no longer share single advertising, business, and circulation departments.

In sum, the "Failing Newspaper Bill" was given the sweeter-sounding label, "Newspaper Preservation Act," and was ultimately signed into law in mid-summer of 1970 by President Rich-

Marshall Harlan and Potter Stewart dissented. Mr. Justice Abe Fortas took no part in this decision.

[85] Citizen Publishing Co. v. United States, 394 U.S. 131, 89 S.Ct. 927 (1969).

[86] See, e. g., Editor & Publisher, March 15, 1969, p. 9.

[87] For text of Senate Bill 1312, see Subcommittee on Antitrust and Monopoly of the Committee on the Judiciary, United States Senate, 90th Congress, First Session, The Failing Newspaper Act, Part 1, July 12–14, 18–19, 25–26, 1967, at p. 2. These extensive hearings are a valuable storehouse of information on antitrust law and lore affecting the mass media. The original Failing Newspaper Bill was introduced by the late Senator Carl Hayden of Arizona. Despite opposition from Senator Philip A. Hart of Michigan, chairman of the Subcommittee on Antitrust and Monopoly, a revised bill was reported favorably by the Senate Judiciary Committee. However, this bill came out of committee too late to receive action on the Senate floor; hearings on a similar measure (H.R.19123) in the House of Representatives had not been completed when the 90th Congress adjourned. There the matter rested until the 91st Congress was galvanized into action by publishers' complaints following the March 10, 1969, Supreme Court decision in Citizen Publishing Co. v. United States.

ard M. Nixon. How one views the Newspaper Preservation Act depends on one's individual view of what is rhetoric and what is reality. The problem here, in part, is that everyone says similar things, but evidently says them with quite different objects in mind. The United States Department of Justice, which brought the antitrust case against Tucson's Citizen Publishing Company, spoke out against illegal combinations in restraint of trade in the news business. So did Justice Douglas's opinion deciding the *Tucson* case. But then, publishers and members of Congress argued that the *Tucson* decision could not be allowed to stand; without an antitrust exemption, 44 newspapers in 22 cities could no longer continue to gain economies through their joint operating agreements, and some of these newspapers, losing such savings in operating costs, might be forced out of existence. So it was that both the proponents and the opponents of the Newspaper Preservation Act argued that they were in favor of preserving "an independent and competitive press."[88]

The Newspaper Preservation Act says:

NEWSPAPER PRESERVATION ACT

(15 U.S.C.A. Sections 1801–1804)

Section 1801. Congressional declaration of policy.

In the public interest of maintaining a newspaper press editorially and reportorially independent and competitive in all parts of the United States, it is hereby declared to be the public policy of the United States to preserve the publication of newspapers in any city, community, or metropolitan area where a joint operating arrangement has been heretofore entered into because of economic distress or is hereafter effected in accordance with the provisions of this chapter.

Section 1802. Definitions.

As used in this chapter—

(1) The term "antitrust law" means the Federal Trade Commission Act and each statute defined by section 44 of this title as "Antitrust Acts" and all amend-

---

88 Cities with daily newspapers in joint operating agreements include: Albuquerque, N. M.; Bristol, Tenn.-Va.; Charleston, W. Va.; Columbus, Ohio; El Paso, Tex.; Evansville, Ind.; Fort Wayne, Ind.; Franklin-Oil City, Pa.; Honolulu, Hawaii; Knoxville, Tenn.; Lincoln, Neb.; Madison, Wis.; Miami, Fla.; Nashville, Tenn.; Pittsburgh, Pa.; Saint Louis, Mo.; Salt Lake City, Utah; San Francisco, Calif.; Shreveport, La.; Tucson, Ariz., and Tulsa, Okla.

ments to such Act and such statutes and any other Acts in pari materia.[89]

(2) The term "joint newspaper operating arrangement" means any contract, agreement, joint venture (whether or not incorporated), or other arrangement entered into by two or more newspaper owners for the publication of two or more newspaper publications, pursuant to which joint or common production facilities are established or operated and joint or unified action is taken or agreed to be taken with respect to any one or more of the following: printing; time, method, and field of publication, allocation of production facilities; distribution; advertising solicitation; circulation solicitation; business department; establishment of advertising rates; establishment of circulation rates and revenue distribution: *Provided*, That there is no merger, combination, or amalgamation of editorial or reportorial staffs, and that editorial policies be independently determined.

(3) The term "newspaper owner" means any person who owns or controls directly, or indirectly through separate or subsidiary corporations, one or more newspaper publications.

(4) The term "newspaper publication" means a publication produced on newsprint paper which is published in one or more issues weekly (including as one publication any daily newspaper and any Sunday newspaper published by the same owner in the same city, community, or metropolitan area), and in which a substantial portion of the content is devoted to the dissemination of news and editorial opinion.

(5) The term "failing newspaper" means a newspaper publication which, regardless of its ownership or affiliations, is in probable danger of financial failure.

(6) The term "person" means any individual, and any partnership, corporation, association, or other legal entity existing under or authorized by the law of the United States, any State or possession of the United States, the District of Columbia, the Commonwealth of Puerto Rico, or any foreign country.

---

[89] "In pari materia" means "upon the same matter or subject;" Black's Law Dictionary, 4th Rev.Ed., p. 898. Statutes *in pari materia* are to be construed together.

Section 1803.   Antitrust exemption.

(a) It shall not be unlawful under any antitrust law for any person to perform, enforce, renew, or amend any joint newspaper operating arrangement entered into prior to July 24, 1970, if at the time at which such arrangement was first entered into, regardless of ownership or affiliations, not more than one of the newspaper publications involved in the performance of such arrangement was likely to remain or become a financially sound publication: *Provided,* That the terms of a renewal or amendment to a joint operating arrangement must be filed with the Department of Justice and that the amendment does not add a newspaper publication or newspaper publications to such arrangement.

(b) It shall be unlawful for any person to enter into, perform, or enforce a joint operating arrangement, not already in effect, except with the prior written consent of the Attorney General of the United States. Prior to granting such approval, the Attorney General shall determine that not more than one of the newspaper publications involved in the arrangement is a publication other than a failing newspaper, and that approval of such arrangement would effectuate the policy and purpose of this chapter.

(c) Nothing contained in this chapter shall be construed to exempt from any antitrust law any predatory pricing, any predatory practice, or any other conduct in the otherwise lawful operations of a joint newspaper operating arrangement which would be unlawful under any antitrust law if engaged in by a single entity. Except as provided in this chapter, no joint newspaper operating arrangement or any party thereto shall be exempt from any antitrust law.

Section 1804.   Reinstatement of joint operating arrangements previously judged unlawful under antitrust laws.

(a) Notwithstanding any final judgment rendered in any action brought by the United States under which a joint operating arrangement has been held to be unlawful under any antitrust law, any party to such final judgment may reinstate said joint newspaper operating arrangement to the extent permissible under section 1803(a) of this title.

(b) The provisions of section 1803 of this title shall apply to the determination of any civil or criminal action pending in any district court of the United States on July 24, 1970, in which it is alleged that any such joint operating agreement is unlawful under any antitrust law.

Nixon

The Newspaper Preservation Act was passed despite strenuous objections from the Antitrust Division of the Department of Justice. The governments' attorneys expressed fear that if profit pooling or price fixing laws were relaxed to aid newspapers, "many publishers will opt for that way [joint operating agreements] even though they might be capable of remaining fully independent, or of finding other solutions to the difficulties which preserve competition."[90] Weekly newspapers, small dailies, and the American Newspaper Guild strongly and repeatedly urged against passage of a failing newspaper act, often complaining that joint advertising rates provide newspapers in a joint operation situation with an advantage which competitors simply cannot overcome.[91] Senator Philip Hart of Michigan, chairman of the subcommittee which held hearings on the bill, declared that propping up a failing large or middle-sized newspaper might put competing small dailies or weeklies in the same area at an insuperable disadvantage.[92]

John H. Carlson, writing in the Indiana Law Journal, expressed dismay about the antitrust exemption for so-called failing newspapers.[93]

> The Newspaper Preservation Act of 1970, while purporting to advance the public interest of "maintaining a newspaper press editorially and reportorially independent * * *" is another step toward the disturbing trend of special legislation following governmental antitrust victories.

Carlson contended that the Newspaper Preservation Act's antitrust exemption is justifiable only when there is a clear showing that such exemption is "essential to the preservation of an independent and competitive press." However, he declared that the

[90] Statement of Donald F. Turner, assistant attorney general, Antitrust Division, Department of Justice, before the Senate Judiciary Committee, Subcommittee on Antitrust and Monopoly, on S. 1312, April 1968, p. 18.

[91] See, e. g., The Guild Reporter, Sept. 8, 1967, p. 8; "Failing Newspaper Bill Assailed," Associated Press dispatch in Wisconsin State Journal, Madison, Sec. 1, p. 8, April 17, 1968.

[92] Wisconsin State Journal, loc. cit.

[93] John T. Carlson, "Newspaper Preservation Act: A Critique," Indiana Law Journal 46:392 (Spring, 1971).

Newspaper Preservation Act, which legalized the *Tucson* arrangement as well as similar operations elsewhere, allowed newspapers which were nowhere close to failing financially to dodge antitrust laws.[94]

> Newspaper chains participate in fifteen out of the twenty two present joint newspaper operating agreements, wherein recent transactions by those chains indicated considerable financial strength. An example of profits earned by newspaper chains is provided by two joint operating agreement newspapers: Madison Newspapers, Inc., in Madison, Wisconsin, and the Journal-Star Publishing Co. in Lincoln, Nebraska. These two arrangements earned a 22 and a 16.4 per cent return on owners' equity respectively in 1968.

> *   *   *   *   *   *   *   *   *

> In terms of antitrust policy, it is incumbent upon those seeking antitrust exemption to clearly establish the necessity. Since the proponents of the NPA have not shown a clear economic need for this exemption, having failed to demonstrate that a substantial number of newspapers would fail without it, the Congressional conclusion that the antitrust exemption embodied in the NPA is necessary for the preservation of independent and competing sources of news is unwarranted.

> *   *   *   *   *   *   *   *   *

> Joint operations enable the participating newspapers to eliminate the costly duplication of printing facilities, distribution points, delivery vehicles, circulation departments, advertising departments, and business departments. Cost savings from these joint arrangements make the establishment of competing newspapers difficult since they must duplicate these facilities, thus bearing proportionately higher costs.

Just as Carlson's critique of the Newspaper Preservation Act first appeared in print in the spring of 1971, publisher Bruce Brugman of the *San Francisco Bay Guardian* offered his own critique in the form of a challenge to the Act's constitutionality. *The Bay Guardian*, a monthly with a circulation of 17,000, saw itself in a tough competitive situation. *San Francisco's Chronicle and Examiner* had tied themselves into a joint newspaper operating agreement some years before, in September of 1965. Under that agreement, one newspaper—*The News-Call-Bulletin* —was put to death, and the two remaining dailies carved up the

94 Ibid., pp. 397–399, 400.

morning (*Chronicle*) and evening (*Examiner*) markets. Printing for the *Chronicle* and the *Examiner* is done by a jointly owned subsidiary, the San Francisco Newspaper Printing Company. The two remaining daily papers' editorial staffs are kept independent, although the two newspapers jointly publish a unified Sunday edition. Profits from all operations are shared half-and-half. As a result, the *Chronicle* and *Examiner* have achieved a highly profitable monopoly position in San Francisco's daily newspaper market.[95]

Publisher Brugman and the *Bay Guardian* contended that the Newspaper Preservation Act is unconstitutional because it unfairly encourages such a journalistic monopoly. The effect of the Act, they contended, causes it to violate the press freedom guarantee of the First Amendment.

Chief Judge Oliver J. Carter summed up the *Bay Guardian's* arguments:[96]

> The plaintiffs are the owners and publishers of a small paper that has been a bimonthly paper and is now monthly. They contend that the defendants' monopoly position in the San Francisco market enables the defendants to destroy or weaken any potential competition. They contend that the profit sharing, joint ad rates, and other cooperative aspects of the joint operating agreement enable the defendants to establish and perpetuate a stranglehold on the San Francisco newspaper market. The plaintiffs contend that the Act is unconstitutional because it unfairly encourages this journalistic monopoly.

Judge Carter, however, was not persuaded by such arguments. He ruled that the simple answer to the plaintiffs' contention is that the Act does not authorize any conduct. He added that the Newspaper Preservation Act is a narrow exception to the antitrust laws for newspapers in danger of failing, and that the Act is "in many respects merely a codification of the judicially cre-

---

[95] Bay Guardian Co. v. Chronicle Publishing Co., 344 F.Supp. 1155, 1157 (D. C.Cal.1972). This court confrontation did not represent a full-dress trial. The plaintiffs originally sought a declaratory judgment that the Act was unconstitutional, but "such an action could not be maintained for technical jurisdictional reasons." See 340 F.Supp. 76 (Feb. 24, 1972). Then, the defendants —including the *Examiner* and the *Chronicle*—"answered the antitrust portions of the complaint by asserting the Act in two affirmative defenses to those claims." Plaintiffs—*Bay Guardian Co.*—then moved to strike those defenses on grounds that the Newspaper Preservation Act is unconstitutional on its face.

[96] 344 F.Supp. 1155, 1157 (D.C.Cal.1972).

ated 'failing company' doctrine." [97]   Although he upheld the Act's constitutionality, Judge Carter's words were not particularly kind to the legislation: [98]

> *   *   *   [T]he Act was designed to preserve independent editorial voices. Regardless of the economic or social wisdom of such a course, it does not violate the freedom of the press. Rather it is merely a selective repeal of the antitrust laws. It merely looses the same shady market forces which existed before the passage of the Sherman, Clayton and other antitrust laws.

John H. Carlson, writing about San Francisco's joint-operation newspapers after passage of the Newspaper Preservation Act but before the *Bay Guardian* lawsuit reached the courtroom, was even more scathing in his remarks about the Act: [99]

> Section 2 [of the Newspaper Preservation Act] states that once the eligibility requirements of Section 4(a) and (b) have been satisfied, it is the policy of the Newspaper Preservation Act to preserve the editorial and news reporting independence of the newspaper publications participating in joint operations. It is questionable whether in fact the NPA [Newspaper Preservation Act] achieves this objective. In San Francisco, the performance of the *Examiner* in reporting the *Chronicle's* struggle to obtain renewal of its broadcasting license reveal that little editorial independence can be expected on issues in which either of the participating newspapers have [sic] a vested interest. The *Examiner's* coverage of this controversy, culminating in the FCC's announcement to withhold renewal of the *Chronicle's* license, was delayed and minimal. Since the public relies upon local newspapers for detailed and complete news reports, the preservation of joint newspaper operating agreements, such as found in San Francisco, does not serve the public interest.

Such recriminations aside, the importance of the Newspaper Preservation Act should not be overestimated. As Professor Paul Jess of the University of Michigan has noted, the Act did little more than legalize the 22 joint operating agreements already in existence at the time the Act was passed. There has been no scramble to add to the number of joint operating agreements as such agreements are outlined by the act. The text of

---

[97] Ibid.

[98] Ibid., p. 1158.

[99] Carlson, op. cit., p. 409.

the Newspaper Preservation Act indicates that to enter a joint operating agreement now requires that at least one of the two newspapers must be "failing", or "in probable danger of financial failure." Any new joint operating agreement, furthermore, must be undertaken only after receiving written consent from the Attorney General of the United States. The Attorney General must determine that at least one of the newspapers applying for joint operation is "failing" or "in probable danger of financial failure." [1]

SEC. 111. CONSENT DECREES

Negotiated settlements, which settle antitrust proceedings without a formal trial, are coming into increasing use in cases affecting the mass media.

Court decisions, however, are only a part of the antitrust story affecting the communications media. In fact, court-adjudicated cases may be becoming less important in antitrust law than the instrument which is now receiving much use: *consent decrees.* Consent decrees—also sometimes called consent judgments—are negotiated final legal settlements between the government and a business. Consent decrees have the force of law once they have been approved by a judge. Such consent decree settlements can take place in civil, but not criminal, antitrust cases.[2]

Where a newspaper or broadcasting station is concerned, an antitrust consent decree works in the following fashion. First, civil antitrust suit is filed by the Antitrust Division of the Justice Department against the owners of a newspaper or broadcasting station. In the opinion of the Justice Department, the communications medium involved may have been engaging in anti-competitive business practices. Or, a certain ownership may, in the eyes of the Justice Department, have acquired too many media units—newspaper and broadcasting—in one market, according to the antitrust laws as they have been interpreted by the courts.

---

[1] Telephone interview with Dr. Paul Jess, Department of Journalism, University of Michigan, Ann Arbor, Mich., March 22, 1973. See also Newspaper Preservation Act, 15 U.S.C.A. §§ 1802(5) and 1803(b).

[2] As Prof. Lorry Rytting of the University of Utah has said, the Justice Department is sensitive to charges that criminal antitrust suits might be filed, in effect, to force the signing of civil consent decrees. Current justice department policy discourages the use of concurrent criminal and civil antitrust complaints. Rytting, "Antitrust Consent Decrees: A Threat to Freedom of the Press?", unpublished paper, School Of Journalism, University of Wisconsin, 1967.

Second, the owners may decide that it will do them no good to fight the antitrust suit. The owners' attorneys may see that a court battle is almost certain to result in defeat. So, in order to avoid lengthy and expensive trial, attorneys for the owner will sit down with attorneys from the Antitrust Division of the Justice Department. Once a consent agreement is worked out, it means that the owners have promised to stop certain business practices or to divest themselves of certain media units. After the agreement is reached, it is made final by being formalized before a federal district judge.

Consent decrees have the advantage of allowing a defendant to settle a suit without admitting a violation of law. An example of this was the sale, late in 1968, of WREX-TV in Rockford, Ill., by the Gannett Company of Rochester, New York. In that year, the Antitrust Division of the Department of Justice has filed a civil antitrust suit against the Gannett Company, which owned, in addition to WREX-TV, also owned the Rockford Newspaper, the Morning Star and the Register-Republic. Gannett had acquired the two newspapers in 1967, and had purchased WREX-TV in 1963 for $3,500,000. Under the consent decree, the Gannett Company agreed to divest itself of the television station to James S. Gilmore, Jr., president of Gilmore Broadcasting Co., for $6,850,000.[3]

Earl A. Jinkinson, formerly chief of the Midwest Office in Chicago of the Department of Justice's Antitrust Division, has summarized some of the differing ways consent decrees are viewed.[4]

> The term "consent decree" has been defined in a number of ways. Judge Igoe, when faced with the necessity of finding the meaning of a consent decree after a lengthy trial * * * finally observed that one of his greatest difficulties was that consent decrees are "all things to all men." His observation was somewhat accurate, depending of course on the viewpoint. To the Government attorneys the consent decree is an act of grace granted in order to give the attorneys and the entire staff more time to attend to other ever-pressing and sometimes more important matters. On the other hand, many defense counsel at least profess to believe, erroneously I might add, that the consent decree is a governmental device for winning cases, thrust upon an unwilling defendant which, to adopt the words of Seth

3 The Gannetteer, magazine of the Gannett Co., January 1969, p. 3.

4 Earl A. Jinkinson, "Negotiation of Consent Decrees," Antitrust Bulletin, Vol. 9: Nos. 5–6 (Sept.–Dec., 1964), pp. 673–690, at pp. 676–677.

Dabney, is like "Bryon's maiden who strove and re-
pented, but ultimately consented." To attorneys for
private parties injured because of the violation [of antitrust statutes], the consent decree is an abrogation of
the duty of the Department of Justice to protect their
client's rights. As a matter of fact the wails of an-
guish from the lips of plaintiff counsel in treble damage suits barely falls short of accusing Government
counsel of a complete sell-out to defense counsel.

In 1947, Zechariah Chafee warned that consent decrees could
increase the danger to press freedom through heavy use of the
antitrust laws. Consent decrees are reached without trials, after secret proceedings. Evidence presented in reaching these decrees is not made public. Furthermore, such decrees are as legally binding as the decision of a federal court, and may be enforced with contempt-of-court sanctions if they are not obeyed.[5]

It has been suggested that the government, which has begun
—or which has indicated that it soon may begin—an antitrust
action is very much in the driver's seat against the defendant,
which may feel compelled to "settle" by way of a consent decree.
True, if an owner decides that the terms insisted on by the Antitrust Division violate his rights, he may halt the negotiations for
a consent decree and demand a full trial. Trials, however, are
expensive, lengthy, and may carry with them publicity which the
media owners find damaging.[6]

Whether consent decrees are a threat to press freedom or a
boon to media owners which allows them to avoid full-dress antitrust trials, the fact remains that such decrees affecting the
mass media have been issued with increasing frequency in recent years.[7]

[5] Chafee, op. cit., Vol. 2, p. 670.

[6] Rytting, op. cit.

[7] See, e. g., United States v. Wichita Eagle Publishing Co., Inc., 1959 Trade
Cases, Para. 69,400; United States v. Western Newspaper Union, 1960 Trade
Cases, Para. 69,709; United States v. Stamps Conhaim Whitehead, Inc., 1963
Trade Cases, Para. 70,857; United States v. Metro Associated Services, Inc.,
1964 Trade Cases, Para. 71,078; United States v. Greater Buffalo Press, 1965
Trade Cases, Para. 71,479; United States v. Lima News, 244 F.Supp. 592
(1965), and United States v. Lindsay-Schaub Newspapers, Inc., 1967 Trade
Cases, Para. 72,085.

Chapter 16

TAXATION AND LICENSING

SEC. 112. TAXATION

The mass media are constitutionally protected from discriminatory or punitive taxation.

Taxation has long been a fighting word to the press. Taxes on the press instituted in England in 1712 were called "taxes on knowledge," because they raised the purchase price of pamphlets or other printed materials beyond the means of most persons. In American history, taxation of the press has long been hated and feared. The Stamp Act of 1765 imposed great hardships on printers, taxing newspapers, advertisements, and pamphlets, as well as many legal documents [1] and became a great rallying cry for colonists who resisted British authority. Such a storm of protest arose in the colonies through both newspapers and pamphlets, to say nothing of mobs which forced British stamp agents to resign, that Parliament repealed the Stamp Act taxes as they affected printer-editors.

If American colonists hated the Stamp Act taxes because they infringed on "the liberty of the press" and "free inquiry," American memories were also very short. In 1785, only two short years after the War of Independence officially ended, the state of Massachusetts passed a newspaper stamp tax. If the Massachusetts legislature had a short memory, printers and publishers did not. Howls of protest reminiscent of the Stamp Act disturbances of 1765 soon echoed from the columns of Massachusetts newspapers. One writer who called himself "Lucius" declared that the tax on newspapers was a *"stab to the freedom of the people."* He acknowledged that Massachusetts newspapers were full of scurrilous articles, and admitted that the tax of a penny on each copy seemed small. But "Lucius" added that "tyranny begins small," and that the tax of even a half-penny on each newspaper copy could be a precedent for a tax of £100 on each issue.[2] Protests such as these led to the repeal of the Mas-

---

[1] Arthur M. Schlesinger, Prelude to Independence: The Newspaper War on Great Britain, 1763–1776 (New York: Knopf, 1958) p. 68.

[2] Massachusetts Centinel, May 28, 1785.

636

sachusetts stamp tax on newspapers later in 1785, although the Massachusetts legislature shortly thereafter enacted a tax upon newspaper advertisements.[3] The tax on advertisements was not repealed until 1788.[4]

Newspapers and other units of the mass media of communications are businesses. As such, the media are not immune from taxation just like other business enterprises, as long as the taxes fall with a more or less even hand upon the press as well as other businesses. *Discriminatory* or *punitive* taxation, however, raises quite different issues. The classic case in United States constitutional law occurred during the 1930s and involved the flamboyant Huey "Kingfish" Long, the political boss and governor of Louisiana who entertained dreams of someday becoming President. The Supreme Court decision in Grosjean, Supervisor of Accounts of Louisiana, v. American Press Co., Inc.[5] effectively halted a Huey Long-instigated attempt to use a punitive tax to injure newspapers which opposed Long's political regime.

During the 1930s, Louisiana's larger daily newspapers were increasingly expressing opposition to Long's political machine. Louisiana's larger newspapers' sniping at Governor Long's dictatorial posturings soon brought about retaliation. The Louisiana legislature passed a special two per cent license tax on the gross receipts of all newspapers, magazines, or periodicals having a circulation of more than 20,000 copies per week.[6] Of Louisiana's 163 newspapers, only 13 had circulations of more than 20,000 per week. Of these 13 newspapers to which the tax applied, 12 were opponents of Long's political machine.[7] This transparent attempt to silence newspaper critics was challenged in the courts by nine Louisiana newspaper publishers who produced the 13 newspapers then appearing in the state which had circulations of more than 20,000 copies a week.

Newspapers subject to the gross receipts tax were required to file a report every three months showing the amount of the tax and the gross receipts. When such reports were filed, the tax for each three month period was to be due and payable. Failure to report or to pay the tax was made a misdemeanor, subject

[3] Ibid., July 6, July 30, 1785.

[4] Clyde Augustus Duniway, Freedom of the Press in Massachusetts (New York, 1906) p. 137.

[5] 297 U.S. 233, 56 S.Ct. 444 (1936).

[6] 297 U.S. 233, 240, 56 S.Ct. 444, 445 (1936).

[7] J. Edward Gerald, The Press and the Constitution 1931–1947 (Minneapolis, University of Minnesota Press, 1948) p. 100; William A. Hachten, The Supreme Court on Freedom of the Press: Decisions and Dissents (Ames, Iowa: Iowa State University Press 1968) p. 77; 297 U.S. 233, 56 S.Ct. 444, 445 (1936).

to a $500 fine. In addition, an officer of a publishing company which failed to file a report and pay the gross receipts tax could be sentenced to not more than six months in jail.

In declaring the Louisiana tax unconstitutional, a noted conservative—Justice George Sutherland—spoke for a unanimous Supreme Court. Justice Sutherland, a man not revered for his felicity of expression, may indeed have had some able assistance in writing what has come to be known as "Sutherland's great opinion in *Grosjean*." It has been asserted that Sutherland's opinion included a proposed concurring opinion which had been drafted by the famed liberal Justice Benjamin Nathan Cardozo, and which the Court wished to add into Justice Sutherland's opinion.[8]

Whether assisted by Cardozo or not, the Sutherland opinion in Grosjean remains noteworthy. Justice Sutherland began with a historical overview of government-imposed dangers to freedom of expression, including reference to John Milton's 1644 "Appeal for the Liberty of Unlicensed Printing" and to the end of the licensing of the press in England in 1695. As Sutherland noted, "mere exemption from previous censorship was soon recognized as too narrow a view of the liberty of the press." Sutherland wrote:[9]

> In 1712, in response to a message from Queen Anne (Hansard's Parliamentary History of England, vol. 6, p. 1063), Parliament imposed a tax upon all newspapers and upon advertisements. * * * That the main purpose of these taxes was to suppress the publication of comments and criticisms objectionable to the Crown does not admit of doubt. * * * There followed more that a century of resistance to, and evasion of, the taxes, and of agitation for their repeal. * * * [T]hese taxes constituted one of the factors that aroused the American colonist to protest against taxation for the purposes of the home government; and that the revolution really began when, in 1765, that government sent stamps for newspaper duties to the American colonies.
>
> These duties were quite commonly characterized as "taxes on knowledge," a phrase used for the purpose of describing the effect of the exactions and at the same time condemning them. That the taxes had, and were

---

[8] Irving Brant, The Bill of Rights: Its Origin and Meaning (New York: Bobbs-Merrill, 1965) pp. 403–404.

[9] 297 U.S. 233, 249, 56 S.Ct. 444, 449 (1936).

intended to have, the effect of curtailing the circulation
of newspapers, and particularly the cheaper ones whose
readers were generally found among the masses of the
people, went almost without question, even on the part
of those who defended the act.   May (Constitutional
History of England, 7th ed. vol. 2, p. 245), after discussing the control by "previous censure" [licensing
and prior restraint], says: *   *   *   a new restraint
was devised in the form of a stamp duty upon newspapers and advertisements,—avowedly for the purpose of
repressing libels.   This policy, being found effectual in
limiting the circulation of cheap papers, was improved
upon in the two following reigns, and continued in high
esteem until our own time."   Collett [History of the
Taxes on Knowledge] (vol. I, p. 14), says: "Any man
who carried on printing or publishing for a livelihood
was actually at the mercy of the Commissioners of
Stamps, when they chose to exert their powers."

Sutherland quoted Thomas Erskine's great speech in defense
of Thomas Paine, when Erskine said: " 'The liberty of opinion
keeps governments themselves in due subjection to their duties.' "
The Justice asserted that if taxes had been the only issue,
many of England's best men would not have risked their careers
and their lives to fight against them.   The issue in England for
many years, however, involved discriminatory taxation designed
to control the press and silence criticism of government.   The
Grosjean opinion added:[10]

The framers of the First Amendment were familiar
with the English struggle, which had then continued
for nearly eighty years and was destined to go on for
another sixty-five years, at the end of which time it
culminated in a lasting abandonment of the obnoxious
taxes.   The framers were likewise with the then recent
[1785–1788] Massachusetts [stamp tax] episode; and
while that occurrence did much to bring about the
adoption of the amendment, the predominant influence
must have come from the English experience.

Justice Sutherland rejected the State of Louisiana's argument
that the English common law in force when the Constitution
was adopted forbade only prior restraints on the press and said
nothing about forbidding taxation.[11]   In reply, Sutherland quoted from a great 19th century American constitutional scholar,

10 297 U.S. 233, 247–248, 56 S.Ct. 444, 448 (1936).

11 297 U.S. 233, 249, 56 S.Ct. 444, 449 (1936).

Judge Thomas Cooley, and declared that Cooley had laid down the test to be applied:[12]

> The evils to be prevented were not the censorship of the press merely, but any action of the government by means of which it might prevent such free and general discussion of public matters as seems absolutely essential to prepare the people for an intelligent exercise of their rights as citizens.

Application of this test led Justice Sutherland to rule that the Louisiana gross receipts tax on its larger newspapers was an unconstitutional abridgement of the First and Fourteenth Amendments. Sutherland declared:[13]

> It is not intended by anything we have said to suggest that the owners of newspapers are immune from any of the ordinary forms of taxation for support of the government. But this is not an ordinary form of tax, but one single in kind, with a long history of hostile misuse against the freedom of the press.
>
> [12] The predominant purpose of the grant of immunity here invoked was to preserve an untrammeled press as a vital source of public information. The newspapers, magazines, and other journals of the country, it is safe to say, have shed and continue to shed, more light on the public and business affairs of the nation than any other instrumentality of publicity; and since informed public opinion is the most potent of all restraints upon misgovernment, the suppression or abridgement of the publicity afforded by a free press cannot be regarded otherwise than with grave concern. The tax here involved is bad not because it takes money from the pockets of the appellees. If that were all, a wholly different question would be presented. It is bad because, in the light of its history and of its present setting, it is seen to be a deliberate and calculated device in the guise of a tax to limit the circulation of information to which the public is entitled in virtue of the constitutional guaranties. A free press stands as

---

12 297 U.S. 233, 249, 56 S.Ct. 444, 449 (1936), quoting 2 Cooley's Constitutional Limitations (8th ed.) p. 886.

13 297 U.S. 233, 250–251, 56 S.Ct. 444, 449 (1936). Accord: See City of Baltimore v. A. S. Abell Co., 218 Md. 273, 145 A.2d 111, 119 (1958). It was held that Baltimore city ordinances imposing taxes on advertising media were unconstitutional in that they discriminatorily taxed newspapers and radio and television stations. About 90 per cent of the impact of the taxes was on those businesses.

one of the great interpreters between the government and the people. To allow it to be fettered is to fetter ourselves.

In view of the persistent search for new subjects of taxation, it is not without significance that, with the single exception of the Louisiana statute, so far as we can discover no state during the one hundred fifty years of our national existence has undertaken to impose a tax like that now in question.

The form in which the tax is imposed is in itself suspicious. It is not measured or limited by the volume of advertisements. It is measured alone by the extent of the circulation of the publication in which the advertisements are carried, with the plain purpose of penalizing the publishers and curtailing the circulation of a selected group of newspapers.

Despite these ringing words, it should be noted again that the communications media are not exempt from paying non-discriminatory general business taxes. A case in point involved *The Corona Daily Independent,* a California newspaper which challenged a $32-a-year business license tax imposed by the City of Corona. The newspaper, which had paid the tax in a number of previous years, in 1951 refused to pay the tax. The newspaper went to court, arguing that the tax violated freedom of the press as guaranteed by the First and Fourteenth Amendments. However, the California Appellate Court ruled:[14]

There is ample authority to the effect that newspapers and the business of newspaper publication are not made exempt from the ordinary forms of taxes for the support of local government by the provisions of the First and Fourteenth Amendments.

*   *   *   *   *   *   *   *   *

In Tampa Times Co. v. City of Tampa * * * an ordinance imposed an annual business license tax upon newspapers, magazines, and other periodicals or publications, based upon gross receipts, with a minimum tax of $10 per annum upon receipts from all sales and advertising, both wholesale and retail. The tax was applied equally to all lines of business. There was no

---

[14] City of Corona v. Corona Daily Independent, 115 Cal.App.2d 382, 252 P.2d 56 (1953), cert. den. 343 U.S. 833, 74 S.Ct. 2 (1953). See also Giragi v. Moore, 48 Ariz. 33, 64 P.2d 819 (1937) (general sales tax law placing a one per cent tax upon businesses' sales or gross income not unconstitutional as applied to newspapers); Arizona Publishing Co. v. O'Neil, 22 F.Supp. 117 (D.C.Ariz.1938), affirmed 304 U.S. 543, 58 S.Ct. 950 (1938).

claim that the ordinance was arbitrary or harsh in nature. There the court held that the ordinance was one for revenue; that the question was one of whether or not a newspaper was immune from the burden of taxation to maintain government; and declared that it had no knowledge of any case where a newspaper had been held immune from all forms of taxation. The court stated that a tax in any form is a burden, yet that alone does not impair freedom of the press any more than an *ad valorem* tax will destroy freedom of speech. On appeal to the Supreme Court of the United States, the action was dismissed for want of a substantial Federal question.

The phrase "power to tax is the power to destroy" is without application to the issue here presented. There is no allegation or showing by defendant that the amount levied was arbitrary or harsh in nature, or oppressive or confiscatory, or that defendant's freedom to disseminate news and comment has been actually curtailed or abridged by the requirement that it shall pay a tax of $8 per quarter for publishing its newspaper. Nor is there any showing that the imposition of the tax was for the purpose of regulating defendant's business.

While the ordinary business tax here in issue is levied in form upon the privilege of engaging in or transacting business, it is, on its face and in fact, a tax for revenue purposes only, and does not grant or take away any right to do business, does not subject business to withdrawal or control by the city, is not regulatory in any manner, and in substance has been recognized and upheld by the weight of authority.

We conclude that a nondiscriminatory tax, levied upon the doing of business, for the sole purpose of maintaining the municipal government, without whose municipal services and protection the press could neither exist nor function, must be sustained as being within the purview and necessary implications of the Constitution and its amendments.

The general rule to be drawn from cases such as Grosjean v. American Press Co. and Corona Daily Independent v. City of Corona seems to be this: the media are not exempt from nondiscriminatory taxation. More broadly, the media are businesses and are subject to general laws which regulate business. As it

was said by the Supreme Court of the United States in 1939 in
Associated Press v. National Labor Relations Board:[15]

> The business of the Associated Press is not immune
> from regulation because it is an agency of the press.
> The publisher of a newspaper has no special immunity
> from the application of general laws. He has no spe-
> cial privileges or immunities to invade the rights and
> liberties of others. He must answer for libel. He may
> be punished for contempt of court. He is subject to the
> anti-trust laws. Like others he must pay equitable and
> nondiscriminatory taxes on his business.

SEC. 113.   LICENSING

**When licensing power over expression amounts to prior censor-
ship, it is constitutionally forbidden.**

Older than discriminatory taxation (although often closely related to it) is the ignoble control over the press known as licensing. Licensing, to journalists and legal scholars, calls up visions
of that most hated of all controls over the press: prior censorship. Licensing in England in the 16th and 17th centuries, for
example, meant that only licensed printers—persons who had
the approval of government or of powerful persons closely tied
to the establishment—were allowed to print.

England's authoritarian licensing system was allowed to ex-
pire in 1695,[16] but battles for freedom are never really won once
and for all. The recurring battles for free expression by Jehovah's Witnesses were waged in large measure against municipal
ordinances which involved license taxes. The struggles of the
Jehovah's Witnesses during the 1930s and 1940s were noteworthy: time and again, they fought their cases all the way to the
Supreme Court of the United States and ultimately succeeded.

---

[15] Associated Press v. National Labor Relations Board, 301 U.S. 103, 132–
133, 57 S.Ct. 650, 656 (1937). See Lee Enterprises v. Iowa State Tax Commission, 162 N.W.2d 730, 734, 754–755 (Iowa 1969). Ten corporations, including newspapers, radio and television broadcasters, advertising agencies and
firms engaged in retail merchandising and in the auto business challenged an
Iowa tax law known as Section 25 of Division VII, Iowa House File 702.
With that measure, the Iowa General Assembly had amended the state's revenue statutes, including as taxable "the gross receipts of * * * "director-
ies, shoppers guides and newspapers whether or not circulated free or without charge to the public, magazine, radio and television advertising * * *."
The Iowa Supreme Court held that the tax does not violate freedom of the
press as guaranteed in either the United States or Iowa Constitutions because the law was of general application and not discriminatory.

[16] Fredrick S. Siebert, Freedom of the Press in England, 1476-1776 (Urbana,
Ill.: University of Illinois Press, 1952) pp. 260-263.

This religious sect, as Professor William A. Hachten has noted, endured great suffering. The American Civil Liberties Union reported, for example, that in one six-month period of 1940, "1,488 men, women and children in the sect were victims of mob violence in 355 communities in 44 states."[17] As Professor J. Edward Gerald has pointed out, the Jehovah's Witnesses made themselves unpopular with their refusal to salute the American flag; their contempt for most if not all organized religion, and with their denunciations of the Catholic Church. Likewise, their persistent street sales of literature and doorbell ringings for their cause often raised hackles among non-believers.[18]

The Jehovah's Witness cases are useful reminders that the right of freedom of expression belongs not only to media corporations but also to the people. Furthermore, the landmark case of Lovell v. City of Griffin is crucially important, as Professor Hachten has emphasized, because it explicitly gives constitutional protection to distribution of literature as well as to publication.[19]

Alma Lovell, a Jehovah's Witness, was convicted in a municipal court in Griffin, Ga., and sentenced to 50 days in jail when she refused to pay a $50 fine. Her crime? She had not received written permission from the City Manager of Griffin to distribute her religious tracts. The city ordinance provided:[20]

> That the practice of distributing, either by hand or otherwise, circulars, handbooks, advertising, or literature of any kind, whether said articles are being delivered free, or whether same are being sold, within the limits of the City of Griffin, without first obtaining permission from the City Manager of the City of Griffin, such practice shall be deemed a nuisance, and punishable as an offense against the City of Griffin.

Alma Lovell simply could not be bothered with such "technicalities." She regarded herself as a messenger sent by Jehovah, and believed that applying to the City Manager for permission would have "been 'an act of disobedience to His commandments.' " The Supreme Court, however, regarded the City of Griffin's ordinance as far more than a mere technicality. Speaking for an undivided court, Chief Justice Charles Evans Hughes denounced the ordinance:[21]

17 Hachten, op. cit., p. 73; see also Gerald, op. cit., pp. 136–137.

18 Gerald, p. 137.

19 303 U.S. 444, 58 S.Ct. 666 (1938); Hachten, p. 74.

20 Lovell v. City of Griffin, Ga., 303 U.S. 444, 447, 58 S.Ct. 666, 667 (1938).

21 303 U.S. 444, 451–452, 58 S.Ct. 666, 669 (1938). Mr. Justice Cardozo took no part in this decision.

We think that the ordinance is invalid on its face. Whatever the motive which induced its adoption, its character is such that it strikes at the very foundation of the freedom of the press by subjecting it to license and censorship. The struggle for the freedom of the press was primarily directed against the power of the licensor. It was against that power that John Milton directed his assault by his "Appeal for the Liberty of Unlicensed Printing." And the liberty of the press became initially a right to publish "without a license what formerly could be published only *with* one." While this freedom from previous restraint upon publication cannot be regarded as exhausting the guaranty of liberty, the prevention of that restraint was a leading purpose in the adoption of the constitutional provision. * * * Legislation of the type of the ordinance in question would restore the system of license and censorship in its baldest form.

The liberty of the press is not confined to newspapers and periodicals. It necessarily embraces pamphlets and leaflets. These indeed have been historic weapons in the defense of liberty, as the pamphlets of Thomas Paine and others in our own history abundantly attest. The press in its historic connotation comprehends every sort of publication which affords a vehicle of information and opinion. * * *

The ordinance cannot be saved because it relates to distribution and not to publication. "Liberty of circulating is as essential to that freedom as liberty of publishing; indeed, without circulation, the publication would be of little value." Ex parte Jackson, 96 U.S. 727, 733, 24 L.Ed. 877.

Since the ordinance of the City of Griffin was not limited to " 'literature' that is obscene or offensive to public morals or that advocates unlawful conduct," the ordinance could not be upheld.[22] In Schneider v. New Jersey, the Supreme Court reviewed four cities' ordinances. Three of these anti-littering ordinances in effect punished distributors should the recipient of a leaflet throw it to the ground. The Supreme Court held that such ordinances were unconstitutional.

[22] 303 U.S. 444, 451, 58 S.Ct. 666, 668 (1938).

Referring to its opinion in Lovell v. Griffin, the Court handed down this ruling in Schneider:[23]

> [W]hatever the motive [behind the ordinance at issue in Lovell v. City of Griffin], the ordinance was bad because it imposed penalties for the distribution of pamphlets, which had become historical weapons in the defense of liberty, by subjecting such distribution to license and censorship; and that the ordinance was void on its face, because it abridged the freedom of the press. Similarly in Hague v. C. I. O., 307 U.S. 496, 59 S.Ct. 954, 83 L.Ed. 1423 [1939], an ordinance was held void on its face because it provided for previous administrative censorship for the exercise of the right of speech and assembly in appropriate public places.
>
> The Los Angeles, the Milwaukee, and the Worcester ordinances under review do not purport to license distribution but all of them absolutely prohibit it in the streets, and, one of them, in other public places as well.
>
> *   *   *   *   *   *   *   *   *
>
> We are of opinion that the purpose to keep the streets clean and of good appearance is insufficient to justify an ordinance which prohibits a person rightfully on a public street from handing literature to one willing to receive it. Any burden imposed upon the city authorities in cleaning and caring for the streets as an indirect consequence of such distribution results from the constitutional protection of the freedom of speech and press. This constitutional protection does not deprive a city of all power to prevent street littering. There are obvious methods of preventing littering. Amongst these is the punishment of those who actually throw papers on the streets.

In this same decision, the Supreme Court also dealt with an ordinance of the Town of Irvington, New Jersey, which denied street distribution or house-to-house calls to anyone who did not have written permission from the chief of police. The Irvington ordinance also required that any person distributing circulars or seeking contributions had to restrict his canvassing to hours between 9 a. m. and 5 p. m. Also, the canvasser had to have with him a permit, including a photograph of himself, which had to be shown to a police officer or other person upon request.[24]

23 Schneider v. State of New Jersey (Town of Irvington), 308 U.S. 147, 161–162, 60 S.Ct. 146, 151 (1939).

24 308 U.S. 147, 157–158, 60 S.Ct. 146, 149 (1939).

In declaring the Irvington ordinance unconstitutional, Mr. Justice Owen Roberts wrote: [25]

> If it [the ordinance] covers the petitioner's activities [in making house-to-house calls], it equally applies to one who wishes to present his views on political, social or economic questions. The ordinance is not limited to those who canvass for private profit; nor is it merely the common type of ordinance requiring some form of registration or license of hawkers, or peddlers. It is not a general ordinance to prohibit trespassing. It bans unlicensed communication of any views or the advocacy of any cause from door to door, and permits canvassing only subject to the power of a police officer to determine, as a censor, what literature may be distributed from house to house and who may distribute it. The applicant must submit to that officer's judgment evidence as to his good character and as to the absence of fraud in the "project" he proposes to promote or the literature he intends to distribute, and must undergo a burdensome and inquisitorial examination, including photographing and fingerprinting. In the end, his liberty to communicate with the residents of the town at their homes depends upon the exercise of the officer's discretion.

> As said in Lovell v. City of Griffin, supra, pamphlets have proved most effective instruments in the dissemination of opinion. And perhaps the most effective way of bringing them to the notice of individuals is their distribution at the homes of the people. On this method of communication the ordinance imposes censorship, abuse of which engendered the struggle in England which eventuated in the establishment of the doctrine of the freedom of the press embodied in our Constitution. To require a censorship through license which makes impossible the free and unhampered distribution of pamphlets strikes at the very heart of the constitutional guarantees.

> Conceding that fraudulent appeals may be made in the name of charity and religion, we hold a municipality cannot, for this reason, require all who wish to disseminate ideas to present them first to police authorities for their consideration and approval, with a discretion in the police to say some ideas may, while others may not,

---

[25] 308 U.S. 147, 163–165, 60 S.Ct. 146, 152 (1939).

be carried to the homes of citizens; some persons may, while others may not, disseminate information from house to house. Frauds may be denounced as offenses and punished by law. Trespasses may similarly be forbidden. If it is said that these means are less efficient and convenient than bestowal of power on police authorities to decide what information may be disseminated from house to house, and who may impart the information the answer is that considerations of this sort do not empower a municipality to abridge freedom of speech and press. We are not to be taken as holding that commercial soliciting and canvassing may not be subjected to such regulation as the ordinance requires. Nor do we hold that the town may not fix reasonable hours when canvassing may be done by persons having such objects as the petitioner. Doubtless there are other features of such activities which may be regulated in the public interest without prior licensing or other invasion of constitutional liberty. We do hold, however, that the ordinance in question, as applied to the petitioner's conduct, is void, and she cannot be punished for acting without a permit.

Jehovah's Witnesses were to have many other days in court, defending the freedoms of religion, speech and press guaranteed by the First Amendment and protected from state encroachment by the Fourteenth Amendment. Even though the Court's 1938 Lovell v. Griffin decision had overturned a license tax, the case of Jones v. City of Opelika, Alabama, brought the issue back to the Court in slightly different form. In some respects, the Opelika ordinance looked quite innocuous: a $10 per annum license fee for engaging in business as a "Book Agent." [26] Although he gave some stirring judicial language to the concept of freedom of expression, Justice Stanley Reed, writing for the majority in this 5–4 decision, upheld the Opelika ordinance. Reed wrote: [27]

One man, with views contrary to the rest of his compatriots, is entitled to the privilege of expressing his ideas by speech or broadside to anyone willing to listen or read. Too many settled beliefs have in time been rejected to justify this generation in refusing a hearing to its own dissentients. But that hearing may be limited by action of the proper legislative body to times, places and methods for the enlightenment of the com-

[26] Jones v. City of Opelika, 316 U.S. 584, 586, 62 S.Ct. 1231, 1234 (1942).
[27] 316 U.S. 584, 594–595, 62 S.Ct. 1231, 1238 (1942).

munity which, in view of existing social and economic conditions, are not at odds with the preservation of peace and good order.

This means that the proponents of ideas cannot determine entirely for themselves the time and place and manner for the diffusion of knowledge or for their evangelism, any more than the civil authorities may hamper or suppress the public dissemination of facts and principles to the people. The ordinary requirements of civilized life compel this adjustment of interests.

In 1942, Justice Reed thus held that nothing in the collection of *nondiscriminatory* license fees—from persons selling Bibles, books, or papers—abridged freedom of worship, speech or press.[28] Justice Reed's opinion dismissed as unsubstantial the Jehovah's Witness complaint that the license tax of Opelika could be a dangerous weapon of censorship because the license could be revoked at will by city officials.[29]

Some eleven months later, however, after more Jehovah's Witness cases has been heard, the Supreme Court reversed itself and vacated its ruling that the Opelika ordinance was constitutional.[30] By this action, the Court adopted, as its majority position, the 1942 dissent in Jones v. Opelika written by Chief Justice Harlan Fiske Stone.[31] Stone's opinion held:

> The ordinance in the Opelika case should be held invalid * * * the requirement of a license for dissemination of ideas, when as here the license is revocable at will without cause and in the unrestrained discretion of administrative officers, is likewise an unconstitutional restraint on those freedoms.

Chief Justice Stone insisted that speech and religion are freedoms which hold a "preferred position" in the framework of constitutional values. He wrote:[32]

> The First Amendment is not confined to safeguarding freedom of speech and freedom of religion against discriminatory attempts to wipe them out. On the con-

[28] 316 U.S. 584, 598, 62 S.Ct. 1231, 1240 (1942).

[29] 316 U.S. 584, 599, 62 S.Ct. 1231, 1240 (1942).

[30] 319 U.S. 103, 63 S.Ct. 890 (1943). See also other Jehovah's Witness cases, Martin v. City of Struthers, 319 U.S. 141, 63 S.Ct. 862 (1943); Douglas v. City of Jeannette, 319 U.S. 157, 63 S.Ct. 882 (1943); Murdock v. Pennsylvania, 319 U.S. 105, 63 S.Ct. 870 (1943), all decided May 3, 1943.

[31] 316 U.S. 584, 600, 62 S.Ct. 1231, 1240–1241 (1942).

[32] 316 U.S. 584, 608, 62 S.Ct. 1231, 1244 (1942).

trary the Constitution, by virtue of the First and Fourteenth Amendments, has put those freedoms in a preferred position. Their commands are not restricted to cases where the protected privilege is sought out for attack. They extend at least to every form of taxation which, because it is a condition of the exercise of the privilege, is capable of being used to control or suppress it.

The victories of the Jehovah's Witnesses before the Supreme Court in cases such as Lovell v. City of Griffin and Jones v. City of Opelika are still worth savoring. A relatively small—and often unpopular—religious sect fought hard to defend freedoms guaranteed to all Americans. In so doing, Jehovah's Witnesses helped greatly to fend off ancient threats to the press revived in modern times: licensing and taxation.

Appendix A

ABBREVIATIONS

A.	Atlantic Reporter.
A.2d	Atlantic Reporter, Second Series.
A.C.	Appeal Cases.
A.L.R.	American Law Reports.
Aff.	Affirmed; affirming.
Ala.	Alabama;—Alabama Supreme Court Reports.
Am.Dec.	American Decisions.
Am.Jur.	American Jurisprudence, a legal encyclopedia.
Am.Rep.	American Reports.
Am.St.Rep.	American State Reports.
Ann.Cas.	American Annotated Cases.
App.D.C.	Court of Appeals, District of Columbia.
App.Div.	New York Supreme Court, Appellate Divisions, Reports.
Ariz.	Arizona; Arizona Supreme Court Reports.
Ark.	Arkansas; Arkansas Supreme Court Reports.
Bing.	Bingham, New Cases, Common Pleas (England).
C.D.	Copyright Decisions.
C.J.	Corpus Juris, a legal encyclopedia.
C.J.S.	Corpus Juris Secundum, a legal encyclopedia.
Cal.	California; California Supreme Court Reports.
Can.Sup.Ct.	Canada Supreme Court Reports.
Cert.	Certiorari, a legal writ by which a cause is removed from an inferior to a superior court.
C.F.R.	Code of Federal Regulations.
Colo.	Colorado; Colorado Supreme Court Reports.
Conn.	Connecticut; Connecticut Supreme Court of Errors Reports.
Cranch	Cranch, United States Supreme Court Reports; United States Circuit Court Reports.
Cush.	Cushing (Massachusetts).
D.C.App.	District of Columbia Court of Appeals Reports.
Dall, Dal.	Dallas, United States Supreme Court Reports; Pennsylvania Reports.
Del.	Delaware; Delaware Supreme Court Reports.
Edw.	Edward; refers to a particular king of England; which king of that name is indicated by the date; used to identify an act of Parliament.
Eng.Rep.	English Reports (reprint).
F.	Federal Reporter.
F.2d	Federal Reporter, Second Series.
F.C.C.	Federal Communications Commission Reports.
F.R.D.	Federal Rules Decisions.

F.Supp.	Federal Supplement.
Fed. Cases, Fed.Cas. **or F.Cas.**	Reports of United States Circuit and District Courts, 1789–1879.
Fla.	Florida; Florida Supreme Court Reports.
Ga.	Georgia; Georgia Supreme Court Reports.
Ga.App.	Georgia Appeals Reports.
How.St.Tr.	Howell's State Trials.
Hun	Hun, New York Supreme Court Reports.
Ibid.	Ibidem, the same, in the same volume, or on the same page.
Ill.	Illinois; Illinois Supreme Court Reports.
Ill.App.	Illinois Appellate Court Reports.
Ind.	Indiana; Indiana Supreme Court Reports.
Ind.App.	Indiana Appellate Court Reports.
Johns.Cas.	Johnson's Cases (New York).
K.B.	King's Bench Reports (England).
Kan.	Kansas; Kansas Supreme Court Reports.
Ky.	Kentucky; Kentucky Court of Appeals Reports.
L.J.	Law Journal (England).
L.R.Q.B.	Law Reports, Queen's Bench (England).
L.R.A.	Lawyers Reports Annotated.
L.R.A.,N.S.,	Lawyers Reports Annotated, New Series.
L.R.Ex.	Law Reports, Exchequer (England).
L.T.	The Law Times (England).
La.	Louisiana; Louisiana Supreme Court Reports.
La.Ann.	Louisiana Annual Reports.
Mass.	Massachusetts; Massachusetts Supreme Judicial Court Reports.
Md.	Maryland; Maryland Court of Appeals Reports.
Me.	Maine; Maine Supreme Judicial Court Reports.
Mich.	Michigan; Michigan Supreme Court Reports.
Minn.	Minnesota; Minnesota Supreme Court Reports.
Miss.	Mississippi; Mississippi Supreme Court Reports.
Mo.	Missouri; Missouri Supreme Court Reports.
Mo.App.	Missouri Appeals Reports.
Mont.	Montana; Montana Supreme Court Reports.
N.C.	North Carolina; North Carolina Supreme Court Reports.
N.D.	North Dakota; North Dakota Supreme Court Reports.
N.E.	Northeastern Reporter.
N.E.2d	Northeastern Reporter, Second Series.
N.H.	New Hampshire; New Hampshire Supreme Court Reports.
N.J.	New Jersey; New Jersey Court of Errors and Appeals Reports.
N.J.L.	New Jersey Law Reports.

N.M. ---------------- New Mexico; New Mexico Supreme Court Reports.

N.W. -------------- Northwestern Reporter.

N.W.2d ----------- Northwestern Reporter, Second Series.

N.Y. -------------- New York; New York Court of Appeals Reports.

N.Y.S. ------------ New York Supplement Reports.

Neb. -------------- Nebraska; Nebraska Supreme Court Reports.

Nev. -------------- Nevada; Nevada Supreme Court Reports.

Ohio App. --------- Ohio Appeals Reports.

Ohio St. ----------- Ohio State Reports.

Okl. --------------- Oklahoma; Oklahoma Supreme Court Reports.

Ops. -------------- Opinions, as of Attorney General of the United States, or a state.

Or., Ore., Oreg. ---- Oregon; Oregon Supreme Court Reports.

P. ---------------- Pacific Reporter.

P.2d -------------- Pacific Reporter, Second Series.

P.L. & R. ---------- Postal Laws and Regulations (1948 ed.)

Pa. --------------- Pennsylvania; Pennsylvania Supreme Court Reports; Pennsylvania State Reports.

Pa.D. & C. --------- Pennsylvania District and County Court Reports.

Pa.Super. ---------- Pennsylvania Superior Court Reports.

Paige ------------- Paige, New York Chancery Reports.

per se ------------ In itself or by itself; used in connection with words actionable *per se*, libelous *per se*, or slanderous *per se*.

Phila. (Pa.) ------- Philadelphia Reports.

Pick. ------------- Pickering, Massachusetts Reports.

Q.B. -------------- Queen's Bench.

R. ---------------- Rex king; regina, queen.

R.C.L. ------------ Ruling Case Law.

R.C.P. ------------ Rules of Civil Procedure.

R.I. --------------- Rhode Island; Rhode Island Supreme Court Reports.

R.R. -------------- Pike & Fischer Radio Regulations.

S.C. -------------- South Carolina; South Carolina Supreme Court Reports.

S.D. -------------- South Dakota; South Dakota Supreme Court Reports.

S.E. -------------- Southeastern Reporter.

S.E.2d ------------ Southeastern Reporter, Second Series.

S.W. -------------- Southwestern Reporter.

S.W.2d ------------ Southwestern Reporter, Second Series.

Sandf. ------------ Sandford, New York Superior Court Reports.

Sec. -------------- Section.

So. --------------- Southern Reporter.

So.2d ------------- Southern Reporter, Second Series.

Stark. ------------ Starkie, English Reports.

S.Ct. ------------- Supreme Court Reporter.

T.L.R. ------------ Times Law Reports (England).

Tenn. --------------- Tennessee; Tennessee Supreme Court Reports.

Tex. --------------- Texas; Texas Supreme Court (and the Commission of Appeals) Reports.

Tex.Civ.App. -------- Texas Civil Appeals Reports.

Tex.Cr.R. ----------- Texas Court of Criminal Appeals Reports.

U.S.C. -------------- United States Code.

U.S.C.A. ------------ United States Code Annotated.

U.S.P.Q. ------------ United States Patents Quarterly.

V. ----------------- Volume.

Va. ---------------- Virginia; Virginia Supreme Court of Appeals Reports.

Vt. ---------------- Vermont; Vermont Supreme Court Reports.

W.Va. ------------- West Virginia; West Virginia Supreme Court of Appeals Reports.

Wash. ------------- Washington; Washington Supreme Court Reports.

Wash.L.Rep. -------- Washington Law Reporter, Washington, D. C.

Whart. ------------ Wharton (Pa.)

Wheat. ------------ Wheaton (U.S.)

Wis. --------------- Wisconsin; Wisconsin Supreme Court Reports.

Wyo. -------------- Wyoming; Wyoming Supreme Court Reports.

Appendix B

SELECTED COURT AND PLEADING TERMS

Action

A formal legal demand of one's rights made in a court of law.

Action in personam

An action against a person, founded on a personal liability.

Action in rem

An action for a thing, or for the recovery of a thing possessed by another person.

Actionable per quod

Words not actionable in themselves may be defamatory when special damages are proved.

Actionable per se

Words that need no explanation in order to determine their defamatory effect.

Amicus Curiae

A friend of the court or one who interposes and volunteers information upon some matter of law.

Answer

The pleading of a defendant against whom a complaint has been filed.

Appeal

An application by an appellant to a higher court to change the order or judgment of the court below.

Appellant

The person or party appealing a decision or judgment to a higher court.

Appellee

The party against whom an appeal is taken.

Banc

Bench, or the place where a court sits. A "sitting in banc" means the meeting of all the judges of a court, as distinguished from the sitting of a single judge.

Bind over

To hold on bail for trial.

Brief

A written or printed document prepared by counsel to file in court, normally providing both facts and law in support of his case.

Cause of action

The particular facts on which an action is based.

Certiorari

A writ commanding judges of a lower court to transfer to a higher court records of a case so that judicial review may take place.

Change of venue

Removing a civil suit or criminal action from one county or district to another county or district for trial.

Code

A compilation or system of laws, arranged into chapters, and promulgated by legislative authority.

Common law

The law of the decided cases, derived from the judgments and decrees of courts. Also called "case law." Originally, meant law which derived its authority from the ancient usages or customs of England.

Complaint

The initial proceeding by a complainant, or plaintiff, in a civil action.

Contempt of court

Any act calculated to embarrass, hinder, or obstruct a court in the administration of justice, or calculated to lessen its dignity or authority. Contempts are of two kinds: direct and indirect. Direct contempts are those committed in the immediate presence of the court. Indirect contempts refer to the failure or refusal to obey a lawful order.

Courts of record

Those whose proceedings are permanently recorded, and which have the power to fine or imprison for contempt. Courts not of record are those of lesser authority whose proceedings are not permanently recorded.

Damages

Monetary compensation which may be recovered in court by a person who has suffered loss, detriment, or injury to his person, property, rights, or business, through the unlawful or negligent act of another person or party.

De Novo

Anew, afresh. A trial de novo is a retrial of a case.

Due Process

Law in its regular course of administration through the courts of justice. The guarantee of due process requires that every man have the protection of a fair trial.

Equity

That system of jurisprudence which gives relief when there is no full, complete and adequate remedy at law; based originally upon the custom of appealing to the King or chancellor when the formality of the common law did not give means for relief.

Estoppel

An admission which prevents a person from using evidence which proves or tends to prove the contrary.

Ex parte

By or concerning only one party. This implies an examination in the presence of one party in a proceeding and the absence of the opposing party.

Ex post facto

After the fact.

Habeas corpus

Latin for "you have the body." A writ issued to an officer holding a person in detention or under arrest to bring that person before a court to determine the legality of the detention.

Indictment

A written accusation of a crime prepared by a prosecuting attorney and presented for the consideration of a grand jury.

Information

A formal, written accusation of a crime prepared by a competent law officer of the government, such as a district or prosecuting attorney.

Injunction

A judicial order in equity directed against a person or organization directing that an act be performed or that the person or organization refrain from doing a particular act.

Judgment

The decision of a court of law.

Nelson & Teeter Mass Com.2d Ed. F.P.—42

Jury
> A group of a certain number of men, selected according to law and sworn to inquire into certain matters of fact, and to declare the truth from evidence brought before them. A *grand jury* hears complaints and accusations in criminal cases, and issues bills of indictment in cases where the jurors believe that there is enough evidence to bring a case to trial. A *petit jury* consists of 12 (or fewer) persons who hear the trial of a civil or criminal case.

Mandamus
> An extraordinary legal writ issued from a court to a corporation or its officers, to a public official, or to an inferior court commanding the doing of an act which the person, corporation, or lower court is under a duty to perform. A writ of mandamus may also demand the restoration of some right or privilege which is being denied to a complainant.

Motion to dismiss
> A formal application by a litigant or his counsel addressed to the court for an order to dismiss the case.

Nol pros, nolle prosequi
> A formal notification of unwillingness to prosecute which is entered upon the court record.

Obiter dictum; plural, obiter dicta
> An opinion by the court given aside from the main issue, or a saying by the way.

Plaintiff
> The person (including an organization or business) who initiates a legal action.

Pleading
> The process in which parties to a lawsuit or legal action alternately file with a court written statements of their contentions. By this process of statement and counterstatement, legal issues are framed and narrowed. These statements are often termed "pleadings."

Preliminary hearing, preliminary examination
> A person charged with a crime is given a preliminary examination or hearing before a magistrate or judge to determine whether there is sufficient evidence to hold that person for trial.

Reply
> The pleading of the plaintiff in response to the "answer" of the defendant.

Res adjudicata or res judicata

    A thing decided.

Respondent

    A party who gives an answer to a bill in equity; also, one who opposes a party who has taken a case to a higher court.

Stare decisis

    To stand by the decisions, or to maintain precedent. This legal doctrine holds that settled points of law will not be disturbed.

Venue

    The particular county, city, or geographical area in which a court with jurisdiction may hear and decide a case.

Verdict

    The decision of a jury as reported to the court.

Writ

    A legal instrument in the judicial process to enforce compliance with orders and sentences of a court.

Appendix C

BIBLIOGRAPHY

Amdur, Leon H., Copyright Law and Practice. New York, 1936.

Angoff, Charles, Handbook of Libel. New York, 1946.

Anonymous Note, "The Regulation of Advertising," Columbia Law Review Vol. 56:7 (Nov., 1956) pp. 1019–1111.

Anonymous Note, "Developments in the Law—Deceptive Advertising." Harvard Law Review Vol. 80:5 (March, 1967) pp. 1005–1163.

Barron, Jerome A., "Access to the Press: A New First Amendment Right," Harvard Law Review Vol. 80 (1967).

Barron, Jerome, Freedom of the Press for Whom? Bloomington, Ind., 1973.

Berns, Walter, Freedom, Virtue and the First Amendment. Baton Rouge, 1957.

Blackstone, William, Commentaries on the Law of England, Vol. IV, adapted by Robert Malcolm Kerr, Boston, 1952.

Bower, George Spencer, A Code of the Law of Actionable Defamation. London, 1923.

Bowker, Richard Rogers, Copyright, Its History and Its Law. Boston & New York, 1912.

Burdick, Francis M., The Law of Torts, Albany, New York, 1926.

Button, Wilfred Alan, Principles of the Law of Libel and Slander. London, 1935.

Chafee, Zechariah, Jr., Freedom of Speech. New York, 1920.

Chafee, Zechariah, Jr. Free Speech in the United States. Boston, 1941.

Chafee, Zechariah, Jr., Government and Mass Communications, 2 vols. Chicago, 1947.

Cooley, Thomas M., A Treatise on the Law of Torts. Chicago, 1930.

Cooley, Thomas M., Constitutional Limitations (8th ed.) Boston, 1927.

Cooper, Thomas, The Law of Libel and the Liberty of the Press. New York, 1830.

Devol, Kenneth S., Mass Media and the Supreme Court. New York, 1971.

Drone, Eaton S., A Treatise on the Law of Property in Intellectual Productions in Great Britain and the United States. Boston, 1879.

660

Duniway, Clyde Augustus, The Development of Freedom of the Press in Massachusetts. Cambridge, 1906.

Emerson, Thomas I., The System of Freedom of Expression. New York, 1970. (Elaborates *Toward a General Theory*)

Emerson, Thomas I., David Haber, and Norman Dorsen, Political and Civil Rights in the United States. 2 vols. Boston, 1967.

Emery, Walter B., Broadcasting and Government: Responsibilities and Regulations. East Lansing, Mich., 1961.

Ernst, Morris L., The First Freedom. New York, 1946.

Ernst, Morris L. and Alexander Lindey. The Censor Marches On. New York, 1946.

Folkard, Henry C., The Law of Slander and Libel (7th ed.) London, 1908.

Fox, Sir John C., The History of Contempt of Court. Oxford, 1927.

Fraser, Sir Hugh, Libel and Slander (7th ed.) London, 1936.

Gatley, Clement, Libel and Slander in Civil Action. London, 1938.

Gerald J. Edward, The Press and the Constitution, 1931–1947. Minneapolis, 1948.

Gillmor, Donald M., Free Press and Fair Trial. Washington, D. C., 1966.

Gillmor, Donald M., and Jerome Barron, Mass Communication Law. St. Paul, Minn., 1969.

Goldfarb, Ronald L., The Contempt Power. New York, 1963.

Griswold, Erwin N., The Fifth Amendment Today. Cambridge, 1955.

Hachten, William A., The Supreme Court on Freedom of the Press: Decisions and Dissents. Ames, Iowa, 1968.

Haight, Anne Lyon, Banned Books (rev. 2d ed.). New York, 1955.

Hanson, Arthur B., Libel and Related Torts, 2 vols. New York, 1969.

Harper, Fowler V. and James Fleming, Jr., The Law of Torts (3 vols.) Boston, 1956.

Head, Sydney W., Broadcasting in America. Boston, 1956.

Hocking, William E., Freedom of the Press. Chicago, 1947.

Hudon, Edward G., Freedom of Speech and Press in America. Washington, 1963.

Hyde, H. Montgomery, ed., Privacy and the Press. London, 1947.

Jolliffe, John, The Constitutional History of Medieval England (2d ed.) London, 1947.

Kaplan, Benjamin, and Ralph S. Brown, Jr., Cases on Copyright. Brooklyn, 1960.

Keir, David, The Constitutional History of Modern Britain. London, 1938.

Kinsley, Philip, Liberty and the Press. Chicago, 1944.

Konvitz, Milton R., First Amendment Freedoms. Ithaca, 1963.

Ladas, Stephen Pericles, The International Protection of Literary and Artistic Property. New York, 1938.

Levy, Leonard W., ed., Freedom of the Press from Zenger to Jefferson. Indianapolis, 1966.

Levy, Leonard W., Legacy of Suppression. Cambridge, 1960.

Lockhart, William B., and Robert C. McClure, "Censorship of Obscenity: The Developing Constitutional Standards," Minnesota Law Review Vol. 45:1 (Nov., 1960) pp. 5–121.

Lockhart, William B., and Robert C. McClure, "Literature, The Law of Obscenity, and the Constitution," Minnesota Law Review Vol. 38:4 (March, 1954).

McCormick, Robert R., The Freedom of the Press. New York, 1936.

May, T. E., Constitutional History of England. New York, 1872.

Meiklejohn, Alexander, Free Speech and Its Relation to Self Government. New York, 1948.

Meiklejohn, Alexander, Political Freedom: The Constitutional Power of the People. New York, 1960.

Michigan Law School. Communications Media. Ann Arbor, 1954.

Mock, Frank R., Censorship, 1917. Princeton, N. J., 1941.

Nelson, Harold L., ed., Freedom of the Press from Hamilton to the Warren Court. Indianapolis, 1967.

Nelson, Harold L., Libel in News of Congressional Investigating Committees. Minneapolis, 1961.

Newell, Martin L., The Law of Slander and Libel in Civil & Criminal Cases. Chicago, 1924.

Nicholson, Margaret, A Manual of Copyright Practice. New York, 1945.

Nimmer, Melville B., Copyright. St. Paul, 1971.

Odgers, W. Blake, A Digest of the Law of Libel and Slander (6th ed.). London, 1929.

Paterson, James, Liberty of Press, Speech and Public Worship. London, 1880.

Patterson, Giles J., Free Speech and a Free Press. Boston, 1939.

Paul, James C. N., and Murray L. Schwartz, Federal Censorship: Obscenity in the Mail. New York, 1961.

Pember, Don R., Privacy and the Press. Seattle, 1972.

Phelps, Robert H., and E. Douglas Hamilton, Libel. New York, 1966.

Pilpel, Harriet and Theodora Zavin, Rights and Writers. New York, 1960.

Prosser, William L., The Law of Torts. 4th ed., St. Paul, 1971.

Rembar, Charles, The End of Obscenity. New York, 1968.

Rourke, Francis E., Secrecy and Publicity. Baltimore, 1961.

St. John-Stevas, Norman, Obscenity and the Law. London, 1956.

Schwartz, Louis B., Free Enterprise and Economic Organization. Brooklyn, 1952.

Seelman, Ernest P., The Law of Libel and Slander in the State of New York. New York, 1941.

Seldes, George, Freedom of the Press. Cleveland, 1935.

Shapiro, Martin, Freedom of Speech: The Supreme Court and Judicial Review. Engelwood Cliffs, N. J., 1966.

Siebert, Fredrick S., Freedom of the Press in England, 1476–1776. Urbana, Ill. 1952.

Simon, Morton J., Public Relations Law. New York, 1969.

Smith, James Morton, Freedom's Fetters: The Alien and Sedition Laws and American Civil Liberties, Ithaca, 1956.

Solberg, Thorvald, Copyright Enactments of the United States, 1783–1906. Washington, 1906.

Solberg, Thorvald, Copyright in Congress, 1789–1904. Washington, 1904.

Stansbury, Arthur J., Report of the Trial of James H. Peck. Boston, 1833.

Starkie, Thomas, The Law of Slander, Libel, Scandalum Magnatum and False Rumors, with the Practise and Pleadings. London, 1813; 4th ed. by Henry C. Folkard, with notes and references to American Cases by Horace G. Wood. New York, 1877.

Sullivan, Harold W., Contempts by Publication. New Haven, 1940.

Swindler, William F., Problems of Law in Journalism. New York, 1955.

Taswell-Langmead, T. P., English Constitutional History (9th ed.) London, 1929.

Thayer, Frank, Legal Control of the Press, 4th ed. Brooklyn, N. Y., 1962.

Warren, Samuel D. and Louis D. Brandeis, "The Right of Privacy," Harvard Law Review, Vol. 4 (1890).

Wittenberg, Philip, Dangerous Words. New York, 1947.

Wittenberg, Philip, The Law of Literary Property. New York, 1957.

Wolff, Robert Paul, Barrington Moore and Herbert Marcuse, A Critique of Pure Tolerance. Boston, 1965.

Wortman, Tunis, Treatise Concerning Political Enquiry, and the Liberty of the Press. New York, 1800.

Yankwich, Leon R., It's Libel or Contempt if You Print It. Los Angeles, 1950.

Additional Reference Material

American Digest System, Decennial Digests, valuable for lists of cases and points adjudicated.

American Jurisprudence, a legal encyclopedia.

Annotated Report System, selected reports and annotations, together with summaries of arguments of counsel.

Compilation of Laws Affecting Publications, such as Wisconsin Laws Affecting Newspapers, published by the Wisconsin Daily Newspaper League. Refer to managers of various state press associations.

Corpus Juris, a legal encyclopedia. See title desired.

Corpus Juris Secundum, a legal encyclopedia.

Law Dictionaries. Black's Law Dictionary, Ballentine's Law Dictionary, Bouvier's Law Dictionary, and the Cyclopedic Law Dictionary are standard law dictionaries.

Law Reviews. Among the outstanding law reviews published under the direction of law schools are Columbia Law Review, Cornell Law Quarterly, Harvard Law Review, Illinois Law Review, Michigan Law Review, Wisconsin Law Review, and Yale Law Journal.

National Reporter System, giving reports of cases in the various jurisdictions, as the Atlantic Reporter, the Northeastern Reporter, the Northwestern Reporter, the Pacific Reporter, the Southeastern Reporter, the Southern Reporter, the Southwestern Reporter, the Federal Reporter, the Supreme Court Reporter, and the New York Supplement.

Restatement of the Law of Torts, covering libel and privacy. Published by the American Law Institute, Philadelphia.

Ruling Case Law, a legal encyclopedia.

Words and Phrases, a legal encyclopedia based on definitions of terms as used in statutes and by the courts.

Appendix D

LIBEL INSURANCE*

By

Richard A. Ek **

Publishers, broadcasters, motion picture companies and producers, advertisers, and advertising agencies run the occupational risk that some element of their product will involve them in a lawsuit. To guard against this threat, there exists what is known as libel insurance. Actually, this insurance also covers slander, invasion of privacy, unfair competition, piracy, plagiarism, and copyright infringement. Not all media have equal need for coverage on all these torts, but the libel insurance policies for the several media write them as a blanket inclusion. Except for appropriate comment on inter-relationships, discussion here will center on libel as it applies primarily to the print and broadcast news media because most of the message traffic runs there.

It is of initial interest that during the earlier free-swinging days of American journalism, nobody worried about trying to insure himself against the rash of libel suits that plagued every publisher willing to print what he believed. Of course, the publisher of yore stood at least as much chance of receiving a punch in the nose from the target of his barbs as he did notice that a lawsuit had been filed against him. Often publishers ran marginal operations which made them poor prospects for collection even if judgments were entered against them, a hazard that tended to diminish as courts became more liberal and exposes of rampant corruption defeated suits.[1]

* Copyright © Richard A. Ek, 1973. The author, Richard A. Ek, is professor in and former chairman of the Mass Communications Department at California State University, Chico. He received his Ph.D. in Communications in 1964 from the University of Southern California.

(Author's note—The following discussion is a generalized, simplified treatment of a complex subject, and it assumes a rudimentary knowledge of libel law. The material was gathered directly from underwriting companies and several leading attorneys specializing in this type of litigation.)

** The author is particularly indebted for assistance to: Carleton Eldridge of the firm of Coudert Brothers in New York City; Arthur B. Hanson of the Mutual Insurance Company Limited; Charles Kenady of the firm of Cooper, White, and Cooper in San Francisco; Anthony Liebig of the firm of Lillick, McHose, Wheat, Adams, and Charles in Los Angeles; Thomas Mackin of the Seaboard Surety Company; Garrett Redmond of the Firemen's Fund American; and Larry Worrall of the Employers Reinsurance Corporation.

1 Frank Luther Mott, American Journalism (New York: The Macmillan Company, 1962, 3rd ed.), particularly pp. 147, 451, 508–509.

Just what force, or coalescing of forces, brought about the birth of libel insurance in the 1930's remains a matter for conjecture. Both the publishing and insurance industries had developed early in this century to the point where a business relationship could be mutually beneficial. The larger newspaper and magazine enterprises had become business institutions that showed interest in controlling risks, and aggressive insurance companies with growing resources showed a readiness to underwrite publishing risks because they believed money could be made on policy premiums. Further, network radio with its uncontrolled ad-lib dangers and the highly realistic talking motion pictures came along during this time, and they in turn stimulated a heavy volume of innovative advertising. The time was ripe for a protective arrangement.

The insurance that has evolved during the brief intervening decades represents much trial and error effort, and policy terms are under constant review by insurer and insured. Unlike maritime or life insurance, for example, libel coverage has a comparatively short history, and there hasn't been enough time for case examples to build an extensive body of law that can interpret every nuance of all policy provisions. That fact, coupled with intense recent activity in the First Amendment field, produces a changing environment where the underwriting companies and the media must continue to feel their way. Similarly, a generalized description of the insurance scene at any given point in time can at best be sketchy, superficial, and temporarily accurate.

Insurance Underwriters

A great deal of the publisher's and broadcaster's liability insurance is written by three domestic firms.[2] They are major insurance companies that conduct multiple-line businesses and consider libel insurance a high-risk,[3] specialty sideline that is not particularly profitable. In spite of energetic sales efforts through brokers,[4] the companies do not generate a corresponding increase in business volume. They hesitate to assign a

[2] Although quite a number of companies are listed in such key insurance literature as Agent's and Buyer's Guide (26th edition, Cincinnati: Compiled by The Fire, Casualty & Surety Bulletins, The National Underwriting Company, 1973) and The Insurance Market Place (9th edition, Indianapolis: The Rough Notes Co., Inc.) as participating in such coverage, the bulk of the libel policy business is channeled by brokers to the three specializing companies described here.

[3] This type of insurance carries high risk classification because losses may be catastrophic. In addition, major media operations are virtually certain to run into lawsuits periodically, a fact that is not necessarily true of, say, fire insurance because a large concern may never have a fire.

[4] The underwriters themselves do not canvass the field except through direct mail. Independent brokers make the actual media contact and then go to the insurer on behalf of the applicant.

cause-and-effect relationship, but the landmark case of New York Times v. Sullivan [5] in 1964 and related cases that have since extended its free speech protection to the media may well have convinced some budget-minded media operators that libel protection is an unnecessary expense.

Each of the underwriters began with a particular medium but came to write other outlets because of policyholder subsidiary ownerships that cut across the lines of print, broadcast, and film. Thus each used a different door, but all ended up in the same business chamber.

The Fireman's Fund American, with headquarters in San Francisco, found that its West Coast location led it into early specialty with the motion picture industry. Movie companies at first insured only their stars and casts, but they later painfully came to realize the existence of libel danger when theater patrons often thought they saw themselves or someone they knew in the supposedly fictional characters so vividly dramatized on the living screen.[6] The Fund does not insure book publishers but does have such contract through movies based on book rights and their extended plots. In addition to print and broadcast coverage, the Fund undertakes advertising liability.

The Employers Reinsurance Corporation, with headquarters in Kansas City, Mo., pioneered newspaper underwriting—and possibly the libel insurance field in the United States—in 1930 and still specializes in that type of business, although now it includes magazines and books. Located as it is in the Midwest, it received encouragement from William Allen White, the legendary editor of the *Emporia Gazette,* to write such insurance as a need of the maturing institutional press as opposed to the earlier party or personal press.[7]

---

[5] 376 U.S. 254, 84 S.Ct. 710 (1964).

[6] Suits came, of course, despite the tactical disclaimer in film title and credit leaders that any resemblance between persons living or dead was purely coincidental.

[7] White wrote a letter that read as follows:

Gentlemen: September 5, 1930

I have your letter and have talked to your Representative, Mr. Warner A. Cory, about newspaper insurance against libel. The idea is good; being new it must be worked out carefully. But certainly newspapers should have insurance against libel as the publishers have insurance against fire or tornado or any other devastating agency.

In this modern day the newspaper business is not so liable to damage for libel arising out of newspaper controversies or political feuds as it is through those damaging misstatements which must necessarily arise when one has to make quick decisions in the newspaper business upon sometimes inadequate facts, or when one's reporters in the haste to avoid the deadline are unable to go carefully into all the implications of any fact which they may

The Seaboard Surety Company, with headquarters in New York City, formed early post-World War II liaison with advertisers and advertising agencies, radio networks, and book publishers concentrated on the East Coast. It specialized in advertising, particularly,[8] and broadcasting, including motion pictures produced expressly for television, but continues to underwrite publishing houses. Seaboard's coverage centers on major outlets in the major cities.

In addition to the above domestic companies, there are two foreign underwriters. The Mutual Insurance Company Limited of Hamilton, Bermuda began offering group libel coverage in 1963 to member daily newspapers of the American Newspaper Publishers Association, and any weekly, bi-weekly, or tri-weekly newspaper they might own or control. This exclusive coverage grew as an offshoot of the strike insurance program set up earlier for members of the A.N.P.A. As an unregulated, foreign-based operation dealing only with newspapers on a mail order basis, it can slash costs and impose relatively few restrictions in its policies.

The second foreign underwriter is Lloyd's of London. The famous Lloyd's international operation has the popular reputation of being willing to insure anything for anyone anywhere for the right premium price. This widely accepted notion is not entirely correct, but it "is more nearly correct of Lloyd's underwriters than of any other insurer in the world."[9] In point of number of

deal with. This danger is real and is becoming more and more acute every day. Insurance against that should be a part of every man's budget.

I welcome your company's entrance into this field. If I can help you in any way, let me know how.

Sincerely yours,
W. A. White

[8] It writes nearly all of the nation's top 45 advertising agencies. Agencies and their client advertisers often buy insurance from the same company due to the difficulty in establishing the party responsible for offending material. This practice avoids recovery tensions between insurance companies. Agency-client problems arise because an advertisement represents a joint venture. The advertiser supplies the basic material, but the agency supplies music, animation, pictures and other such "gloss" needed to finish the product. When the line of who supplied what actionable material under whose prompting becomes blurred, the fragile agency-client relationship may become strained. Agencies, especially, operate on good will, and that's why such a high percentage of the bigger operations buy insurance protection.

[9] The statement is made every year in "Lloyd's Diary", printed and issued annually by the Corporation of Lloyd's, London, England. For historical insights into the intriguing operation at Lloyd's, dating to the seventeenth century, see Charles Wright, A History of Lloyd's (London: Macmillan and Company, 1927). Lloyd's itself does not sell policies but operates as an international syndicated insurance market. Some 260 individual syndicates of varying sizes accept insurance from 250 firms of Lloyd's brokers on behalf of their insurance connections in all parts of the world. It is very difficult

policies, Lloyd's is not a strong contender in the American market, but the policies outstanding are substantial ones in network broadcasting, motion picture production, and advertising.

It should be remembered that Lloyd's does not generally underwrite libel protection as a distinct class of insurance or issue a standard policy for it. The rule with Lloyd's is that there is no rule, and a policy written from among the syndicates of Lloyd's underwriters may or may not occur again, depending upon given circumstances. Protection for libel and related torts is likely to be found in a policy offering broader coverage for a number of things.

Lloyd's, which came into the field in the late 1950's, is somewhat restricted because of state "majority of market" rules discouraging purchase of insurance from a foreign company if the same class of insurance is available from a domestic company. Although these rules lack ironclad force because they are loosely written, Lloyd's is technically supposed to sell only to buyers who can't obtain insurance inside the United States. Such buyers may pose risk hazards, and their premium rate with Lloyd's would reflect that risk.

Lloyd's also reinsures insurance companies—as does Employers Reinsurance Corporation; such reinsurance means a United States company may write a libel insurance policy, and Lloyd's then takes over a portion of the risk. Employers Reinsurance also follows this share-the-risk practice on other lines but sells libel insurance directly.

The Insurance Buyers

Libel coverage obviously is an exotic type of insurance offered to a relatively small, specialized pool of potential buyers. No one knows exactly how much of the total mass media field is

to trace the form and amount of libel coverage Lloyd's clears because each syndicate underwriter only writes a portion of a risk that binds his particular group.

It is of related interest that libel settlement abroad is somewhat a matter of face-saving, and settlements are comparatively low. As opposed to practice in the United States, however, the prevailing party in a libel action in England recovers as his "costs" his own counsel fees, investigation expense, etc., which can turn a nominal recovery into a heavy burden for the losing (paying) party. Corrections and retractions play prominently with the injured party taking token money mostly as a public gesture. Since constitutionally guaranteed First Amendment rights are an American phenomenon, the foreign press makes little fanfare over who can say what; corrections and public apology often redress the personal insult of libel. In Great Britain, the Newspaper Society writes libel insurance for about 40 per cent of the newspaper press. The Society reports (March 14, 1972) that 30 per cent of the remaining newspapers carry insurance through Lloyd's, and the remaining 30 per cent are uninsured.

blanketed, but estimates range around the 50 per cent mark. Newspapers and broadcast stations carry the bulk of the policies, of course, with newspapers buying because they tend to deal in breadth and depth with hot public issues. Radio and television fulfills not only the news function—in less depth, to be sure—but also the entertainment function with its hazards of satire, ad-lib, the probing camera, and legal use of creative property. All the networks and most big-city broadcasters and publishers carry some type of policy. All significant motion picture operations supplying either straight production budget or front money to independents use insurance. About 80 per cent of the major advertising agencies carry policies, and most big advertisers buy some protection.

Non-subscribers either don't know about insurance or for one reason or another don't think they need it. A small, rural "coffee pot" radio station operator using wire service news for rip-and-read reporting probably neither knows nor cares, and he is reasonably safe with the teletype copy provided he doesn't do any creative editing. Some media giants such as *The New York Times* prefer to go uninsured because they retain large staffs of specialized legal talent to serve their many needs, libel considerations being only one. However, other large media operations carry libel insurance in spite of the fact that they retain large legal staffs. Others who think they don't need insurance are those presenting only bland material that affords little chance of offending anyone, financially marginal operators who think libel insurance costs too much, and the group already referred to that mistakenly believes no libel threat exists in the wake of recent Supreme Court rulings extending press freedom.

Additionally, there are media outlets unable to buy insurance, at least through the United States underwriters. Although a few larger university newspapers carry policies, for example, most student media would not qualify because they produce with untrained and sometimes unpredictable staffs who pose prohibitive risk potential.[10] Somewhat similarly, trade maga-

---

[10] High school newspapers and yearbooks often present problems, particularly when gossip columns or April Fool jokes backfire. These publications can be covered if a specific provision naming them is written into the district's general liability policy. Usually such a provision must be added to the policy and may not win approval by all insurance companies. Broadcasters and publishers may find a comparable situation with the comprehensive general liability policies they can buy from almost any company to cover anything from problems in the parking lot to someone who slips on the foyer rug. A personal injury addition for libel and related torts may be tacked onto these everyday policies to cover acts of employees. However, most often this coverage excludes what is printed or broadcast. For example, a reporter may slander a news source while trying to get a story. That slander would be

zines, newspapers, or other publications edited by organization people rather than professional journalists usually classify as unacceptable risks as do those publications catering to underground or special interest audiences with an axe to grind. Some community antenna television franchise holders also find themselves beyond the pale in no-insurance land because their local agreements provide for a certain number of public access channels. These carriers find it difficult to legally censor material prior to presentation, yet they run an undeniable risk with the unpredictable messages of extremist groups.[11]

All such excluded enterprises don't qualify under what can best be described as the "errors and omissions" concept. This concept holds that the general, overground mass consumption media in the United States are run by professionals who employ their polished skills within a well organized structure. They should rarely make mistakes. When they do, their mistakes can be classified as either errors or omissions caused primarily by deadline pressures. Mass circulation magazines—with the exception of weekly news magazines—deal not so much with hot but with cold information, so to speak, in that they enjoy ample time for careful preparation. When they err, the situation may represent management misjudgment. The same reasoning applies to books and motion pictures and to a lesser extent to the painstakingly prepared accounts of advertising agencies.

Unfortunately, hard-hitting or crusading media may qualify from point of view of highly skilled staff operating in a tightly organized manner but still fail in bids to buy coverage because they often pose unacceptably high risks. Their transgressions frequently fall not within the errors and omissions concept but within the realm of deliberate action on dangerous ground. The appraising insurance eye understandably looks upon muckraking and dirtdigging as the potential not for possible but for probable trouble. Those media, especially newspapers and magazines, that conduct worthwhile but dangerous editorial campaigns will

covered under the personal injury addition. But what is published or broadcast as a result of the reporter's aggressive efforts would usually require coverage under a separate publisher's or broadcaster's liability policy.

11 Congressional action on a total CATV control package might in some way solve this problem, as well as unravel the CATV copyright fee tangle. The alternative on the public access libel situation could well be some future companion case for the 1959 landmark case of Farmers Educational & Cooperative Union of America v. WDAY, Inc., 360 U.S. 525, 79 S.Ct. 1302 (1959) which freed broadcasters from the threat of libel action over material they had to carry under the equal time provisions of the Federal Communications Act.

It is of tangential interest that regular "hot line" radio programs can play safe with both insurability and qualified privilege by employing a playback device.

usually find they must pick up most of the expenses from the trouble they start.[12]

Any applicant for libel insurance can expect investigation when he applies. His past in some ways becomes prologue as the underwriters comb over old copy, audio tapes, video tapes, records, files, etc. to determine editorial policy and how business is conducted. The examiners show particular interest in the chain of command and its procedures in clearing material for public presentation. Key personnel come under close scrutiny for job experience and qualification because it is under their hands that the final product takes shape. With magazines, for example, the editor is of crucial importance. Past and pending lawsuits against the applicant and their current standing or disposition provide a significant item of record in the screening process that decides risk potential.

Terminology

Libel insurance operates under principles commonly found in other liability coverage. The insured pays for his protection through a yearly premium. His policy specifies a liability limit, which is the top dollar amount the insurance company pays off for court-awarded damages.[13] The policy often specifies a deductible figure, which is the amount the insured must pay before the insurer comes to his aid. For the sake of illustration, suppose a broadcaster with a $5,000 pure loss deductible and $50,000 liability limit policy suffered a $60,000 court judgment. The broadcaster would pay the $5,000 deductible amount before his insurance paid the next $45,000 up to the policy liability limit; then the insured would need another $10,000 from his own pocket or some loaning source to pay off the remainder needed to satisfy the $60,000 judgment. To complicate but complete the illustration, the policy might include a second deductible figure applying to the cost of legal defense. If the defense deductible were for $5,000, and defense costs totaled $10,000, the insured would have to find yet another $5,000 to be clear of obligation. Sometimes policies are written so that expenses incurred in defending against any lawsuits filed can either be included in the loss deductible or as a separate deductible. Obviously this loss and/or defense provision can be advantageous to the insured, depending on disposition of the case. Also, policies may be written with no deductibles because the insured wants to be free of

[12] The Mutual Insurance Company, which includes only newspapers under its protective mantle, is tolerant of bold editorial policy.

[13] The Insurance companies will not pay fines or penalties arising out of a libel action.

any financial responsibility. Deductibles range all the way from $1,000 in the smaller media up to $200,000 or even more on metropolitan operations. An applicant may request a high deductible for reasons of his own—such as an exchange for his right to hire outside counsel of his own choice—or the insurance company may impose one upon him as a high risk candidate. In general, low deductibles carry high premiums and vice-versa.

The limit of liability, like the deductible, is a matter of reasoned choice between the insured and the insurer. Limits range from a low of $25,000 to a high of $3,000,000. The most frequently found amount is between $50,000 and $100,000, but this range is not as much an indicator of true danger as it is representative of a popular package that scales premium cost against the variables of business health (rate card, circulation, or gross business), deductible, and limit of liability.

One further dimension of liability limit requires explanation. The liability figure represents the amount that cannot be exceeded during the calendar year before the policy comes up for renewal. Under some policies, the total amount may be exhausted early through the aggregate stacking of claims related to one libelous occurrence or item. In others, the policy provides more coverage money in that each separate claim relating to the same liberlous occurrence carries its own full liability limit of protection. Suppose for a moment that a business magazine in one article libeled the president of a corporation as a business thief and at the same time said he had maneuvered the board of directors into a course of action that violated the anti-trust laws. From this one article, or occurrence, two suits, or claims, could result: one from the president who was called a thief and one from the corporation that was called an anti-trust lawbreaker. The aggregate policy would lump *both* claims together under the specified policy limit, while the non-aggregate policy would separate the claims with *each* protected to the full policy limit.

The above simplification for the sake of illustration makes the advantage of a non-aggregate policy appear obvious, but insurance forms differ. Actually, it is common to find a single occurrence limit along with a multiple occurrence limit in the form of, say, $100,000/$300,000. The first limit would be applicable to one offense or offending item, regardless of the number of times it was repeated by other media picking it up or the number of claimants. Above this figure is the second or aggregate limit that can be claimed in any one year.

Premium rates depend on the type of media being insured. Unfortunately, libel insurance does not lend itself readily to actuarial description; although all the underwriters publish scaled rate tables, it should be borne in mind that the tables frequently serve as a departure point for negotiation based on investigation by which premiums are set. A brief look at general guidelines for premiums may be helpful.

Total verified circulation provides the main determinant for newspapers, periodicals, and books. The larger the circulation, of course, the higher the premium.[14] With local station broadcasters, the premium varies by scale against the highest hourly one-time Class "A" advertising rate charged by the individual applicant station. Advertising agencies pay according to gross annual billing, while the index for advertisers is total annual advertising expenditure. Motion pictures present a varied case with audience size and subject being the important factors.[15]

Premium costs within the broad spectrum of media vary so widely that representative examples are elusive. Premiums also may not remain static. At the close of the policy year, the insured's performance and legal troubles come under review for possible premium re-negotiation or even coverage severance at the wish of one or both parties. Again, premiums vary widely and depend primarily on provisions made for deductible, defense, and maximum liability, and each insurance candidate represents a risk that is specifically rated.

At this point it will be useful to deal with the concept of the supplemental policy. A standard policy protects the insured in his regular operations but not in any unusual or sideline operations. Suppose a large regional television station or group owner carrying standard coverage on what it broadcasts from its own transmitter, decides to produce original program material for broadcast and subsequent purchase and viewing by other stations. This creative syndication sideline calls for a separate tailor-made policy called a producer's or syndicator's policy; it

[14] The premium for books is based on a flat circulation rate per million sales, depending on the type of book. Biography, autobiography, and professional texts cost the most to insure with novels, plays, and poetry running about half as much.

[15] Select audience films shown with no expectation of financial return pay a flat rate. Feature films with fictional plots intended for profitable theater distribution to general audiences carry a negotiated premium, and premium cost rises slightly if exhibition includes an expanded audience via television. Rates vary on factual, or non-fiction, films because each situation is different. Setting the rate depends primarily on portrayal of the central character and his/her supporting cast. Since the characters are "real," collaboration by all parties with a part in story line, producing and direction, and acting to portray the character(s)—including whether living or dead—is important in determining risk and rate.

comes with a tailor-made premium price tag to match and supplements the standard broadcaster policy.

Networks also carry specially designed multiple-situation policies that are unique. These blanket policies are drawn to suit the diversification of network overall business operations. As the idea implies, the primary object of customized policies is to cover a lot of peculiar risks over a very wide variety of situations.

A great many standard policies have what is called a "save and hold harmless" provision. This provision protects the contractual agreement made by the insured to hold the licensee-user blameless and indemnify him from legal responsibility for problems arising from use of the insured's product. If our large example television station earlier referred to produced a news or feature story on film that was of national interest, it would need to give a hold harmless agreement to cover distribution and subsequent broadcast risks. The "buyer" would insist on the agreement so that if the film libeled anyone, invaded anyone's privacy, or made unauthorized use of copyrighted material, the producer station rather than the "buyer" or the program sponsor would accept ultimate legal responsibility.

To illustrate differently, if an author sells a novel to a publisher, he would at the same time agree to hold the publisher harmless should a lawsuit develop because the author turns out not to be the real author or an evil "fictional" character turns out to be real, etc. Later the hardback publisher might contract with a paperback publisher and sign a hold harmless agreement on the transfer of publishing rights. To extend the illustration, the paperback publisher would require hold harmless agreements on illustrative material he planned to include in the paperback version as well as on agency handling of promotional advertising. All those "saving" others would probably in turn be saved by insurance. Further ramifications could be added, but the complexities possible in save and hold harmless agreements should already be clear.

Defense and Settlement

Most libel claims end up settled within the deductible amount. Many complaints that are filed do not constitute a good cause of action, but nobody can keep an irate party from suing, regardless of the merits. The trouble is that the party named in the complaint must defend against it or be judged in default. Defending against a groundless suit not only costs money but poses a continuing source of anxiety and irritation pending disposition. Many plaintiffs (injured party) rely on this gadfly element to bring the defendant (media) to terms, even if the settlement is to be a small one. Neither insurance companies nor media pay off on groundless complaints simply because to do so runs counter to principle, but they may negotiate settlement of small nuisance claims where investigation reveals the complaint has some merit.[16] Such a course of action can be cheaper in the long run than going to court, depending upon the case.

Serious cases often conclude with defense costs running higher than the award handed down. Most underwriter experience reflects that most of the money they pay out goes for defense costs and investigation. For that and sound procedural reasons the insurance companies customarily reserve certain rights. Insurers demand to be notified immediately at the first sign of trouble so that a prompt investigation can determine their exposure.[17] They may also suggest or insist upon retraction or correction, depending upon policy terms covering the situation. Additionally, when preliminary maneuvers prove fruitless, the insuring company may wish to exercise its right to buy out of what it judges to be a losing fight. The insurer buys out by paying the difference between the deductible amount and the lowest acceptable settlement figure obtainable from the plaintiff. The insured can then continue in the case if he wishes, but he now stands alone and must bear all liability and expense. Looking at the other side of the coin, the insured may disengage himself from a suit he wants no further part of, and the insurance company would then continue alone. This latter turn-around situation is a possibility on appeal when the insured is willing to nurse his bruises but the insurer seeks to recover from a heavy trial court loss.

The foregoing explanation should not suggest that an adversary relationship exists between insurer and insured. There may be an adversary relationship between these parties on one side and the third party who presents a claim on the other, but the insurance companies and their indemnified media usually try to work out a mutually satisfactory approach once confronted by

---

[16] If the party who wants to sue has a complaint with some merit, he can usually find a lawyer willing to take the case on a contingent fee instead of a retainer. This arrangement means the lawyer takes an agreed-upon amount, usually ranging from 30 to 50 per cent of the court award, provided there is an award. The percentage goes up in relation to the amount of difficulty encountered in getting an award. However, the contingent fee arrangement does cost the plaintiff something; he will have to pay such costs as medical exams, filing fees, jury fees, witness travel, and deposition expense.

[17] In actual practice, notification often comes slowly. The insured may think he is only faced with a threat and tries to calm the troubled waters himself.

a suit. A good example of cooperation with the establishment of an important legal principle at stake was the Rosenbloom v. Metromedia case.[18] The insured and insurer (Fireman's Fund) carried the fight up through the United States Supreme Court at a cost of close to $100,000. In this instance, both the media and the insurance industry stood to gain by persistence; the final decision represented a giant stride toward establishing the rule that a libeled party, even though private, connected to a controversial public issue must prove actual malice in order to collect. The case thus extended the *"Times* rule" [19] requiring proof of actual malice (recklessness or calculated falsity) to establish claim legitimacy in suits involving public officials, public figures, or public issues.

Proof of actual malice can lead to punitive damages, of course, and punitive damages can run very high. Therefore, the position of each underwriter with respect to specific coverage for awards of such "punishment" money—intended to teach the libeler a lesson he won't soon forget—is worth examining. Fireman's Fund and Seaboard Surety exclude punitive damages on the grounds that covering them would be contrary to the public interest. They reason that before punitive damages can be awarded, there must be malice, and malice customarily constitutes a wanton act of gross negligence or intentional wrong. Therefore, it cannot be in the public interest to pay someone for doing something he knew was wrong. Employers Reinsurance policies do not expressly exclude punitive damages; this insurer simply agrees to pay all damages without differentiating them. Employers justifies its approach as based on the principle of vicarious action: the employee did something that got his employer into trouble, and the acts of employees are covered in the policy. The underwriting by Lloyd's is similar in philosophy, but policies written through Lloyd's will often expressly cover punitive awards. The Mutual Insurance Company policy also expressly states that it pays punitive damages; Mutual believes the public interest concept belongs in the criminal realm, but gross negligence in libel must be viewed in its civil identity.

Legal rationales aside, the insured dealing with hot issues under time pressures that could bring accusations of recklessness enjoys broader protection if he is in fact covered for punitive

18 403 U.S. 29, 91 S.Ct. 1811 (1971).

19 The *"Times* rule" popularly refers to the definition of malice established in the case of New York Times v. Sullivan (supra) and those falling under its purview as expanded in more recent related cases. It would probably be fair to say that *"Times* rule" has now become a catch-all term that really applies to the qualified privilege available to the publisher when he reports on public officials, public figures, and matters of public interest.

damages. It should be noted, however, that some states do not allow punitive damages on the reasoning that the injured party should recover only to the extent that he has suffered injury, and in such jurisdictions the coverage is meaningless. All the underwriters pay special damages, which must be proved in detail, and compensatory (or general) damages, which are presumed but usually tied to somewhat reasonable parameters of balm for injured reputation or occupation. Such damages may run high but most frequently remain modest.

As a means of cutting defense and liability costs, the insurers like to see an out-of-court settlement whenever it is possible and feasible, considering the interests of both insured and insurer. Their reasoning: (1) trials cost lots of money, (2) many juries seem to show more sympathy toward the plaintiff than toward the defendant, and (3) many juries fail to understand malice, even when the judge's instructions are good; after inferring malice from some ramification of falsity, such juries at times award large punitive damages or mask a punitive award in a high "pain and suffering" general award. The first point is simply an expensive fact. The other two lead directly into the additionally costly appellate arena where more legal specialists may occasionally enter the case, and they, of course, must investigate for vulnerable points of law.

Because defamation does not lend itself to "standard" settlements, members of a jury can differ widely in what they believe constitutes a fair award to a plaintiff. A jury may in practice average the disparate amounts thought fair by its individual members. If several jurors think punitively, and their quantified influence results in a large compensatory award, an underwriter that does not specifically pay punitive damages may thus end up paying what amounts to some punitive damages. It is the unpredictable conduct and secret thinking of jurors that makes awards and their coverage hard to describe in absolutes.

As a practical matter, the insured and insurer who suffer in the court of first instance usually find more favorable disposition in the court of appeals where no jury is involved. Some policies leave the option to appeal with the insurer, but there is usually no difference of opinion on the wisdom of appealing a trial court decision.[20]

When negotiated settlement maneuvers fail, the insurance companies and their insured media frequently enter a defense

[20] Employers Reinsurance says it has never lost a case on appeal, but the cost of legal expertise necessary to make that statement comes high. Also, every case where a judgment is entered against an insured may not be appealed.

motion for summary judgment. This strategy is the most useful at their disposal and comprises an attempt to persuade the judge to decide the case without resort to a formal courtroom trial by jury. The lawyer for the defense argues to the judge that there really is no dispute as to facts between the two parties— there just seems to be a dispute. If the judge agrees there is no dispute on facts, the case is then decided on points of law. At that juncture the defense in a news-related case would probably try to show some form of qualified or absolute privilege of reporting; that is, the reporter had a legal right to print or broadcast the material in question. The judge then listens to opposing arguments. If he decides afterward to grant the motion, both sides go home, and the case is closed. The better and more experienced the lawyer, the better his chances of winning summary judgment, but insureds without defense provisions in their policies may be unwilling or unable to help themselves with expensive lawyers.[21]

The jury during trial, however, never knows that the defendant carries libel insurance. The legal rules of evidence prohibit information about such coverage from introduction into evidence. Knowledge that the defendant is insured not only can't be connected to the trial issues through relevancy but is considered so prejudicial that the judge will usually order a mistrial— so that the case will have to be tried all over again before a new jury—if the plaintiff's lawyer somehow places it before the jury.[22]

Assessment and Possible Trends

The trend of the law in recent years is favorable to the libel insurance business because it allows ever more privilege to the media in First Amendment rights. In addition, judges show an inclination to restrain juries that wish to make punitive awards.[23] Judges are also showing increasing willingness to en-

[21] When the policy carries a defense deductible, the insurer hires the lawyer(s). Smaller media sometimes feel more comfortable with a known local lawyer, but he may experience only that one libel case in his entire professional life and come up a loser.

[22] According to Alfred F. Conard (ed.) in Conference on Aims and Methods of Legal Research, p. 169 (University of Michigan Press, 1957), work with experimental juries in moot trials has shown that damages increased when the jury learned the defendant carried insurance. Damages increased even more when the fact of insurance coverage came out, but the judge expressly told the jury to disregard it. The experiments were in connection with automobile liability, and whether the damages principles carry over into the personal injury libel field may be debated.

[23] It lies within the power of the judge to reduce damages if he thinks them unreasonable or excessive.

tertain motions for summary judgments. Some jurists might well argue that today's media-favorable libel law makes summary judgment less a discretionary matter and more a virtual requirement under a sort of procedural First Amendment. Finally, about 10 per cent of the suits filed ever get to court, and of the few won by the plaintiff in trial court, most are overturned on appeal. These factors together have produced a decided drop in the severity of insurance losses over the last half dozen years that will probably continue unless recent U.S. Supreme Court appointees influence some landmark anti-media decisions. Following these factors so advantageous to the insurance industry, however, is a contrary force: if the courts are going to protect free speech, an increasing number of media may come to decide they don't need insurance protection too.

Considering the somewhat conservative cast of the present Supreme Court, the legal pendulum could in some way swing away from the more absolute view of unhampered press freedom toward a compromise guaranteeing closer watch on individual rights. The switch could occur in the libel area, but that would require changing a good deal of law. A more likely testing ground appears to be the area of individual privacy rights where there is currently a lot of controversy and no Supreme Court precedent other than Time, Inc. v. Hill,[24] which protected the media by applying the *"Times* rule" to privacy. Thirty-two states now extend protection to privacy either by statute or case law, and a number of lower court decisions since Hill show more sympathy for the individual in his relationship with the media. The significant implications here for libel insurance policies through their privacy coverage provisions appears clear; although at present it is not common for libel plaintiffs to file joint actions in privacy, such procedure could gain ground with encouragement through higher court decisions. Two lances directed at the same target stand a better chance of striking home, and no guidelines restrict the size of privacy awards other than what the court will allow.

Countering present pro-media tendencies in the libel arena is the fact that people nowadays are less forgiving than they used to be, and they sue for fantastic amounts at the drop of a comma. Unhappily, it would appear the media contribute to their own state of legal distress by head-lining large suit filings but playing down or burying settlement or suit drops, thus fueling the popular notion that a good way to sock the mistrusted media is to make them pay plenty through a suit the whole world can

---

[24] 385 U.S. 374, 87 S.Ct. 534 (1967).

read and hear about.[25]   Pending litigation with accompanying ballyhoo can in many instances exercise the same chilling effect on editorial policy as an adverse court ruling.

These attitudes point up the emerging importance of defense assistance over loss coverage with the need focusing on non-conditional and non-deductible defense payment provisions at reasonable price for the media too small to retain specialized consultive counsel.   Although such provisions would undoubtedly serve the best interests of the policy holder, the hazard here for the libel insurance industry lies in the threat that accumulated legal fees for all counsel—not just assigned expensive specialist lawyers—would outstrip income from allowable premiums.   Although premiums between insurer and insured are negotiated, they must remain realistically close to the tables filed by the companies for approval with the several states where they operate through state insurance regulating agencies.   Filling the defense need in view of these limitations and on terms suitable to the insurance industry, the media, and the legal profession should provide an interesting challenge in the years ahead.

[25] Employers Reinsurance says it notices that juries drawn from one-newspaper towns see most hostile to their single publication because they are members of a captive audience; hostility apparently decreases in some sort of crude ratio to the number of alternatives.   Thus TV viewers with many available channels for switching tend toward leniency as do periodical subscribers or prospective buyers from ads because they exercise a choice.

Appendix E

SOME ISSUES IN MUNICIPAL REGULATION
OF CABLE TELEVISION

(The following is a summary of a much longer analysis of deficiencies as found by a specialist, Prof. William B. Blankenburg of the University of Wisconsin-Madison, in the cable ordinance of Madison, Wis.)

SUMMARY

The following is intended to point out some deficiencies in the existing City of Madison ordinance for Community Antenna Television.

A.   No definitions are provided in the ordinance.   On several occasions "franchise" and "license" are used apparently interchangeably.   The ordinance provides only for "community antenna television"—defined by the FCC as only off-the-air television.   "Cablecasting"—also defined by the FCC—is not mentioned in the ordinance.

Definitions are necessary.

B.   The ordinance is non-exclusive.   However, experience indicates that cable is a natural monopoly.   There is no evidence of two successful "parallel" cable systems in the U.S.   Complete Channel Television [the Madison franchisee] has argued that to grant another franchise would not be in the public interest, in effect asking for an exclusive grant.

C.   Alternative types of ownership—for example part city or non-profit, community corporation ownership—should be studied in the future.   Provision should be made in the franchise for possible city purchase of any existing cable system.   Splitting the system with several franchises in various parts of the city could be considered.

D.   Revocation procedures—if necessary—or any other form of milder "penalty" for non-performance are not clearly stated in the ordinance.

E.   The city apparently has no power to control any sale or transfer of control of the company.   In fact, the ownership of Complete Channel has changed substantially twice since 1965.

F.   Provisions should be considered to retain as much local ownership as possible.

683

G.   The timetable for construction is unclear in the amendment to the ordinance.

H.   City review of plans and overseeing of technical standards are unsettled. For example, the Coaxial Committee was told (by Buildings and Inspections) that the city could only inspect the house connection. On the other hand, the City Attorney's office told the committee that the city should review the total plans (including all services, programming, etc.) before allowing franchisees to proceed with construction. The City Council has previously approved the plans of Complete Channel with only minimal review.

I.   Many items for consumer protection are not provided in the ordinance such as guarantee of prompt and careful service, an office to receive complaints, switchback devices so subscribers can use their antennae as well as the cable, and the like.

J.   There appear to be no provisions in the ordinance for protection of any private property that might be damaged during construction or maintenance of the system.

K.   The city should seek to insure as complete service as possible for viewers. Thus, the city should explore requirements for specific types of local programming. Such requirements should include establishment of neighborhood channels and studios, as well as carrying as many off-the-air signals as possible. Further, the city could require specific channels be reserved for future educational and public service use.

L.   Subscriber rates may be only part of a mix of fees in cable. The city should specify that it has the right to examine and approve rates for advertising, pay-TV, and all other cable service.

M.   The city should have complete access to all records of the franchisee—including all FCC records—and should require annual reports filed with the city indicating services, all financial data, and the like.

N.   There should be provisions for coordination of educational programming, and some provision for programming on the government and access channels. It is not entirely clear that this coordination and programming should be left to franchisees.

O.   Many matters are not covered by the existing franchise in addition to those listed above: privacy, pay-TV, emergency (disaster) use, and the like.

P.   The city should consider—in any revisions of the existing ordinance, or in creating any new ordinances—the possibility of cooperating with surrounding communities to insure interconnection, adequacy of service for all citizens of the area, wide diversity of programming, reduced costs to subscribers, and the like. The need for regional planning is now obvious to the City of Madison in many areas—the airport, bus transportation, highway planning. Planning for a larger area is just as important in the case of cable TV.

*

TABLE OF CASES

References are to Pages

C

INDEX

INDEX

END OF VOLUME

KERR KEVIN WILLIAM DUBOIS HALL ROOM #301 HAMOTON HAMPTON 7 3663